The Medieval Translator

Traduire au Moyen Âge

The Medieval Translator

Traduire au Moyen Âge

VOLUME 20

General Editor

Catherine Batt

Editorial Board

Catherine Batt (University of Leeds, UK)
Michèle Goyens (KU Leuven, Belgium)
Ian Johnson (University of St Andrews, UK)
Tamás Karáth (Pázmány Péter Catholic University, Budapest,
Hungary; Comenius University, Bratislava, Slovakia)
Alessandra Petrina (Università degli Studi di Padova, Italy)
Denis Renevey (University of Lausanne, Switzerland)
Christiania Whitehead (University of Lausanne, Switzerland,
co-ordinating editor)
Alessandro Zironi (Alma Mater Studiorum,
Università di Bologna, Italy)

MEDIEVAL TRANSLATIONS
AND THEIR READERS

Edited by

Pavlína Rychterová and
Jan Odstrčilík

BREPOLS

© 2023, Brepols Publishers n.v., Turnhout, Belgium.
All rights reserved. No part of this publication may be reproduced,
stored in a retrieval system, or transmitted, in any form or by any
means, electronic, mechanical, photocopying, recording, or otherwise
without the prior permission of the publisher.
D/2023/0095/32
ISBN 978-2-503-59190-2
e-ISBN 978-2-503-59192-6
DOI 10.1484/M.TMT-EB.5.121719
ISSN 1293-8750
e-ISSN 2566-0292
Printed in the EU on acid-free paper.

Table of Contents

Preface   7

Introduction   9
    Pavlína Rychterová

Authors and Readers   19

Gothic Texts   21
    Translations, Audiences, Readers
        Alessandro Zironi

Translating Latin in the Medieval North   43
    Agnesar Saga and its Readership
        Maria Teresa Ramandi

The Old Swedish Pentateuch Translation and its Reflective Model Reader   65
        Jonatan Pettersson

Old Czech Biblical Prologues   87
    A Medieval Reader's Gateway to the Study of the Bible
        Andrea Svobodová, Kateřina Voleková and Pavlína Rychterová

Reader and Public in a Fourteenth-Century French Translation   111
    Jean le Long and his Readership
        Marco Robecchi

From Devotion to Censure   127
    Hans Tucher's and Bernard of Breydenbach's Pilgrim Accounts and their Two
    Medieval Czech Translations
        Jaroslav Svátek

Educating Laymen and Nuns in the Late Middle Ages in German-
Speaking and Dutch Environments   147
        Katrin Janz-Wenig

Dissemination of Knowledge   165

Miscellaneity in Practice   167
    A Further Look at the English Text Known as the *Lay Folks' Catechism*
        Elisabeth Salter

Old Material and New Perspectives　　　　　　　　　　　　　　　185
   Master Ingold's 'Golden Game'
      Jörg Sonntag

Jan Hus, *The Daughter*　　　　　　　　　　　　　　　　　　205
   Religious Education between Translation and Adaptation
      Pavlína Rychterová

Unbearable Lightness of Multilingual Sermons?　　　　　　　　223
   The So-Called Wilhering Adaptation of Three Czech Sermons of Jan Hus
      Jan Odstrčilík

Religious Education in Transition　　　　　　　　　　　　251

The Fifteenth- and Sixteenth-Century Croatian Translations of the Latin
Liber de modo bene vivendi ad sororem　　　　　　　　　　　253
      Andrea Radošević

Early Readers' Responses to the English Translations of Richard Rolle's
Emendatio vite　　　　　　　　　　　　　　　　　　　　　277
      Tamás Karáth

Predestination and Free Will in the Old French and Middle English
Versions of the *Elucidarium* and in the Middle English *Chastising of
God's Children*　　　　　　　　　　　　　　　　　　　　　299
      Takami Matsuda

The *Boke of Gostely Grace* and the *Orcherd of Syon*　　　　　317
   Revelations of *approuyd wymmen* and their Readership in Fifteenth-Century
   England
      Naoë Kukita Yoshikawa

The Social Function of a Translation　　　　　　　　　　　　337
   Earl Rivers, William Caxton, and the *Dicts and Sayings of the Philosophers*
      Omar Khalaf

Index　　　　　　　　　　　　　　　　　　　　　　　　　　355

Preface

Thirty years ago, Roger Ellis organized the first Cardiff conference on medieval translation. In the years since then, it has become an institution and its remit as a platform for discussion for all scholars interested in the great variety of questions relating to translation in the Middle Ages is more pertinent than ever. The last decade in particular has seen the growth of an interdisciplinary interest in translation. Scholars from all branches of the humanities, from linguistic and literary studies and philology to historiography, philosophy, theology and cultural studies, see the potential for translation studies to break down traditional disciplinary barriers and to reconfigure principles of comparison, along with other methodological and theoretical approaches, so as to do justice to the great variety of medieval texts, establishing fresh means for understanding them and the societies that produced them.

The Cardiff Conference series provides an interdisciplinary forum for the discussion of all aspects of translation in the Middle Ages. Our principal interest in organizing the Eleventh Cardiff Conference on the Theory and Practice of Translation in the Middle Ages in Vienna, March 15–18, 2017, was to cover as broad a scope as possible, to facilitate multilayered exchanges between scholarly topics, methods and cultures. The research topics were diverse, discussed in twenty-seven sessions, eighty-one papers and four key-note lectures in total. Some of the clusters mirrored strong research areas defined by textual material – for example, there were four sessions on Bible translation, two sessions on translations of religious didactic texts and several papers on the translation of scientific texts. Many papers engaged with the special strand of the conference, on translations and their readers. In addition, there was interest in topics such as literary genres, relations between individual languages, especially Latin and the vernaculars, the political dimension of textual cultures in multilingual societies and translation and gender. A traditional focus of the Cardiff conferences, on Western European vernaculars (in particular, medieval English and French), was partially maintained, but a significant number of papers addressed Eastern central European and Eastern European languages (for example, German, Polish, Czech, Hungarian and Croatian). Several sessions were devoted to translation practices in non-European medieval societies.

The present volume gathers papers from the special strand of the conference, 'Medieval Translations and their Readership'. The focus is on the role of the reader in the translation process, on communities of readers and on their active participation in the choices translators make, as well as on the relationship between texts and their recipients in general and on translation as a dialogue between author, text and reader. The conference was hosted by the Austrian Academy of Sciences, Institute for Medieval Research, Vienna, Austria organized by the ERC Starting Grant OVERMODE – Origins of the Vernacular Mode. Regional Identities and European Networks in Late Medieval Europe,

Grant Agreement 263672, COST Action 1301 New Communities of Interpretation: Contexts, Strategies and Processes of Religious Transformation in Late Medieval and Early Modern Europe, and by the Editorial Board of *The Medieval Translator* series (Brepols). The conference received full financial support from the ERC Starting Grant OVERMODE and the COST Action 1301 New Communities of Interpretation.

Pavlína Rychterová, Jan Odstrčilík

Introduction

Pavlína Rychterová

Institute for Medieval Research, Austrian
Academy of Sciences

Translations of works of theology and religious education, the focus of the majority of the contributions to this volume, constitute excellent material for research into medieval lay audiences, their expectations, demands, and experiences.[1] Professional as well as lay authors who translated and adapted Latin and vernacular texts tried to engage their readers, to accommodate their expectations, educate and sometimes even manipulate them. In the case of many extant religious educational texts – some very prominent in literary studies on account of their exceptional aesthetic qualities – we know neither their authors nor their copyists. Moreover, we can identify neither their historical nor even their hypothetical readers. But, even if we do know both a text's author and its primary recipient, we may find that this knowledge does not help us further. The textual strategies that the authors used to engage their readers, to make the works (usually originally in Latin) accessible and understandable to them, are not primarily autobiographical and may only be partially understood through knowing the educational and/or social status of a particular reader. Furthermore, in the majority of cases, these textual strategies cannot be defined as the result of specific regional, and/or linguistic-national conditions. In religious educational texts extant in medieval European languages, individual authors resorted to similar techniques, whether to meet the challenges of translation, to fulfil the educational aims of pastoral theology, or to relate to their readers.[2] These similarities of style demonstrate the degree to which translators had in common a Latin education that promulgated a particular understanding of language, as well as similar literary traditions and an interest in pastoral care. Extant religious educational European vernacular texts from the thirteenth to the sixteenth cen-

---

1 On medieval readership especially, see the approach of Sabrina Corbellini and the work of the COST Action IS 1301 'New Communities of Interpretation: Contexts, Strategies and Processes of Religious Transformation in Late Medieval and Early Modern Europe'. For the approach to religious readership, see *Cultures of Religious Reading*, ed. by Corbellini; *Discovering the Riches of the World*, ed. by Corbellini, Hoogvliet, Ramakers; Corbellini, 'Creating Domestic Sacred Space', pp. 295–309.

2 This issue is directly addressed in a collaborative monograph, containing critical editions of all known medieval vernacular translations of a very popular Franciscan prophetic tract: *John of Rupescissa*, Vademecum in tribulatione, ed. by Lerner, Rychterová.

turies show a great deal of conformity, even those which were evidently the products of heterodox and/or church reform movements, such as the *Devotio moderna* in the Low Countries, English Lollardy or even the Bohemian Hussite movement, the most radical church reform movement in late medieval Latin Europe.

The relative homogeneity of religious educational literature in medieval vernaculars may easily be obscured by the former necessarily varied scholarly treatment of such material at the hands of nationally defined philological and historiographical modes of investigation. Today, research into Middle English pastoral and devotional literature and the conditions of its production dominates scholarly work in the field. This is understandable, given the large number of scholars specializing in English literary studies and Middle English philology.[3] Religious texts in many other vernaculars have until now received little attention, and that attention has been mainly confined to the evidence they offer the linguistic historian, or the literary scholar reading them as premodern expressions of particular modern national identities. The research into late medieval Czech religious educational literature is an exceptional case in this respect and at the same time it displays the typical fate of textual material where research into it has been conducted in languages other than the dominant scholarly ones. Given the strong interest in Hussitology, many religious educational texts have in the past been analysed in detail primarily as sources for the history of the Hussite revolution. This focus has yielded valuable insights into the communication strategies of the leaders of the movement and their followers, but the research has been conducted mainly in the Czech language, and until recently it has not been available outside of Czech historiographical, philological and literary studies, despite the great importance of this material for research into late medieval vernacularisation and especially for what it reveals of how lay people were involved in the Church's political decision-making in general. Discussing this material in English may significantly enrich other research, espe-

---

3 Even in recent scholarship respectful of cultural diversity, the genres of Middle English texts are often regarded as representative of European production as a whole. See, for example, *A Companion to Medieval Translation*, ed. by Beer, which, despite the general title concentrates on Middle English texts, in particular, well-known translations such as Chaucer's. *Prodesse et delectare*, ed. by Kössinger, Wittig, shows a more balanced approach to the variety of European vernaculars, containing contributions on Italian, German, English, French, Scandinavian and Dutch vernaculars. But, as is often the case in Anglophone essay collections, it does not include medieval vernacular literatures originating from areas now polities of the so-called former Soviet Eastern Bloc. The East-West divide remains strong in the scholarship even thirty years after the fall of the Berlin Wall. The rich Iberian tradition (including Castilian and Catalan) is also unrepresented. On a global approach to medieval cultures of translation, see the cluster 'Ideologies of translation' in the individual issues of the open-access journal *Medieval Worlds* (http://www.medievalworlds.net/medieval_worlds?frames=yes, accessed on 3.11.2022), and in particular the individual contributions to issue 11, prefaced Rychterová, 'Instead of an Introduction', pp. 2–16.

cially into Middle English Lollard texts of religious instruction.[4] Careful comparative analysis of relevant vernacular texts across Europe, then, is important to the formulation of a truly European approach to their research and understanding.

This comparative approach may begin with the simple observation of similarities between texts in various vernaculars, as mentioned above; this means abandoning the search for uniqueness among the contributions of individual authors, groups, milieux and 'nations'. In concentrating on similarities between individual texts, we have to ask not only where exactly these similarities originated (as we have suggested, mainly with the shared linguistic and theological education of the individual authors), but how identical and/or similar theological material and linguistical resources and strategies were chosen and organised by individual translators and compilers. To answer this question, we have to consider not only authors but readers, as the latter must also be understood as instrumental in the production of the texts concerned.

Readers shaped the production of texts of vernacular religious instruction in many ways. Already in their choice of language authors anticipate a particular readership; very often, those who wrote these texts were also their first readers and they composed them from the point of view of a student, not a teacher. Readers of Latin texts acted as creative translators, adapting Latin treatises according to the expectations of their readers – sometimes people whom they personally knew, and whose reading material they also knew equally well, being a part of the same network of religious instruction. This is true for lay readers as well as for members of religious orders, who both sometimes belonged to the same readers' network. Members of lay female orders as well as well-to-do lay women highly literate in their own vernaculars with considerable proficiency in spiritual learning were very often either the individually or collectively targeted recipients of many sorts of educational religious texts. Taking a gendered approach to these texts is, nevertheless, not always easy. In most cases it is not possible to decide if particular textual strategies are gender specific, although they may have been understood as such by their authors and/or their readers. It is in any case necessary to regard each textual witness as unique in this respect, both in its approach and in the hypothetical responses of its readers. Respecting each source in the analysis of the similarities and concentrating on the participation of readers in the process of making vernacular catechesis and theology may help us to understand better which textual strategies were used for which purpose (and which were *not* used), and how their authors and readers interacted.

Individual contributions in this volume approach precisely these questions through the use of historiographical, philological and linguistic methods, as well as literary scholarly approaches. They discuss texts extant in many European vernaculars, including Slavonic works usually ignored in Anglophone treat-

---

4 A comparative study of Lollard and Hussite movements in general may help us formulate new approaches and contextualize better both the bodies of work produced. See, for example, *Wycliffism and Hussitism*, ed. by Ghosh and Soukup.

ments, although the situation is constantly improving in this respect and the Medieval Translator series in general, for example, recognizes the great diversity of vernacular languages in medieval Latin Europe.

The first section, 'Authors and Readers', brings together articles examining the idea of a model reader as expressed in translations of biblical texts and texts of religious instruction. Using linguistic methods, Alessandro Zironi analyses in detail the Gothic translations in the so-called Wulfila-bible, pursuing the question of how translators anticipated the needs and educational horizons of their hypothetical readers: 'The approach adopted by Wulfila and his team reveals the intention of having a final product which can be open to the understanding of the common people to be converted and to ensure the integrity of the recently adopted Christian faith' (p. 32–3). Zironi discusses the reception history of the translation, highlighting various functions of the text, beginning with its hypothetical aural reception in the fifth century through to its 'scholarly' reading in the ninth century, and argues for a wider definition of the term 'reader' to include also 'listeners'.

Maria Teresa Ramandi approaches the problem of cultural translation in her examination of the old Norse translation of a twelfth-century Latin Legend of St Agnes. The careful rendering of the Latin text into Norse includes the conscious elaboration of passages describing the social realities of classical Antiquity and their adaptation to the contemporary Icelandic situation. Ramandi argues, from detailed linguistic analysis, that one should take into account the character of the cultural context as being very important for the evaluation of each translation, which can never render the original text perfectly. Rather, one should assess a translation from the point of view of its 'first' readers, among whom the translator must also be counted because of their shared horizon of experience.

Jonatan Pettersson concentrates on an Old Swedish translation of the Pentateuch from the second half of the fourteenth century, a high point for European Bible translation. The translator (or translators) employed various textual strategies to make the text understandable for their target lay readership; they worked especially with explanatory notes and commentaries in order to contextualize the Old Testament within the vernacular discourse of Swedish late medieval society and to offer a basic guide to (already fairly advanced) vernacular exegetical interpretation of the Scripture. The guide aims to eliminate any possibility of a lay heterodox interpretation, so may more properly be read as 'edifying preaching' (p. 82) for lay people who were nevertheless regarded as being able to read and interpret the bible independently in a number of ways.

A Czech translation of both the Hebrew Bible and the New Testament is contemporary with the Swedish one, as a result of widespread efforts to cater for the spiritual aspirations of new lay intellectual elites. Svobodová, Voleková and Rychterová concentrate on the prologues to individual biblical books, either translated from Latin models or independently composed by translators. These prologues address various complex linguistic and translational issues and anticipate and discuss readers' responses in a similar fashion to the commentaries in the Swedish Pentateuch. Nevertheless, the Czech Bible had a very specific reception in the Bohemian Reformation, during which the reading of the bible gained enormous importance as the sole principle of the *reformatio Ecclesiae*. As in Sweden and elsewhere in Europe, biblical translations played a key role in the development of vernacular literary language, in religious instruction, and in the transformation of theological discourse in general: 'A close look at the biblical prologues', the authors stress, 'allows us to understand better all these processes and to formulate important questions for future research'. (p. 106) Biblical prologues may allow a valuable insight into the self-understanding of the translators, into the expectations of their readers, and into the discursive positioning of the biblical translations in individual theological discussions.

The articles of Marco Robecchi and Jaroslav Svátek both discuss medieval travel-writing, its translation into vernacular languages and transformations in its functions with respect to its target audiences. Again, we may observe here great similarities in the way that individual authors employed textual strategies to meet and, at the same time, to shape, the expectations of their recipients. According to Robecchi, the French compilation made in the middle of the fourteenth century by Jean le Long, of a number of well-received Latin works of travel literature, elaborated especially on the 'scientific' and 'marvellous' aspects of its individual sources, resulting in, arguably, a new text. The authors of Czech travelogues, translations from Latin and German models from the middle of the fifteenth century, employ similar strategies in order to achieve several aims – to entertain the reader, to satisfy his or her 'scientific' curiosity, and to define anew any religious message. Originating in confessionally-divided Bohemia, the texts targeted readers regardless of their creed, and their authors reworked their models in order to avoid any polemical interpretations. In this way these translators negotiated seemingly non-negotiable issues. Research into the textual strategies making such a negotiation possible represents an important contribution to the debate about the transformation of religious and social identities in Latin Europe.

Katrin Janz Wenig undertakes a comprehensive analysis of the vernacular reception of the tract *De dilectione Dei et proximi* ascribed to Helwicus Theutonicus (d. 1263), prior of the Dominican convent at Strasbourg, and of the so-called *Sermones Socii*, a collection of sermons written by the Cistercian monk Conrad of Brundelsheim at the beginning of the fourteenth century. Five compiled translations were made from this textual material over the following decades, for a number of identified groups of readers. The article analyses textual strategies employed by the individual authors who compiled vernacular texts of religious instruction based on the Latin models in order to accommodate the educational horizons of their various readers. This careful contextualizing of material constitutes a valuable contribution to research on medieval readers, especially for future comparative approaches.

The contributions in the section on the 'Dissemination of Knowledge' focus on how translators addressed readers, how people read and how they used the manuscripts and printed books made for them. The target audience or model reader of the first section is here put into perspective with the help of discussions of reading practices. Elisabeth Salter considers how late medieval people used the written text as part of their devotional lives, by means of a study of the impact of textual variability in manuscript culture. She looks at manuscript contexts for witnesses of the Middle English *Lay Folks' Catechism* circulating amongst both laity and clergy in compilations of vernacular works of religious instruction. Again, a focus on similarities is important here. Salter discusses the methodological problem of how to establish whether or not a text (or its use) is orthodox. As is also the case with many fifteenth-century Czech texts, the line between an orthodox and a heterodox reading can only seldom be determined for sure. A Wycliffite-Hussite or Wycliffite-Lollard reading of a particular text does not depend solely on its theological contents, which in many cases may display only very subtle differences from orthodox writings, but rather on the active interpretation of the reader which we can only occasionally grasp. It is important to know that for fifteenth-century people reading texts and using manuscripts, miscellanies in particular, 'the line between an orthodox and a Lollard version might be quite blurred'. (p. 181)

Pavlína Rychterová, in her article on the devotional tract for devout women, *The Daughter*, written by Jan Hus in 1413, asks a very similar question. For the greater part, the text comprises a translation of the Sermon for Easter Monday, on Luke 24.13 by John Wyclif embedded into the structure outlined by Bernard of Clairvaux in his *Meditationes piisimae de cognitione humanae conditionis*. Hus died at the stake as a condemned heretic in accordance with the decision of the council of Constance; the council also condemned the writings of Hus's teacher Wyclif. But the reception history of this particular tract, and of several other vernacular works Hus wrote, was not uniquely heterodox; shortly after his death, his vernacular works became part of his commemorative liturgy within the utraquist-hussite Church. Utraquist burghers as well as noble Catholic ladies also read and interpreted his works of religious instruction according to their own needs.

The character of the Latin-Czech macaronic translation of the *Czech Postil* of Jan Hus, extant from the second half of the fifteenth century, provides further evidence for this type of devotional practice. Jan Odstrčilík focuses especially on the character of the language, as well as the practice of code switching and the character of medieval Latin as a metalanguage in the Middle Ages: 'This word-for-word translation [of Hus's *Czech Postil*] preserves all of the major syntactical features of the Czech language, including Czech expressions. The Czech language has not been simply "translated" into Latin but rather has been "encoded". Here, the Latin language adopts the role and a quality of a metalanguage, in which the Czech original is closely preserved so that it may have been turned very quickly back into Czech (including its various dialects) or into another, syntactically similar, vernacular language'. (p. 234) This particular material, then, may be seen as evidence that we should consider Latin and vernacular discourses as intertwined, influencing one another in ways that we do not yet fully understand.

Jörg Sonntag discusses the late medieval German *Puechlein vom Guldin Spil* (*Book of the Golden Game*), written by the Dominican Master Ingold of Basel around the year 1432. The text represents an interpretation of several Latin models, especially of the *Liber de moribus hominum et officiis nobilium ac popularium super ludo scacchorum* (*Book of Chess*), written by the Dominican Jacobus de Cessolis around the year 1300. Ingold's interpretation of the Latin material concentrated on the concept of *ecclesia ludens* and employed the well-established religious technique of interpreting the game in spiritual terms. By doing this, and by using very popular material in a rather original way, Ingold placed his treatise at the heart of contemporary devotional literature. It accommodated the expectations and needs of religious women and men practising the so-called *via perfectionis* by using different techniques of imitation. These people themselves then became prominent models for others to imitate and so became an integral part of the interpretation of the text.

The last section, 'Religious Education in Transition', comprises contributions which focus on textual material from the period when printed books gradually changed the relationships between languages, texts, authors, and readers, robbing them step by step of their 'handwritten' complexity. At the same time, vernacular religious literature grew more and more ambitious in parallel with the advancing quality of spiritual education and with the increasing expectations of devout men and women in and outside of religious orders; people who belonged for the most part to the more affluent sector of flourishing urban societies in the individual realms of Latin Europe.

Andrea Radošević analyses the so-called *Books of Blessed Bernard*, two late medieval Croatian translations of the Latin treatise *Liber de modo bene vivendi ad sororem*, the first from the fifteenth century written in a Glagolitic script, the other from the sixteenth century. The first translation, linguistically grounded firmly within Church Slavonic linguistical discourse, targeted male members of religious orders, by contrast with the Latin model which was intended for nuns. Radošević provides a detailed semantic analysis of the Glagolitic-Croatic translation, demonstrating its elaborate approach to spiritual instruction via the careful choice of theologically-loaded terms. The younger compilation targeted lay readers and, together with the older one, provided a basis for early modern Croatian religious educational literature.

We meet a similar discourse-oriented approach to a theological translation in Tamás Karáth's analysis of the fifteenth-century translation and adaptation of *Emendatio vitae* by Richard Rolle. Like Radošević in her analysis of the Croatian adaptation of *Liber de modo bene vivendi*, Karáth discusses the theological changes to the spiritual teaching of Rolle made by the translators, whom Karáth understands as interpreters, as well as by its readers who were drawn from religious orders and the clerical milieu, as well as from among lay people. Instruction on advanced meditation of the kind found in Rolle's text was already quite common in the religious vernacular literature of the continent, and readers' responses share a considerable resemblance. As Karáth puts it precisely in the conclusion of his article: 'The fifteenth-century readers of these manuscripts may share important aspects of their uses of, and attitudes to, the text' (p. 292). This is not only true for the English readers but also for French, German, Czech or Croatian ones.

Takami Matsuda's article targets the possibilities inherent in the vernacular translation of highly complex theological issues, in this case predestination. The concept was elaborated in one of the most popular works of late medieval devotional literature, the *Elucidarium*, a compendium of Christian doctrine usually attributed to Honorius Augustodunensis. The work was translated into many European vernaculars. Matsuda concentrates on its Old French and Middle English translations, taking into account manuscript copies as well as printed versions of the texts. Although the main principle of translation used by the individual authors, copyists and readers to tackle the problem of predestination is simplification, the individual texts nevertheless show some ambition – developing elaborate metaphors in order to make the issue clear to a reader who was untrained in Latin philosophical and theological terminology. We meet this type of simplification and replacement of terms by metaphors once again in vernacular devotional readings across medieval Europe.

Naoë Kukita Yoshikawa examines the *Boke of Gostely Grace* and the *Orcherd of Syon*, adaptations of Mechthild of Hackeborn's *Liber specialis gratiae* and Catherine of Siena's *Dialogo*. Both are religious texts for devout nuns at Syon Abbey, one of the most interesting European centres of vernacular theology. The Abbey maintained the legacy of Birgitta of Sweden in England, whose revelations and *vita* were used and misused in polemics following the Great Western Schism of 1378. Yoshikawa concentrates on the networks of readership which emerged around Syon Abbey, mostly comprising nuns and their female relatives from among the English-speaking nobility. Again, similarities between the texts are thematised, in particular the textual strategies employed by authors and translators alike. Yoshikawa highlights the function of shared metaphors in religious devotional material. Vernacular production connected with Birgittine centres of learning beyond Syon, for example in Vadstena or Prague, offers ideal material for testing methodological approaches to pan-European comparison of religious educational literature.

Finally, Omar Khalaf discusses the *Dicts and Sayings of the Philosophers* by Earl Rivers, one of the Middle English versions of an originally Arabic and Latin compilation of proverbs, maxims, and teachings attributed to philosophers and legendary figures of the past. The work, extant in many versions and in many European languages, was very popular and, as such, quickly found its way into print. The *Dicts* represent an important textual witness originating just at the beginning of the dissemination of printed books. Khalaf elaborates on the many functions of early incunabula and the textual as well as personal networks that originated around the new technology; he also explores how it marked a departure from manuscript culture leading to the emergence of new reading cultures.

Bibliography

Beer, Jeanette Mary Ayres, ed., *A Companion to Medieval Translation*, ARC Humanities Press Companions (Amsterdam: Amsterdam University Press 2019)

Corbellini, Sabrina, 'Creating domestic Sacred Space. Religious Reading in Late Medieval and Early Modern Italy', in *Domestic Devotions in Early Modern Italy*, ed. by Maya Corry, Marco Faini, Alessia Meneghin, Intersections 59 (Leiden: Brill, 2019), pp. 295–309

Corbellini, Sabrina, ed., *Cultures of Religious Reading in the Late Middle Ages. Instructing the Soul, Feeding the Spirit and Awakening the Passion*, Utrecht Studies in Medieval Literacy 25 (Turnhout: Brepols 2013)

Corbellini, Sabrina, Margriet Hoogvliet, Bart A. M. Ramakers ed., *Discovering the Riches of the World. Religious Reading in Late Medieval and Early Modern Europe*, Intersections 38 (Brill: Leiden 2015)

Ghosh, Kantik, Pavel Soukup ed., *Wycliffism and Hussitism, Methods of Thinking, Impact, Writing, and Persuasion, c. 1360–1460*, Medieval Church Studies 47 (Turnhout: Brepols 2021)

John of Rupescissa, Vademecum in tribulatione *Translated into Medieval Vernaculars*, ed. by Robert Lerner, Pavlína Rychterová, Ricerche, Storia, Dies nova: Fonti e studi per la storia del profetismo 4, (Milano: Vita & Pensiero, 2019)

Kössinger, Norbert, Claudia Wittig ed., *Prodesse et delectare: Case Studies on Didactic Literature in the European Middle Ages / Fallstudien zur didaktischen Literatur des europäischen Mittelalters*, Das Mittelalter. Perspektiven Mediävistischer Forschung. Beihefte 11 (Berlin: De Gruyter Berlin 2019)

Rychterová, Pavlína, 'Instead of an Introduction: Medieval Europe Translated', *Medieval Worlds*, 11 (2020), pp. 2–16

AUTHORS AND READERS

Gothic Texts

Translations, Audiences, Readers

Alessandro Zironi

Alma Mater Studiorum
Università di Bologna

The oldest translation of the Bible into a Germanic language comes from the Goths, specifically the Visigoths. In this essay, I investigate the reasons for translating the sacred text and how readers and audiences approached this work from the fourth century, when the Bible was translated into Gothic, up to the Carolingian age, when the translation was last used.[1] I will first consider the relationship between the Christianization of the Goths and their resulting liturgical needs, then examine some earlier translations and the connections between translation, audience, and oral tradition, before concluding with the role of the Gothic version in the study of the Bible and the subsequent transfer from public audiences to private readings, as the Gothic Bible was no longer used for liturgical purposes after the vanishing of Arianism.

Christianization of the Goths and the Reason for the Translation

During the fourth century, the Goths were divided into two main groups: the Tervingi (which later became the Visigoths) and the Greuthungi (the future Ostrogoths).[2] The Tervingi, who were settled along the Danube, were in direct contact with the Roman Empire, to which they were bound in an alliance whereby the Romans paid the barbarians tributes. The Tervingi, for their part, had to defend the Empire from any external attacks or raids.[3] It is obvious that the Goths and the Greeks of the Eastern Roman Empire were in touch with each

---

[1] In 2015 Andrei Vinogradov and Maksim Korobov published five inscriptions in Gothic letters and language engraved as graffiti discovered in Magup (Crimea). They dated them between the ninth and the eleventh centuries, but the question is still open. See Vinogradov and Korobov, 'Gotskie graffiti iz Mangupskoj baziliki' pp. 57–75; Korobov and Vinogradov, 'Gotische Graffito-Inschriften aus der Bergkrim', pp. 141–57; Zironi, 'La letteratura gotica', pp. 46–48; Dolcetti Corazza and Falluomini, *I Goti*, pp. 158–59.

[2] Heather, *The Goths*, pp. 52–53.

[3] Wolfram, *History of the Goths*, p. 62.

other. Such was the case of the Gothic community, as it existed in Constantinople during the fourth century (it is worth remembering how many barbarians were already in the Roman army) and some of its members were Christian.[4]

The Christian period for the Goths began in the third century, when some Goths dwelling along the Danube shores not far from the Black Sea were converted to Christianity as a result of contacts with inhabitants of the Empire and some Christian captives whom the Goths kept during raids and pillages in the Roman provinces.[5] The existence of some structured Christian communities at the very beginning of the fourth century is confirmed by the presence of the Gothic Bishop Theophilus at the First Council of Nicaea in 325.[6] Very soon afterwards, the large majority of the Christianized Goths turned to the Arian heresy. Arianism was professed by influential members of the Church who encouraged missions among the Germanic tribes on the other side of the Roman *limes*.[7] Inside the borders of the Roman Empire, some orthodox Gothic communities were well rooted. Arian or orthodox, the Goths had the same needs. With the spread of Christianity among the Goths, many of them living beyond the frontier, there was a need for non-Greek speakers to understand the word of God. The greatest obstacle was the liturgy, conducted in Greek, the language in which the New Testament was written.[8]

In the last decades of the fourth century, two surviving documents evidence the interest in the Christian Gothic community of Constantinople by the Patriarch John Chrysostom. Intent on suppressing the Arian heresy largely adopted by the Goths, John himself tried to convert them to orthodoxy with the help of a translator and assigned a church to the Goths of Constantinople in which Gothic-speaking priests could preach and people could worship in their own language:

> It was perceived by John that the Scythians were involved with the Arian net; he therefore devised counter contrivances and discovered a means of winning them over. Appointing presbyters and deacons and readers of the divine oracles who spoke the Scythian tongue, he assigned a church to them, and by their means won many from their error. He used frequently himself to visit it and preach there, using an interpreter who was skilled in both languages, and he got other good speakers do the same. This was his constant practice in the city, and many of those who had been deceived he rescued by pointing out to them the truth of the apostolic preaching.[9]

---

4 Schäferdiek, 'Germanenmission', col. 496.

5 Schäferdiek, 'Germanenmission', col. 498.

6 *Patrum Nicaenorum nomina Latine, Graece, Coptice, Syriace, Arabice, Armeniace*, ed. by Gelzer and others, p. lxiv.

7 Schäferdiek, 'Germanenmission', cols 503–04; Gheller, *'Identità' e 'arianesimo gotico'*, pp. 111–12.

8 Greek was for a long time the only liturgical language; Latin was adopted during the papacy of Damasus (d. 384): Klauser, 'Der Übergang der römischen Kirche', p. 473.

9 Theodoret of Cyrus, *The Ecclesiastical History*, ed. by Jackson, p. 152.

In a letter probably written in 404, John refers to the Ἐκκλησίᾳ τῶν Γότθων ('the Church of the Goths').[10] The granting of a specific church to the Gothic community seems to have started in the year 399; on the occasion of the Eastern liturgy, a Gothic homily was given, followed by a sermon delivered by Patriarch John.[11]

Can we infer that during the liturgy in the Gothic church in Constantinople the scriptures were read in a language other than Greek?[12] And was it Gothic? We cannot be sure, but it would sound a little odd if the Gothic language were not used in a church attended by Goths.[13] Two other pieces of data must also be considered. First, Pope Damasus (366–84) decided that Latin could be used as a liturgical language.[14] Second, in the same years, Paul's First Epistle to the Corinthians was the topic of a theological discussion, in particular Chapter 14, in which the Apostle exhorts preachers to be readily understandable by using the language spoken by the congregation. Commenting on that passage, a still anonymous author known as Ambrosiaster asserted that foreign languages did not permit the union of the community, as the biblical text remained obscure and thus called for the presence of a translator.[15] To summarize, in the second half of the fourth century, the growth in the number of Christians urged for solutions regarding the linguistic gap between the biblical text in Greek and

---

10 John Chrysostom, *Epistulae*, ed. by Migne, col. 727.

11 John Chrysostom, *Homiliae*, ed. by Migne, cols 499–510.

12 Mayer, *The Homilies of St John Chrysostom*, pp. 493–94.

13 Gros, *Les Wisigoths et les liturgies occidentales*, p. 126.

14 Klauser, 'Der Übergang der römischen Kirche', p. 473.

15 'Si ergo nesciero virtutem vocis, ero ei cui loquor barbarus, et is qui loquitur mihi barbarus. non utique id studendum monet, ut invicem per incognitam linguam barbari sibi videantur; sed quia concordiae res est, his nitendum est, ut per unanimitatem intellectus communi laetitia glorientur'; Ambrosiaster, *Commentarius*, XIV. 11, ed. by Vogels, p. 152 ('but if I do not know the meaning of the language, I shall be a foreigner to the speaker and the speaker a foreigner to me. Paul is saying that people should not appear as strangers to one another by using unknown tongues, but in the search of harmony should rejoice with a shared joy in a common understanding'; Ambrosiaster, *Commentaries*, ed. and trans. by Bray, p. 185). 'Sive enim lingua quis loquitur, per duos, ut multum tres; et in particulatim, ut unus interpretetur. hoc est duo aut tres, plus non linguis loquantur, sed singuli, non simul omnes, ne insanire viderentur; ideo ergo ut multum tres, ne occuparent diem linguis loquentes et interpretes illorum et non haberent profetae tempus scripturas disserendi, qui sunt totius ecclesiae inluminatores'; Ambrosiaster, *Commentarius*, XIV. 27, ed. by Vogels, pp. 158–59 ('If any speak in a tongue, let there be only two or at most three, and each in turn; and let one interpret. Two or three people may speak in tongues, but not more, and each one must speak in turn, so as not to appear to be mad. In limiting the number to three at the most, Paul is saying that he does not want these people to take up the whole day and leave insufficient time for prophets, who are the sources of illumination for the whole church, to expound the Scriptures'; Ambrosiaster, *Commentaries*, ed. and trans. by Bray, p. 185). Klauser, 'Der Übergang der römischen Kirche', p. 476.

people speaking and understanding other languages, such as Gothic.[16] In some communities Gothic probably became the language of at least part of the liturgy.[17]

Gothic Translation and its Antecedents

It is widely known that Arian Visigothic Bishop Wulfila and his assistants undertook the translation of the Bible into Gothic in the last decades of the fourth century, but the path that led to this translation began earlier and was closely linked to oral tradition.[18] The Goths, like all other Germanic groups, transmitted their literature orally.[19] This cultural attitude facilitated the approach to the new faith, which practised evangelization by way of direct verbal contact as its first

---

16 Vogel, *Introduction aux sources*, ed. by Botte, pp. 243–45.

17 Traces of liturgies in Gothic language are scant and can be deduced logically. This is the case of a passage from an altercation between Augustine and Pascentius, a *comes domus regiae* about Arianism, and here reference is made to the uses in the barbarian church of the Vandals, which was presumably the same as that of the Goths: 'Latine enim dicitur, *Domine, miserere*. Sola ergo haec Misericordia ab ipso uno Deo Patre et Filio et Spiritu sancto lingua debet hebraea vel graeca, aut ipsa ad postremum postulari latina, non autem et barbara? Si enim licet dicere, non solum Barbaris lingua sua, sed etiam Romanis, *Sihora armen*, quod interpretatur, *Domine, miserere*'; Auctor incertus (Vigilius Tapsensis?), *Epistola XX*, ed. by Migne, col. 1162 ('In fact, in Latin it is said: *Domine, miserere*. Therefore, should this mercy be requested in the Hebrew or Greek language to one God, Father, Son, and Holy Spirit, or can this same mercy be asked in Latin and also in a barbarous language? If, in fact, it is permissible for the Romans to speak in their own language, then in the barbarian language the expression *Domine miserere* corresponds to *Sihora armen*'). About the *altercatio*: Sumruld, *Augustine and the Arians*, pp. 78–84. Salvian of Marseilles remembers in a passage of his *De gubernatione Dei* that the Visigoths during the Eucharistic rite read three lectures, one from the Prophets, one from the Apostles and one from the Gospels: 'Etiamsi a paganis lex diuina non exigat ut mandata faciant quae non sciunt, certe ab haereticis exigit, qui sciunt. Eadem enim etiam illos legere, quae nos legimus, eosdem apud illos prophetas Dei, eosdem apostolos, eosdem euangelistas esse'; Salvien de Marseille, *Du gouvernement de Dieu* V. II. 5, ed. and trans. by Lagarrigue, p. 314 ('Even if the divine law does not exact of the pagans that they keep commandments they do not know, it certainly does exact this of the heretics who know them; for they read the same books we do; they have the same prophets, the same apostles, the same evangelists'; Salvian of Marseilles, *On the government of God*, trans. by Sanford, p. 134). On the Vandalic words: Tiefenbach, 'Das wandalische "Domine miserere"', pp. 251–68.

18 The bibliography on Wulfila and the Gothic translation of the Bible is copious and can be found in Petersen, *Bibliographia gotica amplificata*. The question can be approached through a book by Scardigli, *Die Goten*, pp. 95–132, followed by Stutz, *Gotische Literaturdenkmäler*, pp. 9–14 and more recently Gheller, *'Identità' e 'arianesimo gotico'*, pp. 77–110.

19 Dunphy, 'Oral Traditions', pp. 103–18.

approach to Christianizing people. For instance, Philostorgius reported that Arius, the founder of the heresy many Goths followed, composed strophes and songs to be sung by the simple folk of Constantinople:

> He says that Arius, after his secession from the church, composed several songs to be sung by sailors, and by millers, and by travellers along the high road, and others of the same kind, which he adapted to certain tunes, as he thought suitable in each separate case, and thus by degrees seduced the minds of the unlearned by the attractiveness of his songs to the adoption of his own impiety.[20]

We do not know exactly what happened, but perhaps the popularity of the passage referring to the Apostles who went along the streets of Jerusalem speaking all languages after receiving the Holy Spirit (Acts 2. 4–11) influenced Philostorgius.

The Case of the *Pater Noster*

We know that the first experiences of Christian faith come through daily prayers, like the *Pater Noster*, which is one of the first texts to be translated into many Germanic languages. The Lord's Prayer is a clear example of the relationship between a translated text and its audience. The translation of the *Pater Noster* immediately reveals the problem with any new version of the Holy Scriptures: fidelity to the prayer taught by Jesus and the double effort to respect the syntactic rules of the Gothic language while at the same time having a text which the audience can easily learn by heart. The Greek version surely facilitates memorization by closing lines 2–4 with the possessive pronoun σου ('your') and the same mnemonic practice is repeated by the Gothic text (*þein*). Though the Greek version is colloquial, in Gothic the oral approach is emphasized in order to have a more personal relationship with God. In the first line, the Greek article ὁ used with a pronominal function ('him') is substituted by the personal pronoun *þu*:

Πάτερ ἡμῶν ὁ ἐν τοῖς οὐρανοῖς·	Atta unsar **þu** in himinam,
ἁγιασθήτω τὸ ὄνομά **σου**·	weihnai namo **þein**.
[10]ἐλθέτω ἡ βασιλεία **σου**·	[10]Qimai þiudinassus **þeins**.
γενηθήτω τὸ θέλημά **σου**[21]	Wairþai wilja **þeins**[22]

Obviously, we are not sure about the oral form of the Gothic *Pater Noster* before the linguistic features it assumed in the written translation by Wulfila, but we

---

20 Philostorgius, *The Ecclesiastical History*, ed. by Walford, p. 434.
21 Matthew 6. 9–10: *Novum Testamentum Graece*, ed. by Nestle and others, p. 13.
22 Matthew 6. 9–10: *Die gotische Bibel*, I, ed. by Streitberg, p. 7.

certainly suspect a previous circulation of an oral version of the text. After all, the conversion of the Goths to Christianity had begun earlier than the translation activity undertaken by Wulfila. Some Goths were already in the Roman army from at least the end of the third century, as in the following century the Goths had reached high military ranks.[23] Christianity reached the barbarians in the same years as a result of contacts between soldiers, and among Goths, captives, merchants, and deserters.[24] As this happened, the first engagement with the new religion occurred with the learning of the principal prayers, the first being the *Pater Noster*. Moreover, in Wulfila's time, the conversion of the Goths to Christianity was very recent and still needed to be confirmed. Hence, the translators' group directed by the Visigothic bishop knew very well that it was impossible to imagine an individual reading the Bible, because of the almost complete illiteracy among the Germanic tribes and the high cost of manuscripts, so a largely oral version of the biblical text also had to be considered. At the same time, the evangelic texts presented some difficulties for languages like Gothic, which did not have a sufficient lexicon in specific semantic fields such as philosophy, religious speculation, or the environment and culture of countries of the Near East which had customs, plants, animals and so on mentioned in the Bible but unknown to the majority of the Germanic people.[25]

The Question of Orality

There was also a communicative question to be solved: how could fidelity to the Greek text (which comes from God) be squared with avoidance of obscurity in the Gothic translation? In other words, if you must respect the voice of God manifest even in the order of the words, you are in danger of producing a translation that will be largely obscure for an audience which has to follow the text by ear alone, without any written help. Imagine hearing this:

---

23 Scardigli and Scardigli, 'I rapporti fra Goti e Romani', p. 263 and p. 287.

24 Scardigli and Scardigli, 'I rapporti fra Goti e Romani', p. 283. Some loanwords from Gothic into Latin confirm those contacts: Restelli, 'I più antichi imprestiti gotici del latino', pp. 229–46. The contrary can also have happened: some Latin words particularly used in military context were loaned by Germans: examples can be Gothic *kapillon* (I Corinthians 11. 6), **militon* (Luke 3. 14), etc. It is doubtful that such words can evoke the influence of Latin on the translation of the Bible into Gothic. Germanic speakers could have adopted words pertaining to the military semantic field during the contacts with the Roman Empire before the fourth century and many of them were already used in Greek: Scardigli, *Die Goten*, pp. 84–86. Moreover, the large majority of Latin loanwords in Gothic should have been adopted by Goths in the first three centuries of the Christian era, so before the translation of the Bible: cf. Corazza, *Le parole latine in gotico*, pp. 8–72.

25 For a useful list of semantic domains in the Old and New Testament, see De Waard and Nida, *From One Language to Another*, pp. 178–81; see also Zironi, 'The Evangelic Text as Translation and Interpretative Experience', pp. 124–25.

> [1]Though I speak with the tongues of men and of angels, and have not charity, I am become as sounding brass, or a tinkling cymbal. [2]And though I have the gift of prophecy, and understand all mysteries, and all knowledge; and though I have all faith, so that I could remove mountains, and have not charity, I am nothing.[26]

If we were Goths, we would immediately have some difficulties in understanding what is meant by 'cymbal', 'mystery', and 'knowledge', which in Greek here is *gnosis*. Moreover, the second verse is syntactically complex:

> 1 Ἐὰν ταῖς γλώσσαις τῶν ἀνθρώπων λαλῶ καὶ τῶν ἀγγέλων, ἀγάπην δὲ μὴ ἔχω, γέγονα χαλκὸς ἠχῶν ἢ κύμβαλον ἀλαλάζον.
> 2 καὶ ἐὰν ἔχω προφητείαν καὶ εἰδῶ τὰ μυστήρια πάντα καὶ πᾶσαν τὴν γνῶσιν, καὶ ἐὰν ἔχω πᾶσαν τὴν πίστιν ὥστε ὄρη μεθιστάναι, ἀγάπην δὲ μὴ ἔχω, οὐθέν εἰμι.[27]

In Greek, three hypothetical clauses introduced by ἐὰν ('though') are used together with a consecutive introduced by ὥστε ('so that') and a hypothetical clause of reality with an adversative value by δὲ ('and have'), and finally, the main clause that ends the sentence by οὐθέν εἰμι ('I am nothing'). We should also remember that this passage from Paul is defined as a hymn and therefore has almost poetic patterns that are revealed in Greek by the adoption of a cumulative technique adding clauses introduced by the conjunction καὶ ('and'). The Gothic translation adopts this anaphora but to more fluent effect:

> 1 [...] aiþþau klismo klismjandei.[28]
> 2. jah jabai habau praufetjans jah witjau allaize runos jah all kunþi jah habau alla galaubein, swaswe fairgunja miþsatjau, iþ friaþwa ni habau, in waihts im.[29]

This solution avoids in one case the use of the subordinating conjunction ἐὰν / *jabai* ('though') and prefers in every circumstance the present optative form of the verb (endings in *-au*), repeating five times *habau* ('have'), three times *witjau* ('understand'), and *miþsatjau* ('remove'), thus giving rhythm to the verse. This choice meets the requirements of oral communication so that the assembly attending the liturgy could easily follow the reading.[30] Particular emphasis is also given to the text by the conjunction *iþ* ('if'): breaking the rhythm given by the succession of the conjunction *jah* ('and') plus the optative verbs, the attention of the audience converges upon the main clause, which reveals the answer to all the previous sentences. At the same time, the presence of the two negative adverbs *ni* produces a double trisyllabic expression, *ni habau* and then *in waihts*

---

26 I Corinthians 13. 1–2: *The Bible*, ed. by Stirling, p. 183.

27 I Corinthians 13. 1–2: *Novum Testamentum Graece*, ed. by Nestle and others, pp. 462–63.

28 The first part of the verse in the Gothic translation is lost.

29 I Corinthians 13. 1–2: *Die gotische Bibel*, I, ed. by Streitberg, p. 267.

30 De Waard and Nida, *From One Language to Another*, pp. 25–30; Ong, *Orality and Literacy*, pp. 64–68.

im, that definitively closes the verse. It has already been suggested that many choices made by Wulfila in his translation took into account the finalities of the text, which had to be read in front of an assembly, whence the use of alliteration and other linguistic devices which could help the 'acoustical substance' of words.[31] Therefore, the alliteration of *klismo klismjandei* is not casual but rather normative, in the metrics of Germanic poetry, and also in many poetical formulaic expressions.

The centrality of the audience in the production of the translation is also demonstrated by many individual words, especially those which do not have a clear counterpart in Gothic. The intention of the translators is to make the meaning clear, so that on many occasions they rejected the possibility of using loanwords which ran the high risk of remaining obscure and instead they enlarged the meaning of the Gothic lexicon so that the sense of the Greek term can be comprehensible through a common word. I would like to present two examples. The first one concerns the couple μυστήρια – *runos* in the previous passage by Paul, which has been already discussed.[32] In that passage, with the word μυστήρια the Apostle speaks of 'the secrecy of God's plans'. A very difficult theological concept, which is made comprehensible by choosing the word *runa*. Why? Because the composition of a runic text was rather complex and required the presence of an expert: the runic text could be read right-to-left and vice-versa; at the same time, every single rune could stand for its phonetic value or for its name. For instance, the rune Þ means the unvoiced fricative dental sound /θ/ or its name, Germanic **þurisaz* ('giant', 'monster') (*þurs* in Old Norse) but *þorn* ('thorn') in Old English.[33] Consequently, the reader has to choose between the two interpretations. It is evident that such competence was acquired by few and perceived as a sort of secret knowledge, which one could gain only after an initiatory experience. As a result of using the word *runa*, the Goths linked the idea that even if a man had a secret store of knowledge, without charity he was nothing, and thus the understanding would not have been so different from the meaning of Greek *mysterion*.

Another example can be taken from another passage of the First Epistle to the Corinthians (I Corinthians 10.19–21), in which Paul warns his disciples not to sacrifice to idols as Gentiles do, because you cannot partake of Jesus's Eucharistic table and idolatry:

> [19] What say I then? that the idol is any thing, or that which is offered in sacrifice to idols is any thing? [20] But I say, that the things which the Gentiles sacrifice, they sacrifice to devils, and not to God: and I would not that ye should have fellowship with devils. [21] Ye cannot drink the cup of the Lord, and the cup of devils: ye cannot be partakers of the Lord's table, and of the table of devils.[34]

---

31 Scardigli, *Die Goten*, p. 124.

32 Meli, *Alamannia Runica*, pp. 64–69.

33 Page, *An Introduction to English Runes*, p. 67; Düwel, *Runenkunde*, p. 198.

34 I Corinthians 10. 19–21: *The Bible*, ed. by Stirling, p. 181.

The difficulty in this group of verses lies in some complex concepts. In particular, since the Germans performed sacrifices in their pagan rites, few problems should have arisen in comprehension; it was more complicated to decode what the word 'idol' means. Finally, the idea of evil spirits must be explained. Here is the Greek version and the translation into Gothic:

> [19] τί οὖν φημι; ὅτι εἰδωλόθυτόν τί ἐστιν, ἢ ὅτι εἴδωλόν τί ἐστιν; [20] ἀλλ' ὅτι ἃ θύουσιν, δαιμονίοις καὶ οὐ θεῷ θύουσιν, οὐ θέλω δὲ ὑμᾶς κοινωνοὺς τῶν δαιμονίων γίνεσθαι. [21] οὐ δύνασθε ποτήριον κυρίου πίνειν καὶ ποτήριον δαιμονίων· οὐ δύνασθε τραπέζης κυρίου μετέχειν καὶ τραπέζης δαιμονίων.[35]
>
>> ([19] hva nu qiþam? þatei þo galiugaguda hva sijaina aiþþau þatei galiugam saljada hva sijai? [20] [ni þatei þo galiugaguda waihts sijaina,] ak þatei saljand þiudos, skohslam saljand, jan-ni guda. Ni wiljau auk izwis skohslam gadailans wairþan. [21] ni maguþ stikl fraujins drigkan jah stikl skohsle; ni maguþ biudis fraujins fairaihan jab-biudis skohsle.)[36]

The first problem comes from the compound noun εἰδωλόθῦτον ('sacrifice (to the idols)'). The Gothic language, like all other Germanic idioms, uses composite forms without difficulty, but in this case the translator prefers to ignore the word θῦτον ('sacrifice') and simply gives the word for 'idol' which in turn is a compound noun: *galiug-guþ. Galiug means 'lie', 'falsehood', and guþ, nominative plural in the text, is 'god', namely 'the false gods'. The solution adopted by Wulfila reflects the customs of pagan Germanic culture in which the veneration of the gods goes as far as the action of sacrifice even if we do not know whether the rites were made in the presence of an iconographical representation of a deity.[37] Idols and sacrifices are intimately linked in Germanic pagan practice; thus the overlap of meanings between 'idols' and 'sacrifice' is easily explicable.[38] Hence, the Gothic bishop uses the form for 'idol' intending 'sacrifice', also taking into account that the Greek word intimates the presence of both meanings. What is remarkable in Wulfila's translation is the neologism he adopted for 'idol', namely the compound *galiug-guþ. He uses the same kind of composition, *galiug* + noun for other words where the Greek text has the same structure, *ψεῦδος* + noun:[39]

---

35 I Corinthians 10. 19–21: *Novum Testamentum Graece*, ed. by Nestle and others, p. 457.

36 I Corinthians 10. 19–21: *Die gotische Bibel*, I, ed. by Streitberg, p. 263.

37 Simek, 'Opfer', pp. 311–13.

38 A good example can be found in a sermon delivered by the Anglo-Saxon Abbot Aelfric (c. 955–c. 1010) known as *De falsis diis* in which he used the expression *hǽðengyld*, literally 'tribute to the gods', namely 'sacrifice', to denote 'idols': Ælfric, *De Falsis Diis* XXI. 72, ed. by Pope, p. 680.

39 All forms compare here in the nominative singular case.

ψευδοαπόστολος	galiugaapaustaulus	false apostle	II Corinthians 11. 13
ψευδάδελφος	galiugabroþar	false brother	John 2. 4; II Corinthians 11. 26
ψευδοπροφήτης	galiugapraufetus	false prophet	Mark 13. 22; Luke 6. 26
ψευδόμαρτυρ	galiugaweitwoþs	false witness	I Corinthians 15. 15
ψευδόχριστος	galiugaxristus	false Christ	Mark 13. 22

Having adopted the technique of the linguistic calque, Wulfila expands it to include the translation for 'idols' as well, whenever the Greek language has the specific term εἴδωλόν:

εἴδωλόν	galiugaguþ

It should also be recalled that the letter 'a' at the end of the noun is the connecting vowel between the first and the second word of the compound. The presence of 'a' after a long-syllable word denotes that the composition is a new-coined word which did not exist before the translation of the Bible.[40] In this way, the Gothic translator creates and marks with the recurrent word *galiug-a-* something linked to falsehood and to the idols which are false deities, as many of the Goths could have seen in Roman and Greek statues and images, but also in their own old representations of the heathen gods.

The Gothic verb for 'to sacrifice' is *saljan*. It comes from the Indo-European root **sel-* ('to sell') which in Proto-Germanic languages has the causative meaning of 'to cause to take'. Therefore, it is very different in its semantic meaning from the Greek θύω ('I let smoke', consequently: 'I sacrifice'). The Germanic attitude pays attention to the relation with the recipient of the offering, while the Greek verb mentions the result of the sacrifice which is burnt for the beneficiary.[41] In this case, the translator uses his own lexical material, which is obviously understood by the audience.[42]

The last case to be examined in this passage by Paul has to do with the translation of the Greek δαιμόνιον ('devil'). The choice is for the word *skohsl*, which in Gothic translates δαίμον, δαιμόνιον, but the Gothic translator also uses *unhulþa* (masculine) and *unhulþo* (feminine) for the same Greek words. *Unhulþalo* likewise translates the Greek διάβολος and σατανᾶς, where the feminine is preferred in passages in which evil spirits are exposed to physical torments and possessions.[43] A similar meaning seems to be conveyed by the neuter noun

---

40 Kroesch, 'The Formation of Compound', p. 4.

41 Pokorny, *Indogermanisches etymologisches Wörterbuch*, I, '3. sel-', p. 899 and '4. dheu-', p. 262; Klein, *A Comprehensive Etymological Dictionary*, 'sell', p. 670.

42 The verb *saljan* is discussed by Üçok, *Über die Wortgruppen weltanschaulichen und religiösen Inhalts in der Bibelübersetzung Ulfilas*, pp. 71–72.

43 Üçok, *Über die Wortgruppen weltanschaulichen und religiösen Inhalts in der Bibelübersetzung Ulfilas*, p. 24.

skohsl. This word is less frequent than *unhulþa* (fifteen occurrences) or *unhulþo* (forty occurrences) as it is used only on three occasions, the first in Matthew 8. 28–31, where the demons coming out of the body of a possessed man ask Christ to send them into the bodies of pigs.[44] Moreover, *skohsl* appears as a gloss to the word *unhulþo* in Luke 8. 27 where the same episode is narrated. Finally, it occurs in the Epistle which we are analysing. Particularly thought-provoking is this gloss written in the Codex Argenteus, the invaluable manuscript probably copied in Ravenna during the reign of the Ostrogoth Theoderic in Italy (493–526).[45] In this case, the glossator wanted to create a link to the passage in Matthew in which *skohsl* is applied: he did not need *skohsl* as *interpretamentum* of the word *unhulþo*, easily understood by the Goths. *Unhulþs* and the correlated Teutonic forms were already in common use in the Germanic languages in religious contexts; without the negative prefix *un-*, it can denote a benevolent domestic spirit (see for instance Old High German *holdo* ('spirit', 'servant', 'friend').[46] With the prefix *un-* unclean spirits are designated, thus the frequency in use of the term is no surprise. On the other hand, the scarcity of occurrences for the word *skohsl* suggests a specific use, which can be retraced through its etymology. The Indo-European root is **skek-* ('to spring, to move quickly'), but only in Gothic does the word assume the meaning of 'fiend', 'demon', differing from the other Germanic forms, in which the common denotation is 'someone/something who/which springs or hurries' or similar situation of rapid motion.[47] References to the semantic field of ghosts and/or demons can be traced only in the Old Irish word *scāl* ('supernatural being', 'phantom').[48] The question is: why did the Gothic translator use this particular word in those

---

44 *Die gotische Bibel*, I, ed. by Streitberg, p. 15: '²⁸jah qimandin imma hindar marein in gauja Gairgaisaine, gamotidedun imma twai daimonarjos us hlaiwasnom rinnandans, sleidjai filu, swaswe ni mahta manna usleiþan þairh þana wig jainana. ²⁹ jah sai, hropidedun qiþandans: hva uns jah þus, Iesu, sunau gudis? qamt her faur mel balwjan unsis? ³⁰ Wasuh þan fairra im hairda sweine managaize haldana. ³¹ iþ þo skohsla bedun ina qiþandans: jabai uswairpis uns, uslaubei uns galeiþan in þo hairda sweine' (*The Bible*, ed. by Stirling, p. 14: '²⁸And when he was come to the other side into the country of the Gergesenes, there met him two possessed with devils, coming out of the tombs, exceeding fierce, so that no man might pass by that way. ²⁹And, behold, they cried out, saying, What have we to do with thee, Jesus, thou Son of God? art thou come hither to torment us before the time? ³⁰And there was a good way off from them and herd of many swine feeding. ³¹So the devils besought him, saying, If thou cast us out, suffer us to go away into the herd of swine').

45 The *Codex Argenteus* is a deluxe manuscript, which was probably in use in the palace's church of the Gothic court in Ravenna: Cavallo, 'La cultura scritta a Ravenna', p. 87; Munkhammar, *La Bibbia dei Goti*.

46 Feist, *Vergleichendes Wörterbuch der gotischen Sprache*, 'hulþs', p. 274.

47 Grienberger, 'Untersuchungen zur gotischen Wortkunde', 'skohsl', p. 190; Pokorny, *Indogermanisches etymologisches Wörterbuch*, 'skek-', pp. 922–23.

48 For a discussion of the Celtic words see Vendryès, *Lexique étimologique*, 'scāl', p. 30 and O'Brien, 'Varia', pp. 89–90.

two passages alone? Presumably, he wanted to convey a specific representation of this kind of demon, cited in Matthew's passage and in Paul's Epistle to the Corinthians. The distinctive aspect which *skohsl* should convey is that of uncontrolled and quick motion, which characterizes possessed bodies. In pagan times, this can be connected to the imagination of evil beings embodied by wild animals like wolves, and the same attitude was adopted by the Nordic *berserkir*.[49] The furious and unrestrained conduct of *berserkir* was also the consequence of ritual meals during which parts of wild animals (wolves and similar predators) were eaten in order to take on their qualities.[50] This kind of mutation, known as *berserkergang*, had particular corporeal manifestations. Howard Fabing, reporting the words of the nineteenth-century historian Peter Andreas Munch, gives this explanation:

> This fury, which was called berserkergang, occurred not only in the heat of battle, but also during laborious work. Men who were thus seized performed things which otherwise seemed impossible for human power. This condition is said to have begun with shivering, chattering of the teeth, and chill in the body, and then the face swelled and changed its colour. With this was connected a great hot-headedness, which at last gave over into a great rage, under which they howled as wild animals, bit the edge of their shields, and cut down everything they met without discriminating between friend or foe. When this condition ceased, a great dulling of the mind and feebleness followed, which could last for one or several days.[51]

No evidence of similar physical reactions and rites is known among the Goths, but the coincidence of uncontrolled motion of the body associated also with animals, which emerges from Matthew's episode, and the connection to a ceremonial meal (the ritual drinking alluded to by Paul) open the possibility to customs practised by pagans and easily identified by the audience. If this explanation is convincing, the use of the word *skohsl* instead of the more frequent *unhulþ-* reflects a conscious choice on the part of translators who thus convey a particular idea of evil whose connection to heathen behavioural patterns emerges clearly.

The examples which I have analysed, though they could be more copious, should sufficiently show the attention of the Gothic Bible's translators in rendering the Greek text, as they took into account the cultural background of the receptors of the translation.[52] The approach adopted by Wulfila and his team

---

49 De Vries, *Altgermanische Religionsgeschichte*, I, pp. 264–67; Chiesa Isnardi, *Storia e cultura della Scandinavia*, p. 170.

50 Literary examples have been collected by Chiesa Isnardi, *Storie e leggende del Nord*, pp. 136–38.

51 Fabing, 'On Going Berserk', p. 234. On the *berserkergang* cf. Høyersten, 'Berserkene', pp. 3247–50.

52 The use of the term 'receptor' in translation studies can be deduced from De Waard and Nida, *From One Language to Another*, pp. 33–34.

reveals the intention of having a final product which can be open to the understanding of the common people to be converted and to ensure the integrity of the recently adopted Christian faith. As far as possible, all cultural obstacles have to be removed and the translator facilitates comprehension of situations and value-systems alien to the Germanic tradition. The *modus operandi* of Wulfila is not that far from some instructions given during the second Vatican Council about the use of vernacular languages in the liturgy:

> 21. Especially in the translations intended for peoples recently brought to the Christian Faith, fidelity and exactness with respect to the original texts may themselves sometimes require that words already in current usage be employed in new ways, that new words or expressions be coined, that terms in the original text be transliterated or adapted to the pronunciation of the vernacular language.[53]

Thus, the problems of evangelizing the Germanic tribes in the fourth century were not so different from those of the current Catholic Church when it decided to translate sacred texts from Latin into vernacular languages. The concern of the Congregation for the Divine Worship, which delivered the rule for having texts which were both respectful of the original version but also comprehensible to people, was the same that animated the intentions of the Gothic translators. They searched for an equilibrium between fidelity to the orthodoxy of God's word and its transmission and comprehension in other cultural milieus. Moreover, the Goths had a special awareness of their mainly illiterate public, who received the texts through oral performances. The auditory finish of the translation was not a subordinate aspect, which interfered in the translation's choices, but over the course of the centuries, even the Gothic version of the Bible, originally conceived to be read aloud, became a text also intended for personal reading.

From Orality to Personal Reading

By the turn of the century, both Visigoths and Ostrogoths migrated from Eastern Europe to settle in France and Italy, respectively.[54] During this period, we have no mention of further translations or revisions of Wulfila's version, apart from a commentary on the Gospel of John known to scholars as *Skeireins*, which was likely produced during their settling in the area of the Eastern Roman Empire, as it is a translation from Greek into Gothic.[55] However, when they were in Western Europe, Latin writers immediately related the activity of the Gothic Arian clergy to the biblical texts. Salvian of Marseilles, in his *On the Government of God*, attacked the Visigothic Christians because they only

---

53 Congregation for the Divine Worship and the Discipline of the Sacraments, *Fifth Instruction*, II, 21.

54 Wolfram, *History of the Goths*, pp. 150–71 and 278–84.

55 Bennett, *The Gothic Commentary on the Gospel of John*.

knew what they heard from their priests and teachers.[56] Hence, the diffusion and evangelization of Christianity among the Goths still depended on oral teaching, confirming that illiteracy was the normal condition for the majority of the Germanic people. But Salvian also asserted that they read the sacred texts even if these were manipulated and corrupted by heresy. He was referring to the clergy who had an organization similar to the Orthodox Church: lecturers, deacons, priests, and bishops.[57] We know of a priests' community in Ravenna by the church of St Anastasia where a large number of them signed a deed of sale; one of them, named Wiljariþ, refers to himself as *bokareis*, or a copyist.[58] At the turn of the fifth century, in Ravenna, there was a bookshop managed by a Goth named Uiliaric, perhaps the same man who signed the deed.[59] During the Ostrogoth's Kingdom in Italy (489–553) many biblical manuscripts were copied, and parts of them have survived as palimpsests.[60] One of them, known as *Codex Carolinus*, now in Wolfenbüttel Library, has parallel texts: Gothic on the left and Latin on the right. It was probably used by an Arian community, perhaps in Verona where both languages were practised but – due to its position on the page – with a preference for Gothic.[61] These are years of immersive contact with Latin culture, which largely overrides the Greek influence on which the Bible's translation has depended.[62] In some Gothic cultural centres, namely Ravenna and Verona, the Bible text was studied and emended. So, the translation into Gothic of the Bible is a sort of work in progress, where the Greek text is compared with the Latin and Gothic versions without any passive or overly reverent attitude. In other words, the Gothic

---

56 'Barbari quippe homines, Romanae immo potius humanae eruditionis expertes, qui nihil omnino sciunt nisi quod a doctoribus suis audiunt, quod audiunt hoc sequuntur; ac sic necesse est eos, qui totius litteraturae ac scientiae ignari sacramentum diuinae legis doctrina magis quam lectione cognoscunt, doctrinam potius retinere quam legem'. Salvien de Marseille, *Du gouvernement de Dieu* V. II. 8, ed. by Lagarrigue, p. 316 ('The barbarians, indeed, lacking the Roman training or any other sort of civilized education, knowing nothing whatever unless they have heard it from their teachers, follow blindly what they hear. Such men, completely ignorant of literature and wisdom, are sure to learn the mysteries of the divine law through instruction rather than reading, and to retain their masters' doctrines rather than the law itself'; Salvian of Marseilles, *On the Government of God*, trans. by Sanford, p. 135).

57 About the ecclesiastical organization of the Arian clergy during the Germanic Kingdoms see Mathisen, 'Barbarian "Arian" Clergy', pp. 158–69.

58 Tjäder, *Die nichtliterarischen lateinischen Papyri Italiens aus der Zeit 445–700*, pp. 91–104; Zironi, *L'eredità dei Goti*, p. 27; Francovich Onesti, *I nomi degli Ostrogoti*, p. 362, 'Uiliaric' p. 364, 'Wiliarit', pp. 110–11.

59 Cavallo, 'La cultura scritta a Ravenna', pp. 84–86.

60 Stutz, 'Codices gotici', pp. 52–60; Zironi, *Il monastero longobardo di Bobbio*, pp. 53–68; Lo Monaco, 'De Fatis Palimpsestorum', pp. 53–62.

61 Falluomini, *Der sogenannte Codex Carolinus*, pp. 150–52.

62 Falluomini, *The Gothic Version of the Gospels*. pp. 101–12.

translation has the same dignity, and all three languages can help arrive at the correct interpretation of the sacred texts.[63] It is evident that the native speaking Gothic clergy involved in this kind of study was bilingual with Latin, and in some cases could also read Greek. This process of improvement on the Gothic version of the Bible is demonstrated by a preface written by Gothic grammarians during the Ostrogothic reign in Italy and attached to another manuscript, a Latin version of the Gospels, part of the *Vetus Latina* group known as the *Codex Brixianus*. Scholars agree in considering the *Brixianus* the Latin part of a Gothic-Latin bilingual transmission.[64] The Preface, even if it was not originally part of the manuscript, explains how the Gothic grammarians meant to proceed in their studies. This is their practice; they gloss the Gothic text with the term *wulþrs* when they see the necessity of creating a reference to a Greek or Latin form.[65] The result of this declaration of intent is evident in the *Brixianus*, where the Latin text contains *lectiones* from the *Vulgate* but also from the Gothic text.[66]

The example of the interest of Goth grammarians in the biblical text also reveals a transformation in the need for its translation into Gothic. When the Goths finally settled in Italy and France, their version of the Bible had become part of the Arian liturgy in countries in which many of the barbarians they met were already native Latin speakers or, more generally, in a condition of imperfect bilingualism (where Latin had obviously prevailed). Therefore, the necessity of having both Gothic and Latin texts for the liturgy arose, and this was the occasion to revisit not only the translation without compromising the word-order but also the Latin version, which could also be changed where the Gothic version was considered better than the Latin one. Hence, we can affirm that after a first pioneering phase characterized by the evangelization of the Goths, with all the implications of the particular strategies of oral communication, during the kingdoms of the Goths in Western Europe the role of the Gothic translation changed. It became a matter of philological speculation and eventually a personal relationship with the text; from general, widespread oral use to individual, personal reading.

The ensuing story of the Goths and their language can be briefly summarized; during the second half of the sixth century, the use of Gothic rapidly disappeared and the Arian church dissolved in the same years.[67] The Gothic language persisted in Italy until the year 680 with the Lombards, who are suspected of having used Gothic texts for Arian liturgies: the Lombards were Germanic speakers, so it seems likely that they would have privileged manuscripts

---

63 Zironi, 'La letteratura gotica', p. 43.

64 On the *Codex Brixianus* cf. Burkitt, 'The Vulgate Gospels and the "Codex Brixianus"', pp. 129–34.

65 Scardigli, *Die Goten*, p. 185; Botto, 'La "Praefatio" del "Codex Brixianus"'.

66 Francini, *Edizione sinottica del Vangelo*, pp. 17–19 and 254–55.

67 Zironi, *L'eredità dei Goti*, pp. 17–24 and 26–29.

translated into a Germanic language instead of Latin texts.[68] With the conversion to orthodoxy in 680 and the disappearance of the Lombard language by the latest in the very first decades of the eighth century, Gothic texts became useless and some of them were erased.[69] But other manuscripts must have survived. During the Carolingian age, between the very last years of the eighth century and the first half of the ninth century, an interest in Gothic texts grew among the scholars who surrounded Charlemagne, in particular those who were of Visigothic origin.[70] Following the cultural programme of the Emperor to support and increase the use of vernacular languages in connection with Christian rituals (such as baptism, daily prayers, homilies) some scholars looked back to the past Gothic experience.[71] The Gothic translation could be useful in the first attempts at translation into other Germanic languages, first and foremost into Old High German, the language of the Emperor. We know of examples of this intention thanks to two manuscripts, Vienna, Österreichische Nationalbibliothek, Cod. 795, fol. 20^{r-v} and Paris, Bibliothèque nationale de France, Cod. lat. 528, fol. 71^v, which contain notes for learning and pronouncing Gothic with examples taken from the translation of the Gospels.[72] In these cases, the Gothic translation has the role of an educational instrument for learning the language in order to correctly read and pronounce it. The Gothic translation is practised by the lone scholar, in a personal linguistic acquisition of a foreign language which will be useful for future translations from Latin into other vernacular idioms.

---

68 Scardigli, 'Appunti longobardi', pp. 93–94.

69 About the Lombard Arianism cf. Fanning, 'Lombard Arianism Reconsidered', pp. 241–58; Scardigli, 'Die drei Seelen der Langobarden', pp. 426–29; Pohl, 'Deliberate Ambiguity', pp. 53–58; Sergi, 'Dai Goti ai Longobardi', pp. 217–19.

70 Zironi, *L'eredità dei Goti*, pp. 70–75.

71 The bibliography on the Carolingian Renaissance is constantly expanding. As far as the liturgical use of vernacular languages is concerned, a good reference can be found in two volumes by McKitterick, *The Carolingians and the Written Word*, pp. 20–22 and *Charlemagne*, pp. 237–43 and Haubrichs, *Die Anfänge*, pp. 229–56. The interest in the Gothic language involved the cultural milieu, which had at its centre Charlemagne, with his strategy of connecting his political power to the most famous Germanic kingdom, namely, the Ostrogothic reign of Theoderic the Great. Together with the figure of Theoderic, the Gothic language was also rediscovered thanks to the prestige of the Goths and to their translation of the Bible which was still mentioned in some monastic educational texts. More specifically, Alcuin, Arno of Salzburg, and Theodulf of Orléans devoted particular attention to the Gothic language, the first of his linguistic interests. The second was in intimate contact with Alcuin and his experience in the monastery of St-Amand-les-Eaux allowed him to pay special attention to grammatical and rhetorical questions. The third, Theodulf of Orléans, of Visigothic origin, was the most famous of a large community of Visigothic scholars who took part in the intellectual life of Charlemagne's entourage. See Zironi, *L'eredità dei Goti*.

72 Zironi, *L'eredità dei Goti*, pp. 91–179.

Conclusion

The history of the Gothic translation of the Bible begins in the fourth century and continues until the Carolingian age, roughly 500 years, or half a millennium. I consider this lengthy period of time a good means for investigating in a larger sense how the same translation can change its role across the years. In late Antiquity and the early Middle Ages, the reasons for having a text translated generally relate to the demands of a community and thus take into account the widespread illiteracy of the people then living. Normally, a translation may be made to be orally declaimed and/or to be used in small communities of scholars and therefore destined for very restricted circulation. The case of the Gothic translation suggests another possibility, the modification of the function for the same translation when social and cultural conditions change, in particular with the abandonment of Arianism and the disappearing of Gothic-speaking communities. It is controversial to justify a possible usage of the translated text to evangelize other pagan Germanic-speaking peoples. It has been suggested that the Goths pursued missionary activities among barbarians, in particular those dwelling in Bavaria; some Bavarian words seem to be loanwords from Gothic terms, but the question is highly controversial.[73] Consequently, the translations of the Bible exhaust their liturgical function and become instrument for scholarly knowledge. When it comes to the influence of readers on translations, with regard to the early Middle Ages we have to stretch the idea of readership, to include also those who listened to the reading of a translated text. Finally, the boundary between reading and hearing must be obviated as personal and silent reading is an interior rehearsal of a text that becomes audible in our mind, as were the oral readings of the Bible for the first Christian communities of the Goths.

Bibliography

Primary Sources

Ælfric, *De falsis diis*, in *Homilies of Ælfric: A Supplementary Collection*, ed. by John C. Pope, Early English Text Society, 260 (London: Oxford University Press, 1967–68), II (1968), pp. 667–724

Ambrosiaster, *Commentaries on Romans and 1–2 Corinthians*, ed. and trans. by Gerald L. Bray, Ancient Christian Texts (Downers Groove, IL: IVP Academic, 2009)

---

[73] It was Friedrich Kluge, in 1909, who asserted the influence of the Gothic language on Bavarian due to Arian missions (Kluge, 'Gotische Lehnwörter im Althochdeutschen') and his opinion was particularly supported by scholars during the 1930s. In the following years, Kluge's arguments have been rebutted in many works: cf. Schäferdiek, 'Gab es eine gotisch-arianische Mission im süddeutschen Raum?'; and Stutz, 'Die germanistische These vom "Donauweg" gotisch-arianischer Missionare im 5. und 6. Jahrhundert'.

——, *Ambrosiastri qui dicitur Commentarius in Epistulas Paulinas, Pars II, In Epistula ad Corinthios*, ed. by Heinrich Joseph Vogels, Corpus Scriptorum Ecclesiasticorum Latinorum, 81/2 (Vienna: Hoelder – Pichler – Tempsky, 1968)

Auctor incertus (Vigilius Tapsensis?), *Epistola XX, sive, uti Corbeiensis codex aliique Mss. praeferunt, Collatio Beati Augustini cum Pascentio ariano, habita in domo Anicia Hippone-Regio, praesente Laurentio judice delecto a Pascentio viro spectabili (Altercatio Augustini cum Pascentio)*, ed. by Jacques-Paul Migne, Patrologiae Cursus Completus: Series Latina, 33 (Paris: Migne, 1865), cols 1156–62

The Bible: Authorized Version, ed. by John Stirling (London: British and Foreign Bible Society, 1962)

Die gotische Bibel, ed. by Wilhelm Streitberg†, with a supplement by Piergiuseppe Scardigli, 2 vols, 7th edn (Heidelberg: Universitätsverlag C. Winter, 2000), I

John Chrysostom, *Epistulae*, ed. by Jacques-Paul Migne, Patrologiae Cursus Completus: Series Graeca, 52 (Paris: Migne, 1862)

——, *Homiliae*, ed. by Jacques-Paul Migne, Patrologiae Cursus Completus: Series Graeca, 63 (Paris: Migne: 1862)

Novum Testamentum Graece, ed. by Eberhard Nestle and others, 26th edn (Stuttgart: Deutsche Bibelgesellschaft, 1979)

Patrum Nicaenorum nomina Latine, Graece, Coptice, Syriace, Arabice, Armeniace, ed. by Heinrich Gelzer and others, Scriptores sacri et profani, 2 (Leipzig: Teubner, 1898)

Philostorgius, *The Ecclesiastical History*, in *The Ecclesiastical History of Sozomen, Comprising a History of the Church, from A.D. 324 to A.D. 440, Also the Ecclesiastical History of Philostorgius, As Epitomized by Photius, Patriarch of Constantinople*, trans. by Edward Walford, Bohn's Ecclesiastical Library (London: Bohn, 1855), pp. 425–521

Salvien de Marseille, *Du gouvernement de Dieu*, ed. and trans. by Georges Lagarrigue, Sources Chrétiennes, 220: Œuvres, 2 (Paris: Editions du Cerf, 1975)

Salvian of Marseilles, *On the Government of God*, trans. by Eva M. Sanford (New York: Columbia University Press, 1930)

Theodoret of Cyrus, *The Ecclesiastical History*, trans. by Blomfield Jackson, in *A Select Library of Nicene and Post-Nicene Fathers of the Christian Church*, 2nd series, III: *Theodoret, Jerome, Gennadius, Rufinus: Historical Writings*, etc., ed. by Philip Schaff and Henry Wace (New York: The Christian Literature Company, 1892), pp. 33–159

Secondary Works

Bennett, William Holmes, *The Gothic Commentary on the Gospel of John: 'skeireins aiwaggeljons þairh iohannen': A Decipherment, Edition, and Translation*, The Modern Language Association of America, Monograph Series 21 (New York: Modern Language Association of America, 1960)

Botto, Fernando, 'La "Praefatio" del "Codex Brixianus"', *AION – Filologia germanica*, 19 (1976), pp. 143–61 (pt. 1); 20 (1977), pp. 133–49 (pt. 2); 21 (1978), pp. 137–49 (pt. 3)

Burkitt, Francis Crawford, 'The Vulgate Gospels and the "Codex Brixianus"', *Journal of Theological Studies*, 1 (1899), pp. 129–34

Cavallo, Guglielmo, 'La cultura scritta a Ravenna tra antichità tarda e alto medioevo', in *Ecclesiologia, cultura e arte*, ed. by Antonio Carile, Storia di Ravenna, 2: Dall'età bizantina all'età ottoniana, 2 (Venice: Marsilio, 1992), pp. 79–125

Chiesa Isnardi, Gianna, *Storia e cultura della Scandinavia: Uomini e mondi del Nord* (Milan: Bompiani, 2015)

———, *Storie e leggende del Nord* (Milan: Rusconi, 1977)

Corazza, Vittoria, *Le parole latine in gotico*, Atti della Accademia Nazionale dei Lincei: Memorie: Classe di Scienze morali, storiche e filologiche, 8/14, fasc. 1 (Rome: Accademia Nazionale dei Lincei, 1969)

De Vries, Jan, *Altgermanische Religionsgeschichte*, Grundriss der germanischen Philologie, 12, 3rd edn (Berlin: De Gruyter, 1970), I

De Waard, Jan and Eugene A. Nida, *From One Language to Another: Functional Equivalence in Bible Translating* (Nashville, TN: Nelson, 1986)

Dolcetti Corazza, Vittoria and Falluomini, Carla, *I Goti: Percorsi storici, letterari e linguistici*, Istituzioni e società, 26 (Spoleto: Fondazione centro di studi italiano sull'alto medioevo, 2020)

Dunphy, Graeme P., 'Oral Traditions', in *Early Germanic Literature and Culture*, ed. by Brian Murdoch and Malcom Read, Camden House History of German Literature, 1 (Rochester, NY: Camden House, 2004), pp. 103–18

Düwel, Klaus, *Runenkunde*, Sammlung Metzler, 72, 4th edn (Stuttgart: Metzler, 2008)

Fabing, Howard D., 'On Going Berserk: A Neurochemical Inquiry', *Scientific Monthly*, 83/5 (1956), pp. 232–37

Falluomini, Carla, *Der sogenannte Codex Carolinus von Wolfenbüttel (Codex Guelferbytanus 64 Weissenburgensis): Mit besonderer Berücksichtigung der gotisch-lateinischen Blätter (255, 256, 277, 280)*, Wolfenbütteler Mittelalter-Studien, 13 (Wiesbaden: Harrassowitz, 1999)

———, *The Gothic Version of the Gospels and Pauline Epistles: Cultural Background, Transmission and Character*, Arbeiten zur Neutestamentlichen Textforschung, 46 (Berlin: De Gruyter, 2015)

Fanning, Steven C., 'Lombard Arianism Reconsidered', *Speculum*, 56/2 (1981), pp. 241–58

Feist, Sigmund, *Vergleichendes Wörterbuch der gotischen Sprache mit Einschluss des Krimgotischen und sonstiger zerstreuter Überreste des Gotischen*, 3rd edn (Leiden: Brill, 1939)

Francini, Marusca, *Edizione sinottica del Vangelo di Giovanni in gotico del 'Codex Argenteus'* (Bergamo: Sestante Edizioni, 2009)

Francovich Onesti, Nicoletta, *I nomi degli Ostrogoti* (Florence: Firenze University Press, 2007)

Gheller, Viola, *'Identità' e 'arianesimo gotico': Genesi di un topos storiografico*, DiSCi: Storia antica, 4 (Bologna: Bononia University Press, 2017)

Grienberger, Theodor von, 'Untersuchungen zur gotischen Wortkunde', *Sitzungsberichte der kaiserlichen Akademie der Wissenschaften: Philosophisch-Historische Classe*, 142 (1900), pp. 1–272

Gros, Michel, 'Les Wisigoths et les liturgies occidentales', in *L'Europe héritière de l'Espagne wisigothique: Colloque international tenu à la Fondation Singer-Polignac (Paris, 14–16 mai 1990)*, ed. by Jacques Fontaine and Christine Pellistrandi (Madrid: Casa de Velázquez, 1992), pp. 125–35

Haubrichs, Wolfgang, *Die Anfänge: Versuche volkssprachiger Schriftlichkeit im frühen Mittelalter (ca. 700–1050/60)*, Geschichte der deutschen Literatur von den Anfängen bis zum Beginn der Neuzeit, 1: Von den Anfängen zum hohen Mittelalter, 2nd edn (Tübingen: Niemeyer, 1995)

Heather, Peter, *The Goths*, The People of Europe (Oxford: Blackwell, 1998)

Høyersten, Jon Geir, 'Berserkene – hva gikk det av dem?', *Tidsskrift den norske lageforening*, 24 (2004), pp. 3247–50

Klauser, Theodor, 'Der Übergang der römischen Kirche von der griechischen zur lateinischen Liturgiesprache', in *Miscellanea Giovanni Mercati, I, Bibbia, letteratura cristiana antica* (Vatican: Biblioteca Apostolica Vaticana, 1946), pp. 467–82

Klein, Ernest, *A Comprehensive Etymological Dictionary of the English Languages: Dealing With the Origin of Words and their Sense Development Thus Illustrating the History of Civilization and Culture*, 2 vols (Amsterdam: Elsevier Publishing Company, 1971)

Kluge, Friedrich, 'Gotische Lehnwörter im Althochdeutschen', *Beiträge zur Geschichte der deutschen Sprache und Literatur*, 35 (1909), pp. 124–60

Korobov, Maksim and Andrei Vinogradov, 'Gotische Graffito-Inschriften aus der Bergkrim', *Zeitschrift für deutsches Altertum*, 145 (2016), pp. 141–57

Kroesch, Samuel, 'The Formation of Compound Words in Gothic', *Modern Philology*, 5 (1908), pp. 377–82

Lo Monaco, Francesco, 'De Fatis Palimpsestorum Bibliothecae Sancti Columbani Bobiensis', in *El palimpsesto grecolatino como fenómeno librario y textual*, ed. by Ángel Escobar, Collección Actas Filología (Saragossa: Institución Fernando el Católico, 2006), pp. 53–62

Mathisen, Ralph W., 'Barbarian "Arian" Clergy, Church Organization, and Church Practices', in *Arianism: Roman Heresy and Barbarian Creed*, ed. by Guido M. Berndt and Roland Steinacher (Farnham: Ashgate, 2014), pp. 145–91

Mayer, Wendy, *The Homilies of St John Chrysostom – Provenance: Reshaping the Foundations*, Orientalia Christiana Analecta, 273 (Rome: Pontificio Istituto Orientale, 2005)

McKitterick, Rosamond, *The Carolingians and the Written Word* (Cambridge: Cambridge University Press, 1989)

——, *Charlemagne: The Formation of a European Identity* (Cambridge: Cambridge University Press, 2008)

Meli, Marcello, *Alamannia Runica: Rune e cultura nell'alto medioevo* (Verona: Libreria Universitaria Editrice, 1988)

Munkhammar, Lars, *La Bibbia dei Goti: Ravenna e Teoderico. Un antico manoscritto il 'Codex Argenteus'* (Ravenna: Longo, 2016)

O'Brien, Michael A., 'Varia', *Ériu*, 11 (1932), pp. 86–93

Ong, Walter J., *Orality and Literacy: The Technologizing of the Word*, New Accents (London: Methuen, 1982)

Page, Raymond I., *An Introduction to English Runes*, 2nd edn (Woodbridge: Boydell Press, 1999)

Petersen, Christian T., *Bibliografia Gotica Amplificata*, Gotica Minora, 5 ([Hanau]: Syllabus, s.d.)

Pohl, Walter, 'Deliberate Ambiguity: The Lombards and Christianity', in *Christianizing Peoples and Converting Individuals*, ed. by Guyda Armstrong and Ian N. Wood, International Medieval Research, 7 (Turnhout: Brepols, 2000), pp. 47–58

Pokorny, Julius, *Indogermanisches etymologisches Wörterbuch*, 2 vols, 4th edn (Basel: Francke, 2002), I

Restelli, Giuseppe, 'I più antichi imprestiti gotici del latino', in *Conoscenze etniche e rapporti di convivenza nell'antichità*, ed. by Marta Sordi, Contributi dell'Istituto di storia antica, 6: Scienze storiche, 21 (Milan: Vita e pensiero, 1979), pp. 229–46

Scardigli, Barbara and Piergiuseppe Scardigli, 'I rapporti fra Goti e Romani nel III e IV secolo', *Romanobarbarica*, 1 (1976), 261–95

Scardigli, Piergiuseppe, *Die Goten: Sprache und Kultur* (Munich: Beck, 1973)

——, 'Appunti longobardi', in *Filologia e critica: Studi in onore di Vittorio Santoli*, ed. by Paolo Chiarini, Carlo Alberto Mastrelli, Piergiuseppe Scardigli, and Luciano Zagari, I (Roma: Bulzoni, 1976), pp. 91–131; repr. in Piergiuseppe Scardigli, *Goti e Longobardi: studi di filologia germanica*, Studi e ricerche, 3 (Rome: Istituto italiano di studi germanici, 1987), pp. 191–246

——, 'Die drei Seelen der Langobarden: Eine Skizze', in *Germanische Religionsgeschichte: Quellen und Quellenprobleme*, ed. by Heinrich Beck, Ergänzungsbände zum Reallexikon der germanischen Altertumskunde, 5 (Berlin: De Gruyter, 1992), pp. 413–33

Schäferdiek, Knut, 'Germanenmission', in *Das Reallexikon für Antike und Christentum*, X, (Stuttgart: Hiersemann, 1950–), x (1978) cols 492–547

——, 'Gab es eine gotisch-arianische Mission im süddeutschen Raum?', *Zeitschrift für Bayerische Landesgeschichte*, 45 (1982), pp. 239–57

Sergi, Giuseppe, 'Dai Goti ai Longobardi: I segnali di cambiamento e il problema religioso', in *Il viaggio della fede: La cristianizzazione del Piemonte meridionale tra IV e VIII secolo: Atti del Convegno Alba, Bra, Cherasco, 10–12 dicembre 2010*, ed. by Silvia Lusuardi Siena, Bruno Taricco, and Edoardo Gautier di Confiengo (Alba: Carrù, 2013), pp. 229–39

Simek, Rudolf, 'Opfer', in Rudolf Simek, *Lexikon der germanischen Mythologie*, Kröners Taschenausgabe, 368 (Stuttgart: Kröner, 1984), pp. 311–13

Stutz, Elfriede, 'Codices gotici', in *Reallexikon der germanischen Altertumskunde*, ed. by Heinrich Beck, Dieter Geuenich, and Heiko Steuer (Berlin: De Gruyter, 1973–), v (1984), pp. 52–60

——, 'Die germanistische These vom "Donauweg" gotisch-arianischer Missionare im 5. und 6. Jahrhundert', in *Die Völker an der mittleren und unteren Donau im fünften und sechsten Jahrhundert*, Veröffentlichung der Kommission für Frühmittelalterforschung, 4 (Vienna: Österreichische Akademie der Wissenschaften, 1980), pp. 207–23

——, *Gotische Literaturdenkmäler*, Sammlung Metzler, 48 (Stuttgart: Metzler, 1966)

Sumruld, William A., *Augustine and the Arians: The Bishop of Hippo's Encounters with Ulfilan Arianism* (London: Associated University Presses, 1994)

Tiefenbach, Heinrich, 'Das wandalische "Domine miserere"', *Historische Sprachforschung*, 104 (1991), pp. 251–68

Tjäder, Jan-Olof, *Die nichtliterarischen lateinischen Papyri Italiens aus der Zeit 445–700: II (Papyri 29–55)*, Skrifter utgivna av Svenska Institutet i Rom, 19/2 (Stockholm: Åströms, 1982)

Üçok, Necip, *Über die Wortgruppen weltanschaulichen und religiösen Inhalts in der Bibelübersetzung Ulfilas* (Heidelberg: Winter, 1938)

Vendryès, Joseph, *Lexique étymologique de l'irlandais ancien, Lettres R-S* (Dublin: Institute for Advanced Studies; Paris: CNRS, 1974)

Vinogradov, Andrej and Maksim Korobov, 'Gotskie graffiti iz Mangupskoj baziliki', *Srednie veka* 76 (2015), pp. 57–75 ['ГОТСКИЕ ГРАФФИТИ ИЗ МАНГУПСКОЙ БАЗИЛИКИ', *Средние века*, 76 (2015)]

Vogel, Cyrille, *Introduction aux sources de l'histoire du culte chrétien au Moyen-Âge*, ed. by Bernard Botte, Biblioteca Studi Medievali, 1 (Spoleto: Centro italiano di studi sull'alto medioevo, 1975)

Wolfram, Herwig, *History of the Goths* (Berkeley, CA: University of California Press, 1990)

Zironi, Alessandro, *Il monastero longobardo di Bobbio: Crocevia di uomini, manoscritti e culture*, Istituzioni e società, 3 (Spoleto: Fondazione centro italiano di studi sull'alto medioevo, 2004)

———, *L'eredità dei Goti: Testi barbarici in età carolingia*, Istituzioni e società, 11 (Spoleto: Fondazione centro italiano di studi sull'alto medioevo, 2009)

———, 'La letteratura gotica', in *Le civiltà letterarie del Medioevo germanico*, ed. by Marco Battaglia, Manuali universitari, 183 (Rome: Carocci, 2017), pp. 31–54

———, 'The Evangelic Text As Translation and Interpretative Experience: The Paradigm of the Germanic Languages', in *The Garden of Crossing Paths: the Manipulation and Rewriting of Medieval Texts, Venice, October 28–30, 2004*, ed. by Marina Buzzoni and Massimiliano Bampi, Dipartimento di Scienze del Linguaggio, Atti, 1 (Venice: Cafoscarina, 2005), pp. 119–37

Websites

Congregation for the Divine Worship and the Discipline of the Sacraments, *Fifth Instruction 'For the Right Implementation of the Constitution on the Sacred Liturgy of the Second Vatican Council' (Sacrosantum Concilium, Art. 36), Liturgiam Authenticam: On the Use of Vernacular Languages in the Publication of the Books of the Roman Liturgy* (Vatican, 2001): online: <https://www.vatican.va/roman_curia/congregations/ccdds/documents/rc_con_ccdds_doc_20010507_liturgiam-authenticam_en.html> [accessed 3 November 2022]

Translating Latin in the Medieval North

Agnesar Saga and its Readership

Maria Teresa Ramandi

Independent scholar

'Translation rests on a paradox: while it arises from a recognition of difference, its aim is to replicate, to match form and substance in another language'.[1] Nevertheless, a translation, whether it is free or literal, always causes some sort of change in the transposition of the text from source language into target language, with the inevitable loss of subtle meanings and nuances. This happens because a translation is never just a language translation: it is simultaneously a cultural translation, in which the text written within the culture of the source language is adapted (whether deliberately or unconsciously) by the translator, acting as a filter, into the culture of the target audience. The process of translation is also never objective, as it is influenced by the translator's personal knowledge of the language and culture he is translating and also by his time and by his aim. When reading a translation, one therefore needs to be aware that one is not looking exactly at the original text, but instead at a reflection of it after it has passed through the translator's mind, rather like looking at something through a kaleidoscope or a coloured lens. Obviously, one can be aware of the translator's choices only if the source text is still available to allow comparison with its translation. Unfortunately, though, in most cases the texts used by medieval translators have not survived. And this is particularly true for most of the medieval translated literature in Old Norse-Icelandic, especially that translated from Latin. In fact, very little medieval material in Latin survives to the present day in Iceland, despite the fact that Icelandic medieval libraries must have been well-stocked with books in Latin, as we learn from church inventories.[2] A large part of the corpus of Icelandic literature translated from Latin consists of the sagas of many of the numerous foreign saints, whose cults were introduced to Iceland in the period after the official conversion to Christianity (AD 1000).[3] The

---

1 Copeland, 'The Fortunes of "non verbum pro verbo"', p. 17.

2 Cf. Olmer, *Boksamlingar på Island, 1179–1490*.

3 *Heilagra Manna Søgur*, ed. by Unger, is still the most comprehensive edition of the corpus, although it is now a bit outdated. More recent editions of single manuscripts or of single lives are slowly becoming available. See, for instance, the facsimile editions *Lives of the Saints, Perg. fol. nr. 2, in the Royal Library, Stockholm*, ed. by

exact date when these saints' lives were translated is unknown, and although some fragments preserving them are amongst the oldest remnants of Old Norse-Icelandic literature, the palaeographic evidence alone is not enough to date the actual original translations with precision, as the oldest manuscripts may not have survived.[4] Nevertheless, the existence of such old manuscripts proves that translations of saints' lives were already circulating in the mid-twelfth century. This impression is confirmed by the *First Grammatical Treatise* (*FGT*), which lists among the extant literature of the time, *þýðingar helgar* ('sacred translations'), probably including saints' lives as well.[5] This means that by the time the *FGT* was written (*c.* 1150), translated saints' lives were an established genre. It does not come as a surprise that translations of hagiographies and other religious works were among the first literary works to be produced in Icelandic; in fact, they were probably needed to establish the principles of the Christian faith and present suitable moral models to follow, even amongst people who did not know Latin. Moreover, it seems probable that the early twelfth century was a fertile time to start doing this: Iceland had by this time been Christian for a hundred years and, more importantly, a class of Icelanders learned in Latin was developing following the establishment of the first schools in Iceland during the previous century.

The average student of such schools usually belonged to the wealthiest families of the country; in fact, since the conversion, it was mostly men of high rank who were educated and ordained priests. The only chance for poorer people to study was if they were economically supported by a rich farmer.[6] This could happen if a farmer was in need of a priest for the church in his homestead, in which case, he could choose to have a person taught for this purpose, but, as is

---

Foote, and *Codex Scardensis*, ed. by Slay; the edition of Copenhagen, Det Arnamagnæanske Institut, AM 429 12mo, in *A Female Legendary from Iceland*, ed. by Wolf; the edition of the *Saga heilagrar Önnu*, of *The Old-Norse Icelandic Legend of Saint Barbara*, and of *The Icelandic Legend of Saint Dorothy*, all ed. by Wolf; the edition by Van Deusen, 'The Old Norse-Icelandic Legend of Saints Mary Magdalene and Martha'. The most complete analysis of the cult of saints in Iceland is found in Cormack, *The Saints in Iceland*. A useful and up-to-date instrument for navigating the extant scholarship about Old Norse prose saints' lives is Wolf, *The Legends of the Saints in Old Norse-Icelandic Prose*.

4 The oldest extant manuscript preserving saints' lives, AM 655 4to IX, dates to 1150 and contains *Plácidús saga*, *Blasíus saga* and *Mattheus saga postola* (Bekker-Nielsen, 'On a Handlist of Saints' Lives in Old Norse', p. 323).

5 *The First Grammatical Treatise*, ed. by Benediktsson, p. 208.

6 An alternative would be to enter the religious life in a cloister, as Laurence is said to have taught many students, both the sons of rich men and of poor, in *Laurentius saga* (*Biskupa sögur*, III, ed. by Grímsdóttir, p. 318). On the other hand, in Denmark and Sweden, at least in the late Middle Ages, there were town schools – institutions founded by the city councils but funded by the church as well – which provided an elementary education (reading, writing, and basic arithmetic) for the ordinary children of the town (Bagge, 'Education', p. 153).

stated in *Grágás*, he was bound to provide him with education, fostering, vestments, and books for his profession if no other agreement had been made with the family of the priest in training.[7] From the same law we learn that there was no standard age to be put to school and that students could start even after the age of sixteen. Furthermore, Latin was represented as the core of the education of a priest but also as a difficult skill to acquire. In fact, if the priest in training disliked studying it, he was to be put to other work. Additionally, the frequent shortages of priests in Iceland may have led to the accelerated training of some of them – maybe by the former priest of the church which they were going to be put in charge of –, with very little or no emphasis given to Latin, so that they could be ordained priests as soon as possible.[8] This would explain why many priests were barely able to read Latin, as the future Bishop Laurence, acting as a *visitator* in Iceland on behalf of the archbishop of Níðaros, discovered during his inspection of Icelandic priests.[9] In addition to illiterate priests, the majority of lay people – with the possible exception of a handful of wealthy laymen who were educated and had travelled abroad – had very limited or no knowledge of Latin.[10] Consequently, the only way to make relevant Latin texts available to the wider audience was to translate them into the vernacular. Given that religion played a central part in medieval society, even in Iceland, and that the learned men able to translate were usually clerics, it is unsurprising that many of the texts selected for translation from Latin were religious works, of which a large part consisted of saints' lives. Indeed, such translations were considered edifying for the soul, as well as providing a helpful instrument that illiterate priests could use to prepare their sermons or to read on a specific saint's feast day.

---

7 *Grágás*, ed. by Finsen, pp. 17–18.

8 A survey carried out by Bishop Páll Jónsson reveals that, in his day, Iceland needed 290 priests for its 220 churches (*Biskupa sögur*, II, ed. by Egilsdóttir, p. 313).

9 *Biskupa sögur*, III, ed. by Grímsdóttir, p. 273.

10 *Grágás* states that every man and woman must know the *Pater Noster* and the *Credo in Deum*, otherwise they could be sentenced to lesser outlawry (*Grágás*, ed. by Finsen, p. 7). However, even if we allow that ordinary people understood the actual meaning of the words in those prayers, their knowledge of Latin probably did not go much beyond that. As for women, little is known about their education. From the scanty evidence in the sources, it seems that at least women belonging to wealthy families were educated, probably at home. An example is Halla, Bishop Páll's daughter, who was said to be skilled 'verknaði ok bókfræði', that is 'in working and book-knowledge' (*Biskupa sögur*, II, ed. by Egilsdóttir, p. 316). Nonetheless, some women did attend schools and studied together with men, as the case of Ingunn shows: according to *Jóns saga Helga*, she was a young woman who studied and then taught *grammatica* in the school at Hólar, proving to be second to none in book learning and turning many people into good scholars thanks to her teachings. She read numerous books in Latin and used to let her students read while she was embroidering the lives of the saints (*Biskupa sögur*, I, ed. by Steingrímsson, Halldórsson, and Foote, pp. 219–20). Furthermore, it is highly likely that nuns received an education too, cf. Sigurðardóttir, *Allt hafði annan róm aður í páfadóm*, p. 52.

Moreover, translated saints' lives functioned as models for the Icelanders to write down their own literature. In fact, as Turville-Petre remarks, 'it is unlikely that the sagas of kings and of Icelanders, or even the sagas of ancient heroes, would have developed as they did unless several generations of Icelanders had first been trained in hagiographical narrative'.[11] Therefore, we should 'look upon the translators of the oldest period as founders, but of course not the only founders, of Old Norse prose'.[12]

In light of such comments, the present work will be devoted to the analysis of one of these translated saints' lives, namely *Agnesar saga*, the Old Norse-Icelandic translation of the Latin legend of St Agnes.

From Rome to Iceland: The Legend of St Agnes

St Agnes, whose name comes from the Greek ἁγνή meaning 'pure, chaste', was a Roman martyr who is presumed to have lived between the third and the fourth century. As is the case with many other early Christian martyrs, her story, although recorded in literary sources, is shrouded in legend. It is therefore difficult, if not impossible, to place her within a precise timeframe. Even the date of her martyrdom is uncertain, although traditionally it is thought to have happened on 21 January, which therefore became her feast day. As for the year, it is likely she was executed during the great persecutions against Christians perpetrated by Emperor Diocletian in the year 304, when so many Christians were killed after innumerable tortures that that period became known as 'the martyrs' age'.[13]

It has been claimed that Agnes was the first female saint to be venerated in Rome and that she was one of the earliest holy women to have a substantial cult throughout the empire.[14] Whether this is true or not, what is certain is that in Rome, her cult is proven to be relatively ancient and an interest in her is attested as early as the fourth century, with her name recorded in the earliest Roman calendar, the mid-fourth century *Depositio Martyrum*, which also attests to the celebration of her feast day at the Nomentana site along with twenty-three other

---

11 Turville-Petre, *Origins of Icelandic Literature*, p. 142.

12 Bekker-Nielsen, 'On a Handlist of Saints' Lives in Old Norse', p. 328.

13 In March 304, in fact, Emperor Diocletian issued an edict stipulating that all Christians within the Roman Empire must sacrifice to the Roman gods, which paved the way to a more intense hunt for Christians (Frutaz, *Il complesso monumentale di Sant'Agnese*, p. 20). There are, however, scholars who suggest that Agnes' martyrdom instead took place during the persecutions carried out by Valerian in 256/7, on the grounds that Aspasius, the man who acted as judge in Agnes' trial, might conceivably be identified as Aspasius Paternus, the judge who exiled Cyprian of Carthage during the Valerianic persecutions (Jones, 'Agnes and Constantia', p. 132).

14 Grig, *Making Martyrs in Late Antiquity*, p. 80.

martyrs.[15] Dating to the same century are the Constantinian basilica of St Agnes together with the adjacent mausoleum of St Constance on the Nomentana, which was erected by Emperor Constantine's daughter, Constantina, on the site of St Agnes' grave, thus inevitably strengthening the link between the Nomentana area and the cult of St Agnes.[16] Agnes' cult in Rome was so strong, and also so embedded in the geography of the city, that by the eighth century, a second cult site connected to Agnes had been established within the city walls. This was located in the very spot where it was believed that the brothel where Agnes had been kept was, near the stadium of Domitian (now Piazza Navona), where the church of Sant'Agnese in Agone now stands.[17] Obviously, as Grig remarks, the intercessory power of a saint plays an extremely important role in the cult of saints: the more the saint is considered to be a good intercessor before God, the more he or she is venerated; and certainly, the fact that Agnes possessed the double virtue of being both a virgin and a martyr made her appear an extremely powerful intercessor in the eyes of the believer.[18] Soon her cult spread beyond Rome and Agnes became one of the most venerated female saints in the Christian world. Undoubtedly, the circulation of her legend, which depicted her as a powerful intercessor, significantly contributed to the diffusion and strengthening of her cult.

The legend of St Agnes comes to us in several variants, thus testifying to the fact that the oldest accounts were probably derived from varying, initially oral traditions.[19] The oldest account telling her story is an epitaph by Pope Damasus (366–84) engraved on the paving of St Agnes' basilica in Rome. Not much later than Damasus's epitaph, in 377, Ambrose, bishop of Milan (374–97), composed the *De Virginibus*, a work of exhortation to virginity in three books. One of the examples of virginity presented to the reader in the first book is that of St Agnes.

---

15 Jones, 'Agnes and Constantia', p. 121. The *Depositio martyrum* was published in 354, although it had probably existed since the 330s (Salzman, *On Roman Time*, p. 1990). Agnes' name is also recorded in the *Martyrologium Hieronymianum* (c. sixth century, but based on fifth-century martyrologies), which provides no further information than her feast day (Jones, 'Agnes and Constantia', p. 122).

16 The complex of buildings on the Via Nomentana (St Agnes' basilica and St Constance's mausoleum), now known as Saint Agnes Outside the Walls, was built on land owned by the imperial family, but it has been suggested that, at some point before this land was purchased, it must already have been used as the site for what was believed to be Agnes' grave (Jones, 'Agnes and Constantia', p. 121). Indeed, the site was the location of two sets of catacombs, dating respectively to the second century and to the late third or early fourth century, and it was thought that Agnes' original grave was located in the latter set (Phillips, 'Materials for the Study of the Cult of St Agnes of Rome in Anglo-Saxon England', p. 252).

17 Grig, 'The Paradoxical Body of St Agnes', p. 111. The extant church of Sant'Agnese in Agone, where St Agnes' skull now rests, was built only in the second half of the seventeenth century and is mostly the work of Francesco Borromini (1599–1667). However, it is believed that it stands on the site of an older chapel dedicated to St Agnes.

18 Grig, *Making Martyrs in Late Antiquity*, p. 84.

19 Grig, 'The Paradoxical Body of St Agnes', p. 113.

Agnes is additionally the subject of another work, the fourth-century hymn *Agnes beatae virginis*, which is also attributed to Ambrose of Milan.[20] Ambrose was in all probability known to the Christian poet Prudentius (*c.* 348–413), who seems to have used his works as a source for his elaboration of Agnes' legend in *Peristephanon* XIV.[21] All of these texts were shadowed by a prose legend, the *Passio Agnetis*, composed at the beginning of the sixth century by an anonymous author for convenience identified as Pseudo-Ambrose, which enjoyed a larger diffusion and soon became the main reference for Agnes' story.[22]

The *Passio Agnetis* (*BHL* 156) eventually also reached the westernmost outpost of medieval Christianity, Iceland, where it was translated into the vernacular and became known as *Agnesar saga*.[23] Due to the scantiness of surviving Icelandic manuscripts in Latin, it is difficult to ascertain whether other works about St Agnes circulated in Iceland. It seems, however, that Ambrose's sermon (*BHL* 158c) and Maximus of Turin's sermon (*BHL* 158a), whose inclusion in Paul the Deacon's homily book assured them a wide circulation in the Middle Ages, were also known in Iceland, and indeed they feature in an Icelandic lectionary in Latin from the mid-thirteenth or mid-fourteenth century, the Oslo, Riksarkivet, Lat. Fragm. 678.[24] The *Legenda aurea* by Jacobus de Voragine reached Iceland too, although it is unclear exactly when – the inventory made for Bishop Jón Þorkelsson Vídalín (1666–1700) in 1704 reveals that the cathedral library at Skálholt possessed three printed copies of the *Historia Lombardica*.[25]

---

20 *De S. Agnete*, ed. by Migne, PL 17, cols 1210–11. The attribution of this hymn to Ambrose has been questioned by Franchi de' Cavalieri, *S. Agnese nella tradizione e nella leggenda*, p. 6, on the ground of the discrepancy between the hymn and the prose account given in the *De Virginibus* (cf. *S. Ambrosii De Virginibus*, ed. by Geyer and Zellinger).

21 As with Ambrose the story of St Agnes was taken outside Rome. With Prudentius, a native of Northern Spain, we have confirmation that Agnes was already renowned outside Italy, in the outer part of the Roman Empire.

22 The *Passio Agnetis*, *Bibliotheca Hagiographica Latina Antiquae et Mediae Aetatis* (henceforth *BHL*), 156.

23 Widding, Bekker-Nielsen, and Shook, 'The Lives of the Saints in Old Norse Prose', p. 298 identified in their hand-list *Agnesar saga* as a translation of *BHL* 156. But in fact Unger, in his edition of *HMS*, had already realized that it was a translation of the Pseudo-Ambrosian *Passio Agnetis* (*BHL* 156) as it was edited by Surius in his *De probatis sanctorum historiis* (*Vita sanctae virginis et martyris Agnetis*, ed. by Surius, pp. 507–11). Later, Foote, *Lives of the Saints*, p. 27 suggested that it was a translation of 'the Pseudo-Ambrosian Passio, *BHL* 156, in a version closer to that printed in *Acta Sanctorum* Jan. II 715–18 than in Migne, PL 17, cols 813–21', but 'PL extant Icelandic text is slightly abridged, and the epilogue is omitted'. Wolf agrees with Foote (*A Female Legendary from Iceland*, ed. by Wolf, p. 40 and *The Legends of the Saints in Old Norse-Icelandic Prose*, p. 20).

24 Dr Astrid Marner, University of Bergen, personal communication.

25 Kalinke, *The Book of Reykjahólar*, p. 34. The *Legenda aurea* was commonly known as *Historia Lombardica*.

The fact that it was not translated into Icelandic, despite its popularity, leads one to think that it arrived when most of the saints' lives had already been translated into vernacular from earlier sources. Therefore, *BHL* 156 remains the only known text about St Agnes to have been translated into Old Norse. When exactly *BHL* 156 arrived in Iceland cannot be determined with certainty, nor can the date of its translation. However, given Agnes' importance in the Western Church, it seems plausible to imagine that her Latin legend might have been included in the books that the foreign missionary bishops must have brought with them to Iceland in the period after the official conversion in order to teach the foundations of Christianity and to train local priests. Moreover, taking into account that at this time, being educated meant receiving a clerical education, it seems reasonable to suggest that the first Icelanders who went to study abroad must have become acquainted with the *Passio Agnetis* in the course of their studies.[26] Certainly in most monastic institutions, saints' lives were usually read at meal times, for the commemoration at chapter of a particular saint, and as part of the Night Office on a saint's feast day, in addition to being regarded as suitable material for personal devotion.[27] It is, however, highly likely that knowledge of the legend of St Agnes at this early stage remained limited solely to the most learned clergy who were able to access texts in Latin, and indeed there is no evidence of the contrary.

The first concrete evidence of interest in St Agnes in Iceland appears in 1179, when her feast day was made a holy day of obligation by Bishop Þorlákr Þórhallsson of Skálholt (1178–93), along with those of St Ambrose (7 December) and St Cecilia (22 November).[28] This event is recounted both in *Þorláks saga*[29] and in *Guðmundar saga*,[30] although the latter dwells in more detail on the circumstances

---

26 The first Icelander who is known to have been educated abroad after the conversion is Ísleifr Gizurarson, the first Icelandic bishop. His son, Gizurr, like his father, was sent to study at Herford in Westfalia. And it seems it was common practice among the wealthiest Icelandic families to send their offspring to be educated abroad. Even when good centres of learning were established in Iceland, still many went abroad to complete their studies at universities or other major centres of culture. According to what the sagas relate, among the most popular destinations were France, especially Paris, and England. For instance, Jón Ǫgmundarson, in his youth, before being consecrated bishop, travelled firstly to Norway and Denmark, and then down to Rome (ÍF XVb, p. 184). St Þorlákr stayed in Paris until he acquired all the knowledge he wanted, and thereafter he moved to Lincoln in England, where he was able to further increase his learning (*Biskupa sögur*, II, ed. by Egilsdóttir, p. 52). And his nephew, Bishop Páll Jónsson, also studied in England (*Biskupa sögur*, II, ed. by Egilsdóttir, p. 298).

27 Lapidge, 'Editing Hagiography', pp. 240–41.

28 Holy days of obligation (*löghelgir dagar*) were days on which the faithful were obliged to attend mass and abstain from work. As a holy day of obligation, Agnes' feast day features in the list of obligatory feasts (about three dozen) provided in calendar order in the Christian Laws section of *Grágás*, ed. by Finsen, p. 30.

29 *Biskupa sögur*, II, ed. by Egilsdóttir, p. 181.

30 *Guðmundar sögur biskups*, ed. by Karlsson.

of this measure by presenting the bishop's decision as a consequence of his learning that St Agnes and God had appeared in a vision to one Guðmundr Kárhǫfði. It is not unlikely that in the attempt to promote the cult of these three saints, Bishop Þorlákr also had their Latin legends translated into Icelandic, so that he had material available in the vernacular to read in church or to facilitate the less learned clergymen in the preparation of homilies on the occasion of these saints' feast days. Indeed, it is not impossible to imagine that the bishop himself translated some of the texts. In addition to being fluent in Latin, thanks to his years spent studying abroad, we learn from *Þorláks saga* that Þorlákr was always busy writing holy books, after the example of the Apostle Paul, who said in an epistle that he only wrote things which it is was most necessary to read and to know.[31]

As part of his efforts to promote her cult, Þorlákr possibly chose Agnes as one of the patron saints of the church at Bær in Borgarfjörður, which he himself consecrated.[32] The *máldagar* tell us that she was also co-patron in the church at Þerney, not too far from Bær, along with Sts Mary, James, Nicholas, Þorlákr, and Mary Magdalene.[33] Other places which seem to have had an interest in the saint were the church of Miðbæli under Eyjafjöll, which owned a copy of *Agnesar saga*, and the convent at Kirkjubær, which counted among its possessions an image of St Agnes.[34] All these places are located in southwest Iceland, within the diocese of Skálholt.[35] There is no information about the status of Agnes' cult in the diocese of Hólar, so there is no way to know whether her feast day was ever a holy day of obligation there.[36] Nonetheless, the fact that her feast is listed in *Grágás* among the obligatory feasts enables us to think that it was.[37] From the distribution of the churches dedicated to her and of the places owning her saga or image, it seems that her cult was concentrated in the southwestern part of the country. Even then, however, it is unclear whether Agnes' cult ever actually became popular among believers even within the diocese of Skálholt, or whether it survived after Þorlákr's episcopacy. The fact that there is no evidence of the name Agnes among lay people, when other female saints' names were widely used, probably means that she was not so popular.[38] As a further

---

31 *Biskupa sögur*, II, ed. by Egilsdóttir, p. 161.

32 Cormack, *The Saints in Iceland*, p. 75.

33 Cormack, *The Saints in Iceland*, p. 75.

34 Cormack, *The Saints in Iceland*, p. 75.

35 Iceland was divided into two dioceses, Hólar in the North and Skálholt in the South.

36 Cormack, 'Saints of Medieval Hólar', pp. 7–37.

37 Cormack, *The Saints in Iceland*, p. xix and p. 19, claims that, as the bishop of Hólar had not been present at the Althing in 1275, the older Christian law continued to be in use in the northern diocese up to 1354, whereas at Skálholt it was replaced by new regulations in 1275.

38 The name *Cecilía*, for instance, is widely attested since as early as the twelfth century (Cormack, *The Saints in Iceland*, p. 88). Another popular name was *Margrét*, after

confirmation of the low popularity of her cult, less than a hundred years later, in 1275, Bishop Árni Þorláksson of Skálholt issued new regulations for the churches in his diocese, according to which the feasts of St Agnes, Ambrose, and other less popular saints were omitted from the holy days of obligation.[39]

Despite the apparently low popularity of St Agnes' cult, however, manuscript evidence shows that not only did the text of *Agnesar saga* keep being copied years after her feast day was removed from the holy days of obligation, but it was also revised, expanded, or abridged to suit different purposes and audiences, so that it is appropriate to distinguish between four different redactions of the saga, rather than talking of just one text.

Agnesar saga has been handed down to us in seven Icelandic manuscripts: Copenhagen, Det Arnamagnæanske Institut, AM 238 fol. I (*c.* 1300), AM 238 fol. II (*c.* 1300–50), AM 233a fol. (*c.* 1350–75), AM 235 fol. (*c.* 1400), Stock. Perg. 2. fol. (*c.* 1425–45), AM 238 fol. XV (*c.* 1450–1500), and AM 429 12mo (*c.* 1500).[40] Unfortunately, most of these manuscripts preserve the saga only in a fragmentary form, with the exception of AM 429 12mo, where the saga is preserved in its entirety.

Four different redactions of *Agnesar saga* can be identified: *Agnesar saga meyjar I* (AM 238 I fol., AM 235 fol., Stock. Perg. 2 fol., AM 429 12mo), *Agnesar saga meyjar II* (AM 233a fol.), *Agnesar saga meyjar III* (AM 238 XV fol.), and *Agnesar saga meyjar IV* (AM 238 II fol.).[41] The identification of different redactions of the saga is mainly based on a comparison of its final section in the various manuscripts, which is in a majority of cases the only surviving section of the text, and on its degree of fidelity to the Latin source. Redaction II, III, and IV are not independent translations of the Latin *Passio*, but merely rewritings by means of abridgement or expansion of the text of *Agnesar saga meyjar I*, which represents the closest redaction to what must have been the original translation of the Latin legend of St Agnes. *Agnesar saga meyjar I* is also the only redaction whose text has been preserved in full, at least in one manuscript, AM 429, paradoxically the latest one.

A comparison with the *Passio Agnetis*, the Latin legend of St Agnes, shows how the Icelandic translation was a close rendering of its Latin source, without however being a strict word-for-word translation moulded on the sentence structure and grammar of the source text. It is also evident that the original translator translated rather closely from the original, without omitting long sections of text. The only main difference between the Latin text and the Norse translation lies in the conclusion. Whereas the Latin text ends with a long epilogue featuring the name of Ambrose, who tells the reader that he found the story of St Agnes

---

St Margaret of Antioch, which is attested for the first time in the mid-twelfth century and very frequently thereafter (Cormack, *The Saints in Iceland*, p. 122).

39 Cormack, *The Saints in Iceland*, p. 75.

40 These manuscripts are all collections of saints' lives.

41 For a detailed discussion on the classification of the redactions of *Agnesar saga*, see Ramandi, 'Reassessing "Agnesar saga"', pp. 91–119.

in some 'concealed volumes', to enhance the authenticity of the *Passio*, the Norse translation instead ends with a brief doxological formula. The absence of the Ambrosian epilogue has generally been seen as an abridgment or omission – allegedly by the Icelandic translator.[42] However, recent studies on the Latin legend carried out by Lanéry show that, although the Ambrosian epilogue figures in the oldest manuscripts of the *Passio*, it is absent in many manuscripts dating from after the end of the ninth century (with particular frequency in legendaries dating from between the eleventh and the thirteenth centuries) and linked to certain areas.[43] Some of these manuscripts lacking the Ambrosian epilogue end just with *palmam acquirant*; others instead add a short doxological formula to the end of the *Passio*, often in the form 'martyrizata est autem beatissima Agnes virgo Dei apud urbem Romam die XII kal. Febr. sub Simpronio prefecto regnante. Amen' or 'per Deum dominum nostrum qui vivit et regnat in unitate spiritus sancti per omnia saecula saeculorum. Amen' (cf. *BHL* 156a), the latter being very similar to that in the Norse translation ('fyrir dróttin várn Jesum Kristum, þann er lífir ok ríkir með feðr ok helgum anda, guð um allar alldir verallda. Amen'). In the light of this, it is probably more correct to assume that the version on which our translator was working did not have the Ambrosian epilogue in the first place but must have ended with a doxological formula, as in the *recensio* of the *Passio* represented by *BHL* 156a.

Clearly, the translator always had in mind his audience, prioritizing a general understanding over fanciness of style, and taking the greatest care to render the source text as clearly and naturally as possible in the target language. This includes avoiding untranslated Latin terms in the target text and occasionally leaving out elements for which there was no corresponding word in Old Norse or which would not be particularly clear without a further explanation disrupting the narrative. This is the case, for instance, with the following sentence:

> Cumque pater diceret, in fascibus constitutum se praefecturam agere, et idcirco sibi, quamvis illustrissimum, minime debere praeferre.
>
> > (However, the father said that, appointed *in fasces*, he held the prefecture, and therefore [no one], even if the most illustrious [man] ought to be preferred to him in the smallest degree.)

The sentence was completely omitted in the Norse translation probably because its content would not be easily understandable by his audience, not too familiar with Roman offices and customs, and it would be difficult to render in Norse.

In other cases, in the translation, the Icelandic translator tries to use words or concepts more familiar to his audience, hence, for instance, the Roman god-

---

42 See *Lives of the Saints*, ed. by Foote, p. 27 and *A Female Legendary from Iceland*, ed. by Wolf.

43 As the *recensio* of the *Passio Agnetis* without the Ambrosian epilogue is well attested in several manuscripts, it is now classified (since 1986) as *BHL* 156a, in order to distinguish it from *BHL* 156, which contains the epilogue (Lanéry, *Ambroise de Milan Hagiographe*, p. 350).

dess Vesta undergoes the process identified by Mattias Tveitane as *interpretatio norræna*, becoming the Norse goddess Gefjon.[44] The translation of Roman gods and goddesses into Norse ones is not limited to *Agnesar saga* but recurs in most of the translated sagas mentioning Roman divinities, apart from a few instances where the names of the Roman gods are left in Latin.[45] Simonetta Battista paralleled it with the concept of *interpretatio romana*, first adopted by Tacitus when, describing the Germanic divinities in chapter XLIII of his *Germania*, he used for them the names of those gods of the Roman Pantheon which he judged to possess similar traits, in order to facilitate the understanding of his audience.[46] Vesta was the Roman virgin goddess of the domestic hearth; her fire was kept burning day and night in her temples, attended by her priestesses, the Vestals, who were sworn to chastity. By contrast, Gefjon seems to be associated with plowing and fertility, although sources provide a conflicting description of her. Her name (also appearing in the form *Gefjun*) is probably etymologically connected to the verb *gefa* ('give') and hence also to Gefn, one of the names for Freyja, the Norse goddess of fertility, although there has been some controversy on this matter. The controversy extends also to the conflicting description of her provided by the sources. Whereas in *Gylfaginning* XXXV she is presented as one of the Æsir, a virgin goddess who is attended by all who die virgins, in *Gylfaginning* I she is said to have had four sons with a giant, the four oxen that she used to plough up in a day and a night the land that the Swedish king Gylfi promised to her in return for her favours, thus creating Zealand. Her representation as a virgin is limited to *Gylfaginning* XXXV, and in fact in *Ynglinga saga* V, in addition to the myth of creation of Zealand, it is said of her that Oðinn married her off to his son Skjǫldr, the progenitor of the Danish dynasty of the Skjǫldungar. And in *Lokasenna* XX Loki reveals that she slept with a fair youth in exchange for a necklace.[47] It seems as though the information concerning Gefjon is a bit confused, but this is not surprising if one considers that when these myths were written down, Iceland had been Christian for about two hundred years and obviously, strong as the oral tradition was, many things – especially stories about heathen gods no longer worshipped – must have become blurred in the mist of time. The confusion regarding the identity of Gefjon is also reflected in the fact that her name is used to translate a variety of female Roman goddesses' names:

---

44 Tveitane, 'Interpretatio Norrœna', pp. 1067–82.

45 As, for instance, in *Antonius saga*. About this and for an extensive study on the interpretation of the Roman gods in Norse translations see Battista, 'Interpretation of the Roman Pantheon in the Old Norse Hagiographical Sagas', pp. 175–97.

46 Battista, 'Interpretation of the Roman Pantheon', p. 175. The *interpretatio* seems to be exclusively a Norse phenomenon, as other vernacular translations of saints' lives preserve the Latin names of Roman divinities, cf. for instance, *Ælfric's Lives of Saints*, ed. by Skeat.

47 For a full description of the problems associated with Gefjon, see Clunies Ross, 'The Myth of Gefjon and Gylfi and its Function in *Snorra Edda* and *Heimskringla*', pp. 149–65.

besides Vesta, she regularly replaces Diana, the Roman virgin goddess of the hunt and birthing (cf. *Nikolaus saga, Saga af Fídes, Spes ok Karítas*), and in one instance also Venus (cf. *Stjórn*), the goddess of love, fertility, beauty, and prosperity, whose equivalent is usually Freyja. Some of the fluctuation in the use of the same Norse god's name to replace Roman gods with contrasting characteristics might also be due to the fact that not all translators – although well versed in Latin – had a deep knowledge of the Roman Pantheon. Nonetheless, they preferred to substitute them with Norse gods to help the reader. Therefore, the *interpretatio norræna* itself is a sign that these translations were intended for ordinary people, who probably would have no clue about whom Vesta or any other of the Roman gods were. As regards the equivalence of Vesta-Gefjon in *Agnesar saga*, Battista suggests that it may be based on the fact that both goddesses were virgins and were served by virgins.[48]

Just as for the names of Roman gods, the same process of *interpretatio norræna* is undergone by the names of public offices. For example, the Latin *prefectus urbis filius* is rendered by *borgar greifa son*. Now, the office of urban prefect – usually a former consul who acted as a sort of mayor in Rome, a governor in charge of the administration of the town with legal jurisdiction as well – was certainly unfamiliar to the Icelandic audience, whose society was based on isolated farms rather than on villages and towns. The translator in this case could have just borrowed the word for this non-existent office in Iceland from Latin and left it untranslated, or he could have used an Icelandic word indicating an Icelandic prestigious office (for instance, *goði*, 'chieftain').[49] Instead, he opted for a term which still evoked the foreignness of the concept and at the same time was as understandable as possible to his audience by selecting *greifi*, a word of non-Scandinavian origin, usually meaning 'earl, count' (cognate to the Anglo-Saxon *gerêfa*, and possibly borrowed from Old High German *grāvo*).[50] By doing this, he was probably following an established tradition, as *greifi* was usually employed to render Latin *praefectus* in other translated works.

An example of cultural translation in addition to the language translation is as follows:

> Fit repente concursus populorum ad theatrum et varia furentis populi acclamatio.
>
> > (Immediately, there was a gathering of people at the theatre and the exclamations by the raging people were various.)

---

48 Battista, 'Interpretation of the Roman Pantheon', pp. 188.

49 In more than one instance, Old Norse Saints' lives contain Latin words left untranslated when they indicate concepts or things which were not found in the North; for example, in *Vitae Patrum* one finds *crocodillus, collubium, cucumis, pyramis* (Tveitane, *Den lærde stil*, p. 135).

50 Cf. *An Icelandic-English Dictionary*, ed. by Cleasby-Vigfússon, p. 213. For a possible borrowing of Old High German *grāvo* from Greek *grapheus* ('scribe') see *Altnordisches etymologisches Wörterbuch*, ed. by Vries, p. 186.

Þá var kvatt þings ok dreif þangat mikill fjǫldi manna ok varð þræta mikill um guðs mey.

> (Then, an assembly was summoned and a great number of people rushed there and there was a great wrangling about the maiden of God.)

In the Latin text, people gather at the theatre when Agnes is accused of using sorcery to kill her suitor, but in the Norse translation, an assembly is summoned instead. The theatre was an institution which did not exist in Iceland, where the entertainment was centred in the hall, hence there was no word for it. Therefore, the translator, instead of omitting it or explaining it with a periphrasis thus causing disruption in the unfolding of the plot, chose to replace it with something typically Icelandic, the assembly. After all, it would have been normal in Iceland to solve such a controversial matter at an assembly.

The overall result is a text dominated by parataxis, rather simple in structure, with almost no sign of attempts at reproducing the morphosyntactic structure of the Latin in the target text. In most cases, everything seems to be rendered consistently by the most correct structure required by Old Norse in that specific context. For instance, the Latin hortative subjunctive is translated with the typical hortative indicative that is used in Norse when a command to more than one person is given and the speaker is part of the same group. Latin participles, both present and past, are never rendered with a participle in Old Norse, even if they were available in Old Norse grammar. On the contrary, they are translated in four different ways, listed in order of frequency: 1) they originate a temporal subordinate clause introduced by *en er* + verb, if the Latin participle carries such value; 2) they are turned into the main verb of an independent (or coordinate) clause; 3) at times they are rendered by a relative clause; 4) they become an adjective. Though the passive voice is in very frequent use in the Latin text, the active voice is usually preferred in Norse, even if sometimes this means a change in the subject of the sentence (i.e. the Latin agent or object becomes the subject of the Norse sentence). The Latin gerundive is consistently rendered with an adjective corresponding in meaning to it. However, when the gerundive is part of the construction *ad* + gerundive (expressing purpose) – a construction regularly rendered with a consecutive clause –, then it becomes the main verb of the consecutive clause (introduced by *svá at*). The Latin construction *cum* + subjunctive (with a temporal or causal value) is rendered either by a coordinate clause or, when it has a temporal connotation, with a temporal subordinate introduced by *en er* and followed by *þá* at the beginning of the main sentence. Generally, hypotaxis is avoided when possible; therefore, Latin elements such as *fertur* ('it is told') and *factum est* ('it happened') located at the beginning of a sentence are omitted in order to avoid an unnecessary subordinate in translation. The Latin ablative absolute is always turned either into a main clause or into a temporal subordinate. The numerous Latin relatives, which enrich and at the same time complicate the syntax of the text, are often turned into an independent coordinate clause.

The translation of some of these structures is consistent throughout the entire text, and in some cases exactly the same way of translating a Latin construction is found in other Old Norse texts translated from Latin as well, which might be an indication of the fact that they were standard way of translating certain constructs, taught at school. The original translator appears to be a learned person who must have been familiar with the rest of Old Norse translated literature and its Latin counterparts. In fact, he abides by the tradition represented by those works by choosing to translate certain Latin words in the same way as they were translated in other translated works too. For instance, *prefectus* is consistently translated nearly everywhere as *borgargreifi*, *imperator/Augustus* as *konungr*, *virtus* as *krapt*, and *pontifices maximi* as *blótbiskupar*. Probably only in one case, his creativity prevails and he creates a new word, *gǫfganarmenn* ('worshippers', literally 'men of worshipping'), to render the Latin participle *colentes* – sometime used also as substantive, with the meaning of 'reverer, worshipper'.[51] However, the fact that he seems not to understand or understand fully certain words, such as, for example, *subarrhare*, *dextrochirium*, *apodixin*, and possibly also *parasitus*, mostly words pertaining to the classic Roman era rather than to medieval one, indicates that he probably lacked a knowledge of the classical world and classical Latin literature, and hence that his education must have been centred almost exclusively on ecclesiastical works and the medieval Latin spoken at his time.

It would be impossible to call the style of this translation anything other than a popular style, for it lacks all those elements that Nygaard and other scholars who advocated the so-called learned style in saints' lives consider attributes of such style.[52] According to Nygaard, who first identified the learned style in a

---

51 *A Latin Dictionary*, ed. by Lewis and Short, s.v. *colo*. For the creation of the *hapax legomenon gǫfganarmenn* (preserved only in Stock. Perg. 2), which does not occur anywhere else in the entire corpus of Old Norse prose (cf. *Dictionary of Old Norse Prose*, ed. by the Arnamagnæan Commission), the translator added the genitive of *gǫfgan* (f., 'worshipping') – a derivative of the verb *gǫfga*, which he consistently used to translate the Latin *colo*, from which *colentes* derives – to the word *maðr*, this being one of the most frequent techniques used to form nominal compounds in Old Norse. He could have used the more widespread word *blótmaðr* ('heathen worshipper', 48 occurrences in the *Dictionary of Old Norse Prose*) instead of creating a new word, but he probably felt that its connection with the verb *blóta*, which he systematically uses to translate the Latin *sacrifico*, made it unsuitable to render a derivative of the verb *colo*, which he perceives as different from *sacrifico* and associates with the Norse *gǫfga*. Obviously, the scribes copying its translation over time probably did not have the Latin version in front of them, and, to them, the word *gǫfganarmenn* must have seemed odd or too difficult to be understood by their audience, if not incorrect, and therefore at some point someone changed it to *glatanar menn* ('men of perdition', as in AM 429), unconsciously conferring on it a connotation different from what was originally intended.

52 Even though it has been argued that most Old Icelandic medieval religious literature – hagiography in particular – translated from Latin is written in the so-called 'learned style' (Nygaard, 'Den lærde stil i den norrøne prosa', pp. 153–70), this evaluation has been

part of Old Norse-Icelandic literature and then opposed it to the popular style, typical of the native Icelandic sagas and based on the oral style, the learned style is heavily modelled on Latin grammar and style and its features are: a) the use of past and present participles in analogy with the Latin use of them (i.e. with the same function as a subordinate clause but in apposition to a noun); b) the use of inflected relative pronouns; c) reflexive verbal forms with passive meaning; d) Old Norse dative absolute rendering Latin ablative absolute; e) frequent use of hypotaxis.[53] From the list above showing how our translator rendered the various Latin constructions, one can easily see that Latin participles are always translated as something different in Old Norse, indeed, there are hardly any participles in the saga.[54] As for b), inflected relative pronouns (usually the declinable interrogative pronoun, such as for instance in *kona, til hverrar er*) do not appear at all – after all, as Jónas Kristjánsson demonstrated, they were a late phenomenon, absent in older works, where the demonstrative pronoun *sá* followed by the indeclinable *er/sem* was used instead.[55] The same applies for d), as the Latin ablative absolute is usually translated as a temporal clause, as we have seen. And there are very few cases of reflexive forms used with passive meaning, so this cannot become a decisive factor in classifying the style as learned.[56] Again, from the analysis of the saga, it is clear that parataxis, and not hypotaxis, is predominant in the text, which is marked by the constant presence of the conjunctions *ok* and *en*, even when there was hypotaxis in Latin. As for alliteration, also usually regarded as a sign of the learned style, its presence is not large

---

recently reconsidered by many scholars, who on the contrary find that many saints' lives are indeed written in a simple style, the so-called 'popular style', also found in the traditional Icelandic sagas (Turville-Petre, *Origins of Icelandic Literature*; Bekker-Nielsen, 'On a Handlist of Saints' Lives in Old Norse' and 'Legender – Helgensagaer'; Kristjánsson, 'Learned Style or Saga Style?'). According to this more recent school of thought, the learned style was a phenomenon developing later than the first wave of translation of saints' lives, with a peak in the fourteenth century, when learned writers partially rewrote existing lives in the learned style and occasionally expanded their content drawing from different sources (Bekker-Nielsen, 'On a Handlist of Saints' Lives in Old Norse', p. 329).

53 Nygaard, 'Den lærde stil i den norrøne prosa', pp. 153–70.

54 There are three instances of participles which may reflect the Latin use of them, in AM 238 I fol., fol. 2^r: *sagiandi* (line 5); *utgengnir* (line 15); *reisandi* (line 16). Of them, only *utgengnir* (*voru utgengnir*) is modelled on the Latin past participle *egressi* (*fuissent egressi*), while the other two render two Latin indicatives (*dicebat* and *suscitavit*). Here, two solutions are possible: either they were already in the original translation and the scribes of the other manuscripts updated the style, or instead, AM 238 I was a rewriting of *Agnesar saga* in the learned style as it was popular to do in the fourteenth century, from which AM 238 in fact dates.

55 Kristjánsson, 'Sagas and Saints' Lives', p. 135.

56 Besides, as Jónas Kristjánsson argued, instances of reflexive forms, where the reflexive connotation is so close to the passive connotation as to merge with it, are occasionally found in works written in popular style (Kristjánsson, 'Learned Style or Saga Style?', p. 274).

enough to be significant – there are only few examples, such as 'gull, gimsteina ok gessemar' and 'styrk ok staðfæst' – and, in the majority of cases, even the device of variation, although often employed, is not used to create alliteration, as in the learned style.

If we agree with Bekker-Nielsen in dividing the history of Norse hagiography into three periods,[57] the earliest of which (in manuscripts from 1150 onwards) is characterized by a simple and classic style, as opposed to the learned style of the intermediate period (starting in the thirteenth century with a peak in the fourteenth), then the stylistic evidence alone points towards an early dating for the translation of the Latin legend of St Agnes. The same popular style is also found in the other versions of the saga, despite the fact that some of them were produced in the fourteenth century, when the learned style was in fashion. This may be a sign of the fact that while the Latinate style was perhaps preferred among the learned, the popular style, simpler and clearer, was probably still chosen for works aimed at a larger and general audience, especially if they were intended for public reading.

Although the Icelandic translation of the Latin legend of St Agnes (*BHL* 156a) is a close rendering of the Latin, the final result is no longer the same as its original source. In his attempt to make the original text resonate with his audience, the translator created something slightly different. Additionally, one should not forget the role of each scribe or manuscript compiler in the production of a text which is undoubtedly a copy of the same work and yet at the same time something new, tailored to the purpose of the compilation in which the text is included and to its readership. For example, if we look at the four manuscripts transmitting redaction I of *Agnesar saga*, the text of *Agnesar saga I* preserved in Stock. Perg. 2 fol. is a very good copy of what must have been the original translation of the legend of St Agnes, and reflects the erudite nature of its compiler, Ormur Loptsson, who was interested in collecting saints' lives as they were, probably with no other aim than that of having them in his own collection of books and enjoying their reading at family gatherings or making them available for the preparations of sermons at the church at his farm.[58] By contrast, the text of *Agnesar saga I* preserved in AM 429 12mo, is heavily revised and testifies to a will to tailor the content for a specific female audience – in all probability a girl destined for cloistered life – as unsuitable sections of text, likely to cause unclean thoughts or raise unwelcome questions, have been carefully expunged,

---

57 Bekker-Nielsen, 'Legender – Helgensagaer', p. 120.

58 There is evidence that saints' lives were read aloud also in lay environments and social gatherings. For instance, *Þorgils saga skarða* recounts that when Þorgils arrived at Hrafnagil in Eyjafjörd, where he was murdered, he was offered a choice as to what entertainment he would prefer for the evening. The options were sagas or dances; after enquiring about what sagas were available, he chose to read *Tomas saga erkibyskups* (*Þorgils saga skarða*, ed. by Jóhannesson, Finnbogason, and Eldjárn, p. 218). *Hákonar saga Hákonarson* reports that King Hákon Hákonarson of Norway listened to saints' lives in Norse on his deathbed (*Flateyjarbok*, III, ed. by Vígfússon and Unger, p. 229).

while some emphasis seems to have been added to the benefits of being a nun. Finally, the text preserved in AM 235 fol. represents a slightly abridged but still faithful copy of the original translation, where the text was possibly shortened to cater for the brevity required by a liturgical office or public reading. This shows how legendaries, as well as all sorts of liturgical books, as Michael Lapidge remarks, were 'fluid' texts in the Middle Ages, that is to say texts altered or redacted each time they were copied in order to meet the particular needs and preferences of an individual church or religious institution.[59]

***

This essay suggests that the Latin *Passio Agnetis* (*BHL* 156a) was translated into Old Norse in the days of Bishop Þorlákr Þórhallsson, probably just before or just after 1179, when St Agnes' feast day was made a holy day of obligation by the bishop, possibly in an attempt to promote her cult in Iceland and encourage the values she embodied through the diffusion of her story in the vernacular. Nothing is known about the identity of the translator, apart from what emerges from the analysis of his work by means of comparison with the Latin source. In all probability, he was a learned person, highly likely a clergyman, well-versed in Latin language and scholarship as well as in vernacular translated literature. His misunderstanding of certain Latin words pertaining to the classic Roman era reveals that his education must have been focused almost exclusively on medieval works. It has also been argued that, although the Old Norse translation of the Latin *Passio Agnetis* is a close rendering of its Latin source, with no omission of significant sections of text, and the occasional tendency to summarize and avoid repetitions, the final result is no longer the same as its original source. In fact, despite the proficiency of the translator, it would have been impossible for the two texts to be exactly alike, because besides the language difference, they were created in and for two different cultures, on the one hand, late-antique Latin Roman culture and, on the other hand, medieval Icelandic culture. Far from each other both in space and time, the translator brings these two cultures together on his own terms.

Bibliography

Manuscript Sources

Copenhagen, Det Arnamagnæanske Institut, AM 233a fol.
———, AM 235 fol.
———, AM 238 I fol.
———, AM 238 II fol.
———, AM 238 XV fol.

---

59 Lapidge, 'Editing Hagiography', p. 242.

———, AM 429 12mo
Oslo, Riksarkivet, Lat. Fragm. 678
Stockholm, Kungliga Biblioteket, Stock. Perg. 2 fol.

Primary Sources

Acta Sanctorum, ed. by Johannes Bollandus, 60 vols, 3rd edn (Paris: Palmé, 1863–70), II: *Januarii Tomus Secundus* (1863)

A Female Legendary from Iceland: *'Kirkjubæjarbók' (AM 429 12mo)*, ed. by Kirsten Wolf, Manuscripta Nordica, 3 (Copenhagen: Museum Tusculanum Press, 2011)

Ælfric's Lives of Saints: Being a Set of Sermons of Saints' Days Formerly Observed by the English Church, ed. by Walter W. Skeat, Early English Text Society, 76 (London: Trübner, 1881)

Biskupa sögur, ed. by Sigurgeir Steingrímsson and others, 3 vols, Íslenzk Fornrit, 15–17 (Reykjavík: Íslenzka fornritafélag, 1998–2003), I: *Kristni saga: Kristni þættir: Jóns saga helga*, ed. by Sigurgeir Steingrímsson, Ólafur Halldórsson, and Peter Foote, 2 pts (2003); II: *Hungrvaka, Þorláks saga byskups in elzta, Jarteinabók Þorláks byskups in forna, Þorláks saga byskups yngri, Páls saga byskups*, ed. by Ásdís Egilsdóttir (2002); III: *Árna saga biskups, Lárentíus saga biskups, Söguþáttur Jóns Halldórssonar biskups, Biskupa ættir*, ed. by Guðrún Ása Grímsdóttir (1998)

Codex Scardensis, ed. by Desmond Slay, Early Icelandic Manuscript in Facsimile, 2 (Copenhagen: Rosenkilde & Bagger, 1960)

De S. Agnete, ed. by Jacques-Paul Migne, in *Hymni S. Ambrosio Attributi*, Patrologiae Cursus Completus: Series Latina, 17 (Paris: Migne, 1845), cols 1210–11

Flateyjarbok: En samling af norske konge sagaer med indskudte mindre fortællinger om begivenheder i og udenfor Norge samt annaler, ed. by Guðbrand Vígfússon and Carl Rikard Unger, 3 vols (Christiania: Malling, 1860–68), III (1868)

Grágás: Islendernes lovbog i fristatens tid, ed. by Vilhjálmur Finsen (Kjøbenhavn: Berling, 1852)

Guðmundar sögur biskups, ed. by Stefán Karlsson, Editiones Arnamagnæanæ: Series B, 6 (Copenhagen: Reitzel, 1983)

Heilagra Manna Søgur, ed. by Carl Rikard Unger, 2 vols (Christiania: Bentzen, 1877)

Lives of the Saints, Perg. fol. nr. 2, in the Royal Library, Stockholm, ed. by Peter Foote, Early Icelandic Manuscripts in Facsimile, 4 (Copenhagen: Rosenkilde & Bagger, 1962)

S. Ambrosii De Virginibus, in *Florilegium Patristicum*, fasc. 30, ed. by Bernhard Geyer and Johannes Zellinger (Bonn: Hanstein, 1932), pp. 18–78

Saga heilagrar Önnu, ed. by Kirsten Wolf, Rit / Stofnun Árna Magnússonar á Íslandi, 52 (Reykjavík: Stofnun Árna Magnússonar á Íslandi, 2001)

The First Grammatical Treatise, ed. by Hreinn Benediktsson, University of Iceland Publications in Linguistics, 1 (Reykjavík: Institute of Nordic Linguistics, 1972)

The Icelandic Legend of Saint Dorothy, ed. by Kirsten Wolf, Studies and Texts, 130 (Toronto: Pontifical Institute of Medieval Studies, 1997)

The Old-Norse Icelandic Legend of Saint Barbara, ed. by Kirsten Wolf, Studies and Texts, 134 (Toronto: Pontifical Institute of Medieval Studies, 2000)

Þorgils saga skarða, in *Sturlunga saga*, ed. by Jón Jóhannesson, Magnús Finnbogason and Kristiàn Eldjàrn, 2 vols (Reykjavík: Sturlunguútgafan, 1946), II, pp. 104–226

Vita sanctae virginis et martyris Agnetis, per D. Ambrosium episcopum Mediolanensem scripta, ed. by Laurentius Surius, in *De probatis sanctorum historiis* (Cologne: 1576–81), I: *Complectens sanctos mensium Ianuarii et Februarii* (1576), pp. 507–11

Secondary Works

A Latin Dictionary: Founded on Andrew's Edition of Freund's Latin Dictionary, ed. by C. T. Lewis and C. Short (Oxford: Clarendon Press, 1879)

Altnordisches etymologisches Wörterbuch, ed. by Jan de Vries (Leiden: Brill, 1957–61)

An Icelandic-English Dictionary, ed. by Richard Cleasby and Gudbrand Vigfússon (Oxford: Clarendon Press, 1957)

Bagge, Sverre, 'Education', in Medieval Scandinavia: An Encyclopedia, ed. by Philip Pulsiano and others, Garland Encyclopedias of the Middle Age, 1: Garland Reference Library of the Humanities, 934 (New York: Garland, 1993), pp. 152–53

Battista, Simonetta, 'Interpretation of the Roman Pantheon in the Old Norse Hagiographical Sagas', in Old Norse, Myths, Literature and Society, ed. by Margaret Clunies Ross, The Viking Collection, 14 (Viborg: University Press of Southern Denmark, 2003), pp. 175–97

Bekker-Nielsen, Hans, 'Legender – Helgensagaer', in Norrøn Fortællekunst: Kapitler af den norsk-islandske middelalderlitteraturs historie, ed. by Hans Bekker-Nielsen and others (Copenhagen: Akademisk Forlag, 1965), pp. 118–26

——,, 'On a Handlist of Saints' Lives in Old Norse', Mediaeval Studies, 24 (1962), pp. 323–34

Bibliotheca Hagiographica Latina Antiquae et Mediae Aetatis [BHL], ed. by Socii Bollandiani, 2 vols, Subsidia Hagiographica 6, 12 (Brussels: Société des Bollandistes, 1898–1901); III: Supplementum (1911); IV: Novum supplementum, ed. by Henryk Fros, Subsidia hagiographica, 70 (1986)

Clunies Ross, Margaret, 'The Myth of Gefjon and Gylfi and its Function in Snorra Edda and Heimskringla', Arkiv för nordisk filologi, 93 (1978), pp. 149–65

Cormack, Margaret, 'Saints of Medieval Hólar: A Statistical Survey of the Veneration of Saints in the Diocese', Peregrinations: Journal of Medieval Art and Architecture 3/2 (2011), pp. 7–37

——,, The Saints in Iceland: Their Veneration from the Conversion to 1400, Subsidia Hagiographica, 78 (Brussels: Société des Bollandistes, 1994)

Copeland, Rita, 'The Fortunes of "non verbum pro verbo": Or, Why Jerome is Not a Ciceronian', in The Medieval Translator: The Theory and Practice of Translation in the Middle Ages, ed. by R. Ellis (Cambridge: Brewer, 1989), pp. 15–35

Dictionary of Old Norse Prose / Ordbog over det norrøne prosasprog, ed. by the Arnamagnæan Commission (Copenhagen: Arnamagnæanske Kommission, 1983–)

Franchi de' Cavalieri, Pio Pietro, S. Agnese nella tradizione e nella leggenda, Römische Quartalschrift für christlische Alterthumskunde und für Kirchengeschichte: Supplementheft, 10 (Rome: in Commission der Herderschen Verlagshandlung zu Freiburg im Breisgau und der Buchhandlung Spithöver zu Rom, 1899)

Frutaz, Amato Pietro, Il complesso monumentale di Sant'Agnese (Rome: Nova officina poligrafica laziale, 1992)

Grig, Lucy, Making Martyrs in Late Antiquity (London: Duckworth & Co., 2004)

―――, 'The Paradoxical Body of St Agnes', in Roman Bodies: Antiquity to the Eighteenth Century, ed. by A. Hopkins and M. Wyke (London: The British School at Rome, 2005), pp. 111–22

Kristjánsson, Jónas, 'Learned Style or Saga Style?', in Speculum Norrœnum: Norse Studies in Memory of Gabriel Turville-Petre, ed. by U. Dronke, Guðrun P. Helgadóttir, G. W. Weber, and H. Bekker-Nielsen (Odense: Odense University Press, 1981), pp. 260–92

―――, 'Sagas and Saints' Lives', in Cultura classica e cultura germanica settentrionale: Atti del Convegno Internazionale di Studi, Università di Macerata, Facoltà di Lettere e Filosofia, Macerata, S. Severino Marche, 2–4 maggio 1985, ed. by Pietro Janni and others, Quaderni linguistici e filologici, 3 (Rome: Herder, 1988), pp. 125–43

Lanéry, Cécile, Ambroise de Milan Hagiographe, Collection des Études Augustiniennes: Série Antiquité, 183 (Paris: Institut d'Études Augustiniennes, 2008)

Jones, Hannah, 'Agnes and Constantia: Domesticity and Cult Patronage in the Passion of Agnes', in Religion, Dynasty, and Patronage in Early Christian Rome, 300–900, ed. by Kate Cooper and Julia Hillner (Cambridge: Cambridge University Press, 2007), pp. 115–39

Kalinke, Marianne E., The Book of Reykjahólar: The Last of the Great Medieval Legendaries (Toronto: University of Toronto Press, 1996)

Lapidge, Michael, 'Editing Hagiography', in La critica del testo mediolatino, ed. by Claudio Leonardi, Medioevo latino / Biblioteca, 5 (Spoleto: Centro Italiano di Studi sull'Alto Medioevo, 1994), pp. 239–57

Nygaard, Marius, 'Den lærde stil i den norrøne prosa', in Sproglig-historiske Studier tilegnede Professor C. R. Unger (Christiania: Aschehoug, 1896), pp. 153–70

Olmer, Emil, Boksamlingar på Island, 1179–1490, Årsskrift, Göteborgs Högskolas, 8/2 (Göteborg: Zachrisson, 1902)

Phillips, Christine, 'Materials for the Study of the Cult of St Agnes of Rome in Anglo-Saxon England: Texts and Interpretations' (unpublished doctoral dissertation, University of York, 2008)

Ramandi, Maria Teresa, 'Reassessing "Agnesar saga": The Evidence of AM 238 fol. II', in Opuscula XVI, ed. by Annette Lassen and Philip Lavender, Bibliotheca Arnamagnaeana 50 (Copenhagen: Museum Tusculanum Press, 2018), pp. 91–119

Salzman, Michelle R., On Roman Time: The Codex-Calendar of 354 and the Rhythms of Urban Life in Late Antiquity, Transformation of the Classical Heritage, 17 (Berkeley, CA: University of California Press, 1990)

Sigurðardóttir, Anna, Allt hafði annan róm aður í páfadóm, Úr veröld kvenna, 3 (Reykjavík: Kvenna sögusafn, 1988)

Turville-Petre, Gabriel, Origins of Icelandic Literature (Oxford: Clarendon Press, 1953)

Tveitane, Mattias, Den lærde stil: Oversetterprosa i den norrøne versjonen av Vitae Patrum, Årbok for Universitet i Bergen: Humanistisk serie, 2 (Bergen: Norwegian Universities Press, 1967)

―――, 'Interpretatio Norrœna: Norrøne og antikke gudenavn i Clemens saga', in The Sixth International Saga Conference, 28.7.–2.8.1985 (Copenhagen: Det Arnamagnæanske Institut, 1985), pp. 1067–82

Van Deusen, Natalie M., 'The Old Norse-Icelandic Legend of Saints Mary Magdalene and Martha' (unpublished doctoral dissertation, University of Wisconsin-Madison, 2012)

Widding, Ole, Hans Bekker-Nielsen and L. K. Shook, 'The Lives of the Saints in Old Norse Prose: A Handlist', Medieval Studies, 25 (1963), pp. 294–337

Wolf, Kirsten, The Legends of the Saints in Old Norse-Icelandic Prose, Toronto Old Norse and Icelandic Studies, 10 (Toronto: University of Toronto Press, 2013)

The Old Swedish Pentateuch Translation and its Reflective Model Reader

Jonatan Pettersson

Stockholm University, Department of
Swedish Language and Multilingualism

A Swedish translation of the Pentateuch was prepared in, probably, the first half of the fourteenth century.[1] In the late-thirteenth to mid-fourteenth century the Swedish language becomes clearly visible as a literary language for the first time, with translations made of courtly and religious literature; the vernacular is also established as an administrative language, with the writing of legal codes as well as documents and records.[2] Politically, a period of relative stability began when the four-year-old Magnus Eriksson was elected King of Sweden and was also acclaimed King of Norway in 1319 after decades of civil war between members of the Swedish royal family, and during his reign until 1364, there was a reform of the legislation. The Pentateuch translation seems to stem from King Magnus's time, but virtually nothing is known of its origins and its translator, and it might even have been produced as early as the late thirteenth century. It is only preserved in two late medieval manuscripts, one from the beginning of fifteenth century, and another dated to 1526,[3] but we may also see indirect evidence for the translation in an inventory of the royal treasury of Bohus, a Swedish west-

---

1 A recent introduction to the Swedish Pentateuch translation can be found in Ejrnæs, 'The Bible in the Languages of Scandinavia', pp. 242–44, and Pettersson, 'Nordic Bible Translations' pp. 117–20, and the text will be the topic of a future book by the author of this article. The research behind this article has been carried out partly thanks to a postdoctoral grant from Åke Wiberg Foundation within the Nordic collaboration project *Retracing the Reformation: The Dissemination of The Bible in the Medieval Scandinavian Culture*, partly within the Swedish Riksbankens Jubileumsfond (RJ) research programme 2018–25 *Modes of Modification: Variance and Change in Medieval Manuscript Culture*. Special thanks to Ingela Hedström and Tim Bolton for their help with the translation of quotations in Old Swedish to modern English. The translations follow the source text closely even in its minor mistakes, like, for instance, when the source text breaks the rules of sequence of tenses.

2 The history of vernacular literacy in Swedish begins earlier, and if runic writing is included it stretches back to the beginning of the early European Middle Ages, but there seems to have been a breakthrough of writing in Swedish in the fourteenth century. See Larsson, *Pragmatic Literacy and the Medieval Use of the Vernacular*.

3 The manuscripts are introduced below.

coast royal castle, from 1346, which mentions *unum grossum librum biblie in swenico* ('a large book with the bible in Swedish') and in a note in the vita of St Bridget of Sweden from 1373, where it says that she read a vernacular Bible.[4] However, there is no substantial evidence that allows us to safely set the early history of the Pentateuch translation within a specific historical context, but, nevertheless, it is clearly part of a European history of vernacular Bible translation, which seems to have evolved in the late thirteenth and fourteenth centuries. This study will address the presupposed reader in the Swedish Pentateuch translation in an effort to approach the reading culture it was intended for. The analysis will begin with a more detailed presentation of the Pentateuch translation in relation to the European Bible translation history as a whole, and then turn to some aspects of the rich commentary that accompany the translation to get closer to its intended reader, and then finally discuss the observations in relation to a wider European vernacular Bible reading culture.

The Old Swedish Pentateuch Translation and the Scandinavian Bible Works

The Old Swedish Pentateuch translation belongs to a text collection which is commonly known as *Medeltidens bibelarbeten* I (*Medieval Bible Works* I) from its first modern edition, *Svenska medeltidens bibel-arbeten* (henceforth *MB* I).[5] In the manuscripts, a historical overview of the first six ages of biblical history and two theological expositions based on the *Summa theologiae* of Thomas Aquinas were included accompanying the Pentateuch translation.[6]

As can be seen in Table 1, the different parts are of quite different lengths and with the Pentateuch translation being the longest. The historical overview is a rather brief narration, beginning with the Creation and continuing up to the birth of Christ, with a focus on the genealogy of Jesus and with a special interest in the Babylonian Captivity. There is no known source for this text, but it is usually assumed that it is a translation of an older Latin biblical narrative. The two theological expositions mainly comprise translations of excerpts taken from Thomas Aquinas's *Summa theologiae*, and the first one is thematically connected to the first chapters of the Genesis with a focus on the Creation and the original sin, while the other is connected to the later part of the Pentateuch with its focus

---

4 For references to these sources, see the next section.

5 The translation is also called *Pentateukparafrasen* (*The Pentateuch Paraphrase*), but here the Pentateuch translation is preferred in line with the open definition of the concept and category of translation within Translation Studies. There are also late fifteenth-century Swedish translations of Joshua, Judges, Judith, Esther, Ruth, Maccabees 1–2, and Revelation, which is edited in the second volume of *Svenska medeltidens bibel-arbeten*, also ed. by Klemming, but these are not discussed further in this article.

6 For a more detailed description, see the editions in *Svenska medeltidens bibel-arbeten*, I, ed. by Klemming, pp. 208.25–209.3 and *Fem Moseböcker på fornsvenska enligt Cod. Holm. A 1*, ed. by Thorell.

Table 1: Content of *MB* I

Part	Content	No. of pages in *MB* I	No. of pages in the *Vulgate*
1	Historical overview of the first six ages of history	28	
2	Theological exposition I, mainly concerning the creation, partly based on Thomas of Aquinas's *Summa theologiae*[7]	120	
3	Commentated translation of the Pentateuch	275	
	Genesis	118	73
	Exodus	83	60
	Leviticus	22	41
	Numbers	44	58
	Deuteronomy	8	52
4	Theological exposition II, mainly concerning the old law, based on Thomas of Aquinas's *Summa theologiae*	71	

on the Old Testament Law. I have argued elsewhere that it is clear that the two expositions were created together with the Pentateuch translation as an intended whole, I therefore abstain from discussing this issue here.[8]

The translation itself can be described as a relatively free translation of the Vulgate text with glosses and commentary. In some parts the source was translated quite closely whereas other parts were rendered more or less freely. While this may be regarded as a general pattern common to many medieval translations, it can, nevertheless, vary considerably from one translation to another. Some specific kinds of material in the source text were systematically omitted from the translation. The most conspicuous omissions concern, firstly, repetitions in general, and, secondly, rules and regulations concerning Jewish religious practices.[9] The translator did not avoid the non-narrative parts as a rule, which would otherwise have been a natural omission if the audience was expected to be interested primarily in an entertaining narrative. Instead, the translator kept the non-narrative accounts such as genealogies, the histories of Jewish tribes,

---

7 For the use of the *Summa theologiae* in *MB* I, see *Fem moseböcker på fornsvenska enligt Cod. Holm. A 1*, ed. by Thorell, pp. xxxi–xxxiv.

8 Pettersson, 'De teologiska utredningarna'.

9 The translation principles underlying the Pentateuch translation are briefly described, with examples, in Pettersson 'De teologiska utredningarna', pp. 69–71, and they will be thoroughly discussed in a future book on the Pentateuch translation by the same author.

the catalogue of campsites, parts concerning secular law, etc.[10] He did, however, very consistently omit God's instructions about how and what to sacrifice, how to arrange and decorate the tabernacle, which days to celebrate, etc. The relevance of such religious instructions for Christians is actually explicitly questioned in the second theological exposition following the Pentateuch translation; the omissions therefore show an internal correspondance between the exposition and the translation.

Some of the biblical books, such as Leviticus, were cut to almost half their lengths in the translation – religious instructions constitute a major part of Leviticus, and these were omitted in their entirety. Others were cut even more significantly, with Deuteronomy filling eight pages in the translation compared to the fifty-two pages in the Vulgate, but in this case the cuts concern repetitions. As Deuteronomy is almost entirely a retelling of the three previous books, therefore not much of it is left in the translation.[11]

However, the translator seems to have had the production of a complete translation of the Bible in mind. On numerous occasions he promises the reader to return to certain topics later, but only the Pentateuch translation is known to have been completed out of this grand project.[12]

MB I survived in two relatively closely-related manuscripts: København, Det Kongelige Bibliotek, MS Thott 4 4o, from the first decades of the fifteenth century and Stockholm, Kungliga biblioteket, MS A 1, dated to 1526. Both are connected to the Birgittine Vadstena monastery in central-southern Sweden, and they share some common mistakes inherited from their exemplar, a previous manuscript which was itself also a copy.[13] They do however differ from each other considerably. The older one (MS Thott 4 4o) had been linguistically modernized into fifteenth-century Swedish, whereas the more recent one (MS A 1) renders a fourteenth-century Swedish, but with a lot of misreadings.[14]

It is the language of MS A 1 that motivates the dating of the translation to the first half of the fourteenth century, but the mention of 'a large book with the Bible in Swedish' in the inventory from the Bohus castle 1346 may also pro-

---

10 The fact that religious instructions are omitted while other non-narrative parts are retained has not been observed in previous research, which often characterize the translation as being focused on the narrative and the story, as in Ejrnæs, 'The Bible in the Languages of Scandinavia', p. 243, p. 249.

11 The content of Deuteronomy is consciously and skilfully rearranged in *MB* I, which will be described in a future publication, as previously mentioned (see footnote 1).

12 The fact that translations of Joshua and other books of the Old Testament were produced later in the fifteenth century (see footnote 4) suggests that the *MB* I translator never went beyond the Pentateuch. See Pettersson, 'De teologiska utredningarna', pp. 67–68.

13 Thorell, *Fem moseböcker på fornsvenska*, pp. 1–2.

14 The rewriting in MS Thott 4 4o is recently analysed in Faymonville, 'Om variationen i Codex Thott 4 4:o'. The language in MS A 1 is thouroughly analysed in Thorell, *Fem moseböcker på fornsvenska*.

vide a possible *terminus ante quem*.[15] No information in the work itself sheds any light on its origins and the identity of the translator, with the exception that the translator claims to have been to Trier and, in one comment, he seems to include himself among those who lead the service and offer the Eucharist.[16] It has often been suggested that it was St Birgitta of Sweden (1302/3–73) who commissioned *MB* I, based on a note in her vita where it is said: 'Cum vero vacabat a labore manuum, continue relegebat vitas sanctorum et bibliam, quam sibi in lingua sua scribit fecit'.[17] ('When she rested from manual work, she continually read the lives of the holy and a/the Bible, which she had made someone to write for herself in her own language'). The formulation that she had 'someone to write [the Bible] ... in her own language' can mean that she had translated it, but it can also mean that she commissioned a translation or ordered a copy of an existing translation.[18] A closer analysis of the relation between *MB* I and the revelations of St Birgitta would perhaps elucidate her role in history of *MB* I.

Given the traditional dating of *MB* I, it was made at about the same time as a translation of Genesis-Exodus 18 in Norway, commissioned by King Hákon V Magnússon (d. 1318). This translation belongs to a group of Norwegian-Icelandic translations of biblical books which in post-medieval sources and in modern editions are called *Stjórn*, meaning 'governance'. Together they form a translation from Genesis to Kings, and are connected in the extant manuscripts although they are of different age.[19] The Genesis-Exodus 18-translation (in editions called *Stjórn* I) is reminiscent of the Pentateuch translation in *MB* I in its general strategy of combining a free rendering of the Bible text with glosses and comments.

No direct connection between the Swedish and Norwegian translations may be established; it is, however, very likely that the Swedish translation was inspired by the Norwegian example. Magnus Eriksson, who became King of Sweden and Norway in 1319, was the son of the Norwegian princess Ingeborg and the Swedish

---

15 The charter is published in *Svenskt diplomatariums huvudkartotek* (*SDHK*), no. 5311.

16 In one comment he says he has seen relics of the manna of Exodus 12 in the Trier cathedral, and in another he speaks of 'we [...] who tread first of all to God's altar [...] and handle his holy sacrament which he is part of himself', see *Svenska medeltidens bibelarbeten*, I, ed. by Klemming, p. 324.24–26, p. 330.17–20. Previous research on the authorship is related in *Fem moseböcker*, ed. by Thorell, pp. xxxvi–xlv.

17 *Acta et processus canonizacionis Beate Birgitte*, ed. by Collijn, p. 617.

18 For a discussion, see *Fem Moseböcker*, ed. by Thorell, pp. xxxvi–vii.

19 The different parts of the translations are named and numbered *Stjórn* I–IV from their position in the canonical Bible. *Stjórn* I is thus the Genesis – Exodus 18 translation from the time of King Hákon V Magnússon (1299–1319). *Stjórn* II is a translation of Exodus 19 – Deuteronomy, of uncertain date. *Stjórn* III is a Joshua to Kings translation, which is generally believed to stem from around the middle of thirteenth century, but may possibly have an older predecessor. *Stjórn* IV is a translation of Petrus Comestor's part on Joshua in his *Historia scholastica*. For an overview of the texts and the manuscripts, see Óskarsdóttir, 'Heroes or Holy People?'.

Duke Erik Magnusson. To celebrate their union, Ingeborg's mother, the Norwegian Queen Eufemia of Rügen, had three courtly verse-tales translated into Swedish, the so-called *Eufemiavisor* (*Songs of Eufemia*), which mark the beginning of Swedish as a literary language.[20] These translations were partly based on already existing prose translations of European courtly texts into Old Norse, which at that time already had a history of almost a century in Norway and Iceland. It would therefore not be surprising if the idea of making a Swedish translation of the Bible also came from Norway, which apart from the Genesis-Exodus 18-translation had a history of producing Bible translations dating back to the thirteenth century.

From a wider European perspective, these Nordic Bible translations can be connected with a tradition of vernacular biblical narratives, which render the source freely and supply the reader with glosses and commentary.[21] Of central importance for this tradition is the Latin *Historia scholastica* of Petrus Comestor from late twelfth century, which became the base for many of the vernacular texts, among them the hugely successful *Bible historiale* of Guyart des Moulin from 1295/7.[22] The *Historia scholastica* is also a main source for the Norwegian Genesis-Exodus 18-translation, but it takes a less prominent role in the Pentateuch translation in *MB* I. The Swedish translation, here meant as a unit of the translated biblical text and the commentaries, leans on Thomas Aquinas's *Summa theologiae*, and a wide range of sources. In the following, their content and function will be discussed.

The Commentaries in the Old Swedish Pentateuch Translation

The commentaries accompanying the translated text are an important key to understanding the Old Swedish Pentateuch translation and its history. They comprise glosses, commentaries, and additions, among them few interpolations from other narrative sources. These comments (ranging from just a few words through to very long explications of up to almost 700 words) are spread throughout the Pentateuch, with the notable exceptions of Leviticus and Deuteronomy.[23]

Bible exegesis came to be systematized in the scheme of the four-fold senses, as presented, for instance, in Thomas of Aquinas's *Summa theologiae* I, q. 1, a. 10: the historical or literal sense, the allegorical sense, the tropological or moral sense, and the anagogical sense. In practice, these categories were not stable in the Middle Ages because the terminology shifted, as did the number of categories.[24]

---

20 For a recent discussion of this text, see *The Eufemiavisor and Courtly Culture*, ed. by Ferm and others.

21 A discussion on the Nordic translations in comparison with European history can be found in Pettersson, 'Nordic Bible Translations'.

22 Lobrichon, 'The Story of a Success'.

23 See the discussion following Table 1 above.

24 Cf. de Lubac, *Medieval Exegesis*, II, trans. by Macierowski, pp. 33–37.

The four-fold taxonomy distinguishes between different kinds of meanings present beneath the text's surface and connects its content to different epistemologies. The choice of what fields of knowledge the commentary brings forward for the reader is interesting in itself and might be used to locate the work within exegetical traditions, as well as the aims and intended purpose of a text. As Laurel Amtower notes: '[T]hough medieval commentary addressed what one might call the hidden meaning of a text, its purpose lay not so much in interpreting or understanding the text as in casting it for some other agenda'.[25] Amtower primarily discusses classical texts, but the same applies to biblical exegesis, and the different parts of the four-fold scheme were sometimes conceived as being proper or useful for different readers/listeners or purposes.[26] For lay readers of the vernacular Bible, the literal or the historical sense was considered both necessary and sufficient, whereas the different mystical meanings were a concern for learned recipients.

The extra-biblical material in the Pentateuch translation approaches all four of the categories. The *literal* or *historical sense* concerns the historical settings in the text, and it can be associated with a great number of the comments, for instance, explanations of historical circumstances, provision of missing information, clarifications and amplifications, as, for instance, in the following example from Genesis 15. 29–33 with the comment underlined:[27]

> Nw komber en dagh swa til/ at iacob redde til sin mat/ oc esau komber hem modher aff skogher/ oc bidher sin brodher giwa sik æta mz sik/ oc sigher sik wara mykith modhan/ Æn thz war sidher i them æwum oc i them landom/ at ældre son skulle hawa mykla wyrdhning fore sinom sytzkenom/ oc thy swarar iacob esau Jak giwer thik wæl æta mz mik/ æn thu later mik the wyrdhning som thik bör til/ for thy at thu wast för födder aff modher liwe.[28]

> (Now one day it happens that, when Jacob cooked his food, and Esau comes home from the woods worn out, and asks his brother to share his meal with him, and he claims to be very exhausted. And it was the custom in those times and in those lands that the older son should have greater honour than his siblings, and because of that Jacob answers Esau: 'I will share my meal with you if you leave to me the mark of honour that fell to you because you were first born of the womb'.)

Here, the commentary clarifies the implications of Jacob's offer to Esau. Such explanations of specific historical and cultural circumstances are not very common, but comments that elucidate a particular situation or event in a more general way appear more frequently, such as the explanation given for the raven

---

25 Amtower, *Engaging Words*, pp. 87–88.
26 Cf. Smalley, *The Study of the Bible in the Middle Ages*, p. 244.
27 Murdoch, *The Medieval Popular Bible*, p. 5.
28 *Svenska medeltidens bibel-arbeten*, I, ed. by Klemming, pp. 208.25–209.3.

that Noah let free when the rain had stopped never returning because it had found meat floating in the water.[29] Additional information that helps the reader to understand and accept the story as narrated appears in many forms, whether as glosses or additions or becoming a part of the commentary. There are numerous examples of explanations of, for instance, the linguistic meaning of biblical names (which more often resembles a gloss), and amplifications of the thoughts and feelings of the biblical characters (which more often resembles general additions).[30] Clarification is a typical feature of translation in general, and medieval Swedish vernacular readers could certainly do with some help when integrating the long-ago and far-away stories of the Israelites into their own horizon of experiences.

There are also quite a number of examples of the second type of comment, which concerns the *allegorical meaning* of the biblical text. About a tenth of all instances of extra-biblical material concern symbolic comparisons between someone or something in the Old Testament and someone or something else in the New Testament. One example of such a comment relates to the battle between the Israelites and the Amalekites in Exodus 17. 8–16, where the victory of the Israelites depended on Moses stretching out both arms to each side:

> Hwi bödh war herra hælder scriwa til aminnilse thenna sigher æn margha andra Vtan for thy/ at thenne sigher/ han teknar oppenbarlika/ wars herra sigher a korseno [...] Vtan war herra wille tekna fore them/ hurw gudz son skulle rækkia sina arma a korseno/ tha han stridde sigher aff allom sinom owinom.[31]

> (Why did our Lord record this victory instead of many others, if not because this victory openly signifies our Lord's victory on the cross [...] if not that our Lord wanted to show them how God's son would stretch out his arms on the cross when he took victory from all of his enemies.)

The comparison between Moses stretching out his arms and the crucified Christ is a well-known allegorical interpretation, which is presented here in a somewhat rhetorically-emphasized form. Some further examples are when Joseph is compared with Christ,[32] that the burning bush is said to correspond to Mary, mother of Jesus,[33] and when the twelve fountains of water at a campsite in Exodus 15. 27 are compared with the twelve apostles.[34]

---

29 *Svenska medeltidens bibel-arbeten*, I, ed. by Klemming, p. 171.8–10.

30 Explanations of the linguistic meaning of words and names are listed and discussed in Pettersson, 'De teologiska utredningarna'. Additions which bring forth the feelings of the biblical characters can, for instance, be found in the rendering of Genesis 22, when God ordered Abraham to sacrifice Isaac, see *Svenska medeltidens bibel-arbeten*, I, ed. by Klemming, pp. 199.21–202.17.

31 *Svenska medeltidens bibel-arbeten*, I, ed. by Klemming, p. 326.3–12.

32 *Svenska medeltidens bibel-arbeten*, I, ed. by Klemming, pp. 253.13–254.3.

33 *Svenska medeltidens bibel-arbeten*, I, ed. by Klemming, pp. 281.15–282.2.

34 *Svenska medeltidens bibel-arbeten*, I, ed. by Klemming, p. 322.5.

Furthermore, there are other allegorical comparisons which are made with referents other than the New Testament characters, referring instead, especially, to the Church, to Christians, and to contemporary society. Some examples are when the marriage between Moses and his Ethiopian woman is compared with Christ and the Church,[35] or when the stave of Moses which is used to part the Red Sea is compared with the stave of bishops in contrast to the sword of kings,[36] or when the mourning lasting for thirty days after Aron's death is linked with customs contemporary to the translator.[37] Allegorical interpretation is an important characteristic of the commentary in the Pentateuch translation, and the translator/commentator even reflects on this by discussing the process, technique and problems of allegorical comparison on several occasions.[38]

The third part of the four-fold scheme concerns the *tropological* or *moral meaning*, which accounts for spiritual guidance for our behaviour. In this case, one should distinguish between a 'simple morality' on the one hand and a mystical moral meaning on the other, and it is the later, mystical or spiritual meaning which is considered to be the true type of the tropological category.[39] The simpler type is, instead, regarded as a form of historical meaning and refers to expositions of literally understood models.[40] One such example is a comment added to Genesis 50. 1–3 in which Jacob dies and Joseph ritually treats his body with herbs: 'Oc hawom wi her æpterdöme at æra oc hedhra godha manna likama oc been sidhan the ære dödhe' ('And we have here a model to honour and venerate the body and bones of good men after they are dead').[41] Comments about such moral models exist, but they are not very common.[42]

A tropological exegesis, in which guidance for behaviour is based on symbolical and mystical interpretation, can be seen in the next comment, expanding on the motive of the scouts sent into the land of Canaan by the Israelites in Numbers 13. 17–20:

> Swa skulom wi/ Mædhan wi ærom a wæghenom til himerikis/ i iordhrike/ sænda speiara fore os til himerike/ thz ær wart eghit hiærta/ som wi skulom opta læta lidhukt/ oc thænkia hwilkit himerike ær/ fram fore iordhrike/ hwilkith folk ther ær fore os/ swa som ængla/ oc patriarcha/ oc

---

35 *Svenska medeltidens bibel-arbeten*, I, ed. by Klemming, p. 399.9–32.

36 *Svenska medeltidens bibel-arbeten*, I, ed. by Klemming, p. 316.20–23.

37 *Svenska medeltidens bibel-arbeten*, I, ed. by Klemming, p. 410.23–26.

38 *Svenska medeltidens bibel-arbeten*, I, ed. by Klemming, p. 308.22–311.2, p. 397.3–11.

39 de Lubac, *Medieval Exegesis*, II, trans. by Macierowski, pp. 127–34.

40 de Lubac, *Medieval Exegesis*, II, trans. by Macierowski, p. 130.

41 *Svenska medeltidens bibel-arbeten*, I, ed. by Klemming, p. 269.9–11.

42 For instance, Abraham's hospitality towards the three men in Genesis 18, or Moses praying for the Pharaoh in Exodus 8. 12, see *Svenska medeltidens bibel-arbeten*, I, ed. by Klemming, pp. 188.29–189.2 and p. 298.19–20.

propheta/ apostoli/ martires/ confessores/ oc iomfrwr/ oc frwghur Hwilkin fæste ther ære swa stark/ at ængin owin ma in koma/ oc landit siælfft swa skipath/ at ther ær ænkte nakrom afat/ som honum ma lysta til.[43]

> (In the same way, we should, when we – still here in the earthly realm – are on our way to Heaven, send scouts before us to Heaven, that is our own heart, which we should often release and think about what Heaven is like in comparison with the earthen realm, what people there are ahead of us, like the angels, patriarchs, prophets, apostles, martyrs, confessors, and maidens and wives, what fortress there is that is so strong that no enemy may enter, and the land itself is created in such a way that there is no lack of anything that one would long for.)

Here, the exegesis aims at providing moral edification, taking its cue from a symbolic interpretation of the respective Old Testament passage. There are quite a few clearly identifiable examples of this, as many of the comments are also aimed, if indirectly, at moral edification. That is to say, moral exhortations are occassionally included in comments which also have another exegetical orientation. It is clear, however, that one of the principal aims of the Pentateuch translation was to provide moral guidance for the reader.

The fourth and final approach in the four-fold scheme is the *anagogical meaning*, which points to the heavenly world and the future. Here, as with the tropological meaning, one can distinguish between simpler and more complex variants. The first, simpler type is exemplified by a comment on Genesis 13. 18 when Hebron is described as the place where several saints are buried and 'ther som domadagh skal wara' ('where the Last Judgement will be').[44] This comment refers to the heavenly future but is closely connected to historical facts and does not enfold any concealed inner meaning in the text. An example of anagogical interpretation may be found in the comment to Numbers 17. 10 when the staff of Aaron, which had begun to sprout, was brought into the tabernacle.

> Swa wiisadhe oc war herra/ at warfrv fördhis tha hon war dödh til himerikis/ som ær særdelis gudz hws/ ther til at hon skal wara os til aminnilse/ oc tröst/ oc at wi skulom til henna om siidher/ oc at hon skal minnas ther aldra thera/ som henne minnas her.[45]

> (In this way, our Lord showed that our Lady, after she had died, was brought to Heaven, which is God's own house, where she will remind and comfort us, and so that we will come to her in due time, and so that she shall remember their lives there who remember her here.)

Clear examples of this category are not very common, but they do appear occasionally, as when Pharaoh's soldiers who try to escape the waves in Exodus 14

---

43 *Svenska medeltidens bibel-arbeten*, I, ed. by Klemming, p. 400.16–26.
44 *Svenska medeltidens bibel-arbeten*, I, ed. by Klemming, p. 180.2–6.
45 *Svenska medeltidens bibel-arbeten*, I, ed. by Klemming, p. 407.8–13.

are compared with those sinners who regret their misdeeds too late for the Last Judgement,[46] or when the shining horns of Moses (after he has received the Ten Commandments a second time in Exodus 34) lead the commentator to expand on how the bodies of men will be lighter than the sun after the Last Judgment.[47] The collected comments, therefore, address all four of the exegetical categories, and the translator/commentator moved freely between them.

The Function of the Commentary and the Intended Reader

The commentator had to make fundamental decisions regarding the level of learning that their intended reader had at his or her command. Was the reader, for instance, expected to know what a *Pharaoh* is, or would it be necessary to explain it? In the Old Swedish Pentateuch translation, the commentator apparently regarded such basic explanations as being necessary (the comment is underlined):

> Nw komo the i egipto land oc gaff gudh them mykla nadher fore pharao konunge/ <u>Oc ær pharao almennelikt konungx nampn i thy lande</u>.[48]
>
> (Now they came to the land of Egypt and God gave them much mercy in front of Pharaoh the king. <u>And Pharaoh is the common name of a king in that country</u>.)

Exactly what manner of information may be described as 'basic facts' is not self-evident, but it is hard to imagine that an explanation such as the example above would have been called for had the intended reader been an academically educated person. The very first verse of the Pentateuch offers another such example (the comment is underlined):

> Aff ophowe skapadhe gudh aff alzængo himil oc iordh <u>Ey aff sik siælwom/ som fadher födher son/ Oc ey aff nakro æmpne/ som smidher gör yxe</u>.[49]
>
> (In the beginning, God created heaven and earth from nothing; <u>not from himself, as the father gives life to a son, and not from any matter, as the smith makes an axe</u>.)

The comment, concerning the added phrase *af alzængo* ('from nothing'), provides the reader with examples drawn from everyday experience. One might contrast this very matter-of-fact comment with that of the West Nordic *Stjórn*. Here, the comment based on the *Historia scholastica* and other sources to the

---

46 *Svenska medeltidens bibel-arbeten*, I, ed. by Klemming, p. 317.16–20.

47 *Svenska medeltidens bibel-arbeten*, I, ed. by Klemming, pp. 354.26–355.24.

48 *Svenska medeltidens bibel-arbeten*, I, ed. by Klemming, p. 178.14–16, which includes translation of Genesis 12. 11–16.

49 *Svenska medeltidens bibel-arbeten*, I, ed. by Klemming, p. 155, ll. 1–4, which includes translation of Genesis 1. 1.

first verse of Genesis extends to five pages in the modern edition.[50] The Old Swedish text is clearly directed at a reader who is not expected to take an interest in the theological discourse, but rather one who needs relatively simple instruction in the basic issues of Christian mystery.

The comments in *MB* I are more reminiscent of the language of vernacular homiletics than that of learned theological exposition or instructions for advanced meditation – both of which may be found among vernacular productions in late medieval Europe. On the other hand, the comments still also presuppose a certain degree of intellectual capability on the intended recipient's behalf, as several of them are quite demanding. In the following example, the principles of allegorical interpretation are discussed, with particular reference to Miriam, the sister of Moses, who in some ways represents the Old Testament type of the Virgin:

> Ænkte thing ær andro swa liikt/ at the hawa ey nakan skilnath/ eller warin the badhin eet thing/ oc ey tw Oc fore thy sigx i the boklist ther thæsskyns pröwar/ at i olikom thingom/ skal man leta liknilse oc i likom thingom skilnath/ Fore thy hawa wiise klærka fore ordhqwædhe/ at ængin liknilse rinder allom fyrom fotom/ thy at et thing ær andro liikt/ fore een skæl/ eller tw/ eller flere/ æn aldre alzstingx som nw war sakt.[51]

> (No thing is so similar to another that they would not have any differences, or else they both would be one thing and not two. And therefore, it is said in sciences of that kind that examine these sorts of things, that in different things one should look for similarities and in similar things for differences. Therefore, wise clerics have a saying that no simile runs on all four feet, because one thing is similar to another for one reason or two or more but never in everything, as was now said.)

The discussion takes place on a fairly advanced level, but it is still not explicitly integrated into the learned discourse any further than through the use of simplified expressions such as *i the boklist ther thæsskyns pröwar* ('in the sciences of that kind that examine those sorts of things') and *wiise klærka* ('wise clerics'). The knowledge that is conveyed in the commentary of the Pentateuch translation, then, is not deeply integrated into the academic discourse, and even where there are references to the *auctores*, they are not very common. Of the fifty-two explicit references made in *MB* I, only six belong to the commentary of the Pentateuch translation, whereas most of them accompany the theological expositions that frame the translation in the manuscripts.[52] In any case, it seems that the intended reader of the translation was a person with no academic education but was acquainted to some degree with the existence of a learned tradition.

---

50 *Stjórn*, I, ed. by Astås, pp. 13–18.

51 *Svenska medeltidens bibel-arbeten*, I, ed. by Klemming, p. 397.3–11.

52 The references to Christian, Jewish, and Classical *auctores* are listed in *Svenska medeltidens bibel-arbeten*, I, ed. by Klemming, pp. 582–83.

Commentary Regarding Problematic Acts and Deeds

One fairly large group of comments had the goal of preventing the misinterpretation or questioning of biblical characters, the authority of the biblical text, or even of the authority of the Church. The first example of this type concerns Exodus 2. 11–12 (the comment is underlined):

> Nw sidhan han kom helbrigdho heem til egipto land/ oc war helbrigdho mz konungenom/ tha sa han sinna ætmanna nödh/ oc om en dagh tha wardh han war at en hedhin egipto man slo oc bardhe en hebreiskan man sik nærskyldan Moyses gat ey tholt gudz wanhedher oc sinna ætmanna oc sa sik om kring görla/ æn naghar waare nær som witna matte gen honum/ æn han hæmpdis/ oc slo thaghar i hæl hedhningan oc iordhadhe i sandenom <u>Oc tho war han ey mandrapare/ vtan hælder en rætter domare Thy at gudh siælwer hafdhe lyst fore honum/ at han skulle wara höffdhinge oc rættare ower hebreisko mæn/ oc thy bar honum rætter til at döma oc hæmpnas.</u>[53]

> (Now as he was safely returned home to the land of Egypt and prospered beside the king, then he saw distress among his own kindred, and one day he saw a heathen Egyptian man beat a Hebrew man, closely related [to Moses]. Moses could not bear the dishonour to God and his kindred, and looked around himself carefully, if someone was close who would be able to bear witness against him, and he took revenge and quickly beat the heathen to death and buried him in the sand. <u>Nevertheless, he was no killer but rather a rightful judge, because God himself had chosen him to be chieftain and foreman of the Hebrew men, and therefore it was right for him to judge and take revenge.</u>)

The comment does not explain the exegetical meaning of the passage, but instead *defends* the actions of Moses on juridical and moral grounds. The commentator tries to ensure that the reader does not take a critical stance towards Moses. The passage was often discussed by the authorities, albeit not in the *Historia scholastica*'s rendering of this chapter. Augustine provides what is perhaps the most influential discussion of it in his *Contra Faustum* (XXII. 70); he describes the deed as the result of a quality in a man who is later to be used by God, and he compares Moses to Paul. This relatively complex discussion is rendered in the West Nordic *Stjórn* together with a comment on Acts 7, seemingly drawn from the *Historia scholastica*, which contains a speech by Stephen who touches upon this passage, and legitimizes Moses' actions.[54]

Another example gives a very clear indication about how important it was for the commentator that their readers would not end up drawing the wrong moral and juridical conclusions. It concerns the story of the silver and golden

---

53 *Svenska medeltidens bibel-arbeten*, I, ed. by Klemming, p. 280.1–14.

54 *Stjórn*, I, ed. by Aståas, pp. 384.16–387.6. Petrus Comestor, *Historia scholastica*, ed. by Migne, cols 1663–64.

treasures that the Israelites brought with them during the exodus from Egypt (Exodus 12. 35–36). The passage in the Vulgate reads thus:

> [12. 35:] feceruntque filii Israhel sicut praeceperat Moses et petierunt ab Aegyptiis vasa argentea et aurea vestemque plurimam [12. 36:] dedit autem Dominus gratiam populo coram Aegyptiis ut commodarent eis et spoliaverunt Aegyptios.
>
>> (And the children of Israel did as Moses had commanded, and they asked the Egyptians for silver and golden vessels and a large amount of clothing raiment. Also the Lord gave favour to the people in the sight of the Egyptians, so that they lent/gave unto them, and they plundered the Egyptians.)

This passage is also well-known in biblical exegesis where it is used to justify the role of classical *auctores* within a Christian learned culture; the silver and gold that the Israelites brought from Egypt are compared to the bringing of treasures from the learning of Classical Antiquity into Christian theology in the Middle Ages. The moral and juridical problem in the text is, of course, that the Israelites are actually committing theft, a very serious crime in the Middle Ages. It is emphasized in the *Historia scholastica* that the Lord takes responsibility for the action and that it is motivated by the mistreatment of the Israelites and their liturgical needs (the comment is underlined):

> et petierunt vasa ab Aegyptiis vestemque plurimam, et spoliaverunt Aegyptios <u>ex praecepto Domini; tum pro mercede laboris, qua fraudati erant, tum ut inde fieret tabernaculum.</u>[55]
>
>> (and they asked the Egyptians for vessels and very much raiment, and they plundered the Egyptians <u>at the instruction of the Lord, partly as wage for their work, which they had been cheated of, partly so that it could be used for the tabernacle.</u>)

In this case, the West Nordic *Stjórn* follows the *Historia scholastica* almost verbatim.[56] When we turn to the Old Swedish text, we find a much more verbose comment, which is arranged in three sections:

> [Bible text:] Jsraels sönir togho gulkar oc silffkar oc godha görsæme at lane aff egipto landz folke.
> [Comment:] Oc skulom wi her vnderstanda/at ængin ma mz swikom kænnas at sins ærwodhis lönom/ oc giælla sik siælwer aff annars honum ospordhom/ vtan hwath som gudh siælwer biwdher thz ma syndalöst göras/ æn tho at thz ware ællæs synd Thy at han ma all skipilse omskipta som skapadhe oc skipadhe Oc hafdhe han nakath thz budhit/ som han hawer nw forbudhit/ oc nakath thz forbudhith/ som han hawer nw budhit/ tha waare thz wæl giort som nw ær synd/ oc thz synd som nw ær wæl giort/ swa ær gudz wili alz waldogher.

---

55 Petrus Comestor, *Historia scholastica*, ed. by Migne, col. 1155.
56 *Stjórn*, I, ed. by Astås, p. 425.8–15.

Han hafdhe oc giwith gull oc silff egipto mannom/ som giwer allom hwath som the ægha/ oc hafdhe the forgiort widh han liiff oc gotz fore otro skuld/ oc thy giordhe waar herra enkte a mot them ræt som han skipadhe/ vtan hælder mz oc galt thera giæld som the waaro skyldoghe/ them ther ærwodhat hafdho fore them.
Wi maghom oc vnderstanda mz görsæme godhan kænnedom/ oc wiis ordh/ oc mz egipto mannom hedhna mæstara/ som scriffwadho margha böker/ oc blandath ordh mz wiisdom oc hægumma/ mz wantro oc godhom kænnedom Oc hwilken tima wi faam at læsa thera böker eller höra/ tha skulom wi fæsta mz os thera wiiso ordh oc godhan kænnedoom/ oc ower fara blundande thera wantro oc hagomma Tha taghum wi at lane gulkar oc silffkar oc latom them qwarra sina lergrytor.

([Bible text:] The sons of Israel took gold and silver vessels and great treasures as a loan from the people of the Egyptian land.

[Comment:] And here we shall understand that no one should claim wages for his labour through deceit and repay himself from someone who is not informed about it, but what God himself orders might be done without sin, even if it would be a sin otherwise. Because he who created and shaped everything can reshape everything. And if he [then] had ordered something which he has now forbidden, and had something forbidden [then] which he has now ordered, then that, which now is a sin, was well done then, and that which was a sin then, is now well done. In this way, God's will is almighty.

He had also given gold and silver to the Egyptians, he who gives to all what they own, and, in his eyes, they had wasted their life and goods because of their unfaithfulness, and therefore our Lord made nothing against the law he had created, but rather paid their debt which they owed to them [the Israelites] who had worked for them.

In the case of the treasures, we might also understand them as good knowledge and wise words, as in the case of the Egyptian men [who were] heathen masters who wrote many books and who mixed words of wisdom and nonsense, of superstition and of good knowledge. And when we read their books or listen to them, we should pay attention to their wise words and good knowledge and ignore with closed eyes their superstition and nonsense. Then we borrow golden bowls and silver bowls and leave them their clay pots.)

First, we might note that the Old Swedish translation of the Bible text uses the rather mild expression *togho at lane* ('they borrowed'), the motivation for which may have been the Latin verb *commodarent* as used in the Vulgate ('they offered them/borrowed to them'), but which then also is contradicted by the verb *spoliaverunt* ('they plundered') in the next clause.[57] In the third step of the interpreta-

---

57 See the quotation of Exodus 12. 36 above.

tion at the end of the comment, the Old Swedish text goes on with the same mild expression: *Tha taghum wi at lane* ('Then we should borrow'). The commentator was obviously actively trying to downplay the issue.

It is, however, striking that the comment begins with a discussion of the juridical and moral issues at stake, with the question of whether one might be justified in robbing someone as compensation for unpaid wages. The theft is often justified in exegesis on account of the unpaid wages, as e.g. in the *Historia scholastica* (see above), but the comment in the Old Swedish text explicitly defines it as being an absolute exception ordered by God and warns the reader to understand it as an example to follow. In the last section, the commentator turns to the learned interpretation of the gold as heathen knowledge which he then summarizes neatly and with great understanding. This passage shows that the commentator was able to render the rather complex interpretations in a manner which also made them accessible for an unlearned reader.

Similar moral and juridical issues do not dominate the commentary, but they recur in the translation whenever the biblical characters perform actions which are not up to the moral standards shared by the translator and their (hypothetical) readers. This sensitivity can be illustrated by the passage when Jacob lies to his father to make him bless Jacob instead of his brother Esau (Genesis 27. 18–19):

> Ysaac spör/ hwilkin hans son ær thz/ Æn iacob sigher sik wara esau eldre brodher/ <u>oc ey liwgher han tha æn han swa sighir/ thy at han hafdhe köpt ældre brodherins wördhning oc mz wyrdhninginne nampnith mz hans ia/ oc wiste oc thz aff sinne modher at thz war thæs hælgha andz wili oc raadh</u>.[58]
>
> > (Isaac asks which son of his it is, and Jacob says it is Esau, the elder brother, <u>and he is not lying when he says that, because he had bought the honour of his older brother and together with the honour also the name [i.e. 'Esau'] for his [i.e. Esau's] assent, and he also knew from his mother that it was the wish and advice of the Holy Spirit</u>.)

The comment follows immediately after Jacob's quite striking lie, in which the comment insists on Jacob's innocence and transfers the responsibility to the Holy Spirit. In the *Stjórn*, the story of Isaac and Jacob is first told in full, and only then followed with a long comment which raises similar excuses for Jacob's behaviour.[59] It is as if the commentator in the Old Swedish translation preferred to act directly when a problem appeared, reacting immediately to the anticipated doubts of the future reader.

There are also other issues beyond the moral or juridical ones which are also addressed in a similar way in the commentary. Similar comments concern linguistic issues, as when God changes between singular and plural second person

---

58 *Svenska medeltidens bibel-arbeten*, I, ed. by Klemming, p. 213.24–30.
59 *Stjórn*, I, ed. by Astås, pp. 250.5–251.22.

pronouns in a speech made to the Israelites,[60] or to explain unclear passages such as why it was necessary for trumpets to signal the break-up of the Israeli camp when the cloud pillar could already gather the Israelites,[61] or why Israelites were so passive in their confrontation with King Edom and his people.[62] The commentator goes to great lengths to identify and address any kind of possible obscurity. It is as if anything in the Bible text that might cause a reader to object must be disambiguated and any potential for misinterpretation removed. Moses did *not* do wrong when he slew the Egyptian; it is *not* right to rob someone for unpaid wages; Jacob was *not* a liar, etc. Whereas the commentary in the West Nordic *Stjórn* might sometimes expose contradictory solutions to a problem, the Swedish text is unambiguous.

To sum up, an important part of the commentary focuses on a variety of interpretative problems which could be created through an unguided perusal of the Bible. Most conspicuous of these are those comments which address the behaviour of biblical characters, when these behaviours were amoral or even criminal from the point of view of Christian ethics in the fourteenth century. These figures certainly commit a fair share of the cardinal sins among everything else. The vigilant commentator took responsibility for them: he did not omit the respective passages, which at first sight might have seemed an easy way out of the situation, but after all he was working with a text which was communicated to mankind by God. He instead, then, took pains to make the problematic passages acceptable for a reader who was able to cope only with the historical (literal) meaning of the text. In this way, he took control of the reading and of the process of interpretation.

An Epilogue: The Readers of the Old Swedish Pentateuch Translation in a European Perspective

The Old Swedish Pentateuch translation is one of the European vernacular Bible translations, paraphrases, re-narrations and commentaries which appear in increasing amounts from the thirteenth century onwards, and which are generally believed to have been made mainly for lay readers and audiences. The rich history of medieval Bible translation has for a long time been less well-known and overshadowed by the misconception that in general the Church would have oppressed and opposed vernacular translation that was undertaken prior to the Reformation.[63] This is not to say that were no harsh reactions to heterodox

---

60 *Svenska medeltidens bibel-arbeten*, I, ed. by Klemming, p. 367.17–24, commenting Leviticus 19. 29–32.

61 *Svenska medeltidens bibel-arbeten*, I, ed. by Klemming, p. 388.24–389.14, commenting Numbers 10. 1–10.

62 *Svenska medeltidens bibel-arbeten*, I, ed. by Klemming, p. 409.30, commenting Numbers 20. 21.

63 The traditional view is discussed critically in Gow, 'Challenging the Protestant Paradigm', see also Liere, *An Introduction to the Medieval Bible*, pp. 177–78. Lay reading of

interpretations – and certainly there were local bans on vernacular Bibles – but Bible translations were produced all over Europe, in many cases commissioned by secular rulers, and representatives of the Church hierarchy also encouraged lay people to read biblical texts.[64] The final discussion here will bring the strands together regarding what type of reader and which ways of reading the translator of the Swedish Pentateuch might have had in mind. I shall then put these findings into a broader European perspective.

The intended reader was not, it would seem, expected to be theologically educated – and clerics and members of religious orders would have had to read the relevant texts in Latin.[65] Nevertheless, the commentator made use of each of the levels of fourfold exegesis; however, while the commentary may be described as edifying preaching for lay people, it has little in common with academic exegesis.

The commentator's additions made to morally ambivalent passages connect his text with a long discussion on vernacular bible translation and the risks of heresies arising from lay reading of the Scriptures. An awareness of the problem is explicitly expressed in the Swedish Pentateuch translation, when the commentator launches an attack upon heretic critics of the Church in a comment on the first commandment.[66] Similar concerns might also lie behind the consistent omission of religious instructions. As previously mentioned, the central theme of the second theological exposition in *MB* I is to distinguish the regulations in the Old Law that apply to Christians from those that pertain only to Jews.

The danger of heterodoxy, however, was only one of the problems that the translators of the Old Testament had to manage. Around the year 1000, the monk Ælfric of Eynsham (d. *c.* 1010) had already expressed hesitancy towards translating the Old Testament, especially Genesis, for the lay audience, as uneducated

---

biblical texts in the Middle Ages has been subject to a growing amount of interest among researchers, e.g. *Cultures of Religious Reading in the Late Middle Ages*, ed. by Corbellini, *Vernacular Bible and Religious Reform in the Middle Ages and the Early Modern Era* and '*Wading Lambs and Swimming Elephants*', both ed. by François and den Hollander, *Form and Function in the Late Medieval Bible*, ed. by Poleg and Light.

64 The problem was not translation in itself, but rather preaching outside of the established institutions, see Liere, *An Introduction to the Medieval Bible*, pp. 190–94. Rich overviews of European vernacular Bibles are provided in Hunter and others, 'The Vernacular Scriptures', pp. 338–491, and various chapters in *The New Cambridge History of the Bible*, II, ed. by Lampe.

65 Another possible vernacular reading group would be members of a female order, for whom many vernacular Bible translations were also produced in the Middle Ages. However, the specific orientation of the translation and comments towards lay society in the commentary makes such a conclusion seem less plausible.

66 *Svenska medeltidens bibel-arbeten*, I, ed. by Klemming, p. 331.3–332.20. Such concerns are also visible in other Bible translations, like in the 1361 Middle Dutch History Bible, which was made for a lay person, and which provides evidence for a specific interest in preventing the reader from drawing heretical conclusions from its reading, see Kors, *De Bijbel voor Leken*, pp. 57–59.

readers might come to the conclusion that the text legitimized deeds and acts which were quite the opposite to those that secular and religious authorities accepted – sins such as murder, theft, incest, polygamy, etc.[67] Similar concerns also appear in connection with the vernacular Bibles which were produced later on in the Middle Ages.[68] The Swedish commentator's explanatory additions to morally and juridically questionable acts in the Pentateuch translation seems to be a response to the same question, a concern to save readers from those narratives of the Bible that could be perilous and which could lead the reflective reader astray, not only from the authority of the Church but from moral and legal behaviour in general.

The use of such a discursive strategy to confront and neutralize problematic issues can be interpreted as the efforts of a hegemonic authority to control their readers, but this would be a simplification which then obscures the more interesting view of the reader and his/her way of reading. If the commentator took pains to address particular interpretative issues, then it also means that he presupposed that the reader would be able to make those kinds of critical reflections in their own reading, and also that the text could be read without the supervision of a theologically educated person. This does not say that the empirical readers actually read the text in such an independent way, but that such a literate context was anticipated as a possibility by the author of the translation.

The intended reader, therefore, can be described as a lay person with sufficient intellectual resources to appreciate the moderately advanced discussion in some of the comments while also taking a reflective, critical stance towards the text. It is a picture close to how recent research describes lay practices of religious reflective reading in the European high and late Middle Ages.[69]

It is also important to stress that the majority of the commentaries comprise spiritual guidance and theological exposition covering a wide and deep range of matters. They address the readers' personal faith and describe how the Old Testament connects to and stands as a model for contemporary medieval society. For instance, attributes of Moses are said to mirror those of Christian bishops, and the roles of the king, knights and peasants as well as that of the Church are measured by Old Testament patterns.[70] The text aimed to guide both individuals and society, and to strengthen the position of the Church. The Old Testament books provided models for society and the State, and the Old Swedish translation invited the reader to draw such parallels.[71]

The question, then, is who the intended readers actually were, that is, what real, empirical readers could the translator have had in mind. We know almost nothing about readers in early fourteenth-century Sweden, and only a little about

---

67 Liere, *An Introduction to the Medieval Bible*, pp. 187–89.

68 Liere, *An Introduction to the Medieval Bible*, p. 195, p. 198.

69 See footnote 65.

70 For examples of such commentary, see *Fem Moseböcker på fornsvenska*, ed. by Thorell, pp. xxxix–xlii.

71 There is a connection between the West Nordic King's Mirror (*Konungs skuggsjá*) and *Stjórn*, cf. *Stjórn*, I, ed. by Astås, pp. xxvi–xxx.

the society in general, so the only way to approach an answer to the question is via comparisons with related European examples. There is, for instance, a possible historical link to the *Bible historiale* by Guyart des Moulins and a possible parallel between their respective readers. In 1335 King Magnus Eriksson married Blanche of Namur, who was of the house of Dampierre and related to the French royal family. Blanche was connected, both geographically and socially, with the groups that we know could well have been in possession of Guyart's work, and even if we know nothing about her literary education, it is quite possible that her family either owned a copy of the *Bible historiale* or knew about it or, at least, some of the other French Bible translations. Guyart explicitly addressed lay readers in his preface, but only a wealthy group, like the nobility to which Blanche belonged, could possibly afford to buy the voluminous work. To judge from the numerous surviving copies of his work, it reached a large number of such readers.[72]

The idea of producing a commented Bible in Swedish vernacular might have been initiated or strengthened by personal contact within the European nobility. The French and the Swedish bibles originated within groups of the same social standing. The 1346 inventory from Bohus castle, which speaks about 'a large book with the Bible in Swedish', also mentions that the King had given a German Bible to one of the knights in the council, Ulf Abjörnsson; and, as already mentioned, St Birgitta, who belonged to the highest stratum of the nobility, is said to have owned a Swedish Bible.[73] This evidence, although rather erratic, shows the presence of and interest in Bible translations within the network of nobility surrounding King Magnus. It seems very likely, therefore, that the translator of the Swedish Pentateuch wrote his text just for these or similar recipients.

Both Ulf Abjörnsson and St Birgitta's father, Birger Pettersson, took an active part in the far-reaching legislative reforms during the first half of the fourteenth century, which eventually led to the first Swedish common Country Law and City Law dating to around 1350. This legislative work, which resulted in a synthesis of a number of Provincial Laws being written, must have involved a large part of the nobility during that period. In such circumstances – and with such possible readers – it is perhaps no wonder that the translator/commentator addressed the many juridical and moral problems in the text with the greatest care.

Bibliography

Manuscript Sources

København, Det Kongelige bibliotek, MS Thott 4 4o
Stockholm, Kungliga biblioteket, MS A 1

---

72 Liere, *An Introduction to the Medieval Bible*, p. 195.
73 See footnote 14.

Primary Sources

Acta et processus canonizacionis Beate Birgitte. Efter Cod. A 14 Holm., Cod. Ottob. Lat. 90 o. Cod. Harl. 612 med inledning, person- och ortregister, ed. by Isak Collijn, Svenska fornskriftssällskapet, Serie 2: Latinska skrifter, 1 (Uppsala: Almqvist & Wiksell, 1924–31)

Fem Moseböcker på fornsvenska enligt Cod. Holm. A 1, ed. by Olof Thorell, 3 pts, Samlingar utgivna av Svenska fornskriftsällskapet, Serie 1, Svenska skrifter, 212, 218, 223 (Uppsala: Almqvist & Wiksell, 1955–59)

Petrus Comestor, *Historia scholastica*, ed. by Jacques-Paul Migne, Patrologiae Cursus Completus: Series Latina, 198 (Paris: Migne, 1855), cols 1049–1721

Stjórn: Tekst etter håndskriftene, ed. by Reidar Astås, 2 vols, Norrøne tekster, 8 (Oslo: Riksarkivet, 2008)

Svenska medeltidens bibel-arbeten, ed. by Gustav E. Klemming, 2 vols, Samlingar utgivna av Svenska fornskriftsällskapet, Serie 1, Svenska skrifter 6 (Stockholm: Norstedt, 1848–55), I (1848)

Secondary Works

Amtower, Laurel, *Engaging Words: The Culture of Reading in the Later Middle Ages*, The New Middle Ages (New York and Hampshire: Palgrave, 2000)

Cultures of Religious Reading in the Late Middle Ages: Instructing the Soul, Feeding the Spirit and Awakening the Passion, ed. by Sabrina Corbellini, Utrecht Studies in Medieval Literacy, 25 (Turnhout: Brepols, 2013)

Ejrnæs, Bodil, 'The Bible in the Languages of Scandinavia', in *The New Cambridge History of the Bible*, ed. by James Carleton Paget and others, 4 vols (Cambridge: Cambridge University Press, 2012–16), II: *From 600 to 1450*, ed. by Richard Marsden and E. Ann Matter (2012), pp. 239–50

Faymonville, Louise, 'Om variationen i Codex Thott 4 4:o – ett tolkningsförslag', *Arkiv för nordisk filologi*, 132 (2017), pp. 153–78

Form and Function in the Late Medieval Bible, ed. by Eyal Poleg and Laura Light, Library of the Written Word, 27 (Leiden and Boston: Brill, 2013)

Gow, Andrew, 'Challenging the Protestant Paradigm: Bible Reading in Lay and Urban Contexts of the Later Middle Ages', in *Scripture and Pluralism: Reading the Bible in the Religiously Plural Worlds of the Middle Ages and Renaissance*, ed. by Thomas J. Heffernan and Thomas E. Burman, Studies in the History of Christian Traditions, 123 (Leiden and Boston: Brill, 2005), 161–91

Hunter, M. J. and others, 'The Vernacular Scriptures', in *The Cambridge History of the Bible, II: The West from the Fathers to the Reformation*, ed. by G. W. H. Lampe (Cambridge: Cambridge University Press, 1975), pp. 338–491

Kors, Mikel, *De Bijbel voor Leken: Studies over Petrus Naghel en de Historiebijbel van 1361*, Encyclopédie Bénédictine (Turnhout: Brepols, 2007)

Larsson, Inger, *Pragmatic Literacy and the Medieval Use of the Vernacular: The Swedish Example*, Utrecht Studies in Medieval Literacy, 16 (Turnhout: Brepols, 2009)

Liere, Frans van, *An Introduction to the Medieval Bible*, Introduction to Religion (Cambridge: Cambridge University Press, 2014)

Lobrichon, Guy, 'The Story of a Success: The "Bible historiale" in French (1295–ca. 1500)', in *Form and Function in the Late Medieval Bible*, ed. by in Eyal Poleg and

Laura Light, Library of the Written Word, 27: Manuscript World, 4 (Leiden and Boston: Brill, 2013), pp. 307–32

de Lubac, Henri, *Medieval Exegesis*, 2 vols (Grand Rapids, Michigan: William B. Eerdmans Publishing Company / Edinburgh: T&T Clark, 1998–2009), II: *The Four Senses of Scripture*, trans. by Edward M. Macierowski (2000)

Murdoch, Brian, *The Medieval Popular Bible: Expansions of Genesis in the Middle Ages* (Cambridge: Brewer, 2003)

Pettersson, Jonatan, 'De teologiska utredningarna i Medeltidens bibelarbeten 1', *Arkiv för nordisk filologi*, 134 (2019), pp. 107–48

———, 'Nordic Bible Translations in Medieval and Early Modern Europe', in *Vernacular Bible and Religious Reform in the Middle Ages and Early Modern* Era, ed. by Wim François and August den Hollander, Bliotheca Ephemeridum Theologicarum Lovaniensium, 287 (Leuven, Paris, and Bristol, CT: Peeters, 2017), pp. 107–48

Smalley, Beryl, *The Study of the Bible in the Middle Ages*, 3rd edn (Oxford: Blackwell, 1983)

Svanhildur Óskarsdóttir, 'Heroes or Holy People? The Context of Old Norse Bible Translations', in *Übersetzen im skandinavischen Mittelalter*, ed. by Vera Johanterwage and Stephanie Würth, Studia Medievalia Septentrionalia, 14 (Vienna: Fassbaender, 2007), pp. 107–21

The Eufemiavisor and Courtly Culture: Time Texts and Cultural Transfer: Papers from a Symposium in Stockholm, 11–13 October 2012, ed. by Olle Ferm, Ingela Hedström, Sofia Lodén, Jonatan Pettersson, and Mia Åkestam, Konferenser, 88 (Stockholm: Kungliga Vitterhets historie och antikvitets akademien, 2015)

The New Cambridge History of the Bible, ed. by James Carleton Paget and others, 4 vols (Cambridge: Cambridge University Press, 2012–16), II: *From 600 to 1450*, ed. by Richard Marsden and E. Ann Matter (2012)

Thorell, Olof, *Fem moseböcker på fornsvenska: En språklig undersökning på grundval av de bevarade handskrifterna*, Nordiska texter och undersökningar, 18 (Stockholm: Hugo Gebers/Köpenhamn: Levin & Munksgaard, 1951)

'*Wading Lambs and Swimming Elephants': The Bible for the Laity and Theologians in the Late Medieval and Early Modern Era*, ed. by Wim François and August den Hollander, Bibliotheca Ephemeridum Theologicarum Lovaniensium, 257 (Leuven, Paris, and Bristol: Peeters, 2012)

Vernacular Bible and Religious Reform in the Middle Ages and the Early Modern Era, ed. by Wim François and August den Hollander, Bibliotheca Ephemeridum Theologicarum Lovaniensium, 287 (Leuven, Paris, and Bristol: Peeters, 2017)

Website

Svenskt diplomatariums huvudkartotek (*SDHK*), no. 5311, online: <https://sok.riksarkivet.se/sdhk?SDHK=5311&postid=sdhk_5311> [accessed 3 November 2022]

Old Czech Biblical Prologues

A Medieval Reader's Gateway to the Study of the Bible

Andrea Svobodová

Institute for Czech Language, Czech Academy of Sciences

Kateřina Voleková

Institute for Czech Language, Czech Academy of Sciences

Pavlína Rychterová

Institute for Medieval Research, Austrian Academy of Sciences

Biblical prologues have accompanied biblical texts in manuscripts of the Latin Vulgate since Late Antiquity, although they did not constitute an integral part of the biblical canon.[1] They introduced individual biblical books or larger sections of the Bible, such as the Epistles, the Four Books of Kings, or the Pentateuch.[2] A considerable number of biblical prologues were written at the beginning of the fifth century by Jerome, the author of the Latin translation of the Bible known as the Vulgate. Jerome's Bible prologues are frequently based on his expositions of his own biblical translations into Latin or on his Bible commentaries, as well as on his Epistles. In these texts he often summarizes the content of a particular biblical book, defends his Latin translation, and discusses the biblical canon. From the sixth century onwards Jerome's prologues, as well as

---

1 The research underlying this article was supported by the Czech Science Foundation, Project No. 15-06405S (*Old Czech Biblical Prologues*), carried out at the Czech Language Institute of the Czech Academy of Sciences.

2 On the prefaces in the Medieval Latin Bibles, see De Bruyne, *Prefaces to the Latin Bible*; Light, 'Non-Biblical Texts in Thirteenth-Century Bibles', pp. 169–83.

those of Pseudo-Jerome, sporadically appeared in Latin biblical manuscripts; they became more frequent in the eighth and ninth centuries in the course of the so-called Carolingian renaissance.[3] Moreover, new prefaces, both original texts and adaptations of older textual material, began to appear in the High Middle Ages. The prologues, although of secondary status, as indicated by rubrics and decoration, were then copied along with the biblical text as its integral, formalized part.[4] Their formal constitution varied in Latin Bibles, as did their number and content, until the appearance of the so-called *Paris Bible* or *exemplar Parisiense*.[5]

The term *exemplar Parisiense* denotes Bibles produced in Paris in the thirteenth century. Individual biblical manuscripts from this period possess a significant number of common characteristics: they were Pandects (complete collections of all books of the Bible in one codex), and the books were arranged according to a new order that closely followed the historical chronology of biblical history, and also included the apocryphal books (Ezra 3, Prayer of Manasseh, Baruch including the Epistle of Jeremiah). Furthermore, the text of the *Paris Bible* was divided into numbered chapters; *capitula* or *breves (libri)*, chapter summaries, which had been an integral part of biblical manuscripts up until then, disappeared, and a new set of prologues, based on Jerome's texts, was added, often together with *Interpretationes Hebraicorum nominum*, a list of Hebrew names, accompanied by short explanations in Latin. The *Paris Bible* contained sixty-four introductions and prefaces to the biblical books, including six newly written prologues, which cannot be found in manuscripts of the unglossed Vulgate before the thirteenth century and which are connected to the *Glossa ordinaria*.[6] Thanks to the productive Parisian scriptoria and active booksellers, the *Paris Bible* became widely popular among the newly founded mendicant and preaching orders and quickly spread all over Christian Europe, including Bohemia, where it became the model for the earliest translation of the Bible into the medieval (Old) Czech vernacular.[7]

This essay focuses on the biblical prologues, a topic which has been neglected in Czech philological and literary studies. Our analysis concerns three closely related issues: first, the efforts of the translators and authors of the prologues

---

3 The occurrence of prologues in the earliest Latin manuscripts is discussed by Berger, 'Les Préfaces jointes aux livres'.

4 Light, 'Non-Biblical Texts in Thirteenth-Century Bibles', p. 171.

5 The first list of prologues was created by Donatien De Bruyne (cf. De Bruyne, *Préface de la Bible latine*, the second edition with an English commentary: *Prefaces to the Latin Bible*). Fridericus Stegmüller endeavoured to make a list of biblical prologues in medieval Latin Bibles, listing 558 items (cf. *Repertorium Biblicum*, I, ed. by Stegmüller, pp. 253–310). For the Paris Bible see Van Liere, 'The Latin Bible', p. 103.

6 Van Liere, 'The Latin Bible', pp. 104–05; Light, 'The Thirteenth Century and the Paris Bible', pp. 380–91; Light, 'French Bibles c. 1200–30', pp. 155–68.

7 The term 'Old Czech' represents a translation of the Czech terms 'staročeský' – 'staročeština' designating written medieval Czech languages as extant in the sources.

to cope with the linguistic issues they had to solve during their work; secondly, the impact of biblical translation on the development of written/literary language in late medieval Bohemia, and thirdly, the varying understandings of the authority of a biblical text written in the vernacular. The reception of the Czech Bible in the fourteenth and fifteenth century was very multifaceted; the extant sources are numerous, as they comprise over 200 manuscripts and manuscript fragments. Currently, we are working with a hypothesis of three redactions of the Czech Bible, as formulated in the 1980s by Vladimír Kyas, a leading authority in medieval Bohemian studies. His hypothesis was based in particular on surviving complete Bibles, on partial translations and on fragmentary texts; however, he only selectively considered the biblical translations contained in vernacular theological, catechetic, and homiletic texts. A close look at these translations will enable us to draw a more complex picture of the late medieval vernacularization of the Bible in Bohemia.

Prologues in the Medieval Czech Bible

Evidence of vernacular biblical translations in Bohemia is attested by twelfth-century glossed Latin texts. These glosses are rather sporadic but they provide valuable evidence for a discourse of Bible translation in the Czech vernacular.[8] One of the oldest Czech translation glosses, found in Jerome's prologue to Jeremiah in a Latin Old Testament from the twelfth century, testifies to the interest of an unknown scholar.[9]

The Psalter and Gospel lectionaries were very probably the first biblical books translated into Czech at the end of the thirteenth century. The oldest textual witnesses originate from the Benedictine milieu: the *Seitenstetten Evangeliary* (Seitenstetten, Stiftsbibliothek, Cod. 272) and the *Vienna Evangeliary* (Vienna, Österreichische Nationalbibliothek, Cod. 4733). The *National Museum Glossed Psalter* (Prague, Knihovna Národního muzea, MS XIV D 13) was made in the Benedictine female monastery of St George; this prayer book belonged to an unknown nun of noble origin. The Latin *Wittenberg Psalter* from the same time contains an interlinear Czech translation and also served as a prayer book for a noble woman.[10] Intended as prayer books and liturgical manuals, the oldest Czech Psalters and Gospel lectionaries had no prefaces.[11]

The first Czech translation of the entire Bible was made in the 1350s. For the translation of the Psalter, the authors drew on previous Czech material, while it seems that other biblical books were translated anew. In the biblical material

---

8 Cf. *Jagić's Glosses*, Vienna, Österreichische Nationalbibliothek, Cod. 1190.

9 Olomouc, Zemský archiv v Opavě, pobočka Olomouc, Sbírka rukopisů Metropolitní kapituly, MS CO 400, fol. 1[ra–vb]. Cf. *Staročeské biblické předmluvy*, ed. by Voleková and Svobodová, pp. 105–06.

10 Vintr, *Die älteste tschechische Psalterübersetzung*, p. 46.

11 Vintr, *Die ältesten tschechischen Evangeliare*, p. 146.

which originated from before 1500, we identify three distinct versions of this translation, referred to as redactions or recensions in Czech philology, preserved in more than a hundred manuscripts and in more than a hundred fragments.[12] They are often accompanied in their respective manuscripts by various apparatus for biblical exegesis, for preaching or for the liturgical use of the Bible. The most common among these texts in the Old Czech biblical manuscripts are lists of pericopes and biblical prologues.

The first redaction of the medieval Czech Bible, as attested in the so-called *Dresden Bible*, was produced by two groups of translators who worked independently of each other, as may be determined from the different vocabulary they employed for particular terms.[13] It would seem that individual translators in both groups dealt with the source text (some exemplar of the *Paris Bible*) at their own discretion (we can identify their individual work through slight differences in style and vocabulary), and for some reason most of them omitted the prologues preceding individual biblical books. So, for example, the Gospel of Luke begins in the first redaction with the fifth verse of the first chapter, because the first four verses, which form Luke's introduction to his work, were formally set apart as a prologue in the *Paris Bible* (Luke 1. 1–4). The Czech translator of the Gospels then intentionally omitted it and the Gospel of Luke in the first-redaction manuscripts therefore begins with the words 'Byl jest za dnóv Herodových, krále židovského, jeden pop, jménem Zachař' ('There was in the days of Herod, Jewish king, a certain priest named Zacharias').(Fig. 1)

In general, the surviving copies of the first redaction of the Czech Bible contain a relatively small number of prologues. The majority of these prologues accompany the Apostolic Letters – both the summarizing introduction and the short prefaces

---

12 On the conception of the three Old Czech translations of the Bible, see Kyas, *Česká bible*; also cf. Pečírková, 'Czech Translations of the Bible', p. 1171; Sichálek, 'European Background', p. 75.

13 Cf. Kyas, *Česká bible*, p. 43; Pytlíková, 'Průzkum překladové a překladatelské stránky první redakce staročeského biblického překladu', pp. 54–146; Sichálek, 'European Background', p. 76. For example, Latin *sacerdos* ('priest') was translated with the older Czech lexeme *pop* (an early loanword from medieval Greek **pappas* through Old High German **pfaffo*) by one group and with the word *kněz* (an early loanword from Germanic **kuningaz*) by the other – cf. Rejzek, *Český etymologický slovník*, p. 311, p. 538. The *Dresden Bible* was destroyed in 1914 (Dresden, Sächsische Landesbibliothek, MS Mscr. Dresd. Oe.85). However, the recto sides of the folios were photocopied in 1914; for the facsimile, see *Die alttschechische Dresdener Bibel*, ed. by Rothe and Scholz; some biblical books were copied by hand by Josef Vraštil (a photocopy of Vraštil's transcript is stored in the Department of Language Development, Czech Language Institute of the Czech Academy of Sciences, Prague). The revision of the first redaction survives in the *Litoměřice-Třeboň Bible* from 1414 (I and II: Litoměřice, Oblastní archiv v Litoměřicích, collection Biskupské sbírky Litoměřice, MS BIF 3.2 and MS BIF 3.1; III: Třeboň, Státní oblastní archiv v Třeboni, MS A 2) and in the *Olomouc Bible* from 1417 (Olomouc, Vědecká knihovna, MS M III 1/I–II). Parts of the first translation can also be found in a few compiled Bibles dating from the fifteenth century.

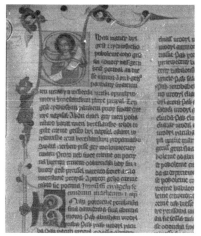

Figure 1: Prologue to the Gospel of Matthew, *Dresden Bible*, Dresden, Sächsische Landesbibliothek, MS Dresd.Oe.85, fol. 541[r]. Microfilm copy stored at the Institute of Czech Literature of the Czech Academy of Sciences.[15]

to individual Pauline Epistles. Another prologue precedes the Gospel of Matthew; the same text (perhaps the direct model for the Prologue in the first redaction) is also included in *St Matthew's Gospel with Homilies* containing a Czech translation of the Gospel with selected exegetical commentaries, among them one ascribed to Emperor Charles IV.[14] The two other prologues – to the Book of the Genesis and to the Acts of the Apostles – do not build on any known Latin text, but may be original works by one of the translators known as *Dominicanus*.[16]

Dominicanus's prologue to the Book of Genesis shows the purpose and concerns of the translator, something the translated prologues of Jerome reveal only to a limited extent. It seems that Jerome's prologues were regarded as 'historical' texts by the translators. The resume of Jerome's prologue to the Pentateuch, included in the so-called *Prague Bible* from 1488, a revised version of the first-redaction prologue, laconically states:

> Here ends the prologue to the five books of Moses by Saint Jerome, in which Saint Jerome apologizes and talks about the reason why after seventy translations of the Old Testament a new one was necessary; answering all his enemies who scolded him because of that and called his work unnecessary and useless, he announces and explains broadly the need and use of this translation.[17]

---

14 Prague, Národní knihovna České republiky, MS XVII A 4.

15 For the catalogue, see *Ústav pro českou literaturu, Staročeská sbírka (lístkový katalog)*, online: <https://starocech.ucl.cas.cz/retrobi/domu> [accessed 3 November 2022].

16 *Staročeské biblické předmluvy*, ed. by Voleková and Svobodová, pp. 240–41, pp. 452–53. See also Kyas, *Česká bible*, p. 39, pp. 47–48, pp. 62–64.

17 *Staročeské biblické předmluvy*, ed. by Voleková and Svobodová, p. 239. The translations of Czech textual quotes were made by the authors of this article.

The translators of the first redaction did not connect Jerome's efforts with their own work, nor did they use his example as an argument to legitimize their own translation, which other contemporary Czech translations of exegetical and catechetic works would do.[18] In his own prologue, *Dominicanus* did not emphasize the fact that he and his colleagues were translating a holy text into the vernacular. He instead sought to prevent basic misunderstandings that might occur when theologically unlearned people were confronted with a biblical text. This indeed is very remarkable, considering that the first redaction of the Czech Bible was mostly received in monastic and clerical milieus – at least as evidenced by the extant manuscripts. It instead indicates that the intended reader was probably a lay person and that the (supporting) clerical user had to be warned to interpret the biblical text with great care. *Dominicanus* starts with a quotation from Aristotle's metaphysics: 'All men by nature desire knowledge'.[19] He therefore defines the Czech Bible as an epistemological project:

> In this way the human reason is made that it goes further and further, higher and higher, it asks and longs for answers where everything originated, how the things are connected, and to which end each thing comes.[20]

Following this statement, the significance of which is not immediately clear or explicitly discussed, the author delineates the boundaries of the (self-)educational efforts of a (lay) Bible-reader, presupposing his/her questions: 'Wanting to know which beginning this world had in its creation, we should know where the Lord was before he created something'. A lengthy quotation from Augustine's *Enarrationes in Psalmos* follows, in which the idea of God's self-sufficiency is summarized, and which is also supplemented by the same definition in a dialogical form. This doubling of the answer indicates that the author was not quite confident in the ability of the intended reader to understand the quotation properly. He then moves on to another crucial question that this imagined reader might ask: 'Why was man created?' Augustine's authority, together with that of Thomas Aquinas and Hugh of Saint Victor, again helps at least to show the reader, if not to clarify this very complex problem, at which exact point he/she should stop to ask:

> And therefore everything which is around the world was created for the use of man so that man knowing God would serve Him with all this [which is around the world in the world]. Through this service the divinity will not be more but human longing, improving in good works, fulfilling his salvation.[21]

---

18 Rychterová, 'Preaching, Vernacular, and the Laity', pp. 297–330.

19 Aristotle, *Metaphysics* I. 1. 980a. 22.

20 *Staročeské biblické předmluvy*, ed. by Voleková and Svobodová, p. 240.

21 *Staročeské biblické předmluvy*, ed. by Voleková and Svobodová, p. 241.

The other of *Dominicanus*'s original prologues from the first redaction introduces the Acts of the Apostles. In contrast to Jerome's prologue to the Acts, which was translated and copied in most of the Czech Bibles (the original prologue appears only in the *Dresden Bible* and in the *Litoměřice-Třeboň Bible*), *Dominicanus* opens his introduction with the Pentecost miracle:

> About the holy apostles as well as about all God's scholars it is written that when they were filled with the Holy Spirit, they started to speak. In the way Jesus Christ revealed the new status of the Holy Scripture, it was announced and disseminated in the whole world, which is described here in these books on the Acts of Apostles. Therefore the Saviour said in the Gospel of St Marcus: 'Go into all the world and preach the gospel to all the creation' [Mark 16. 15]. And this clarion anouncement of the holy faith in all the world happened through the reinforcement of the Holy Spirit.[22]

The Pentecost miracle, together with the gifts of the Holy Spirit described in Chapter 16 of Mark's Gospel, is the key narrative in the New Testament defining the peoples who were the target of the Christian message which was delivered them in their own language and, as such, forms the strongest argument for the translation of Holy Scripture into vernacular languages. However, *Dominicanus* does not develop this theme further in an apologetic or didactic way; instead he paraphrases Acts 2, reminding the reader of how St Peter and St John first revealed the Scripture to Jewish people amongst whom three thousand were then baptized subsequently.

In both his prologues, *Dominicanus* actually adressess the key issues of the vernacular translation of the Bible: the authority of a vernacular translation of the Scripture and the danger of misunderstanding the text if it were read and speculated on by readers who were not theologically educated.[23] Nevertheless, he abstains from profoundly discussing the issue, which would perhaps push boundaries of the genre, although the polemical tenor represents the dominant feature in the most popular of Jerome's prologues. However, it is very possible that at this point the thin red line between indvidual concepts of textual authority lies: the authority of Jerome, Augustine and Thomas Aquinas was regarded as sufficient for all those who had to instruct the lay readers.

Biblical Discourse and the Bohemian Reformation

Only a few extant manuscripts with biblical material from this period were made for the personal devotion of the laity: translations of the Psalter and Books of Hours, as well as translations and adaptations of biblical paraphrases such as the *Legenda aurea* by Jacobus de Voragine, the *Historia scholastica* by Petrus

---

[22] *Staročeské biblické předmluvy*, ed. by Voleková and Svobodová, p. 451.

[23] The persecution of rigorous biblicist Valdensians reached its peak in Bohemia at that time. See on this Patschovsky, *Die Anfänge*.

Comestor, or Pseudo-Bonaventure's *Meditationes vitae Christi*.[24] However, at the beginning of the fifteenth century, the situation had changed. Members of the higher nobility became interested in the vernacular Bible and commissioned expensive illuminated manuscripts (such as the so-called *Litoměřice-Třeboň Bible* also known as Zmrzlík's Bible). The nobles were most probably emulating the bibliophilic interests of King Wenceslas IV, who in the late fourteenth century had commissioned many exclusive codices of works written in German, among them the magnificently illuminated German Bible.[25] His courtiers followed his example. In addition, pastoral care became more elaborate and sophisticated in the last decades of the fourteenth century, a development which was connected with the ambitious church politics of Johannes of Jenstein, Archbishop of Prague, as well as with the increasing importance of pastoral theology at the University of Prague. At that time, several Latin preaching aids and exegetical texts were translated into Czech, such as the the extensive exposition on the Gospel of Matthew from Nicolas de Lyra's *Postilla litteralis*.[26]

The authority of the Bible related to the question of its translation was an issue at the university at the same time. Sometime at the end of the fourteenth century Jan of Mýto called *Sophista* (d. c. 1402), one of the first theologians at the University of Prague and teacher of Jan Hus, propounded *questio* on the authority of the Bible and the writings of Church Fathers.[27] At first, he stresses that the authority of the Bible has to be regarded higher than the authority of Church Fathers. They erred as we may see on some examples of contradictory sentences contained in their writings. We may therefore assume, Jan concludes, that not everything they wrote has to be regarded as inspired by Holy Spirit.[28] The focus on the *Sentences* of the Fathers led the philologist Václav Flajšhans, who wrote the seminal essay on Jan of Mýto, to the hypothesis that the *questio* represents an introductory opening lecture for a series of *lectionum* on Peter of Lombard's Sentences.[29] We may assume in any case that the occasion was in this or another way prominent.[30] Defining in this way the superior authority of the

---

24 See on these works Vidmanová, 'K původní podobě', pp. 16–45; *Život Krista Pána*, ed. by Stluka; *Staročeský hlaholský Comestor*, ed. by Pacnerová.

25 Vienna, Österreichische Nationalbibliothek, Cod. 2759–64 (the so-called *Wenceslas Bible*). Cf. Kyas, *Česká bible*, pp. 56–57, pp. 66 and 100.

26 *Výklad Mikuláše Lyry*, ed. by Homolková and Svobodová.

27 Nechutová, 'Autorita Bible', 510–14. Arguments in favor of the authority of Vulgate were quite common at the time, Henry Totting of Oyta, professor of Paris, then Prague and finally Vienna Universities, authored a very influential questio *De sacra scriptura et de veritatibus catholicis* which was very probably known at the University of Prague when Jan of Mýto formulated his own treatise. See on this Lang, 'Henrici Totting de Oyta quaestio', pp. 5–9.

28 Nechutová, 'Autorita Bible', p. 511.

29 Flajšhans, 'Jan z Mýta', pp. 437–43.

30 The question is extant in two copies, Wroclav, Biblioteka universitecna, I F 244, fol. 264v–265v and I F 285, fol. 295v–298v.

Bible Jan turns to the problem of its translations. He stresses that each translation originates in specific cultural and linguistic context and that it is not possible to maintain the original meaning of a text in any translation. Only Jerome's Latin translation may be used without concerns, because it was inspired by Holy Spirit; as such it is not less trustworthy than the Hebrew original version but even more. Jerome's prologue to the pentateuch, *Desiderii mei*, serves here as the main evidence. Translations 'in German and other vernaculars', however, made for kings and princes, were dangerous enterprises for the translators as well as their readers, Jan of Mýto concludes. Only the gift of Holy Spirit allows one, according to him, to translate biblical texts not only word-by-word but sense-by sense, as Saint Jerome did. Interestingly Jan closes his reasoning rather abruptly here: *Sed hec pro nunc de illo sufficiant* (But for now it is enough). He does not offer any proposal about how the institutional church and/or scholastic theology should deal with this particular problem. As said above, at the time he tackled the issue, biblical translations into both vernaculars of the realm were very popular, especially among the nobility and at the royal court, i.e. among important financial and political suporters of the university. Alongside, the answer to the question of who may preferably receive the Gift of the Holy Spirit was by no means clear. Influential theologians of the time advocated the idea that the uneducated lay people were more worthy to receive the Gift than many high skilled theologians who were guilty of the deadly sin of (intellectual) pride. In any case Jan of Mýto promotes in his *quaestio* the same *sola scriptura* principle which some time later became the main ideological pillar of the Hussite reformation.

Increasing demand, as well as the efforts of theologians, among them in particular the adherents of Wycliffite reform, for the dissemination of the vernacular Bible among lay people, were probably the main reasons for the revision of the first translation of the Bible at the beginning of the fifteenth century. The aim of this revised translation was to linguistically 'modernize' the version that was already fifty years old. It may have been considered an insufficient text, as massive changes occurred to the Czech language, its phonology, morphology, and vocabulary in the second half of the fourteenth century. These changes came along with, and were caused by, the increasing degree of literacy among the Czech speaking population and by the subsequent rise in the use of the Czech language as a language of literature. Literary genres were heavily influenced by the Latin and German literatures which had been received on a large scale in Bohemia.[31] Soon after the second revision, a thoroughly reworked third redaction of the text was prepared. According to Kyas, the anonymous author, probably from the University of Prague, translated the Latin original as accurately as possible consequently avoiding the rather volatile vocabulary that had been used in the previous redactions.[32]

The attribution of surviving Czech biblical texts to the second or third redaction is not always possible as the surviving material is often hybrid. The individual texts display a high number of modifications and revisions, as may be

---

31 Kyas, *Česká bible*, p. 66.

32 Kyas, *Česká bible*, pp. 100–02.

Figure 2: *Litoměřice Prologues*, Litoměřice, Oblastní archiv v Litoměřicích, collection Biskupské sbírky Litoměřice, MS BIF 3.1, fol. 144[r].

seen, for example, in several exemplars of the Czech New Testament which were produced in the second half of the fifteenth century. These texts originated in the Utraquist Church, a Christian confession that arose from the Hussite reform movement of the first half of the fifteenth century. The confession's most important theological and liturgical deviation from mainstream Catholicism was communion under both kinds for lay people, which was approved by the Council of Basel in 1437 after two decades of religious wars. A rigorous *sola scriptura* principle inspired by Wyclif characterized the Hussite reform movement from the beginning, and during the religious wars the vernacular Bible became a symbol of the reform. Hussite warlords took the pocket exemplars of the vernacular bible into the battle, the Law they fought for contained in it.[33] The extant Bibles of the second and third redactions contain varying numbers of prologues. The majority of these prologues were copied from the so-called *Old Czech Collection of Biblical Prologues*, which had been translated by an anonymous author at the beginning of the fifteenth century from various Latin models. Some extant Old Czech vernacular Bibles take the *Paris Bible* as their model.[34] (Fig. 2)

With the introduction of print, the revision of the vernacular Czech Bible gained new momentum. The first complete printed Czech Bible, the so-called *Prague Bible* from 1488, includes only four prologues.[35] Three of them, written by Jerome, appear here in a new translation that differs significantly from the texts contained in the bibles of the second and third redaction: a general prologue (*Frater Ambrosius*),[36] a prologue to the Pentateuch (*Desiderii mei*),[37] and

---

33 Rychterová, 'Preaching, Vernacular, and the Laity'.

34 Cf. *Staročeské biblické předmluvy*, ed. by Voleková and Svobodová, pp. 54–62.

35 *Pražská bible* (1488).

36 *Repertorium Biblicum*, I, ed. by Stegmüller, no. 284.

37 *Repertorium Biblicum*, I, ed. by Stegmüller, no. 285.

the prologue to the four Gospels (*Plures fuisse*).[38] The fourth preface represents an original Czech exposition on the new translation of the Psalter. It addresses the difficulty of translating this metaphorical poetic text, defends the approach that was taken with the new translation of the Psalter into Czech, and discusses some obscure passages in the Latin *Psalterium iuxta Hebraeos*:

> In some places, where it [the sense] had been obscured, I consulted the Psalter translated by St Jerome from Hebrew, although this interpretation is not in general use. Then I sometimes used St Jerome's exegesis in place of the generally used version to clarify the meaning [of the biblical word], without impairing or altering the ideas of the prophet.[39]

The anonymous author addresses several problems of biblical translation, all of them departing from the idea that an understanding of the biblical text may be achieved only through the gift of Holy Spirit. The prophets spoke obscurely in order to let the readers seek *refugium* through praying to God, asking him to open their reason, and not doubting that the weakness of human reason would be unable to approach the message without special grace. Those people in the past and present who read and continued to read the Scripture without this grace, could not and cannot understand it. Moreover, all the idioms and sayings which are included in the biblical text may be comprehensible only in the language which the prophets used; translated into another language, they confuse the human mind even more.[40] The verse form of the psalms (which here are actually defined as David's prophecies) represents, according to their translator, the next obstacle to their proper understanding. But to ignore the verse form and aspire only for the message of the text would mean producing an interpretation which is something other than a translation. It is instead necessary to pay attention to each word and to the word order. In particular, nothing should be abridged, i.e. the sense should not be 'shortened', because especially in these speeches various senses are contained.[41] The translator clearly had the principles of exegesis in mind, and his goal was very ambitious: to create such a translation which would preserve the fourfold sense of the Scripture, giving the reader the possibility of understanding God's message in all its aspects – with the condition that it was understood with the assistance of the Holy Spirit, of course.

The four prologues of the *Prague Bible* can also be found in several other incunabula and in printed Bibles and New Testaments from the sixteenth century, with

---

38 *Repertorium Biblicum*, I, ed. by Stegmüller, no. 596.

39 *Prologue to the Book of Psalms* in the first printed psalter, *Staročeské biblické předmluvy*, ed. by Voleková and Svobodová, p. 277. For the English translation of the complete text see *Prologue to the Book of Psalms in Old Czech Printed Bibles*, ed. and trans. by Svobodová and others, online: <https://mecz.kreas.ff.cuni.cz/publication/first-printed-psalter/> [accessed 3 November 2022].

40 Here we paraphrase the text in *Staročeské biblické předmluvy*, ed. by Voleková and Svobodová, p. 276.

41 *Staročeské biblické předmluvy*, ed. by Voleková and Svobodová, pp. 276–77.

some variety in their appearance (and also in wording). No 'traditional', i.e. medieval, prologues may be found in the Czech translation of the New Testament of 1533, made by the Humanist authors Beneš Optát and Petr Gzel, who did not follow the tradition of the Vulgate, but instead used Erasmus's new Latin translation as well as his commentaries.[42] The same is true for the so-called *Kralice Bible*, a translation of the entire Bible from textual materials in the original languages (Hebrew and Greek). It was made by scholars, members of the Unity of Brethren, a Christian confession that arose from the radical wing of the Hussite reform movement in the second half of the fifteenth century. This Bible was first published in six volumes between 1579 and 1594, then re-published in a single volume in 1613. Due to its exceptional linguistic qualities it became instrumental in the codification of the modern Czech language as described and systematized in the early nineteenth century by the founders of modern Czech linguistics, philology, and literary studies.[43]

The Old Czech Collection of Biblical Prologues

At the beginning of the fifteenth century, an extensive collection of Czech biblical prologues was produced (henceforth *The Collection*), by an unknown translator who drew on various Latin models. It was probably motivated by the revision of the earliest biblical translation and may be regarded as part of the efforts of anonymous editors to complement the Czech Bible with prologues according to the Latin Vulgate manuscripts, especially the *Paris Bible*. *The Collection* contains prologues to almost all the books of the Bible or its larger divisions, offering one or more prefaces for every biblical book. It comprises more than a hundred items; in addition to the sixty-four prefaces to the *Paris Bible*, it contains nearly another forty introductory texts translated from the previous Latin Bibles. The Czech translator seems to have also used the *Glossa ordinaria*. Both extant copies of the collection appear in manuscripts together with the Czech translation of the *Interpretationes Hebraicorum nominum* (*Interpretations of Hebrew Names*), a popular exegetical handbook that formed part of the *Paris Bible* and which preachers may have used as an inspiration for the exegesis of biblical proper nouns. *The Collection* is preserved in two copies from the first quarter of the fifteenth century. The first copy, the so-called *Litoměřice Prologues*, is contained in the second volume of the *Litoměřice-Třeboň Bible* (dated to 1414).[44] Based on many pieces of evidence (identical copyist errors and proof-reading marks) we may regard this manuscript as the direct source for the other existing copy, the *St Vitus Metropolitan Chapter Prologues*.[45]

---

42 *Nový testament všecek již nejposléze a pilně od Erazma Roterodámského*; cf. Dittmann and Just, *Biblical Humanism in Bohemia and Moravia*, pp. 122–23.

43 *Biblí české díl první až šestý*, 6 vols (1579–94); cf. Dittmann and Just, *Biblical Humanism in Bohemia and Moravia*, p. 257.

44 Litoměřice, Oblastní archiv v Litoměřicích, collection Biskupské sbírky Litoměřice, MS BIF 3.1, fols 144^r–73^r.

45 Prague, Archiv Pražského hradu, Knihovna Metropolitní kapituly u sv. Víta, MS A 127, fols 1^r–34^v.

Translations of the biblical text into vernacular languages had to meet two main requirements: accuracy and comprehensibility. The prologues are different in this respect; they are mostly scholarly texts containing elaborated pastoral, literary-historical, and linguistic explanations, and a plethora of terms for which the Czech language did not have any established equivalents in the early fifteenth century. In particular, the translator of *The Collection* faced a demanding task, as he closely followed the Latin text and translated the prologues word-for-word. However, sometimes he did not understand Latin properly and corrupted the sense of the text. When interpreting his model and searching for appropriate expressions, he resorted to several methods. For some terms, he used the Czech equivalents as proposed by Bartoloměj of Chlumec, called *Claretus*, a scholar and canon of St Vitus Cathedral in Prague, in his Latin-Czech dictionaries from the 1350s. These dictionaries were intended for university students and, therefore, contain basic Latin terms and expressions with their Czech equivalents pertaining to all the seven liberal arts. Bartoloměj of Chlumec also coined many new Czech words, but only some of these new terms were accepted in the long run.[46] The author of *The Collection* used, for example, Bartoloměj's neologism *čtena* derived from the verb *čísti* ('to read') for Latin *littera*, a word which otherwise did not gain general acceptance.[47] In some cases, the translator introduced his own neologisms. For example, in order to distinguish between the Latin words *astronomus* and *astrologus*, he used the current Czech word *hvězdář* ('astronomer') for *astronomus*, whereas for *astrologus* he coined a new word from the same root *hvězd-* (cf. Latin *astrum* = Old Czech *hvězda*), but with a different suffix: *hvězdovník* ('astrologer'). Again, this was a word which was not generally accepted.[48] Most frequently, he used current Czech words in new contexts, providing them with a new semantic field: for example, *částka*, originally 'a small part' (a diminutive form of the Old Czech lexeme *čiest* 'a part'), is used in the prologues for 'pericope', i.e. a section of the biblical text'.[49] He preserved Greek expressions which were in the Latin model and added an explanatory note based on Latin commentaries to the Bible. Here he probably drew on the exposition to the biblical prologues *Expositiones prologorum Bibliae* composed by William Briton (*Guillelmus Brito*) at the end of the thirteenth century. For example, in the third prologue to the Book of Job, the translator annotated the Greek word ἐσχηματισμένος in accordance with the definition given in Brito's *Expositiones*:[50]

---

46 Cf. Michálek, *Česká slovní zásoba*; Sichálek, 'European Background', p. 71.

47 Cf. Kyas, *Česká bible*, p. 51, p. 63.

48 Cf. Kyas, *Česká bible*, p. 64.

49 Cf. Kyas, *Česká bible*, p. 64.

50 *Scematismenos, id est defectus modi communis loquendi* ('Scematismenos, i.e. insufficient in the general manner of speaking'). Brito, *Expositiones*, Prague, Národní knihovna České republiky, MS IX C 9, fols 26ʳ–95ᵛ, here fol. 59ᵛ.

Obliquus [...] totus liber fertur et lubricus et quod grece rethores vocant *ἐσχηματισμένος*.[51]
Celé tyto knihy zkřiveny sú a plzké, a jakož krásnořeci řecky dějí scematismenos, točižto nedostatečné v uobecném obyčeji mluvenie.[52]

> (These whole books are distorted and indecent, and what orators in Greek call *ἐσχηματισμένος*, i.e. insufficient in the general manner of speaking.)

As has already been noted, the oldest extant copy of *The Collection* constitutes a part of the second volume of the *Litoměřice-Třeboň Bible*. This is a large, carefully written, and richly illuminated manuscript, commissioned and owned by a prominent Czech nobleman, Petr Zmrzlík of Svojšín, the mint master of King Wenceslas IV. Immediately after its completion, the codex was submitted to a proof-reader who checked the transcription and corrected the copyist's errors. He evidently compared the text to the Latin Vulgate, corrected imprecise translations, and added the translation of those passages which had been omitted by the translator, both in the biblical text and in the text of the prologues.

The proof-reader aimed to make the text as close as possible to the Latin original; he interfered, therefore, with the translation to a great extent. He deleted (erased, underlined, or crossed through) expressions which he identified as erroneous or regarded as inadequate and replaced them with his own translations. For example, he erased the word *spravedlivé* ('fair') at the beginning of the prologue to the First Epistle to the Corinthians *Epistola prima ad Corinthios multas causas diversasque complectitur*[53] ('The First Epistle to the Corinthians contains numerous and diverse disputes') and replaced it with the word *mnohé* ('many'): 'Epištola prvá k Korintským mnohé [spravedlivé *orig.*] pře a rozličné osahuje'.[54] In this he followed the Latin original, which used the word *multas* ('many, numerous'), and which had probably been misread by the translator as *iustas* ('fair'). The original, incorrect translation *spravedlivé* also appears in some of the other extant manuscripts. These copies therefore drew on a copy of the collection of prologues which had not been corrected. As there are a number of Czech Bibles which contain prologues that stem from the original version of *The Collection*, we may therefore assume considerable dissemination of the original text (the hypothetical archetype) of *The Collection* in Bohemia. (Fig. 3)

---

51 Prologue to Job, *Cogor per singulos*, see *Repertorium Biblicum*, I, ed. by Stegmüller, no. 344. *Biblia Sacra*, IX, pp. 70–71.

52 *Litoměřice Prologues*, Litoměřice, Oblastní archiv v Litoměřicích, collection Biskupské sbírky Litoměřice, MS BIF 3.1, fol. 152^v; Staročeské biblické předmluvy, ed. by Voleková and Svobodová, p. 269.

53 *Repertorium Biblicum*, I, ed. by Stegmüller, no. 690.

54 *Litoměřice Prologues*, Litoměřice, Oblastní archiv v Litoměřicích, collection Biskupské sbírky Litoměřice, MS BIF 3.1, fol. 167^v; Staročeské biblické předmluvy, ed. by Voleková and Svobodová, p. 408.

Figure 3: The proof-reader's emendation in the *Litoměřice Prologues*, Litoměřice, Oblastní archiv v Litoměřicích, collection Biskupské sbírky Litoměřice, MS BIF 3.1, fol. 167ᵛ.

Some features in the proof-reader's version of *The Collection* allow us to regard this version as a fair copy of the text. The translator often used two or more Czech equivalents for one Latin expression – a common translational practice in many languages, not only in Czech. This feature may be found not only in 'unfinished' texts but also in elaborated illuminated Bibles. In *The Collection*, the translator tried to outline the semantic field of individual Latin terms as accurately as possible with the help of more than one vernacular equivalents in his translation. For example, he translated the polysemantic Latin verb *edere* ('render, proclaim, state, quote') with the help of three Czech verbs *složiti* ('compose'), *učiniti* ('create'), and *přidati* ('add'). The proof-reader largely crossed out or underlined those alternative translations and explanations which could not be found in the Latin prologues. In general, from the contemporary perspective, his interventions improved the translation. Nevertheless, he did not always succeed. For example, he removed the explanations of Greek words (which were missing in the Latin model) without replacing them with Czech translations of the Greek term and, as a result, the meaning of the term would have remained unclear for lay readers.

Individual prologues of *The Collection* were sometimes copied unchanged into codices containing the Czech Bible, while sometimes the copyists significantly reworked them. The changes were mainly lexical; less common words were replaced by more common lexemes. Some copyists reworked the text according to the Latin original they had at their disposal, which contained variant wording. Consequently, the prologues underwent numerous changes during the fifteenth century.

Some prologues were extensively reworked by the Utraquist authors.[55] Due to the rigorous Hussite biblicism, the Utraquist version of Czech Bible, prologues included, addressed two goals: firstly, to stay as close as possible to the

---

55 Cf. *Staročeské biblické předmluvy*, ed. by Voleková and Svobodová, pp. 72–75.

Latin model and, secondly, to be perfectly understandable for a lay reader with respect to contemporary developments in the spoken language. Continuous adjustments made to the wording of the text, especially concerning lexical, as well as morphological and syntactic features, are therefore characteristic for Utraquist Czech Bibles although many (confessionally neutral) copies of other vernacular texts from the period also show some degree of such reworking. The Utraquist authors took even very small, inconspicuous shifts of meaning seriously – for example, the verb *popsati* in the sense of 'write, compose' was replaced with *napsati*, a verb with a different prefix (*po-* × *na-*) but with practically the same meaning; *pravidlo* for Latin *linea* ('principle, rule') replaced the former equivalent *řád* ('order', 'rule'), very probably on account of the polysemantic character of the word *řád*. Sometimes, most likely because of the efforts to render the wording of the Latin text as accurately as possible, Czech words were replaced by Czechized Latinisms which then prevailed, which then also replaced the former Czech words used in spoken language. In this way, the proof-readers replaced *křivitel* ('a crook') with *falšieř* for Latin *falsarius* ('fabricator, distorter, falsifier'). They also removed some of the neologisms from the original translation, it would seem because these had not found their way into spoken language. These include, for instance, the compound *svieconošě* ('taperbearer') for Greek-Latin *acolythus* ('acolyte'). This neologism (invented by the author of *The Collection*) was based on the description of the function of this particular office – an acolyte assisted in a religious service by bearing candles during processions and liturgical entrances. It was the Czechized form of the Latin term, *akolyta*, as introduced by the Utraquist authors which prevailed in the long term.

New Translations of the Latin Prologues

The copyists of Czech biblical manuscripts often worked with incomplete codices, were selecting a preferred version from the competing options, and combined the textual variants which were available to them.[56] Many manuscripts therefore contain prologues with the wording of the first redaction and prologue collection, while they have new translations as well. A case in point is a text written by the scribe 'Matěj z Prahy' for the *Litoměřice-Třeboň Bible*. The opening prologue in this three-volume codex is not Jerome's letter to Paulinus (*Frater Ambrosius*),[57] which can be found in most manuscripts of the second and third redaction, but a text with the incipit *Zdá mi se dobré* ('It seems good to me'). In this prologue, its author, the scribe Matěj, provides instructions on how to handle this codex because the biblical books in the *Litoměřice-Třeboň Bible* are not arranged as usual but in the order in which Matěj had received the material to copy. First, he provides an overview of the division of the Bible into the Old Testament and the New Testament, selectively including the Hebrew, Greek,

---

56 Cf. Kyas, *Česká bible*, p. 43, p. 66.
57 *Repertorium Biblicum*, I, ed. by Stegmüller, no. 248.

Latin, and Czech names for the individual biblical books.[58] He then describes the unusual array of the books in the first volume (I and II Maccabees, Proverbs-Ecclesiasticus, Acts, James-Jude, Matthew-John, Genesis-Ruth), and explains briefly the title and the content of each biblical book. He quotes the number of its chapters and states how many pages the reader must turn to find a certain book; for example, 'You will find the beginning of this book once you have turned fifty six folios' ('počátek těch knih nalezneš převrha šest a padesát listóv').[59] The search for the beginning of a particular book is also facilitated by a numerical entry written after each paragraph that refers to the folio number of the book in question: 'You should also know that, in addition to the mentioned number of the folios that you need to turn, all folios are numbered in red ink to avoid mistakes during the search' ('také to věz, žeť to, cožť sem velel listy v počet přemietati, k tomu máš počet dole na každém listu psaný rubrikú, aby sě po něm zpravoval bez omyly').[60] The preface is primarily intended as a guide to help readers find their way through this unusually arranged biblical compilation.

In several fifteenth-century Czech Bibles, where it is unclear if they were produced by Catholics or Utraquists, there are new translations of several Old Testament Latin prologues. How these prologues approach the hypothetical lay reader and what they consider to be important information for him/her is remarkably similar to the way that these issues were handled by the authors of the first biblical redaction.[61] We encounter here explanatory notes to the proper nouns (e.g. *quattuor scelera Damasci, Gazae, Tyri, Idumeae*,[62] 'hřiechy Damaška, Gazy, Tira a Idumea, měst tak řečených',[63] 'sins of Damascus, Gaza, Tyre, and Edom, cities of those names'), which indicates that the authors did not expect their readership to be knowledgeable in the subject matter.

The four Prologues of the first printed Czech Bible, the so-called *Prague Bible* of 1488, were translated anew in the linguistic vein of the Utraquist biblical translations: their authors avoided neologisms, archaic and cumbersome expressions, and unusual Latin and Greek words. This new translation became popular, at least, with printers from the end of the fifteenth century, and it can

---

58 The source of this translation may be the prologue to the Books of Kings (*Viginti et duas*, see *Repertorium Biblicum*, I, ed. by Stegmüller, no. 323), which was translated for the prologue collection, included in the second volume of the *Litoměřice-Třeboň Bible* (Litoměřice, Oblastní archiv v Litoměřicích, collection Biskupské sbírky Litoměřice, MS BIF 3.1).

59 Litoměřice, Oblastní archiv v Litoměřicích, collection Biskupské sbírky Litoměřice, MS BIF 3.2, fol. 1ᵛ; *Staročeské biblické předmluvy*, ed. by Voleková and Svobodová, p. 229.

60 Litoměřice, Oblastní archiv v Litoměřicích, collection Biskupské sbírky Litoměřice, MS BIF 3.2, fol. 2ᵛ; *Staročeské biblické předmluvy*, ed. by Voleková and Svobodová, p. 230.

61 Cf. Kreisingerová, 'Vysvětlivky ve staročeském biblickém překladu', pp. 214–16; *Staročeské biblické předmluvy*, ed. by Voleková and Svobodová, pp. 66–72.

62 *Biblia Sacra*, XVII, p. 9.

63 *Staročeské biblické předmluvy*, ed. by Voleková and Svobodová, p. 320.

be found, in reworked versions, in printed Bibles from the sixteenth century onwards. Printed Bibles from the sixteenth century, however, show significant changes concerning the purpose of the prologues. For example, the first printed Czech Bible of the sixteenth century, the so-called *Venice Bible*, published in Venice in 1506, contains a new general introduction written by the publishers explaining the enterprise to the reader and praising their own product in comparison with the Bibles which had previously been published. The apparatus, especially, are highlighted, which were added by them to facilitate basic orientation in the text through summaries of individual chapters and concordances in the margins. Such authorial prefaces became common in printed Bibles produced at that time, becoming increasingly elaborated, and with some being more popular than others. The preface of the humanist scholar Sixt of Ottersdorf (*c.* 1500–83) was printed repeatedly in various Bibles by several publishers.

The New Testament as printed by the member of the Unity of Brethren, Mikuláš Klaudyán (*Claudianus*) (d. 1521) in 1518 is an exception here, as he ignored all the changes which had been introduced by contempory printers and with the four Gospels returned to the archaic wording of the medieval Czech translation. This was an unusual move in comparison to the efforts of the majority of other publishers who were trying to keep pace with the development of spoken language, as their first and foremost concern was to satisfy the readers who wanted the Bible in a language which they were intimate with.[64] Klaudyán writes:

> I noted some time ago, informed by other [men], learned in the Holy Scripture, great deficiency in the Czech [translation] of the New Testament; in some places words are changed, in some places the forms, in some places the sense of the text. And this [may be found] especially in the printed Bibles or Testaments which are in accordance neither with the Latin Scripture nor with the ancient translations into Czech language. [...] Instead of words of God, human words were introduced in some places, and instead of reason, faith, and sense of the Holy Spirit human adverse [reason] was introduced in some places, so the people reading it, would believe, it originates in God; some people may regard it as more suitable, clearer, more reasonable, and so the belief and the truth may be transformed into a falsehood.[65]

Leaning on the argument made in Deuteronomy 4. 2 ('Do not add to what I command you and do not subtract from it, but keep the commands of the Lord your God that I give you') the publisher reveals the reasons for his decision to return to a linguistically antiquated version of the New Testament and then explains further how he had found out about the history of changes that had been made in the Czech translation of the New Testament. An older copy of the Czech New Testament from his personal library allowed him to compare the

---

64 *Staročeské biblické předmluvy*, ed. by Voleková and Svobodová, pp. 81–86.
65 *Zákon Nový*, fols A2ᵛ–A3ᵛ.

original translation with the printed bibles on the market (he mentions two different prints, one from Prague and other from Kuttenberg) and to trace all the linguistic innovations back to what he believed to be their origins. He saw the replacement of the Czech past perfect tense with the simple past – a change which had taken place roughly a hundred years earlier – as being an especially grave error, because, as he stressed, without the past perfect tense the Latin wording could not be correctly rendered. He highlights the accurate German translations printed in Augsburg and Nuremberg as models to follow in this respect, which could be found in the print shops with which he regularly collaborated:

> Do not misunderstand me [reader], as if I would give Germans preference in the issue of truth. I wish them as all the peoples in Christ's love the insight and the use of truth, but the most Czech people and those [people] in it who are closer to the truth [because of their adherence to the practice of the communion] under both kinds.[66]

Klaudyán regarded the accuracy of the translation as necessary for maintaining the authority of the biblical text. His particular focus on the usage of the past tense not only reveals his personal linguistic sensitivity but also the fact that there was a considerable number of readers who shared his approach. He announced his return to the archaic language in the title on the cover of the book as a main element of marketing. We may assume that he targeted the members of the Unity of Brethren, whose obsession with the *sola scriptura* principle determined their approach to the biblical text. When the bishop of the Unity, Lukáš of Prague, translated the New Testament anew in 1525, he tried to preserve even the syntax of the Latin text, and following Klaudyán he returned to the use of archaic verb forms in past perfect. The effort made to convey God's original message as accurately as possible also stands behind the Czech translation of the *Erasmus Bible*, and likewise behind the most brilliant achievement of the Unity, the *Kralice Bible* (see above).

Denominational diversity was multifaceted in sixteenth-century Bohemia: Catholics, Utraquists, and the Unity of Brethren were joined by various factions of Protestants in the 1520s, although these latter were mostly German speaking and therefore did not belong, at first, to the target customers of the Czech publishers. In any case, the majority of these publishers strove to sell their bestselling product, the Bible, without any constraints. They therefore tried to put texts on the market which would be suitable for anybody, not only for members of one particular confession. The printing culture had two effects in the process of producing vernacular bibles. During the first decades the printers, as we have seen, used the materials which were at their disposal, made some changes and some additions, and then found out whether their potential customers would respond positively. For a short time, manuscript and print cultures were in balance until the latter prevailed.

---

66 *Zákon Nový*, fol. A4^v.

Epilogue

Prefaces are the most commonly attested para-biblical texts in the Old Czech biblical manuscripts of the fourteenth and fifteenth centuries. Their main aims were to familiarize the reader with the issues raised in the respective biblical section or book, summarize its contents, and outline the modes of their interpretation. They may be found in many of the extant Czech Bibles, although their numbers fluctuate and they do not appear in all. The first few prefaces appear in the earliest biblical translation from the mid-fourteenth century. The translation of the whole prologue collection, based on a set of sixty-four texts known from the *Paris Bible* and augmented by a further forty introductions drawn from other Latin sources, dates from the beginning of the fifteenth century. At the same time, the vernacular Bible advanced from being a mere tool for aiding the basic understanding of the Latin text, which then alone was the object of interpretation, through to an independent object of exegesis.

Czech prologues were copied into numerous manuscripts; their wording was frequently changed, as was the wording of the biblical texts which they accompanied, with revisions ranging from small changes concerning graphemes and morphology to significant changes of vocabulary and syntax. The copyists adjusted the texts according to developments in spoken language. These revisions motivated by efforts to grasp God's message as precisely as possible in the constantly changing language of the people resulted in new translations. Sometimes these returned to the archaic language of the first medieval translations in the belief that this would more accurately mirror God's message. Biblical translations played a key role in the development of the vernacular literary language, in the religious communication of confessionally divided late medieval Bohemia, and in the transformation of theological discourses in general. A close look at the biblical prologues therefore allows us to understand better all these processes and to formulate important questions for future research.

Bibliography

Manuscripts and Early Prints

Biblí české díl první až šestý, 6 vols (Kralice: print-shop of the Unity of Brethren, 1579–94)
Dresden, Sächsische Landesbibliothek, MS Mscr. Dresd. Oe. 85 (destroyed in 1914)
Litoměřice, Oblastní archiv v Litoměřicích, collection Biskupské sbírky Litoměřice, MS BIF 3.1
——, MS BIF 3.2
Nový testament všecek již nejposléze a pilně od Erazma Roterodámského (Náměšť nad Oslavou: Matěj Pytlík of Dvořiště, 1533)
Zákon Nový: Najposléze po mnohých jiných vytištěný, kdež cos jest v jiných poopuštěno, jako concordancie, předmluvy a jiné věci, to v tomto dosti spravené najdeš: Cum gratia et privilegio Reverendissimi Generalis in ordine (Mladá Boleslav nad Jizerou: Mikuláš Klaudyán, 1518)

Olomouc, Vědecká knihovna, MS M III 1/I–II
———, Zemský archiv v Opavě, pobočka Olomouc, Sbírka rukopisů Metropolitní kapituly Olomouc, MS CO 400
Prague, Archiv Pražského hradu, Knihovna Metropolitní kapituly u sv. Víta, MS A 127
———, Knihovna Národního muzea, MS XIV D 13
———, Národní knihovna České republiky, MS IX C 9
———, MS XVII A 4
Pražská bible (Prague: s.n., 1488)
Seitenstetten, Stiftsbibliothek, Cod. 272
Třeboň, Státní oblastní archiv v Třeboni, MS A 2
Vienna, Österreichische Nationalbibliothek, Cod. 1190
———, Cod. 2759–64
———, Cod. 4733

Primary Sources

Biblia Sacra iuxta Latinam vulgatam versionem ad codicum fidem iussu Pauli P.P. VI cura et studio monachorum abbatiae pontificiae sancti Hieronymi in Urbe ordinis sancti Benedicti edita (Rome: Typis Polyglottis Vaticanis, 1926–), ix (1951), xvii (1987)

Die alttschechische Dresdener Bibel: Drážďanská anebo Leskovecká bible: Fascimile, aufgrund der photographischen Aufnahmen von 1914 nach dem verbrannten Original aus dem 14. Jahrhundert, ed. by Hans Rothe and Friedrich Scholz, Biblia Slavica, 1 (Paderborn: Schöningh, 1993)

Henrici Totting de Oyta Quaestio de sacra scriptura et de veritatibus catholicis, ed. by Albert Lang (Opuscula et textus historiam ecclesiae eiusque vitam atque doctrinam illustrantia. Series scholastica 12, Münster: Monasterii Westfalorum in aedibus Aschendorf, 1953)

Staročeské biblické předmluvy, ed. by Kateřina Voleková and Andrea Svobodová (Prague: Scriptorium, 2019)

Staročeský hlaholský Comestor, ed. by Ludmila Pacnerová, Práce Slovanského Ústavu AV CR, Nová Řada, 11 (Prague: Slovanský Ústav Akad. Věd České Republiky – Euroslavica, 2002)

Výklad Mikuláše Lyry na evangelium sv. Matouše: Kritická edice staročeského překladu, ed. by Milada Homolková and Andrea Svobodová (Dolní Břežany: Scriptorium, 2018)

Život Krista Pána, ed. by Martin Stluka (Brno: Host, 2006)

Secondary Works

Berger, Samuel, 'Les Préfaces jointes aux livres de la Bible dans les manuscrits de la Vulgate', *Mémoires présentés par divers savants à l'Académie des inscriptions et belles-lettres de l'Institut de France, A, Sujets divers d'érudition*, 16 vols (Paris: Imprimerie nationale, 1844–1975), xi/2 (1904), pp. 1–78

De Bruyne, Donatien, *Prefaces to the Latin Bible: Introductions by Pierre-Maurice Bogaert and Thomas O'Loughlin*, ed. by Pierre-Maurice Bogaert and Thomas O'Loughlin, 2nd edn with English commentary, Studia Traditionis Theologiae, 19 (Turnhout: Brepols, 2015); 1st French edn: *Préface de la Bible latine* (Namur: Godenne, 1920)

Dittmann, Robert, and Jiří Just, *Biblical Humanism in Bohemia and Moravia in the 16th Century*, Europa Humanistica, 18: Répertoires et Inventaires, 1 (Turnhout: Brepols, 2016)

Kreisingerová, Hana, 'Vysvětlivky ve staročeském biblickém překladu prorockých knih', *Linguistica Copernicana*, 2/6 (2011), pp. 211–22

Kyas, Vladimír, *Česká bible v dějinách národního písemnictví*, Edice Studium, 96 (Prague: Vyšehrad, 1997)

Van Liere, Frans, 'The Latin Bible, c. 900 to the Council of Trent, 1546', in *The New Cambridge History of the Bible*, ed. by James Carleton Paget and others, 4 vols (Cambridge: Cambridge University Press, 2012–16), II: *From 600 to 1450*, ed. by Richard Marsden and E. Anne Matter (2012), pp. 93–109

Light, Laura, 'French Bibles c. 1200–30: a New Look at the Origin of the Paris Bible', in *The Early Medieval Bible: Its Production, Decoration and Use*, ed. by Richard Gameson, Cambridge Studies in Palaeography and Codicology (Cambridge: Cambridge University Press, 1994), pp. 155–76

———, 'Non-Biblical Texts in Thirteenth-Century Bibles', in *Medieval Manuscripts, their Makers and Users: A Special Issue of Viator in Honour of Richard and Mary Rouse*, ed. by Christopher Baswell (Turnhout: Brepols, 2011), pp. 169–83

———, 'The Thirteenth Century and the Paris Bible', in *The New Cambridge History of the Bible*, ed. by James Carleton Paget and others, 4 vols (Cambridge: Cambridge University Press, 2012–16), II: *From 600 to 1450*, ed. by Richard Marsden and E. Anne Matter (2012), pp. 380–91

Michálek, Emanuel, *Česká slovní zásoba v Klaretových slovnících* (Prague: Academia, 1989)

Patschovsky, Alexander, *Die Anfänge einer ständigen Inquisition in Böhmen: Ein Prager Inquisitoren-Handbuch aus der ersten Hälfte des 14. Jahrhunderts*, Beiträge zur Geschichte und Quellenkunde des Mittelalters, 3 (Berlin: De Gruyter, 1975)

Pečírková, Jaroslava, 'Czech Translations of the Bible', in *Interpretation of the Bible*, ed. by Jaroslava Pečírková (Ljubljana and Sheffield: Slovenska akademija znanosti in umetnosti – Sheffield Academic Press, 1998), pp. 1167–1200

Pytlíková, Markéta, 'Průzkum překladové a překladatelské stránky první redakce staročeského biblického překladu' (unpublished doctoral thesis, Palacký University Olomouc, 2011)

Rejzek, Jiří, *Český etymologický slovník* (Prague: Leda, 2015)

Repertorium biblicum medii aevi, ed. by Fridericus Stegmüller, 11 vols (Madrid: Consejo Superior de Investigaciones Científicas, Instituto Francisco Suárez, 1950–), I: *Initia biblica, Apocrypha, Prologi*, (1950; 2nd edn 1981); IV: *Commentaria: Auctores N – Q* (1954), 2nd edn (1989)

Rychterová, Pavlína, 'Preaching, Vernacular, and the Laity', in *A Companion to Jan Hus*, ed. by Michael van Dussen and Pavel Soukup, Brill's Companions to the Christian Tradition, 90 (Leiden and Boston: Brill, 2020), pp. 297–330

Sichálek, Jakub, 'European Background: Czech Translations', in *The Wycliffite Bible: Origin, History and Interpretation*, ed. by Elizabeth Solopova, Medieval and Renaissance Authors and Texts, 16 (Leiden and Boston: Brill, 2016), pp. 66–84

Vidmanová, Anežka, 'K původní podobě a textové tradici staročeského Pasionálu', *Listy filologické / Folia philologica*, 108/1 (1985), pp. 16–45

Vintr, Josef, *Die älteste tschechische Psalterübersetzung: Kritische Edition* (Verlag der Österreichischen Akademie der Wissenschaften: Wien, 1986)

——, *Die ältesten tschechischen Evangeliare: Edition, Text- und Sprachanalyse der ersten Redaktion*, Slavistische Beiträge, 107 (Munich: Sagner, 1977)

Websites

Prologue to the Book of Psalms in Old Czech Printed Bibles, ed. by Andrea Svobodová, trans. by Andrea Svobodová, Sarah Gráfová, and Jan Čermák, *MECZ: Database of MEdieval CZech Textual Sources in Translation*, online: <https://mecz.kreas.ff.cuni.cz/publication/first-printed-psalter/> [accessed 3 November 2022]

Ústav pro českou literaturu, Staročeská sbírka (lístkový katalog), online: <https://starocech.ucl.cas.cz/retrobi/domu> [accessed 3 November 2022]

Reader and Public in a Fourteenth-Century French Translation

Jean le Long and his Readership

Marco Robecchi

Free University of Bozen

In 1351, Jean le Long d'Ypres, abbot of the monastery of Saint-Bertin in the town of Saint-Omer, translated into French six works concerning the Near East and Asia. All of them were written in the first half of the fourteenth century. The first is a re-translation of the Latin *Flos historiarum*, originally written in French by Hayton of Coricus (*La Flor des estoires de la terre d'Orient*), and translated into Latin by Nicole Faucon. It contains a description of the fourteen kingdoms of Asia, a history of the Mongol Empire, and a history of Arabian conquests. The second is the *Liber peregrinationis* written by the Florentine Dominican Riccoldo da Monte di Croce, containing basically a description of the Middle East. The third is the famous *Relatio*, written by the Franciscan Odorico da Pordenone, describing the Far East. The fourth is the *Liber de quibusdam ultramarinis partibus et praecipue de Terra Sancta* written by the German Dominican Wilhelm von Boldensele, describing the Egyptian kingdom and the Holy Land. The fifth are the letters exchanged between Khan Toghon Temür and Pope Benedict XII and the sixth is short anonymous treatise transmitted under the title *De statu, conditione ac regimine magnis Canis*.[1] All these texts represent travel accounts and geographical treatises, and the last two of them informs us about the Mongol Empire's relations with the papacy and about the Franciscan mission in Cathay. While translating these works, Jean le Long created what we could call a *summa geographica* containing that era's knowledge of the Orient, the friars' mission in the East, and the Mongol Empire.

---

[1] For Hayton, the original French and Latin translation are edited by Kohler, see Hayton of Corico, *La Flor des Estoires de la Terre d'Orient*, pp. 111–253. Jean le Long's French translation is edited by Dörper, *Die Geschichte der Mongolen*. For Riccoldo, see Robecchi, *Riccold de Monte di Croce, 'Liber peregrinationis'*. For Odorico, the Latin text has been edited by Marchisio, see Odorico da Pordenone, *Relatio*; Jean le Long's French translation is edited by Andreose and Ménard, *Le voyage en Asie d'Odoric de Pordenone*. For Boldensele, see Deluz, 'Guillaume de Boldensele'. For the letters, see Concina, 'Da Pechino ad Avignone', pp. 139–48. The Latin *De statu* has been edited, by Gadrat, '"De Statu, conditione ac regimine magni Canis"', pp. 355–71; the French translation is still unpublished.

In fact, we do not know why he chose these six texts. He translated books kept in monastic libraries between Flanders and the Northwest region of Germany.[2] In his Latin *Chronicon monasterii sancti Bertini*, Jean le Long explicitly mentions Marco Polo. Several formulations in his text indicate that he perhaps knew texts such as Giovanni da Pian del Carpine's *Historia Mongalorum*, or even Jean de Joinville's *Life of Saint Louis*. Jean le Long had as it seems knowledge of texts dealing with the Orient exceeding the six he translated. We may therefore assume that he chose them deliberately.[3]

My aim is to examine the role of the intended reader (the *lecteur*, the commissioner, and/or the target reader) in Jean le Long's choices as a translator, as well as the role of the factual reader (further readers) in the subsequent reception of the work, extant in six copies.[4] The first question is: to whom did Jean le Long address his translations? In contrast to other translators and medieval authors, Jean le Long did not write a general prologue to his work where he would reflect upon his method of translation or mention the commissioner or sponsor (*commanditaire*), so that we would be able to identify the primary addressee. This lack of information obliges us to look for traces of the 'target reader' in the texts, for example in additions, omissions and other types of modification the translator made to his Latin sources. As none of the surviving manuscripts is dedicated to a named addressee, we must consider the extant manuscripts as belonging to 'further readers'.

In order to understand the aims of the translator, we have to clarify several issues at first. The text or the *corpus* of texts the translator chose can reveal much about his/her personality if we look closely at all the auctorial interventions in the text of the model. The reception history of the model may reveal social and textual networks of which the translator was part. All this information contributes also to the idea of a 'target reader' the translator had in mind. A detailed analysis of extant copies of the translation may allow us to reconstruct the groups of recipients who actually read the text. In the following essay the translation of Jean le Long will be examined in order to shed more light on these questions.[5]

---

2 See especially, Robecchi, 'Riccoldo, Jean le Long e la sua raccolta' and its bibliography.

3 See Robecchi, *Riccold de Monte di Croce, 'Liber peregrinationis'*, pp. 23–25. Jean le Long affirms in his *Chronicon*: 'illarum partium multa mirabilia vidit [Marco Polo], de quibus postea librum in vulgari Gallico composuit quem librum mirabilium cum pluribus similibus penes nos habemus' ('[Marco Polo] saw wonders in those regions, that he reports in a French book of wonders that we own [in our library] with other similar books').

4 For this distinction, see Brandenberger, 'Una traduccion bajomedieval y su publico', pp. 75–94 and more recently Buridant, 'Esquisse d'une traductologie au Moyen Âge', p. 328. Similar reflexions in Lefèvre, 'Les acteurs de la traduction', p. 188, who distinguishes between 'les traducteurs et leurs premiers destinataires, le plus souvent commanditaires du travail [et le versant] de la reproduction et de la diffusion des livres traduits' ('the translators and their first addressees, often sponsors of the work, and the aspect of reproduction and diffusion of translated texts').

5 The first condition concerning the translator's choice and the philological relationships with his sources has already been analysed, see Robecchi, 'Riccoldo, Jean le Long e la sua raccolta'.

Identifying the 'Target Reader'

Studying a translation, we have to consider that a translator can intervene in a text in three different ways: He can omit parts of the source-text; he can add new passages to the source-text; he can transform or re-formulate individual passages and adjust them for his purpose.

Although Jean le Long respects his source, he omits few passages, notably the episodes where Riccoldo in his *Liber peregrinationis* expresses his deep religious and emotional feelings. For instance, the passage where the pilgrim invokes Christ is missing in the translation:

> et venimus juxta mare et cantavimus ibi Evangelium 'Ambulans Jhesus juxta mare Galilee'. Ibi rogavi Christum quod me ad suum discipulatum vocaret et faceret me piscatorem hominum.
>
> > ([I. 17:], and we came to the seaside and read the Gospel 'Jesus Walked Upon the Sea of Galilee'. There I invoked Christ so that he called me as a disciple and made me a fisher of men.)

In the same way Jean le Long shortens the narrative of the encounter of the pilgrim with his brothers in Baghdad:

> Venimus autem per fluvium rectu cursu usque Baldacum civitatem mirabilem: ibi occurrerunt nobis fratres nostri ordinis extra civitatem, quos cum vidimus tantus erat fletus et inundacio lacrimarum pro gaudio quod paucis verbis explicari non posset.
>
> > ([XIX. 14:] We came straight to Baghdad on the river [Tigris]: our brothers came towards us and we cried and shed tears, so that I cannot explain this in few words.)

This passage is simplified in the French translation, because Jean le Long omits the tears and the emotion of the source-text:

> 'Et vinrent à l'encontre de nous jusques au dehors de la cité les freres de nostre ordene des freres precheurs qui là demeurent, et nous receurent à tres grant joye'
>
> > ('our brothers of the Dominican Order came towards us outside the city, and received us with great joy'.)

As we can find these passages in all the Latin manuscripts, we can regard this type of intervention as the choice of the translator, who was not interested in personal feelings of the pious friar. On the other hand, Odorico's bravery and boldness are highlighted in the translation because Jean le Long omits the passages which may have diminished it.[6] This does not necessarily correlate (Ric-

---

6 See *Le voyage en Asie d'Odoric de Pordenone*, ed. by Andreose and Ménard, p. cxvi: 'Jean le Long est allé plus loin en faisant disparaître partout le compagnon d'Odoric, au moment de l'incendie, puis dans la scène de la tempête'. For Riccoldo's, see Robecchi, *Riccold de Monte di Croce, 'Liber peregrinationis'*, pp. 123–51.

coldo's personality subdued at the expense of Odorico's personality), but as an expression of a desire of the translator to underline the adventurous character of the narrative at the expense of the issues of religiosity.

Additions are far more important than omissions in Jean Le Long translation. They provide us with explicit information about the translator's choices. When Riccoldo cites the miracle of the Marriage of Cana and finds the 'puteum unde ministri hauserunt aquam implentes ydreas' ('the well where the servants took the water'), Jean le Long specifies 'les VI caves d'eaue que Nostre Seigneur converty comme dit est' ('the six pots full of water that Jesus transformed, as [the Gospel] says').[7] When Riccoldo talks about Akeldama's field, where Judas Iscariot hanged himself, Jean le Long explains that 'les Juys achetterent des xxx deniers dont Dieux fu venduz, comme tesmoingne l'Evangille' ('Jews bought the field for 30 denarii, the price of God, as the Gospel witnesses'). The same statement is found in Boldensele's account 'vers midy est celle campaigne Acheldemath, *qui fu acatez des xxx deniers dont Diex fu venduz*' ('toward the South there is the field Akeldama, *bought with the 30 denarii, price of God*').[8] When Riccoldo, Odorico, and Boldensele mention the cities of Sodom and Gomorra, Jean le Long clarifies this, adding the following passage to the original Latin text: 'que Diex confondi par feu et soulphre plouvant dou chiel, et les ardy pour les granz pechiez des gens qui y habitoient' ('that God destroyed with fire and sulphur falling from the sky, and burned them because of the great sins of their inhabitants') in Riccoldo's account and 'Et aussi en la pugnition sus ditte soloient jadis y estre en celui lieu où est ores celui lac puant celle meir morte qui encores est bien hideuse en detestation de celui pechiet' ('the city is now set, for that punishment, where there is that stinking lake, the Dead Sea, and it is still horrible as damnation for that sin') in Boldensele's account.[9] He adds a similar passage when Odorico mentions the city of Soldania (that he calls *Sodoma*):

> [Soldania] n'est mie Sodoma, l'une des V citez sur quoy Dieux fist plouvoir feu et souffre du ciel en venjange de pechiez contre nature qui rengnoit en eulz, comme dist la Sainte Escripture. Car ces V villes furent jadis en la Sainte Terre de Promission, en ce lieu qui est ore la Mer Morte. Et ceste Sodoma, dont nous parlonz yci, scient ens où roiaulme de Persie.
>
> > (is by no means the Sodom that was one of the five cities upon which God threw fire and sulphur falling from the sky, to avenge the sins against nature that affected them, as the Bible testifies. These five cities were in olden times in the Promised Land, where

---

[7] Robecchi, *Riccold de Monte di Croce, 'Liber peregrinationis'*, p. 197; de Backer, *L'Extrême Orient*, p. 259.

[8] Robecchi, *Riccold de Monte di Croce, 'Liber peregrinationis'*, p. 207; de Backer, *L'Extrême Orient*, p. 265; Deluz, 'Guillaume de Boldensele', p. 340.

[9] Robecchi, *Riccold de Monte di Croce, 'Liber peregrinationis'*, p. 209; de Backer, *L'Extrême Orient*, p. 271; Deluz, 'Guillaume de Boldensele', p. 342. Jean le Long's sources are the Holy Bible and its commentaries.

presently there is the Dead Sea. This other Sodom, of which we speak here, is set in the Kingdom of Persia.)[10]

Finally, translating Riccoldo's chapters on the Jacobite and Nestorian heresies, Jean le Long adds some long explanations of their principles and doctrine. Riccoldo, addressing his fellows, did not need to develop his exposition in this direction as his brothers probably knew the subject.

In general, Jean le Long did not rewrite his source-text in a didactic and moralistic way, as most religious translators did at this time, but limited his additions to information useful for a lay reader or to rhetorical embellishment which would make the narrative more attractive and entertaining. For example, he expanded Odorico's account of the Martyrdom of Thane, the four Franciscans brutally killed in India in 1321 or Riccoldo's narrative on the first adventure of Genghis Khan.[11] He modified the syntax, and added a hint of suspense.[12] He rendered the brief passage from the *Flos historiarum* about the rebellion of a Syrian knight against the sultan of Babylon ('Et cum esset in campo altrinsecus imminente pugna, dixerunt ad invicem: "Nonne sumus omnes Sarraceni? Pugnare ad invicem et occidere non licet"') as follows:

> Avint que les II hostz furent assamblez et ordonnez par leurs batailles l'une contre l'autre pour tantost ferir ensamble. Quant il se virent en tel estat, il envoierent coureurs messagier li un à l'autre en disant: 'Nous sommes tous freres, nous sommes tous Sarrasin! Il ne loist point que nous nous combatonz ensamble et que nous nous entretuons'.
>
>> (The two armies were ready for battle, one against the other, to defeat each other. But the two sides sent messengers one to the other, saying: 'We are all brothers, we are all Muslims! Our religion does not allow us to fight and kill each other'.)[13]

To the passage of *Flos historiarum* on Alexander the Great, one of the greatest heroes in medieval imagination ('[...] ex parte septentrionis per longum est magnum desertum Indie, ubi tot serpentes et animalium diversitates imperator Alexander dicitur invenisse, ut in ipsius ystoriis plenius continetur' – 'towards the North there is the Great Indian Desert, where King Alexander found snakes and every kind of animal, as we can read in his histories'), Jean Le Long added details making the narrative more adventurous:[14]

---

10 *Le voyage en Asie d'Odoric de Pordenone*, ed. by Andreose and Ménard, p. 5.

11 For these two passages, see respectively Robecchi, 'Un traducteur au XIVe siècle', pp. 73–74 and *Le voyage en Asie d'Odoric de Pordenone*, ed. by Andreose and Ménard, p. 112.

12 See Robecchi, 'Un traducteur au XIVe siècle'.

13 Robecchi, *Riccold de Monte di Croce, 'Liber peregrinationis'*, p. 315; de Backer, *L'Extrême Orient*, does not publish this part of Riccoldo's text.

14 *Die Geschichte der Mongolen*, ed. by Dörper, p. 197. We do not know where Hayton took this information, but we suggest some texts like Walter of Châtillon's *Alexandreis* or the famous pseudo-Aristotle's *Secretum secretorum*.

> Vers nort a le grant desert d'Inde où tant a de serpens et de cruelz bestes que c'est grant merveilles. En celi desert fu mené par faulz conduisseurs li grans rois Alixandres pour lui et tout son host faire tuer des serpanz. Et furent ces faulx meneurs là croisez, comme on treuve en ses istoires.
>
>> (Towards the North there is the Great Indian Desert, full of snakes, dragons, and ferocious animals: awful things! King Alexander the Great has been led in this Desert by deceitful guides that let Alexander and his army be killed by the snakes. These deceitful guides have been condemned, as we can read in histories and romances.)[15]

He refers to an episode that contemporary readers probably knew from some *romances* about Alexander the Great popular at the time. Some references to familiar and daily life seem to refer to a well-known reality of the 'target reader'. Some examples: Jean le Long mentions tailors with a word, *parmentier*, that was more known in Picardy and East France.[16] Translating Odorico's text he uses the adjective *lanu* ('woolen'), 'un terme technique du commerce des toisons utilisé dans les échanges entre les ports normands et picards et l'Angleterre'.[17] Finally, he uses some locutions typical of the Picard dialect as 'taster au pauch' ('verify the reality of a thing by the touch', probably used by merchants), 'tout mis en tacz et en bloque' ('in a great confusion') and 'ainsi que Robin dansse' ('to make an effort without results').[18]

These and other features of the text show a particular direction. Previous scholars already proposed some considerations on Jean le Long's style. Philippe Ménard declares: 'Jean le Long [...] sait donner du mouvement et de la vie à son texte [...] Il a le sens du pathétique, le goût du merveilleux, le désir de dramatiser les grands moments du récit' ('Jean le Long gives movement and life to his text. He feels the touching aspects, he has a taste for the wonders, he wants to dramatize the great moments of the story').[19] Christine Deluz states that Jean le Long translates Boldensele's travel account aiming to satisfy the curiosity of his contemporaries who were discovering a new, wider world.[20] With his narrative style, he transformed a rather dry Latin travel account into a pleasant French tale. We

---

15 *Die Geschichte der Mongolen*, ed. by Dörper, p. 197. We do not even know Jean le Long's source, as the text does not give sufficient details.

16 Cf. 'parementier', in *Dictionnaire du Moyen Français*, online <https://www.atilf.fr/dmf> [Version 2020] and Godefroy, *Dictionnaire de l'ancienne langue française et de tous ses dialectes du IXe au XVe siècle*, v, col. 758b (Picardy, Lorraine, Northern Champagne, Wallonia).

17 Roques, 'Compte rendu à Andreose-Ménard', p. 251.

18 Robecchi, Robecchi, *Riccold de Monte di Croce, 'Liber peregrinationis'*, p. 137 and the 'Glossaire'.

19 Ménard, 'Jean le Long "translateur" et interprète d'Odoric', p. 48.

20 Deluz, 'Traité de l'état de la Terre sainte', p. 1000: 'Jean le Long [...] mit en roman un certain nombre de récits de voyage et de pèlerinage afin de satisfaire la curiosité crois-

may therefore suppose that he did not translate the Latin text into French for his monastic peers, but for lay people, north-eastern French merchants, lay bourgeois, well educated people actually, who did not necessarily know and read Latin. Ypres, Ghent, Bourges, Arras, and Saint-Omer were the richest merchant centres at the time. Serge Lusignan recently stressed the distance between feudal and chivalric literature on the one side and the urban and bourgeois production on the other side. There was a common literary life in the city of North-eastern France.[21] Although Jean le Long was a Benedictine, his monastery of Saint-Bertin was deeply involved in the urban life in the region and the fact that he wrote book for lay customers should not surprise us.

Identifying the 'Further Readers' in the Manuscripts

Jean Le Long's French translations have been transmitted in seven manuscripts and in a sixteenth-century printed edition.[22] The most ancient manuscript, Besançon, Bibliothèque Municipale, MS 667 (= *A*), was copied in 1368, seventeen years after Jean le Long's translation (dated 1351). It was probably made in the Abbey or in the city of Saint-Omer, the town where the translator was abbot, as we can extrapolate from a little note concerning the translator: '[…] et ad present abbé d'icellui lieu 1368' ('and currently abbot of this monastery Anno Domini 1368').[23] This note was probably added by the copyist, someone who perhaps lived in the abbey or in its vicinity and was acquainted with it. This manuscript does not seem to be a dedication copy, so we cannot identify a 'target reader', but only a 'further reader'. It contains only the six translations, and seems to reflect Jean Le Long's original plan to translate these six texts together. It is a modest manuscript, with a simple illustration on the first page and a few decorations here and there. We may nevertheless identify one anonymous reader of the manuscript with the help of several notes in the margins. In what follows, the left column quotes passages that received a note, added in the right margin and marked in italic:

---

sante de ses contemporains pour un monde que l'on commençait à découvrir plus vaste et plus divers qu'on ne l'avait imaginé jusqu'alors'.

21 Lusignan, *Essai d'histoire sociolinguistique*, pp. 256–57: 'vocation urbaine et bourgeoise de la littérature arrageoise et sa mise à distance de la culture féodale et chevaleresque, comme le reflète la production littéraire locale'; 'la participation des villes du Nord à une culture communale partagée'.

22 I gave a presentation on the Latin, Italian, and French manuscripts in Robecchi, 'Riccoldo after Riccoldo'; here I focus exclusively and in greater depth on the French manuscripts. We will not talk about the seventh manuscript from Moskau (copied in the 19th century) in the present article.

23 Besançon, Bibliothèque Municipale, MS 667, fol. 1[r].

- three notes show generic interest in European issues and personalities:

Text	Note
'Quant les Turquemans qui avoient esté subgiz aus Sarrasins et tributaries virent que il furent raempli de tres granz richesse' [fol. 10va, fol. 16] ('when the Turcs have been submitted to the Saracens and they paid taxes, they saw that they gained a lot of riches')	nota pro Francia ('note, advantage for France')
'pour celluy Edouart roy d'Angleterre faire tuer par un assaxin' [fol. 43ra, l. 19] ('[they tried] to kill Edward king of England by an assassin')	de Edoart roy Angloys ('about Edward, King of the English')
'elle [Damietta] a esté II fois prinse de Crestiens [...] la seconde fois par Monseigneur Saint Loys' [fol. 45va, ll. 4–7] ('the city has been conquered twice by the Christians [...] the second time by the King Saint Louis')	des crestiens par Saint Loys ('about the Christians by [the intervention of] Saint Louis')

— some notes show interest in saints or biblical sites:

Text	Note
'En ceste cité de Trapesonde est li corps Saint Anastasius' [fol. 85rb, l. 16] ('the body of Saint Anastasius is in the city of Trabzon')	nota de quicumque ('note about someone')
'Saint Thomas l'appostre' [fol. 92rb, ll. 5–6] ('Saint Thomas Apostle')	de Saint Thomas Apoustre ('about Saint Thomas Apostle')
'sus lequel est l'Arche Noe' [fol. 85va, l. 8] ('[on the mount] there's the Ark of Noah')	de Archa Noe ('about Noah's Ark')
'Dont fu Job' [fol. 85va, l. 23] ('where Job came from')	de Job ('about Job')
'on dist est le Secq Arbre' [fol. 85va, l. 1] ('we call it Secq Arbre')	de l'Abre Sec ('about the Abre sec')

— two notes show interest in Mongols' habits:

Text	Note
'couronnent de la peel de leur ami, et à ce ressamblent aus deables' [fol. 60rb, l. 4] ('[the Mongols] use crown made of the skin of this animal [the owl that helped them] and they look like devils')	de inimico humani generis ('about the enemy of the humanity')
'vous ont mestier sur toute rien, c'est obeisance au prince et concorde' [fol. 60rb, l. 22] ('moreover they obey to the prince and they have harmony')	de obediencia et concordia ('about obedience and harmony')

These short notes are not sufficient to identify the reader's dialect (even though *abre* could be a Picard form). He was interested in the issues of secular rulership as it seems; furthermore, he seems to know Latin.

There is another manuscript containing marginal notes, Paris, Bibliothèque nationale de France, MS fr. 1380 (= *C*). This manuscript, which contains only Jean le Long's translations, was copied during the first decade of the fifteenth century in Paris. Unfortunately, there is no indication of the manuscript's owner. Analysis of the fifty-five notes written by a mid-fifteenth-century hand convey an idea of one of the readers (or maybe the only reader) of this manuscript. His interests do not differ very much from the interests of the reader of *A*:

— one note shows the reader's interest in Mongols:

Text	Note
'Et je Aycones chevalier fu meismes present au couronnement de deux de leurs Canis, mais pour certain ilz tindrent du tout leur anciene guise. Premierement firent assembler tout le peuple, puis firent le siege du roy dessoubz un paveillon et estendirent sur la terre un feultre tres noir' [fol. 16vb] (I, Knight Ayton, attendend the crowning of two Khans, and for certain they followed their ancient custom. First, they assembled the whole people, then they made the throne under a pavillon and spread a black felt [carpet] out on the ground')	nota icy de la maniere du gouvernement du grans Canis de Tartarie qui est leur empereur ('about the custom of governance of the Khan, that is their emperor')

— some notes show interest in saints and biblical sites:

Text	Note
'Ce royaume est moult grant et y a de grandes citez et terres' [fol. 103va] ('this kingdom is wide and there are big cities and countries')	le corps saint Thomas à Monbarum ('the body of Saint Thomas lays in Monbarum')
'Le corps saint Jehan Bouche d'Or' [fol. 120vb] ('the body of Saint John Chrysostom')	Nota de saint Jehan Bouchedor ('note about saint John Chrysostom')
'En Ephesim la cité là où saint Jehan tout vif se mist en son sepulcre' [fol. 121ra] ('in Ephesim, the city where Saint John, still alive, entered in his sepulchre)	Icy se mist saint Jehan en sepulture ('here Saint John entered in his sepulchre')

— one note shows interest in diplomatic relations with Europe:

Text	Note
'À la seconde requeste disons que nous voulons que payx et perpetuelle' [fol. 24vb] ('to the second request, we answer that we want peace, eternal peace')	nota de la paix entre les crestiens et les tartres ('note about the peace between Christians and Mongols')

- some notes show interest in geography:

Text	Note
'Tyr, qui est une ancienne cité' [fol. 121vb] ('Tyre is an ancient city')	la cité de Tyr ('the city of Tyre')
'De Acre vins en IIII jorus par terre [...] Gasan [...] villes de Philistins' [fol. 122ra] ('I travelled from Acre for three days to Gasan [...] cities of Philistines')	le païs des Philistins en Palestine ('the city of Philistines in Palestine')

- numerous notes show interest in *mirabilia* as for example the following ones:

Text	Note
'Les souris y·ssont aussi grandes que sont chiens' [fol. 97vb] ('mices are as big as dogs')	les souris y sont grans comme chiens ('mices are as big as dogs')
'Entour ce fleuve treuve on ligement aloes' [fol. 123vb] ('around this river there is the wood aloe')	icy se treuve le bons aloes ('here you can find good aloe')
'C'est une best moult duisable' [fol. 124ra] ('this is a docile animal')	nota de l'elefant ('note about the elephant')
'Comme on dist est le Sec Arbre' [fol. 96ra, similar to A's note] ('as we call it, the Sec Arbre')	nota ici est le Sec Arbre ('note, here the Sec Arbre')

The readers of these two manuscripts were probably educated lay people, but there are no further identifying clues. The reader of *A* has had some knowledge of Latin, so that he could switch codes; even though the reader of *C* did not write in Latin, and his clumsy letters seem to indicate a non-professional intellectual, he was well acquainted with Jean le Long's translation. Again, we can find in both manuscripts the ambivalent interest in the Orient, as a political entity on one side, and as a place of marvels and strange things on the other side.

MS *D*, London, British Library, MS Cotton Otho D II, is a 'sibling' of MS *C*. It was copied in the first decade of the fifteenth century, too; the scriptorium in which the manuscripts were copied and decorated seems to be the same, but the magnificent illustrations of MS *D* were surely made by the *Maître de l'Épître d'Othéa* between 1404 and 1410.[24] After the 1430s the Cotton MS belonged to Jacquette of Luxembourg, but she cannot be its commissioner, as she had not yet been born when the manuscript was produced.[25] It is, once again, a *recueil homogène*, that is, a multi-text book which is physically one; further-

---

24 Robecchi, 'Le *Roman de Mélusine* du ms. BL Cotton Otho D II', pp. 324–27; see also Meiss, *French Painting in the Time of Jean De Berry*, pp. 338–89 and Ouy, Reno, and Villela-Petit, *Album Christine de Pizan*, pp. 131–42.

25 The *ex libris* was burnt in the fire of the British Museum in October 1731, but Thomas Smith's ancient catalogue of 1696 informs us about the possessor, see Smith, *Catalogus Librorum Manuscriptorum Bibliothecæ Cottonianæ*, p. 74.

more, it contains Jean d'Arras's *Roman de Mélusine*.[26] On the one hand, this association emphasizes the 'pseudo-historical' role of the Crusade fought by the sons of Melusine against the Muslims; but, on the other hand, it highlights the fictional and wondrous character of Jean le Long's work.

MSS *C* and *D* belong to the same sub-group of the textual family (β); the other sub-group is formed by Paris, Bibliothèque nationale de France, MS fr. 2810 (*E*), containing the famous *Livre des merveilles* (*Book of Wonders*), and the mid-fifteenth-century Bern, Burgerbibliothek, MS 125 (*F*).

MS *E* was commissioned by the powerful John the Fearless, Duke of Burgundy, who presented it to his uncle, the influential bibliophile John, Duke of Berry, in 1413[27]. They were two of the most powerful men in fifteenth-century France, relatives of the Kings of France. The Bern MS *F* was probably commissioned by Charles, Duke of Orléans, the famous poet who was imprisoned in England between 1415 and 1450. The manuscript can be dated to the middle of the fifteenth century, after the Duke was freed.[28]

MSS *E* and *F* differ from the other four in their content and structure. The text order in the MSS *ABCD* is: 1) Hayton, 2) Riccoldo, 3) Odorico, 4) Boldensele, 5) *Lettres*, 6) *De statu*. In the MSS *EF* the order is slightly different: 1) Odorico, 2) Boldensele, 3) *Lettres*, 4) *De statu*, 5) Hayton, which appears here in the original French version, not in Jean le Long's translation, 6) Riccoldo. Marco Polo's *Devisement du monde* (7) and John of Mandeville's *Livre des merveilles* or *Livre des voyages* (8) follow in both manuscripts.

The Bern MS (*F*) is a very interesting one. It is a *recueil composite organisé*, that is, a collection containing pieces written in different times and/or places and compiled according to a recognizable set of criteria. The three works, Marco Polo's *Devisement*, Mandeville's *Livre des merveilles*, and the six Jean le Long's translations, have been copied in three different codicological units at three different times: Mandeville at the beginning of the fifteenth century, Jean le Long next to Marco Polo in the middle of the fifteenth by the same scribe, Bertrand Richart, a courtly scribe as it seems. He also copied the duke-poet's lyrics.[29] Charles of Orléans probably assembled the three different units on his own.[30] Marie de Clèves, the wife of Charles of Orléans, inherited the MS, and placed her *ex libris* on the cover. The last known medieval owner was a member of the Pons de Saint Maurice family. We do not know how this beautiful MS came to his possession, but he erased the previous coats of arms in the *lettrines* and added his own.

---

26 The most recent edition is Jean d'Arras, 'Roman de Mélusine', ed. and trans. by Vincensini; see also Robecchi, 'Le *Roman de Mélusine* du ms. BL Cotton Otho D II' about the links between the *Roman de Mélusine* and Jean le Long's translations.

27 For this manuscript, see now Mourgues, *La poétique du voyage*.

28 For the identification of Charles of Orléans as the patron and of his wife Marie de Clèves as owner see Robecchi, 'Le ms. 125 de la Burgerbibliothek de Berne', pp. 157–92.

29 See especially Carpentras, Bibliothèque Municipale, MS 375.

30 See Robecchi, 'Le ms. 125 de la Burgerbibliothek de Berne', pp. 182–83.

The insertion of Marco Polo and Mandeville can be seen as a clue to the reception of Jean le Long's work in this, in many regards, exclusive cultural milieu. Marco Polo's work is usually entitled *Le devisement du monde* ('The Description of the World'), a title that recalls the encyclopaedic tradition and suggests a scientific interpretation of the world. In the two manuscripts the titles are telling: in the Parisian one, it is entitled *Le livre de Marc Paul des merveilles d'Asie la grant et d'Inde la Majour et Mineur et des diverses regions du monde* (fol. 1^r), while in the Bern MS *F* it is entitled *Le grant Kan qui devise les grans merveilles qui sont en la terre d'Ynde* (fol. 1^r), and *Le rommans du grant Kaan de la grant cité de Cambalut* (fol. 94^r). These titles highlight the marvellous. Moreover, the Bern MS also indicates the genre: a *roman*, a term that at this time designates fictional narratives. Unfortunately, Mandeville's work lacks a title in both manuscripts, but it is usually known as *Livre des merveilles*, as it is called in a number of other manuscripts. It is possible that the two different compilers of the Paris and Bern MSS decided to insert Hayton's original version of *La Flor des estoires de la terre d'Orient* because Jean le Long's translation omits a part of the fourth book, which describes the organization of a crusade against the Muslims with the support of the Mongols. The compilers' aim would be in that case to create a collection not only dedicated to a description of Eastern countries, but also to the Holy War against the infidels and to the organization and undertaking of a new Crusade. This would go along with the renewal of interest in the idea of a crusade and the dream of conquest that emerged during the fifteenth century. Although this interpretation may well be possible, the reason for including Hayton could also be that the Parisian workshop knew this version and decided to insert it as an *antigraphe*, perhaps ordered by the commissioner, John the Fearless.

The renewal of interest in the Crusades in the fifteenth century followed the Fall of Constantinople to the Turks in 1453. Paris, Bibliothèque nationale de France, MS fr. 12202 (= *B*), which belongs to the same textual family as *A*, was copied in the North-eastern region of France at the end of the fifteenth century, or, to be more precise, in Picardy between 1480 and 1490.[31] It is a modest manuscript (as *A* is) copied as a *recueil homogène*. After the six translations of Jean le Long follows an excerpt from Vincent de Beauvais's *Speculum historiale* concerning the life and death of Mahomet (fols 172^v–73^r), and the so-called *Anonymus Pisanus*, an anonymous translation of the Latin legend of Mahomet and the rise of Islam.[32] This manuscript may be regarded as an evidence of a new understanding of Latin Christianity's relationships with Islam. After the Fall of Constantinople, thanks to Nicolas of Cusa and his works *De pace fidei* and *Cribratio Alcorani*, knowledge of Islam became necessary to launch a new wave

---

31 The watermarks are Briquet 6056 *étoile à huit rayons* (Namur 1482/3, Arras 1485, Rouen 1490, Paris 1498) and Briquet 8215 *lettre G* (Sens 1485, Douai 1489).

32 For this text, see Robecchi 'Une légende de Mahomet inédite dans le ms. fr. 12202 de la BnF', online: <https://romane.hypotheses.org/492> [accessed 3 November 2022], and Mancini, 'Per lo studio della leggenda di Maometto in occidente'.

of crusades.[33] There are some analogies between this and some Latin manuscripts that preserve Riccoldo's *Liber peregrinationis*, such as Turin, Biblioteca Nazionale, MS H.II.33, copied between the end of the fifteenth and the beginning of the sixteenth century. The whole manuscript is dedicated to Islam, as it contains a translation of the *Qur'an* by Robert of Ketton, the *Doctrina Muhamet* by Herman of Carinthia, and Riccoldo's *Contra legem Sarracenorum*.

There is another manuscript from the late fifteenth century extant containing Riccoldo's *Liber peregrinations*, Paris, Bibliothèque nationale de France, MS lat. 6225. It contains, among other texts, John of Castiglione's *Exhortatio in Turchos*, Riccoldo's *Contra legem Sarracenorum*, Herman of Carinthia's *Doctrina Muhamet*, and Peter the Venerable's letters about Islam.

Jean le Long's translations remained popular during the sixteenth century, they were among those medieval texts which made it into the printed culture which meant a dramatic transformation of their readership. In 1529, Jean de Saint-Denys printed in Paris a collection of the six translations as if they formed a unique text and he entitled it *L'hystore merveilleuse, plaisante et recreative du grand Empereur de Tartarie seigneur des Tartres nommé le grand Can*. He clearly wanted to market it as a *roman* of wonders and delight, and not as a learned encyclopaedia.[34]

Conclusion

Regarding the style of the translation and the auctorial modifications, one can deduce that Jean le Long seriously considered the documentary and 'scientific' message of his work. The six works were originally written in Latin by missionaries and members of religious orders for their peers. For example, Riccoldo wrote for his fellow friars, Hayton for Pope Clement V, and Wilhelm of Boldensele for Cardinal Hélie de Talleyrand-Périgord. Jean le Long took these texts and changed their assignment and purpose: the rich Picard bourgeoisie probably represented the 'target reader' of his translations. This unfortunately has to stay a hypothesis, as no substantial evidence can confirm it.

The 'further readers' took advantage of two different aspects of the work, irreconcilable at the first sight: the 'scientific' (especially AB) and the marvellous (especially $CDEF$). The two α manuscripts, A and B, even if originating in different milieux and different periods, seem to testify to and to emphasise the interest in the 'scientific'. By contrast, the four β manuscripts were owned by noble families, and the fact that three of them contain the *Roman de Mélusine* by Jean d'Arras, the *Devisement du monde* by Marco Polo (also *Livre des merveilles* or *Roman du grant Kaan*), and Mandeville's *Livre des merveilles* may be seen as an evidence of the entertaining and marvellous reading of Jean le Long's works in this particular milieu. Nevertheless, it is important to remember that

---

33 See the classic account by D'Ancona, 'La leggenda di Maometto'.

34 There is no study yet of this printed edition.

the genre categories we operate with are often ahistorical, and that travel literature did not in fact exist as a genre in the Middle Ages. One must also consider the complexity of networks that underlie medieval *recueils*: readers' interests were probably much more complex than we can imagine.[35]

Jean le Long's translation represents an interesting case for the question on various levels of reception of medieval translations. The elaborate conceptual frame and the inner coherence of the text based on six different models demonstrates the deep engagement of the translator with his subject. Unfortunately, he did not reveal whom he had in mind as a reader when he drafted his work, but the analysis we have made with the help of a handful of samples can offer some clues for a better understanding of the multi-layered message that a text and its individual copies contain, as well as the multiple facets of reception that a text can receive, in accord with and beyond the translator's (hypothetical) aims.

Bibliography

Manuscript Sources

Bern, Burgerbibliothek, MS 125 (= *F*)
Besançon, Bibliothèque Municipale, MS 667 (= *A*)
Carpentras, Bibliothèque Municipale, MS 375
London, British Library, MS Cotton Otho D II (= *D*)
Paris, Bibliothèque nationale de France, MS fr. 1380 (= *C*)
——, MS fr. 2810 (= *E*)
——, MS fr. 12202 (= *B*)
——, MS lat. 6225
Torino, Biblioteca Nazionale, MS H.II.33

Primary Sources

de Backer, Louis, *L'Extrême Orient au Moyen Âge d'après les manuscrits d'un flamand de Belgique, moine de Saint-Bertin à Saint-Omer, et d'un prince d'Arménie, moine de Prémontré à Poitiers* (Paris: Leroux, 1877)

Concina, Chiara, 'Da Pechino ad Avignone ed oltre: La corrispondenza tra Benedetto XII, il "Qaghan" Toghon-Temür e i principi Alani nella traduzione francese di Jean le Long (1351)', *Itineraria* 17 (2018), pp. 109–60

Deluz, Christiane, 'Guillaume de Boldensele, Liber de quibusdam ultramarinis partibus et praecipue de Terra sancta (1336) suivi de la traduction de frère Jean le Long (1350)', (unpublished doctoral thesis, Université Paris IV, 1972)

Gadrat, Christine, '"De statu, conditione ac regimine magni Canis": L'original latin du "Livre de l'estat du grant Caan" et la question de l'auteur', *Bibliothèque de l'École des Chartes*, 165/2 (2007), pp. 355–71

---

35 Azzam, Collet, and Foehr-Janssens, 'Les manuscrits littéraires français', p. 657: 'entretissage de réseaux tantôt participatifs, tantôt concurrents'.

Die Geschichte der Mongolen des Hethum von Korykos (1307) in der Rückübersetzung durch Jean le Long: Traitiez des estas et des conditions de quatorze royaumes de Aise (1351), ed. by Sven Dörper, Europäische Hochschulschriften, 13: Französische Sprache und Literatur, 236 (Frankfurt am Main and New York: Lang, 1998)

Hayton of Corico, *La Flor des Estoires de la Terre d'Orient*, ed. by Charles Kohler, in *Recueil des Historiens des Croisades: Documents arméniens*, II (Paris: Imprimerie nationale, 1906), pp. 111–253

Jean d'Arras, *Roman de Mélusine*, ed. and trans. by Jean Jacques Vincensini, Le livre de poche, 4566, Lettres gothiques (Paris: Librairie Générale Française, 2003)

Le voyage en Asie d'Odoric de Pordenone traduit par Jean le Long OSB, ed. by Alvise Andreose and Philippe Ménard, Textes littéraires français, 602 (Genève: Droz, 2010)

Mancini, Augusto, 'Per lo studio della leggenda di Maometto in occidente', *Rendiconti della Reale Accademia Nazionale dei Lincei*, 10/6 (1934), pp. 325–49

Odorico da Pordenone, *Relatio de mirabilibus orientalium Tartarorum*, ed. by Annalia Marchisio, Edizione Nazionale dei Testi Mediolatini d'Italia, 41 (Firenze: SISMEL – Edizioni del Galluzzo, 2016)

Robecchi, Marco, *Riccold de Monte di Croce, 'Liber peregrinationis', traduit par Jean le Long d'Ypres*, Travaux des littératures romanes: Études et textes romans du Moyen Âge (Strasbourg: ELiPhi, 2020)

Secondary Works

Andreose, Alvise, *La strada, la Cina, il cielo: Studi sulla* Relatio *di Odorico da Pordenone e sulla sua fortuna romanza*, Medioevo Romanzo e Orientale: Studi, 17 (Soveria Mannelli: Rubbettino, 2012)

Astell, Ann W., 'On the Usefulness and Use Value of Books', in *Medieval Rhetoric: A Casebook*, ed. by Scott D. Troyan, Routledge Medieval Casebooks, 36 (London: Routledge, 2004), pp. 41–62

Azzam, Wagih, Olivier Collet, and Yasmina Foehr-Janssens, 'Les manuscrits littéraires français: Pour une sémiotique du recueil médiéval', *Revue belge de philologie et d'histoire* 83/3, *Langues et littératures modernes – Modernetaal en litterkunde* (2005), pp. 639–69

Brandenberger, Tobias, 'Una traduccion bajomedieval y su publico', in *Essays on Medieval Translations in the Iberian Peninsula*, ed. by Tomás Martínez Romero and Roxana Recio, Estudis sobre la traducció 9 (Castelló and Omaha, NE: Publicaciones de la Universitat Jaume I – Creighton University, 2001), pp. 75–94

Buridant, Claude, 'Esquisse d'une traductologie au Moyen Âge', in *Translations Médiévales: Cinq siècles de traductions en français au Moyen Âge (XIe–XVe siècles): Étude et Répertoire*, ed. by Claudio Galderisi, 3 vols (Turnhout, Brepols, 2011), I: *De la translatio studii à l'étude de la translatio*, pp. 325–81

D'Ancona, Alessandro, 'La leggenda di Maometto in occidente', *Giornale storico della letteratura italiana* 13 (1889), pp. 199–281

Deluz, Christiane, 'Traité de l'état de la Terre sainte', in *Croisades et pèlerinages: Récits, chroniques et voyages en Terre sainte, XIIe–XIVe siècle*, ed. by Danielle Regnier-Bohler, Bouquins, 1 (Paris: Laffont, 1997), pp. 996–1028

Godefroy, Frédéric, *Dictionnaire de l'ancienne langue française et de tous ses dialectes du IXe au XVe siècle*, 10 vols (Paris: Vieweg, 1881–1902)

Lefèvre, Sylvie, 'Les acteurs de la traduction: commanditaires et destinataires: Milieux de production et de diffusion', in *Translations Médiévales: Cinq siècles de traductions en français au Moyen Âge (XIe–XVe siècles): Étude et Répertoire*, ed. by Claudio Galderisi, 3 vols (Turnhout: Brepols, 2011), I: *De la translatio studii à l'étude de la translatio*, pp. 147–206

Lusignan, Serge, *Essai d'histoire sociolinguistique: Le français picard au Moyen Âge*, Recherches littéraires médiévales, 13 (Paris: Classiques Garnier, 2012)

Meiss, Millard, *French Painting in the Time of Jean De Berry: The Limbourgs and their Contemporaries*, 2 vols (London: Thames & Hudson, the Pierpont Morgan Library, 1974)

Ménard, Philippe, 'Jean le Long "translateur" et interprète d'Odoric', in *Culture, livelli di cultura e ambienti nel Medioevo occidentale, Atti del IX Convegno della Società Italiana di Filologia Romanza, Bologna, 5–8 ottobre 2009*, ed. by Francesco Benozzo and others (Roma: Aracne, 2012), pp. 25–48

Mourgues, Priscilla, *La poétique du voyage dans le* Livre des merveilles *(ms. Paris, BnF, fr. 2810)*, (unpublished doctoral thesis, Université de Bordeaux, 2022)

Ouy, Gilbert, Christine Reno, and Inès Villela-Petit, *Album Christine de Pizan*, Texte, Codex & Contexte, 14 (Turnhout: Brepols, 2012)

Robecchi, Marco, 'Riccoldo after Riccoldo: The "Liber peregrinationis" and its Vernacular Translations', forthcoming in the issue of the conference *Riccoldo da Monte di Croce († 1320): Missionary to the Middle East and Expert on Islam (7–8 September 2017)* (Stockholm: The Royal Swedish Academy of Letters, History and Antiquities, 2021)

——, 'Le *Roman de Mélusine* du ms. BL Cotton Otho D II: Questions textuelles, extratextuelles et contextuelles', *Romania* 138 (2019), pp. 353–427

——, 'Un traducteur au XIVe siècle: Réflexions pour l'étude du recueil de Jean le Long', *Le Moyen Français*, 84 (2019), pp. 67–78

——, 'Le ms. 125 de la Burgerbibliothek de Berne: De Charles d'Orléans à Jacques Bongars (en passant par Marie de Clèves)', *Medioevi*, 3 (2017), pp. 157–92

——, 'Riccoldo, Jean le Long e la sua raccolta odeporica: traduttore o editore?', in *Atti dell'XI convegno della Società Italiana di Filologia Romanza*, ed. by Antonio Pioletti and Stefano Rapisarda (Soveria Mannelli: Rubbettino, 2016), pp. 431–46

Roques, Gilles, 'Compte rendu à Andreose-Ménard', *Le voyage en Asie: Revue de Linguistique Romane*, 75 (2011), pp. 237–57

Smith, Thomas, *Catalogus Librorum Manuscriptorum Bibliothecæ Cottonianæ* (Oxford: Sheldonian Theatre, 1696); facsimile edn: *Catalogue of the Manuscripts in the Cottonian Library, 1969*, ed. by Colin G. C. Tite (Cambridge: Brewer, 1984)

Websites

Dictionnaire du Moyen Français (*DMF*), ATILF – CNRS & Université de Lorraine, online: <https://www.atilf.fr/dmf> (Version 2015) [accessed 3 November 2022]

Robecchi, Marco, 'Une légende de Mahomet inédite dans le ms. fr. 12202 de la BnF', in *Billets*, section romane de l'IRHT, 29 August 2016, online: <https://romane.hypotheses.org/492> [accessed 3 November 2022]

From Devotion to Censure

Hans Tucher's and Bernard of Breydenbach's Pilgrim Accounts and their Two Medieval Czech Translations

Jaroslav Svátek

Centre for Medieval Studies, Institute of Philosophy, Academy of Sciences, Prague

The texts discussed in this essay originated in Bohemia at the end of the fifteenth century. At this time, the kingdom of Bohemia was the only realm in Latin Europe where three Christian churches co-existed: the Catholics, the Utraquists, and the radical Unity of Brethren. The two latter churches fulfilled several tasks in the eyes of their members, people who had left the Catholic church. Their specific ecclesiological, liturgical, and theological settings especially accommodated the wishes of lay people for closer participation in the future direction of the Church, understood as a community of believers. Such a wish was not uncommon in Europe at this time, and individual Church authorities tried to meet it in various ways, carefully (or not-so-carefully) balancing encouragement and integration on the one side and exclusion and repression on the other.[1] The accelerated vernacularization of pastoral or even theological literature very probably represents the most visible aspect of this very important social phenomenon. In Bohemia, lay participation in those Church issues which surpassed the sphere of pastoral care was formulated by elite theologians active at the University of Prague in the first decades of the fifteenth century. These men let their flock share in their massive critique of schismatic papacy as well as their ideas for theology and liturgy for leading the faithful in their journey to salvation. The new teachings as formulated by John Wyclif – who sought to solve the post-schism crisis of Church hierarchy through stronger participation of secular ruling elites in ecclesiastical decision making and in a poor Church which had been freed of earthly possessions – received a strong response in Bohemia. After the execution of Jan Hus in 1415, the leader of the church critical movement which emerged from the theological and pastoral debate, the movement then transformed into a Christian sect which claimed to be the true Church of Christ. As the king of Bohemia, Wenceslas IV, died unexpectedly in 1419, the

---

1 John Van Engen, 'Multiple Options', pp. 257–84.

situation escalated quickly and the realm was split between the Catholic and Utraquist parties, with the latter winning the upper hand on account of having very flexible military forces which were able to defy several of the subsequent crusades which were launched by the papacy and Emperor Sigismund of Luxembourg, who was the actual heir to the Kingdom of Bohemia. Following two decades of religious wars, the Bohemian estates concluded a peace with the Roman Church in 1436, which recognized *nolens volens* the Utraquist teaching which was also acknowledged by Sigismund who then took up rule over the kingdom. Bohemian society lived under a fragile peace in the second half of the fifteenth century, which František Šmahel characterizes as 'a tolerance out of sheer necessity'.[2] Catholic and Utraquist leaders found themselves invovled in never-ending polemics against each other, with both parties anxiously watching the activities of the Unity of Brethren. But below the surface of these openly staged animosities and declared hostilities, the social as well as religious life of the lay population very often crossed confessional boundaries, whether in interconfessional marriages or in the reading of shared vernacular pastoral and entertaining literature.[3]

By the end of the fifteenth century, the importance of book printing was appreciated at first by the Catholic Church, the Utraquists and the Unity of Brethren followed two decades later. All three of the religious communities, recognized the usefulness as a polemical weapon but also as a means for the less spectacular but all the more effective 'evangelization' of new adherents. Alongside vernacular bibles (which were mostly confessionally indifferent, because they were mainly printed for economical profit), a number of other religious works also appeared, consisting largely of liturgical handbooks and (semi-)theological tractates. The number of religious prints compared to the overall number of books printed in Bohemia in the period was quite high, however, to date only a few of them have been analysed in detail.[4] This essay will focus on the Czech translations and adaptations of two German and Latin texts belonging to a very popular genre of travelogues to Palestine. In these texts, religious instruction was usually paired with geographic description of exotic regions and the thrilling narratives of an adventure novel. As such, travelogues relating to Palestine represented a promising merchandise which could fulfil several aims at once – entertaining the reader, instructing them in the geography of the known world, and facilitating the transfer of a more or less polemical religious message. The following analysis will search for an answer to the question of how the controversies between Utraquists, the Unity of Brethren, and Catholics shaped these basically uncontroversial books of knowledge about exotic lands.

---

2 Šmahel, 'Svoboda slova, svatá válka a tolerance z nutnosti v husitském období', pp. 644–79.

3 Rychterová, 'Preaching, the Vernacular, and the Laity', pp. 297–330.

4 Just, 'Printed Books in the Bohemian Reformation', pp. 220–21.

Mikuláš Bakalář and his Workshop

In 1498, two books were printed in the workshop of Mikuláš Bakalář (Nicholas 'Bachelor') in the town of Pilsen, western Bohemia. Traditionally titled *The Treatise on the Holy Land* (*Traktát o zemi svaté*) and *The Life of Mohamed* (*Život Mohamedův*), these incunables can be viewed from several different perspectives. Most of the scholarly attention given to these books so far, has focused on examining their place within the contexts of the origins of the printing press in late medieval Bohemia.[5] Mikuláš Bakalář, known also as Mikuláš Štětina, was probably born in Upper Hungary (today's Slovakia), studied at the University of Cracow – hence his cognomen 'Bachelor' – and by the end of the 1480s had settled in Pilsen, where he was to become one of the first known printers in the Czech Lands.[6] We know of approximately thirty titles edited by him by the turn of the sixteenth century. With one exception, they were printed in Czech and comprised popular literature, calendars, and travelogues.[7]

The *Treatise on the Holy Land* belongs to a vast corpus of late medieval pilgrimage accounts of Jerusalem. As the number of readers in Bohemian society grew overall, there was an increasing interest for this type of literature, which was promoted by the printing activity of Mikuláš Bakalář.[8] The other text, the *Life of Mohamed*, fits perfectly into the enduring tradition of polemics against Islam and Eastern Christianity. Until the end of the fifteenth century, works of this genre were only accessible in Bohemia in Latin. Both of the texts considered here are translations, which have been attributed traditionally (but inconclusively) to the printer himself.[9] My aim in this article is to analyse the translation strategies employed in the two texts, in particular: how were both adaptations made and how did the translator treat his sources? How do both texts reflect the specific religious situation in the Czech lands called the 'Kingdom of the Two People'?

---

5 The life and activities of Mikuláš Bakalář have been thoroughly investigated in the collective volume *Mikuláš Bakalár Štetina*, ed. by Kohút. For the most recent study, which presents an overview of his prints, see Voit, 'Mikuláš Bakalář jinak'.

6 The mention of his geographical origin appears in the explicit of *The Life of Mohamed*: 'Virgo Theutunicis multum celebrata sacellis, Virgo, quam Ungari maximo thure colunt, hac de gente ortus, precor sanctissima, me ope recepto ruere haud sinas' ('Virgin, who are venerated in many German shrines, Virgin, greatly revered by the Hungarians, I, originating from their country, pray you, oh most holy [one], give me strength and do not let me perish!'), Prague, Knihovna Premonstrátské kanonie na Strahově, DR IV 37/3, fol. 30r.

7 See Voit, 'Mikuláš Bakalář jinak', pp. 95–99.

8 Productions from his workshop include the translations of John Mandeville's bestseller (two different editions: *Knížka o putování jeho po světě, po zemi i po moři*, 1510; *Cesta po světě*, 1513) and Amerigo Vespucci's treatise on the New World (*Spis o nových zemiech a o Novém světě*, 1508) edited in Pilsen only seven years after the expedition. See Voit, 'Mikuláš Bakalář jinak', pp. 98–99.

9 Sokol, 'Život Mohamedův z r. 1498 a jeho předloha', p. 40; Koutníková, 'Český prvotisk', p. 195.

The Treatise on the Holy Land and its Model

The *Treatise on the Holy Land* (henceforth *The Treatise*) survives in only two exemplars: Prague, Knihovna Národního muzea, MS 25 E 8, and Prague, Knihovna Premonstrátské kanonie na Strahově, MS DR IV 37/5 (in fragments).[10] It is a relatively short book of thirty-two folios *in octavo* with twenty lines per page. On the rare occasions when scholars have paid attention to *The Treatise*, it has been considered to be a partial translation of Bernard of Breydenbach's pilgrimage account, *Peregrinatio in Terram Sanctam*.[11] Edited and first printed in 1486 in Latin, the detailed encyclopaedic account in the *Peregrinatio* became widely dispersed across Europe, and was translated in its entirety into many languages, including German,[12] French, Spanish, Dutch, and Italian.[13] In consideration of the number of editions, particularly those produced in sixteenth-century Venice, and their distribution (to date more than fifteen exemplars have been identified in Czech libraries alone, of prints in German, Latin, and French), Breydenbach's *Peregrinatio*, then, may be regarded as a real bestseller of the genre.[14] It provided an updated and practical travel guide, accompanied by fine illustrations, tables with alphabets of oriental languages, and other practical instruction for late medieval pilgrims in the Holy Land. It may also have served as an instrument of anti-Islamic propaganda.[15]

The Treatise, however, exhibits so many differences when compared with the *Peregrinatio* that the question of its original model needs to be reconsidered. The author of *The Treatise* translated only a part of Breydenbach's travelogue, as shown in the following scheme:

---

10 The text of this travelogue was recently edited in an appendix to my study Svátek, 'Traktát o zemi svaté (1498)', pp. 121–38. While the first incunable lacks two folios (9 and 16), only 11 folios survive in the Strahov exemplar.

11 Koutníková, 'Český prvotisk', pp. 191–96; Voit, 'Mikuláš Bakalář jinak', pp. 98–99; *Gesamtkatalog der Wiegendrucke*, no. GW0508210N, online: <www.gesamtkatalogderwiegendrucke.de> [accessed 3 November 2022]; Urbánková, *Soupis prvotisků českého původu*, pp. 157–59 (no. 38); Šimáková and Vrchotka, *Katalog prvotisků Knihovny Národního muzea*, p. 104 (no. 477).

12 The German version was edited simultaneously with the Latin original, 14 February 1486.

13 Bernhard von Breydenbach, *Peregrinatio in Terram sanctam* (*Gesamtkatalog der Wiegendrucke*, no. GW05075, online as above). Since the Latin original of Breydenbach's account has not yet been edited, all references in this article are taken from the digitized exemplar in Darmstadt, Universitäts- und Landesbibliothek, Inc. IV/98, online: <http://tudigit.ulb.tu-darmstadt.de/show/inc-iv-98> [accessed 3 November 2022]. On the textual tradition and composition of this account, see Timm, *Der Palästina-Pilgerbericht des Bernhard von Breidenbach*, pp. 89–97; the editions of Breydenbach's account are listed in *Europäische Reiseberichte des späten Mittelalters*, I, ed. by Paravicini and Halm, pp. 203–06.

14 *Europäische Reiseberichte*, I, ed. by Paravicini and Halm, p. 205.

15 Timm, *Der Palästina-Pilgerbericht des Bernhard von Breidenbach*, pp. 79–80 and pp. 328–50; Meyers, 'La Peregrinatio in terram sanctam de Bernhard von Breidenbach (1486) comme instrument de propagande', pp. 365–74.

Bernard of Breydenbach's *Peregrinatio in Terram sanctam*	Czech translations
dedication to Berthold of Henneberg, archbishop of Mainz (fol. 2ʳ)	
preface (fol. 4ᵛ)	
Part I: Pilgrimage to Jerusalem (fol. 8ʳ; split into subchapters)	Treatise on the Holy Land (without internal division into chapters)
Compendiosa terre sancte descriptio et singulorum locorum[16] (fol. 36ʳ)	
De moribus, ritibus et erroribus eorum qui sancta loca inhabitant (fol. 55ʳ; for detailed analysis, see below)	The Life of Mohamed (see below)
Luctuosa oratio super desolatione Terre Sancte (fol. 88ᵛ)	
Part II: Pilgrimage to Sinai (Egypt) (fol. 98ᵛ)	
Annexes: List of islands from Venice to Rhodes (fol. 129ʳ)	
Latin – Arabic dictionary (fol. 130ʳ)	
Historias prefatiuncula (fol. 131ʳ)	
De regimine peregrinatium in transmare (fol. 143ʳ)	

My recent research into the possible source texts for *The Treatise* points instead towards a travelogue written by Hans Tucher, a merchant of Nuremberg, who, together with a handful of companions, visited Palestine, Sinai, and Egypt in 1479/80.[17] His account, entitled *Die Reise ins Gelobte Land*, went through six print editions between 1482–86 which were printed in different workshops in Augsburg, Strasbourg, and Nuremberg.[18] Being one of the first printed travelogues, Tucher's text probably met the demands and expectations of late-fifteenth-century readers, especially those who were planning a pilgrimage to Palestine in addition to basic information concerning the holy sites, the book also includes geographical information and practical advice, such as information about the *regimen sanitatis* and medical prescriptions for travellers adapted from the *Rezeptbuch* (prescription book) of Hartmann Schedel, a Nuremberg physician and the later author of a

---

16 This is an adaptation of the geographical guide to the Holy Land written by Burchardus de Monte Sion at the end of thirteenth century. This has been edited as *Burchardi de Monte Sion Descriptio Terrae Sanctae*, ed. by Laurent, pp. 1–94.

17 For a detailed analysis, see Svátek, 'Traktát o zemi svaté (1498)', pp. 94–120.

18 Herz, *Die 'Reise ins Gelobte Land' Hans Tuchers des Älteren (1479–1480)*; on the dissemination of Tucher's account in the later Middle Ages and in the Modern period, see Herz, *Studien zur Drucküberlieferung der 'Reise ins Gelobte Land'*.

famous encyclopaedic *Weltchronik*.[19] The success of Tucher's work is confirmed by the fact that it was used by the travellers Konrad Beck and Felix Fabri, who visited the Holy Land in 1483 and wrote their own accounts. Tucher's travelogue was also used at least once in the account of Sigmund Thungers, dating to the middle of the sixteenth century.[20] Despite these well-known recipients, the dissemination of *Die Reise ins Gelobte Land* was not that spectacular in comparison with Breydenbach's *Peregrinatio*, which was printed four years later and gained much more attention.

Although there is no evidence that Tucher's travelogue was read in Bohemia, the similarities between *Die Reise ins Gelobte Land* and *The Treatise* are striking, Mikuláš Bakalář took wording from the preface which described the achievements of its author, Hans Tucher (passages translated word for word are highlighted in bold in the German text):[21]

Treatise on the Holy Land (Prague, Knihovna Národního muzea, 25 E 8, fols 1ᵛ–2ʳ)	Hans Tucher, *Die Reise ins Gelobte Land* (ed. by Herz, pp. 339–40)
*Léta od porodu panenského tisícého CCCC. LXXXII. v pondělí **dne šestého měsiece máje**, my, kněz **Mikuláš**, kanovník řezenský, a **Jan**, měštěnín normberský, vyjeli sme z Normberka ve jméno božie tiem úmyslem prostě pro milého boha a spasenie našie duše a pro žádnú marnú chlúbu ani s které všetečnosti, abychom ohledali svatá miesta, a zvláště ty miesta a krajiny, v nichž pán Ježíš v svém svatém člověčenství obyt měl a divy činil a potom veliké a ukrutné muky trpěl a umřieti pro naše spasenie ráčil. A zvláště k **božiemu hrobu do Jeruzaléma** a dále do Jericho a k Jordánu až do Mrtvého moře tu jiezdu vzeli sme předse a splnili i dokonali s pomocí boží a zase se vrátili do Normberga.*	*Nach Cristi vnsers lieben Heren gepurt M cccc lxxix jar am dorstag,* **der do was der sechst tag deß monetz may***, pin jch* **Hanns Tucher, burger** *vnd die zeyt einer deß kleineren ratz* **der stat Nuremberg***, meines alter einvndfunfczig jare vnd funf wochen,* **doselbst außgezogen jn dem namen des almechtigen Gottes jn willen vnd meynung alleyn vmb Gotes ere vnd meiner sele selikeyt vnd keÿnes rumes, furwiczes noch ander leichtuertikeyt willen, die heiligen stete vnd besunder die ende, do** *Christus* **Jhesus** *vnser* **seligmacher jn seiner heiligen menschheit sein leben vnd wesen gehabt, gewandelt, gotliche wunderwerck erzaigt vnd, vmb vnsers hails willen, sein manigueltigs piners leiden, marter vnd tod geliden***, vnd sein erlich leiplich begrebnuß erwelt vnd gehabt hat,* **besunder sein Heiliges Grab zu Jherusalem***, vnd furbaß andere seiner lieben heiligen rastung zubesuchen.*

---

19 Hartmann Schedel, *Weltchronik 1493*.

20 This unedited work is preserved in the manuscript Munich, Bayerische Staatsbibliothek, MS Cgm 954, where the prologue may be found on fol. 19ʳ (see also Herz, *Die 'Reise ins Gelobte Land'*, p. xiv).

21 Breydenbach's travelogue is dedicated in the prologue to Bertold of Henneberg, Archbishop of Mainz, and does not contain any element relating to the prefaces which are presented here. See Bernhard von Breydenbach, *Peregrinatio in Terram sanctam*, fols 2ʳ–3ʳ.

> [In the year after the virgin birth, 1482, on a Monday, the sixth day of the month of May, we, a priest, Nicolaus, Canon of Regensburg, and Jan, Burgher of Nuremberg, departed from Nuremberg in the name of God with the intention, for the dear God and the salvation of our soul, but not for vain glory, nor out of some nosiness, of visiting holy places and especially those places and regions in which Lord Jesus in his holy humanity stayed and performed miracles and then suffered great and cruel pains and died for our salvation. And we went especially to the Holy Sepulchre in Jerusalem, and further, to Jericho and Jordan, and the Dead Sea and accomplished [our] journey and returned to Nuremberg.]

While the identification of the source text helps us to understand the creative process behind the adaptation, new interpretative problems also emerge. The prologue to the Czech adaptation introduces two pilgrims by name. We may identify a certain 'John, burgher of Nuremberg' (*Jan, měštěnín normberský*) as Hans Tucher himself, but the other man, a canon from Regensburg named Nicholas (*Mikuláš, kanovník řezenský*), does not appear in the German source at all. The hypothesis (set out by L. Koutníková) that these two men were invented by the translator does not seem persuasive.[22] Firstly, she only compared *The Treatise* with Breydenbach's bestseller and paid no attention to Tucher's text. Secondly, this would be a unique occurrence for such an invention to be made by the printer, as Mikuláš Bakalář did not invent any other authorial figures for any of his other travelogue editions (Amerigo Vespucci, John Mandeville).

Along with the additional persona of Nicholas, the prologue in the Czech version also includes a different date – Monday, 6 May 1482 (*Léta od porodu panenského T[isícého] CCCC. LXXXII. v pondělí dne šestého měsiece máje*). Conversely, the German original gives the date as 'Thursday, 6 May 1479' (*M cccc lxxix jar am dorstag, der do was der sechst tag deß monetz may*). Although the two versions are set in different years, both dates are chronologically accurate: 6 May did fall on a Thursday in 1479 and on a Monday three years later. In order to reconstruct the genesis of the Czech version we must, hypothetically, assume the historical existence of Nicholas of Regensburg, who set out for Jerusalem three years after Hans Tucher had, and then, on his return, he drew on Tucher's recently published, pre-existing source text when writing the account of his travel. If this speculative reconstruction is correct, then the Czech translator would have worked from Nicholas's version, rather than Tucher's original.

---

22 Koutníková, 'Český prvotisk', p. 195.

On the one hand, this hypothesis is supported by the way that the adaptor abridges the German original. The overall situation can be seen in the following scheme:[23]

Hans Tucher, *Die Reise ins Gelobte Land* Nuremberg, Stadtarchiv, E 29 (FA Tucher)/III, Nr. 11 in: Herz, *Die 'Reise ins Gelobte Land'*, pp. 327–638	*The Treatise on the Holy Land* Prague, Knihovna Národního muzea, 25 E 8 in: Svátek, 'Traktát o zemi svaté (1498)', pp. 91–143
Prologue (fol. 1^r)	Prologue (fols 1^r–2^r)
Part I: Pilgrimage to Jerusalem (fols 3^r–22^v)	
from Nuremberg to Venice (fol. 3^r)	
from Venice to Jaffa (fol. 7^v)	from Venice to Jaffa (fols 2^r–5^r)
stay in the Holy Land (fols 22^v–79^v)	stay in the Holy Land (fols 5^r–32^v)
from Jaffa to Jerusalem (fol. 22^v)	from Jaffa to Jerusalem (fol. 5^r)
stay in Jerusalem (fol. 27^r)	stay in Jerusalem (fol. 7^r)
comparison of the Church of the Holy Sepulchre with church of St Sebald in Nuremberg (fol. 33^r)	description of the Church of the Holy Sepulchre (fol. 10^v)
other holy places in and around Jerusalem (fol. 45^v)	other holy places in and around Jerusalem (fol. 18^r)
the ride to Bethlehem (fol. 57^v)	the ride to Bethlehem (fol. 25^r)
the ride to Jordan (fol. 70^r)	the ride to Jordan (fol. 28^r)
a treatise on theriac (fol. 72^v)	a treatise on theriac (fol. 29^v)
description of holy sites in Hebron, Galilea, on the coast and in Damascus (fol. 75^r)	description of holy sites in Hebron, Galilea, on the coast and in Damascus (fol. 30^v)
Chronicle of the Kingdom of Jerusalem (fols 80^r–86^v)	
regimen sanitatis and prescriptions of Hermann Schedel (fols 87^r–91^v)	
Nuremberg-Jerusalem itinerary by land (fols 92^r–93^r)	
instructions for the route to Saint Catherine's monastery (fols 93^v–98^r)	
Part II: Pilgrimage to Saint Catherine's monastery (fols 98^v–172^r)	
Return from the Holy Land (fol. 159^r)	

---

23 Neither *Die Reise* nor *The Treatise* contain internal titles. The structure of Tucher's travelogue is similar to that of the divisions in Breydenbach's compendium.

Hans Tucher, *Die Reise ins Gelobte Land* Nuremberg, Stadtarchiv, E 29 (FA Tucher)/III, Nr. 11 in: Herz, *Die 'Reise ins Gelobte Land'*, pp. 327–638	*The Treatise on the Holy Land* Prague, Knihovna Národního muzea, 25 E 8 in: Svátek, 'Traktát o zemi svaté (1498)', pp. 91–143
Appearance of the Holy Sepulchre (fol. 171^r) Keyserthum vnd xx cristenliche Kunigreich (itineraries in Europe and Near East) (fols 172^v–75^r) instructions for travel from Venice to Jerusalem (fols 175^v–83^r) contract with the shipowner (fol. 183^r–85^v)	

The Czech text focuses only on the parts of the pilgrimage to Palestine, and the visits to Jerusalem, Bethlehem, and the river Jordan, while neither Tucher's visit to Saint Catherine's Monastery on Mount Sinai, nor his stays in Cairo and Alexandria, are included. Each of the passages in which the merchant of Nuremberg describes his personal experience is also reduced; while Tucher, for example, relates his imprisonment in Jerusalem and the preparatory arrangements made by his group for their travel across Sinai, these testimonies are missing in the Czech adaptation.[24] Specialists on early printing in Bohemia have previously assumed that the abbreviations in the Czech version were due to economic limits at Mikuláš Bakalář's workshop in Pilsen.[25] While this hypothesis can be accepted as being plausible, in general, it does not, however, solve the question of the specific features of the Czech adaptation discussed above: the shift in chronology and the alleged co-traveller Nicholas, canon of Regensburg.

On the other hand, the pilgrim Nicholas of Regensburg cannot be confirmed in any other extant source.[26] The sole surviving account of the pilgrimage to Jerusalem made in 1482 (per the date given in *The Treatise*), the itinerary of friar Paul Walther von Güglingen, makes no mention of such a name, even though it contains a long list of the names of those people who were aboard the pilgrims' galley.[27] Nor does the itinerary of Güglingen's journey correspond in detail to

---

24 Cf. Herz, *Die 'Reise ins Gelobte Land'*, pp. 443–45 and *Traktát o zemi svaté*, fol. 28^r in Svátek, 'Traktát o zemi svaté (1498)', p. 136.

25 Voit, 'Mikuláš Bakalář jinak', pp. 82–83; *Mikuláš Bakalář Štetina*, ed. by Kohút, p. 36.

26 The only documented canon of this name living in Regensburg at this time was a certain Nicholas Sturm of Staffelstein (near Bamberg) who became a regular canon in Our Lady at Old Chapel (*Unsere Liebe Frau zur Alten Kapelle*) in 1492, see *Die Urkunden-Regesten des Kollegiatstiftes U. L. Frau zur Alten Kapelle in Regensburg*, I, ed. by Schmid, no. 1390 (17 March 1494), no. 1421 (7 March 1496), no. 1589 (29 May 1507) and Schmid, *Die Geschichte des Kollegiatstiftes U. L. Frau zur Alten Kapelle*, p. 123.

27 *Fratris Pauli Waltheri Guglingensis Itinerarium*, the list of participants appears on pp. 67–68.

the list of places which were allegedly visited by two pilgrims from Nuremberg and Regensburg as related in *The Treatise*. If the hypothetical Nicholas did make a pilgrimage to the Holy land in 1482, then, it was presumably as part of another group for which no other record survives. It is not possible, therefore, to reconstruct the precise manner that Mikuláš Bakalář reutilized Hans Tucher's German travelogue (and/or its hypothetical reworkings by the likewise hypothetical Nicholas). Nevertheless, we can certainly say that the *Treatise on the Holy Land* was adapted from Tucher's *Die Reise ins Gelobte Land* and not from the Breydenbach's *Peregrinatio in Terram Sanctam*. The travelogue of the Nuremberg merchant may well have been the textual basis for the description of another journey which took place three years later in 1482. However, the circumstances of this journey and the identity of the travellers mentioned in the Czech text remain unknown.

The Life of Mohamed

The second incunable discussed here survives in a single exemplar in Prague Strahov library (DR IV 37/3). It originally comprised thirty folios (three of which, fols 7–9, are now missing) *in octavo* format, and reveals many similarities with the previous book – beyond just having been edited in the same year. Unlike *The Treatise*, *The Life of Mohamed* does represent an adaptation from Breydenbach's *Peregrinatio*.[28] Specifically, it reproduces only one part of Breydenbach's compendium, entitled *De moribus, ritibus et erroribus eorum qui sanctam inhabitant terram*, which concerns the life of the Prophet, the principles of Islam, and the customs of various inhabitants of Jerusalem, who are divided into categories according to their creed.[29] As Frederike Timm has pointed out, this part assumes a central position in Breydenbach's compendium, dividing the first descriptive part about the pilgrimage to the Holy Land from the depiction of the pilgrimage sites in the second part which describes the way to Mount Sinai, to Saint Catherine's Monastery, and to other sanctuaries in Egypt.[30] The *De moribus, ritibus et erroribus* was inspired by several authoritative texts such as the *Speculum historiale* (part of *Speculum maius*) by Vincent of Beauvais or the *Dialogus contra Judeos* by Petrus Alphonsi. However, Breydenbach did not write the *De moribus, ritibus et erroribus* himself, but it was instead written by the Dominican theologian Martin Rath. Breydenbach, as the *auctor principalis* and commissioner of the whole editing project, authorized him to compile this particular chapter and undertake its rhetorical design.[31] The Czech adaptation, known as *The Life of*

---

28 This was stated for the first time by Sokol, 'Život Mohamedův z r. 1498 a jeho předloha'.

29 Bernhard von Breydenbach, *Peregrinatio in Terram sanctam*, fols 55ʳ–88ʳ.

30 Timm, *Der Palästina-Pilgerbericht des Bernhard von Breidenbach*, p. 79.

31 Detailed analysis may be found in Timm, *Der Palästina-Pilgerbericht des Bernhard von Breidenbach*, pp. 95–96.

Mohamed, therefore mirrors a long textual tradition of anti-Islamic polemics, although we can assume that Mikuláš Bakalář was not aware of it in detail.

The Life of Mohamed is divided into two parts. The first focuses on the life of the Prophet and on the principles of the Islamic religion. As can be seen from the following overview of titles introducing its internal divisions and chapters, it shows some structural differences from the original *Peregrinatio*:

Bernhard von Breydenbach: *Peregrinatio in Terram sanctam*	*The Life of Mohamed*
De ortu et origine Mahumeti	O narození Mahumetovém ('On Mohamed's Birth')
De detestabili vita et conversatione Mahumeti	O mrském životě Mahometovém ('On Mohamed's Perfidious Life')
De tempore et modo, quo M. sectam suam incepit	O času, v kterém Mahumet blud svój počel ('Of the Time When Mohamed's Heresy Began')
De misera et infelici morte Mahumeti	missing fols 7–9[32]
De articulis in Alkorano seu lege mahumetice contentis cum eorum compendiosa improbationes propter vulgares	O artikulech v zákoně Machometovém položených ('On the Articles of Mohamed's Law')
Sequitur de Sarracenis deque eorum moribus et erroribus	O Saraceniech a o mravech jejich ('On Saracens and their Manners')
1) de eius secte initio seu inchoatione	-
2) de falsis et ficticiis huius recte fundamentis	-
3) de variis erroribus et viciis multiplicibus in lege Mahumeti contentis	O rozličných bludech u zákoně Machometovém položených ('On Diverse Heresies in Mohamed's Law')
	Že Mahumet blúdí při tom, což jest přikázal činiti ('That Mohamed Errs in his Commandments')
	Že Machomet blúdí při tom, čeho se naděje ('That Mohamed Errs in What He Hopes')
4) cur ad eam sectam [...] tanta conflixerit hominum multitudo	-
5) de diuturnitate durationis illius secte	-

---

[32] A note remarking on this lacuna on the empty fol. 7ʳ, which was supplied to replace the missing part, was added while the book was being rebound, probably at the beginning of the twentieth century. See online: <www.manuscriptorium.com> [accessed 3 November 2022] where the following folios are wrongly numbered (fol. 8 in the database corresponds to fol. 11 marked in pencil in the volume itself).

The Czech translator occasionally expanded the text – as can be seen in the third part of the section detailing the errors and customs of Muslims, which is itself further divided into three subsections – and he deliberately omitted several chapters (although the translation of the chapter *De misera et infelici morte* may originally have been included on the now-missing folios 7–9). Following the section on errors and customs, Breydenbach's text then presents a series of commentaries on the Islamic religion, adapted from the *Dialogus* by Petrus Alphonsi, which the Czech adaptor omitted completely.

The other part of *The Life* concerns the 'nations' of Jerusalem, i.e., the various religious communities of Christians and Jews. This kind of division appears in almost all descriptions of the Holy Land. It is usually placed in the part describing the Church of the Holy Sepulchre whose interiors were (and still are) shared by these communities.[33] Breydenbach's treatise presents this topic separately, and the intentions underlying his description appear to be uniquely encyclopaedic. The individual religious communities are defined ethnically and culturally, with the book providing the reader with engravings which depict each of them in their typical attire, as well as with samples of their scripts and reproductions of alphabets. These images are missing in the Czech version, and the corresponding chapter, entitled 'A Treatise on Various Peoples' (*Traktát o rozličných národech*),[34] is not illustrated in this manner. Mikuláš Bakalář did not have such printing options in his rather modest workshop, least of all a set of sophisticated printing blocks.[35] A close examination of the chapter headings reveals that the Latin contents of the original are more faithfully reproduced than in the previous section, even if they are arranged in a different order. This suggests some appreciation by the Czech translator of the encyclopaedic qualities in Breydenbach's original text:

---

33 Hans Tucher's aforementioned travelogue, and its Old Czech adaptation, are not exceptional; the *Treatise on the Holy Land* typically circulated in a different and much shorter version, comprising about two folios. For comparison, see Herz, *Die 'Reise ins Gelobte Land'*, pp. 405–10 and Svátek, 'Traktát o zemi svaté', pp. 129–30.

34 Although the reader can learn some general basic facts about these ethnic groups, the word 'nation' (*národ*) in this context may be better taken as denoting their religious aspects, as the descriptions essentially concern the religious practices of these communities.

35 The only image in the *Life of Mohamed* is a woodcut on the title page (Prague, Knihovna Premonstrátské kanonie na Strahově, DR IV 37/3, fol. 1ʳ) depicting Mohamed teaching his disciples who are sitting around at school desks. Although its origin is unclear, it certainly comes from the German-speaking area. See on the printing workshops in Bohemia in the given time Voit, 'Limity knihtisku v Čechách a na Moravě 15. a 16. století', p. 120.

Latin original [without title]	Old Czech adaptation *Traktát o rozličných národech* ('The Treatise on Various Nations')
De iudeis, quorum etiam plerique hisce temporibus Hierosolimis manent	
De Grecis, quorum etiam plures sunt in Hierusalem	untitled
De Surianis, qui Hierosolimis et locis illis manentes etiam se asserunt esse christianos	*Tuto čti o Surianech* ('On Syrians')
De Jacobitis et eorum erroribus	
De Nestorianis et eorum erroribus	*O Nestorianiech* ('On Nestorians')
De Armenis et eorum erroribus	*O Armeniech* ('On Armenians')
De Georgianis et eorum moribus et ritibus	*O Georgianiech* ('On Georgians')
De Abasinis sive Indianis et eorum cerimoniis	*O Indianiech* ('On "Indians"')
	O Jakobitiech ('On Jacobites')
De Maronitis et eorum reditu abolim ad ecclesiam rhomanam	*O Maronitiech* ('On Maronites')
Sequitur disputatio quedam necessaria ad predicta	
De causis varietatis errorum et sectarum multiplicium	
De Latinis qui sunt in Hierusalem	*O Latiniech* ('On Latins')
	O Židech ('On Jews')

Original Additions to the Czech Version

The Czech *Life of Mohamed* is characterized by a shortening of its source-text, similar to the approach previously witnessed in *The Treatise*. While the corresponding part from Breydenbach's original compendium fills more than thirty pages of *in folio* format, with forty-four lines per page, its Czech adaptation is approximately a quarter of this length. Although, in general, the translator abbreviates the source material, on occasion he also rather deftly compiles various parts of the original into new pieces, while inserting several of his own additions. Thus, the chapter entitled 'That Mohamed Errs in his Commandments' (*Že Machomet blúdí při tom, čeho se naděje*) features a very offensive and obscene story about Mohamed and a donkey.[36] This passage appears at the end of the chapter *De articulis in Alkorano* in Breydenbach's original, and reproduces the responses of Petrus Alphonsi, which as a whole is omitted in the Czech

---

36 Prague, Knihovna Premonstrátské kanonie na Strahově, DR IV 33/3, fols 15ᵛ–16ʳ.

adaptation; however, the translator makes sure to pick up this brief and racy story, using it to underline the perfidious character of the Prophet's religion.[37]

The passage on the Latins which appears in the second part, *The Treatise on Various Nations*, also received a similar treatment. Here, the Czech translator inserted into a description of Mount Zion an account of a donation of 1000 florins made to Jerusalem by the Duke of Burgundy, which features at an earlier point in Breydenbach's text.[38] The translator, therefore, clearly had access to a complete copy of Breydenbach's treatise, as he was able to select various passages from throughout according to what he considered fitting for inclusion in his Czech adaptation.

The Czech adaptation's deliberate omission of certain details in the *Peregrinatio*'s description of the different *nationes* in Jerusalem is particularly striking. While it is true that the translator also skipped several statements about the Greeks (regarding the theological reasons for their secession from the Church) and the Jews (including a subchapter on usury, *De excrescentia iudaice usure*), the only other parts which he systematically and rigorously left out were those concerning the sacrament of communion under both kinds as practiced by the individual religious communities in Jerusalem (passages missing from the translation are marked bold):[39]

---

[37] Bernhard von Breydenbach, *Peregrinatio in Terram sanctam*, fol. 62ᵛ: 'Cum etiam de ipso vestro seductore legatur cum quodam tempore iter faceret mulierem que sibi casu obviam venit in via opprimere voluit qui quem facinus horrens restitit, asinam suam porcus ille impurissimus sodomitaque fedissimus est aggressus, dicens pro sui excusatione ad socios que mulier illa coitum sibi negando amplius peccavisset quod si centum homines occidisset pro eo que ipse eam cum propheta dei impregnasset'.

[38] Prague, Knihovna Premonstrátské kanonie na Strahově, DR IV 33/3, fol. 28ᵛ; Bernhard von Breydenbach, *Peregrinatio in Terram sanctam*, fol. 26ᵛ.

[39] This aspect is also referred to by Sokol, 'Život Mohamedův z r. 1498 a jeho předloha', pp. 39–42.

Peregrinatio in Terram Sanctam	Život Mohamedův
(De Grecis): *Sabbatum multum colunt more pene iudeorum numquam in eo ieiunantes (sabbato sancto pasche solo excepto) sed et carnes in eo comedunt splendide semper epulantes. Sacramentum preterea confirmationis paruulis suis mox post baptismum conferunt per simplices sacerdotes contra ecclesie vetitum.*	*Sobotu velmi ctie vedlé obyčeje židovského. Nikdy se vín nepostiece, ale maso jedie kromě v sobotu před velikú nocí. Dietky jejich hnedky po křstu kněžie biřmují proti přikázání církve svaté.* (They observe the sabbath according to Jewish custom. They do not refrain from wine drinking, but they eat meat, except on the Saturday before Easter. Their children are confirmed by the priests immediately after baptism, against the orders of Holy Church.)
Nam et sacramentum eukaristie eisdem [parvulis] tribuunt sub utraque specie non solum adultis. Amplius in fermento conficiunt contra ecclesie prohibitionem et Christi institutionem. (fol. 77^v)	*V kvasném hlebie posvěcují proti přikázání církvie svaté a pána našieho Ježíše Krista ustavení.* (fols 18^v–19^r) (They consecrate leavened bread, against the orders of Holy Church and the commandments of our Lord Jesus Christ)
(De Jacobitis): *Isti etiam heretici jacobite uno solummo se digno signant in modum crucis quos Greci et Suriani predentes asserunt ideo facere, que tantum unam in Christo confitentur naturam.* **Ipsi etiam parvulos suos adhuc ad ubera pendentes sub utraque specie communicant, in hoc Grecis et Surianis conformes.** *Ipsi diuersis utuntur ydiomatibus sicut in diuersas prouincias in quibus habitant.* (fol. 80^r)	*Tito také jakobité žehnají se křížem svatým jedním prstem.* (These Jacobites cross themselves with one finger.) *Mají také svú zvláštní literu a řeč.* (fol. 27^r) (They also have special letters and language.)
(De Nestorianis): *Preterea hii nestoriani in fermentato pane conficiunt instar Grecorum atque* **sub utraque specie communicant eucharistie sacramentum parvulis et adultis** *et alia multa abusiua ac sancte romane ecclesie contraria et erronea obseruant, de quibus singillatim dicere longum esset nimis. Caldaica utuntur littera et lingua in officiis diuinis [...]* (fol. 80^v)	*Tito také nestoriáni posvěcují v kvasném hlebě obyčejem řeckým.* (These Nestorians consecrate leavened bread, according to Greek custom.) *Při přisluhování kaldejského užívají jazyka.* (fol. 21^v) (When celebrating mass, they use the Chaldean language).
(De Abasinis): *Nam in fermentato conficiunt, instar Grecorum* **sub utraque specie sacramentum conferunt parvulis et adultis** *et illos per simplices sacerdotes faciunt confirmari adhuc infantes.* (fol. 82^v)	*Také posvěcují v kvasném hlebie obyčejem řeckým.* [They consecrate leavened bread] *Dietky jejich sprostí kněžie biřmují.* (fol. 25^{r-v}) (Ordinary priests confirm their children)

The practice of Communion under both kinds, common to all the religious communities of eastern Christians in the Holy Land, was frequently remarked on by travellers from Latin Europe, including Bernhard von Breydenbach. However, Mikuláš Bakalář deliberately skipped over these passages. This liturgical practice was the main distinguishing feature of the Utraquist Church in Bohemia, and as such it was the key issue addressed in the polemics between Utraquists and Catholics. We may almost certainly assume that Mikuláš Bakalář deliberately avoided mentioning Communion under both kinds in his translation: he lived and worked in Pilsen, a stronghold of the Catholic party, and his main customers were, likewise, Catholic priests and laics. It is possible, therefore, that the reason Mikuláš Bakalář introduced this 'censorship' was simply that he wanted to avoid any controversial debates, and any suspicion of him having an affinity with the 'Hussite heretics', as the Utraquist church was usually called by the Catholics. Conversely, it may have been that he resisted the temptation to use this liturgical particularity to declare his own Catholic position – very probably in consideration of the potential Utraquist customers whose goodwill might well be forfeit in this way. While scholars consider Breydenbach's text to be, among other things, a tool of (anti-Islamic) propaganda, as mentioned above, the Czech adaptation refocuses the intentions of the text onto a different level. Where the Dean of Mainz wanted to convey detailed information about oriental and exotic communities, the printer of Pilsen is more careful not to offend the 'true' (Catholic) faith. Bakalář's text also mirrors the fierce polemical discourse, which concentrated on the liturgical issues and which dominated public debate in Bohemia at the time. Within it, for example, 'Indians' (Abyssinians) are labelled as 'heretics' (*kacieři*, fol. 24ᵛ) and 'despicable people' (*biedni lidé*, fol. 25ʳ), whereas in the Latin original it simply claims that these people 'can be susceptible to certain errors in faith' (*a certis pravis erroribus non sunt alieni neque immunes*).

The Readers

Bakalář's activities, specifically his adaptation of Tucher's travelogue, for which he used a version that had been printed in Nuremberg in 1483, attest to the renewal of the trade links between Pilsen and Nuremberg which had been interrupted during the religious wars between 1419 and 1434.[40] The two incunables provide an interesting case study in terms of translation strategies. If we accept the hypothesis that the translator was the printer Mikuláš Bakalář himself, then we can see an effort being made to offer engaging, entertaining books of immediate interest to a public which originated from the late medieval Bohemian Catholic milieu. Bakalář, with the intent of increasing sales, applied his translation techniques to that purpose. On the one hand, he condensed voluminous compendia into a booklet which could be produced within the scope of his modest

---

40 Voit, 'Role Norimberku při utváření české a moravské knižní kultury', pp. 389–457.

workshop, and which would be affordable for his readers. On the other hand, by omitting the 'communion *sub utraque*' issue, he increased how attractive his product would be to a wider audience.

This initiative on the part of the Catholic printer becomes more evident when compared with another adaptation of Breydenbach's text which was produced some thirty years later, in which only the section on the 'various peoples' of Jerusalem is translated.[41] Entitled *Nine Divisions of Christians Living in the Holy Land from the Treatise of Peter* [!] *of Brayndenbuch* (*Devět rozdíluov křesťanuov v zemi zaslíbené z traktátu Petr z Brayndenbuchu*) the text was drafted by Adam Bakalář, a notary in Litomyšl (eastern Bohemia), and first printed in 1539 then, again, in 1542 by Alexander Oujezdecký of Pilsen.[42] Both editions contain an appendix, a travel account describing the journey of Martin Kabátník, a member of the Unity of Brethren, to Jerusalem and Egypt in 1491–92.[43] The description of the religious communities in Jerusalem appears here, then, in a new context: Adam Bakalář was a member of the local Brethren community in Litomyšl, and the titles printed by Alexander Oujezdecký were often produced in this milieu.[44] These new editions make even more radical abridgements of Breydenbach's original text than the translation of Mikuláš Bakalář had. *Nine Divisions of Christians* covers only three folios and omits the section about Jews. In contrast to *The Life of Mohamed*, the *Nine Divisions of Christians* respects the order of the communities as they are set out in the *Peregrinatio in Terram sanctam*. Most importantly, in this new adaptation Adam Bakalář leaves the passages on Communion under both kinds as they are in the original text.[45]

We can therefore consider *The Life of Mohamed* and the *Nine Divisions of Christians* to be two independent translations, undertaken in order to adapt a part of a popular compendium to the needs of different confessional groups in late medieval Bohemia. In addition to the economic reasons, it is evident that

---

41 Sokol, 'Život Mohamedův z r. 1498 a jeho předloha', pp. 40–42.

42 Adam Bakalář is also known as Adam Šturm of Hranice. His nickname arises from his bachelor degree, gained from the Prague University in 1519.

43 Martin Kabátník, *Cesta z Čech do Jerusalema a Kaira r. 1491–92*, ed. by Prášek and the latest edition, Martin Kabátník, *Cesta z Čech do Jeruzaléma a Egypta r. 1491–1492*, ed. by Vajdlová. The print of Kabátník including the *Nine Divisions of Christians* treatise survives today in two exemplars: Dresden, Sächsische Landesbibliothek – Staats- und Universitätsbibliothek, 4 A 1029 (edition from 1539), and Stockholm, Kunglia biblioteket, Teol. Reform. Luther 173 Dd. The Dresden exemplar has been fully digitized at <https://digital.slub-dresden.de/werkansicht/dlf/55789/1/> [accessed 3 November 2022].

44 The list of Alexander's prints is published in Voit, *Český knihtisk mezi gotikou a renesancí*, II, pp. 457–76.

45 This can be illustrated with the quotation of the part about Greeks (cf. the table above): '[…] Sobotu světí a maso jedí ten den. Dětí kněží prostí potvrzují. **Svátost těla a krve páně velikým i malým rozdávají podobojí způsobau**, kvašený chléb posvěcují, při posvěcení vody k vínu nepřilívají.', Dresden, Sächsische Landesbibliothek – Staats- und Universitätsbibliothek, 4 A 1029, fol. 73r (marked by JS).

religious motives influenced the textual decisions made by Mikuláš Bakalář, or whoever actually prepared the translation if not him, in 1498. The scant survival of copies in both cases (one of *The Life of Mohamed* and one of each edition of the *Nine Divisions of Christians*) precludes any hypothesis on the impact of these works on their readers. The same can also be said of the *Treatise on the Holy Land*, which originated in the same publishing context and survives in only two copies. These publications provide evidence, primarily, for how carefully balances were made in the confessionally divided late medieval Bohemian society between the varying interests and sensitivities there, and how cautiously the actual religious-political discourses and vocabularies were handled, in attempts to avoid any escalations which might destroy the hard won, peaceful coexistence. Indeed, this was a tolerance of a sheer necessity. Further research into the textual materials from fifteenth- and sixteenth-century Bohemia may teach us how well the society then learned to negotiate around seemingly non-negotiable issues. Increasing scholarly consciousness with regard to the emergence and transformations of this particular feature of social communication is not without gain – it may represent an important contribution to the debate on the processes of confessionalization in the sixteenth and seventeenth centuries, and on the transformation of religious and social identities in Early modern Europe as a whole.[46]

Bibliography

Manuscript and Old Print Sources

Darmstadt, Universitäts- und Landesbibliothek, Inc. IV/98
Dresden, Sächsische Landesbibliothek – Staats- und Universitätsbibliothek, 4 A 1029
Munich, Bayerische Staatsbibliothek, MS Cgm 954
Prague, Knihovna Národního muzea, 25 E 8
Prague, Knihovna Premonstrátské kanonie na Strahově, DR IV 37/3
——, DR IV 37/5
Stockholm, Kungliga biblioteket, Teol. Reform. Luther 173 Dd

Primary Sources

Bernhard von Breydenbach, *Peregrinatio in Terram sanctam* (Mainz: Erhard Reuwich, 1486)
Burchardi de Monte Sion Descriptio Terrae Sanctae, ed. by J. C. M. Laurent, in *Peregrinationes medii aevi quatuor* (Leipzig: Hinrichs Bibliopola, 1864), pp. 1–94
Fratris Pauli Waltheri Guglingensis Itinerarium ad Terram sanctam et ad Sanctam Catharinam, ed. by Matthias Sollweck (Tübingen: Litterarischer Verein, 1892)

---

[46] The research leading to these results received funding from the European Research Council under the European Community's Seventh Framework Programme (FP/2007) / ERC Grant Agreement No. 263672.

Martin Kabátník, *Cesta z Čech do Jerusalema a Kaira r. 1491–92*, ed. by Justin V. Prášek (Prague: Otto, 1894)

———, *Cesta z Čech do Jeruzalém a Egypta r. 1491–1492*, ed. by Miloslava Vajdlová (Prague: Arbor vitae, 2019)

Hartmann Schedel, *Weltchronik 1493. Kolorierte und kommentierte Gesamtausgabe*, ed. by Stephan Füssel (Köln: Taschen, 2001)

Die Urkunden-Regesten des Kollegiatstiftes U. L. Frau zur Alten Kapelle in Regensburg, ed. by Joseph Schmid, 2 vols (Regensburg: Habbel, 1911–12)

Secondary Works

Europäische Reiseberichte des späten Mittelalters, ed. by Werner Paravicini and Christian Halm, 3 vols, Kieler Werkstücke: Reihe D, 5 (Frankfurt am Main: Lang, 1994–2001), I: *Deutsche Reiseberichte*, 2nd rev. edn (2001)

Herz, Randall, *Die 'Reise ins Gelobte Land' Hans Tuchers des Älteren (1479–1480): Untersuchungen zur Überlieferung und kritische Edition eines spätmittelalterlichen Reiseberichts*, Wissensliteratur im Mittelalter, 38 (Wiesbaden: Reichert, 2002)

———, *Studien zur Drucküberlieferung der 'Reise ins Gelobte Land' Hans Tuchers des Älteren*, Quellen und Forschungen zur Geschichte und Kultur der Stadt Nürnberg, 34 (Nuremberg: Stadtarchiv, 2005)

Just, Jiří, 'Printed Books in the Bohemian Reformation', in *From Hus to Luther: Visual Culture in the Bohemian Reformation*, ed. by Kateřina Horníčková and Michal Šroněk, Medieval Church Studies, 33 (Turnhout: Brepols, 2016), pp. 219–30

Koutníková, Lenka, 'Český prvotisk: "Traktát o zemi svaté"', *Časopis čs. knihovníků*, 3 (1924), pp. 191–96

Meyers, Jean, 'La Peregrinatio in terram sanctam de Bernhard von Breidenbach (1486) comme instrument de propagande: À propos d'un ouvrage récent', *Le Moyen Âge: Revue d'histoire et de philologie*, 115 (2009), pp. 365–74

Mikuláš Bakalár Štetina: štúdie a materiály o živote a diele slovenského prvotlačiara v Plzni, ed. by Leo Kohút (Bratislava: SAV, 1966)

Rychterová, Pavlína, 'Preaching, the Vernacular, and the Laity', in *A Companion to the Hussites*, ed. by Michael van Dussen and Pavel Soukup, Brill's Companions to the Christian Tradition, 90 (Leiden and Boston: Brill, 2020), pp. 297–330

Schmid, Joseph, *Die Geschichte des Kollegiatstiftes U. L. Frau zur Alten Kapelle in Regensburg* (Regensburg: Manz, 1922)

Sokol, Vojtěch, 'Život Mohamedův z r. 1498 a jeho předloha', *Listy filologické*, 50 (1923), pp. 35–42

Svátek, Jaroslav, 'Traktát o zemi svaté (1498): staročeská adaptace cestopisu norimberského měšťana Hanse Tuchera', *Listy filologické*, 140/1–2 (2017), pp. 91–141

Šimáková, Jitka and Jaroslav Vrchotka, *Katalog prvotisků Knihovny Národního muzea v Praze a zámeckých a hradních knihoven v České republice* (Prague: Národní muzeum, 2001)

Šmahel, František, 'Svoboda slova, svatá válka a tolerance z nutnosti v husitském období', *Český časopis historický*, 92 (1994), pp. 644–79

Timm, Frederike, *Der Palästina-Pilgerbericht des Bernhard von Breidenbach und die Holzschnitte Erhard Reuwichs: Die Peregrinatio in terram sanctam (1486) als Propagandainstrument im Mantel der gelehrten Pilgerschrift* (Stuttgart: Hauswedell, 2006)

Urbánková, Emma, *Soupis prvotisků českého původu*, Edice Sektoru Služeb a Speciálních Oddělení (Prague: Státní knihovna ČSR, 1986)

Van Engen, John, 'Multiple Options: The World of the Fifteenth-Century Church', *Church History*, 77 (2008), pp. 257–284

Voit, Petr, 'Limity knihtisku v Čechách a na Moravě 15. a 16. století', *Bibliotheca Strahoviensis*, 8–9 (2007), pp. 113–40

——, 'Role Norimberku při utváření české a moravské knižní kultury první poloviny 16. století', *Documenta Pragensia*, 29 (2010), pp. 389–457

——, 'Mikuláš Bakalář jinak', in *Kniha 2012: Zborník o problémoch a dejinách knižnej kultúry*, ed. by Miroslava Domová (Martin: Slovenská národná knižnica, 2012), pp. 68–106

——, *Český knihtisk mezi gotikou a renesancí*, 2 vols (Prague: Academia, 2013–), II: *Tiskaři pro víru i tiskaři pro obrození národa 1498–1547* (2017)

Websites

Darmstadt, Universitäts- und Landesbibliothek, online: <http://tudigit.ulb.tu-darmstadt.de> [accessed 3 November 2022]

Dresden, Die Sächsische Landesbibliothek – Staats- und Universitätsbibliothek, Digitale Sammlungen, online: <http://digital.slub-dresden.de> [accessed 3 November 2022]

Gesamtkatalog der Wiegendrucke, online: <www.gesamtkatalogderwiegendrucke.de> [accessed 3 November 2022]

Manuscriptorium, online: <www.manuscriptorium.com> [accessed 3 November 2022]

Educating Laymen and Nuns in the Late Middle Ages in German-Speaking and Dutch Environments

Katrin Janz-Wenig

State and University Library Hamburg,
Carl of Ossietzky

Introduction

This essay concerns textual material from the fourteenth and fifteenth century in Germany, Switzerland, and the Low Countries. The goal is to show how Latin sermons were translated, re-interpreted, adapted, and transformed in different vernacular discourses. I will focus on one of the sermons used for the first Sunday after Pentecost on I John 4. 16 *Deus caritas est*, from a widely diffused sermon collection known as the *Sermones Socci*.[1] Five different medieval German versions of the sermon have been preserved. These vernacular translations, the oldest in Middle High German, the most recent in Middle Dutch, were made and compiled for different audiences and readers.[2] Indeed, the text was received in the Franciscan environment, in Benedictine and Dominican nunneries, and it may be found in books for lay and private readers, mostly women.

The *Decem gradus amoris*

The *Sermones Socci* were probably compiled around 1300 by Conrad of Brundelsheim (d. 1321), abbot of the Cistercian monastery of Heilsbronn (Franconia).[3]

---

1 For the collection *Sermones Socci*, cf. Janz-Wenig, *Decem gradus amoris deutsch*, pp. 61–90.

2 The article is based on a more comprehensive study, which also provides the corpus of the central texts in critical editions, cf. Janz-Wenig, *Decem gradus amoris deutsch*, with further literature.

3 For the collection see Worstbrock, 'Konrad von Brundelsheim', cols 151–52; Janz-Wenig, 'Konrad von Brundelsheim'. Conrad of Brundelsheim is considered to be the author or editor of the collection only on the basis of various indications; he cannot be proven with certainty to be the author.

The collection was widely distributed,[4] valued, and immensely influential,[5] especially in the German-speaking areas, along with the *Sermones dormi secure* by Johannes of Werden,[6] the sermons of Peregrinus of Opole,[7] and those of the so-called *Discipulus*.[8] The *Sermones Socci* consists of two volumes of sermons for every Sunday of the year and a volume of sermons for the feast days of the saints. They offer a number of texts for every Sunday and the saints' days.[9] Characteristic of the transmission is the extraordinary homogeneity and consistency of individual sermons which were copied in various textual contexts. They were intended for monastic audiences and served, just like theological treatises or patristic texts, the reading and study purposes of the friars. They are shaped above all by Cistercian thought and reflect the mysticism of Bernard of Clairvaux. Entirely missing are *exempla*. The prologue presents a topos common to sermon collections, stating that the sermons do not contain any new theological ideas and thoughts, but bring together theological knowledge in a large compilation. In terms of form, the sermons are scholastic throughout, with multi-unit *partitiones* and *distinctiones*. Every sermon in the temporal cycle is preceded by a biblical pericope; in the case of the saints' sermons, the pericope is chosen freely. The language is based on the rhetorical style of Bernard of Clairvaux and corresponds to *sermo humilis*. In addition to Bernard and the Holy Scripture,

---

4 So far more than 300 witnesses have come to light. More than 100 manuscripts contain a complete volume of the sermon cycle. Only rarely is a complete collection in all three volumes transmitted as a coherent unit. Two-thirds of the codices transmit single sermons in other sermonaries or ascetic-theological miscellany manuscripts. Moreover, the sermons are also shortened into excerpts, cf. Janz-Wenig, *Decem gradus amoris deutsch*, pp. 71–82.

5 That the *Sermones Socci* were highly esteemed in the late Middle Ages can be seen in a whole series of wills and legacies of the time. Also, high prices reflect an interest in the collection. In addition, some of the codices still preserved today reflect the value attributed to the collection, as can be seen by the selection of parchment as writing material or by features such as high-quality bindings. This is extraordinary for sermon manuscripts and manuscripts in regular use. The *Sermones Socci* were present in almost every monastery, regardless of religious order; and in parish and collegiate churches as well as in domestic private libraries.

6 Johannes of Werden (d. 1437), *Sermones dominicales dormi secure de tempore et de sanctis*; probably the most widely disseminated sermon collection of the late Middle Ages. The collection was printed in a total of twenty-five editions, seventeen of which appeared before the year 1500; for more details see Worstbrock, 'Johannes von Werden (de Verdena)'.

7 Peregrinus de Opole OP (d. after 1333), *Peregrinus de tempore et de sanctis*; cf. Schneyer, *Repertorium der lateinischen Sermones*, IV, pp. 548–74; see furthermore among others Worstbrock, 'Peregrinus von Oppeln (from Ratibor) OP'.

8 Johannes Herolt OP (d. 1468), also called *Discipulus*, prior and lector in the Nuremberg Dominican Convent. His sermons were printed forty-six times in total before the year 1500; for more details see Worstbrock, 'Herolt, Johannes (Discipulus)'. On the phenomenon of preaching as a mass medium of the Middle Ages cf. Steer, 'Bettelordens-Predigt als "Massenmedium"'.

9 Johannes Baptist Schneyer lists a total of 379 individual sermons for the *Sermones Socci*, cf. Schneyer, *Repertorium der lateinischen Sermones*, I, pp. 716–47.

Augustine and Gregory the Great are quoted, as well as ancient authors such as Ovid and Cicero. Albertus Magnus, Bonaventure, and ideas from early and high scholasticism also found their way into the compilation.[10]

Another source was found during the research for the study underlying this publication: The model for the sermon *Deus caritas est* is a self-contained section, *De decem gradibus amoris* from the treatise *De dilectione Dei et proximi* ascribed to Helwicus Theutonicus (d. 1263), prior of the Dominican convent at Strasbourg.[11] Until now twenty-two manuscripts have been identified transmitting the text, which was written shortly after the middle of the thirteenth century.[12]

The sermon *Deus caritas est*, is divided into three parts.[13] First, the question of the love of God is posed generally. The second section asks how this love can be nourished by man, and finally, a highly detailed third section describes how the believing soul can ascend to God in ten steps.[14] These are presented from different thematic points of view in varying levels of detail and are subdivided according to the scholastic model of the text. The indications of the steps are precisely adopted from the Latin source. In the sermon not only are passages from the treatise by Helwicus Theutonicus reproduced word-for-word, but also passages from the works and sermons of Bernard of Clairvaux, Gregory the Great, and Saint Augustine. The occasional very long citations originate not in popular compilations such as florilegia or encyclopedias but are, it seems, taken directly from the works of the authors mentioned.[15]

---

10 Detailed and comprehensive research into the sources of the *Sermones Socci* is still pending. In the hitherto rather modest research into the *Sermones Socci*, the focus has been on the unusual name of the collection. It can be assumed that this name is similar to a modern brand name and thus a sign of the popularity of the collection. See some pure speculations about the naming in Worstbrock, 'Konrad von Brundelsheim', pp. 149–51; Janz-Wenig, *Decem gradus amoris deutsch*, pp. 70–71.

11 For a long time this text was attributed to Thomas Aquinas. The attribution to a Dominican named Helwicus is found in some manuscripts and medieval library catalogues. For reasons of content Martin Grabmann supposes Helwicus Theutonicus as author, cf. Grabmann, 'Helwicus Theutonicus O.Pr. (Helwic von Germar?)'.

12 Further information on the author, and on the text and its transmission cf. Janz-Wenig, *Decem gradus amoris deutsch*, pp. 15–59; edition, ibid., pp. 169–204, cf. Janz-Wenig, 'Helwicus Theutonicus'.

13 Janz-Wenig, *Decem gradus amoris deutsch*, p. 206, ll. 3–6: 'Ideo proposito themate exigente sermonem de caritate, prout Dominus dederit, exordiamur. Sunt ergo hic tria per ordinem dicenda: Primo, quid per caritatis nomen dicatur. Secundo, in anima religiosi hominis quomodo nutriatur. Tercio, quibus gradibus in ea ascendatur'.

14 Ibid, p. 209, ll. 42–47: 'Primus ergo est, in quo caritas facit languere utiliter. Secundus, in quo querere incessanter. Tercius, in quo operari indesinenter. Quartus, in quo sustinere infatigabiliter. Quintus, in quo appetere inpatienter. Sextus, in quo currere uelociter. Septimus, in quo audere uehementer. Octauus, in quo stringere inamissibiliter. Nonus, in quo ardere suauiter. Decimus, in quo assimilari totaliter'.

15 Cf. Janz-Wenig, *Decem gradus amoris deutsch*, p. 84, p. 166.

The *Sermones Socci* were used as a preaching aid and as a homiletic manual. Indices are evidence of this, consistently attached to the collection as they are, and offering a very precise indexing of the content of the sermons. The user thus had fast and easy access to the theological topics dealt with in the various texts. This also seems to explain the extraordinary popularity of the collection and its widespread use. This widely disseminated sermon collection as well as individual sermons from it served as model sermons and as source for sermons transmitted in the vernacular.

The Vernacular Transmission

All in all, five independent vernacular versions of the sermon *Deus caritas est* have been identified, which date from the fourteenth and fifteenth centuries. All have the same Latin source: the *Predigt von der Minne zu Gott* (*Sermon on the Love of God*), a double sermon from the corpus of the so-called *Engelberger Predigten*, the *Predigt von den zehn Graden der Liebe* (*Sermon on the Ten steps of Love*), the *X trapkijns vander mynnen* (*Ten Steps of Love*), and the *Staffel göttlicher Lieb* (*Stages of Divine Love*), which are also disseminated as part of a proverb collection on divine love.[16]

The first four versions are complete, self-contained, and thoughtfully conceived texts, which take over the structural outline of ascending steps – sometimes precisely and sometimes with minor variations – from the Latin original. The short text *Staffel göttlicher Lieb* only refers to the first two steps of the Latin source. All of the vernacular texts belong to the most common types of spiritual literature of the late Middle Ages. Likewise, the method and manner of adapting and revising the Latin source corresponds to the frequently observed translation conventions of the time. The texts in question offer very illustrative examples of the characteristic translator strategies of the fourteenth and fifteenth centuries: they show word-for-word translations, paraphrases, compilations up to almost completely new texts by merely adopting the structure, and some thoughts of the source text. The different reworkings and elaborations allow us to draw conclusions about the respective context of how they were adopted, the ways they were used, as well as about the spiritual discourse of the target audience.

The *Predigt von der Minne zu Gott*

The shortest of the vernacular sermons is the *Predigt von der Minne zu Gott*.[17] It does not begin with a comprehensive pericope, but paraphrases the biblical

---

16 Cf. Stöllinger-Löser, 'Zehn Staffeln der Gottesliebe'; Janz-Wenig, 'Zehn Staffeln der Gottesliebe'; in more detail and with editions of the individual texts cf. Janz-Wenig, *Decem gradus amoris deutsch*, pp. 91–161, pp. 233–314.

17 Transmission: Gießen, Universitätsbibliothek, MS 879, fols 11ʳ–16ᵛ; München, Bayerische Staatsbibliothek, Cgm 132, fols 24ᵛ–30ᵛ; <http://www.handschriftencensus.de/

Educating Laymen and Nuns in the Late Middle Ages 151

verse from the Epistles (I John 4. 16) *Deus caritas est* as a theme, followed by a short *introductio thematis*. The aim of the sermon is to provide instructions on how to reach God taking the nine steps through the true love of God. A *divisio thematis* preceding the statements is missing. The steps correspond largely to the Latin model, with the eighth step omitted. The *dilatatio thematis*, i.e. the explanation of the respective steps, is normally very short and in some respects only translated literally, along with some brief commentary.[18] The topic here is 'the illness', or respectively 'the sin'. Necessary for the ascent to God is a correspondingly humble attitude and man's predilection for good things and works. If the soul has this attitude, it seeks God without ceasing. The omnipotence of God is represented by a paraphrase of the Creed and the hymn *Veni creator spiritus*. A concrete instruction follows, on how the seeker of God can make progress on his way: He should not dwell with the vices, with pride, worldly pleasures, or unholy things, but he should observe and obey God's commandments. A first biblical example is cited, taken over from the Latin model, with Mary Magdalene, who sought Christ on Easter morning. In the next step, the person is required to do good things to please God. This section is translated almost directly from the Latin source and is followed by a reference to inner attitude, which manifests itself in modesty and patience. This attitude is necessary for the act of devotion described, for which the person must now suffer the contempt of others. The soul should enter into a complete emulation of Christ and be ready to give up everything for God. The author (preacher) indicates repeatedly the difficulty of this undertaking. He addresses directly the listener or reader with the admonishment not to despair and to be patient and introduces the actual pericope of the sermon which is explained with regard to the attributes of the love of God as a noble virtue.

The fifth step describes an impatient desire for God, which is explained along with his distance from the human soul and the overcoming of sins. The deer thirsting for water in the forty-first Psalm as well as Rachel's heartfelt desire for children; these biblical motifs serve as illustrations of desire. As a consequence of this desire, the soul emulates God. As a result, with the next higher step the

---

werke/1046> [accessed 3 November 2022]; cf. Janz-Wenig, *Decem gradus amoris deutsch*, pp. 95–104; edition: ibid., pp. 239–45.

18 For example, the first step (also for the further footnotes: the text translated from Latin is always underlined): Janz-Wenig, *Decem gradus amoris deutsch*, pp. 209–10, l. 48, ll. 62–64: 'Primus ergo gradus est, in quo caritas facit languere utiliter. […] 3° mutat gustum, ut amarescat anime peccatum, quod prius libuit, sapiat aliquantulum summum bonum, quod ante non sapuit'; ibid., p. 239, ll. 8–10: 'Dev erst ist nvzzev chranchait. Daz ist, daz der mensche niht svnden wil, noch vor der vil lieb, di er hat zv got, niht enmage, daz dem menschen vor ist pitter gewesen, daz wirt im denne suzze'. The second grade is formulates similarly

ibid., p. 211, l. 69: Secundus gradus est, in quo facit querere incessanter.'; ibid., p. 240, l. 15: 'Dev ander staphel ist, daz man got an vnderlazze svche'.

ibid., p. 212, l. 95: '3us gradus est, in quo amor facit operari indesinenter.'; ibid., p. 241, l. 29: 'Der dritte staphel ist chreftigiv vnd starchiv arbeit in gotes dienst'.

soul becomes courageous and demands to kiss God. Through this desire a fire has now been kindled in the ascending soul, which, according to its progress in the love of God, lets people experience fervent love in three different ways. Some are only warmed internally by the love of God, others, in turn, experience a more heated love, but the perfect ones burn with love for God. In a final step, the soul now becomes equal to God in gentleness, mercy, and purity. The conclusion is a short summary of the sermon, the usual *unitio*, in which it is again repeated that the lovers of God do not leave him, even if this should mean death for them. At the end we have the usual *clausio*.

The text was probably written to teach the basic articles of faith. Often, simple allegorical interpretations of basic tenets can be found, e.g. the Creed, the Ten Commandments, or the biblical commandment of the love for God and one's neighbour. The target audience was certainly not very educated in either religious matters or in Latin. The vocabulary of the text is simple and the syntax easily understood as main clause parataxis, as well as main and relative subordinate clause constructions prevail. We find biblical examples and quotations, each of which is explained. The listening or reading audience is addressed both indirectly and generally as an individual and directly through appeals. The preacher also gives concrete instructions that clarify what has been said. In addition, the author can be recognized as a thoroughly well-educated theologian and a skilful compiler: We find in the text plentiful references to patristic concepts that go back to Bernard of Clairvaux, Dionysius the Areopagite, and Gregory the Great, added by the translator. Moreover, Gregory's three *habitus* of the beginning, progressing, and the perfect state are cited several times to explain each individual step. Also striking is the appearance of images, which are also transmitted in the *Seven Stages of Prayer* of David of Augsburg. Perhaps this connection to the work of David argues for the origin of the text in a Franciscan milieu, which is also underlined by texts copied in the two codices that transmit the sermon together with the vernacular sermon. The text was written, based on the dating of the manuscripts and of the Bavarian language used, probably in the first half of the fourteenth century and is thus the first piece of evidence regarding the reception of the corresponding sermon from *Deus caritas est* in the *Sermones Socci*.

A Double Sermon from the Corpus of the So-Called *Engelberger Predigten*

The *Sermones Socci* are also an important source for the collection known as the *Engelberger Predigten*.[19] Sixteen of its fifty-four collected sermons written in the South Alemannic language are based on models from *Sermones Socci*. The *Engelberger Predigten* were completed in the third quarter of the fourteenth century as a compilation of sermons to be read to the Benedictine nuns of the double monastery of Engelberg in Switzerland. Their use as instructions for the

---

19 For a general survey and introduction see Beck, 'Engelberger Prediger'.

lay brothers is also conceivable. The texts are formulated in figurative language, with frequent concrete references to the monastic life. The collection belongs to the great vernacular preaching works and is to be placed on par with that of Berthold of Regensburg, the collections of the so-called *St Georgener Predigten*, the sermons of the *Schwarzwälder Predigten*, and the *Paradisus anime intelligentis*.[20] The question of authorship remains unresolved.[21] Theologically, the collection upholds the tradition of Dominican mysticism influenced by Meister Eckhart, Johannes Tauler, and Henry Suso. Mystical elements and statements are embedded in the frame of ascetic discussions and expositions on the love of God. Individual sermons usually have a clearly defined theme and a clear structure, with many distinctions. They display a relatively simple sentence construction as well as recurring figures or images that are calculated to approach the target readers, who want to understand and moreover experience how the ascent to God is possible.

The double sermon *Ignis ante ipsum praecedit* preserves the entire three-part structure of its Latin template.[22] As a theme, however, it does not take over the epistle of the pericope (I John 4. 16), but instead picks up the psalm verse *Ignis ante ipsum praecedit* (Psalm 96. 3). It follows the Latin template in the *introductio thematis* as well as in the *divisio thematis*, distinguishing between the two kinds of love, *caritas accidentalis* (*zůvallent minn*) and *caritas substantialis* (*wesliche minn*). In the second section, the sermon sets down how Love needs to be properly nourished. The first six stages of the love of God follow in the third section of the first sermon. The other text of the double sermon proceeds in a similar way: the theme is introduced, the *introductio thematis* and the *divisio thematis* are adopted, followed by the summary of the steps presented in the first sermon, before explaining stages seven through ten. Both texts together take over the

---

20 For a summary of the collection: Janz-Wenig, *Decem gradus amoris deutsch*, pp. 105–09, with further literature. In greater detail, see Stauffacher, 'Untersuchungen zur handschriftlichen Überlieferung des "Engelberger Predigers"'; Wetzel and Williams-Krapp, 'Engelberger Prediger', p. 252.

The study by Stauffacher provides detailed information on the transmission of the sermons and was intended to be a preparatory study for a critical edition of the entire collection. Unfortunately, the dissertation was not published promptly nor did the planned edition come to fruition. The research project *MüBiSch: Mündlichkeit – Bildlichkeit – Schriftlichkeit*, which was launched in 2005 at the University of Geneva by René Wetzel and Fabrice Flückiger, announce a critical edition of the entire collection online: <www.muebisch.ch> [accessed 3 November 2022], where there is also other literature on the subject; see as well: <http://www.handschriftencensus.de/werke/824> [accessed 3 November 2022].

21 So far, different authors have been proposed. For a summary cf. Janz-Wenig, *Decem gradus amoris deutsch*, pp. 108–09.

22 Transmission of the two sermons (Sigla: Ea 15, Ea 16): Engelberg, Stiftsbibliothek, MS 335, fols 129r–45r; Strasbourg, Bibliothèque nationale et universitaire, MS 2801, fols 94ra–101ra; cf. Janz-Wenig, *Decem gradus amoris deutsch*, pp. 109–12; edition: ibid., pp. 249–74.

steps of the Latin sermon; only the second and third steps are reversed in the order. The author of the sermon was certainly a cleric familiar with the preaching theories of his time and very well trained in rhetoric.

If the author has completely taken over the structure of the source, he nevertheless freely filled the individual sections, partly by added *distinctiones*, partly by stringing together mostly biblical quotations, which are interpreted using exegetical models. Characteristic of this author's style are the many references to the world of the expected readers. A number of monastic offices are named: *meistrin, portnerin, siechmeistrin, kelnerin*.[23] By mentioning familiar everyday issues, the author creates an appropriate closeness to his audience. He also speaks about his office as a preacher, a noteworthy contemporary self-disclosure. The language shows rhetorical aspirations. The corpus of the *Engelberger Predigten* stands in the tradition of the spiritual teaching of Meister Eckhart and Johannes Tauler, but also in the tradition of the so-called sister-books, in which the nuns reported their visionary and mystical experiences. In these two sermons the audience often is addressed directly. Latin biblical verses, which appear only in the first sermon, are translated. The text reveals the author's will to create a high rhetorical standard; skilfully he transfers passages from the Latin template into German and integrates them into his text.[24]

Predigt von den zehn Graden der Liebe

The most elaborate of the vernacular versions of the sermon *Deus caritas est* from a theological point of view is the *Predigt von den zehn Graden der Liebe*.[25] It probably originated around the middle of the fifteenth century in the spiritual environment of the female Dominican monastery in Nuremberg and presupposes that the readers and listeners have knowledge of Latin and a certain theological education.

---

23 Ibid., p. 257, ll. 137–43: *abbess, doorman, infirmaria, cellaria*.

24 Ibid., p. 211, ll. 76–79: 'Super hunc gradum anima pedem ponit, cum diligenti et frequenti discursu rationis inquirit dicens: *In lectulo meo quesiui per noctem, quem diligit anima mea. Surgam et circuibo ciuitatem,* id est omnium creaturarum uniuersitatem, *per uicos et plateas* [Song of Songs 3. 1–2]'.

Ibid., p. 258, ll. 152–56: 'Hie suochet die sele iren geminten in allen creaturen, vnd si vindet sin nút als si selber sprichet: *Jn lectulo meo quesiui per noctem, quem diligit anima mea et non inueni illum. Vocaui et non respondit mihi.* Jch suochte minen geminten in der nacht vnd ich vant sin nút. Jch ruofte ime vnd er entsprach mir nút. [Song of Songs 3. 1]'.

25 Transmission: Berlin, Staatsbibliothek, Mgq 1133, fols 20^r–28^v; Eichstätt-Ingolstadt, Universitätsbibliothek, MS sm 214, pp. 267–95; München, Bayerische Staatsbibliothek, Cgm 750, fols 2^r–14^r; Nürnberg, Stadtbibliothek, MS Cent. VI, 43b, fols 44^r–55^r; <http://www.handschriftencensus.de/werke/6201> [accessed 3 November 2022]; cf. further Stöllinger-Löser, 'Zehn Staffeln der Gottesliebe'; Janz-Wenig, *Decem gradus amoris deutsch*, pp. 119–32; edition: ibid., pp. 279–99.

The *Predigt von den zehn Graden der Liebe* is the only one of the vernacular adaptations of the sermon *Deus caritas est* that takes over both the biblical pericope of the original *thema* as well as the steps to God, which are translated literally.[26] The thoughts about the love of God at the beginning of the Latin sermon are not included in the vernacular sermon. After a short *introductio thematis*, the *divisio* follows with a first enumeration of the steps. In the subsequent *dilatatio thematis* further distinctions are elaborated. While in the first few stages the progression of the soul seeking God is described in great detail, from the sixth step onwards the explanations become shorter. The explanation of the last step consists of just two sentences. The sermon ends with a usual *clausio*. The text is full of theological implications. It conveys theological knowledge through the numerous quotations from the Church Fathers – as can be found in the Latin source. Likewise, we find echoes of the allegorical language of Dominican mysticism. The language, an early modern High German version of the Bavarian dialect, is simple, with many enumerations, interjections, salutations, and even appeals to the reader or listener. Biblical examples place mainly female figures at the centre. The text was certainly designed as a reading sermon for a female convent, such as that of the Dominican nuns at Nuremberg. This text is most striking in that, in addition to the Latin *sermo*, other entries or translations from the *Decem gradus amoris* of the text from Helwicus Theutonicus can also be found. However, since the vernacular text also shows translations that are contained only in the sermon *Deus caritas est* and not in the *Decem gradus amoris*, both sources must have been available to the author or compiler of this text.

The four manuscripts that transmit the *Predigt von den zehn Graden der Liebe* are manuscripts for everyday use containing short spiritual texts in the vernacular intended for private reading or table readings in the refectory. They were written in southern Germany in the second half of the fifteenth century, very probably in the context of the religious reform in the Dominican nunneries.[27]

---

26 Ibid., pp. 209–10, ll. 48–54: 'Primus ergo gradus est, in quo caritas facit languere utiliter. Hic languor nil aliud est nisi displicentia peccati et dolor de conmissis. Cantico: *Nuntiate dilecto, quia amore langueo* [Song of Songs 5. 8]. Psalmo: *Oculi mei*, id est intelligentia, *languerunt pre inopia meritorum* [Psalm 87. 10]. Super hunc gradum anima pedem affectus ponit, cum primum Deum amare incipiens a peccato languescit. Sed Dominus cum medicinali oleo sue misericordie occurrit, anime languenti dicens: *Hec infirmitas non est ad mortem* [John 11. 4], nisi ad mortem mortis, scilicet peccati mortalis'.

Ibid., pp. 279–80, ll. 12–19: 'Die außlegung dez ersten gradus. Dye lieb in dem ersten grad macht sich vnd kranck nützlich. Da von spricht Salomon in dem puch von der lib in der person der begirlichen sele: *Verkündiget meinem libhaber, wänn ich kranck bin.* Auf disen stapfel setzt dy sel die füß ir begird, wenn sie ymm anuang anhebend got zu liben, swach vnd kranck wirt zu den sünden. Dise kranckhait ist nit zu dem leiplichen tode, alz Ihesus sprach von Lazaro, sunder in diser kranckait styrbet dy sel allen totsünden, vnd alle fleyschlich begyrd vergencklicher ding wirt getött in ir'.

27 Cf. among others Willing, *Die Bibliothek des Klosters St Katharina zu Nürnberg*, pp. xcii–xcix. In addition, a Dominican provenance of the Berlin manuscript can be assumed.

X trapkijns vander mynnen

The Middle Dutch text *X trapkijns vander mynnen* was written in the second half of the fifteenth century and represents the youngest vernacular adaptation of the sermon from the *Sermones Socci*.[28] This text is, unlike the previous three vernacular versions, not a sermon but a treatise on the love of God. It is transmitted within a miscellany of edifying texts containing a Book of hours and several texts of mystical and ascetic content. The edifying devotional book contains ownership marks from the sixteenth century, and is written largely for female lay readers. The differences between the Latin sermon *Deus caritas est* from the *Sermones Socci* and this particular adaptation reveal an influence of the *Devotio moderna* and clearly appeal to a female audience.

The manuscript conforms to late medieval piety in the way common in the circles of the *Devotio moderna*. Such miscellaneous manuscripts were handed down many times and, in the case of the manuscript in question, we may describe it as a *Volksbuch und Frömmigkeitsfundament des Laien* ('folk book and foundation of lay piety').[29] The codex, a semi-liturgical prayer book, includes a collection of private prayers.[30] In the first part it focuses on the presentation of different paths to God, reflections on the love of God, the virtues and the works of mercy, and the Passion of Christ. Many other texts in the codex deal with topics of the sermon *Deus caritas est*, such as, for example, the section on the *Doctrine of the Three Spiritual Ways to God*.[31]

The short treatise *X trapkijns van der mynnen* is the only known vernacular version of the *Decem gradus amoris* outside the Upper German language area. The text stands in the tradition of Rhenish mysticism, it takes over the structuring of the ascension of the soul to God in ten steps (the terms for the steps are usually translated literally), but omits the second step and adds a new tenth step, which identifies union with the beloved as the ultimate goal. In terms of content, the textual material from the sermon *Deus caritas est* is barely used; only in the first step do we find material from the template.[32] Although the pericope is not quoted, it is found indirectly as a paraphrase at the beginning of the treatise.

---

28 Transmission: Den Haag, Koninklijke Bibliotheek, MS KA 37, fols 189ra–93ra; Janz-Wenig, *Decem gradus amoris deutsch*, pp. 133–52; edition, ibid., pp. 303–09.

29 Achten, *Das christliche Gebetbuch im Mittelalter*, p. 32.

30 Cf. Moschall, *Marien Voerspan of Sapeel*.

31 Cf. on this manuscript, Janz-Wenig, *Decem gradus amoris deutsch*, pp. 134–45.

32 Ibid., pp. 209–10, l. 48, ll. 62–64: 'Primus ergo gradus est, in quo caritas facit languere utiliter. […] 3° mutat gustum, ut amarescat anime peccatum, quod prius libuit, sapiat aliquantulum summum bonum, quod ante non sapuit'.

Ibid., p. 303, ll. 9–13: 'Dat eerste traphkijn vander mynnen gods. Die eerste is orberlic te quellen, dat is siec te wesen inwendelic van mynnen. ¶ Dat is also te verstaen: Een mensche, die lichaemlic siec is, die verhest sijn smaec, dat hem welneer, wel plach te smaken, dat smaect hem qualic ende bitter ende dat hem qualic plach te smaken, dat smaect hem nu wel'.

The general remarks about love, which are found in the Latin sermon, were not included in the text.

The aim of the ascension is not simply the vision of God, but the *unio mystica*, which is described in the language of bridal mysticism. This becomes particularly apparent in the newly added tenth step. The path of the soul proceeds from being sick with love, turning away from sin, heartfelt prayers, good works, enduring tireless suffering, longing, and searching for the ever-withdrawing lover, until the soul as bride is finally received, comforted, and kissed by her bridegroom. The recurrent disappearance of the beloved requires patience and fuels an even greater desire, which makes the soul equal to the beloved in his humanity, gentleness, humility, and thus in all of his virtues. Only now can the soul, as a bride, fully unite with Christ, her bridegroom. What happens to the soul on its way, and how it comports itself, is described, for example, in the well-known 'Lives of Grace of the Nuns'.[33]

The recurring emphasis on the healing power of Christ's blood – the bleeding arms that surround the soul – is striking. It calls for a forceful and bloody imitation of Christ, one that focuses on suffering as the only true means of mystical union. Only through suffering can the redemptive work of Christ and the deification of the soul be made possible. Similar to the way wounds feature in the revelations of Elsbeth of Oye, the wounds which the soul receives on its way to God are already a sign of its coalescence with God. Pain is perceived as the presence of God, which, according to the text, the God-loving and God-seeking soul can recognize.[34]

The text is written in a relatively simple language. It offers enumerations of the experiences of the soul that make the described issues more compelling and vivid, as well as interjections that create a closeness to the spoken language and address the readers directly.[35] Direct biblical quotations are few; more frequent are indirect biblical references through paraphrases. Biblical examples are completely missing. Authorities are rarely cited: St Augustine only once and Gregory the Great twice. This treatise does not deal with the teaching of theological knowledge or the transmission of religious beliefs, but rather with the spiritual edification of lay people (the content of the manuscript indicates this). The text is also characterized by motifs of love or bridal mysticism, as well as by the so-called suffering and blood mysticism typical of the Upper Rhine sister-books.

The Latin sermon *Deus caritas est* is reinterpreted in the *X trapkijns vander mynnen* in terms of popular mystical piety, which promises salvation through the Imitation of Christ. Certainly, the widespread and well-known work by

---

[33] Cf., for example, Ringler, *Viten- und Offenbarungsliteratur in Frauenklöstern des Mittelalters*, pp. 298–99.

[34] Gsell, 'Das fließende Blut der "Offenbarungen" Elsbeths von Oye', pp. 462–65.

[35] Janz-Wenig, *Decem gradus amoris deutsch*, pp. 305, ll. 55–57: 'Ay, leiden niet een woert, en moghen verdraghen of enen slach of enen wonde, om die mynne haers brudegoms. Ja, dat meer is, wi en moghen niet een lelic op sien verdraghen'.

Thomas Hemerken of Kempen, the *Imitatio Christi*, had at least an indirect influence on it.[36]

Since the text of the *X trapkijns vander mynnen* reproduces only the structure of the Latin sermon *Deus caritas est*, it is conceivable that the author had only a shortened version of the Latin sermon at his or her disposal.[37] For the definition of the text as a kind of treatise and not as a sermon, the codicological context has to be taken into account.[38] The *X trapkijns vander mynnen* are transmitted in a rather private devotional book containing short reflections, treatises, and prayers.[39]

The Proverbial Collection *Staffel göttlicher Lieb*

In addition to the vernacular versions of the Middle Latin sermon *Deus caritas est* already presented, there is also a heavily abbreviated German version of the Latin text transmitted as a part of the proverbial collection *On Divine Love*.[40]

This proverb collection is transmitted in a twofold way: a) independently in miscellanies of mystical-ascetic content, and b) in the context of the so-called *Prayer Book I for Elisabeth Ebran*.[41] The latter was compiled for Elisabeth Ebran in 1426 by Johannes of Indersdorf, monastic reformer, provost of the Augustinian canonry of Indersdorf, and later confessor to Duke Albert III the Pious of Bavaria-Munich.[42] In his comprehensive analysis of the treatise *The Three Kinds*

---

36 Detailed analysis in Janz-Wenig, *Decem gradus amoris deutsch*, p. 151.

37 The shortened versions of the sermon, cf. Janz-Wenig, *Decem gradus amoris deutsch*, pp. 86–87, 221–32.

38 Cf., for example, *Medieval Monastic Preaching*, ed. by Muessig, p. 5: '[…] Furthermore, the form and style of sermons could come in various packages, sometimes appearing to be treatises, letters, biblical commentaries, and saints' lives, adding further confusion to what constitutes the content of preaching'.

39 Cf. Schiewer and Schiewer, 'Predigt im Spätmittelalter', p. 729.

40 Transmission: München, Bayerische Staatsbibliothek, Cgm 29, fol. 47^{r-v}; Cgm 105, fols 181^{r}–82^{r}; Cgm 255, fol. 53^{r-v}; Cgm 372, fol. 140^{r-v}; Cgm 763, fol. 64^{r-v}; Cgm 4285, fols 188^{v}–89^{v}; Cgm 4484, fols 313^{v}–15^{v}; Cgm 4698, fols 109^{v}–11^{r}; Clm 7596, fols 26vb–27ra; <http://www.handschriftencensus.de/werke/2908> [accessed 3 November 2022]. Stöllinger-Löser, 'Zehn Staffeln der Gottesliebe', col. 1517; Janz-Wenig, *Decem gradus amoris deutsch*, pp. 153–58; edition, ibid., pp. 313–14.

41 Haimerl, *Mittelalterliche Frömmigkeit im Spiegel der Gebetbuchliteratur Süddeutschlands*, pp. 152–60; Haage distinguishes two prayerbooks for Elisabeth Ebran; cf. on the author and his works Haage, 'Johannes von Indersdorf' und 'Der Traktat "Von dreierlei Wesen der Menschen"', above all pp. 74–97.

42 Cf. on the structure Haimerl, *Mittelalterliche Frömmigkeit im Spiegel der Gebetbuchliteratur Süddeutschlands*, pp. 153–55; Haage, 'Der Traktat "Von dreierlei Wesen der Menschen"', pp. 49–59, p. 77, p. 530. The section of the text containing the *Staffeln göttlicher Liebe* is found under the siglum IV. 4.

of Man by Johannes of Indersdorf, Bernhard Haage offers an overview of the manuscripts that transmit the *Prayer Book I*.[43] As is often the case with prayer books, the instability of the texts is reflected in a correspondingly large divergence between the manuscripts. Thus, not all the manuscripts cited by Haage include the section on 'Divine Love' (IV. 4).

In the proverb collection *On the Divine Love*, a short excerpt from the *Staffel göttlicher Lieb* immediately follows statements on the love of God and of one's neighbour reminiscent of the corresponding biblical commandments on love as well as a paraphrase of chosen passages from Augustine's *Confessiones*. Then the description of the first step follows, a free translation of St Bernard's quotation *Magna res est amor, sed sunt in ea gradus*, as we know it from the sermon *Deus caritas est*.[44]

The source for the short vernacular text must have been the Latin sermon that is transmitted within the *Sermones Socci*, with regard to the closeness of the excerpt to the Latin text. The author changes only occasionally the wording of his model and then only slightly. In two places he distances himself a little from the source by adding more in his own words to clarify the message. He shortens the text by summarizing individual thoughts, dropping most of the biblical and patristic quotations, and by omitting the scholastic *distinctiones*. The two steps of love thus presented can therefore be understood without any in-depth theological knowledge, but they also lack any rhetorical embellishments and references to the everyday devotional routine of the intended reader.

The goal of the ascension is formulated here as the attainment of true divine love and not as the ascension into the divine homeland. The first step is the sickness of the soul. However, the German translation lacks the idea of purpose which is emphasized in the Latin source. The *conmissis* of the source, that is, the offences or guilt as a description of the sickness, are more generally presented as pain of the heart because of time badly spent. The author summarizes the start of the second step in a simplifying way. He reduces the three possibilities or ways of searching described in the Latin sermon to just one: the eager hearing of the holy word of God. The appeal to meditate on why one does not

---

43 Haage, 'Der Traktat "Von dreierlei Wesen der Menschen"', pp. 49–59, pp. 533–34.

44 Janz-Wenig, *Decem gradus amoris deutsch*, pp. 209–10, ll. 48–54: 'Primus ergo gradus est, in quo caritas facit languere utiliter. Hic languor nil aliud est nisi displicentia peccati et dolor de conmissis. Cantico: *Nuntiate dilecto, quia amore langueo* [Song of Songs 5. 8]. Psalmo: *Oculi mei*, id est intelligentia, *languerunt pre inopia meritorum* [Psalm 87. 10]. Super hunc gradum anima pedem affectus ponit, cum primum Deum amare incipiens a peccato languescit. Sed Dominus cum medicinali oleo sue misericordie occurrit, anime languenti dicens: *Hec infirmitas non est ad mortem* [John 11. 4], nisi ad mortem mortis, scilicet peccati mortalis'.

Ibid., p. 313, ll. 4–7: 'Dy erst staffel macht den menschen kranck, aber dy kranckayt ist nicht anders dann ein missuallen der sundt vnd ein smercz des herczen vmb dy vbel verczerten zeyt. An dy staffel seczt der mensch seynen fues, wen er Got von erst lyeb hat vnd trawrig ist inwendig in der sel'.

find God, even though one is looking for Him, is connected to the well-known example of Mary Magdalene at the tomb, which is also mentioned in the Latin source.

Through his addition, the translator emphasizes Mary's perseverance, which does not let her be diverted from the search, even if other people could distract her. The description of the first two steps concludes with a quotation from Gregory the Great, which actually belongs to the third step of the Latin source. The language is simple, Latin keywords are translated with two synonymous German expressions. A tendency to rank or enumerate the individual arguments is evident. A homiletic tone characterizes the majority of contemporaneous translations of Latin edifying literature into the vernacular.

Summary

The texts presented in this article all share the same structure: the soul's rise to God in up to ten steps. The starting point on this path of knowledge is the treatise *Decem gradus amoris* by the Dominican Helwicus Theutonicus. A Latin sermon, *Deus caritas est*, is based on one part of this treatise. The sermon is transmitted in a collection called *Sermones Socci*, which was very popular in the fourteenth and fifteenth centuries. The sermon *Deus caritas est* forms the starting point for the various vernacular appropriations of the exposition on the rise of the soul to God.

The texts, structured by the outlines formulated in the Latin text, are supplemented and shaped in each case with further pastoral and edifying thoughts, exempla, allegories, and other digressions. The connection between individual adaptations can only by seen in the structure of the sermon *Deus caritas est*. Each author created a new text based on the Latin template and thus his own individual interpretation of the path the soul has to follow towards God, a path dependent on a given spiritual context and target audience.

The vernacular texts were probably written primarily for female readers and communities: The *Predigt von der Minne zu Gott* conveys basic catechetic teachings in plain language and includes primarily Augustinian and Franciscan thoughts, which are reflected both in the text itself and in the contexts of their transmission.

For the Benedictine nuns of Engelberg monastery in Switzerland, a linguistically elaborate double sermon was conceived on the basis of the Latin model, including references to the daily routine of the nuns in the monastery. The spiritual tenor of the text is similar to the mysticism of Meister Eckhart and even more to the teachings of Johannes Tauler. Exemplary female figures from the Bible and saints' lives are thematized to guide the female reader.

The *Predigt von den zehn Graden der Liebe* most likely originated in the spiritual environment of the Nuremberg Dominicans. For its readers the text required knowledge of Latin and at least some theological knowledge. The author of this reading sermon also went back to the treatise of Helwicus Theutonicus, in addition to the texts from the *Sermones Socci*.

The youngest vernacular version of the sermon *Deus caritas est* is the Middle Dutch treatise on the *X trapkijns vander mynnen*. It is transmitted within an edifying miscellany with an attached Book of Hours and it represents one of several texts of ascetic-mystagogical content in the manuscript. The changes to the Latin template reveal a marked influence of the *Devotio moderna* movement.

Within the proverbial collections on the love of God, only shortened versions of the first two steps of the ascension of the soul to God as described in the sermon *Deus caritas est* are adopted. Particularly interesting is the version adopted into the so-called *Prayer Book I for Elisabeth Ebran*.

All these texts treated above may be seen as examples of the close intertwining of Latin and vernacular edifying literature in the late Middle Ages. The reception of the Latin sermon *Deus caritas est* varied greatly. Stable texts in Latin were deliberately re-written and re-interpreted during their transition into the vernacular. The resulting vernacular treatises have only the original basic structural features in common. One cannot speak of translations in the strict sense in the case of any of these texts. They should rather be called compilations in which paraphrases or free vernacular transmissions of sections of the Latin template are interwoven in multiple ways with other thoughts and quotations from various sermons, legends, and exempla. The decomposition of the Latin templates down to its smallest parts is characteristic of the processes of rewriting of religious educative texts in the late Middle Ages. The history of the vernacular reception of the sermon *Deus caritas est* represents an example of vernacular text reception of the time, whose main principle seems to lie in variation and compilation. New text formations emerged, which can sometimes be described as highly artistic compositions and compilations. These give us not only a fascinating insight into the working methods of late medieval authors and compilers, but also a better understanding and a better knowledge of the reality of everyday life, the practice of piety, and the spirituality of the late Middle Ages.[45]

Bibliography

Primary Sources

Janz-Wenig, Katrin, *Decem gradus amoris deutsch: Entstehung, Überlieferung und volkssprachliche Rezeption einer lateinischen Predigt im ausgehenden Mittelalter: Untersuchung und Edition*, Texte des späten Mittelalters und der frühen Neuzeit, 56 (Berlin: Schmidt, 2017), pp. 165–314

---

45 For thorough proofreading of the English text as well as the helpful and critical comments, I would like to thank Michael Durgin very much.

Secondary Works

Achten, Gerard, *Das christliche Gebetbuch im Mittelalter: Andachts- und Stundenbücher in Handschrift und Frühdruck. Ausstellung Bonn-Bad Godesberg, Wissenschaftszentrum, 11.2.–10.4.1988*, 2nd rev. edn, Staatsbibliothek Preussischer Kulturbesitz: Ausstellungskataloge, 13 (Wiesbaden: Reichert, 1988)

Beck, Sigisbert, 'Engelberger Prediger', in *Die deutsche Literatur des Mittelalters: Verfasserlexikon*, ed. by Kurt Ruh and others, 14 vols, 2nd edn (Berlin: De Gruyter, 1978–2008), II: *Comitis, Gerhard – Gerstenberg, Wigand* (1980), col. 408

Grabmann, Martin, 'Helwicus Theutonicus O.Pr. (Helwic von Germar?), der Verfasser der pseudothomistischen Schrift "De dilectione Dei et proximi"', in *Mittelalterliches Geistesleben*, ed. by Martin Grabmann, 3 vols (Munich: Hueber, 1926–56), II (1936), pp. 576–85

Gsell, Monika, 'Das fließende Blut der "Offenbarungen" Elsbeths von Oye', in *Deutsche Mystik im abendländischen Zusammenhang: Neu erschlossene Texte, neue methodische Ansätze, neue theoretische Konzepte: Kolloquium Kloster Fischingen 1998*, ed. by Walter Haug und Wolfram Schneider-Lastin (Tübingen: Niemeyer, 2000), pp. 455–82

Haage, Bernhard Dietrich, 'Der Traktat "Von dreierlei Wesen der Menschen"' (dissertation, University of Heidelberg, 1968)

——, 'Johannes von Indersdorf', in *Die deutsche Literatur des Mittelalters: Verfasserlexikon*, ed. by Kurt Ruh and others, 14 vols, 2nd edn (Berlin: De Gruyter, 1978–2008), IV: *Hildegard von Hürnheim – Koburger, Heinrich* (1983), cols 647–51

Haimerl, Franz Xaver, *Mittelalterliche Frömmigkeit im Spiegel der Gebetbuchliteratur Süddeutschlands*, Münchener Theologische Studien, 1/4 (Munich: Fink, 1952)

Medieval Monastic Preaching, ed. by Carolyne Muessig, Brill's Studies in Intellectual History, 90 (Leiden, Boston, and Cologne: Brill, 1998)

Moschall, Joachim, *Marien Voerspan of Sapeel: Eine mittelniederländische Bearbeitung der 'Goldenen Schmiede' des Konrad von Würzburg*, ed. by Joachim Moschall, Erlanger Studien, 40 (Erlangen: Palm & Enke, 1983)

Ringler, Siegfried, *Viten- und Offenbarungsliteratur in Frauenklöstern des Mittelalters: Quellen und Studien*, Münchner Texte und Untersuchungen, 72 (Munich: Artemis, 1980)

Schiewer, Regina D., *Die deutsche Predigt um 1200: Ein Handbuch* (Berlin: De Gruyter, 2008)

——, and Hans-Jochen Schiewer, 'Predigt im Spätmittelalter', in *Textsorten und Textallianzen um 1500*, ed. by Mechthild Habermann and others (Berlin: Weidler, 2009), I: *Literarische und religiöse Textsorten und Textallianzen um 1500*, ed. by Alexander Schwarz, Franz Simmler and Claudia Wich-Reif, Berliner Sprachwissenschaftliche Studien, 20 (2009), pp. 727–71

Schneyer, Johannes Baptist, *Repertorium der lateinischen Sermones des Mittelalters für die Zeit von 1150–1350*, 11 vols, Beiträge zur Geschichte der Philosophie und Theologie des Mittelalters, 43 (Münster: Aschendorffsche Verlagsbuchhandlung, 1969–90)

Stauffacher, Mathias, 'Untersuchungen zur handschriftlichen Überlieferung des "Engelberger Predigers"', 3 vols (dissertation, University of Basel, typescript, 1982)

Steer, Georg, 'Bettelordens-Predigt als "Massenmedium"', in *Literarische Interessenbildung im Mittelalter: DFG-Symposion 1991*, ed. by Joachim Heinzle, Germanistische Symposien: Berichtsbände, 14 (Stuttgart: Metzler, 1993), pp. 314–36

Stöllinger-Löser, Christine, 'Zehn Staffeln der Gottesliebe', in *Die deutsche Literatur des Mittelalters: Verfasserlexikon*, ed. by Kurt Ruh and others, 14 vols, 2nd edn (Berlin: De Gruyter, 1978–2008), x: *Ulrich von Lilienfeld – 'Das zwölfjährige Mönchlein'* (1999), cols 1515–17

Wetzel, René and Williams-Krapp, Werner, 'Engelberger Prediger', in *Killy Literaturlexikon: Autoren und Werke des deutschsprachigen Kulturraumes*, ed. by Wilhelm Kühlmann (Berlin: De Gruyter, 2009–), III (2009), p. 252

Willing, Antje, *Die Bibliothek des Klosters St Katharina zu Nürnberg: Synoptische Darstellung der Bücherverzeichnisse*, 2 vols (Berlin: Akademie, 2012)

Worstbrock, Franz Josef, 'Johannes von Werden (de Verdena)', in *Die deutsche Literatur des Mittelalters: Verfasserlexikon*, ed. by Kurt Ruh and others, 14 vols, 2nd edn (Berlin: De Gruyter, 1978–2008), IV: *Hildegard von Hürnheim – Koburger, Heinrich* (1983), cols 811–13

———, 'Konrad von Brundelsheim', in *Die deutsche Literatur des Mittelalters: Verfasserlexikon*, ed. by Kurt Ruh and others, 14 vols, 2nd edn (Berlin: De Gruyter, 1978–2008), V: *Kochberger, Johannes – 'Marien-ABC'* (1985), cols 147–53

———, 'Peregrinus von Oppeln (von Ratibor) OP', in *Die deutsche Literatur des Mittelalters: Verfasserlexikon*, ed. by Kurt Ruh and others, 14 vols, 2nd edn (Berlin: De Gruyter, 1978–2008), VII: *'Oberdeutscher Servatius' – Reuchart von Salzburg* (1989), cols 402–04; XI: *Nachträge und Korrekturen* (2004), col. 1187

———, 'Herolt, Johannes (Discipulus)', in *Die deutsche Literatur des Mittelalters: Verfasserlexikon*, ed. by Kurt Ruh and others, 14 vols, 2nd edn (Berlin: De Gruyter, 1978–2008), III: *Gert van der Schüren – Hildegard von Bingen* (1981), cols 1123–27

Websites

Janz-Wenig, Katrin, 'Konrad von Brundelsheim', in *Verfasser-Datenbank: Autoren der deutschsprachigen Literatur und des deutschsprachigen Raums: Von den Anfängen bis zur Gegenwart* [10.1515/vdbo.vlma.2357, published 13 November 2017]

———, 'Helwicus Theutonicus', in *Verfasser-Datenbank: Autoren der deutschsprachigen Literatur und des deutschsprachigen Raums: Von den Anfängen bis zur Gegenwart* [10.1515/vdbo.vlma.1726, published 13 November 2017]

———, 'Zehn Staffeln der Gottesliebe', in *Verfasser-Datenbank: Autoren der deutschsprachigen Literatur und des deutschsprachigen Raums: Von den Anfängen bis zur Gegenwart* [10.1515/vdbo.vlma.4971, published 13 November 2017]

Handschriftencensus: Eine Bestandsaufnahme der handschriftlichen Überlieferung deutschsprachiger Texte des Mittelalters, online: <http://www.handschriftencensus.de/> [accessed 3 November 2022]

MüBiSch: Mündlichkeit – Bildlichkeit – Schriftlichkeit, online: <www.muebisch.ch> [accessed 3 November 2022]

DISSEMINATION OF KNOWLEDGE

Miscellaneity in Practice

A Further Look at the English Text Known as the *Lay Folks' Catechism*

Elisabeth Salter

University of Hull

Introduction

This essay comes about from ongoing research on popular religion and the evidence for the ways that late medieval people used written text as part of their devotional lives.[1] In general, in my research, I make a case for looking closely at manuscripts, in order to further our understandings of the experiences and practices of those who used, owned, and read the texts being discussed.[2] Medieval manuscripts often do not comply with the rules that have been set by later editions of the texts that they contain. Medieval manuscripts often give us a picture of extensive variability in terms of the content of a text, rather than adherence to a specific version that may have been used as the base text for a modern scholarly edition. And texts appear in numerous differing manuscript contexts that are often classed as 'miscellaneous' in terms of theme(s) and purpose(s).[3] Whilst scholarly editions are extremely valuable, as they provide important tools for carrying out scholarship, often providing comparative examples, I am particularly interested in the impact of the variability of manuscript culture on the medieval individuals who read, used, and owned these texts.

---

1 (I am grateful to COST Action IS1301 for stimulating ongoing research and discussion).

2 See, for example, Salter, *Popular Reading in English, c. 1400–1600*.

3 On medieval miscellaneous manuscripts in general see *Insular Books*, ed. by Connolly and Radulescu; for a recent consideration of miscellaneous manuals of religious instruction see, for example, McKeon, 'Diversity and Similitude in Middle English Ten Commandments Texts' and *Collecting*, ed. by Corbellini, Murano, and Sognore.

Lay Folks' Catechism

Some of the most widely circulated texts of late medieval English popular religion are what we might class as 'works of religious instruction'. These are often found in manuscripts that have been identified as 'miscellanies'. The Lincoln Thornton manuscript (Lincoln, Cathedral Library, MS 91) is one example, compiled by Robert Thornton in the mid-fifteenth century and containing charms, prayers, romances, spiritual and devotional tracts, recipes, and didactic works.[4] Another example is Cambridge, University Library, MS Ff.2.38, a mid-fifteenth-century compendium of saints' lives, prayers, catechetical works, and treatises on merchant behaviour. It is largely in English and includes 'works of religious instruction' as well as other moral and didactic works.[5] This essay takes the group of short catechetical texts known as the *Lay Folks' Catechism* as its main example. This is one amongst very many collections which fit into the class of 'works of religious instruction', or pastoral manuals as they are sometimes described.[6] I examine a small group of manuscripts that have been identified as containing *Lay Folks' Catechism* texts (complete texts or extracts) with the purpose of exploring how late medieval people may have used and experienced these versions of the text. I am interested in the ways that the miscellaneity of manuscript culture may relate to a set of broader cultural issues that we might call 'miscellaneity in practice'.[7]

As with much medieval English literature, the work carried out by the Early English Text Society (EETS) has been formative in our understanding of what material a medieval text contains. This is certainly the case for the *Lay Folks' Catechism* as a key parallel text edition was printed by EETS in 1901.[8] The EETS editors of *The Lay Folks' Catechism* took two English versions, the first identified as 'Archbishop Thoresby's Instruction or Catechism for the People', which is preserved in the Bishop's Register. The second version, which the editors identify as a 'Wycliffite Adaptation', is taken from London, Lambeth Palace Library, MS 408. As with many religious texts of this era, the extent to which MS 408 is clearly Wycliffite has come into question in more recent years and that will form part of the discussion later in this essay. Changes in critical perspective notwithstanding, the EETS edition remains a very valuable first port

---

4 For the facsimile edition of this manuscript see *The Thornton Manuscript (Lincoln Cathedral MS 91)*, intr. by Brewer and Owen; Thompson, 'Another Look at the Religious Texts in Lincoln Cathedral Library, MS 91', pp. 172–73 for specific consideration of reading tastes.

5 *Catalogue of the Manuscripts Preserved in the Library of the University of Cambridge*, II, ed. by Hardwick, pp. 404–08. For a codicological description of this manuscript see, for example, McSparran, 'Introduction'.

6 Gillespie, '"Doctrina and Predicacio"', pp. 36–50.

7 I use the term 'miscellaneity' in accord with Ralph Hanna III, 'Miscellaneity and Vernacularity', p. 37.

8 *The Lay Folks' Catechism*, ed. by Simmons and Nolloth.

of call for familiarizing oneself with the *Lay Folks' Catechism*. The indicative content proposed in the EETS edition is as follows:[9]

Preamble / Prologue 'The Need for Instruction'[10]

'Six Things':[11]

The Fourteen Points of Belief (Articles of the Faith)

The Ten Commandments

The Seven Sacraments

The Seven Deeds of Mercy

The Seven Virtues

The Seven Deadly Sins

Additional matter preceding the 'Six Things' (edited from the 'Wycliffite Adaptation', London, Lambeth Palace Library, MS 408):[12]

Pater Noster

Ave Maria

The Apostles' Creed

The Five Senses

The *Lay Folks' Catechism* and Linguistic Translation

The *Lay Folks' Catechism* presents a significant case study of linguistic translation with some evidence for the ways that the translation process was perceived and orchestrated by medieval contemporaries. Although the detail of linguistic translation is not the core concern of this essay, it makes sense to pause on this issue, here, as it provides important contextual evidence for the wider discussion. The issue of translating religious text from Latin to vernacular languages in the fourteenth and fifteenth century is highly charged. As Vincent Gillespie noted:

> Thoresby's instructions are not remarkable for their contents which are commonplace and rudimentary, but because they mark a significant stage in the evolution of the vernacular pastoral manual by conferring official approval on and encouraging the circulation of a vernacular version of his Latin original.[13]

---

9 *The Lay Folks' Catechism*, ed. by Simmons and Nolloth, pp. 2–99. The indicative content is taken from the running headers of the edition.

10 *The Lay Folks' Catechism*, ed. by Simmons and Nolloth, pp. 2–6.

11 *The Lay Folks' Catechism*, ed. by Simmons and Nolloth, pp. 20–99.

12 *The Lay Folks' Catechism*, ed. by Simmons and Nolloth, pp. 7–19.

13 Gillespie, '"Doctrina and Predicacio"', p. 43.

In his consideration of evidence for the origins of the *Lay Folks' Catechism*, Robert Swanson focused on an additional document, a letter (in Latin) sent from Archbishop Thoresby to J. de Gaitrik/Gaytring (the translator). The letter provides instructions about the proposed translation.[14]

> [Thoresby requested translation of the] full compendium articles of the faith, the precepts of the Decalogue, and other things (contained in a certain schedule which we send to you closed under our seal) [...] that these should be made known diligently in the vulgar tongue among the subjects of our diocese and province aforesaid by rectors, vicars, parochial chaplains, or any other having cure of souls, on every Sunday under certain penalties [...] And indeed, on account of the lack of care of certain priests (which has not been what it ought) to take good care lest any occasion for error should be left to them in any words touching on the fundamentals of the said faith.[15]

It is clear that linguistic translation allows for the formation of a different text rather than simply rendering of the same text in a different language.[16] In the context of the *Lay Folks' Catechism* this difference has been discussed by Vincent Gillespie, who observes a changed tone and emphasis in the English version of the *Catechism* compared to the original Latin. Gillespie identifies that the modifications and expansion of the English version include a 'movement to a greater flexibility of usage'.[17] Gillespie also notes that the opening homiletic preamble to the English version is more specific than its Latin counterpart in its identification of the church's role in teaching. He concludes:

> The directness is understandable in a work which was to be used primarily for the instruction of the laity who could not be relied upon to know or understand the basic premises of the Church's attitude to teaching and salvation.[18]

Where Gillespie observes a directness, which we might consider to represent a more didactic tone, Swanson's examination of the Thoresby letter invites us to consider the possibility that the directness of tone might be an interest in clarity of meaning at the expense of 'stylistic elegance'. Swanson cites this passage from the letter:

> [...] you roughly translate the aforesaid schedule with all possible speed, seeking clarity of meaning rather than stylistic elegance, since it is intended for the informing of the laity, so to speak. Farewell.

---

14 Swanson, 'The Origins of "The Lay Folks' Catechism"', pp. 92–100.

15 Swanson, 'The Origins of "The Lay Folks' Catechism"', pp. 99–100.

16 See for example, Ellis and Evans, 'Introduction', pp. 2–10; *The Idea of Vernacular*, ed. by Wogan-Browne and others, pp. 10–12.

17 Gillespie, '"Doctrina and predicacio"', p. 43.

18 Gillespie, '"Doctrina and predicacio"', p. 44.

([...] debite recensita contenta in eadem grosso modo cum celeritate possibili transferatis, plus querentes in tralnslacione ipsa, cum sit ad laicorum informacionem, ut dicitur, ordrinata, intellectum patulum quam ornatum. Valete.)[19]

Whether for clarity, didacticism, or because of a disinterest in producing a stylistically elegant vernacular text, these discussions lead to the conclusion that the vernacular translation of the *Lay Folks' Catechism* forms a new text that is distinct from its Latin predecessor. The focus on the impact of linguistic translation on a text such as the *Lay Folks' Catechism* is an important staging post in advancing our understandings of the nature of the texts of religious instruction that were circulated in the vernacular in the late fourteenth and fifteenth centuries. However, a key issue for discussion in this essay is the extent to which it is helpful to identify a text which is categorically a *Lay Folks' Catechism* as distinct from the many types of vernacular religious instruction that were in circulation during this time. A look at the surviving manuscripts identified as *Lay Folks' Catechism* texts tends to suggest that this was a very variable corpus. The manuscript case studies in the second half of this essay explore some of that variability.

Diversity and Complexity

One of the interesting aspects of the *Lay Folks' Catechism* (and the broader context of the miscellaneous manuscripts containing works of religious instruction) is their potential to be altered and reformed because they are made up of a number of short units of text. Those units are part of a numbered sequence of catechetical instruction; the 'Six Things' in the vocabulary of the *Lay Folks' Catechism*. This is an issue that Ralph Hanna has alluded to where he states:

> In the absence of a full *Lay Folks Catechism*, manuscript compilers had to reconstruct an analogous document from fragments.[20]

At the same time, however, and central to the nature and role of the religious instruction, is their highly programmatic structure often using numbering devices for the different sections.[21] The combination of re-formable units and the programmatic structure creates an interesting tension between variability and proscription. This, I suggest, has a direct impact on how we understand the medieval reader's experience of miscellaneity. What I mean here is that the medieval individual would have been accustomed to variability in these central tenets of the Christian church – this is perhaps best illustrated by imagining a medieval layperson who encountered certain preaching about the catechetic basics from

---

19 Swanson, 'The Origins of "The Lay Folks' Catechism"', pp. 99–100.

20 *The Index of Middle English Prose*, XII, ed. by Hanna.

21 Thompson, 'Another Look at the Religious Texts in Lincoln Cathedral Library, MS 91', p. 177.

his or her parish priest, but also had access to, or witness of, a written text (perhaps this was chained in the church for common use) and alongside this, he or she regularly saw those parts of the Catechism that were inscribed on the church wall. Each of these examples of contact with the catechetic basics could have been slightly different – embellished or summarized, for example, or emphasizing differing specific aspects of the basic Christian teaching. All of this experience leads to an understanding of variability amidst a strong sense of a clear programme of religious instruction that encouraged little flexibility in terms of belief and practice.

The diversity and complexity of the surviving texts of the *Lay Folks' Catechism* is widely acknowledged by scholars who have discussed them. In her 'new look' at the group of surviving manuscripts, for example, Anne Hudson divides the texts (she lists twenty-five manuscripts in all) into three groups: firstly, complete versions (twelve texts); secondly, extracts (seven texts); thirdly, significantly reworked texts (six texts). As she notes, the division between the second and third group is 'to some extent arbitrary'.[22] A key concern of Hudson in her discussion of the manuscripts is the possibility, and nature, of Lollard versions of the text. As she comments at the outset of the article, it has become a 'critical commonplace' to identify two versions of the *Lay Folks' Catechism*: one orthodox and one Lollard.[23]

Assumptions about the existence of the two versions of the *Lay Folks' Catechism* (orthodox and Lollard) arise from the EETS edition and its ascription of Lambeth MS 408 as the Lollard (Wycliffite) version of the catechism. But Hudson does not include the Lambeth manuscript in her list of twenty-five surviving texts, describing it as 'idiosyncratic' and questioning whether the scribes of Lambeth MS 408 saw any connections between the material they were copying and Thoresby's catechism.[24] Her final assessment of Lambeth MS 408 is that the 'prominence it has gained by its appearance and categorisation in the EETS edition is out of all proportion to its intrinsic importance'.[25]

Gillespie discusses the *Lay Folks' Catechism* in the context of the 'design and function' of a range of pastoral manuals, including the *Speculum Christiani*.[26] Gillespie's focus is less on the manuscripts and more on the tone of the vernacular text in comparison to Thoresby's Latin version. This includes the *Lay Folks' Catechism*'s emphasis on the numbering of the items (the 'Six Things') and its focus on the responsibility of the laity (as well as the clergy) to teach the unlearned these rudiments of the faith. He uses the EETS edition as his source, and does not consider the possibility of varied tone in the different manuscript

---

22 Hudson, 'A New Look at the "Lay Folks' Catechism"', p. 247.
23 Hudson, 'A New Look at the "Lay Folks' Catechism"', p. 243.
24 Hudson, 'A New Look at the "Lay Folks' Catechism"', p. 249.
25 Hudson, 'A New Look at the "Lay Folks' Catechism"', p. 258.
26 Gillespie, '"Doctrina and Predicacio"', p. 36, and quoting from the title of the article.

versions.[27] Sue Powell's discussion of the 'transmission and circulation of the *Lay Folks' Catechism*' gives a detailed description of the genesis and nature of the text, with consideration throughout of the dialectical evidence for northern and southern versions.[28] Powell, writing soon after Hudson, slightly emends Hudson's list of manuscripts, specifically the second and third categories (extracts and significantly reworked texts) with one feature being to include Lambeth MS 408 as a 'significantly reworked' text, rather than disregarding it.[29]

Each of the contributions by Hudson, Swanson, Gillespie, and Powell opens up questions about the possibility (or not) of the circulation of a *Lay Folks' Catechism* text prior to Archbishop Thoresby's injunctions, and the instruction to John de Gaytring to make the translation from Latin into English. Swanson's discovery of the letter from Thoresby to Gaytring is taken to prove that the translator was working to a commission, as discussed above. An implication derived from this and asserted by Powell is that Gaytring's work, therefore, 'was not circulating independently beforehand'.[30] Hudson also raises questions about the circulation of the sequence of catechetical material in advance of the Gaytring translation.[31]

As Gillespie's consideration of the *Lay Folks' Catechism* is set in the context of a discussion about the variety of preaching manuals in circulation it presupposes circulation of the kind of material found in the *Lay Folks' Catechism* as part of the general context of vernacular religious texts in circulation in the late fourteenth and fifteenth centuries. And, although I appreciate the interest of defining a moment in which a new translation came about, and the significance of the injunction, my approach to the *Lay Folks' Catechism* is also to appreciate it as part of the context of a diverse range of versions of similar vernacular material circulating amongst laity and clergy. With this in mind, it is interesting to note the reasons that Hudson gives for dismissing Lambeth MS 408. She describes Lambeth MS 408 as an 'assemblage of diverse materials drawn together in an eclectic fashion' which seems to imply that there were other versions that were less of an assemblage and more explicitly structured texts.[32]

While some of the manuscripts discussed by Hudson (and Powell) do follow a specific pattern (the 'Six Things') and have significant correspondence between them, the significance of this definable form for the fifteenth-century reader is not clear. The potential for variability of a sequence is slightly greater in the

---

27 Gillespie, '"Doctrina and Predicacio"', p. 50, n. 36.

28 Powell, 'The Transmission and Circulation of the "Lay Folks' Catechism"', pp. 67–84.

29 Powell, 'The Transmission and Circulation of the "Lay Folks' Catechism"', p. 73 n. 24.

30 Powell, 'The Transmission and Circulation of the "Lay Folks' Catechism"', p. 72 n. 20.

31 Hudson, 'A New Look at the "Lay Folks' Catechism"', p. 249.

32 Hudson, 'A New Look at the "Lay Folks' Catechism"', p. 257.

manuals that are identified as 'miscellaneous' than in those that are more particularly identified as specifically the *Lay Folks' Catechism*. However, in the culture of miscellaneity where our imagined medieval individual is accustomed to experiencing – hearing, using, witnessing – variations in the catechetical texts, it is not immediately clear why one format of catechetical instruction, such as that known as the *Lay Folks' Catechism*, would be particularly noticeable in the general context of multiple versions. Indeed, there is much variability even amongst those texts which are considered to be complete and faithful copies of the *Lay Folks' Catechism*. Additionally, in terms of the reading experience, the versions regarded as faithful copies are embedded in differing manuscript contexts, which, I would propose, alone suggests a differing variety of reading experiences even if the *Catechism* texts themselves are strongly similar.[33]

In terms of a reader's access to the catechetical instruction, it is difficult to define an absolute distinction between the sequence of instructional texts in the miscellany manuscript Cambridge, University Library, MS Ff.2.38 (mentioned above) and that found in a text designated as a *Lay Folks' Catechism* in the research. MS Ff.2.38, like numerous other English devotional compilations, contains the following sequence of religious instruction:

The Ten Commandments

The Seven Works of Mercy (bodily)

The Seven Works of Mercy (ghostly)

The Five Bodily Wits

The Five Ghostly Wits

The Seven Deadly Sins

The Seven Virtues Contrary to the Seven Deadly Sins

The Twelve Articles of Belief

The Seven Sacraments Shortly Declared of St Edmund of Pontigni[34]

One of the issues at stake in this essay is the manuscript evidence for the stability (or conversely the variability) of texts that have been categorized as the *Lay Folks' Catechism*. So how does the variability of the *Lay Folks' Catechism* manifest in manuscript culture? What might have been the impact of this miscellaneity in practice on the users and readers of these texts in the fifteenth century? I will explore these questions with reference to two case studies. The purpose of these examples is to see how far we can draw conclusions about the contemporaneous experience of using, reading, and owning a book that contains the *Lay Folks' Catechism*. I use the EETS edition as a base text for comparison, partly because it is, rightly, an important reference point for scholarship, and I have

---

33 The issue of manuscript context is discussed at length in Salter, *Popular Reading, 1400–1600*.

34 See Salter, 'Evidence for Devotional Reading in Fifteenth-Century England', p. 92.

also been guided by another important source, Robert Raymo's entry for 'Works of religious instruction' in *A Manual of the Writings in Middle English, 1000–1500*, in order to define the small group of texts here considered.[35] The group of manuscripts I have examined is all those identified by Raymo as *Lay Folks' Catechism* texts that are housed in the British Library, London. I have used a couple of comparative examples to augment this exploration, the 'complete' text in the Thornton manuscript (Lincoln MS 91), and those printed in EETS.[36] The first manuscript case study takes up the point made by Gillespie regarding the significance in the English translation of the preamble and examines this with reference to the group of manuscripts I have outlined. The second case study examines the question of defining heterodox or orthodox versions, discussed by Hudson, and looks at this with regard to the same group of manuscripts, focusing in particular on one example from that group.

The Didactic Preamble

As noted, one of the key textual elements that defines a text as specifically a *Lay Folks' Catechism* rather than a similar-looking sequence of religious instruction is the 'preamble'. This opening section of the sequence makes reference to Archbishop John Thoresby, who instigated the translation of the catechetical sequence from Latin into English at the convocation of clergy in November 1357. For example, in the preamble of the Bishop's register edition, which forms the primary source for the EETS volume, reference is made to:

> Oure Fadir the Ercebishop that god almighten save [...]
> Will that al men be saufe and knawe god almighten [l. 42 and l. 44].[37]

And in the opening to the delineation of the 'Six Things' we read:

> Our fadir the Ercebisshop of his godenesse
> has ordained and bidden that thai be shewed
> openly on inglis o-monges the folk [ll. 74–76].[38]

But whether all the versions that have been described as *Lay Folks' Catechisms* actually included this version of the preamble (or the preamble at all) is worth exploring. For my purposes, the important question to ask from this evidence is what was the impact on its readers and users if the preamble was not included, or included in a revised or partial form, or attached to varied catechetical texts? Certainly, if the didacticism of the *Catechism* is significant, then one would

---

35 Raymo, 'Works of Religious Instruction', pp. 2279–2331 and pp. 2492–2540.

36 See Hudson, 'A New Look at the "Lay Folks' Catechism"', pp. 246–47; *The Thornton Manuscript (Lincoln Cathedral MS 91)*, intr. by Brewer and Owen.

37 *The Lay Folks' Catechism*, ed. by Simmons and Nolloth, p. 4. In the EETS edition the preamble occupies ll. 1–53.

38 *The Lay Folks' Catechism*, ed. by Simmons and Nolloth, p. 22. In the EETS edition, the introduction to the 'Six Things' occupies ll. 51–76.

expect some sort of explanatory preamble for the reasons that Gillespie has outlined.

As Gillespie identified, in the opening sections of the texts considered to be most complete, there is a clear emphasis on explaining the purpose of the *Lay Folks' Catechism* for teaching the laity. This is clearly seen in two places at the outset of these versions: the first section which is identified as 'Preamble or Prologue' and given the additional heading of 'The Need for Instruction' in the EETS, and the opening lines of the section labelled as the 'Six Things'. In the York register version and the Thornton manuscript, both of which are written in prose, there is no clear division between the Preamble and the opening to the 'Six Things' – the division has come about from the format of the EETS edition in which there is a gap after the preamble because of the extensive additional material at this point printed in the parallel text of Lambeth MS 408.

Being guided by the layout in both 'Thornton' and 'Register' means we can take the EETS 'Preamble' (ll. 1–52) and the introductory lines of the 'Six Things' (ll. 52–76) as one sequence. Here, we find a description of the *Lay Folks' Catechism* specifically as an aid for instructing the laity[39] and an enumeration of the 'Six Things', which asserts the role of the clergy in ensuring that all their parishioners know them, and teach them to their children.[40] Taken together (that is ll. 42–76), this preamble reads as follows:

> Oure fadir the Ercebishop, that god almighten save
>
> That als saint Paule sais of Iesu crist
>
> – Paulus ad Thimotheum secundo ca –
>
> Will that al men be saufe and knawe god almighten
>
> And namely thas underloutes that to him langes
>
> Has treted and ordayned for for commune profet
>
> Thurgh the conseile of his clergie
>
> That ilkans that undir him has kepynge of saules
>
> Openly on Inglis opon sonondaies
>
> **Teche and preche thaim, that thai have cure of**
>
> **The lawe and the lore to knawe gold almighten**
>
> **That principali mai be shewed in this sex thinges**[41]
>
> In the fourteen poyntes that falles to the trouthe
>
> In the ten comandementez that god has gyven us

---

39 *The Lay Folks' Catechism*, ed. by Simmons and Nolloth, ll. 42–50, p. 4, p. 6.
40 *The Lay Folks' Catechism*, ed. by Simmons and Nolloth, ll. 51–76, p. 20, p. 22.
41 *The Lay Folks' Catechism*, ed. by Simmons and Nolloth, ll. 51–53 in bold.

A Further Look at the English Text Known as the Lay Folks' Catechism   177

In the seven Sacramentes that er in hali kirke
In seven dedis of merci until oure even-cristen
In the seven vertues that ilk man sal use
And in the seven dedely sinnes that man sal refuse
And he commands and bids in all that he may
That all that haves kepyng or cure under him
Enioygne thair parochiens and thaire sugettes
That thai here and lere this ilk sex thinges
And oft sithes reherce tham til that thai kun thaime
And sithen teche tham their childir, if thai have any
What tyme so thai er of eld to lere tham[42]
And that parsons and vikers and al paroche prestes
Enquire diligently of their sugettes, in the lentyn tyme
Whan thai come to shrift, whethir thai kun this sex thinges
And if it be funden that thai kun thaim noght
That thai enjoyne tham opon his behalve
And of payne of penaunce for to kun tham
And forthi that nane sal excuse tham
Thurgh unknalechyng for to kun tham
Our fadir the Ercebisshop of his godenesse
Has ordained and bidden that thai be shewed
Openly in inglis o-monges the folk.[43]

Gillespie identified that the education process is encouraged at home alongside being part of the clergy's responsibilities as expressed in ll. 63–65 of the quotation above.[44] And, he proposes that the Gaytring translation changes the nuance regarding culpable ignorance of the clergy that is found in the Thoresby (Latin) version from which the *Lay Folks' Catechism* is translated. Gillespie also identified some other changes of tone and emphasis in the English version, all of which point towards a translation which 'transforms an episcopal directive into

---

42 *The Lay Folks' Catechism*, ed. by Simmons and Nolloth, ll. 63–65 in bold.

43 *The Lay Folks' Catechism*, ed. by Simmons and Nolloth, ll. 42–76, p. 4, p. 6, p. 20, p. 22; See also Gillespie, '"Doctrina and Predicacio"', n. 38.

44 Gillespie, '"Doctrina and Predicacio"', p. 45.

a real, pragmatic and helpful manual'.[45] But what happens, given the miscellaneity of manuscript culture, if we look at the group of manuscripts in the British Library? Do they all contain these lines, and if they do not, does that matter?

Both London, British Library, MS Arundel 507 and MS Harley 6615, each identified by Hudson as a 'significantly reworked text', contain the preamble sequence faithfully and they therefore set up the aims in the clear and didactic manner to which Gillespie refers. Indeed, it is difficult to ascertain any significant 'reworking' taking place in this opening preamble. The catechetical material in manuscripts Arundel 507 and Harley 6615 just happen to be reworked (differently), so they prepare their readers exactly in the Gaytring manner but continue with slightly different material. The differences in each of these versions are interesting because they do not remove or replace any elements of the *Lay Folks' Catechism*. Both versions represent all Six Things. The version in MS Arundel 507 tends to embellish the text; this is particularly noticeable in the Ten Commandments, where most precepts have an additional line augmenting that found in the EETS edition. These additions do not fit with the kind of additional material one might expect in a text categorized as 'Lollard'; they simply add an extra example, usually at the end of the precept text as found in the EETS edition and occurring almost entirely word for word in MS Arundel 507. The differences in MS Harley 6615 tend towards abridgement; again taking the example of the Ten Commandments, the precepts are given in their summary version; the approximate equivalent of just two of the EETS lines for each precept (although set out in prose).

The manuscript contexts of these two *Catechisms* are also different, as far as it is possible to tell, given that MS Arundel 507 is a composite book, with textual units ranging in date from the early thirteenth to the later fourteenth century. MS Harley 6615, which is described in the catalogue of Harleian manuscripts as a 'collection of devotional treatises' gives, in contrast, the appearance of a manuscript written in one hand. Alongside the *Catechism*, MS Harley 6615 contains various devotional and instructional texts including the *Chastising of God's Children*, the *Revelations of St Bridget* (Birgitta of Sweden), various remedies against temptation, and the story of St Gregory.[46] The booklet in which the *Catechism* is found in MS Arundel 507 (fols 21^r–91^v) contains a number of texts in Latin with a focus on moral precepts, instructions for monastic behaviour and prayers. (It was probably compiled by a monk called Richard Sedgebrook in the late fourteenth century). The English contents of MS Arundel 507 include *Four Things Needs Man to Know*, *Upon the Love of God*, *Meditations Upon the Passion*, and a *Treatise Upon the Value of Time and its Proper Employment*. While the English texts of MS Arundel 507 are, therefore, from a similar pool of English didactic and moralizing devotional texts as those found in MS Harley 6615,

---

45 Gillespie, '"Doctrina and Predicacio"', p. 45.

46 Cf. *Catalogue of Illuminated Manuscripts of the British Library*, online: <https://www.bl.uk/catalogues/illuminatedmanuscripts/record.asp?MSID=5135> [accessed on 3 November 2022]; *The Lay Folks' Catechism* is on folds 127^r–40^v.

the extent of the Latin texts in MS Arundel 507 and its provenance in a monastic environment imply a different intended use and likely readership from those manuscripts such as MS Harley 6615, which are dominated by English texts and translations.

MS Harley 1022, which is identified by Hudson as a complete text, begins at l. 83 of the EETS edition thereby omitting the opening preamble and therefore its didactic emphasis. As Hudson notes, manuscript evidence does not clearly point to a loss of the first 82 lines, so it may simply be that this text was copied without the didactic preamble.[47] The *Lay Folks' Catechism* in MS Harley 1022 therefore begins with '*Th*e fyrst poynt *th*at we sal trow of *th*e godhed'.[48] London, British Library, MS Add. 25006, listed as one of the complete versions by Hudson, is an interesting example. It opens with a faithful rendition of the preamble in a prose style layout and then proceeds with the 'Six Things' in a verse layout. At several places in this manuscript, the numbered sequences are emphasized by simple notes *in margine*, adding to the didactic impression of the text. It is not clear where the copyist for MS Add. 25006 took the idea of using both prose and verse layouts for his version of the *Catechism*, or if, indeed, he instigated this layout. As this manuscript is just one booklet from what was probably a larger manuscript it is not possible to solve this question.

The 'significantly reworked' versions MS Arundel 507 and MS Harley 6615, both of which include the preamble, although quite different from each other in terms of length, offer all the same basic reading experience. The embellishments found in MS Arundel 507 furnish the reader with more examples, and more material for his or her wider consideration of the practical applications of the 'Six Things', whereas the MS Harley 6615 tendency towards summarizing gives the reader a snappier, perhaps more easily memorized, version of the same set of tenets. The difficulty of ascertaining whether MS Harley 1022 deliberately omits the preamble, thereby dismissing the value of that didactic introduction, or if the material is simply lost, has been noted. If the preamble is what distinguishes a *Lay Folks' Catechism* from the many works of religious instruction, and MS Harley 1022 did begin at l. 83, then this is the least complete, or faithful, of this group so far. The interesting addition to this exploration is MS Add. 25006, with its transition from the prose preamble to the verse of the 'Six Things'. This manuscript, I suggest, most strongly indicates the perception of the didactic preamble as something distinct and separate from the series of tenets found in so many texts in the category of 'works of religious instruction'.

Manuscript Example 2: The Heterodoxy Issue

One other major area of investigation for the *Lay Folks' Catechism* is the orthodox, heterodox, and Lollard (Wycliffite) context. As noted above, this has in part been stimulated by the EETS version that printed an 'orthodox' version in paral-

---

47 Hudson, 'A New Look at the "Lay Folks' Catechism"', n. 13.

48 London, British Library, MS Harley 1022, fol. 66[r].

lel with a 'Wycliffite' version. The ideological affiliations of these texts have been unpicked more recently (along with much work on heterodoxy where manuscript studies have played an important part), and this has included consideration of fine nuances of tone and the use of specific words regarded in the research as ideologically distinct.[49] An important intervention in the scholarship relating to *Lay Folks' Catechism* has been Anne Hudson's 'New Look'. Hudson proposed that the commonplace of identifying two distinct versions of *The Lay Folks' Catechism*, one orthodox and the other Wycliffite/Lollard, has a 'grain of truth to several of error or at least to several of oversimplification'.[50] One manuscript from this case study group that highlights the complexities is London, British Library, MS Add. 24202, identified by Hudson as including an 'extract' of the text.[51] MS Add. 24202 contains just three pages of *Lay Folks' Catechism* (fols 35ᵛ–36ᵛ); these pages incorporate two sections, 'The Seven Sacraments' and 'The Seven Virtues'. Each of these two sections has very clear rubricated headings such as the title 'Here begynnes *The* Seven Sacramentis' at the top of fol. 35ᵛ which begins this extract. The second of the two items ends abruptly.

If we take both the *Lay Folks' Catechism* material and the manuscript context into account, this manuscript provides valuable evidence for the problems that can arise with assigning a label of either 'Lollard' (Wycliffite) or 'orthodox' to some versions of the text. The version of 'The Seven Sacraments' in MS Add. 24202 includes th ('orthodox') version of the fourth sacrament as follows:

> *Th*e furthe is *th*e sacrament of the aulter Cristis owne body under fourme of brede right as he toke it of *th*e blessed mayden. *Th*e whiche iche man *th*at of elde is owes to reseyve onys in the yeer. *Th*at is to say at Paske as holy churche usest whann *th*ei ben clene of synes yerowe penaunce.[52]

This is clearly non-Lollard according to the criteria set by Hudson in which she states that:

> Two parts of the section would have been repugnant to anyone with Lollard sympathies: those on the Eucharist and on penance [...] the instruction to receive [the sacrament] once a year at Easter after confession clearly implies, by its repetition of the 1215 Lateran Council provision, the acceptance of the orthodox doctrine which the Lollards disputed.[53]

However, the manuscript context for MS Add. 24202, other texts in this manuscript, written in the same hand as *The Lay Folks' Catechism*, is clearly Lollard/

---

49 See, for example, Peikola, '"And after All, Myn Ave Marie Almost to the Ende"', p. 290.

50 Hudson, 'A New Look at the "Lay Folks' Catechism"', p. 243.

51 Hudson, 'A New Look at the "Lay Folks' Catechism"', p. 246.

52 London, British Library, MS Add. 24202, fol. 36ʳ.

53 Hudson, 'A New Look at the "Lay Folks' Catechism"', p. 255.

Wycliffite. This includes, for example, the *Tretise of Miraclis Pleying* which is one of the well-known Wycliffite tracts in circulation in fifteenth-century England.[54] But just to confuse matters, MS Add. 24202 also shares some direct correspondences with Lambeth MS 408 (the text which Simmons and Nolloth described as a Lollard version of *The Lay Folks' Catechism*). For example, the last lines of the second of the seven virtues of MS Add. 24202 have an additional line not present in the Register and Thornton versions but present in Lambeth MS 408:[55]

London, British Library, MS Add. 24202

For wi*th* outen gode dedis come we nev*er* to hevene
and specialy but if we kepe *th*e biddyngis of god.[56]

London, Lambeth Palace Library, MS 408

For wi*th* oute goode dedys we come never to hevyn
And but we holde specialy *th*e biddyng of god.[57]

What this example demonstrates is that for fifteenth-century people reading and using manuscripts such as MS Add. 24202, the line between an orthodox and a Lollard teaching might be quite blurred, i.e. the effort of the research to distinct between orthodox and heterodox Christian teaching may sometimes obscure the rather complex character of religious experience in the given time and place. Specifically with regard to the extract of the *Lay Folks' Catechism* in this manuscript, while the content of that extract has been identified as part of the orthodox version (and indeed definitely non-Lollard according to Hudson's classification), the experience of reading and using this manuscript was heterodox. This serves as a good example for the miscellaneity of manuscript culture more generally, and also gives a demonstration of the ways that the extractability of *The Lay Folks' Catechism* makes it particularly able to appear in a variety of manuscript contexts with differing nuances on the orthodoxy/heterodoxy spectrum.

Conclusion

The purpose of this essay is to open up some possibilities for understanding the ways that medieval people may have experienced the miscellaneity of manuscript culture, with particular reference to the vernacular texts that were most available

---

54 London, British Library, MS Add. 24202, fol. 14[r]–21[r] (mistake on the BL website: the treatise ends on fol. 21[r]) and noted by Hudson, 'A New Look at the "Lay Folks' Catechism"', p. 5, n. 18: 'The other contents of this manuscript are Lollard or show some sympathy with Lollardy'. See *Selections from English Wycliffite Writings*, ed. by Hudson.

55 Lincoln, Cathedral Library, MS 91, fol. 217[r] (from facs).

56 London, British Library, MS Add. 24202, fol. 36[v].

57 *The Lay Folks' Catechism*, ed. by Simmons and Nolloth, ll. 1196–97, p. 81.

to the widest spectrum of society, 'works of religious instruction'. I have taken the *Lay Folks' Catechism* as a useful test case because this enables an exploration of the ways that the culture of manuscript variability may have had an impact on the reading experience of this officially approved programme of vernacular religious instruction. The example of the *Lay Folks' Catechism* also enables a consideration of the scholarly inheritance of a valuable comparative textual edition – that found in the Early English Text Society. The two examples I discussed encourage us to ask questions about the relevance of the experience of the medieval reader for defining this group of *Catechism* texts as identifiably different from the many other works of religious instruction being translated and in circulation at this time as well as for defining the distinction between orthodox and heterodox teaching in general. The manuscripts discussed in this essay are indicative of the ways we might consider the impact of miscellaneity in the context of the production and reproduction of English vernacular works of religious instruction in the late Middle Anges.

Bibliography

Manuscript Sources

Cambridge, University Library, MS Ff.2.38
Lincoln, Cathedral Library, MS 91
London, British Library, MS Add. 24202
———, MS Add. 25006
———, MS Arundel 507
———, MS Harley 1022
———, MS Harley 6615
London, Lambeth Palace Library, MS 408

Primary Sources

The Lay Folks' Catechism or the English and Latin Versions of Archbishop Thoresby's Instruction for the People: Together with a Wycliffite Adaptation of the Same and the Corresponding Canons of the Council of Lambeth, ed. by Thomas Frederick Simmons and Henry Edward Nolloth, Early English Text Society: Original Series, 118 (London: Kegan Paul, Trench, and Trübner, 1901)

The Thornton Manuscript (Lincoln Cathedral MS. 91), introduction by Derek S. Brewer and Arthur Ernest Bion Owen (London: The Scolar Press, 1975)

Secondary Works

Catalogue of the Manuscripts Preserved in the Library of the University of Cambridge, ed. by Charles Hardwick and Henry Richards Luard, 5 vols (Cambridge: Cambridge University Press, 1856–67), II, ed. by Charles Hardwick

Ellis, Roger and Ruth Evans, 'Introduction', in *The Medieval Translator 4: Proceedings of the Conference, Held at Cardiff, 1993*, ed. by Roger Ellis and Ruth Evans (Exeter: Exeter University Press, 1994), pp. 2–10

Gillespie, Vincent, '"Doctrina and Predicacio": The Design and Function of Some Pastoral Manuals', *Leeds Studies in English*, 11 (1980), 36–50

Hanna, Ralph III, 'Miscellaneity and Vernacularity: Conditions of Literary Production in Late Medieval England', in *The Whole Book: Cultural Perspectives on the Medieval Miscellany*, ed. by Stephen G. Nichols (Ann Arbor, MI: University of Michigan Press, 1996), pp. 37–52

——, *The Index of Middle English Prose*, 24 vols (Cambridge: Brewer, 1984–2017), *Handlist* XII: *Manuscripts in Smaller Bodleian Collections* (1997)

Hudson, Anne, 'A New Look at the "Lay Folks' Catechism"', *Viator*, 16 (1985), pp. 243–58

Insular Books: Vernacular Manuscript Miscellanies in Late Medieval Britain, ed. by Margaret Connolly and Raluca Radulescu, Proceedings of the British Academy, 201 (Oxford: Oxford University Press, 2015)

McKeon, Sarah, 'Diversity and Similitude in Middle English Ten Commandments Texts', *The Library of Trinity College Dublin: Blog*, 17 January 2017, online: <https://www.tcd.ie/library/manuscripts/blog/2017/01/diversity-and-similitude-in-middle-english-ten-commandments-texts/#more-2429> [accessed on 3 November 2022]

McSparran, Frances, 'Introduction', in *Octavian: Edited from Lincoln, Dean and Chapter Library, MS 91 and Cambridge University Library, MS Ff.2.38*, ed. by Frances McSparran, Early English Text Society: Original Series, 289 (Oxford: Oxford University Press, 1986)

Peikola, Matti, '"And After All, Myn Ave Marie Almost to the Ende": Pierce the Ploughman's Crede and Lollard Expositions of the Ave Maria', *English Studies*, 81/4 (2000), pp. 273–92

Powell, Sue, 'The Transmission and Circulation of the "Lay Folks' Catechism"', in *Late Medieval Religious Texts and their Transmission: Essays in Honour of A. I. Doyle*, ed. by Alastair J. Minnis, York Manuscript Conferences: Proceedings Series, 3 (Cambridge: Brewer, 1994), pp. 67–84

Raymo, Robert, 'Works of Religious Instruction', in *A Manual of the Writings in Middle English, 1000–1500*, 11 vols (Yale: Yale University Press, 1967–2005), VII (1986), pp. 2279–2331 and pp. 2492–2540

Salter, Elisabeth, 'Evidence for Devotional Reading in Fifteenth-Century England: A Comparative Analysis of One English Poem in Six Manuscript Contexts', in *Vernacularity in England and Wales, c. 1300–1550*, ed. by Elisabeth Salter and Helen E. Wicker, Utrecht Studies in Medieval Literacy, 17 (Turnhout: Brepols, 2011), pp. 65–97

——, *Popular Reading in English, c. 1400–1600* (Manchester: Manchester University Press, 2012)

Selections from English Wycliffite Writings, ed. by Anne Hudson (Cambridge: Cambridge University Press, 1981)

The Idea of Vernacular: An Anthology of Middle English Literary Theory, 1280–1520, ed. by Jocelyn Wogan-Browne and others (Exeter: Exeter University Press, 1999)

Thompson, John, 'Another Look at the Religious Texts in Lincoln Cathedral Library, MS 91', in *Late-Medieval Religious Texts and their Transmission: Essays in Honour of A. I. Doyle*, ed. by Alastair J. Minnis, York Manuscript Conferences: Proceedings Series, 3 (Cambridge: Brewer, 1994), pp. 169–87

Swanson, Robert, 'The Origins of The "Lay Folks' Catechism"', *Medium Aevum*, 60/1 (1991), pp. 92–100

Websites

Catalogue of Illuminated Manuscripts of the British Library, online: <https://www.bl.uk/catalogues/illuminatedmanuscripts/record.asp?MSID=5135> [accessed on 3 November 2022]

Old Material and New Perspectives

Master Ingold's 'Golden Game'

Jörg Sonntag

Sächsische Akademie der Wissenschaften,
Projekt: Klöster im Hochmittelalter.
Innovationslabore europäischer
Lebensentwürfe und Ordnungsmodelle,
FOVOG, TU Dresden

This essay examines the rarely studied *Puechlein vom Guldin Spil* (*Book of the Golden Game*) written by the Dominican Master Ingold of Basel around the year 1432. In the context of the current boom of research on the culture of the game, the *Puechlein* represents an exceptional source containing detailed information on the broad variety of forms and characters of medieval games.[1] Ingold not only combined different games and their interpretation in a unique way; he also introduced one of their first known taxonomies. My analysis concentrates on the role the interpretation of games played in the vernacular religious discourse; on the transformations of theological conceptualization of games; and on Ingold's idea of two playing societies both in Heaven and on Earth, a concept based on the exegetical interpretations formulated by the individual authors of the so-called Upper-German mysticism of his time.

Games and Moralizing Treatises – Some Introductory Remarks

The medieval terms *ludus* and *iocus*, were present in various discourses in the Moiddle Ages: both terms could mean fun and enjoyment, while *ludus*, far more than *iocus*, also meant a particular game. In extant texts *ludus* may denote several varieties of physical exercise, dancing, gambling, lay and religious theatre, singing, bathing, solving riddles, reciting poems, having sexual intercourse, or engag-

---

1 Scholarly research on games and game playing overcame the Enlightenment view of the body-despising, non-playful Christian Middle Ages several decades ago. However Walter Endrei in his book about games continues to depart from this assumption. See Endrei, *Spiele und Unterhaltung im Alten Europa*, p. 8. Prominent figures who have a hostile opinion of games in the Middle Ages include, incidentally, Friedrich Schiller and Friedrich Nietzsche. See for instance Leutzsch, 'Der tanzende Christus', pp. 101–02.

ing in any activity with uncertain results. Scholars often struggle to define the discursive context of the term. Furthermore, overlapping semantic fields in the case of terms as game, gambling, play and physical exercise, complicate the scholarly discussion on the problem.[2] According to Johan Huizinga, playing/toying (*spielen*, *jouer*, *giocare*) can be identified as a basic anthropological component of human existence which is older than any culture.[3] Huizinga defined games as voluntary actions played within restricted boundaries of space and time, accompanied by a common awareness of 'otherness', of doing something different, in a sort of parallel universe.[4]

Roger Caillois has underlined the non-productive character of games: they do not create anything new since the players return to their 'status quo' once the game is finished, as it has no influence on 'normal' life.[5] Games, often played in a group, can be played for enjoyment (in itself) or as a profession. Sometimes they follow specific scenarios, sequences of actions, out of which – if a group is playing – common normative rules may develop. These codes of action can result from the specific character of a particular game, from its rules, or from a shared wish to act in concert. Games can therefore be defined as special cases of social communication, although they seem to be excluded from the ordinary space and time frame of social interaction.[6]

Certainly, the game remains a complex phenomenon which is structurally anchored in everyday life, not only in antiquity and today, but also in the Middle Ages. From the fourteenth century onwards, especially, there is more evidence than for the earlier period of both positive and negative assessments of games. It is no coincidence that French and Italian scholars studying games have identified a late medieval *invasion ludique*, and have marked the society of the fifteenth century as a ludic one.[7] In particular, religious people, preachers and pastors, had to face this phenomenon when they addressed the social focal points involving games. For a long time the *religiosi*, monks and nuns, were pioneers in the religious interpretation of nearly all kinds of game and play as shall be discussed below. By moralizing about them and by adopting their terminologies to describe issues of individual moral conduct, the mendicant orders in particular provided every member of medieval society with helpful advice in this respect.

From the late thirteenth century onwards, a great many morality books were published. The most prominent example, one of the earliest and most discussed

---

2 In German for example *Spiel* means activities described in English as game, gambling, play, or sport. See, for instance, Buland and Schädler, 'Einleitung zur Buchreihe Ludographie', pp. 7–8.

3 Huizinga, *Homo ludens*. On this theory, see Flitner, 'Johan Huizingas Homo ludens', p. 20.

4 Flitner, 'Johan Huizingas Homo ludens', pp. 21–22, pp. 45–46, pp. 212–13.

5 Caillois, *Les jeux et les hommes*, pp. 31–40.

6 Cf. Sonntag, 'A Matter of Definition?', pp. 335–36 and p. 355.

7 See, for instance, Mehl, 'Les jeux de dés et des tables et les ordres religieux', p. 174 and Rizzi, *Ludus/ludere*, passim.

by historians, is the *Liber de moribus hominum et officiis nobilium ac popularium super ludo scacchorum*, known as the *Book of Chess*, written by the Dominican Jacobus de Cessolis around the year 1300.[8] In his prologue, Jacobus expounds on the circumstances and reasons for the invention of chess. Chess was, according to him, invented by a pagan master named Xerxes or Philometus of Chaldea for three reasons. The first was to reform the maleficent Evilemordach, son of the Persian King Nebuchadnezzar. Evilemordach lost each chess game and so learnt to control his anger. The second reason was to keep the player from being idle, and the third to indulge the desire for novelty.[9] In the first chapter, Jacobus describes the chessmen on the board; the king, the queen, the elders (that is, the judges, i.e. bishops), the knights, and the rooks (the deputies of the king). Taking many exempla from John of Salisbury and Aegidius Romanus, respectively, Jacobus speaks of good and bad conduct.[10] In the second chapter, he describes the eight pawns. He likens them to eight commoners; the first pawn stands for the farmer, the second for the smith, the third for the clothier and scribe. The fourth pawn represents the merchant, the fifth the physician, the sixth the innkeeper, the seventh the city guard, and finally, the eighth the gambler and courier. Gamblers are characterised very negatively. As Jacobus argues, they stand in the shadow of prostitutes and other immoral people. When they gamble unprofitably and deplorably and lose their money, they become robbers, thieves, arsonists, murderers, and betrayers.[11] In this exposition, Jacobus inserted an exemplum of Bernard of Clairvaux, which went on to become one of the most famous stories of the conversion of gamblers. According to the story Saint Bernard was challenged by a foreign gambler to play for his horse. Although the gambler scored eighteen points with three throws of the dice, Bernard still won. He scored nineteen points, with sixes on two dice; then, through divine intervention, the third dice split into two parts, one showing a six, the other one showing an ace.[12] In the third chapter of his *Book of Chess*, Jacobus discusses different chess openings and moves. He connects every move in a game to the particular performance of a good or bad deed. The reader may imitate these good deeds profitably and with their help lead a good Christian life.[13] Jacobus is highly innovative here. Living in flourishing northern Italian city states, he used the chess game to sketch

---

8 Research on this highly influential book, indeed one of the most copied texts in the late Middle Ages, has extended to the point where it has become barely manageable. To mention just a few representative analyses: Kramer, *Bauern, Handwerker und Bürger*; Plessow, *Mittelalterliche Schachzabelbücher zwischen Spielsymbolik und Wertevermittlung*; Adams, *Power Play*, pp. 15–56 and Mehl, *Des jeux et des hommes dans la société médiévale*, pp. 91–162.

9 Jacobus de Cessolis, *Libellus de moribus*, ed. by Habor, I. 1–2, pp. 6–8.

10 Jacobus de Cessolis, *Libellus de moribus*, ed. by Habor, II. 1–5, pp. 13–72.

11 Jacobus de Cessolis, *Libellus de moribus*, ed. by Habor, III. 1–8, pp. 126–34.

12 The gambler atones for his sins after this miracle and becomes a monk. Cf. Jacobus de Cessolis, *Libellus de moribus*, ed. by Habor, III. 8, pp. 133–34.

13 Jacobus de Cessolis, *Libellus de moribus*, ed. by Habor, IV. 1–8, pp. 135–64.

a social model that, unlike John of Salisbury's *Policraticus*, enhances the positive function of each of society's individual member in the given system, with respect to their individual rights and duties.

The treatise became highly popular very soon after its publication. It was frequently copied, abridged, expanded, commented on, and translated. At least five German versions survived. The most prominent example is the *Schachzabelbuch* written in 1337 by the Benedictine monk Conrad of Ammenhausen who expanded on Jacobus's treatise considerably in his rhymed tract.[14] Of course, there had been moralizing books on games before Jacobus, but none of them had such an impact on European literatures. By the mid fourteenth century, Jacobus's *Book of Chess* represented the most important template for moralizing narratives. Ingold of Basel drew on this well-known material.

The 'Golden Game' – Tradition Meets Creativity

In his *Puechlein vom Guldin Spil*, Ingold develops a highly original classification of games and their place in the struggle between virtues and vices. He describes the origins, natures, and risks, of seven different types of games as well as the prospects of success when playing them. He starts with chess, which is then followed by board games played with flat pieces (*tabulae*), dice games, card games, shooting (including all kinds of ball games and other games characterized by the need to hit a mark), dancing (along with running, swimming, fighting and horseback riding), and harp playing.[15] By playing these games in the right way, the players may transform them into 'golden' games to be set against the seven deadly sins. Chess can be played against pride, board games against gluttony, cards against lust, throwing dice against avarice, shooting against wrath, dancing against sloth, and harp playing against envy and hatred.[16]

As already indicated, the game of chess attracted Ingold's sustained attention. He names his source, the *Book of Chess* by Jacobus de Cessolis.[17] However, following the approach of the German mysticism flourishing in his time in the

---

14 *Das Schachzabelbuch des Jacobus de Cessolis*, ed. by Schmidt. On the book, see Kliewer, *Die mittelalterliche Schachallegorie und die deutschen Schachzabelbücher*. On Jacobus's reception, see Plessow, *Mittelalterliche Schachzabelbücher*, pp. 46–95 and Adams, *Power Play*, pp. 15–56 and 173 (note 12).

15 *Das Goldene Spiel von Meister Ingold*, ed. by Schröder, p. 3.

16 *Das Goldene Spiel von Meister Ingold*, ed. by Schröder, p. 1.

17 *Das Goldene Spiel von Meister Ingold*, ed. by Schröder, p. 1: 'das ein prediger was der hieß pruoder Jacob Tessali, der hat dar über geschriben, dar auss ich vil han genomen, auch han ich vil genomen auß der gescbrift und vil auß meinem aygen sinn und auch von sagen'. ('that there was a preacher named Brother Jacob Tessali, who wrote on this [chess game]. I took a lot from this [treatise], from the Holy Scripture, from my own eyes, and from hearsay').

Upper Rhine region, Ingold re-interpreted Jacobus' exposition into a theologically sophisticated account of salvation.

Ingold created a twofold interpretative scheme for the chessboard, which referred on the one hand to the joyful *Ecclesia triumphans*, the Church triumphant in Heaven, ruled by Christ, and on the other hand, to the *Ecclesia militans* fighting on Earth. Ingold depicts the *Ecclesia triumphans* as a heavenly playground, with Christ as the best player ever – a king ruling the whole world. The queen on this playground is Mary, his mother and ruler over all the angels and heavenly armies.[18] The characterisation of Mary as Chess Queen, and of Christ as Chess King, may not have been unusual, but as already pointed out, Ingold's detailed depiction of heavenly society (including the Holy Spirit) as a chess game represented a completely new approach.[19] Ingold notes that this almighty Queen will never lose a game nor will she ever leave her King. The bishops on the chessboard embody the patriarchs and the holy angels who brought their wisdom to human beings. The knights signify the holy martyrs, 'those of the blood', as well as those known as 'White Martyrs' which may refer to deceased Dominicans.[20] The rooks stand for the apostles and all the poor people who have not found justice on earth. They will judge the twelve Tribes of Israel in the Last Judgement.[21] In keeping with Christ's role as supreme player, the pawns defined by Jacobus as eight commoners are now transformed into the King's courtly officials. Ingold's pawns, then, are first the king's gatekeeper and then his physician (as well as the huntsman, cook, fisherman, and apothecary). The third piece stands for the chancellor (including his scribes), the fourth for the king's confessor, the fifth for the chaplain (and the almsgiver), the sixth signifies the King's standard bearer, the seventh the cupbearer (and the cellarer), and the eighth represents the court marshal (as well as the 'seneschal' and the coachman/charioteer).

---

18 The motif of Mary as Queen of Heaven and her Son's spouse (as well as His mother) was fundamental to medieval mysticism. As Anne J. Duggan has argued, 'the duality of her position in relation to Christ thus made her an ideal model for queens, as wives and mothers of kings'; Duggan, 'Introduction', p. xvii.

19 On Mary as Chess queen, for instance in Gautier de Coinci's *Les Miracles de Nostre Dame*, see Taylor, 'God's Queen', pp. 403–19.

20 On Cyprian's effective distinction between red martyrs of the blood and white martyrs of spiritual labour, see, for instance, Kinnard, '"Imitatio Christi" in Christian Martyrdom and Asceticism', pp. 131–45.

21 *Das Goldene Spiel von Meister Ingold*, ed. by Schröder, pp. 37–40.

The Pawns (according to Jacobus de Cessolis)	The Pawns (according to Ingold of Basel)
1 farmer 2 smith 3 clothier and scribe 4 merchant 5 physician 6 innkeeper 7 city guard 8 gambler and courier	1 the King's gate keeper 2 the King's physician (huntsman, cook) 3 the King's chancellor and scribes 4 the King's confessor 5 chaplain and eleemosynary 6 the King's standard bearer 7 the King's cupbearer and cellarer 8 the King's court marshal, charioteer, and courier

Furthermore, Ingold argued that these eight figures represent eight Gifts, namely, the seven Gifts of Holy Spirit, plus the Gift of prayer.

The Gifts of the Holy Spirit	
Porter	He stands for the gift of divine fear (*goetliche vorcht*) since nobody shall pass through the gate without his permission. Fear is the beginning of all wisdom. There are six different kinds of fear.[22]
Physician, cook, and baker	He stands for the gift of divine charity (*goetliche miltikayt*). The *manna* of the Lord shall be relished by many people. No physician shall treat sick persons who have not confessed their sins before getting spiritual medicine (*sel ertzney*). All officers shall prove their clemency as the King had to do.[23]
Chancellor	He stands for the gift of how to live an upright life among bad people (*poessen unstrauffperlichen*): by means of scripture and seals, the chancellor shall take care of the royal properties enabling both he himself and the king to live in a law-abiding manner.[24]
Confessor	He stands for the gift of divine counsel (*goetlicher rat*). The confessor shall accompany his King in war. He is like a broom that sweeps even the smallest amount of dust away from human souls.[25]

22 *Das Goldene Spiel von Meister Ingold*, ed. by Schröder, pp. 37–38.
23 *Das Goldene Spiel von Meister Ingold*, ed. by Schröder, p. 39.
24 *Das Goldene Spiel von Meister Ingold*, ed. by Schröder, p. 39.
25 *Das Goldene Spiel von Meister Ingold*, ed. by Schröder, p. 40.

Chaplain	He stands for the gift of divine understanding (*goetliche verständlichhayt*) by which Holy Scripture is comprehended. The chaplain must understand what he is praying, singing and reading.[26]
Captain and 'standard bearer'	He stands for the gift of strength (*sterk*). The standard bearer shall only take office if the king himself does not go off to war, because one nation shall not have two heads.[27]
Cupbearer	He stands for the gift of the foretaste of divine wisdom (*fürschmeckende weißhayt gotz*).[28] Here, Ingold integrates the well-known history of Noah as the inventor of wine, and its animal effect on human beings.[29]
Court Marshal and courier	He stands for the gift of devotional prayer (*andächtigs gebet*). The messenger carries the divine coat of arms that is God's love (*goetlichü minn und lieb*).[30]

These eight 'spiritual servants' (*geistlich dienstlüt*), fulfilling the tasks given them by the Holy Spirit, move in the same way as pawns on the chess board and should therefore always go forward towards God, never backwards.[31]

In fact, the description of the heavenly court as a 'playing community' was not completely new. It features most prominently in the *Dieta salutis*, a work which was probably known to Ingold. For a long time, the *Dieta* was attributed to Bonaventure, but was actually composed by his Franciscan confrère William of Lavicea.[32] This moralizing, mystical text was written shortly before 1300 in France and was frequently copied in the course of the fourteenth century, and again towards the end of the fifteenth century. In 1492, Jean Perrin translated it into French. From then until the eighteenth century, the *Dieta* was reprinted many times.[33] Manuscripts of this work often also contain the *Themata dominicalia*, an index of topics suitable for preaching.[34]

However, within the *Dieta*, the heavenly church 'at play' only appears in connection with dancing. As is typical of religious texts of this sort, both negative

---

26 *Das Goldene Spiel von Meister Ingold*, ed. by Schröder, p. 40.

27 *Das Goldene Spiel von Meister Ingold*, ed. by Schröder, pp. 39–40.

28 *Das Goldene Spiel von Meister Ingold*, ed. by Schröder, p. 40.

29 *Das Goldene Spiel von Meister Ingold*, ed. by Schröder, pp. 40–41.

30 *Das Goldene Spiel von Meister Ingold*, ed. by Schröder, p. 41.

31 *Das Goldene Spiel von Meister Ingold*, ed. by Schröder, p. 41.

32 Guyot, La 'Dieta salutis et Jean Rigaud', pp. 360–93.

33 Cf. Haureau, 'Guillaume de Lavicea', pp. 552–55 and Guyot, 'La Dieta salutis et Jean Rigaud', pp. 360–93.

34 See, for instance, Ansbach, Staatliche Bibliothek, MS lat. 13, fols 1r–9r (around 1350) and Jena, Thüringer Universitäts- und Landesbibliothek, MS Bud. f. 367, fols 52v–56v (around 1475).

and positive evaluations of play may be encountered, depending on the context. For example, at the beginning of the chapter concerning the mortal sins, William refers to the playing of games, specifically dice, as one of the heinous sins.[35] However, in the conclusion he talks about the 'three-jump-dance' (*tripudium*) and 'round dancing' (*chorea, ballata*) in the most playful community (*jucundissima societate*) of the heavenly city of Jerusalem. This community and its dancing games become the goal of each good Christian, for there the dancers are Christ (as King) and Mary (as Queen), joined by patriarchs and prophets, apostles, martyrs, popes and Church Fathers, monks and hermits, chaste virgins and faithful married folk, and all the saints. In this arrangement, five privileges of the blessed are discussed, namely predestination, forgiveness of sins, contemplation in devotion, true conversion of the mind, and the performance of good works.[36] Palm branches in the dancers' hands symbolize the fruits of their good works.[37] Christ dances in front of the choir as the *chorealis ductor*. William assigns specific antiphons to Him and His fellow dancers. Christ, as *monarcha praecipuus*, calls to each group and receives a response. Both parts of the antiphons comprise of biblical citations. From time to time William gives an interpretation of them which he frames as coming from the mouth of Christ Himself. The following table contains an overview of the additional texts which accompany the songs:[38]

The dance of the heavenly court in the Dieta Salutis

Dancers	Function within the heavenly society	Call of Christ	Response of the Singers
Mary	Queen of all virgins and sweetest player of the tympanum	John 2. 4. Interpretation: Christ announces that He possesses divinity and humanity, while Mary possesses virginity and fertility.	Luke 1. 45–46. Interpretation: not known.
Angels	Squires (domicelli) of the noblest King	Psalm 102. 20. Interpretation: Angels are Christ's messengers, who follow His commands, and work great wonders.	Apocalypse 7. 12. Interpretation: Christ possesses benediction in His incarnation, enlightenment by His birth,

---

35 William of Lancea, *Dieta salutis*, ed. by Peltier, I. 2, p. 251.

36 William of Lancea, *Dieta salutis*, ed. by Peltier, X. 6, p. 342.

37 William of Lancea, *Dieta salutis*, ed. by Peltier, X. 6, p. 343 (William refers to Song of Solomon 7. 8).

38 This table expands the list offered by Martin Leutzsch ('Christus als Tänzer', p. 149).

Dancers	Function within the heavenly society	Call of Christ	Response of the Singers
			wisdom in His preaching, grace in being the elected one, in His Passion and death; He possesses glory in His resurrection; virtue in His ascension and strength in fulfilling the Last Judgement.
Patriarchs and Prophets	Counsellors of the King. Christ reveals His secrets to them. (collaterales et regis consiliarii, quibus tanquam senioribus expertis revelat ministerium consistorii sui)	Exodus 3. 13 and 15; Exodus 19. 4 and 6. Interpretation: Christ is by seed the chosen one; Egypt is the world of lust; the Red Sea means sin and hell; the promised land is for the ever-living; the eagles' wings are the feathers of angelic contemplation. William mentions some individual prophets and patriarchs.	Apocalypse 5. 8–10. Interpretation: As pointed out in the Credo, Christ deserves to open the seven seals of His Father's book.
Apostles	Seneschals of the King (regis senescali), who possess the plenitude of potency (plenitudo potestatis)	Luke 22. 28–30. Interpretation: Apostles are friends of Christ, their fellow, and source of love. Christ makes them into almighty kings in heaven, participants at the heavenly table where humanity is like food and divinity like drink. The Apostles are actors in the Last Judgement.	John 6. 69–70 (sung by Peter). Interpretation: Christ is anointed by divine consecration; equal to God Father in power, eternity, and majesty.
Martyrs	The most strenuous knights of the King, (strenuissimi Regis milites), who defeat the three kingdoms (of the world, of the flesh and of the devil)	Matthew 5. 10. Interpretation: The burden of martyrdom is heavy. Martyrs do not die because of their sins, but because of justice. The fruits of martyrdom are huge. The realm of heaven is theirs.	II Timothy 2. 11. Interpretation: Labour is one way of enacting the Passion.

Dancers	Function within the heavenly society	Call of Christ	Response of the Singers
Popes, confessors, and Church Fathers (pontifices, confessores,[39] doctores)	Popes as celebrants of the mass; Church fathers as preachers and writers	I Peter 2. 9 (just to the popes). Interpretation: There is a predestined people, a royal priesthood taking care of the laity, holy by tvirtue of perfection, who are very attractive to the people due to their exemplary life and pastoral prudence.	Psalm 65. 12 (sung by popes and Church Fathers). Interpretation: Fire means strength against all enemies, water signifies humility for the blessed, the refrigerium felicitatis stands for misery.
		Matthew 5. 13 (just to the Church Fathers). Interpretation: The Catholic interpretation of the Bible is the spice of holy speech. Food without salt is like biblical words without interpretation. As salt conserves meat against worms, interpretation conserves the flesh against sins.	Jesus answers the chorus, this time with Matthew 11. 28.
Monks and Hermits (monachi et anachoretae)	Praying and psalm-singing folk	Matthew 5. 14 (to all monks, hermits, and confessors): Interpretation: Confessors are the light of the world. As the sun is eight times bigger than the earth so the virtue and grace of such men is eight times higher than others.	
Virgins, chaste widows, faithful married folk	Not known	Wisdom of Solomon 4. 1. Interpretation: Childlessness stands for virginal shamefacedness, chastity of widows and the moderate sexual life of married people. Virgins possess the virtue of integrity	Song of Solomon 1. 1. Interpretation: William points to Proverbs 8. 21, Apocalypse 14. 3, and Matthew 13. 23; these passages are followed by a detailed interpretation of the number of '40'.

---

39 In William's later argumentation, the confessors appear in the next group along with the monks and anchorites. His structure is not clear at this point.

Dancers	Function within the heavenly society	Call of Christ	Response of the Singers
		, widows the virtue of internal devotion; married people possess blessed descendants. All these three groups have excellent reputations.	
All saints	Not known	Matthew 25. 34 and Romans 8. 17. Interpretation: They all are predestined, elected sons and brothers of Christ in eternity.	I Timothy 1. 17. Interpretation: Christ sacrificed himself for all human beings. He is at the same time visible and invisible, almighty, but human.

Each of the participants in this 'truly blessed [...] dance' (*vere beate* [...] *chorea*) wears, like Christ and Mary, white clothes[40] and endeavours, in a specific reference to Matthew 25. 32–33, to dance always on the right side of Christ, and never on the left.[41] The whole group of dancers then concludes this 'inexpressibly great gathering', this 'eternal circle', with 'unimaginably sweet songs': *Sanctus, Sanctus, Sanctus* (Isaiah 6. 3).[42]

The *Dieta* further develops a lengthy exposition of the eternal cosmic spheres, derived from Aristotelian astronomy and the theology of the Church Fathers. Just as Dante would later do in his *Divine Comedy*, the *Dieta* mentions historical persons dancing for joy. An Old-French anonymous prose work that pre-dated the *Dieta*, namely *La Court de Paradis*, formulates a similar concept: describing the Eucharist in heaven as a festival of the singing church.[43] We can already find specific groupings in *La Court de Paradis* (similar to the later *Dieta*), which comprise for example angels (archangels, seraphim, and cherubim), patriarchs (led by Jacob, Moses, and Abraham), apostles (Peter, Thomas, Phillip, and Andrew), martyrs and confessors (among the latter, for example, Sylvester and Nicholas), virgins (Catherine, Agnes, Cecilia, Margaret, and others), and different male and female saints (such as Ambrose, Augustine, Martin, Jerome, Benedict, Francis, Dominic, Bernard).

Ingold's idea of a dancing heavenly family was not so elaborate. He concentrated more on the link between such a playful but solemn pastime in Heaven, and the pastime on Earth. It is for this reason that he relates the chess figures to the earthly *Ecclesia militans* as the other part of the fundamental game of salva-

---

40 Referring to Songs of Solomon 5. 10, see Guilelmus de Lancea, *Dieta salutis*, ed. by Peltier, x. 6, p. 343.

41 William of Lancea, *Dieta salutis*, ed. by Peltier, x. 6, p. 343.

42 William of Lancea, *Dieta salutis*, ed. by Peltier, x. 6, p. 342.

43 *La Court de Paradis*, ed. by Vilamo-Pentti, vv. 24–26, p. 81.

tion. Here, Ingold addresses a variety of socio-political issues, just as Jacobus de Cessolis had done. Ingold, in fact, refers very often to Jacobus's book. borrowing phrases, exempla, and parables from it. He repeats Jacobus' narration regarding the invention of chess, Daniel's vision of the four empires, the exposition on the three ways of becoming a king (by birth, by election, and by usurpation), and the interpretation of Eve as the first Christian queen. In accord with Jacobus he discusses the nine Worthies, as well as the movements of the individual chess pieces on the chessboard: The truthfulness and steadiness that is expected of the elders (bishops), is expressed in their movement along squares of the same colour on the chessboard.[44]

The two *Ecclesiae* refer symbolically to each other. Ingold embellishes the exegetical interpretation with advice to his readers that they should imitate those heavenly and earthly models. Undoubtedly, interlinking heavenly and earthly congregations was popular among the preachers, especially within the religious order to which Ingold belonged. However the motif may have first been used when religious authors were writing about music and the orbital movements of the planets.[45] The author of *Dieta* developed it further. Adding the context of the game of chess, as well as of other games, Ingold certainly broke new ground, as evidenced by his discussion of dancing and shooting games.

Ingold argues here that Christ would have been the best dancer and the best archer of all time, in the same way as He would have been the best chess player. Jesus danced twelve dances according to Ingold:
1. in Mary's womb, when she went to Jerusalem and entered the house of Zacharias and Elizabeth;
2. in Mary's womb, when she went to Nazareth in fear of the Jews;
3. in Mary's womb, when she went from Nazareth to Bethlehem;
4. as he went from Bethlehem to Jerusalem in order to sacrifice in the Temple;
5. during the flight to Egypt;
6. as Jesus returned and preached in the temple at the age of twelve;
7. as he drove the money changers out of the Temple;
8. as he went into the temple on Palm Sunday;
9. as he went into the temple again preaching justice;
10. as he went into the Garden of Gethsemane to pray;
11. as he met his enemies in the Garden;
12. as he walked beneath the weight of the cross up to the hill of Golgotha to die.[46]

---

44 *La Court de Paradis*, ed. by Vilamo-Pentti, p. 2, pp. 5–7, p. 15, and p. 46.

45 The Benedictine Abbot Rupert of Deutz speaks on the overarching cosmic Music of the Spheres. See Rupert of Deutz, *Liber de divinis officiis*, ed. by Haacke, xi. 8, p. 378. On the motif of the music-making God, see Linden, 'Der inwendig singende Geist auf dem Weg zu Gott', p. 377. On the Music of the Spheres, see Miller, *Measures of Wisdom*, pp. 484–521; Hammerstein, *Musik der Engel*, passim, and Rohmann, *Tanzwut*, pp. 109–12.

46 *Das Goldene Spiel von Meister Ingold*, ed. by Schröder, p. 74.

Ingold wrote that whenever men, including monks, are dancing, walking or sitting, they should imitate Him in their minds. The dancer's soul is then invited to participate in a spiritual dance with her bridegroom, Christ.

Dancing is embedded here into a meditation on the life and Passion of Jesus. Ingold deployed similar techniques concerning the *Schiessenspiel*, the game of shooting. After describing the dangers of 'bad' shooting, he then went on to explain how to shoot correctly. This was done, again, in a spiritual way. The character of Clemency (*sanftmut*) loves all human beings. In the shooting game, she punishes them harshly for their sins, but treats the innermost part of their souls with care. An apocalyptic knight (Apocalypse 6. 1–2) astride a white horse and holding a bow signifies Christ, the best shooter of all time. The white horse represents His innocent human nature, while the four horseshoes signify the four elements (fire, air, water, and earth) in His humanity. The saddle symbolises the soul of Jesus. The reins stand for the three unifications *in Christ*: (1) the unification of the divinity with the body of Christ, (2) the unification of the divinity with the soul of Christ (both eternal unifications), and (3) the unification of soul and human body in Christ. With the death of Jesus on the cross, the third of these bonds of unity is torn apart. The knight's bow itself symbolizes the power of God the Father. Christ plays this shooting game every day hitting only his selected people, in reference to Psalm 126. 4: 'Blessed were those, whose hearts were touched by the arrow of God'.[47] Ingold also adds that God not only hits the hearts of adults and children, but also their souls and consciences. He then goes on to argue that all good Christians, being shaped by their devotion, should address their prayers to God in the same way. The *Pater Noster* should be addressed to God alone, since it comes from Him alone. Prayers simply learnt by heart will fail. It is important to love God while stretching the bow, just as He also loved all of His people.[48]

Ingold's mystical imitations obviously do not function via one-to-one copying or physical congruence, but rather within the mind, through an interpretation of diverse role models from the past. The goal of the imitated pattern and the imitating act, then, was seen as being congruent with – while without necessarily being – a physical performance. This technique, of course, is (at least) as old as the four senses of the Holy Scripture and one basic model of monastic rituals. A case in point are the liturgical hours: with their chants, the monks symbolically played on King David's harp; by attributing the different hours to stations of Christ's Passion they brought the ancient event to life once more. The monks imitated David and, above all, Christ by doing something different from what they had previously done.[49]

---

47 Ingold makes no distinction between Jesus and Christ.

48 *Das Goldene Spiel von Meister Ingold*, ed. by Schröder, pp. 77–78.

49 I discuss this phenomenon using the examples of Honorius of Autun and others in Sonntag, 'Tempus fugit', pp. 226–27 and 'The Horror of Flawlessness', pp. 113–15.

Ingold offers several such techniques, including some for board and card games and for dice. Christ, the most famous gambler and harp player, mastered all these games. Again, Ingold's primary goal was mental imitation, which could be achieved through actual playing or from the idea that one was playing. The player, then, always had to imitate Jesus and other models of perfection. As Ingold argued, the one who imitated Christ by playing such a spiritual game with him would experience God and enter the Kingdom of Heaven.[50]

Ingold justified his mystical concept by pointing to the well-known discussion on *eutropolia*, serious cheerfulness, as presented by Aristotle, which had been disseminated by another Dominican, Thomas Aquinas. The message was clear: games (concrete and spiritual games) which helped in acquiring virtues were not only good games but also necessary in order to withstand the rigours of human life. Thomas even argued that God's creation of the world was a game for him. Every man should play in order to imitate Christ, and thus find their way to Him. Consequently, he focused on almost every form of the game (*ludus*) and its outcomes, and evaluated and addressed how they related to the different strata of society.[51]

In fact, gaming and playing as objects of reflection were explicitly developed into a significant and self-contained topic in the fourteenth- and fifteenth-century Dominican milieu. Many morality books referred to Thomas Aquinas. Ingold, however, referred to the work of Thomas and of the others who had written on this subject. He took up Johannes of Rheinfelden's *Ludus cartularum moralisatus* from 1377, which for the first time used the card game in order to teach people proper conduct.[52] Ingold also included *Die vierundzwanzig goldenen Harfen* (*The Twenty-Four Golden Harps*) written by Johannes Nider, and some works by Johannes Herolt.[53] Ingold's *Puechlein vom Guldin Spil* was thus part of a complex Dominican tradition and of an interpretative textual network dealing with games. In fact, such an increasing spiritualization of the game and of its playing had become since the thirteenth century a distinctive part of the typical *dingallegorische Erbauungsliteratur* of the later Middle Ages.[54] The popularity of the chess game and its social comprehensiveness, best suited to explaining cultural contexts and mechanisms, formed

---

50 *Das Goldene Spiel von Meister Ingold*, ed. by Schröder, pp. 72–73.

51 On this point see Breitenstein and Sonntag, 'Das Gewissen und das Spiel', pp. 120–28.

52 On this treatise, see Jönsson, 'Der "Ludus cartularum moralisatus"', pp. 135–47 and 'Card-Playing as a Mirror of Society', pp. 359–73.

53 Johannes Nider, *Die vierundzwanzig goldenen Harfen*, ed. by Abel. In particular, Ingold may have employed Johannes Herolt's treatises *Discipulus de eruditione christifidelium*, *De chorea*, as well as some drafts on dancing and playing dice. See the introduction in *Das Goldene Spiel von Meister Ingold*, p. xxvi.

54 See Schmidtke, *Studien zur dingallegorischen Erbauungsliteratur des Spätmittelalters*, and Schouwink, 'Strip Dice Medieval Style', p. 299.

the cornerstone of Ingold's elaborate mystical concept interconnecting heaven and earth, for the first time, by means of seven games, and – with this – all games. According to this goal and in light of its spiritual imitation techniques, Ingold innovatively took well-established modes of symbolization, in particular those taken from Jacobus de Cessolis and the *Dieta* (concerning chess and dancing) and expanded them to encompass other games and their players.

Conclusion

Ingold's *Puechlein vom Guldin Spil* was arguably produced both as a devotional book for the lower nobility and bourgeois, and as a compendium for preachers. The Dominican used different sources, taken from a reservoir of older materials. For some part of the most prominent one, the *Book of Chess* by Jacobus de Cessolis, he remained true to the original; but other parts (such as the eight pawns) were transformed in their validity and significance. His old material now constituted the fundamental anchor for a mystical concept that, for the first time, integrated all other games into the heavenly cosmos of an *Ecclesia ludens*. In assigning the well-established religious techniques of spiritual imitation to the games, Ingold at the same time placed his treatise at the heart of the contemporary devotional literature which was being shaped by German mysticism, explicitly from the Upper Rhine region. Here, the loving soul (*minnende Seele*) represented the core motif linking all these mystical texts.[55] True love was first and foremost achieved through play – not only through the well-known metaphor of sexual interplay, but concretely through the game of dice or the board game. Unlike Jacobus de Cessolis, however, Ingold's aim was to open a direct gateway to God's transcendence, indeed to find God in one's own heart by both imitating Him during play and by playing with Him. While the Franciscan *Dieta salutis* and other such works had already described the heavenly playground, none of them had addressed this dimension of imitation with such intensity. The religious life was undoubtedly a 'laboratory of innovation' for different techniques of imitation. It is interesting therefore that these techniques also found their way into other areas of medieval life: they were preached, like Ingold's *Puechlein vom Guldin Spil*.

In fact, a fundamental Christianization of play appeared in medieval religious life, not only through new games, but also through a decisive interpretative turn in the conceptualization of the game in general.[56] The Game-discourse was aligned with monastic conditions and needs, games were transformed and purified, were endowed with their own origin-myths, and due to this new, Christian

---

[55] See, for instance, Egerding, Die Metaphorik der spätmittelalterlichen Mystik and Gebauer, Christus und die minnende Seele.

[56] Sonntag, 'Erfinder, Vermittler und Interpreten', pp. 241–74.

interpretation, were made spiritually meaningful. Indeed, it was that new Christian meaning which – by the strong emphasis on the individual conscience and the intention to play – paved the way for the spiritualization of the game in the later Middle Ages. Because religious women and men practised the so-called *via perfectionis* by using different techniques of imitation, they themselves became prominent models to imitate, as well as their use and interpretation of games. In many ways, the *Puechlein vom Guldin Spil* is an expression of this complex cultural phenomenon.

Ingold elevated the games from immanence to a higher spiritual level. In turn, he innovatively transferred well-known ways of mystic communication into the concrete level of immanence. In two respects, then, he brought a new perspective to old material. He translated it not in linguistic terms, but – much more importantly – in the cultural sense, and this was undoubtedly a tremendous 'performance'.

Bibliography

Manuscript Sources

Ansbach, Staatliche Bibliothek, MS lat. 13
Jena, Thüringer Universitäts- und Landesbibliothek, MS Bud. f. 367

Primary Sources

Das Goldene Spiel von Meister Ingold, ed. by Edward Schröder, Elsässische Litteraturdenkmäler aus dem XIV. bis XVII. Jahrhundert, 3 (Strasbourg: Trübner, 1882)

Das Schachzabelbuch des Jacobus de Cessolis, O. P. in mittelhochdeutscher Prosaübersetzung, ed. by Gerard F. Schmidt, Texte des späten Mittelalters, 13 (Berlin: Schmidt, 1961)

Guilelmus de Lancea, *Dieta salutis*, in *Bonaventurae Opera omnia*, ed. by Adolphe C. Peltier, 15 vols (Paris: Vivès, 1864–71), VIII (1866), pp. 247–358

Jacobus de Cessolis, *Libellus de moribus hominum et officiis nobilium ac populorum super ludo scachorum*, ed. by Ann Harbor (microfilm of the University of Austin, MI, 1983)

La Court de Paradis: Poème anonyme du XIIIe siècle, ed. by Eva Vilamo-Pentti, Suomalaisen Tiedeakatemian Toimituksia, Ser. B, 79/1 (Helsinki: Suomalainen Tiedeakatemia, 1953)

Rupert of Deutz, *Liber de divinis officiis*, ed. by Hrabanus Haacke, Corpus Christianorum: Continuatio Mediaevalis, 7 (Turnhout: Brepols, 1967)

Secondary Works

Adams, Jenny, *Power Play: The Literature and Politics of Chess in the Late Middle Ages*, The Middle Ages Series (Philadelphia, PA: University of Pennsylvania Press, 2006)

Breitenstein, Mirko and Jörg Sonntag, 'Das Gewissen und das Spiel: Zwei Innovationsfelder des Mittelalters', in *Denkströme: Journal der Sächsischen Akademie der Wissenschaften*, 17 (2017), pp. 96–133

Buland, Rainer and Ulrich Schädler, 'Einleitung zur Buchreihe Ludographie', in *Alfons X. 'der Weise': Das Buch der Spiele*, ed. by Ulrich Schädler and Ricardo Calvo, Ludographie, 1 (Berlin: LIT, 2009), pp. 7–10

Caflisch, Sophie, *Spielend lernen: Spiel und Spielen in der mittelalterlichen Bildung*, Vorträge und Forschungen, 58 (Ostfildern: Thorbecke, 2018)

Caillois, Roger, *Les jeux et les hommes: Le masque et le vertige* (Paris: Gallimard, 1967)

Duggan, Anne J., 'Introduction', in *Queens and Queenship in Medieval Europe: Proceedings of a Conference Held at King's College London, April 1995*, ed. by Anne J. Duggan (Bury St Edmunds: St Edmundsbury Press, 2002), pp. xv–xxii

Egerding, Michael, *Die Metaphorik der spätmittelalterlichen Mystik* (Paderborn: Schöningh, 1997)

Endrei, Walter, *Spiele und Unterhaltung im Alten Europa* (Hanau: Dausien, 1988)

Flitner, Andreas, 'Johan Huizingas Homo ludens', in *Homo Ludens: Der spielende Mensch*, ed. by Günther G. Bauer, Homo Ludens: Internationale Beiträge des Instituts für Spielforschung und Spielpädagogik, 1 (Munich: Katzbichler, 1991), pp. 19–23

Gebauer, Amy, *Christus und die minnende Seele: An Analysis of Circulation, Text, and Iconography*, Imagines Medii Aevi, 26 (Wiesbaden: Reichert, 2010)

Guyot, Bertrand-Georges, 'La Dieta salutis et Jean Rigaud', *Archivum franciscanum historicum*, 82 (1989), pp. 360–93

Hammerstein, Reinhold, *Die Musik der Engel: Untersuchungen zur Musikanschauung des Mittelalters*, 2nd edn (Bern: Francke, 1990)

Haureau, Barthélemy, 'Guillaume de Lavicea, Frère mineur', *Histoire Littéraire de la France*, 26 (1873), pp. 552–55

Huizinga, Johan, *Homo ludens: Versuch einer Bestimmung eines Spielelementes der Kultur* (Amsterdam: Pantheon, 1939)

Jönsson, Arne, 'Card-Playing as a Mirror of Society', in *Chess and Allegory in the Middle Ages* ed. by Olle Ferm and Volker Honemann, Runica et Mediaevalia (Södertälje: Sällskapet, 2005), pp. 359–73

——, 'Der "Ludus cartularum moralisatus" des Johannes von Rheinfelden', in *Schweizer Spielkarten, I: Die Anfänge im 15. und 16. Jahrhundert*, ed. by Detlef Hoffmann (Schaffhausen: Sturzenegger-Stiftung, 1998), pp. 135–47

Kinnard, Isabelle, '"Imitatio Christi" in Christian Martyrdom and Asceticism: A Critical Dialogue', in *Asceticism and its Critics: Historical Accounts and Comparative Perspectives*, ed. by Oliver Freiberger, Cultural Criticism Series, 1 (Oxford: Oxford University Press, 2006), pp. 131–52

Kliewer, Heinz-Jürgen, *Die mittelalterliche Schachallegorie und die deutschen Schachzabelbücher in der Nachfolge des Jacobus de Cessolis* (Giessen: Chemoprint, 1966)

Kramer, Karl-Sigismund, *Bauern, Handwerker und Bürger im Schachzabelbuch: Mittelalterliche Ständegliederung nach Jacobus de Cessolis*, Forschungshefte des Bayerischen Nationalmuseums München, 14 (Munich: Deutscher Kunstverlag, 1999)

Leutzsch, Martin, 'Der tanzende Christus', in *Tanz und Religion: Theologische Perspektiven*, ed. by Marion Keuchen and others (Frankfurt: Evangelische Verlagsanstalt, 2008), pp. 101–43

Linden, Sandra, 'Der inwendig singende Geist auf dem Weg zu Gott', in *Lyrische Narrationen – Narrative Lyrik: Gattungsinterferenzen in der mittelalterlichen Literatur*, ed. by Hartmut Bleumer and Caroline Emmelius, Trends in Medieval Philology, 16 (Berlin: De Gruyter, 2011), pp. 359–86

Mehl, Jean-Michel, *Des jeux et des hommes dans la société médiévale*, Nouvelle bibliothèque du Moyen Âge, 97 (Paris: Champion, 2010)

——,, 'Les jeux de dés et des tables et les ordres religieux', in *Religiosus Ludens: Das Spiel als kulturelles Phänomen in mittelalterlichen Klöstern und Orden*, Arbeiten zur Kirchengeschichte, 122 (Berlin and Boston: De Gruyter, 2013), pp. 171–86

Miller, James, *Measures of Wisdom: The Cosmic Dance in Classical and Christian Antiquity*, Visio: Studies in the Relations of the Art and Literature, 1 (Toronto: Toronto University Press, 1986), pp. 484–521

Plessow, Oliver, *Mittelalterliche Schachzabelbücher zwischen Spielsymbolik und Wertevermittlung: Der Schachtraktat des Jacobus de Cessolis im Kontext seiner spätmittelalterlichen Rezeption*, Symbolische Kommunikation und gesellschaftliche Wertesysteme, 12 (Münster: Rhema, 2007), pp. 46–95

Rizzi, Alessandra, *Ludus/ludere: Giocare in Italia alla fine del medio evo*, Ludica: Collana di storia del gioco, 3 (Rome: Viella, 1995)

Rohmann, Gregor, *Tanzwut: Kosmos, Kirche und Mensch in der Bedeutungsgeschichte eines mittelalterlichen Krankheitskonzepts*, Historische Semantik, 19 (Göttingen: Vandenhoeck & Ruprecht, 2013)

Schouwink, Wilfried, 'Strip Dice Medieval Style: Christ's Clothes and Other Garments in a Mystic Sermon of the Fifteenth Century', *Fifteenth Century Studies*, 20 (1993), pp. 291–307

Schmidtke, Dietrich, *Studien zur dingallegorischen Erbauungsliteratur des Spätmittelalters*, Hermaea: Germanistische Forschungen, Neue Folge, 43 (Tübingen: Niemeyer, 1982)

Sonntag, Jörg, 'Erfinder, Vermittler und Interpreten: Ordensleute und das Spiel im Gefüge der mittelalterlichen Gesellschaft', in *Religiosus Ludens: Das Spiel als kulturelles Phänomen in mittelalterlichen Klöstern und Orden*, Arbeiten zur Kirchengeschichte, 122 (Berlin: De Gruyter, 2013), pp. 241–74

——, 'A Matter of Definition? Game, Play, and Ritual in Medieval Monasteries', in *Il gioco nella società e nella cultura dell'alto medioevo, Atti della LXV Settimana di studi*, ed. by the Centro italiano di studi sull'alto medioevo (Spoleto: Centro italiano di studi sull'alto medioevo, 2018), pp. 335–56

——, 'Die Wirkmacht der Nachahmung: Tanzende Heilige und tanzende Klosterleute im hohen und späten Mittelalter', in *Tanz der Vormoderne*, ed. by Philip Knäble, Gregor Rohmann, and Julia Zimmermann, Das Mittelalter, 23/2 (Berlin: De Gruyter, 2018), pp. 258–80

——, 'Tempus fugit: La circolarità del tempo monastica nello specchio del potenziale di rappresentazione simbolica', in *Religiosità e civiltà: Le comunicazioni simboliche (secoli IX–XIII), Le Settimane internazionali della Mendola, nuova serie 2007–2011*, ed. by Elisabetta Filippini and Giancarlo Andenna (Milan: Vite et Pensiero, 2009), pp. 221–42

———,, 'The Horror of Flawlessness: Perfection as Challenge of Life in the Middle Ages' in *Experiencing the Beyond: Intercultural Approaches*, ed. by Gert Melville and Carlos Ruta, Challenges of Life, 4 (Berlin and Boston: De Gruyter Oldenbourg, 2017), pp. 107–20

Taylor, Steven M., 'God's Queen: Chess Imagery in the Poetry of Gautier de Coinci', *Fifteenth Century Studies*, 17 (1990), pp. 403–19

Jan Hus, *The Daughter*

Religious Education between Translation and Adaptation

Pavlína Rychterová

Institute for Medieval Research, Austrian
Academy of Sciences

The focus of this essay is the transformation of lay religious education in fifteenth-century Bohemia. This transformation was prompted by the concern of some of the elite Church intellectuals for the salvation of the faithful guided by morally questionable pastors and simoniac schismatic popes. This concern, at first rather unspectacular, expressing itself in moderate moral instruction for pastors and in just as moderate production of vernacular catechetic literature, was deeply serious, and led to an ecclesiological radicalization of some of the leading theologians of the University of Prague. Under the influence of John Wyclif, whose philosophical approach was influential in Prague since the 1390s, these theologians opened the dialogue on the *renovatio ecclesiae* to the lay public. The laics very soon formed a religious movement, a pressure group which participated actively in demonstrations of disobedience, street fights, and public riots. Those university theologians who became leaders of this movement, communicated with their lay followers very carefully, fully aware of their importance for the success of the reform program they formulated. And indeed the reform movement was successful: the mobilization of society led to a revolt, the revolt led to a civil war, and the war after fifteen years to a peace in a land weary with permanent fight. In the second half of the fifteenth century three confessions were well-established in Bohemia, the Catholics, the Utraquists (called after their innovation in the liturgical practice, the communion under both kinds for lay people) and the radical branch of the Utraquists, the Unity of Brethren. The coexistence of these three churches asked for very nuanced interaction with and among the lay adherents. In following sections I will discuss some aspects of this interaction, particularly those so far neglected.

The Daughter: The Transmission History

On the Understanding of the Right Way to Salvation (*O poznání cesty pravé k spasení*), traditionally called by Czech literary scholars *Dcerka* (*The Daughter*) according to the opening sentence appearing at the beginning of each of the ten chapters ('Hear, daughter'), is one of the shorter vernacular tracts by the leader of the Bohemian Church reform movement Jan Hus. It was written at the end of the year 1412 after he was exiled from Prague in May 1412 in the wake of what is known as the indulgences riots.[1] Agreeing with Wyclif, Hus saw in the correctly fulfilled office of the preacher the only remedy for the depraved church of his time.[2] Deprived of daily communication with his lay followers gathered around the Bethlehem Chapel in Prague's Old Town, the passionate preacher Hus decided to write down the core of the reform teaching in the language of his congregation, i.e., in Czech. He wrote three volumes titled *Expositions* (*Výklady*) and a collection of sermons, *Czech Sunday Postil* (*Česká nedělní postila*), in which he discussed in detail the cornerstones of Christian teaching. In these texts he drew extensively on his previous scholarly as well as exhortative work written in Latin.[3] In the same period, Hus produced shorter texts, including an exhortative tract dedicated explicitly to women, written possibly at the request of a (sophisticated and probably noble) woman preparing to take the veil.[4] The tract has been known to the modern Czech literary studies and philology from their inception.[5] They considered it to be 'the most beautiful' tract of Jan Hus and as such, it has been the focus of their aesthetic interest.[6] Historians concentrating on the analysis of Hus's theological thinking have not analysed nor contextualized this catechetic work. Only the theologian Jan Sedlák was able to identify one of the main sources of the text, the sermon on Luke 24.13 by John Wyclif.[7] The other source, Bernard of Clairvaux's *Meditationes piissimae de*

---

1 On the so-called 'indulgences' riots see Soukup, *11.7.1412*, and Šmahel, *Die Hussitische Revolution*, pp. 864–88.

2 Soukup, 'The "Puncta" of Jan Hus', pp. 91–126.

3 On Jan Hus and his vernacular work see Rychterová, 'The Vernacular Theology of Jan Hus', pp. 170–213, 'Theology Goes to the Vernaculars', pp. 231–50, as well as Perett, 'Jan Hus's Productive Exile', pp. 83–107, and 'Jan Hus and Faction Formation', pp. 45–66.

4 In his introduction Hus approaches a female addressee: 'Hear, daughter, who pledged your virginity to Him' (Mistr Jan Hus, *Drobné spisy české*, ed. by Daňhelka, p. 163: 'To slyš, dcerko, jenž si jemu panenstvie zaslíbila'). See below, pp. 212.

5 The first transcription and rudimentary edition of the text was published in 1825 by Václav Hanka, librarian in the Library of the National Museum in Prague and author of the manuscripts of Königinhof and Grünberg (containing forged medieval Czech written poems): *Dcerka M. J. H. aneb poznání cesty pravé k spasení*, ed. by Hanka.

6 See Mistr Jan Hus, *Drobné spisy české*, ed. by Daňhelka, 13. Daňhelka himself describes *The Daughter* as a singular work in formal and stylistic terms because of the anaphora at the beginning of each chapter of the text ('Hear Daughter and bend your ear') leaning on Psalm 44. 1.

7 Jan Sedlák was the most prolific expert on Hus's and Hussite theology and the author of one of two seminal monographs on Jan Hus dating from 1915: *M. Jan Hus*. Like Novotný's work, *M. Jan Hus*, it was written on the occasion of the 500th anniversary of Hus's

cognitione humanae conditionis, was identified by the philologist František Ryšánek several decades later, and reviewed by the historian Amedeo Molnár.[8] Both sources are referred to in the explanatory notes to the critical edition of the tract produced by the philologist Jiří Daňhelka and his team in 1985. The carefully prepared edition unfortunately did not lead to further analytical effort. More recently, *The Daughter* has been discussed by Thomas A. Fudge who heavily criticized the ('unsatisfactory') work of previous generations of Czech scholars and characterized the tract as 'teaching the duty of eschatological disobedience'.[9] He provides little evidence and no analysis of the text to support this speculation.[10]

The full version of *The Daughter* is extant in four manuscripts;[11] two additional manuscripts[12] contain fragmentary versions, and one manuscript is lost.[13] Prague, Knihovna Národního muzea, MS IV C 18, originated in the year 1414; it contains Hus's *Czech Sunday Postil* (fols 1^r–196^r), an anonymous exposition of the Passion of Christ (fols 196^v–200^v, fols 227^v–33^v), Hus's *On the Six Errors* (*O šesti bludiech*, fols 201^r–12^v), and *The Daughter* (fols 213^r–27^v). A colophon on fol. 196^r identifies the scribe: 'These books [i.e. the individual chapters of Hus's *Czech Sunday Postil*] were finished on the Sunday before St Catherine in the year 1414 since God's birth by the hand of Sigmund of Domažlice'.[14] The scribe used a diacritical orthography, new at that time, which Hus according to his own words (there is no autograph of Hus's Czech works extant) used to make the written Czech a more efficient medium.[15] Hus obviously propagated the new orthography among his literate adherents, among whom Sigmund of Domažlice

---

death at the stake in Constance. Sedlák wrote from the Catholic point of view, Novotný from the national and secular point of view. Together they represent the best reconstruction of Hus's life. For Wyclif's sermon, see Sedlák, 'Je Husova "Dcerka" dílo původní?', pp. 359–66.

8 Mistr Jan Hus, *Drobné spisy české*, ed. by Daňhelka, p. 433; Molnár, 'K pramenům Husovy Dcerky', pp. 224–30.

9 Fudge, *Jan Hus between Time and Eternity*, p. 7.

10 Fudge, *Jan Hus between Time and Eternity*, pp. 3–28.

11 Prague, Knihovna Národního muzea, MS IV C 18, fols 213^r–27^r; ibid., MS IV B 15, fols 280^v–97^r; ibid., MS IV E 29, fols 206^v–23^r; Brno, Moravská zemská knihovna, Mk 19, fols 155^r–69^r.

12 Prague, Knihovna Metropolitní kapituly, MS D 82, fols 424^v–32^r (fourth and fifth chapter); Prague, Knihovna Národního muzea, MS IV H 32, fols 155^r–58^v (parts of the first and second chapter).

13 Prague, Knihovna Metropolitní kapituly, MS C 32.

14 All the translations from medieval Czech into modern English are mine.

15 The new orthography using a specific grapheme for each phoneme of the Czech language was space-saving in comparison with the orthography used at that time, which recorded the unique Czech phonemes with a combination of two or more existing graphemes of the Latin alphabet. The programmatic character of Hus's appraisal of the new orthography persuaded modern historians that Hus was an inventor of the new orthog-

may be counted, aiming to increase the impact of the vernacular message among the lay, Czech-speaking population of Bohemia. The manuscript may be regarded as one of the few extant results of the efforts made by the close adherents of Hus, mostly university-educated priests belonging to the lower orders, often in precarious positions, to spread Hus's version of religious education among the laity.

Brno, Moravská zemská knihovna, Mk 19, from the second half of the fifteenth century, represents the next stage in the reception of *The Daughter*. It is an imposing, professionally made and professionally illuminated composite volume with luxurious binding, containing most popular Latin works for advanced meditation: the *Meditationes de interiori homine* of Pseudo-Bonaventure, the Pseudo-Augustinian *Speculum peccatoris* and *Soliloquia*, the *Elucidarius* of Honorius of Autun, the *Imago vitae* of Bonaventure, and the *Synonyma de lamentatione animae peccatricis* by Isidor of Seville. These texts are accompanied by Latin and Czech expositions on the necessity of the communion under both kinds for laics and excerpts from Czech translations of religious educational tracts: the *Paradisus animae* by Albert the Great, the Czech version of the *Speculum peccatoris*, two Czech works by Jan Hus, *The Nine Pieces of Gold* (*Devět kusóv zlatých*), and *The Daughter*.[16] Besides, the book contains quotations from the works of a leading Hussite theologian, Martin Lupáč, and a leading Hussite jurist, Jan of Jesenice. The volume was probably made for a moderate Utraquist (Hussite) theologian active in pastoral care. Jan Hus is called a saint and a martyr of Czech lineage, which means he is counted among Czech patrons, the martyrs Wenceslas, Ludmila, and Adalbert.[17] Czech written works recorded in

---

raphy, which is nevertheless unlikely. See on this recently *Orthographia Bohemica*, ed. by Voleková, pp. xxxv–xxxvi.

16 *The Nine Pieces of Gold* (Mistr Jan Hus, *Drobné spisy české*, ed. by Daňhelka, pp. 420–21), may be described as a very short, idiosyncratic *vade mecum* to salvation. It contains nine concisely formulated theses, in the form of commandments, in which the moderate religious practice and general high moral standards are highlighted as the true emulation of Christ in contrast to excessive penance (like self-flagellation), showy deeds of humility (like pilgrimage or participation in crusades), and especially foundations and capitations bequeathed to church institutions in exchange for (annual) prayers. The critique of church practice of subsidiary penance may be regarded as a specific reformatory trait in Hus's work, but the same critique may easily be found in vernacular religious educative texts written and read decades before Hus was born. Such a critique was very common in Bohemia, especially in the last third of the fourteenth century. See Rychterová, 'Kirchen- und Klerikalkritik im Böhmen des 14. und 15. Jahrhunderts zwischen Latein und Volkssprachen', pp. 291–308.

17 *The Daughter* is introduced in the manuscript as 'Exposition good and redemptory by Master Jan Hus of Holy Memory'; the *Nine Pieces of Gold* are introduced as follows: 'Righteous in Jesus Christ and God's martyr in God's hope and revered Saint Master Jan Hus of Czech lineage wrote these Nine Pieces of Gold which he called "gold" for their great benefit and a magnificent reward in the Heavenly Kingdom' (Brno, Moravská zemská knihovna, Mk 19, fol. 155r: 'Výklad dobrý a spasitedlný Mistra Jana Husi Svaté

the volume originated in the second half of the fourteenth century, and together with the two works by Hus they represent a very modest type of religious education in which no space is open for radical theological ideas, with the exception of the communion under both kinds for lay people. This goal was propagated by a standardized argumentation directed towards a lay audience with the help of preaching and of translations of key texts.[18]

Prague, Knihovna Národního muzea, MS IV E 29 is of a different character. It contains Czech historical works and translations of highly popular historical and apocryphal texts. The first sixty-five folios contain a translation compiled from the chronicles of Martin of Troppau and of Jakob Twinger of Königshofen, the work of a Bohemian nobleman, Beneš of Hořovice, at the end of the fourteenth century.[19] An apocryphal *Life of Adam and Eve* follows, in the so-called 'Solfernus' version[20] (fols 67^r–154^r), and a Czech translation of the *Consolatio peccatorum seu processus Luciferi contra Iesum Christum*, known also under the title *Liber Belial*, written by Jacob of Teramo (fols 154^v–93^v). Then, *The Daughter* follows (fols 206^v–23^r), accompanied by various historical and other notes and by a selective Czech translation of the Compacts of Basel. The *Old Czech Annals* close the volume. *The Daughter* represents the only religious educative text in the collection. The reasons for its selection are unknown. Similar collections, very often personal miscellanies, containing a number of notes and extracts, and displaying historical as well as legal interests, were usually made by educated priests and laics active in the administrative apparatus of the Church as well as in various secular entities.[21]

Prague, Knihovna Národního muzea, MS IV B 15, originated in the third decade of the sixteenth century and is connected with the noble Roupov family. The lords of Roupov were among the many noble Hussite war profiteers; there was a Catholic as well as an Utraquist branch of the family; members of both were active in high offices of the realm at the turn of the sixteenth century. In the manuscript a work written by one member of the Catholic branch of the family, the Carthusian monk Hynek of Roupov, is recorded, as well as several letters addressed by

---

paměti'; ibid., fol. 178^v: 'Poctivý v Kristu Ježíši a v naději boží mučedník a Svatý velebný Mistr Jan Hus z pokolenie českého těchto devět kusóv složil, kteréž jest I zlatými nazval pro jich veliké zaslúženie a odplatu hojnú v královstvie nebeském').

18 On the Utraquist standard argumentation in favour of the communion under both kinds for lay people, see Rychterová, 'Fighting for the Minds of the People', 362–65, and Marek, *Václav Koranda mladší*, pp. 58–98.

19 Dragoun, 'Rukopisy kroniky "Martimiani"', pp. 14–20.

20 *Solfernus*, ed. by Hanzová; Murdoch, *The Apocryphal Adam and Eve in Medieval Europe*.

21 On the phenomenon of composite volumes and personal miscellanies see the individual articles in *Collecting, Organizing and Transmitting Knowledge*, ed. by Corbellini, Murano, and Signore. On the Bohemian and Czech material see the articles of Rychterová, 'The Czech Lay Theologian', pp. 115–30 and Doležalová, 'Late Medieval Personal Miscellanies', pp. 179–96.

him to Lidmila of Klinštejn, a member of another family of war profiteers related to the Lords of Roupov by marriage. MS IV B 15 is a composite volume containing a collection of Czech written religious educative tracts. The intended readers were probably women (perhaps Lidmila of Klinštejn herself) from a network of noble families who were carefully balancing their loyalties between the Catholic and Utraquist factions at the royal court, and swiftly shifting the allegiance to the successive rulers – King George of Podiebrady, the Jagiellonian kings, as well as the first Habsburg ruler Ferdinand I. Beside Hus's *The Daughter* the manuscript contains Czech translations of the *Revelations* of Birgitta of Sweden and of Heinrich Suso's *Horologium sapientiae*, both made by Thomas of Štítné, a layman, translator, and writer of Czech religious literature in the last decade of the fourteenth century.[22] In addition, there is a Czech translation of the so-called *Letters of St Jerome*, originally composed in German on the basis of a Latin model by the chancellor of the Emperor Charles IV, John of Neumarkt,[23] and an anonymous exhortative tract on the Passion of Christ (*Meditations on Sixty Five Woes of Christ*). The primary (female) addressee of the volume seems to have been of the Utraquist confession; passages in Birgitta's *Revelations* concerning the (lay) communion under one kind were re-interpreted in MS IV B 15; here the communion under both kinds is mentioned instead.[24] No other changes were made in the text. Birgitta's *Revelations* as well as Heinrich Suso's *Horologium sapientiae* or the so-called *Letters of St Jerome* were all works written long before the Hussite movement began to emerge. They mediate a sort of moderately ambitious religious educative reading aiming at lay people literate in their own vernacular. *The Daughter* was regarded by the author (or authors) of the collection as a work perfectly suitable for the same purpose: moderately ambitious religious reading material for literate women of noble origin, regardless of their confessional affiliation.

Some of the works copied in MS IV B 15 also appear in Prague, Knihovna Národního muzea, MS IV H 32: the Czech translation of the *Letters of St Jerome* (*O svatém Jeronýmovi knihy troje*: 'Three Books on St Jerome'), the Czech translation of *Horologium sapientiae* by Heinrich Suso as well as *The Daughter*, both copied in excerpts. The book, decorated with modest illuminations, otherwise contains a collection of prayers, suitable for Catholics as well as Utraquists.

Prague, Knihovna Metropolitní kapituly, MS D 82 was written at the beginning of the sixteenth century in the milieu of the radical Hussite faction, called the Unity of Brethren. It contains Czech theological and religious educative texts, mostly works by the most prolific lay theologian of the Hussite reformation and founder of the Unity of Brethren, Petr Chelčický – the manuscript contains the only surviving copies of several of them. *The Daughter* (the fourth and fifth chapters were copied here) appears here again together with the *Nine Pieces of Gold* as is the case

---

22 See on him and his work Rychterová, 'Thomas of Štítné (1330–1400) and his Translation of the "De Septem Itineribus Aeternitatis" by Rudolf of Biberach', pp. 121–44.

23 Černá, 'The Letters of St Jerome of the Prague Chancellor and Notary John of Neumarkt', pp. 47–74.

24 Rychterová, 'The Revelations of St Birgitta in the Holy Roman Empire', p. 257.

in manuscript Mk 19 as well as in other extant manuscripts containing works by Petr Chelčický (Chelčický himself commented on the *Nine Pieces of Gold*).[25]

The transmission history of *The Daughter* caters to a great variety of readers – the text was interesting for ardent followers of Hus; for leading Utraquist theologians interested in concepts of moderate religious education from the pre-Hussite era; for priests relying on the religious educational tracts in their native language in preparing their sermons for their congregation; for laics, maybe urban administrators interested in historiography; for well-educated Utraquist and Catholic noble women, as well as for men (priests as well as laics) interested in the work of the most original and radical lay theologian of fifteenth-century Bohemia. The work could appeal to all these different people and as such become part of very different contexts and interpretative efforts. The community of readers as (hypothetically) revealed in the extant manuscripts was probably even broader. Jan Hus had written a work which was accessible to literally everybody with an understanding of the Czech language.[26]

Jan Hus conceived his Czech body of work as a sort of legacy for his lay followers. In writing his Czech tracts he relied heavily on his own Latin texts and on the work of John Wyclif. He wrote his Czech works as he was banned from Prague far away from the university library. The portable library he took with him contained his own treatises, the most important works by Wyclif as well as various other texts, the number of which should not be overestimated – the majority of authorities quoted by Hus in his Czech texts he took from his own Latin works, as well as from some by Wyclif.

Author and Translator

The Daughter is conceived in ten chapters (probably emulating the Ten Commandments) in which the reader may learn basic tenets of instruction in Christian ethics. First of all, the female and virgin reader, if we take the opening sentence seriously and not as a mere rhetorical ornament, has to perceive human dignity which is a godlike quality residing in Him. Second, she has to contemplate her own conscience; third, the wretchedness of this life; fourth, she has to be on guard against temptation; fifth, she should learn about three enemies of salvation; sixth, atone for her sins; seventh, consider the dignity of the soul; eight, be aware of future judgment and penalty; ninth, contemplate eternal beatitude, and finally, love God above all.[27] The reader has to 'hear with her ears' and 'see

---

25 On the manuscript and on the context of the oeuvre of Petr Chelčický see Boubín, 'Chelčického spisy v kapitulním sborníku', pp. 9–47, here pp. 9–11.

26 In contrast to the second largest work by Hus, the *Czech Sunday Postil*, *The Daughter* probably was not translated into Latin. See on this translation Odstrčilík, 'Translation and Transformation of Jan Hus's Czech Sunday Postil', pp. 153–84.

27 Mistr Jan Hus, *Drobné spisy české*, ed. by Daňhelka, p. 163: '[…] viz, žeť chci, aby poznala sě, vědúc, k komu jsi podobná stvořena. Druhé, aby poznala své svědomie. Třetie,

with reason' which will both lead to understanding.[28] This understanding will secure the acquirement of knowledge and allow to achieve the heavenly reward from Jesus Christ, who was born from a pure virgin and raised the virginal state over all other states: 'This you have to hear, daughter, who pledged your virginity to Him'.[29] This passage seems clearly to indicate that Hus conceived the tract for a nun or nuns or for a beguine and/or a community of beguines. In the first chapter self-awareness is praised because self-knowledge will make the knowledge of God possible, whereas only the knowledge of God makes loving him possible. The idea of self-awareness as defined and further developed in this way is taken from the first chapter of Pseudo-Bernard's *Meditationes*: human memory, reason, and will correspond to God the Father, the Son and the Holy Spirit.[30] Hus directly translated about ten per cent of the text of the first chapter but he basically followed Pseudo-Bernard's argumentation without its terminological interests and detailed clarity. Thus, for example, the reasoning on the character of memory, reason, and will is omitted in Hus's translation although it elucidates further the terms crucial in the first chapter of Hus's exposition:

> Memoriae attribuimus omne quod scimus, etiamsi non inde cogitemus. Intelligentiae tribuimus omne, quod verum cogitando invenimus, quod etiam memoriae commendamus: voluntati, omne quod cognitum et intellectum, bonum et verum esse expetimus.[31]
>
> (We attribute to our memory everything that we know, even if we don't think about it. We attribute to intelligence everything that we find true by thinking, which we also recommend to the memory. To the will, all we desire is that which is known and understood, good and true.)

Pseudo-Bernard's *Meditationes* are subdivided into fourteen chapters which together represent theological analysis and meditation in process, something

---

aby poznala nynějšieho života biedu. Čtvrté, aby poznala zdejšieho přiebytka pokušenie. Páté, aby poznala tři nepřietele. Šesté, aby právě sě kála. Sedmé, aby dóstojenstvie duše vážila. Osmé, aby k budúciemu súdu pilně hleděla. Deváté, aby život věčný vážila. Osmé, aby k budúciemu súdu pilně hleděla. Deváté, aby život věčný vážila. Desáté, aby pána boha nade všechny věci najviece milovala'.

28 Mistr Jan Hus, *Drobné spisy české*, ed. by Daňhelka, p. 163.

29 Mistr Jan Hus, *Drobné spisy české*, ed. by Daňhelka, p. 163: 'To slyš, dcerko, jenž si jemu panenstvie zaslíbila'.

30 Bernard of Clairvaux, *Opera omnia*, ed. by Migne, col. 483: 'Et ita per cognitionem mei valeam pervenire ad cognitionem Dei. Quanto namque in cognitione mei proficio, tanto ad cognitionem Dei accedo. Secundum interiorem hominem tria in mente mea invenio per qua Deum recolo, conspicio, et concupisco. Sunt autem haec tria, memoria, intelligentia, voluntas sive amor'.

31 Bernard of Clairvaux, *Opera omnia*, ed. by Migne, col. 487.

Hus did not want to emulate for his readers.[32] He therefore wrote a text in many ways leaning on the *Meditationes* but entirely different in its ambition and in the character of the instruction.

The most extensive chapter of the tract is Chapter 4, on 'the temptation in this world'.[33] Here, Jan Hus used one of the sermons by John Wyclif (Sermon for Easter Monday, on Luke 24. 13) as his model.[34] The sermon is in fact more of an academic tract, in which the usual and very popular sermon structure developed by Dominican preachers is completely missing and no exhortative aim is evident. At first the two disciples are discussed who were unstable in their faith and were led by Jesus to the truth. Then the question arises whether Jesus Christ consecrated the bread during the meal in Emmaus; Wyclif voices a negative opinion on the church dignitaries in this respect describing their interpretations of the verses if the Scripture concerning the meal in Emmaus as 'dreaming' and themselves as more unstable in their faith as the two disciples of Christ.[35]

The actual topic of the sermon, temptation, follows the thesis that Christ helps in His absence, that His mind radiates more than was the case during His presence on the earth.[36] Hus translated Wyclif's lengthy exposition on temptation almost in its entirety. He nevertheless incorporated his translation as separate passages into his own reasoning. Wyclif had developed his argument in the following steps. At first the character of temptation by God, man, and devil is

---

32 The first chapter *De dignitate hominis* is followed by *De miseria hominis horore mortis et distinctione supremi judicis* [On the misery of man, the dread of death and the distinction of the supreme judge] (2); *De dignitate animae, et vilitate corporis* [On the dignity of the soul and the lowliness of the body] (3); *De praemio patriae coelestis* [On the reward of heavenly homeland]; *De quotidiano sui ipsius examine* [On te daily self-examination] (5); *De attentione orationis tempore habenda* [On the Time to pay attention to prayer] (6); *De custodia cordis, et studio orationis* [On the keeping of the heart and the study of prayer] (7); *De incuriae seu negligentiae inter orandum detestatione* [On the negligence during atonement in prayer (8); *De instabilitate cordis humani* [On the instability of the human heart] (9); *De impatientia correctionis, et accusatione propriorum defectuum ac vitiorum* [On the impatience of correcting and accusing one's own defects and vices] (10); *De individuo comitatu conscientiae nos ubique remordentis* [On the accompanying conscience tormenting us (11); *De tribus inimicis hominis, carne, mundo et diabolo* [On the three enemies of man, flesh, world, and devil] (12); *De impugnatione trium dictorum inimicorum* [On the assault of the three mentioned enemies] (13); *De desiderio patriae coelestis, et summa eiusdem felicitate* [Of the desire of the heavenly homeland and the supreme happiness of the same] (14). Already a simple comparison between this structure and the structure of Hus's tract (see above) reveals a completely different tenor of the two treatises.

33 Mistr Jan Hus, *Drobné spisy české*, ed. by Daňhelka, p. 170: '[…] zdejšieho světa pokušenie […]'.

34 *Johannis Wyclif Sermones*, IV, ed. by Loserth, pp. 66–74 (sermo VII).

35 *Johannis Wyclif Sermones*, IV, ed. by Loserth, p. 68: Unde nostri instabiles qui sompniant quod Christus antequam incepit loqui discipulis regulariter panem quem fregerat consecravit sine fundacione plus quam illi duo discipuli fluctuant in incerto.

36 *Johannis Wyclif Sermones*, IV, ed. by Loserth, p. 68.

defined: [...] 'ut Deus, homo et dyabolus sepe temptant. Deus autem semper bene, quia iuste, homo autem nunc bene nunc male, sed dyabolus semper male'. (God, man and the devil always tempt. But God tempts always well, because he is just, and man tempts now well, now evil, but the devil tempts always evil).[37] Temptation addresses the soul and the will. The devil is able to drive men to despair, he has tempted the Lord thrice and he especially tempts prelates in order to do the greatest damage. To resist the devil man has to be strong and healthy, and he has to renounce exclusive ascetic practices: [...] 'sicut communiter faciunt religiosi stolidi, qui simulant sanctitatem'. (as do stupid religious in general who simulate holiness).[38] Most helpful are the three cardinal virtues, faith, hope, and charity: 'Nichil enim valet contra diabolum in ista materia plus quam fides'.[39] (Nothing is more valuable against devil in this case than faith). Furthermore, man has to avoid solitude: [...] 'sic enim temptavit Evam solitariam atque Christum'. (... for so he tested Eve alone and Christ).[40] Nevertheless, God does not allow the devil to tempt a man overly.[41] We should dwell in the light of God's love and face the devil who is a liar and cannot know who is predestined for damnation and who is not, because God does not reveal that to him.[42] If tempted, man has to trust in God and His love. The devil uses (hu)man's sin to tempt him saying that (any) sin will damn him anyway; Cain, Saul, and many others were damned although they sinned less. This is a lie; only final impenitence can damn a man. Therefore, if we fall into despair, it is our own doing. We have to consider how the devil tries to master human will, but it is necessary to hope in God's help. Then it will be possible to defy temptation, because the acts of the soul are in our power: 'Et tunc possimus faciliter esse beati non obstante quacunque temptacione diaboli, cum plures adiutores sunt nobiscum quam cum toto suo exercitu...' (And then we may be easily blessed, notwithstanding any temptation of the devil, since there are more helpers with us than with his whole army...)[43]

Hus omitted Wyclif's opening exposition on Luke 24.13, and started the fourth chapter on temptation with his usual opening sentence 'Hear Daughter [...] and learn to know the temptation of this world'. Then he translated the sentence: 'Congruum est de temptationibus parum loqui: est autem temptacio active actus temptantis et temptacio passive passio, qua formaliter quis temptatur, et distinguitur secundum variacionem multiplicem temptatoris'. (It is appropriate to speak a little about temptations. Now temptation is the active act of the tempter, and passive temptation is a passion, by which one is formally

---

[37] *Johannis Wyclif Sermones*, IV, ed. by Loserth, p. 69.
[38] *Johannis Wyclif Sermones*, IV, ed. by Loserth, p. 71.
[39] *Johannis Wyclif Sermones*, IV, ed. by Loserth, p. 71.
[40] *Johannis Wyclif Sermones*, IV, ed. by Loserth, p. 71.
[41] *Johannis Wyclif Sermones*, IV, ed. by Loserth, p. 71.
[42] Joh*annis Wyclif Sermones*, IV, ed. by Loserth, p. 72.
[43] *Johannis Wyclif Sermones*, IV, ed. by Loserth, p. 74.

tempted, and is distinguished by the multiple variance of the tempter.)[44] as follows: 'The first temptation is the one with which somebody tempts another person, and the other one is the one with which somebody is tempted'.[45] He did not try to find or invent the equivalents for the Latin terms but interpreted them, transferring them from the philosophical and theological discourse into the pastoral narrative. The next paragraph is translated as follows:

ut Deus, homo et dyabolus sepe temptant. Deus autem semper bene quia iuste, homo autem nunc bene nunc male, sed dyabolus semper male.	Because God tempts, man tempts and devil tempts. God always tempts well [with good intention], because when He tempts He tempts according to justice. Man tempts sometimes well [with good intention] and sometimes badly [with evil intention]. The devil tempts always badly [with evil intention].
Quando autem homo capit occasionem a quocunque non racionali ut de viciis vel creatura aliqua ut intrinsecus sit temptatus, ille pocius se ipsum temptat sive diabolus.	But when man takes anything unreasonable as an excuse, so he is tempted from the inside, he tempts himself, or the devil tempts him through a thing, but the thing does not tempt him.
	As it was [in the case of Eve]; the apple, or whichever fruit it was she ate, did not tempt her but only she did as well as the devil through the fruit,
quam res illa naturalis, que pure facit quod incumbit suo officio naturali.	because each unreasonable thing does nothing else than God commanded it according to its nature.
Supponamus ergo quod Deus quandoque suum predestinatum filium temptat ad meritum	Further you should know that that God tempts His elected son or daughter for [their] benefit, as the Scripture shows, and I wrote much about it elsewhere,
et quandoque prescitum ad dampnacionem ex condignitate prioris demeriti inducit in temptacionem desperacionis finalis.[46]	but the devil tempts to damnation and man sometimes to sin. But the devil's temptation is always evil and the worst of all. Therefore, man has to avoid it most.[47]

---

44 *Johannis Wyclif Sermones*, IV, ed. by Loserth, pp. 68–69.

45 Mistr Jan Hus, *Drobné spisy české*, ed. by Daňhelka, pp. 170: 'jest pokušenie jedno, jímž kto pokúšie jiného, a druhé, jímž kto pokúšien bývá'.

46 *Johannis Wyclif Sermones*, IV, ed. by Loserth, p. 69.

47 Mistr Jan Hus, *Drobné spisy české*, ed. by Daňhelka, p. 170: 'Neb pokúšie bóh, pokúšie člověk a pokúšie ďábel. Bóh vždy pokúšie dobře; neb když pokúšie, tehdy

We may see here how Hus worked with Wyclif's text: he translated complex utterances as accurately as possible, but enriched them with explanatory addenda, mostly referring to known passages from the Old and New Testaments, connecting the educational horizon of his readers with the theological and philosophical discourse of Wyclif. He omitted passages touching on delicate theological subject matters (here the concept of the *presciti*, the 'foreknown'). At the end of the paragraph, he added a short summary of its most important message.

Wyclif's notice about the 'religiosi stolidi, qui simulant sanctitatem', is missing from Hus's argument, as well as the lengthy exposition on the character of God's providence: 'Unde inter alia que Deus vult esse ab homine ignorata hoc est unum precipuum quod homo ignoret dampnacionem propriam, in tantum quod ut dicunt catholici: Deus non potest dampnacionem propriam revelare homini, quia tunc daret culpabiliter occasionem homini ut desperet'. (Hence, among other things that God wants to be unknown to man, this is one of the most important things that a man does not know his own condemnation, inasmuch as, as Catholics say, God cannot reveal his own damnation to man, because then he would at fault give man an opportunity to despair).[48] The last part of Wyclif's sermon, concerning the fall into despair and God's mercy displayed in the Scripture, as well as the summary of the arguments, are also missing in Hus's translation.

Passages on temptation translated from Wyclif's sermon are enriched with Hus's own lengthy additional explanations. The first one concerns the character of the devil's temptation:

> Each sin happens in the will and is orchestrated by the will, as our Saviour means when he says that all evil ideas come from the heart, that means from the will: murders, fornication, theft, false witnesses, blasphemy, and other sins. Therefore, when the devil tempts men with any sin, it never becomes a deadly sin without the consent of man.[49]

Then Hus quotes St Augustine, St Gregory the Great, and Aristotle. Wyclif's passage on the temptation of Christ follows, enriched by Hus's reasoning on the

---

pokúšie spravedlivě. Člověk někdy pokúšie dobře a někdy také zle. A ďábel vždy zle. Ale když člověk vezme sobě příčinu od které kolivěk věci, jenž nenie rozumná, aby ze vnitř byl pokúšen, ten sám sebe pokúšie a neb ďábel ho pokúšie skrze tu věc, ale ta věc ho nepokúšie. Jako Evy jablko, neb které ovoce jest jedla, to jest jie nepokúšělo, ale ona sama sebe a ďábel skrze to ovoce. Neb každá taká věc nerozumná nic jiného nečiní, než co jí bóh v její přirození rozkázal. Dále věz, že bóh svého syna vyvoleného neb dcerky své vyvolené pokúšie k zaslúžení, jakož písmo ukazuje? A o tom psal sem mnoho jinde. Ale ďábel, ten pokúšie k zatracení. A člověk někdy k hřiechu. Ale ďáblovo pokúšenie jest vždy zlé a najhoršie. Protož toho sě má člověk najviece varovati'.

48 *Johannis Wyclif Sermones*, IV, ed. by Loserth, p. 72.

49 Mistr Jan Hus, *Drobné spisy české*, ed. by Daňhelka, p. 170: 'každý hřiech koná sě volí a má hniezdo u vóli, jakož sám spasitel náš praví řka, že z srdce, to jest z vole srdečné pocházějí myšlenie zlá, vraždy, cizoložstva, smilstva, krádeži, křivá svědectvie, rúhanie a tak i jiní hřieši. Protož pokúšie-li člověka ďábel kterým kolivěk hřiechem, tehdy nikdy nenie hřiech smrtedlný, když k němu člověk nepřivolí'.

disappointment of the devil who brought the priests to murder Christ, hoping that he (the devil) would conquer Him in this way. As the devil realized his mistake, he tried to prevent the crucifixion of Christ through Pilate's wife. Wyclif's passage on the devil not knowing who is *prescitus* for damnation is followed by Hus's own exposition of various ways in which the devil tempts men, in the form of the devil's direct speech:

> He tells them [the men]: It is pointless what you do, because you are in deadly sin; [...] you are young, you may enjoy the world, you have enough time to regret your sins; [...] God redeemed you, you are his elected son, you may live as you wish; [...] God's law is too harsh, it is impossible to live according to His commands. [...] And the devil has many such stratagems to deceive men.[50]

The rest of Chapter 4 is filled with lengthy model answers with which the penitent human being has to meet the devil and his various temptations. Here Hus teaches the reader not to fear the devil but to show him his own weakness, the gaps in the logic of his argument and his immense inferiority in comparison with God's love and Providence: there is nothing sweeter and easier than to serve God and to love him. Anybody who has the will, may fulfil God's law: 'I will not follow such a liar as you are but I will hear my beloved father and saviour Jesus Christ, who is the eternal truth'.[51]

This chapter demonstrates how Hus approached people for whom he felt responsible as their pastor. His foremost concern was not to inspire champions of faith who would distinguish themselves in religious exercises, and emulate the saints and Christ Himself. He was not a zealot pushing through the reform by all means available.[52] Hus stresses temperance in all areas of spiritual experience, the most crucial being the three cardinal virtues and God's unconditional love in which man has to trust. Concerning language and style, he avoided any rhetorical figure which would not match the communicative experience of his hear-

---

50 Mistr Jan Hus, *Drobné spisy české*, ed. by Daňhelka, p. 172: 'Ty což učiníš, to vše zle činíš; neb jsi v hřieše smrtedlném. [...] Jsi mlád, požívaj světa, ještě máš dosti času ku pokání; [...] Oč máš péči? Však bóh, za tě trpěv, dosti jest učinil a jsi boží syn vyvolený ke spasení; jistě budeš spasen, bd živ zde, jakož chceš [...] Á, kterak jest vám bóh těžký zákon ustavil! I kto jej móž naplniti [...]? A má ďábel chytrý mnoho jiných lstí, ale těchto zvláště požívá, chtě člověka uvésti k nekání konečnému'.

51 Mistr Jan Hus, *Drobné spisy české*, ed. by Daňhelka, p. 175: 'nebť tebe lháře poslúchati nechci, ale milého otce svého a spasitele Jezukrista, jenž jest věčná pravda'.

52 For example, in the passage in the sixth chapter in which Communion is the issue, Hus stresses that it does not matter how often a Communion is taken, if the person tries to avoid sin and to love God. Considering how prominent the Holy Communion was in the Bohemian reformation this passage appears strange at first glance, but it corresponds only too well with Hus's understanding of pastoral care: 'Eat the bread, daily or every other day, either once a week or once a month, or as God allows you. More importantly, avoid sin and love God as much [as you can]'. Mistr Jan Hus, *Drobné spisy české*, ed. by Daňhelka, p. 78.

ers. This does not mean his message was devoid of complexity – on the contrary, based on the work of Bernard of Clairvaux, it is quite demanding, and presupposes advanced literacy, spiritual commitment, and a good grounding in basic issues of Christian meditation. Although the tract is explicitly directed at female believers, this dedication is missing in the fourth chapter and each and every believer is targeted.[53]

An overall critique of the institutional church and its conduct, a topic very common in Hus's work, Latin and Czech, is hardly present in *The Daughter*. The only passage somehow recalling Hus's usual attacks on the papal curia and the Church hierarchy in general is in the second chapter. Here, Hus writes about conscience, which should not be too 'narrow' and not too 'broad': 'Broad conscience often takes evil for good and sin for no sin. [...] In such conscience many bad priests do dwell who do not consider fornication, greed, and simony deadly sins. As it is in other estates too'.[54]

Hus criticizes all those who disregard God's commandments, but hold their own instruction in high esteem: 'And so do popes, bishops, as well as other prelates and canons, but also princes, lords, and burghers'.[55] According to Hus, priests are liable to the same sins as all the other social groups. Hus does translate Wyclif's point that the devil especially tempts priests and prelates because of the great damage he may cause in this way. He incorporates it into the fourth chapter, but does not extend or comment it in any way.[56] This also applies to the central issue of Wyclif's and Hus's theology and ecclesiology: Hus mentions the Church of the elect in the sermon, but does not seize the chance to explain it in detail to his readers. This does not correspond to Hus's usual treatment of Wyclif's work in his vernacular adaptations – he used them as a template which he commented and extended at will, especially in the passages concerning the reform approach.[57]

---

53 The passage on women in childbed cannot be regarded as proof of specific interest in women because it originates in Wyclif's sermon which does not address women specifically.

54 Mistr Jan Hus, *Drobné spisy české*, ed. by Daňhelka, p. 166: 'Neb svědomie široké často má zlé za dobré, hřiech za nehřiech. [...] Ó co jest zlořečených v tom svědomí mnoho kněží, jenž smilstvie, lakomstvie a svatokupectvie svého za hřiech smrtedlná nepokládají. Též v jiných staviech'.

55 Mistr Jan Hus, *Drobné spisy české*, ed. by Daňhelka, p. 167: 'jakož činie papeži, biskupové a jiní preláti a zákonníci i také kniežata, páni i měštěné'.

56 Mistr Jan Hus, *Drobné spisy české*, ed. by Daňhelka, p. 171: 'A hledá pokušením, kdež by mohl najviece uškoditi. Protož prelátóv a kniežat velikých viece jest pilen, aby je svedl s božie cěsty. Protož také najviece jest pilen mužóv svatých, a zvláště těch, kteříž slovem božím v cierkvi svaté prospievají; neb ti najviece rušie jemu jeho královstvie'. (And he seeks by the means of temptation to cause the greatest damage. Therefore he focuses mostly on prelates and great princes to mislead them from the right path. He focuses therefore on holy men and especially those from whose words [preaching] the church benefits at most, because they tear down his kingdom).

57 Rychterová, 'The Vernacular Theology of Jan Hus', pp. 183–205.

In *The Daughter* Hus handles the topic of sinful prelates and the depravity of the church very cautiously, as he does with the central Wycliffite reform concepts. We may conclude that Hus intentionally avoided Church reform as a topic in this tract.

This is actually quite unusual if we compare *The Daughter* with other vernacular works Hus wrote during his exile before he departed for Constance in the autumn of 1414. The other texts directly address the need for a reform of the Church; in fact, it is the main issue in most of them. *The Daughter* focuses on a rather ambitious programme of spiritual education, but without any ecclesiological or eschatological urgency, which dominates Hus's other writings. He composed the text very carefully, respecting the abilities of his readers. That does not mean the text would be simplistic. Hus brought the vernacular Czech exhortative style to perfection. He did not have to invent it, for he could draw on a relatively rich tradition of Czech religious educative writing. Nevertheless, it is unknown whether and how he used the religious literature written in Czech – there are no known quotes in his works which would originate in the texts of this particular genre. We may observe some similarities, for example, between *The Daughter* and the exhortative tracts directed at women written by Thomas of Štítné (d. after 1400); but they cannot be regarded as a proven source of Hus's tract. All the models identified in his Czech works were written in Latin.

Therefore, we may assume that Hus, an excellent preacher according to contemporaneous witnesses, was well capable of moving between various discourses as well as creatively shaping them. He did not create new (pro-reform) standards of religious education with *The Daughter*, he brought to fruition the existing ones. It is a known fact that Hus relied on his lay followers in his reform efforts – desirous that they share his deep concern for the condition of the Church hierarchy, and his criticism of the way of life of Church dignitaries. Besides, he cared much for the spiritual well-being of his flock, and he was very well able to differentiate between the various demands of his socially heterogenous listeners. There was a number of high-ranking ladies, members of noble families, who were his committed supporters. It is quite possible that the reason for their support was not so much any deep knowledge of and concern for the problems of the hierarchical Church, as the fact that Hus was able to give them what they expected as fitting their high rank: a high-class spiritual teaching written in a high-class literary style in their own vernacular.[58] *The Daughter* is very likely one of the textual witnesses of Hus's communication with this very important circle of supporters. This aspect is also the reason why the text could be adapted in the heterogenous contexts shown by its manuscript transmission. In this regard, we have to complete the picture of Hus's personality that the previous generation of scholars has bequeathed to us: Hus indeed was a great reformer, a great preacher, a great tribune of the people, a man of unshakable principles and of deep trust in God's truth and justice. But he was also a religious teacher capable

---

58 Rychterová, 'Thomas of Štítné (1330–1400) and his Translation of the "De Septem Itineribus Aeternitatis" by Rudolf of Biberach', pp. 121–44.

of approaching sophisticated ladies properly and of inspiring deep loyalty in them. Furthermore, he was a distinguished author of vernacular spiritual literature which would, in the decades to come, be read by Utraquists who turned him into their most venerated martyr, as well as by Catholics who regarded him as the worst of heretics. When in the middle of the 1430s the theologian Jan of Příbram tried to find a middle ground for a religious education suitable for both parties, he chose Hus as his point of departure, and as common ground on which the Czech Christian community could consolidate itself and find a way to a peaceful coexistence. The reception history of *The Daughter* shows that Hus's legacy as a religious teacher for all was indeed appreciated by all in the end.

Jan Hus is one of the historical personalities who are defined through their exceptional deeds and fates by posterity. Hus's role as the leader of an important religious movement determined research on him from the beginning. Historians mainly focused on those sources that bear witness to his ideas and actions as a devoted Church reformer. Those of his works that were less relevant for the questions about Hus's role in the first phase of the Hussite revolution, never received a proper historiographic contextualization and narrative. The purpose of the present essay is to demonstrate that it may be worth of the effort. It becomes clear that Hus was not only a reform theologian, a passionate preacher and a harsh critic of the Church hierarchy, but also a devoted pastor who scrupulously met the spiritual needs of his flock, leaning on well-established traditions of spiritual education.

Bibliography

Manuscript Sources

Brno, Moravská zemská knihovna, Mk 19
Prague, Knihovna Metropolitní kapituly, MS C 32
———, MS D 82
Prague, Knihovna Národního muzea, MS IV C 18
———, MS IV B 15
———, MS IV E 29
———, MS IV H 32

Primary Sources

Bernard of Clairvaux, *Opera omnia*, ed. by Jacques-Paul Migne, Patrologiae Cursus Completus: Series Latina, 184 (Paris: Migne, 1854)

Dcerka M. J. H. aneb poznání cesty pravé k spasení: Z rukopisu 15. století, ed. by Václav Hanka (Prague: Heß, 1825)

Johannis Wyclif Sermones, ed. by Johann Loserth, 4 vols (London: Trübner, 1886–90), IV: *Sermones miscellanei (Quadriganta de tempore: Sermones mixti XXVI)* (1890)

Mistr Jan Hus, *Drobné spisy české*, ed. by Jiří Daňhelka (Prague: Academia, nakl. československé akademie věd, 1985)

Solfernus, ed. by Barbora Hanzová (Prague: Ústav pro jazyk český AV ČR, 2015)

Secondary Works

Boubín, Jaroslav, 'Chelčického spisy v kapitulním sborníku', in Petr Chelčický, *Spisy z kapitulního sborníku*, ed. by Jaroslav Boubín, Sbírka pramenů k náboženským dějinám, 5 (Prague: Historický ústav, 2018), pp. 9–47

Collecting, Organizing and Transmitting Knowledge: Miscellanies in Late Medieval Europe, ed. by Sabrina Corbellini, Giovanna Murano, and Giacomo Signore, Bibliologia, 49, Elementa ad librorum studia et pertinentia (Turnhout: Brepols, 2018)

Černá, Soňa, 'The Letters of St Jerome of the Prague Chancellor and Notary John of Neumarkt: A Transmission History', in *Pursuing a New Order I: Religious Education in Late Medieval Central and Eastern Central Europe*, ed. by Pavlína Rychterová and Julian Ecker, The Medieval Translator / Traduire au Moyen Âge, 17/1 (Turnhout: Brepols, 2018), pp. 47–74

Doležalová, Lucie, 'Late Medieval Personal Miscellanies: The Case of Mattheus Beran (d. 1461), Augustinian Canon of Roudnice nad Labem', in *Collecting, Organizing and Transmitting Knowledge. Miscellanies in Late Medieval Europe*, ed. by Sabrina Corbellini, Giovanna Murano, and Giacomo Signore, Bibliologia, 49, Elementa ad librorum studia et pertinentia (Turnhout: Brepols, 2018), pp. 179–96

Dragoun, Michal, 'Rukopisy kroniky "Martimiani"', in *Staročeská kronika 'Martimiani'*, ed. by Štěpán Šimek (Prague: Scriptorium, 2019), pp. 14–20

Fudge, Thomas A., *Jan Hus between Time and Eternity: Reconsidering a Medieval Heretic* (London: Lexington Books, 2016)

Marek, Jindřich, *Václav Koranda mladší: Utrakvistický administrátor a literát*, Středověk, 3 (Prague: Nakladatelství Lidové noviny, 2017)

Molnár, Amedeo, 'K pramenům Husovy Dcerky', *Listy filologické*, 102 (1979), pp. 224–30

Murdoch, Brian, *The Apocryphal Adam and Eve in Medieval Europe: Vernacular Translations and Adaptations of the Vita Adae et Evae* (Oxford: Oxford University Press, 2009)

Novotný, Václav, *M. Jan Hus: Život a učení*, 3 vols (Prague: Leichter, 1921–23), I–II

Odstrčilík, Jan, 'Translation and Transformation of Jan Hus's Czech Sunday Postil', in *Pursuing a New Order II: Late Medieval Vernacularization and the Bohemian Reformation*, ed. by Pavlína Rychterová and Julian Ecker, The Medieval Translator / Traduire au Moyen Âge, 17/2 (Turnhout: Brepols, 2019), pp. 153–84

Orthographia Bohemica, ed. by Kateřina Voleková (Prague: Akropolis, 2019)

Perett, Marcela, 'Jan Hus and Faction Formation: The Evidence of Hus's Post-1412 Writings', *Kosmas: Czechoslovak and Central European Journal*, 28/2 (2015), pp. 45–66

——, 'Jan Hus's Productive Exile: Writing as Rabble-Rousing', *Husitský Tábor*, 20 (2016), pp. 83–107

Rychterová, Pavlína, 'Fighting for the Minds of the People: Strategies of Argumentation in the Vernacular Discourse on Church Unity in Fifteenth-Century Bohemia', in *Wycliffism and Hussitism: Methods of Thinking, Writing, and Persuasion, c. 1360 - c. 1460*, ed. by Kantik Ghosh, Pavel Soukup (Turnhout: Brepols, 2021, pp. 361–86)

——, 'Kirchen- und Klerikalkritik im Böhmen des 14. und 15. Jahrhunderts zwischen Latein und Volkssprachen', *Rivista di storia del cristianesimo*, 12 (2015), pp. 291–308

——, 'Theology Goes to the Vernaculars: Jan Hus, "On Simony", and the Practice of Translation in Fifteenth-Century Bohemia', in *Religious Controversy in Europe, 1378–1536: Textual Transmission and Networks of Readership*, ed. by Michael van Dussen and Pavel Soukup, Medieval Church Studies, 27 (Turnhout: Brepols, 2013), pp. 231–50

———,, 'Thomas of Štítné (1330–1400) and his Translation of the "De Septem Itineribus Aeternitatis" by Rudolf of Biberach', in *Pursuing a New Order I: Religious Education in Late Medieval Central and Eastern Central Europe*, ed. by Pavlína Rychterová and Julian Ecker, The Medieval Translator / Traduire au Moyen Âge, 17/1 (Turnhout: Brepols, 2018), pp. 121–44

———, 'The Revelations of St Birgitta in the Holy Roman Empire', in *A Companion to Birgitta of Sweden and Her Legacy in the Late Middle Ages*, ed. by Maria H. Oen, Brill's Companions to the Christian Tradition, 89 (Leiden and Boston: Brill, 2019), pp. 247–68

———, 'The Vernacular Theology of Jan Hus', in *A Companion to Jan Hus*, ed. by František Šmahel and Ota Pavlíček, Brill's Companions to the Christian Tradition, 54 (Leiden and Boston: Brill, 2015), pp. 170–213

Sedlák, Jan, *M. Jan Hus* (Prague: Dědictví sv. Prokopa – B. Stýblo, 1915)

———, 'Je Husova "Dcerka" dílo původní?' in *Studie a textu k životopisu Husovu*, ed. by Jan Sedlák, Studie a texty k náboženským dějinám českým 2 (Olomouc: Matice Cyrilometodějská, 1915), pp. 359–66

Soukup, Pavel, 'The "Puncta" of Jan Hus: The Latin Transmission of Vernacular Preaching', in *Pursuing a New Order II: Late Medieval Vernacularization and the Bohemian Reformation*, ed. by Pavlína Rychterová and Julian Ecker, The Medieval Translator / Traduire au Moyen Âge, 17/2 (Turnhout: Brepols, 2019), pp. 91–126

———, *11.7.1412: Poprava tří mládenců: Odpustkové bouře v Praze*, Dny, které tvořily české dějiny, 22 (Prague: Havran, 2018)

Šmahel, František, *Die Hussitische Revolution*, Monumenta Germaniae Historica, Schriften, 43 (Hannover: Hahnsche Buchhandlung, 2002)

Unbearable Lightness of Multilingual Sermons?

The So-Called Wilhering Adaptation of Three Czech Sermons of Jan Hus

Jan Odstrčilík

Institute for Medieval Research, Austrian Academy of Sciences

The old Cistercian monastery at Wilhering, Upper Austria, is home to a late medieval manuscript which contains three intriguing sermons. The three sermons have their origin in the *Czech Sunday Postil* (*Česká nedělní postila*), a famous Czech sermon collection composed by Jan Hus, a reformer found guilty of the Wycliffite heresy and executed at the Council of Constance in 1415. What makes these three sermons unique is their language. While Jan Hus composed the original works in an elaborated and self-confident Czech, an unknown author of the *Wilhering Sermons* translated a substantial number of the Czech words into Latin. The result is a macaronic text, in which parts written in both Czech and Latin may often appear within a single sentence.

In the following essay this historical text will be examined from various perspectives: firstly, its source, the *Czech Sunday Postil*, will be addressed, and then the *Wilhering Sermons*, including the context of their manuscript, their orthography, changes in the content, and most importantly, the interplay between the two languages, possible motivations for the code-switching, basic triggers, and the potential role of 'visual dimorphs'.

The Source: Czech Sunday Postil

There are many sermon collections attributed to Jan Hus[1] but the *Czech Sunday Postil* is the only one he wrote entirely in Czech.[2] He composed it under extraor-

---

1 See in particular: Vidmanová, 'Hus als Prediger', Soukup, 'Jan Hus as a Preacher', and Soukup, *Hus als Prediger*.

2 Jan Hus is also the supposed author of the so-called *Czech Festival Sermons* (*Česká sváteční kázání*). Despite the similar title, this is neither a *Postil*, nor a coherent sermon collection. In fact, these twenty-six sermons originated at different times and many of them under-

dinary circumstances. His long-lasting conflict with the Church resulted in a papal interdict being imposed on Prague in the year 1412, which would last for as long as Jan Hus was staying there. This move finally forced Jan Hus out of the Kingdom's capital and into exile. He left behind his pulpit in Bethlehem Chapel – one of the largest buildings in Prague – from which he had criticized the corruption in the Church and especially the Papal Curia. The *Czech Sunday Postil* became a way of keeping in contact with his followers and expanding the reach of his teaching. Whereas his previous Latin sermon collections were mainly intended for fellow preachers to use as model sermons, the *Czech Sunday Postil* was written especially for the use of lay readers and listeners.[3]

Hus finished the text in October 1413.[4] It features valuable information on his struggle with the Church authorities as well as the core of his fierce critique of the corrupt church hierarchy. It is not surprising therefore that the *Czech Sunday Postil* has been characterized by the acknowledged expert on Hus's written work in Czech, the philologist Jiří Daňhelka, as Hus's most important and most personal work.[5]

The *Czech Sunday Postil* comprises fifty-nine sermons in all, fifty-seven of which are on different Sunday readings of the liturgical year, including two additional sermons for the Octave of Easter and two for the Octave of Pentecost (in both cases for Monday and Tuesday). The two remaining sermons outside the liturgical year are intended for the feast of church consecration. Each sermon is introduced by a biblical reading, which in some copies also includes collections of short interlinear glosses. Hus compiled a comprehensive subject index, which enabled the reader to quickly search for various themes within the sermons and their parts.[6] The same elaborated structure is found in two other Czech works by Hus from the same period: a complex work called *Expositions on Faith, Ten Commandments, and Pater Noster*,[7] and the treatise *On Simony*.[8]

---

went various modifications and alternations during their transmission, and on a scale, which is unusual for others of Hus's work. See the introduction in Jan Hus, *Česká sváteční kázání*, ed. by Daňhelka, see also Rychterová, 'The Vernacular Theology of Jan Hus', pp. 180–82.

3 Hus speaks about those who will 'read it or listen to it', see Jan Hus, *Česká nedělní postila*, ed. by Daňhelka, p. 60.

4 On the dating of the *Czech Sunday Postil*, see Vidmanová, 'Kdy, kde a jak psal Hus českou Postillu'.

5 Jan Hus, *Česká nedělní postila*, ed. by Daňhelka, p. 7.

6 Such an index is not just a simple or neutral subject index. On the contrary, the selection of subjects shows Jan Hus's ideological intentions, e.g. there are only two items covering the 'Pope': *Papežova pýcha veliká* ('The Pope's Great Pride') and *Papežstvie držela jest žena* ('A Woman Was a Pope'), see Jan Hus, *Česká nedělní postila*, ed. by Daňhelka, p. 54. Pavlína Rychterová describes this phenomenon in another of Hus's works, *Expositions on Faith, Ten Commandments, and Pater Noster* see Rychterová, 'The Vernacular Theology of Jan Hus', pp. 184–85. For a more general study on Hus's use of indices, see Šmahel, 'Instead of Conclusion'.

7 Jan Hus, *Výklady*, ed. by Daňhelka.

8 Jan Hus, *Knížky o svatokupectví*, ed. by Molnár [Daňhelka].

The manuscript tradition of the *Czech Sunday Postil* is very coherent. According to Jiří Daňhelka, who has prepared a critical edition of this work, five complete medieval manuscripts contain the same text with only small textual differences between them. This is an unusual feature in the case of vernacular sermon collections, which were frequently reworked rather than accurately copied. Daňhelka interpreted this textual stability as a testimony to the scribes' respect for the text and its author.[9]

This does not mean that there are no variants or adaptations of the extant text at all, however: all concern the Latin translations of the work. Perhaps the most substantial reworkings are the linguistically mixed *Wilhering Sermons*, and a complete Latin translation preserved in Brno, Moravská zemská knihovna, Mk 91, which features occasional Czech glosses and passages.[10] Both adaptations have also significant changes to the contents of the sermons and their overall purpose.[11] This study deals primarily with the *Wilhering Sermons*; when appropriate, they will also be compared with the Latin translation in Mk 91.

Wilhering Sermons

The manuscript containing the *Wilhering Sermons*, Wilhering, Stiftsbibliothek, Cod. IX 122, consists of 158 folios and was originally dated to the beginning of the fifteenth century.[12] Since then, Daňhelka has argued that the orthography of the *Wilhering Sermons* instead points to the second half of the fifteenth century.[13] The manuscript probably belonged originally to the Cistercian monastery in Vyšší Brod/Hohenfurt in Southwest Bohemia, which was founded by Vok I of Rožmberk in 1259.[14] The monastery was located in a German-speaking area,

---

9 See Jan Hus, *Česká nedělní postila*, ed. by Daňhelka, p. 14. This contrasts with the situation found in the *Czech Festival Sermons*, see note 2.

10 See Odstrčilík, 'Translation and Transformation of Jan Hus's Czech Sunday Postil'.

11 It was originally supposed that Brno, Moravská zemská knihovna, Mk 56 contains another major Latin translation of the *Czech Sunday Postil*, see Dokoupil, *Catalogus codicum manu scriptorum Bibliothecae Dietrichsteinianae Nicolspurgensis*, p. 102. However, it is more proper to characterize this text as a free adaptation from multiple sources and the *Czech Sunday Postil* as just one of them, see Jan Hus, *Česká nedělní postila*, ed. by Daňhelka, p. 29 and especially Miškovská, 'Latinské překlady české Postilly v rukopise Mk 91 a Mk 56 a vztah k jejich předlohám', pp. 193–97. See also Martinková, 'Husova staročeská Postila v latinském překladu'. On other minor adaptations, see the introduction in Hus, Jan Hus, *Česká nedělní postila*, ed. by Daňhelka.

12 For the old manuscript description, see: Grillnberger, 'Die Handschriften der Stiftsbibliothek zu Wilhering'. A partially updated manuscript description can be found in *manuscripta.at*, online: http://manuscripta.at/?ID=32659 [accessed 3 November 2022].

13 Jan Hus, *Česká nedělní kázání*, ed. by Daňhelka, p. 38.

14 See Patera, 'Mistra Jana Husi česká kázání na posvěcenie kostela a na sv. Trojici', pp. 355–56.

which was populated by monks from the Wilhering Abbey in Upper Austria, roughly 34 km air distance away.[15] Czech monks were admitted to the monastery later, and from the fourteenth century the community became bilingual.[16]

The manuscript contains numerous religious texts, among them expositions on the Psalms (Cassiodorus, Basilius Magnus, and anonymous tracts), Bonaventure's *De triplici via*, the Pseudo-Augustinian *Speculum peccatorum*, and a tract on the art of preaching called *Aurissa sive de arte predicandi* written by Jacobus de Saraponte.[17] Such company is quite atypical for the *Czech Sunday Postil*. The five manuscripts mentioned above with complete copies of the original Czech text contain either only other Czech works by Jan Hus, or else works by other Utraquist authors (see Prague, Knihovna Národního muzea, MS III B 11).

In the last decade of the nineteenth century Adolf Patera firstly recognized and analysed the relationship between the *Wilhering Sermons* and the *Czech Sunday Postil*.[18] He determined that two of the *Wilhering Sermons* (fols 87^v–93^r and fols 93^r–99^r) on the feast of church consecration correspond to sermons nos 58 and 59 from the *Czech Sunday Postil*, and the last one (fols 99^v–100^v) to sermon no. 33 *On the Trinity* from the same work. However, Patera believed that the *Wilhering Sermons* were actually transcripts of sermons from the beginnings of Hus's preaching activity from c. 1402 to 1407, which Hus later used for his *Czech Sunday Postil* in 1413.[19] As Hus is known mainly for his late Czech works, the linguistically mixed text did not correspond to Patera's image of him as a fervent propagator of the Czech language. He then supposed that somebody else might have used Latin as decoration.[20] Patera also published a diplomatic edition of the sermons in the same article.

The problem of the *Wilhering Sermons* was only lightly addressed afterwards until Jiří Daňhelka's critical edition of the *Czech Sunday Postil*, into which he included also the *Wilhering Sermons*, c. 100 years after Patera's study.[21] In the introduction, Daňhelka summarized the research regarding the sermons and challenged Patera's conclusions. According to Daňhelka, the *Wilhering Sermons* did not originate in the first decade of the fifteenth century but in its second half. The scribe copied Hus's sermons and, while doing this, helped himself in the copying by changing parts of the text into Latin, as it was a language in which he was used to express himself.[22] The appendix of the critical edition of the *Czech*

---

15 Kaindl, *Geschichte des Zisterzienserstiftes Hohenfurt in Böhmen*, pp. 9–10.

16 Bok, 'Literaturpflege im Kloster Vyšší Brod/Hohenfurt vom 13. bis zum 15. Jahrhundert', p. 182.

17 On this tract, see Odstrčilík, 'Jacobus de Saraponte's "Aurissa"'.

18 Patera, 'Mistra Jana Husi česká kázání na posvěcenie kostela a na sv. Trojici'. The article contains the first transcription of the sermons.

19 Patera, 'Mistra Jana Husi česká kázání na posvěcenie kostela a na sv. Trojici', p. 356.

20 Patera, 'Mistra Jana Husi česká kázání na posvěcenie kostela a na sv. Trojici', p. 357.

21 Jan Hus, *Česká nedělní postila*, ed. by Daňhelka, pp. 37–39.

22 Jan Hus, *Česká nedělní postila*, ed. by. Daňhelka, p. 38: 'opisovač [si] vypomáhal latinou, protože byl zvyklý se jí vyjadřovat'.

Sunday Postil prepared by Daňhelka contains an edition of the *Wilhering Sermons*. It is based solely on Patera's previous diplomatic edition, since Daňhelka did not revisit the manuscript.

We know hardly anything about the author of the *Wilhering Sermons*. A small hint may be provided by the fact that he addresses the audience as *pueri* ('children') and speaks about *nos spirituales* ('our clergy'). Unfortunately, however, this is neither unique nor helpful for further identification. Nevertheless, there is an indication that he might be from the monastery of Vyšší Brod. In Sermon no. 58, the author added the following passage to the original text (p. 680, fol. 92r):[23]

> Také z těch slóv stalo sě spasenie a oslavenie dnešní den tomuto kostelu, jehož jako dnes posvěcenie bohu ke cti a jeho miléj matce panně Mariji, jenž jest zvláště dědična tohoto kostela […]
>
>> (And also from these words, salvation and celebration came today into this church, as well as its consecration for the honour of God and his dear mother Virgin Mary, who especially is the heir of this Church […])

The Church of the monastery of Vyšší Brod is dedicated to the Assumption of the Virgin Mary, and it is possible that the author of the *Wilhering Sermons* was actually referring to this particular church.

The text at our disposal contains a small number of scribal errors. On fol. 88r, the scribe mistakenly wrote the word *znati* ('to know') instead of the correct *svati* ('saint'). He noticed his error and immediately corrected the word. The late medieval graphemes 'v' and 'n' can sometimes look almost identical. Similarly, the graphemes 'z' and 's' were very often regarded as being interchangeable by scribes when writing and copying vernacular Czech texts. On fol. 89r the scribe first wrote the word *jedno* ('only') which he then corrected to *jiného* ('another'), for which only the latter reading makes sense in the sentence. Moreover, the word *jedno* appears again on the next line, which would suggest that the scribe had originally skipped the line while copying before noticing his mistake and correcting it.

These transcription errors indicate that the author/scribe had copied the Czech text from a manuscript of the *Czech Sunday Postil*, and confirm that the text as transmitted in the *Wilhering Sermons* was not the result of *reportatio* or *dictatio*. Only modest hints are available as concerns the direct model of the macaronic translation. In in the Sermon no. 59 (fol. 98v) we can find a marginal gloss *cautus* (fol. 98v) that is present in two manuscripts of the *Czech Sunday Postil*.[24] In Prague, Knihovna Národního muzea, MS IV C 18, from the year

---

23 If not otherwise stated, the page refers to the edition of the *Wilhering Sermons* in Jan Hus, *Česká nedělní postila*, ed. by Daňhelka, and folio to the manuscript, Wilhering, Stiftsbibliothek, Cod. IX 122.

24 Jan Hus, *Česká nedělní postila*, ed. by. Daňhelka, p. 458. Cf. also the list of variant readings on p. 582.

1414, the word *cautus* is written as a marginal gloss on fol. 195ᵛ connected with a pair of tie-marks to the Czech word *wystrazny* ('careful', 'cautious') in the main text as in the *Wilhering Sermons*. Similarly, Prague, Národní knihovna České republiky, MS XVII A 11, also contains *cautus*, where it appears as an interlinear gloss on fol. 324ᵛ, written immediately above the said Czech word.

The same sermon (fol. 94ᵛ) contains the reading *homo* ('man') on two occasions, as a replacement for the correct *článek* ('article').[25] However, the author of the *Wilhering Sermons* had obviously misread the original *článek* as *člověk* ('man') and had translated that instead.[26] There are two manuscripts of the *Czech Sunday Postil* which provide the same readings (Prague, Knihovna Národního muzea, MS III B 11, fol. 152ʳ, and Prague, Národní knihovna České republiky, MS XVII G 30, fol. 3ʳ).[27] However, none of these manuscripts appears to be the source for the Wilhering sermons.

As has already been mentioned, Sermon no. 33 is preserved only as a fragment in the *Wilhering Sermons*. A fragment of this sermon in Czech running to almost exactly the same length can also be found in Národní knihovna České republiky, MS VI F 22, fols 267ᵛ–68ʳ. Textual differences between the *Wilhering Sermons* and this particular fragment of the *Czech Sunday Postil* exclude the possibility that the *Wilhering Sermons* would be a copy of the Prague manuscript. It proves, however, that Sermon no. 33 circulated in this abbreviated form independently of the corpus of the *Czech Sunday Postil*.[28]

---

25 *Wilhering Sermons* (fol. 94ᵛ; p. 686): 'A že quilibet **homo** fidelis est verbum domini Iesu, et quod non potest salvari aliquis sine fide, ideo non potest nullus salvari, jedne ač každý **homo** [!] některak aspoň v rozumu bude mieti, a tak jej uchem vnitřním slyšeti'. Cf. Jan Hus, *Česká nedělní postila*, pp. 452–53: 'A že každý **článek** viery jest slovo Ježíšovo a že nemóž nižádný spasen býti bez viery, protož nemóž nižádný spasen býti, jedné ač každý **článek** některak aspoň v rozumu bude mieti a tak jej uchem vnitřním slyšeti'.

26 The typical orthography of the word *článek* would be *članek* while *člověk* would be written as *človiek*. In the word *človiek* the 'v' and 'i' could merge into 'w', a common variant of the letter 'v'. The change of *článek* into *člověk* was probably supported by preceding sentence *najprvé člověk má jíti k Ježíšovi* ('firstly a man should go to Jesus').

27 Neither of the manuscripts has the reading *člověk* in both instances. Prague, Knihovna Národního muzea, MS III B 11, fol. 152ʳ, has the second word *člověk*, which was corrected to *článek*, and Prague, Národní knihovna České republiky, MS XVII G 30, fol. 3ʳ, has the first reading as *člověk* and the second as *článek*. The latter manuscript does not contain the complete text of the *Czech Sunday Postil*, but only Sermon no. 59. What both Czech manuscripts demonstrate, is that such misreadings were rather common.

28 This is, actually, the case with the models for all three of the sermons in the *Wilhering Sermons*. The Czech Sermon no. 58 is preserved in the so-called Dzikowian Manuscript, see Svobodová, 'Komplexní studium Rukopisu dzikovského se zaměřením na grafickou, jazykovou a textovou analýzu české sbírky kázání', pp. 41–42, pp. 474–80, and pp. 673–81. Sermon no. 59 is preserved also in Prague, Národní knihovna České republiky, MS XVII G 30. This shows that all three sermons also circulated independently of the collection of the sermons.

One of the noteworthy differences between the original *Czech Sunday Postil* and the *Wilhering Sermons* is their orthography. Early Czech scribes faced a difficulty in recording specific Czech phonemes with the limited set of Latin letters. They solved the problem by using so-called digraphs, two-letter combinations representing a single phoneme. While this solution was generally accepted it was rather cumbersome, and it hampered the understanding of Czech texts creating ambiguous readings. This was especially an issue for copyists and unskilled readers. In the early fifteenth century, a new orthography for the Czech language was introduced in Bohemia.[29] Czech phonemes were given new graphemes, based on Latin letters and complemented by diacritic signs. This groundbreaking change has traditionally been attributed to Jan Hus. Although it is improbable that he invented the system, it is nevertheless undeniable that he was one of the first users and ardent supporters of this innovation. All the complete Czech manuscripts of the *Czech Sunday Postil* employ (or try to employ) the diacritic orthographic system.[30]

Jan Hus was quite explicit about his wishes regarding the copying of his works. In the introduction to the subject index of the *Czech Sunday Postil*, he explains that he 'wrote it' in the same way he 'spoke', and reminds future copyists not to change anything in his text, including the orthography.[31] Hus's works later became a legacy of the founding martyr of the new Christian confession, and as such they were regarded as 'holy texts'. This may explain why almost all the extant copies of his work display the new diacritic orthography, even if the scribes did not always understand its principles.[32] In general, the new orthography was only gradually accepted during the fifteenth century.[33] While the manuscripts of the *Czech Sunday Postil* use the new orthography, the *Wilhering Sermons* were written in the old way.[34] This indicates that their exemplar was not regarded by the author of the *Wilhering Sermons* as the testament of a holy man, but rather as materials which were open to being reworked according to the needs of individual readers. In the copy at our disposal Jan Hus, the author of

---

29 It is described in the contemporaneous treatise *Orthographia Bohemica*, ed. by Voleková.

30 See *Orthographia Bohemica*, ed. by Voleková, pp. xxvii–xxxix

31 Jan Hus, *Česká nedělní postila*, ed. by Daňhelka, p. 58: 'Protož prosím každého, ktož bude psáti, aby jinak nepsal, než jako sem já psal'.

32 See the discussion of manuscripts in Jan Hus, *Česká nedělní postila*, ed. by Daňhelka, especially pp. 14–20.

33 Unfortunately, there is no detailed study on the spread of the diacritic orthography in fifteenth-century Bohemia. For the general history of diacritic writing, see Šlosar, 'Diakritický pravopis', Voleková, 'Znaménko rozlišovací a zdůrazňovací ve staročeských rukopisech', and *Orthographia Bohemica*, ed. by Voleková, pp. xlix–lxxv.

34 Of course, it is possible that the unknown model of the *Wilhering Sermons* used the digraphic system and that it was lost during the time. E.g. one of the manuscripts of Hus's *Expositions*, Neustadt an der Aisch, Kirchenbibliothek, MS 2888, dated to 1460, is written in digraphic system.

the sermons, is not even mentioned. Passages which refer to him in the original text are omitted from the *Wilhering Sermons*.[35]

The Readers

There are two sets of notes which can be distinguished in the margins of the *Wilhering Sermons* with one set written in black ink and the other in red ink. The notes in black seem to have been written first, since they include (amongst other things) a number of items taken from the margins of the original Czech source, such as references to biblical books and various keywords. The notes in red ink only accompany specific parts of the text and they seem to reflect the interests of some reader of these sermons (e.g., the word *hic*, 'here', in red ink on fol. 88ʳ and fol. 89ʳ). A passage on fol. 98ᵛ is accompanied by the remark *hic pausa* ('here, make a break') in red ink, clearly a reminder to the preacher that they should pause when delivering the sermon.

Some of the notes in the margins are written in Czech, others in Latin, e.g. on fol. 97ᵛ, there is a list of virtues written in black ink which also appears in the margins of the *Czech Sunday Postil*. The marginal note *pokora* ('humility') is translated in the *Wilhering Sermons* into Latin as **humilitas**.[36] The two other marginal notes with virtues are not translated and remain as *spravedlnost* ('justice') and *skrovnost* ('modesty').

The changing of language in the notes can also be observed in the margins of fol. 90ʳ. Here the note written in red ink in the margins reads **peccator penitens** ('a repentant sinner') and it corresponds to the passage in the main text reading **misericors salvator nominat hřiešníka** ('**the merciful saviour names** the sinner').

The *Wilhering Sermons* also contain multilingual notes. The note in black ink in the margins of fol. 92ᵛ states: *nebo Christus praví:* **Domus mea domus oracionis** ('because Christ says: **My house is a house of prayer**'). There is also a bilingual interlinear gloss on fol. 88ᵛ: The list of evident sinners in the text, like prostitutes, dancers, or usurers, ends with the words *jsú* **manifesti peccatores** ('they are evident sinners'). The word *jsú* ('they are') is then glossed in red ink in the interlinear space as *ti* **omnes** ('they **all**'). These linguistically intricate glosses prove that the bilingual character of the *Wilhering Sermons* is a reflection of the bilingualism of their various users, be they the author himself, the scribe or other readers.

---

35 The original Sermon no. 59 included a colophon with date and place, in which Hus finished the work. Sermon no. 58 contained a reference to another sermon from the *Czech Sunday Postil*. The anonymous author did not remove these two passages with the purpose of hiding Hus's authorship; rather, he probably regarded them as being unnecessary for the new purpose of the work. Still, such changes contributed to the decontextualization of the original work and facilitated its new contextualization.

36 However, the word *pokora* in the main body of the text remains untranslated in the *Wilhering Sermons*.

Overall, the content of Hus's texts in the *Wilhering Sermons* remains relatively unchanged. The author of the *Wilhering Sermons* omitted a couple of passages throughout. In Sermon no. 58, a passage criticizing monks who allow dancing in their monasteries, is modified with a statement which avoids the critique of monastic orders (possibly with regard to the Cistercians in Vyšší Brod/Hohenfurth), and focuses instead on the clerics:

> *Czech Sunday Postil:* Též diem i o tanci, jímž v neděli bohu sě rúhají, jako die svatý Bernard, že, ktož v domu přepustí, a zvláště v klášteře mnišie, majíce v něm na své i na cizie hřiechy plakati, písmo svaté čísti a nábožně sě modliti, i učinie z něho jeskyni lotrovú a kurevskú (Jan Hus, *Česká nedělní postila*, ed. by Daňhelka, p. 444).

>> (I say the same on the dance with which they offend God on Sunday as St Bernard says, if somebody allows it in his house and especially the monks in a cloister which should be [a place] to cry for their own sins as well as for the sins of others; [they should] read Scripture, pray religiously in it, but they change it into a den of thieves and whores.)

> *Wilhering Sermons:* Též diem i o tanci, jímž v neděli bohu sě porúhají, jako die s. Bernardus, že, ktož v domu přepustí, **a zvlášť' duchovní**, tance neb kostectvie a nebo smilstvie, **mortaliter peccant, et spirituales plus quam seculares, quia, quod secularibus est veniale, hoc nobis spiritualibus est mortale** (Wilhering, Stiftsbibliothek, Cod. IX 122, fol. 88^v; p. 675).

>> (I say the same on the dance with which they offend God on Sunday as St Bernard says, if somebody, **especially cleric**, allows in his house dance, banquets or fornication, **deadly sins – and clergy more than laymen because for laymen it is an ordinary sin while for us, the clerics, it is a deadly sin.**)

Another passage is also omitted from Sermon no. 59. Here Jan Hus had used the example of the King Antiochus IV, who according to the Books of Maccabees and Josephus Flavius, had pillaged the Temple in Jerusalem and erected an altar for Zeus in it instead:

> *Czech Sunday Postil*: A ten znamená pyšné, jenž v cierkvi svaté mají je lidé jako za modly, ani z pýchy své hubie ty, kteříž nechtie sě modlám těm modliti, a také i knihy pálé, kteréž jsú proti jich zlosti (Jan Hus, *Česká nedělní postila*, ed. by Daňhelka, p. 451).

>> (And he signifies proud men, who are being honoured as idols by people in the Holy Church, and because of their pride, they are killing those who do not want to pray to these idols and they also burn books, which talks against their hate.)

> *Wilhering Sermons*: a ten znamená pyšné, jenž v cierkvi svaté mají je lidé jako za modly, ani pak z pýchy své hubie ty, kteříž nechtie modlám těm modliti (Wilhering, Stiftsbibliothek, Cod. IX 122, fols 93^v–94^r; p. 684).

(And he signifies proud men, who are being honoured as idols by people in the Holy Church, and because of their pride, they are killing those who don't want to pray to these idols.)

It would seem that the omitted passage had already lost its social context by the time that the *Wilhering Sermons* were written, as it refers to the key issue of Hus's conflict with the church authorities, the public burning of the works of John Wycliff, as ordered by the Archbishop of Prague in 1410.[37]

Specifics of the Czech Language

The Czech language employed in the *Wilhering Sermons* is generally the same on linguistic grounds as in the original *Czech Sunday Postil* with only some minor differences. Most notably, there are two rather systematic changes: firstly, vocalization of the syllabic 'r' and 'l' in the positions TrT and TlT and, secondly, the dative and locative singular of feminine adjectives has the ending -*éj* instead of -*é*.

1. Vocalization of the syllabic 'r' and 'l' in the positions TrT and TlT:

Czech Sunday Postil	Wilhering Sermons	English translation
Trhlého	Trihlého	[of] tugged
Naplníte	Napliníte	[you] will fill up
Držení	Drižění	Holding

2. The dative and locative singular of feminine adjectives has the ending -*éj* instead of -*é*:

Czech Sunday Postil	Wilhering Sermons	English translation
k věčné radosti	k věčnéj radosti	for the eternal joy
k tvé vóli	k tvéj vuoli	at your will
o svaté trojici	o svatéj trojici	about the Holy Trinity

At the lexical level, the regular use of the conjunction *ež* ('that') instead of *že* is notable, as is the use of *inhed* instead of *ihned* ('immediately'). We also find two rather archaic forms that are not present in the Czech original: On one occasion *ny* ('us') is used instead of *nás*, and, similarly, the first-person plural ending -*my*

---

37 Hus wrote a treatise on the occasion, *De libris hereticorum legendis*, which starts with the words: *Libri hereticorum sunt legendi, non conburendi, dum in ipsis veritas continetur.* ('The books of heretics should be read, not burnt, if they contain truth.'). See Jan Hus, *Polemica*, ed. by Eršil, p. 21.

in the case of *nemóžemy* ('we can't') is used once in place of the original *nemóžeme*.

While such forms can be found in other contemporary Czech texts, they are not present in the preserved manuscripts of the *Czech Sunday Postil*. For this reason, we can cautiously attribute them to the author of the *Wilhering Sermons*.

Latin Language and the Translation

The Latin text is basically a word-for-word translation with occasional transpositions, smaller omissions, and additions. The following table shows one passage, both in the original version and side by side in its Wilhering adaptation. Latin words are given in bold. Notice that in the *Wilhering Sermons* various short words have been added into the original, and which are therefore missing from the left column:

Czech Sunday Postil (Jan Hus, *Česká nedělní postila*, ed. by Daňhelka, p. 443)	*Wilhering Sermons* (Wilhering, Stiftsbibliothek, Cod. IX 122, fol. 88ʳ; p. 674)	Word-by-word English translation of the version from the *Wilhering Sermons*
A	A	And
tak	tak,	so,
-	**pueri**	children
-	**dilecti,**	dear
v	**in**	in
tomto	**hoc**	this
čtení	**evangelio**	Gospel
ukazuje	**ostendit**	[he] shows
nám	**nobis**	us
svatý	s.	s.
Lukáš	**Lucas**	Lucas
na	**in**	in
-	**domino**	the lord
Ježíšovi	**Iesu**	Jesus
veliké	**magnam**	great
milosrdenstvie,	**misericordiam**	mercy
-	**et**	and
na	**in**	in

Czech Sunday Postil (Jan Hus, *Česká nedělní postila*, ed. by Daňhelka, p. 443)	*Wilhering Sermons* (Wilhering, Stiftsbibliothek, Cod. IX 122, fol. 88[r]; p. 674)	Word-by-word English translation of the version from the *Wilhering Sermons*
Zacheovi	Zacheo	Zacchaeus
pokánie	**penitenciam**	penitence
pravé	**veram,**	real
a	a	and
na	na	in
jiných	jiných	others
-	**eciam**	also
-	**ostendit**	shows
reptánie	reptánie	grumbling
nemúdré.	nemúdré.	unwise

This type of word-for-word translation preserves all of the major syntactical features of the Czech language, including Czech expressions. There are, indeed, many regional flavours of Latin which are heavily influenced by their corresponding vernacular languages. This is one of the reasons behind the multiple 'national' dictionaries of medieval Latin, such as for instance the Latin-Czech *Latinitatis medii aevi lexicon Bohemorum*,[38] whereas classical Latin in comparison has universal dictionaries. However, this particular word-for-word translation is not so simple. The Czech language has not been simply 'translated' into Latin but rather has been 'encoded': Here the Latin language adopts the role and a quality of a metalanguage, in which the Czech original is closely preserved so that it may have been turned very quickly back into Czech (incl. its various dialects) or into another, syntactically similar vernacular language. The *Wilhering Sermons* are not unique in this respect. The Latin translation of the *Czech Sunday Postil* in Mk 91, for example, uses the same 'encoding' method of translation.[39]

This Latin 'code' must be regarded as a rather extreme case of 'Czech' medieval Latin, for which the *Wilhering Sermons* share typical features. The use of *solus* for 'himself' (i.e. classical Latin *ipse*) is typical here, as is *ipse* for 'he'.[40] Also of note is the use of the reflexive pronoun *suus, sua, suum* ('his, her, its') for the Czech reflexive pronoun *svůj, svá, své*, regardless of the grammatical person, although this was not exclusively employed as can be seen in the following example. The pronoun *svůj* is translated once as *tuus*, according to the rules of clas-

---

[38] See *Latinitatis medii aevi lexicon Bohemorum*, online: <http://lb.ics.cas.cz/#cs> [accessed 3 November 2022].

[39] See Odstrčilík, 'Translation and Transformation of Jan Hus's Czech Sunday Postil'.

[40] Cf. *Quadragesimale Admontense*, ed. by Florianová and others, p. xxviii.

sical Latin, but also once as *suus* as would be expected in 'Czech' medieval Latin, and one further occasion it is simply left untranslated.

Czech Sunday Postil (Jan Hus, *Česká nedělní postila*, ed. by Daňhelka, p. 457)	Wilhering Sermons (Wilhering, Stiftsbibliothek, Cod. IX 122, fol. 97ᵛ; p. 691)	Word-by-word English translation of the version from the *Wilhering Sermons*
A	A	And
ihned	inhed	immediately
přikryješ	přikryješ	you will cover
lásků,	lásků,	with love
miluje	**diligens**	loving
pána	**dominum**	the lord
boha	**deum**	god
ze	**ex**	from
všeho	**toto**	all
srdce	**corde**	hearth
svého	**tuo**	your
a	**et**	and
ze	**ex**	from
všie	**tota**	all
duše	**anima**	soul
své	**sua**	your
a	**et**	and
ze	**ex**	from
všie	**tota**	all
mysli	**mente**	mind
své.	své.	your

Both Czech and Latin substantives possess three grammatical genders: masculine, feminine, and neuter. Being different languages, the gender of words with the same meaning is often different which occasionally causes issues in the text. In the first example, a Czech substantive is translated into a Latin word of a different gender, but the adjective in Czech remains in the original gender (fol. 89ᵛ; p. 676 and fol. 95ʳ; p. 686):

(1) prvý   turba
first(M)-NOM.SG. crowd(F)-NOM.SG.
'the first crowd'

(2) domus   tělesný
house(F)-NOM.SG.   physical(M)-NOM.SG.
'the physical house'

In the second example, a Latin substantive assumes the Czech gender. This is especially the case with the Latin word for house, *domus* (feminine), which is used to translate the Czech word *dóm* (masculine): (fol. 90ᵛ; p. 678 and fol. 94ᵛ; p. 685)

(3) in domo   tuo
in house(F)-ABL.SG   your(M)-ABL.SG
'in your house'

(4) domus   spiritualis   primus
house(F)-NOM.SG   spiritual(M/F)-NOM.SG   first(M)-NOM.SG
'first spiritual house'

The fact that the Latin word *domus* is of the second declination could facilitate this transition as this declension mainly comprises substantives in the masculine and neuter genders. However, the author of the *Wilhering Sermons* did know the correct gender of *domus* in Latin, as he used it in phrases such as *secunda domus* ('the second house').

Compound verb forms represent another, even more complicated issue. Czech language uses compound verb forms for the perfect past tense and also, in part, for the future tense, conditional mood, and passive voice. The Latin language often employs simple verb forms to convey the same function. This may constitute a problem for a literal full or partial translation from Czech to Latin that could result in the production of ungrammatical passages. In the *Wilhering Sermons*, the vast majority of compound verb forms is correctly translated, however, we can find two remarkable instances which escaped the translator's attention. In the first case, the Czech auxiliary verb *jest* ('is') remains in place, while the word *odpustil* ('forgave', past or l-participle) is translated with the Latin perfect tense (fol. 88ʳ; p. 673):

(5) jemuž   jest   milostivý   **salvator**
who-DAT.SG   be-AUX.3SG.PRS   merciful-NOM.SG   saviour-NOM.SG.

peccata	dimisit
sin-ACC.PL.	forgive-3SG.PER

'to whom the merciful Saviour forgave the sins'

The second example is similar, except that the auxiliary verb *jest* ('is') is actually translated into Latin as *est* (fol. 94ᵛ; p. 685):

(6) et	posuit	est	založenie
and	lay-3SG.PERF	be-AUX.3SG.PRS	foundation-ACC.SG

'and he laid the foundation'

Both examples clearly show the dominance of the underlying language (Czech) in this translation.

Another feature of the *Wilhering Sermons* is a tendency to slightly expand or enhance *nomina sacra* in Latin in comparison to the original. Jan Hus often just uses simple forms, such as *Ježíš* ('Jesus'), *spasitel* ('saviour'), or *bóh* ('God'). However, in the *Wilhering Sermons* these forms are occasionally expanded:

Czech Sunday Postil (Jan Hus, *Česká nedělní postila*, ed. by Daňhelka)	English translation	Wilhering Sermons (Wilhering, Stiftsbibliothek, Cod. IX 122)	English translation
Ježíš	Jesus	pius Iesus (fol. 90ʳ)	merciful Jesus
viděti Ježíše	to see Jesus	viděti Iesum misericordem (fol. 90ʳ)	to see the merciful Jesus
Spasitel	Saviour	misericors salvator (fol. 90ʳ)	merciful saviour
slovo Ježíšovo	the word of Jesus	verbum domini Iesu (fol. 94ᵛ)	the word of the Lord Jesus

In the case of the biblical quotations, we have to consider two options. In this process, the translator could either retranslate verbatim from the Czech original back to Latin, or use directly the Vulgate variant, hence we have to compare all three wordings (Czech, the *Wilhering Sermons*, Vulgate):

Czech Sunday Postil: A ten bieše knieže zjevných hřiešníkóv a bohatý (Jan Hus, *Česká nedělní postila*, ed. by Daňhelka, p. 443).

Wilhering Sermons: **Et iste erat princeps publicanorum et dives** (Wilhering, Stiftsbibliothek, Cod. IX 122, fol. 88ʳ; p. 674).

Vulgate: **et hic princeps erat publicanorum, et ipse dives** (Luke 19. 2).

In this case, the Czech wording and that of the Vulgate are very close and it is impossible to decide, whether the translator retranslated the Czech version or used the Vulgate. In other cases, however, the Latin translation of biblical quotations in the *Wilhering Sermons* differ significantly from that of the Vulgate:

Czech Sunday Postil: Kto ukradne jednu ovci, navrať čtyři ovce za jednu ovci (Jan Hus, *Česká nedělní postila*, ed. by Daňhelka, p. 448).

Wilhering Sermons: Kto **furatur** unam ovem, **reddat** pro una čtyři ovce (Wilhering, Stiftsbibliothek, Cod. IX 122, fol. 91ʳ; p. 679).

Vulgate: Si quis **furatus fuerit** bovem aut ovem, et occiderit vel vendiderit: quinque boves pro uno bove **restituet**, et quatuor oves pro una ove (Exodus 22. 1).

Here, the most interesting feature is the verb form *furatur*, which is used in the simple present tense rather than the future perfect tense (*furatus fuerit*) as would have been expected, and which would correspond to the form in the Vulgate. Again, the reason for the use of this form seems to be an effort to produce an exact, literal translation of the Czech text. In the Czech language, each verb as a lexical unit has a specific category called aspect that can be either perfective or imperfective. The former one denotes an action in progress, the latter an action as a complete act. This means also that in the Czech language, there are usually verb pairs – verbs with the same meaning but different aspect.[41]

The category of aspect influences also the grammar. If a verb is imperfective, then the future tense is built with an auxiliary verb, 'to be', and an infinitive. If a verb is perfective, then the simple present form with the future meaning is used instead. The present form of perfective verbs is unambiguous since the perfective verbs can never signify an ongoing or present action, but only a whole action in the past or future.

The *Czech Sunday Postil* uses the present form of the perfective verb *ukradne*. Its meaning is unambiguously that 'he/she/it will steal'. The author of the *Wilhering Sermons* seems to have translated it as literally as possible, i.e. in the Latin present tense *furatur*. This proves that the author of the *Wilhering Sermons* did not use the Vulgate in this case but translated directly from Czech.

Translations of biblical quotations in the *Wilhering Sermons* are also not always the same but they vary according to the variations in the Czech original. Thus, we can observe how the original Vulgate is translated in the *Czech Sunday Postil* and further retranslated back with various degrees of language mixing. A good example can be found in the Sermon no. 58 with the biblical quotation from Luke 19. 5. Its original Latin version from the Vulgate is *hodie in domo tua oportet me manere* (Douay-Rheims Bible translation: *for this day I must abide in thy house*). This biblical verse appears in the following versions in the *Czech Sunday Postil* and subsequently in the *Wilhering Sermons*:

---

41 For an easy explanation see, e.g., Naughton, *Czech*, p. 146.

first version:

Czech Sunday Postil: Dnes v domu tvém musiem býti (Jan Hus, *Česká nedělní postila*, ed. by Daňhelka, p. 446).

Wilhering Sermons: Dnes **in domo tuo oportet me esse** (Wilhering, Stiftsbibliothek, Cod. IX 122, fol. 90ᵛ; p. 678).

second version:

Czech Sunday Postil: Dnes musím v tvém domu býti (Jan Hus, *Česká nedělní postila*, ed. by Daňhelka, p. 454).

Wilhering Sermons: **hodie oportet me in domo tua** býti (Wilhering, Stiftsbibliothek, Cod. IX 122, fol. 96ʳ; p. 688).

third version:

Czech Sunday Postil: dnes v domu tvém musiem bydliti (Jan Hus, *Česká nedělní postila*, ed. by Daňhelka, p. 446).

Wilhering Sermons: **hodie in domo tuo oportet me** bydliti (Wilhering, Stiftsbibliothek, Cod. IX 122, fol. 90ᵛ; p. 678).

As Jan Hus himself used various rewordings for the biblical quotation, so the author of the *Wilhering Sermons* took liberty in which words he translated into Latin and which he left untranslated.

Language Mixing

There are *c.* 1311 Latin words spread between *c.* 362 passages of the *Wilhering Sermons*, which constitute *c.* 13 per cent of the text in all.[42] A typical, longer passage from the text can be seen here with the example of Sermon no. 59, in which the words given in Latin have been marked in bold (fol. 95ʳ; p. 686):

A tak, má-li kto býti spasen, musí v Krista věřiti, jeho slovo vnitř **audire** a je skutkem až do smrti plniti. Protož musí pevně dóm cnosti v Kristovi, jenž jest kámen pevný, založiti. Protož i die Kristus v 7. k. s. Mat.: 'Každý, **qui audit** slova má **et facit ea, similis est homini sapienti, edificanti domum suam** na kámen'. Ten kámen jest Kristus, jakož die s. Pavel, **in quo debet** založen **domus spiritualis**; neb jinak by ten dóm proti

---

[42] The exact numbers cannot be determined more precisely because of the nature of the code-switching. Firstly, a number of words are rather ambiguous in their nature. This is especially true in the cases such as proper names (*Lucas*), short interjections (like 'O') and to some extent, the numbers – these could often be counted equally as either Latin or Czech. Secondly, what constitutes a Latin passage? The figure of 345 refers to the number of continuous Latin passages but in many cases a Latin passage might be interrupted by only a single Czech word, like *quod lectum est **tu** dominico post ascensionem domini* ('which is read **that** Sunday after the ascension of the Lord') (Wilhering, Stiftsbibliothek, Cod. IX 122, fol. 100ʳ); pp. 694–695).

pokušení nemohl konečně ostáti, jako **domus** tělesný, nemaje založenie pevného, neostál by před větrem a před povodní.

> (And so, if somebody wants to be redeemed, he has to believe in Christ, **hear** his word inside and fulfil it till death. Therefore, he has to found firmly the house of virtue in Christ, who is a firm rock. Therefore, Christ says in Matthew 7: 'everyone **who hears** these words of mine **and do them, is like a wise man who built his house** on the rock'. And this rock is Christ, as St Paul says, **in which has to** be founded a **spiritual house**; or otherwise could that house not stand against the temptation till the end, as a corporal **house**, because it would not have a firm foundation and therefore it could not stand firmly against the wind and the flood.)

The distribution of the Latin words is very uneven. There are no Latin words in the pericopes, only in the explanatory part of the sermons. In some paragraphs, the Latin words constitute only a very small percentage. While it is admittedly not precise to use the division into paragraphs as introduced in a modern edition, it can still provide a rough overview of the overall pattern: there are no Latin words in the fifth paragraph of Sermon no. 59, while in the following paragraph of the sermon, the percentage of Latin words exceeds 32 per cent. There seem to be no obvious reason for this variation in this case. Both paragraphs are rather similar in their nature.

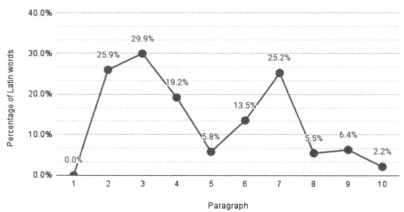

Sermon 59 - Percentage of Latin words

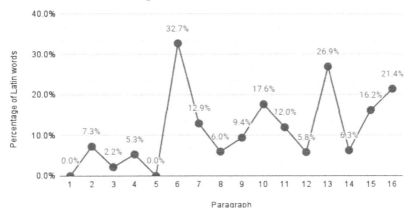

Sermon 33 - Percentage of Latin words

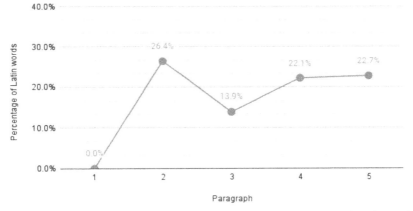

The average length of text that is written continuously in Latin is 3.8 words. Intralinear glosses, i.e. glosses that are integrated into the main body of the text, are very rare, e.g. (fol. 88ʳ; p. 674):

(7) měl	pilnost	velikú,	**quod**
have-3SG.PERF	diligence-ACC.SG	great-ACC.SG	that

videret	– uzřel	**Iesum**	
see-3SG.SBJV.IMPRF	– see-3SG.COND.PRF	Jesus-ACC.SG	

'he had a great diligence **to see** – see **Jesus**'

Since their overall number is very small, it is difficult to identify any specific reason for their incorporation into the text or an overall pattern for their use. However, in the example just given, a role may be played by the word *videret* having a subjunctive mood as a part of the purpose of the clause. The Czech language does not have this mood and instead uses the conditional mood. In the original Czech text, this intent is expressed as follows (p. 443):

(8) jest	měl	pilnost	velikú,	aby
be-AUX.3SG.PRS.	have-3SG.PRF	diligence-ACC.SG.	great- ACC.SG.,	that
uzřel			Ježíše	
see-3SG.COND. PRF			Jesus-ACC.SG	

'he had a great diligence to see Jesus'

Almost all the other Latin words can be labelled as insertions or as parenthetical asides. This means that they do not accompany any specific Czech word or phrase. Instead, they stand independently in their respective sentences. Such insertions can be as long as seventeen words, or, on the contrary, very short. The latter case is especially typical of words such as *salvator* ('saviour', 5x), *Iesus* ('Jesus', 5x), *homo* ('man', 18x). Other solitary words can be also found, and sometimes the text switched back and forth very quickly between languages (fol. 99r; p. 693):

(9) o	němž	die	David	prorok:	**Beati**
about	whom-LOC.SG.	say-3SG.PRS.	David-NOM.SG.	prophet-NOM.SG:	blessed-NOM.PL.
ti,	**qui**	**habitant**	**in**	**domo**	**tua**
they-NOM.PL.	that-NOM.PL.	dwell-3 PL.PRS.	in	house-ABL.SG.	thy-ABL.SG.

'About whom David the prophet says: Blessed are they that dwell in thy house'.

The short switches from Latin back into Czech are especially interesting in the case of conjunctions: *ež* ('that', 2x), *že* ('that'), with *jenž* ('who'), *jímž* ('by what'), *neb* ('because'), and *poňavadž* ('because'), e.g. (fol. 88v; p. 675):

> Ó, milý křesťane, zdali **non scis? Si non scis, tunc iam scias**, ež **dominico celebrare est se a peccatis** zdržeti […]
>
> > (O, dear Christian, don't you know? If **you don't know that, let you then know** that **to celebrate Sunday means to** abstain **from sin.**)

On account of the relatively limited extent of the *Wilhering Sermons*, we can only speculate about the underlying reasons for preserving Czech conjunctions in these cases. However, if the idea of 'encoding' is plausible, then the conjunctions are one of the parts which are the most difficult to convey in Latin in a word-for-word translation. The author may have deemed (either knowingly or unconsciously) that it was important to preserve the Czech conjunctions, *ež* in this case, so as to preserve the original 'Czech' syntax as much as possible. The Latin conjunction *quod* could very well have been used as a translation for *ež / že* (and indeed as it was elsewhere). However, the author of the *Wilhering Sermons* also used this conjunction for the Czech conjunctions *aby* ('in order to') and *kteréž* ('which'), as well as for the pronoun *co* ('what'). This makes *quod* slightly ambiguous, which was perhaps enough motivation to compel the author to preserve the original Czech conjunction here.

Further information on the motivations for the code-switching are revealed if we look at which specific Latin words appear in them. The following table lists those which are most common (given here without lemmatization, and changed to lower-case):

Order	Word	Occurrences	Percentage
1	et	57	4.34%
2	in	48	3.67%
3	homo	42	3.21%
4	est	41	3.13%
5	quod	22	1.68%
6	non	22	1.68%
7	salvator	18	1.38%
8	dicit	12	0.92%
9	qui	12	0.92%
10	sicud	12	0.92%

Generated using *Utilities for Online Operating System*, online: <https://www.online-utility.org/text/analyzer.jsp> [accessed 3 November 2022].

With the possible and prominent exception of the word *homo* ('man'), this would appear to be an expected frequency for any Latin text. However, it is interesting to compare this table against the most commonly used first words as found in the Latin passages:

Order	Word	Occurrences	Percentage
1	homo	34	9.47%
2	in	25	6.96%
3	et	15	4.18%
4	salvator	13	3.62%
5	non	10	2.79%
6	quod	7	1.95%
7	omnes	6	1.67%
8	qui	6	1.67%
9	sicud	6	1.67%
10	domus	5	1.39%

Generated using *Utilities for Online Operating System*, online: <https://www.online-utility.org/text/analyzer.jsp> [accessed 3 November 2022].

As can be seen, the Latin passages themselves tend to start with the most commonly used Latin words in the text as a whole. The recurrence of the word *domus* is influenced by Sermon no. 59 which features a long bilingual exposition on this topic. Again, the most striking feature is the presence of the word *homo*.

One of the basic explanations of the phenomenon can be that short, common, and/or frequent Latin words were triggers of code-switching. In this respect, the *Wilhering Sermons* provide a unique opportunity to look at the visual aspect of code-switching. Its role was first discussed by Laura Wright,[43] when she focused on medieval, Latin-English-Norman business writing from the fifteenth century. She has successfully shown the role of abbreviation in rendering the language of the text ambiguous by obfuscating or hiding language-specific parts, thus enabling various expansions of abbreviations in various languages. She called these elements 'visual diamorphs'.[44] Her methodology was then modified and applied to medieval Irish homiletic literature by Tom ter Horst and Nike Stam.[45] In contrast to the materials which Wright, ter Horst, and Stam worked with, the *Wilhering Sermons* have a well-known underlying model, which allows the close observation of the treatment of specific elements.

The *Wilhering Sermons* contain many ambiguous words, which can be read both as Latin and Czech even when they have not been abbreviated: short particles (*o* and *ai*) and proper names (*Lucas*). Furthermore, we find multiple examples which could be labelled as visual diamorphs, i.e. abbreviations, which can be expanded once more in multiple ways. This can be again the case of proper

---

43 Wright, 'On Variation in Medieval Mixed-Language Business Writing'.
44 Wright, 'On Variation in Medieval Mixed-Language Business Writing', pp. 203–04.
45 ter Horst and Stam, 'Visual Diamorphs'.

names ('*Mat.*') and numbers (*2a žalost hřícha*). However, what is probably the most intriguing element is the expanding of abbreviations regarding Jesus (*ihs*) and Christ (*xps*). The text of the *Wilhering Sermons* contains many Czech equivalents which have been written down in full as *Ježíš* and *Kristus*. This may lead to the assumption that where the abbreviations *ihs* and *xps* and similar have been employed, they should be expanded as Latin words.

If we look closely at Patera's diplomatic edition and Daňhelka's subsequent edition based on it and compare them with the manuscript, then an interesting inconsistency can be found in the way they expand these abbreviations, e.g., Sermon no. 58 (Figs 1, 2):

Patera's edition:	Ai considera, dilecte fidelis Christiane (p. 363)
Daňhelka's edition:	Aj, considera, dilecte fidelis christiane (p. 677)
Transliteration:	Ai ɋſidâ dilcê fidêl x̄ane
English translation:	'See, consider this, beloved faithful Christian'

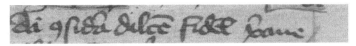

Figure 1: Wilhering, Stiftsbibliothek, Cod. IX 122, fol. 90ʳ.[46]

Patera's edition:	mili homo et fidelis krzeſtane (p. 362)
Daňhelka's edition:	milý homo et fidelis křesťane (p. 697)
Transliteration:	mili hô z fidêl x̄ane
English translation:	'dear man and faithful Christian'

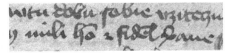

Figure 2: Wilhering, Stiftsbibliothek, Cod. IX 122, fol. 89ᵛ.

As we see, Patera and Daňhelka expand the very same *xane* abbreviations once as a Latin word and once as a Czech word! However, can this abbreviation be expanded as a Czech word at all? Isn't that just the mistake on the side of editors? Luckily, an almost identical case confirms this possibility (Fig. 3):

---

[46] Because of the Covid-19 pandemic at the time this study was being written, it was not possible to obtain images of better quality.

Patera's edition: O fidelis krzeſtanku (p. 365)
Daňhelka's edition: O fidelis křesťánku (p. 679)

Transliteration: O fidêl x̂anku
English translation: 'O faithful little Christian'

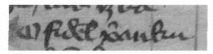

Figure 3: Wilhering, Stiftsbibliothek, Cod. IX 122, fol. 91ʳ.

The abbreviation *x̂anku* used here is unambiguous – it is the diminutive of the word *křesťan* ('Christian'), i.e., *křesťánku*, since there is no Latin word to which this abbreviation could correspond.

This suggests that the abbreviation *x̂ane* is probably a linguistically ambiguous visual diamorph which can be read in both languages as needed – and as Patera and Daňhelka unintentionally proved by their inconsistent transcriptions. I believe that the same is true also for abbreviations for Jesus (*ihs*) and for Christ (*x̂ps*). One could read them either in Latin or in Czech.

However, did the author of the *Wilhering Sermons* use Latin abbreviations just to purposefully introduce such ambiguity? Let us now return to the most common Latin words. What do they have in common? Almost all of them can be abbreviated significantly in late medieval Latin writing. The best example of this is probably the already often-quoted word *homo* ('man'). This word is a common addition made by the author of the *Wilhering Sermons* and serves to address the audience, e.g., (Wilhering, Stiftsbibliothek, Cod. IX 122, fol. 89ʳ; p. 676): *Tu considera, o homo, ež tehdy pán bóh* […] ('And here consider, o man, that at that time the Lord God […]'). The author of the *Wilhering Sermons* did, indeed, know and use the Czech equivalent, *člověk*, elsewhere so why then did he use the Latin word *homo* so often instead?

I would argue that the reason behind this becomes obvious when we look at the abbreviations of these words from fol. 96ᵛ:

 hô (homo)

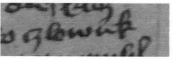 czlowiek (člověk)

In other words, the word *czlowiek* takes much more space, while the word *homo* can be easily abbreviated in the way that it requires only two letters with a superscript line above the 'o'. Similar things can be said also with regard to the other common Latin words. The Czech language (as with other vernacular languages) did not have as many abbreviations and was thus much more literal (*sic!*).

Throughout this study, I have sought to describe some of the orthographical differences found between the main manuscripts of the *Czech Sunday Postil* and the manuscript of the *Wilhering Sermons*. There is one more peculiar point, which may be of importance here. The principal Czech manuscripts make hardly any use of Czech abbreviations, while the *Wilhering Sermons*, even in the Czech text, abbreviate many words:

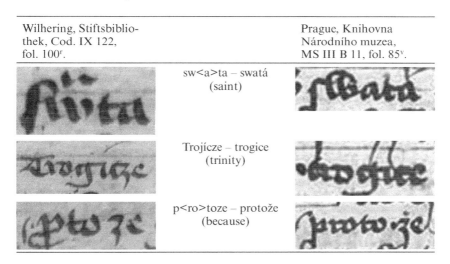

Therefore, we can observe a tendency for higher writing economy in the *Wilhering Sermons*, which is reflected both in the Czech and in the Latin.

Conclusion

The *Czech Sunday Postil* was originally written for lay readers, partly for their education but partly also as a personal testimony of Hus's ideas and struggles. Its importance is reflected in its consistent manuscript tradition, following the 'letter' of his work even in the orthographic system. On the other hand, the *Wilhering Sermons* represent an example of the radical reception and recontextualization of this work. They were intended for and used as model sermons and changes in the content and language correspond to that role. Hus is stripped from the work, sermons are rearranged, put into an unusual manuscript context, the orthography is changed, unsuitable passages are omitted while others, such as addresses to the audience, are added.

The most puzzling feature of the sermons is, however, the mixture of the languages. Latin passages are often direct, word-for-word translations from the Czech. All major syntactical features of the original language are preserved, and the translations enable the quick and swift translation back into Czech (incl. various dialects) or other similar vernaculars if required. The Latin language thus works as a kind of a meta-language, in which the Czech language is 'encoded'. This is not a unique strategy, however, as the Latin translation of the *Czech Sunday Postil* in Mk 91 also has similar features.

Code-switching is frequent, sometimes happening after single words. Some of the Czech conjunctions are left untranslated within Latin passages, perhaps with the intent of preserving the original syntactical structure as much as possible and facilitating rendering the text back in Czech, if necessary. On the other hand, a number of specific words tend to be given in the Latin language, most notably the frequent *homo* ('man'). Moreover, many words, either expanded or abbreviated, can be read both as Czech and Latin.

Motivations for the code-switching seem to vary: the bilingualism of the author or his greater familiarity with Latin than with Czech definitely played a role; however, the most prominent motive seems to be economy of writing. While scribes had developed a very advanced system of Latin abbreviations, for other languages, among them Czech, only a very limited set of abbreviations were used. By using Latin abbreviations in place of Czech, this allowed the author of the *Wilhering Sermons* to write down his sermons more rapidly and more efficiently.

Bibliography

Manuscript Sources

Brno, Moravská zemská knihovna, Mk 91
Neustadt an der Aisch, Kirchenbibliothek, MS 2888
Prague, Knihovna Národního muzea, MS III B 11
———, MS IV C 18
Prague, Národní knihovna České republiky, MS VI F 22
———, MS XVII A 11
———, MS XVII G 30
Wilhering, Stiftsbibliothek, Cod. IX 122

Primary Sources

Jan Hus, *Česká nedělní postila: Vyloženie svatých čtení nedělních* ed. by Jiří Daňhelka, Magistri Iohannis Hus Opera Omnia, 2 (Prague, Academia, 1992)
———,*Česká sváteční kázání*, ed. by Jiří Daňhelka, Magistri Iohannis Hus Opera Omnia, 3 (Prague: Academia, 1995)

——, *Knížky o svatokupectví*, in *Drobné spisy české*, ed. by Amedeo Molnár [Jiří Daňhelka], Magistri Iohannis Hus Opera Omnia, 4 (Prague: Academia, 1985), pp. 187–270

——, *Polemica*, ed. by Jaroslav Eršil, Corpus Christianorum: Continuatio Mediaevalis, 238 (Turnhout: Brepols, 2010)

——, *Výklady*, ed. by Jiří Daňhelka, Magistri Iohannis Hus Opera Omnia, 1 (Prague: Academia, 1975)

Orthographia Bohemica, ed. by Kateřina Voleková, introduction by Kateřina Voleková and Michal Dragoun, trans. by Marcela Koupilová, Ondřej Koupil, and David Livingstone (Prague: Akropolis, 2019)

Quadragesimale Admontense / Quadragesimale admontské, ed. by Hana Florianová, Dana Martínková, Zuzana Silagiová, and Hana Šedinová, Fontes Latini Bohemorum, 6 (Prague: OIKOYMENH, 2006)

Secondary Works

Bok, Václav, 'Literaturpflege im Kloster Vyšší Brod/Hohenfurt vom 13. bis zum 15. Jahrhundert', in *Zisterziensisches Schreiben im Mittelalter: Das Skriptorium der Reiner Mönche: Beiträge der Internationalen Tagung im Zisterzienserstift Rein, Mai 2003*, ed. by Anton Schwob and Karin Kranich-Hofbauer, Jahrbuch für Internationale Germanistik, Reihe A: Kongressberichte, 71 (Bern: Peter Lang, 2005), pp. 179–91

Dokoupil, Vladislav, *Catalogus codicum manu scriptorum Bibliothecae Dietrichsteinianae Nicolspurgensis*, Catalogi codicum manu scriptorum in Bibliotheca Universitatis Brunensis asservatorum, 2 (Prague: Státní pedagogické nakladatelství, 1958)

Grillnberger, Otto, 'Die Handschriften der Stiftsbibliothek zu Wilhering', in *Die Handschriften-Verzeichnisse der Cistercienser-Stifte*, 2 vols (Vienna: Hölder, 1891), II, pp. 1–114

Kaindl, Dominik, *Geschichte des Zisterzienserstiftes Hohenfurt in Böhmen* (Český Krumlov: author's edn, 1930)

Martinková, Michaela, 'Husova staročeská Postila v latinském překladu', *Usta ad Albim Bohemica*, 13/1 (2013), pp. 31–36

Miškovská, Hana, 'Latinské překlady Husovy české Postilly v rukopise Mk 91 a Mk 56 a vztah k jejich předlohám', *Listy filologické / Folia philologica*, 113/3 (1990), pp. 188–99

Naughton, James D., *Czech: An Essential Grammar*, Routledge Essential Grammars (London and New York: Routledge, 2005)

Odstrčilík, Jan, 'Translation and Transformation of Jan Hus's Czech Sunday Postil', in *Pursuing a New Order II: Late Medieval Vernacularization and the Bohemian Reformation*, ed. by Pavlína Rychterová and Julian Ecker, The Medieval Translator / Traduire au Moyen Âge, 17/2 (Turnhout: Brepols, 2019), pp. 153–84

——, 'Jacobus de Saraponte's "Aurissa": Evidence for Multilingual Preaching', *Medieval Worlds*, 13 (2021), pp. 147–76, online: <https://doi.org/10.1553/medievalworlds_no13_2021s147> [accessed 3 November 2022]

Patera, Adolf, 'Mistra Jana Husi česká kázání na posvěcenie kostela a na sv. Trojici', *Věstník Královské české společnosti nauk: Třída filosoficko – historicko – filologická*, 15 (1890 [1891]), pp. 355–85

Rychterová, Pavlína, 'The Vernacular Theology of Jan Hus', in *A Companion to Jan Hus*, ed. by František Šmahel and Ota Pavlícek, Brill's Companions to the Christian Tradition, 54 (Leiden and Boston: Brill, 2015), pp. 170–213

Šlosar, Dušan, 'Diakritický pravopis', in *Dějiny českého pravopisu (do r. 1902): Sborník příspěvků z mezinárodní konference Dějiny českého pravopisu (do r. 1902) 23.–25. září 2010, Brno, Česká republika / History of Czech orthography (Up to 1902): Proceedings of the International Conference History of Czech Orthography (Up to 1902), 23.–25. September 2010, Brno, Czech Republic* (Brno: Host, 2010), pp. 200–05

Šmahel, František, 'Instead of Conclusion: Jan Hus as Writer and Author', in *A Companion to Jan Hus*, ed. by František Šmahel and Ota Pavlíček, Brill's Companions to the Christian Tradition, 54 (Leiden and Boston: Brill, 2015), pp. 370–410

Soukup, Pavel, 'Jan Hus as a Preacher', in *A Companion to Jan Hus*, ed. by František Šmahel and Ota Pavlíček, Brill's Companions to the Christian Tradition, 54 (Leiden and Boston: Brill, 2015), pp. 96–129

——, *Hus als Prediger*, Kohlhammer Urban-Taschenbücher, 737 (Stuttgart: W. Kohlhammer, 2014)

Svobodová, Andrea, 'Komplexní studium Rukopisu dzikovského se zaměřením na grafickou, jazykovou a textovou analýzu české sbírky kázání' (unpublished doctoral thesis, Charles University of Prague, 2016)

ter Horst, Tom, and Nike Stam, 'Visual Diamorphs: The Importance of Language Neutrality in Code-Switching from Medieval Ireland', in *Multilingual Practices in Language History: English and Beyond*, ed. by Päivi Pahta, Janne Skaffari, and Laura Wright, Language Contact and Bilingualism, 15 (Berlin: De Gruyter Mouton, 2018), pp. 223–42

Vidmanová, Anežka, 'Hus als Prediger', *Communio Viatorum*, 19 (1976), pp. 65–81

——, 'Kdy, kde a jak psal Hus českou Postillu', *Listy filologické / Folia philologica*, 112/3 (1989), pp. 144–58

Voleková, Kateřina, 'Znaménko rozlišovací a zdůrazňovací ve staročeských rukopisech', *Slavia Occidentalis. Linguistica*, 75/1 (2018), pp. 133–41

Wright, Laura, 'On Variation in Medieval Mixed-Language Business Writing', in *Code-Switching in Early English*, ed. by Herbert Schendl and Laura Wright, Topics in English Linguistics, 76 (Berlin: De Gruyter Mouton, 2011), pp. 191–218.

Websites

http://manuscripta.at

Latinitatis medii aevi lexicon Bohemorum, online: <http://lb.ics.cas.cz/#cs> [accessed 3 November 2022]

Utilities for Online Operating System, online: <https://www.online-utility.org/text/analyzer.jsp> [accessed 3 November 2022]

RELIGIOUS EDUCATION IN TRANSITION

The Fifteenth- and Sixteenth-Century Croatian Translations of the Latin *Liber de modo bene vivendi ad sororem*

Andrea Radošević

Old Church Slavonic Institute, Zagreb

Introduction

This essay focuses on the so-called *Books of Blessed Bernard*, a late medieval Croatian translation of the Latin treatise *Liber de modo bene vivendi ad sororem* (henceforth *Liber*)[1] written in the twelfth and thirteenth centuries and long attributed to St Bernard of Clairvaux.[2] Although the text is known among scholars of Croatian medieval literature, it has not attracted the attention of historians and it has not yet been analysed and contextualized within its respective textual cultures. I will discuss this particular translation, aiming to contribute fundamental insights into the vernacular reception of the *Liber* in late medieval and early modern northern and western part of Croatian lands. The Grškovic's Miscellany is probably written in Istria. The Petris Miscellay was created somewhere in the northern or northwestern Croatian lands.

The tract, beginning with the words *Carissima in Christo soror*, may be described as the admonition of a nun by her spiritual father. Individual themes organized around Christian virtues and vices provide elaborate exhortations drawing on bible exegesis, especially of the Song of Songs and the Church fathers. Renunciation of the world, mortification of the flesh, rigorous modesty

---

1 Divi Bernardi abbatis ad sororem: Modvs bene vivendi in christianam religionem (1490).

2 The tract was probably written by a member of the Order of Saint Augustine. See *The Manere of Good Lyvyng*, ed. by Mouron, pp. 5–6. The seventeenth-century attribution of the work to Thomas of Froidmont (c. 1150–c. 1225) is still endorsed in some modern research and works of reference, for example, in the following essays: Kuczynski, *Prophetic Song*, pp. 88–100; Newman, 'Flaws in the Golden Bowl', p. 124, pp. 139–40. About the other attributions to Thomas of Froidmont see more in *The Manere of Good Lyvyng*, ed. by Mouron, p. 5. Today, Thomas of Froidmont (Thomas of Beverley) is generally known as the author of the *Vitae of Thomas*; see Pinder, 'The Cloister and the Garden', p. 176; Mouron, 'Praying without Images', p. 301.

in each respect, and constant meditation on earthly tribulations and heavenly delights must accompany the reader on her path to salvation. The text was very popular in the Middle Ages; it was translated into several European vernaculars (see below) and found its way into print before 1500.[3]

Over the last twenty years, the *Liber* has attracted increasing scholarly interest, although it has been well known since the beginning of modern scholarship. Jean Mabillon already doubted the medieval attribution to Bernard and the edition of the text was included in the Patrologia Latina as *dubium*.[4] The text received more attention through research on female spirituality in the Middle Ages. Thirty years ago Barbara Newman referred to it in her essay on twelfth-century female spirituality, and Brian McGuire paid attention to the reception of the *Liber* in the Order founded by the Swedish visionary Birgitta of Sweden.[5] Michael Kuczynski analysed the *Liber* in detail in his study of the medieval exegesis of the Psalter.[6] Janice Pinder, in order to illustrate 'the gender quality of theorizing about the religious life', compared the *Liber* to the *Speculum virginum*.[7] Anne Mouron published several comprehensive essays on the *Liber*, discussing at large the questions of its origin, authorship, content, as well as its literary and social contexts.[8] Thanks to the Middle English translation of the *Liber*, transmitted under the title of the *Manere of Good Lyvyng*, the tract has been focused on significantly in English literary studies. The other extant vernacular translations are mostly discussed by philologists and linguists, but comparative research on the European transmission and reception of the work is still missing.[9]

The *Liber* belongs to the 'literature of formation', that is, to a 'large group of writings concerned with training professed religious in the spiritual life, the practice of virtues, and communal and private discipline'.[10] The flourishing of literature dedicated to pious women in the late twelfth to thirteenth centuries was in

---

[3] The work was translated into several European vernaculars; see for example Dawn, 'La fuerza del prólogo', pp. 349–55.

[4] Bernardus Claraevallensis, *Liber de modo bene vivendi ad sororem*, ed. by Migne, cols 1199–1306.

[5] Newman, 'Flaws in the Golden Bowl', pp. 139–40; McGuire, 'A Benedictine-Cistercian Source?', p. 86; cf. Mouron, 'Praying without Images', pp. 91–92.

[6] Kuczynski, *Prophetic Song*, pp. 88–101.

[7] Pinder, 'The Cloister and the Garden', pp. 159–79.

[8] The *Manere of Good Lyvyng*, ed. by Mouron; Mouron, 'Praying without Images', pp. 91–101; Mouron, '"Listen to me, daughter, listen to a faithful counsel"', pp. 81–106; Mouron, '"Sub mensa Patrum micas collegi"', pp. 25–36; Mouron, '"The Manere of Good Lyvyng"', pp. 300–22.

[9] The *Manere of Good Lyvyng*, ed. by Mouron, pp. 19–37; For studies of texts in Hungarian, Catalonian, and German see, respectively, Korondi, 'A "Liber de modo bene vivendi"', pp. 156–64; Bratsch-Prince, 'La fuerza del prologo', pp. 349–55; Wareham,'"Wann du fromm lebst / so wirst du nimmer trawrig"', pp. 362–79.

[10] This term, as Newman said, includes an 'instruction for novices, commentaries on religious rules; works of guidance for solitaries; letters of direction to individual monks,

response to the growing number of communities of religious women who needed advanced instructions for contemplative life.[11] Likewise, there was a 'growing demand for professionals to provide pastoral care to religious women'.[12] Exhortative spiritual tracts for monks and nuns had similar topics and promoted identical spiritual goals to which their readers were to aspire. Apart from differences in approach to male and female readers, which are mostly seen in the use of particular gendered allusions, the same texts were often used for both male and female monasteries alike.[13] It is not uncommon to find texts which were originally addressed to women then being copied and adapted for male audiences.[14] For example, one version of the *Liber* (Madrid, Biblioteca Nacional de España, MS 871) 'indicates that, at least in the second half of the thirteenth century, the "virginal rhetoric" found on the *De modo* could be considered just as appropriate to man as it was for women'.[15] Furthermore, these treatises were taken up by translators and compilers who adapted them for lay readers by choosing chapters which could be used for their spiritual improvement.[16]

The *Liber de modo bene vivendi* in Croatian Vernacular Literature

The *Liber* is transmitted in two independent Croatian translations. The first translation, the so-called *Books of Blessed Bernard the Abbot* (*Knige blaženago Brnarda Opata*) from the fifteenth century is extant in the so-called Petris' Miscellany (Zagreb, Nacionalna i sveučilišna knjižnica, MS R 4001, fols 1ʳ–23ʳ),

---

nuns and recluses, and treatises dealing with aspects of spirituality and the common life'; Newman 'Flaws in the Golden Bowl', pp. 113–14.

11 The best-known works are the *Letters of Abélard to Heloize*, the *De institutione inclusarum* written by Aelred from Rievaulx, the *Ancrene Wisse*, the *Speculum virginum*, and the *Liber de modo bene vivendi*; Newman, 'Flaws in the Golden Bowl', pp. 112–14; Mouron, '"Listen to me, daughter, listen to a faithful counsel"', p. 93; Newman, 'Liminalities', pp. 379–81.

12 Hotchin, 'Female Religious Life and the "Cura Monialium" in Hirsau Monasticism, 1080 to 1150', p. 59.

13 Pinder, 'The Cloister and the Garden', p. 163; Bos, 'The Literature of Spiritual Formation for Women in France and England, 1080 to 1180', p. 212. Almost all extant manuscripts of the *Speculum virginum* belonged to male monasteries; Newman, 'Flaws in the Golden Bowl', p. 114.

14 There are various versions of the *Ancrene Wisse* that were adapted for monks; Gunn, *'Ancrene Wisse'*, pp. 183–84.

15 Pinder, 'The Cloister and the Garden', pp. 173–74.

16 Gunn, *'Ancrene Wisse'*, p. 3. Adapted parts of the *Ancrene Wisse* and the *Doctrine of the Hert* were widely used by lay readers; Renevey and Whitehead, '"Opyn þin hert as a boke"', p. 144; Gunn, *'Ancrene Wisse'*, p. 183.

written in a Glagolitic script and dated to the year 1468.[17] The other Croatian translation, transmitted under the name *Teachings that Saint Bernard Gave to his Sister* (*Nauci svetog Bernarda sestri svojoj*), dates from the sixteenth century and is extant in several manuscripts written in Latin script (Zagreb, Arhiv Hrvatske Akademije Znanosti i Umjetnosti, MSS I b 55, Iv a 34, I b 83).[18] The *Liber* was highly popular in the fifteenth and sixteenth centuries, probably because the alleged author, Bernard of Clairvaux, was considered at that time to be one of the leading authorities for spiritual teaching.[19] Croatian translations mirror this popularity in many respects.

The translations not only differ in the script in which they are transmitted, but there are also other important differences between them, with regard to their language, length, the rendering of the Latin text, and their intended recipients. Although both translations were written in Croatian, the Glagolitic translator used linguistic archaisms, or more precisely words which were inherited from older Slavonic literature as written in the Croatian redaction of Old Church Slavonic.[20] While the *Books* mostly follows the Latin text faithfully, the translation is significantly shorter, it comprises only the first thirteen chapters of the original seventy-three. Conversely, the *Teachings* contains a rendering of all seventy-three chapters, combining translation with adaptation, and almost all chapters have been modified significantly. Moreover, the *Books* is addressed to a male audience (a community of brothers), while the *Teachings* are addressed to sisters, like its Latin model.

In the *Books* the aim of the translation is addressed in the prologue. The translator explains that this text, originally written for a female audience, has now been reworked into an instructive moral work for clerics.[21] Although the central part of the prologue presents a close translation of the Latin text, the

---

17 The so-called 'Glagoljica' is a Slavic script created according to his legend by St Cyril of Thessaloniki at the request of Moravian Prince Rostisalv in the ninth century. A great part of Croatian medieval vernacular literature is written in Glagolitic script; Radošević, 'Croatian Translation of Biblical Passages in Medieval Performative Texts', p. 224. The so-called Petris' Miscellany is one of the most important literary monuments in Croatia; This Miscellany contains diverse texts translated from Latin; Štefanić, *Glagoljski rukopisi otoka Krka*, pp. 359–60.

18 The MS I b 83 (so-called Lulić's Manuscript) contains only the translation of the twenty-seventh chapter about confession (*Ot ispovidi*). In the MS I b 55 the prologue and the beginning of the first chapter of the *Teachings* are missing.

19 Marko Marulić, Croatia's most significant and well-known humanist author who is also called a 'father of Croatian literature', is in several studies considered to be the translator of the *Techings*. Pandžić, *Nepoznata proza Marka Marulića*, pp. 38–49; Kukuljević, 'Marko Marulić i njegovo doba', p. lxxvi.

20 Radošević, 'Croatian Translation of Biblical Passages in Medieval Performative Texts', pp. 225–26.

21 The prologue begins with an opening instruction: 'Počinu se knige B(la)ž(e)n(a)go Brnarda' ('Here the *Books of Blessed Bernard* begin').

translator's changes and additions at the very beginning and at the end of this section clearly announce that the tenor of the text will differ from that of the Latin original.

In the very first sentence of the opening, the recipient is given advice on how to read and use the text with the help of the metaphor of a mirror:[22]

> Počinu se knige B(la)ž(e)n(a)go Brnarda opata na po(uče)nie vsem' regulnikom' v ke imaû često pozirati kako v zrcalo ke učini za prošnû za svoe sestre na sp(a)senie mnozem.[23]
>
> (Here the *Books of Blessed Bernard the Abbot* begin for teaching all clerics, in which [these books] they should often look, as in the *Mirror*; which [these books] I produced at the request of my sister for the salvation of others.)

In the *Liber* the same metaphor does not appear until the second part of the text.[24] The phrasing is similar to that employed in the *Speculum virginum*, for which there are strong arguments for it having influenced the *Liber*.[25] Many medieval texts use 'mirror' in their titles or rely on the mirror as metaphor.[26] Saint Augustine says in his *Enarratio in Psalmum* 118 that the mirror, i.e. Holy Scripture and God's commandments, provides a model for virtuous and right living.[27] Drawing on his words, Gregory the Great writes that 'Holy Scripture

---

22 More about reading instructions in medieval prologues, see Renevey and Whitehead, '"Opyn þin hert as a boke"', p. 132.

23 Zagreb, Nacionalna i sveučilišna knjižnica, MS R 4001, fol. 1ʳ. This particular opening sentence is very close to the incipit of the *Speculum monachorum* attributed to Blessed Bernard the Abbot in a manuscript from the Iberian Peninsula written in the fifteenth century (fols 6ᵛ–9ʳ): 'Incipit utile et breve speculum Beati Bernardi Abbatis in quo se debet monachus cotidie speculari' ('[Here] begins the useful and short mirror of Blessed Bernard the Abbot about which a monk should reflect every day'). The author was Arnulfus de Boeriis, a twelfth-century Cistercian from the diocese of Louvain; *textmanuscripts / Les enluminures*, online: <https://www.textmanuscripts.com/medieval/bernard-of-clairvaux-60696> [accessed 3 November 2022].

24 Bernardus Claraevallensis, *Liber de modo bene vivendi ad sororem*, ed. by Migne, cols 1199A–B: 'Nunc ergo, charissima soror, hunc librum accipe, et eum ante oculos tuos quasi speculum propone, eumque omni hora velut speculum contemplare. Praecepta namque Dei specula sunt, in quibus se ipsas animae inspiciunt, et in quibus cognoscunt maculas, si quae sunt, foeditatis'. Pinder, 'The Cloister and the Garden', p. 161: 'Now therefore, dearest sister, receive this book, and place it before your eyes like a mirror, and look into it often as into a mirror. For the precepts of God are mirrors, in which souls look upon themselves, and in which they recognize the stain of sin, if there are any'. In general, the mirror metaphor was habitually used in the constant process of self-evaluation and emendation; Pinder, 'The Cloister and the Garden', pp. 160–63.

25 Pinder, 'The Cloister and the Garden', pp. 160–63.

26 Mews, 'Virginity, Theology, and Pedagogy in the "Speculum Virginum"', p. 21.

27 Bradley, 'Background of the Title "Speculum" in Mediaeval Literature', p. 103.

offers a mirror to our spiritual eyes, so that our interior countenance may be seen in it. We recognize in it what is deformed and what is beautiful in ourselves'.[28]

By including this metaphor, the translator formulated a clear instruction to the reader about the proper use of the *Books*, highlighting the importance of everyday scrutiny of their own thoughts and actions in consideration of the instructions in the *Books* on how to lead a good clerical life. For the reader, reading the *Books* should be like looking in a mirror, that is, it should result in introspection and self-examination. The importance of constant observing is also underlined at the end of the prologue in which the translator expands on the instructions about close reading with a further note on close observing: 'read and look again closely and carefully' (*gusto pročitaite i progledaite*). The Croatian verb *progledati* means realizing something after watching or observing it and brings two actions together: observation and comprehension. Within this frame, the translator then proceeds to describe, step by step, the proper reception of the given advice consisting not only of careful reading, but also of what the true comprehension should be, which is given as a precondition for harmonizing the instructions with the reader's actual way of living.[29]

In the final sentences of the prologue, the translator then sums up the meaning of the *Books*. By shortening the text and omitting the eschatological conclusion from the Latin original, the translator strengthens the importance of close reading and deeper reflection, as a means to help everyone recognize their sins and develop their conscience. What is interesting here is that this final instruction, unique to the translation, is very close to the advice given in the chapter *De habitu*, in which the brothers are urged to clean their consciences from all sins and evils:

| Draga bratê, očistitê kon'šenciû vašu ot vsakogo greha i zlobê.[30] (Dear brothers, clean your conscience from every sin and evil.) | Soror dilecta, munda conscientiam tuam ab omni malitia.[31] |

---

28 Gregory the Great, *Moralium libri, sive expositio in librum B. Iob.*, ed. by Migne, b. 2, cap. 1, cols 553–54. English translaton quoted from Bradley, 'Background of the Title "Speculum" in Mediaeval Literature', pp. 110–11.

29 Evans, 'An Afterword on the Prologue', p. 372.

30 Zagreb, Nacionalna i sveučilišna knjižnica, MS R 4001, fol. 15ᵛ (translation of *De habitu*).

31 Bernardus Claraevallensis, *Liber de modo bene vivendi ad sororem*, ed. by Migne, col. 1215C: 'Dear sister, clean your conscience from every evil'.

Zato moê draga brat'ê, knige ove vaše razumom' svet'lim' gusto pročitaite i progledaite, a to es(t) kon'šenciû i grehi vašimi kimi ste raneni.[32]

(Therefore, my dearest brothers, take this book with reason, and then read and look again closely and carefully, for it is the conscience and your sins that wounded you.)

Soror mihi in Christo dilecta, librum istum tua prudentia stuiose percurrat, et peccata mea assidue lugeat ut qui non sum dignus impetrare indulgentiam, saltem tuis orationibus possim consequi peccatorum meorum veniam. Omnipotens Deus custodiat, et ab omni malo te defendat, et cum omnibus tecum Deo pariter servientibus ad vitam perducat aeternam, venerabilis soror. Amen.[33]

Since the *Books* is the first text in the Petris' Miscellany, we have to consider that the prologue (especially the mirror metaphor) may not only refer to the *Books* itself, but instead to all the texts transmitted in the manuscript.[34] Similarly the Latin expression *sub mensa Patrum micas collegi / da pod stolom' meštar mrvice pobrah* (*I collected the crumbs under the table of the Fathers*), with which the author of the *Liber* expresses his approach in gathering different quotations from many authorities, could also be applied to the character of the collection of texts in the miscellany as a whole.

The *Books* contains the translation of the first thirteen chapters of the *Liber*. With the exception of the first two chapters, whose order have been reversed, all the chapters of the *Books* follow that of the *Liber*. Some of the chapters discuss general religious topics (proper faith, charity, love of God), while others are particularly intended for the clergy. The *Liber* contains readings about the nature of faith, about the character of divine grace, the importance of spiritual *affectio*, the cultivation of the fear of God (*De timore Dei*), and the contempt of the world (*De contemptu mundi*).[35] The *Books* ends in the middle of the thirteenth chapter, *De dilectione proximi*. Since this chapter contains some repetitions of a subject (love) already discussed in the fifth (*De charitate*) and, again, in the twelfth chapter (*De dilectione Dei*), the translator may have cut the thirteenth chapter short to avoid further repetition. The other chapter that is significantly shorter than its underlying original is the fourth, about the fear of God, which renders only the first half of the original Latin text. Apart from these two chapters, the largest number of simplifications and omissions can be found in the chapters on

---

32 Zagreb, Nacionalna i sveučilišna knjižnica, MS R 4001, fol. 1ᵛ (translation of *Praefatio*).

33 Bernardus Claraevallensis, *Liber de modo bene vivendi ad sororem*, ed. by Migne, cols 1199B–C.

34 Dürrigl, 'Pogled na Petrisov zbornik kao zrcalo', pp. 101–06.

35 Kuczynski, *Prophetic Song*, p. 88; Mouron, '"Listen to me, daughter, listen to a faithful counsel"', p. 87.

God's mercy and charity. The omissions mostly affect quotations from the Scripture and commentaries on it, especially those from the Song of Solomon.

The *Books*' fourth chapter on the fear of God comprises the first half of the chapter *De timore Dei* and a good part of the chapter *De charitate*, which is then translated again as part of the fifth chapter. As the translator drew twice on the same Latin text, it would be interesting here to see what might have prompted him to make such a decision.

At the beginning of the fourth chapter the translator omits the exposition on Peter Lombard's division of fear into worldly, servile, initial and chaste fears, instead only mentioning the total number of fears. He then describes in more detail only the worldly (*plteni*) and servile (*službeni*) fears, before interrupting the translation of the respective chapter and replacing it with the exposition on initial and chaste fears from the text of the chapter on charity. One of the most obvious differences between worldly and servile fears is their relationship with charity.[36] An imperfect attitude towards love and charity, which is typical of those who are in fear of losing worldly goods, or in fear of the threat of God's punishment, seems to have encouraged the translator to introduce a long explanation of perfect charity, a topic that was of greater concern to the translator.[37]

The paragraph on charity refers to the Song of Solomon, with the fifth chapter opening with an exposition on dissociation of the body and the soul. God's charity dissociates man from worldly things, an idea which connects the charity-theme with the definition of the first fear, that of losing earthly wealth. The next thought, that a man must avoid sins for God's love, briefly summarizes the definition of chaste fear. In the *Liber*'s fourth chapter the translator takes only the explanations for the two deleterious fears which should be avoided. As joining with Christ is the leitmotif of the *Books*, and chaste fear itself refers to this unity, it could be assumed that the translator considered the frequent repetition of this leitmotif to be enough to encourage the reader to take the path of Christian love.

A comparison of the fourth and fifth chapters, containing translations of the same passage from the chapter *De charitate*, shows that there are some differences between them, although they both have the same omissions. The quotation in each taken from the Song of Songs with the motif of female breasts is missing, most likely so as not to arouse carnal desires in a male reader who was a member of a religious order. The text in the fifth chapter on charity follows the Latin original, whereas the same passage in the fourth chapter relating to fear (awe) of the Lord is significantly shorter. In the chapter on fear the translator instead concentrates on giving concise advice and avoiding repetition. The two chapters also differ in how they address the recipient. The repeated addressing of an

---

36 Johnson said that servile fear 'blinded one to charitable nature of divinely judicious discipline and punishment [...] People who feared servilely failed to perceive the love which lay behind the threat of punishment and, thus, the degree and merit fear of God were insufficient', Johnson, "'In dryȝdred and daunger'", p. 55.

37 For more on Peter Lombard's teaching on the four fears, see Colish, *Peter Lombard*, I, p. 178.

individual reader in the chapter on charity shows that the translator was more focused on the individual recipient or, more precisely, on his individual soul, while in the fourth chapter he addresses the community of brothers as a whole.

Recipients of the *Books of Blessed Bernard*

At the beginning of the prologue the intended readers are addressed as 'dear beloved brothers of holy profession' (*draga bratê svetoga profesa*). The use of phrases such as 'none of you' (*nigdore ot vas*), 'one of you', or 'is there any of you' indicates that active participation with the spiritual exercise was expected from each particular member of the community. There are also changes to the chapter headings that contain references to the monastic life, such as in the translation of the eighth chapter (*De habitu*), which is entitled 'Sermon of Saint Bernard the Abbot Appealing to Brothers to Walk Modestly' (*Slovo s(ve)t(a)go Brnarda opata da bi bratê priproĉe hodili*).

In terms of the audience, the earlier translation in the *Books* is not addressed to a female audience, but unlike the Latin original, it is mostly (though not always) addressed in the second person plural. Nevertheless, the translator's attitude towards the recipients cannot simply be explained as a replacement of a female addressee in the singular by male recipients in the plural. As some parts of the *Books* show, the translator's periodic altering of the addressee between the plural ('dear brothers') with the singular ('dear brother') is actually intended. In a translation that is mainly directed at the community of brothers the switch to singular indicates that each and every soul is being addressed individually and directly. This may be seen in the chapter on compunction, where the turtledove stands for faithfulness to Christ and the Church:

> A zato, *bratiê moê*, vazmite priliku ot te grlice [...] *Bratê moi*, imaš' pozor grlice
> [...] Zato, *moi dragi brate*, ne prêstaûĉi plači za grehi tvoe [...] I zato, *dragi brate*, ako grihov' ne budeš plakati [...] *Bratê moê*, ako za bezakoniê vaša plakati ne budête.[38]
>
> > (And therefore, *my brothers*, take the example of that turtledove [...] *My brother*, you have the looks of the turtledove [...] Therefore, *my dear brother*, don't stop weeping for your sins [...] And therefore, *dear brother*, if you don't weep for your sins [...])
>
> Latin original: Igitur, *honesta virgo*, accipe exemplum hujus turturis [...] *Soror venerabilis*, genas habes turturis [...] Igitur, *soror charissima*, indesinenter peccata tua cum lacrymis lava.[39]

---

38 Zagreb, Nacionalna i sveučilišna knjižnica, MS R 4001, fols 18ʳ–19ʳ.

39 Bernardus Claraevallensis, *Liber de modo bene vivendi ad sororem*, ed. by Migne, cols 1218B–1219A: 'Therefore, honourable virgin, take the example of this turtledove [...] Reverent sister, you have the cheeks of the turtledove [...] therefore, dear sister, wash your sins indefinitely with your tears [...] Honourable virgin, if you don't weep for your sins'.

Within this commentary, derived primarily from the Song of Songs (*vox turturis audita est in terra nostra*, 2. 10; *pulchrae sunt genae tuae sicut turturis*, 1. 9), the turtledove represents the true model of *memorandi* and *imitandi*.[40] While the opening, in which the collective is addressed, serves to motivate the brothers to memorize and understand the importance of the admonition, the final part, in which an individual is addressed, admonishes all those refusing to accept the given advice. The translator's switch between the modes of address, especially when alternating between warning and exhortation, suggests that the text was drafted for an oral performance in which a superior gives advice to brothers of holy profession by reading the *Books* aloud.[41] The intention to touch every soul during the written/oral performance is probably best seen in the simultaneous use of both second-person plural and second-person singular in the same address. The use of *verba dicendi* in the second-person plural when delivering the following message while, at the same time, giving the preferred answer in the first-person singular imitates a speech in which the one posing the question to a group or community expects the same answer to be given by each participant:

Tako da istinno morete rêci: 'Ranen esam'.[42]

(So you could truly say: 'I am wounded'.)

Ita ut recte valeas dicere: 'Vulnerata charitate ego sum'.[43]

The Translator's Attitude Towards Gender

Since this translation shifts the emphasis from instructions on the good life for women to teachings on general religious topics and subjects relating to the monastic life, its treatment of gender greatly affects both its content and style. Unlike the Latin original and the later Croatian translation, the *Books* instead offers instructive readings addressed to 'dearest brothers', that is, to clerics, but also includes chapters that could be of some use to a wider audience. Here, 'sister' is only mentioned in the first address to the audience: 'My dear sister in Jesus and my dearest brothers' (*Draga moê sestro va Is(u)h(rst)i i prevzlûblena moê bratê*). The translation does not offer the adjectives that appear in the *Liber* when addressing the female audience (*honestissima, reverendissima soror, soror*

---

[40] The turtle is just one of many members of the book of nature that in the Middle Ages did not appear just as a certain *sensus moralis*, but also served as a mirror in which everyone should look.

[41] Catherine Innes-Parker also thinks that the author of the *Lignum vitae* did not expect all of his audience to be able to read, but he assumed some context of listening, such as oral reading. Innes-Parker, 'Translation, Authorship, and Authority', p. 229.

[42] Zagreb, Nacionalna i sveučilišna knjižnica, MS R 4001, fol. 7ʳ.

[43] Bernardus Claraevallensis, *Liber de modo bene vivendi ad sororem*, ed. by Migne, col. 1208D: 'So you may really say: I am wounded with love'.

in Christo dilecta mihi, soror venerabilis, soror dilecta, soror charissima, soror mihi amabilis).[44] They are either omitted or else are replaced with the expressions *brate* ('brother'), *bratê moê* ('my brothers'), *draga moê bratê* ('my dear brothers'), or rarely as *častna bratê* ('honoured brother'). The Latin expression *sponsa Christi* is translated as 'brother', 'servant of Good' and, rarely, as 'bride' if it refers to the soul. The name of Jesus Christ, which in Latin original often appears as 'bridegroom', is mostly rendered as 'Jesus', 'Jesus the Lord', 'Jesus the King of Heaven', or 'the bridegroom of the man's soul'. Allusions to female imagery or characteristics, such as embracing the bride (*amplexus pulcherrimi sponsi*) or to breasts, were mostly (but not always) omitted or abbreviated. All the passages in which virginity is glorified are removed. Even the text of the Hymn from the *Roman Breviary* is interrupted at the point where the word *virginum* appears and is replaced by angels, patriarchs, prophets, apostles, martyrs, confessors, and others.

> Meû korami anĵ(e)lskimi pêli budêtê emu slat'ke pês'ni kako pisano es(t): ki prêbivaš meû liliumi ograen' tan'ci. *A to es(t) s(ve)timi anĵ(e)li i patriêrhi i proroki i ap(usto)li mučeniki i ispovêdniki i pročimi.*[45]

> (Among choirs of angels you will sing sweet songs to him, as it is written: You feed among the lilies surrounded by a choir. And that is with holy angels and patriarchs and prophets and apostles and martyrs and confessors, and others.)

> atque inter virginum choros cantabis illi dulces hymnos, sicut scriptum est: Qui pascis inter lilia, *Septus choreis virginum, Sponsus decorus gloria.*[46]

The translator also had to resolve issues where biblical quotations were couched grammatically in the feminine, especially those from the Song of Songs. Sometimes the translator made simple grammatical alterations by changing the gender, mostly from the second-person feminine singular to the second-person masculine plural. For example, in the translation of a short anaphoric passage from the chapter *De habitu*, the translator faithfully translated only the first two sentences from the Song of Songs. In the third and fourth sentences, in which the allegorical meaning of the Scripture is explained, the gender of the subject is changed to the masculine plural:

> Ovo ti krasna esi priêtelnice moê. *Ovo ti kras'na esi* va očiû tvoeû golubic'. Kras'ni za pobolšan'e plti i čistoti mišleniê. *Ovo vi kras'ni este* imiûĉi čistotu i smerêno mišlenie v srci.[47]

---

44 The most frequent addressee is *soror*, followed by *sponsa*; *virgo* is the rarest one.

45 Zagreb, Nacionalna i sveučilišna knjižnica, MS R 4001, fol. 22ʳ.

46 Bernardus Claraevallensis, *Liber de modo bene vivendi ad sororem*, ed. by Migne, cols 1222B–C: 'With the choirs of virgins you will sing many sweet songs, as it is written: You feed among the lilies | surrounded by choir of virgins | a bridegroom beautiful with glory'.

47 Zagreb, Nacionalna i sveučilišna knjižnica, MS R 4001, fol. 15ᵛ.

> (Behold thou art fair, my love, *behold thou art fair* [feminine singular], thine eyes are as those of doves. Fair [masculine plural] is to say because of the perfection of the body and purity of thought. *Behold thou art fair* [masculine plural], having a pure and simple intent of heart.)
>
> Ecce tu pulchra es, amica mea; *ecce tu pulchra*: oculi tui columbarum. Pulchra videlicet propter perfectionem corporis, et munditiam cogitationis. *Ecce tu pulchra es*, habens mundam et simplicem intentionem cordis.[48]

Although the translator mostly avoids expressions such as 'bride' or 'bridegroom', there are nevertheless still some parts containing bridal imagery in the chapters concerned with the monastic life.[49] The soul as Christ's bride replaces the expression *sponsa Christi*, thereby allowing traces of bridal imagery to be retained. This is especially evident in the translation of the chapter *De dilectione Dei* in which the interpretation of love for Jesus is based on several quotations from the Song of Songs. By introducing the expression 'our soul' the translator re-interprets those parts of Scripture referring to the bride, while preserving some biblical verses in their original form in the translation:

> I na vsaki dan zovê me *govorêĉi d(u)ši n(a)šei*, 'pridi ot livana vzlûblena moê, pridi ot livana pridi da koruniši se'.[50]
>
> (And every day he calls me *saying to our soul*, 'come from Libanus, my dear, come from Libanus, come and be crowned'.)
>
> Quotidie *vocat me dicens*, 'veni de Libano, sponsa, veni, coronaberis'.[51]

By introducing the word *soul* in the chapter *De compunctione* the translator preserved comparison between the two bridal imageries: one between a turtledove and its mate form the world of nature and the other one between Jesus and the soul, as his particular bride. With this addition it was easier to apply bridal imagery in the text which was addressed to the male audience, and also to highlighten the exemplum (*similitudo*) of turtledove as a perfect model of perseverance.[52]

---

48 Bernardus Claraevallensis, *Liber de modo bene vivendi ad sororem*, ed. by Migne, col. 1215C: 'Behold thou art fair, O my love, behold thou art fair, thine eyes are as those of doves. Fair is to say because of the perfection of the body and purity of thought. Behold thou art fair, having a pure and simple intent of heart'.

49 On this allegory see Newman, 'Gender', pp. 43–44.

50 Zagreb, Nacionalna i sveučilišna knjižnica, MS R 4001, fol. 21ᵛ.

51 Bernardus Claraevallensis, *Liber de modo bene vivendi ad sororem*, ed. by Migne, col. 1221D: 'Daily he called me, "come from Libanus, my spouse, come: thou shalt be crowned"'.

52 The turtledove is medieval symbool of chastity and devotion to a single mate. It appears in the Old Testament, Physiologus and numerous medieval bestiaries.

Zato ûre d(u)še, ka si obručenice H(rsto)va, drži podobstvo grlice i ne otpućai se ot obručenika tvoego dragago i ne iĉi drugoga.[53]

> (*Because of you, soul, who are the bride of Christ*, be like a turtle and do not separate from your dear spouse and do not seek another one.)

> *O sponsa Christi*, assimilare et tu huic turturi, et praeter Jesum Christum sponsum tuum, amatorem non quaeras alterum.[54]

The example here shows that the translator occasionally expresses his closeness with the brothers, implying that he is one of them. Unlike the *Liber*, in which the narrator encouraged the sister to address others in the monastery, in the *Books* the narrator addresses the whole community of recipients by saying *ki sa mnu este* ('who are with me'). In making this identification it then becomes easier for him to stimulate the other brothers to become champions of *bene vivendi*. In the chapter *De contemptu mundi* the exclamatory addressing (*O sponsa Christi*) is replaced with the expression *o, Rabê boži* ('o, servant of God'). After defining the man's relationship with God, the translator then begins, in the second-person singular, to give recommendations about the nothingness of earthly riches. His instructions at the outset are further strengthened through the use of the imperative form *znai* ('you should know').

In the *Books* Jesus is presented as the bridegroom of the soul and the Church. In the chapter *De habitu* the translator emphasizes several times that the brothers should not serve Christ the bridegroom (*Jesu Christo sponso*) as it said in the *Liber*, but rather Christ the heavenly ruler.

> Vzlûbleni, želeû da ot vas' rečet' se to ča v pesneh Solomunih' govorit' se: 'Vsa lepa esi, draga moê, i skvrni ni v tebê'. I oĉe di: 'Pridi ot livana da ukruniši se.' Vistinu b(la)ž(e)na es(t) ona d(u)ša ka Is(u)h(rst)u n(e)b(e)skom ženihu služi bez' griha. Tako i vi, *moê bratê*, b(la)ž(e)ni budêtê *ako Is(u)h(rst)u c(esa)ru* v(a)šemu bez griha služili budêtê.[55]

> (Dearest, I want that it will be said of you ase it is said in Solomon's Songs: 'Thou art all fair, O my love, and there is not a spot in thee'. And it is also said: 'Come from Libanus, come: thou shalt be crowned'. Truly blessed is the soul that serves Jesus Christ, celestial spouse without stain. And so you, *dear brothers*, will be blessed, if you serve *Jesus Christ your Caesar* without sins'.)

> Charissima, opto ut de te dicatur illud quod in Canticis canticorum legitur: 'Tota pulchra *es, amica mea, et macula non est in* te'. Et iterum:

---

53 Zagreb, Nacionalna i sveučilišna knjižnica, MS R 4001, fol. 18ᵛ.

54 Bernardus Claraevallensis, *Liber de modo bene vivendi ad sororem*, ed. by Migne, col. 1218B–C: 'O, spouse of Christ, be like the turtle, and except Jesus Christ your spouse, do not seek for another one'.

55 Zagreb, Nacionalna i sveučilišna knjižnica, MS R 4001, fol. 15ʳ.

'Veni de Libano, veni, coronaberis' [Cantica Canticorum IV. 7. 8]. Vere beata est illa anima quae Jesu Christo sponso coelesti servit sine macula. Sic et tu, soror venerabilis, beata eris, si Jesu Christo sponso tuo sine macula servieris.[56]

Translator as Author

In the *Books* even the minor changes made by the translator serve to modify the effect of the text; a closer look at these modifications may allow us to understand the authorial intentions of the translator in detail. Firstly, we may observe that some omissions from the eschatological arguments of the concluding chapters shift the tone of the whole treatise. In particular, the use of the word 'teaching' (*nauka*) is important: In the chapter *De fide*, the Latin word *moribus* is translated as 'teaching'. For example: 'wholeness of the faith should not be broken by the wrong teachings' (*celost verê ne hotêi razbiti zalimi nauci*). This corresponds to a passage in the translator's prologue: 'I could write you something from Holy Scripture and teachings' (*da bih vam nike riči svetoga pisma i nauka napisal*). Similarly, the use of the term 'sin' is idiosyncratic in the translation.[57] Although the author of the *Liber* discusses sin as a part of his instructions for a better life, he makes far more frequent mention of the mistakes and wrong choices that the addressee (a sister) could make on her path to salvation. In the Croatian text, however, all of these minor and major obstacles in the effort to lead a Christian life are usually translated as 'sins'. Thus, for example, in the chapter on God's mercy, the translator writes of going to Hell or Heaven in terms of 'fall(ing) into sin' or being 'delivered from sin':

> Za *grih'* prvoga č(lovê)ka *vpadosmo v grih'*, a po milosti B(o)ži *izbavleni esmo ot greha i moremo na nebo iziti*.[58]
>
> (For the sin of the first man we descend *into sin*, but by the grace of God we are *saved from sin and we can go to Heaven*.)

---

56 Bernardus Claraevallensis, *Liber de modo bene vivendi ad sororem*, ed. by Migne, cols 1214D–1215A: 'Therefore, my loved sister in Christ, let your richness be good manners, let your beauty be a good life. Dearest, I would like to say of you as it is read *in Canticis*: *Thou art all fair, O my love, and there is not a spot in thee*; and more: *Come from Libanus, come: thou shalt be crown*ed. Truly blessed is the soul that serves Jesus Christ, celestial spouse without stain. So you, venerable sister, will be blessed, if you serve Jesus Christ your spouse without stains'.

57 The idea of sin is represented more in the other parts of the *Liber*, mostly in those chapters whose main topic is a particular vice. The chapters with which the *Liber* begins, that is, the ones that were translated in the *Books*, are directed more towards encouraging the recipients to adopt the preferred virtue and teaching.

58 Zagreb, Nacionalna i sveučilišna knjižnica, MS R 4001, fol. 3ᵛ.

Per *peccatum* primi hominis *in infernum* descendimus; sed per gratiam Dei nos *confidimus ascendere in coelum.*[59]

The word 'sin' sometimes replaces polysemantic words ('bez *griha*' / 'without *sin*' / 'sine *macula*') and appears as an addition in other relevant formulations ('vsakoga *greha i zlobê*' / 'every *sin and malice*' / 'omnis *malitia*').

Another important semantic area is that of reflection as the desired response to the moral teachings.[60] The main condition of good living is reflection on issues that could possibly lead to sin and then, consequently, to perdition. The idea of reflection distinguishes the *Liber* from other similar spiritual guides, such as the very popular *Ancrene Wisse*, which abounds in concrete instructions and examples from everyday life.[61] In the Croatian translation of the *Liber*, such reflection transforms the processes of listening into processes of comprehension: the recipient is motivated to be mindful and actively to receive instruction. Neither reading nor listening should be undertaken without comprehension of and reflection on every single tenet described, since their acceptance is the key to understanding good 'living'. The translator adds or replaces suitable expressions with words relating to the mind and reflection, as in the following passages:

'Draga moê bratê, *vaz'mitê na pamet'* obraz' svetih'[62] / 'My dear brothers, *bear in mind* examples of saints' / Soror mihi in Christo amabilis, *audi* exempla sanctorum';[63] '*razumiimo* ča Solomun di'[64] / '*We should understand* what Solomon says' / '*quid est* quod ait Salomon'.[65]

Paratextual auctorial instructions, which are located between the title and the main text of the individual chapters, are used to describe the intended accomplishments of the reader in terms of reflection and comprehension: 'read properly and understand' (*Čti pravo i razumei*).[66] As Dürrigl said, by using this expression the translator emphasized that the text now contains valuable and important teachings that should be approached rationally but not without love.[67] A similar approach is likewise expressed in the final sentence about the correct

---

59 Bernardus Claraevallensis, *Liber de modo bene vivendi ad sororem*, ed. by Migne, cols 1202B–C: 'For the sin of first men we descend to Hell, by the grace of God we truly ascend to Heaven'.

60 Kienzle, 'Introduction', p. 155.

61 Mouron, '"Listen to me, daughter, listen to a faithful counsel"', p. 90.

62 Zagreb, Nacionalna i sveučilišna knjižnica, MS R 4001, fol. 17ʳ.

63 Bernardus Claraevallensis, *Liber de modo bene vivendi ad sororem*, ed. by Migne, col. 1216D: 'My sister in Christ amiable, listen to the examples of saints'.

64 Zagreb, Nacionalna i sveučilišna knjižnica, MS R 4001, fol. 19ᵛ.

65 Bernardus Claraevallensis, *Liber de modo bene vivendi ad sororem*, ed. by Migne, col. 1219D: 'What is that Salomon said'.

66 Zagreb, Nacionalna i sveučilišna knjižnica, MS R 4001, fol. 1ᵛ.

67 Dürrigl, 'O čitanju, pisanju i kompiliranju u hrvatskoglagoljskom srednjovjekovlju', p. 227.

manner of thinking as given by God, which was added by the translator to the end of the chapter *De habitu*: 'B(og) dai vsakomu *pravu misal*'[68] ('Let God give everyone *the right thought*').

The *Books*, compared to the original, possesses fewer contemplative passages and transmits the urgency of the message by means of imperative forms and cause-and-effect statements. Thus, the emphasis is on comprehension of the received advice and the addressee is constantly prompted to draw connections between the Scripture and the explanation. The most frequent strategy employed when abbreviating and strengthening the text is to introduce cause-effect conjunctions to connect sentences, to shorten lengthy explanations, or else to replace long addresses ('*I zato*'[69] / 'And therefore' / '*Soror in Christo amabilis mihi, sicut superius dixi tibi*'[70]). This approach then underlines the message and compels the reader's attention in the passages which follow. It encourages the recipients to think about consequences and to try to understand causal relations.

The translator employs various strategies for retaining the attention of the reader and to make the message more memorable. He avoids synonyms and does not back away from using frequent repetitions, which makes the text easily memorable and stimulates the reader's contemplation of the subject matter. Thus, in one passage of the *Books* the Latin words *cum*, *per*, *propter*, and *pro* are translated by the Croatian word *skoze* ('because of') which has a cause-and-effect connotation. The repetition of this particular word imitates the punctuation used in the *Liber* between different Bible verses as an impetus for compunction. By introducing a word with these kinds of connotation as a pause mark, the translator in turn forces the recipient to pause and consider the received text. Also, by occasionally introducing anaphora the translator makes the text rhythmic and memorable. Sometimes 'it' refers to the addition of the connector *i* ('and') or *a* ('but'), through which it became possible to take short breaks while reading or listening the text. In the *Books* the tone is more direct and admonitory than in the *Liber*. The admonitory tone is certainly associated with the stronger emphasis placed on reflection in the translation. Sometimes the translator combines rhetorical figures (mostly anaphora) with imperative forms, in order to intensify the effect of the message given in a particular part of the text. For example, he translates Latin *sit* (*budi* / 'to be') and *nihil* (*ne budi* / 'to be not') as positive and negative forms of the imperative of the verb *biti* ('to be'). The effectiveness of the expression is further reinforced at the ends of the chapters where the translator replaces all the subjunctive forms with imperatives: *non delinguas* (*ne hotêi pregrešiti* / 'do not want to make a mistake'); *non polluas* (*ne hotêi oskvrniti* / 'do not want to defile'). The translator's direct style is occasionally evident when sentences paraphrasing the text from the *Liber* begin with verbs.

---

[68] Zagreb, Nacionalna i sveučilišna knjižnica, MS R 4001, fol. 16ᵛ.

[69] Zagreb, Nacionalna i sveučilišna knjižnica, MS R 4001, fol. 12ʳ.

[70] Bernardus Claraevallensis, *Liber de modo bene vivendi ad sororem*, ed. by Migne, col. 1212B.

In order to produce a greater impact on the recipient, the translator occasionally adds exclamations. In the first passage of the chapter *De spe*, which is the first chapter of the *Books*, the translator makes an exclamatory sentence in which he glorifies those who wait in orderly and calm fashion for the justice of God and his mercy. The originally short Latin sentence, in which the expectation of God's mercy is only stated implicitly, is expanded in the translation on several levels. Unlike the *Liber*, in which the sentence appears as the antithesis of the one preceding it, in which it is said that mercy appears as the vain hope of those who persist in evil, in the *Books* it is turned into a strong apostrophe of those who properly expect God's justice and mercy. First, by opening the sentence with the exclamation, and, further, by introducing the couplets, the translator significantly heightens the effect of the poetic qualities of the language. Through these two couplets, the translator glorifies God's mercy and divine justice while underlining the correct attitude towards evil. Furthermore, God's mercy is also joined in this passage by hope, and divine justice is joined with God's mercy. The translator also points out the importance of God's mercy by adding a sentence in which he explains God's merciful attitude towards the man immersed in sin.

A further, specific feature of the text must also be highlighted: In the Glagolitic community,[71] to which the translator belonged, Old Church Slavonic was present as the language of the liturgy. The translator used Church Slavonic to mark certain points or ideas within the text. On occasion, he introduced archaisms from Old Church Slavonic into the biblical quotations. In the following example, the archaic Old Church Slavonic form of the pronoun *az* ('I') – first appears in the quotation from the New Testament, and then again in the explanation of that quotation:

> A to es(t) Is(u)h(rst) ki znameniti govori: '*Az*' esam' cvet polski i liliumi v dol'ci' [...] A to es(t), *az* esam' i is'tina i krepost'.[72]
>
> > (And that is Christ, who said: 'I am the flower of the field, and the lily of the valleys' [...] That is, I am sanctity, goodness, and justice.)
>
> Christus, designat, dicens: '*Ego* flos campi, et lilium convallium' [Song of Songs 2. 1] [...] id est, *Ego* sum sanctitas, bonitas et justitia.[73]

He also favours Old Church Slavonic for creating emphasis, such as in the opening or closing sentences of particular chapters:

> Sliši ča r(e)če b(la)ž(e)ni Paval ap(usto)l ot sebê g(lago)lûĉi: 'Milos'tiû božieû esam' to eže esam'.[74]

---

71 More about Glagolitic reading community in Radošević and Dürrigl, 'Glagoljska čitateljska zajednica na primjeru Drugoga beramskoga brevijara'.

72 Zagreb, Nacionalna i sveučilišna knjižnica, MS R 4001, fol. 4ʳ.

73 Bernardus Claraevallensis, *Liber de modo bene vivendi ad sororem*, ed. by Migne, col. 1203B: 'Namely Christ saying: I am the flower of the field, and the lily of the valleys [...] That is, I am sanctity, goodness, and justice'.

74 Zagreb, Nacionalna i sveučilišna knjižnica, MS R 4001, fols 3ᵛ–4ʳ.

(Listen to what blessed Paul the apostle said speaking about himself saying: 'By the Grace of God I am who I am'.)

Audi Paulum apostolum de se dicentem: 'Gratia Dei sum id quod sum'.[75]

The Sixteenth-Century Compilation

In the sixteenth-century Glagolitic Gršković's Miscellany (Zagreb, Arhiv Hrvatske Akademije Znanosti i Umjetnosti, MS VII 32, fols 185–89, fols 191–95), which was probably written in Istria, we find an excerpt from the *Books* under the title 'A Very Beautiful and Useful Chapter'.[76] It contains the *Books*' fourth chapter 'About the Fear of God' (*Slovo svetago Brnarda ot straha kapitul*) together with an anonymously transmitted short collection of moral sentences from the fifteenth century.[77]

The compilation is addressed to a single, unnamed recipient. Apart from the opening address, where it is said that we should fear God and listen to his commandments, the rest of the passage comprises only quotations from Proverbs, Ecclesiastes, Ecclesiasticus, and the Psalms. The idea that wisdom is the key to the proper reflection which could save the reader's soul is given far more emphasis, predominantly through the introduction of numerous quotations from, again, Proverbs as well as Sirach, and the Book of Wisdom in the final third of the text, which reminds the reader of the dangers of living a reckless life. By adding short moral sentences throughout the text, the compiler made the teachings about wisdom, charity and the fear of God more user friendly. This material boosted the persuasive function of the text, since most of the sentences are formed as appeals or commandments. In the text taken from the *Books*, comprising some two thirds of the compilation, the recipient is encouraged to reflect, not only on the received moral message, but also constantly on how one can relate to God in everyday life. The main message of the compilation is to be mindful and cautious. Instructions addressing the dangers of a reckless life and undesirable acts and manners are framed as warnings and appeals:

---

75 Bernardus Claraevallensis, *Liber de modo bene vivendi ad sororem*, ed. by Migne, col. 1202D: 'Listen to Paul the Apostle by himself saying: But by the grace of God, I am what I am'.

76 Štefanić, *Glagoljski rukopisi Jugoslavenske akademije*, II, p. 51; Radošević, 'Vele lip kapitul i koristan', p. 44.

77 The older version of the sentences is written in the Petris' Miscellany (Zagreb, Nacionalna i sveučilišna knjižnica, MS R 4001, fols 238–39). Radošević, 'Zbirka sentencija iz Petrisova i Grškovićeva zbornika u kontekstu hrvatskoglagoljske refleksivne proze'. The first few lines of this short collection of moral sentences appear in several medieval texts translated into Croatian in the fifteenth century, such as the *story of Akir the Wise* and the translation of the *Disticha Catonis*. Radošević, 'Vele lip kapitul i koristan', p. 52.

Ne imii družbu sa ženu lûkavu da ne izgoriš' ognem ee.[78]

(Do not keep company with a cunning woman if you do not want to be burnt.)

Ne pit vina mnog da te ne povrati v norost'.[79]

(Do not drink much wine so you do not succumb to madness.)

The warning tone at the very end of the compilation stands in opposition to the opening promise taken from Psalm 32. 18 where it is said: 'zač su oči gospodni zvrhu onih' ki se nega boe i na onih' ki ufaû v nega milosrdie' ('behold, the eyes of the Lord are on them that fear him and on them that hope in his mercy').[80] Although the compilation contains a promise of entering Heaven for those that chastely obey the Lord (which is in fact the final sentence taken from the *Books*), it ends with a measure-for-measure motif from Matthew 7. 2. At the end the recipient is forced to consider the nature of his conduct. The aim is to encourage the recipient to reflect on the warning that everyone will be judged according to their acts. It is also significant that, in the penultimate piece of advice that is given, the Gate of Heaven appears in the negative within a consequential sentence in which the predicate is made in the imperative form: 'da gospodin B(og) tebi ne zatvori vrat raiskih' ('so God would not close Heaven's Door to you').[81] In the final sentence *divine justice* is implicitly stated, through reference to a quotation from the Sermon on the Mount: 'i kako budeš miril tako se i tebi mirilo bude' ('with what measure you mete, it shall be measured to you again').[82] The Door of Heaven is open, but miserable deeds may close it.

Since the same verse from Proverbs 9. 10 on the interconnectedness between the fear of God and wisdom appears in both the first and third parts of the compilation, we could say that, by compiling the *Books*' chapter with the anonymous collection of moral sentences, the author augmented the reader's comprehension of, at the least, initial fear, and maybe also of chaste fear. Thus, this compilation went even further than the *Books* had to explain the teachings which required the correct understanding of the fear of God. It is not possible to comprehend the fear of God correctly without the glory of wisdom.

Conclusion

This essay has illuminated the role of the *Liber* in medieval vernacular literature. In the Old Croatian translation and, especially, in the later sixteenth-century compilation, emphasis is laid on the developing of self-awareness, that is, on

---

78 Zagreb, Arhiv Hrvatske Akademije Znanosti i Umjetnosti, MS VII 32, fol. 188ᵛ.
79 Zagreb, Arhiv Hrvatske Akademije Znanosti i Umjetnosti, MS VII 32, fol. 189ʳ.
80 Zagreb, Arhiv Hrvatske Akademije Znanosti i Umjetnosti, MS VII 32, fol. 185ᵛ.
81 Zagreb, Arhiv Hrvatske Akademije Znanosti i Umjetnosti, MS VII 32, fol. 189ʳ.
82 Zagreb, Arhiv Hrvatske Akademije Znanosti i Umjetnosti, MS VII 32, fol. 189ʳ.

training the wise mind to recognize the perils of sin. This contrasts with the *Liber* itself where the concern was with things that could prevent a sister's spiritual growth. By shortening some passages of the texts while simultaneously intensifying causality and effect and highlighting the proper way of reading the book, the translator slightly altered its purpose, or more precisely, he emphasized one particular aspect of the work. Through grammatical means, he also made the didactic function of the text emphatic.

The adaptation of the text to serve a male audience was first and foremost his goal. He occasionally retained certain quotations from the Song of Songs as well as the allegory of the soul as Christ's spouse, at least in the chapters which were closely connected to clerical life as well in the chapter with important advice on how to be a good monk. By drawing on the same Latin text when composing both the fourth and fifth chapters the translator underlined the importance of charity in the context of finally joining with Christ, which is the leitmotif of the *Liber*. Even with the smaller additions, the translator contributed to the expansion of the theological level of the texts: he highlighted the importance of simplicity by introducing it in the heading of one chapter; he highlighted and explained God's mercy on several occasions, and he managed to underline the vow of stability by some procedure of the brothers.

The later compilation is a good example of the *mouvances* of a medieval text that was constantly being changed and whose later audience (the lay public) was completely different from that of the Latin *Liber* that was first written at the request of a still-unknown sister. As the sixteenth-century compilation shows, parts of the *Books* served as a useful source for composing further didactic compilations and instructional commentaries.

Bibliography

Manuscript Sources

Zagreb, Nacionalna i sveučilišna knjižnica, MS R 4001 (Petris' Miscellany)
Zagreb, Arhiv Hrvatske Akademije Znanosti i Umjetnosti, MS VII 32 (Gršković's Miscellany)
Zagreb, Arhiv Hrvatske Akademije Znanosti i Umjetnosti, MS I b 55
―――, MS Iv a 34
―――, MS I b 83 (Lulić's Miscellany)

Primary Sources

Bernardus Claraevallensis, *Liber de modo bene vivendi ad sororem*, ed. by Jacques-Paul Migne, Patrologiae Cursus Completus: Series Latina, 184 (Paris: Migne, 1859), cols 1199–1306D

Divi Bernardi abbatis ad sororem: Modvs bene vivendi in christianam religionem (Venice: per Bernardinum de Benaliis et Mattheum Parmensem, 1490)

Gregory the Great, *Moralium libri, sive expositio in librum B. Iob.*, ed. by Jacques-Paul Migne, Patrologiae Cursus Completus: Series Latina, 75 (Paris: Migne, 1849), cols 509–1162

The Manere of Good Lyvyng: A Middle English Translation of Pseudo-Bernard's 'Liber de modo bene vivendi ad sororem', ed. by Anne E. Mouron, Medieval Women: Texts and Contexts, 30 (Turnhout: Brepols, 2014)

Secondary Works

Bos, Elisabeth, 'The Literature of Spiritual Formation for Women in France and England, 1080 to 1180', in *'Listen, Daughter': The 'Speculum Virginum' and the Formation of Religious Women in the Middle Ages*, ed. by Constant J. Mews, The New Middle Ages (New York: Macmillan, 2001), pp. 201–20

Bradley, Ritamary, 'Background of the Title "Speculum" in Mediaeval Literature', *Speculum*, 29/1 (1954), pp. 100–15

Bratsch-Prince, Dawn, 'La fuerza del prólogo: la traducción catalana del "Liber de modo bene vivendi ad sororem" de Antoni Canals', in *Actas del XI Congreso Internacional de la Asociación Hispánica de Literatura Medieval*, ed. by Armando López Castro and María Luzdivina Cuesta Torre, 2 vols (León: Universidad de León, Secretariado de publicaciones, 2007), I, pp. 349–55

Colish, Marcia L., *Peter Lombard*, 2 vols, Brill's Studies in Intellectual History, 41 (Leiden: Brill, 1994), I

Dürrigl, Marija-Ana, 'O čitanju, pisanju i kompiliranju u hrvatskoglagoljskom srednjovjekovlju', *Slovo*, 60 (2010), pp. 219–34

——, 'Pogled na Petrisov zbornik kao zrcalo', in *Meandrima hrvatskoga glagoljaštva: Zbornik posvećen akademiku Stjepanu Damjanoviću o 70. rođendanu*, ed. by Tanja Kuštović, and Mateo Žagar (Zagreb: Hrvatska sveučilišna naklada, 2016), pp. 95–108

Evans, Ruth, 'An Afterword on the Prologue', in *The Idea of Vernacular: An Anthology of Middle English Literacy Theory, 1280–1530*, ed. by Jocelyn Wogan-Browne, Nicholas Watson, Andrew Taylor, and Ruth Evans (University Park: Penn State UP; Exeter: Exeter University Press, 1999), pp. 371–78

Gunn, Cate, *'Ancrene Wisse': From Pastoral Literature to Vernacular Spirituality*, Religion and Culture in the Middle Ages (Cardiff: University of Wales Press, 2008)

Hericgonja, Eduard, *Srednjovjekovna književnost*, Povijest hrvatske književnosti, 2 (Zagreb: Liber-Mladost, 1975)

Hotchin, Julie, 'Female Religious Life and the "Cura Monialium" in Hirsau Monasticism, 1080 to 1150', in *'Listen, Daughter': The 'Speculum Virginum' and the Formation of Religious Women in the Middle Ages*, ed. by Constant J. Mews, The New Middle Ages (New York: Macmillan, 2001), pp. 59–83

Innes-Parker, Catherine, 'Translation, Authorship, and Authority: The Middle English *Lignum Vitae*', in *In principio fuit interpres*, ed. by Alessandra Petrina and Monica Santini, The Medieval Translator / Traduire au Moyen Âge, 15 (Turnhout: Brepols, 2013), pp. 225–35

Johnson, Eric J., '"In dryȝdred and daunger": The Tradition and Rhetoric of Fear in Cleanness and Patience' (doctoral thesis, University of York, Centre for Medieval Studies, University of York, June 2000)

Kienzle, Beverly Mayne, 'Introduction', in *The Sermon*, ed. by Beverly Mayne Kienzle, Typologie des sources du Moyen Âge occidental, 81–83 (Turnhout: Brepols, 2000), pp. 143–74

Korondi, Ágnes, 'A "Liber de modo bene vivendi" szerzősége és szövegkörnyezetei a késő középkori magyar nyelvű kolostori kódexirodalom tükrében', *Erdélyi Múzeum*, 67 (2005), pp. 156–64

Kuczynski, Michael P., *Prophetic Song: The Psalms as Moral Discourse in Late Medieval England*, The Middle Ages Series (Philadelphia, PA: University of Pennsylvania Press, 1995)

Kukuljević, Ivan, 'Marko Marulić i njegovo doba', in *Marko Marulić: pjesme Marka Marulića, Stari pisci hrvatski*, vol. 1. (Zagreb: JAZU, 1869), pp. i–lxxvii

'Listen, Daughter': The 'Speculum Virginum' and the Formation of Religious Women in the Middle Ages, ed. by Constant J. Mews, The New Middle Ages (New York: Macmillan, 2001)

McGuire, Brian Patrick, 'A Benedictine-Cistercian Source? The Book Brigitta Kept on her Person', *Brigittiana*, 16 (2003), pp. 81–104

Mews, Constant J., 'Virginity, Theology, and Pedagogy in the *Speculum Virginum*', in *'Listen, Daughter': The 'Speculum Virginum' and the Formation of Religious Women in the Middle Ages*, ed. by Constant J. Mews, The New Middle Ages (New York: Macmillan, 2001), pp. 21–40

Mihaljević, Milan, 'Položaj crkvenoslavenskga jezika u hrvatskoj srednjovjekovnoj kulturi', in *Zbornik na trudovi od Megjunarodniot naučen sobir Sveti Naum Ohridski i slovenskata duhovna, kulturna i pismena tradicija (organiziran po povod 1100-godišninata od smrtta na sv. Naum Ohridski)*, ed. by Ilija Velev and others (Skopje: Univerzitetot 'Sv. Kiril i Metodij', 2011), pp. 229–38

Mouron, Anne E., '"Listen to me, daughter, listen to a faithful counsel": *Liber de modo bene vivendi ad sororem*', in *Writing Religious Women: Female Spiritual and Textual Practice in Late Medieval England*, ed. by Denis Renevey and Christiania Whitehead (University of Toronto Press, 2000), pp. 81–106

——, 'Praying without Images', *The Way*, 51/4 (2012), pp. 91–101

——, '"Sub mensa Patrum micas collegi": The Making of the *Liber*', in *In principio fuit interpres*, ed. by Alessandra Petrina and Monica Santini, *The Medieval Translator / Traduire au Moyen Âge*, 15 (Turnhout: Brepols, 2013), pp. 25–36

——, '*The Manere of Good Lyvyng*: The Manner of a Good Translator?', *Medium Aevum*, 78/2 (2009), pp. 300–22

Newman, Barbara, 'Flaws in the Golden Bowl: Gender and Spiritual Formation in the Twelfth Century', *Traditio*, 45 (1989/90), pp. 111–46

——, 'Liminalities: Literate Women in the Long Twelfth Century', in *European Transformations: The Long Twelfth Century*, ed. by Thomas F. X. Noble and John van Engen, Notre Dame Conferences in Medieval Studies (Notre Dame, IN: University of Notre Dame Press, 2012), pp. 354–402

——, 'Gender', in *The Wiley-Blackwell Companion to Christian Mysticism*, ed. by Julia A. Lamm, Blackwell Companions to Religion (Oxford: Wiley-Blackwell, 2012), pp. 41–55

Pandžić, Zvonko, *Nepoznata proza Marka Marulića. O novootkrivenim i novoatribuiranim hrvatskim rukopisima* (Zagreb: Tusculanae editiones, 2009)

Pinder, Janice, 'The Cloister and the Garden: Gendered Images of Religious Life from the Twelfth and Thirteenth Centuries', in *'Listen, Daughter': The 'Speculum Virginum' and the Formation of Religious Women in the Middle Ages*, ed. by Constant J. Mews, The New Middle Ages (New York: Macmillan, 2001), pp. 159–79

Radošević, Andrea, 'Croatian Translation of Biblical Passages in Medieval Performative Texts', *Studies in Church History*, 53 (2017), pp. 223–41

——, 'Vele lip kapitul i koristan – "Liber de modo bene vivendi ad sororem" in "Gršković's Miscellany" from the 16th Century', *Croatica*, 61 (2017), pp. 43–72

——, 'Zbirka sentencija iz Petrisova i Grškovićeva zbornika u kontekstu hrvatskoglagoljske refleksivne proze', *Senjski zbornik*, 48 (2021), pp. 261–86

Radošević, Andrea and Marija-Ana Dürrigl, 'Glagoljska čitateljska zajednica na primjeru Drugoga beramskoga brevijara', *Slovo*, 70 (2020), pp. 191–216

Renevey, Denis and Christiania Whitehead, '"Opyn þin hert as a boke": Translation Practice and Manuscript Circulation in *The Doctrine of the Heart*', in *The Medieval Translator: Traduire au Moyen Âge*, ed. by Jacqueline Jenkins and Olivier Bertrand, The Medieval Translator / Traduire au Moyen Âge, 10 (Turnhout: Brepols, 2008), pp. 125–48

Štefanić, Vjekoslav, *Glagoljski rukopisi otoka Krka*, Djela Jugoslavenske akademije znanosti i umjetnosti, 51 (Zagreb: JAZU, 1960)

——, *Glagoljski rukopisi Jugoslavenske akademije,* 2 vols (Zagreb: JAZU, 1970), II

Wareham, Edmund, '"Wann du fromm lebst / so wirst du nimmer trawrig": Professor Jodocus Lorichius and the Cistercian Nuns of Günterstal', *Oxford German Studies*, 43/4 (2014), pp. 362–79

Websites

textmanuscripts / Les enluminures, online: <https://www.textmanuscripts.com/medieval/bernof-clairvaux-60696> [accessed 3 November 2022]

Early Readers' Responses to the English Translations of Richard Rolle's *Emendatio vite*

Tamás Karáth

Pázmány Péter Catholic University,
Budapest, Hungary and Comenius
University, Bratislava, Slovakia

The Middle English *Emendatio vite* and its Readers: Richard Misyn, O. Carm. and the Version A Translation

The most popular work of Richard Rolle (d. 1349) is the *Emendatio vite* (henceforth *EV*), surviving in 108 manuscripts.[1] The *EV* is a balanced summary of Rolle's guide to contemplation in twelve short chapters ranging from conversion in Chapter 1 to the climax of the contemplative experience in Chapter 12. The Latin tract was translated into Middle English in seven independent versions, attested by sixteen manuscripts.[2] As such it represents the most often translated writing of the mystic. The translations are extant exclusively in fifteenth-century manuscripts, but the earliest full translation may precede 1400, as fragments of an English *EV* have been traced in *Pore Caitif*,[3] a devotional compilation from the late fourteenth century.

The Middle English translations of the *EV* provide numerous instances for the translators' editorial endeavours. Previously, I have investigated the translators' strategies transforming Rolle's mystical authority and experience.[4] As I have demonstrated, the Middle English translations of Rolle's *EV* display a few patterns of the translators' interventions which become even more discernible in a comparison with other translated Rollean texts. The major legacy of the translators of the *EV* is the emergence of new concerns about the theological issues of deification, the Last Judgement, and universal salvation, as well as the revision

---

1 Richard Rolle, *De emendatione vitae*, ed. by Spahl, pp. 21–85.

2 For the full list of the manuscripts containing the Middle English translations, see Allen, *Writings Ascribed to Richard Rolle*, pp. 240–43; Lagorio and Sargent, 'English Mystical Writings', p. 3424; Richard Rolle, *De emendatione vitae*, ed. by Spahl, pp. 133–43; and Hanna, *The English Manuscripts of Richard Rolle*, p. 229. My classification of the manuscripts into versions follows Lagorio and Sargent.

3 Brady, 'The Seynt and his Boke', pp. 20–31.

4 Karáth, 'The Re-Invention of Authority in the Fifteenth-Century Translations of Richard Rolle's "Emendatio Vitae"', pp. 255–74; Karáth, *Richard Rolle*.

of the affective responses to Rolle's mysticism, thus shaping a new model of contemplation.[5] But whether the late medieval readers of the translations were perceptive of the new emphases is perhaps of even more significance to the study of the transformation of Rolle's authority. This chapter will look at the translations from the readers' perspective and will investigate the passages which triggered the particular attention of the readers. I will ask if these passages bear the marks of the overt or covert editing of the translators, and consequently, if readers responded to the translators' revisions rather than to an 'unrevised' Rolle. Whether the readers suspected that these passages were affected by the translation or not cannot be gauged and may even be irrelevant to my purposes. Just as the translations of the *EV* represent individual, though not the typical, ways of interpreting Rolle in the fifteenth century, the annotations of readers and users of these translations, even if very limited in volume and scope, represent the earliest indications of readers responding to the new contemplative ideal of the *EV* shaped partly by the translators' interventions.

While we have an idea of readers who may have read the *EV* translations in the fifteenth and early sixteenth centuries, the actual readers are elusive. Four versions of the English *EV* survive with late medieval users' marginal notes that range from scribal corrections to marginal signs and key-word notes to dense annotations by multiple readers. Marleen Cré and Hugh Kempster did valuable research on the readers (users). Cré prepared the profiles of the readers leaving marginal notes in the Carthusian Amherst MS (London, British Library, MS Add. 37790) containing the translation of *EV* by Richard Misyn, O. Carm. (d. 1462), while Kempster discussed readers' responses in the Version A manuscripts of the *EV*.[6]

The Translation of Richard Misyn, O. Carm.

According to the testimony of all the three copies of Richard Misyn's translation, carefully preserving the translator's prologue and colophons, the translation was written at the instigation of a York anchoress, Margaret Heslington (d. 1439):

> At þe reuerence of oure lorde Ihesu criste, to þe askynge of þi desire, syster Margarete, couetynge a-sethe to make, for encrece also of gostely comfort to þe & mo, þat curiuste of latyn vnderstandes noght, I, emonge lettryd men sympellest, and in lyfynge vnthriftyest, þis wark has takyn to translacion of lattyn to englysch, for edificacyon of many saules.[7]

---

5 Karáth, *Richard Rolle*, pp. 241–44.

6 Cré, *Vernacular Mysticism in the Charterhouse*, esp. Appendix 4: 'Reader Profiles', pp. 321–39; Kempster, 'Richard Rolle, "Emendatio Vitae"', pp. lxxiv–cxix.

7 Richard Rolle, *The Fire of Love, and The Mending of Life or The Rule of Living*, trans. by Misyn, p. 2.

(Explicit liber de Incendio Amoris, Ricardi Hampole heremite, translatus in Anglicum instancijs domine Margarete Heslyngton, recluse, per fratrem Ricardum Misyn, sacre theologie bachalaureum, tunc Priorem Lyncolniensem, ordinis carmelitarum, Anno domini M°.CCCCxxxv^{to} in festo translacionis sancti Martini Episcopi, quod est iiij nonas Iulij, per dictum fratrem Ricardum Misyn scriptum & correctum.)[8]

Misyn's version was, however, read by a larger community of readers besides 'Sister Margaret'. The translator himself dedicated his work to many Christian souls with the probable intention that his text would be disseminated beyond Margaret's own and Misyn's Carmelite circles.

The three manuscript copies of the Misyn translation, indeed, assume three different textual communities. Oxford, Corpus Christi College, MS 236 carries only the two Misyn translations of Rolle's *EV* and *Incendium amoris* (translated as *Fire of Love* by Misyn), and as such, its design may be closest to Misyn's autograph delivering the two translations as devotional readings for Margaret Heslington.[9] The second copy of Misyn's translations – New Haven, Yale University, Beinecke, MS 331 – ends with a verse life of St John of Bridlington, a Northern Augustinian friar and prior canonized in 1401.[10] The presence of the Augustinian saint in the manuscript points at the intersections of Rolle's nascent cult in the North and the growing popularity of an Augustinian saint, certainly targeting readers from within the Augustinian channels of textual dissemination.[11] The third copy of Misyn's translations embedded in the Amherst manuscript, one of the richest anthologies of late Middle English devotional and contemplative texts, has been ascribed to Carthusian production by several scholars.[12] Cré argues that Amherst was not only read, annotated, and possessed

---

8 Richard Rolle, *The Fire of Love, and The Mending of Life or The Rule of Living*, trans. by Misyn, p. 104.

9 For a description of the Corpus Christi MS, see Thomson, *A Descriptive Catalogue*, pp. 120–21 and Hanna, *The English Manuscripts of Richard Rolle*, pp. 179–80.

10 For the description of the Beinecke MS, see Shailor, *Catalogue of the Medieval and Renaissance Manuscripts in the Beinecke Rare Book and Manuscript Library*, II, pp. 153–55 and Hanna, *The English Manuscripts of Richard Rolle*, pp. 121–22.

11 Margaret Laing located the dialect of the manuscript in the area where Lincolnshire, Leicestershire, and Nottinghamshire meet. Laing, 'Linguistic Profiles and Textual Criticism', p. 204. This may be indicative of the provenance of the manuscript (still within the 'homeland' of Richard Misyn); however, the dialect of the manuscript (and probably of the copyist) is no evidence of the actual place of its production.

12 The most detailed study of the manuscript and its design is by Cré, *Vernacular Mysticism in the Charterhouse*. For catalogue descriptions of the manuscript, see the *Catalogue of Additions to the Manuscripts in the British Museum in the Years 1906–1910*, pp. 153–56; Allen, *Writings Ascribed to Richard Rolle*, pp. 223–24, p. 241, pp. 247–48, and p. 260; Hanna, *The English Manuscripts of Richard Rolle*, pp. 80–82, and the discussions in the critical editions of the major texts in Amherst, which Hanna lists on p. 82.

by Carthusians, but the manuscript eventually 'originated [...] in one of the Carthusian houses of England'.[13]

The Amherst manuscript contains a plethora of annotations by its readers. Cré has identified seven annotators of the manuscript, including the Amherst scribe (Annotator 5) and James Grenehalgh, Carthusian monk of Sheen (Annotator 6), whose annotations in various manuscripts and the communication with Johanna Sewell on the margins of several manuscripts have been catalogued and studied by Michael G. Sargent.[14] Four of the seven annotators of the Amherst manuscript have commented on the English *EV* in the manuscript.

To start with the more low-key readers, Annotator 4 marked 'longer passages by writing abbreviated "notae" next to all the lines of the marked passage'.[15] His attention was drawn to two passages on humility and to an exposition of the Trinity.[16] Annotator 3, still very low-key, otherwise leaving profuse notes elsewhere in the manuscript, marked the importance of two passages about the expected mentality of contemplatives. Two further *notae* probably by the same hand confirm that this annotator was interested in the exterior signs that describe the contemplative on his quest for the ultimate truth.[17] Annotator 2 left a dozen definitely identifiable *nota* inscriptions on the margins of the English *EV*, seven of which are related to the last two chapters elaborating on love and on the contemplative fulfilment.[18] Finally, Annotator 1, in a sixteenth-century cursive handwriting, left twenty-two certainly identifiable notes related to the English *EV*. Besides the words *nott*, *notta*, and *nota*, he frequently noted key words of the adjacent passages, especially those providing definitions (as e.g. 'what prayer is' and 'contemplation, what it is' on fol. 15^v, 'grace' and *perfitenes* on fol. 18).[19] The notes of Annotator 1 are quite evenly spread on the margins of the English *EV*, with slightly more focus on the two concluding chapters. One of the passages drawing his attention point out the significance of a claim that the translator, Richard Misyn, himself attempted to make even more articulate through his editorial interventions into Rolle's *EV*: 'hereby it is schewyd that holynes is not in cryinge of the harte or terys or vtwarde warkys'.[20] Misyn's attempts to

---

13 Cré, *Vernacular Mysticism in the Charterhouse*, p. 19.

14 Sargent, *James Grenehalgh as Textual Critic*.

15 Cré, *Vernacular Mysticism in the Charterhouse*, p. 335.

16 Cré, *Vernacular Mysticism in the Charterhouse*, p. 335.

17 Cré, *Vernacular Mysticism in the Charterhouse*, p. 327.

18 Cré, *Vernacular Mysticism in the Charterhouse*, pp. 325–26. In the profile of Annotator 2, Cré has not treated the notes on the *EV* (*Mending of Life*) separately from the notes on the ensuing work in the manuscript, Rolle's *Incendium amoris* in Misyn's translation (*Fire of Love*). As the *Mending on Life* ends on fol. 18, all notes appearing from fol. 18^v (and before fol. 95) belong to the *Fire*.

19 Cré, *Vernacular Mysticism in the Charterhouse*, pp. 321–22.

20 Cré, *Vernacular Mysticism in the Charterhouse*, p. 322.

attenuate the highly affective elements of Rolle's descriptions, as I have shown elsewhere, resonate in the responses of Annotator 1.[21]

The Version A Text

Another Middle English translation of the *EV*, richly annotated by readers, is the Version A text, extant in five copies.[22] Kempster has edited the Version A text on the basis of Dublin, Trinity College, MS 432; he also prepared the diplomatic transcript of one Latin recension (Oxford, Bodleian Library, MS Bodley 54) along with the translations in the Trinity, the Cambridge, and the Douce manuscripts in parallel columns.[23] Kempster's introductory analysis provides a thorough investigation of the early readers of all the five Version A copies on the basis of manuscript evidence. Kempster looks at the translation in the 'cross-section of Rolle's early readership' in the particular context of the Version A copies, i.e. 'a fourteenth-century scribe whose Latin recension is related to the translator's exemplar, a translator, five fifteenth-century copyists, a few correctors, and a handful of other early owners and readers'.[24] Nevertheless, while the relatively frequent sixteenth- and seventeenth-century owners' annotations allow us to reconstruct the early readership of these manuscripts, most of the annotations of scribes and readers are not sufficient to gain any insight into the readers' interpretations.

Two late fifteenth-century sister manuscripts, Bodleian Library, MS Douce 322 and British Library, MS Harley 1706, reveal a very intriguing history of dissemination, but they are far more silent on how the Dominican nuns of Dartford and the Benedictine nuns of Barking were reading the Rolle translations.[25] Several notes of ownership outline a probable lay audience and use of Cambridge, University Library, MS Ff.5.30.[26] Kempster concludes: 'There is insufficient information here to make any firm comment on the early provenance or

---

21 For Misyn's overwriting Rolle's affective language, especially the passages related to sighs and tears, see Karáth, *Richard Rolle*, pp. 121–33.

22 The five manuscripts of the Version A translation are Cambridge, University Library, MS Ff.5.30; Dublin, Trinity College, MS 432; London, British Library, MS Harley 1706; Oxford, Bodleian Library, MS Digby 18; and Oxford, Bodleian Library, MS Douce 322.

23 Kempster, 'Richard Rolle, "Emendatio Vitae"'.

24 Kempster, 'Richard Rolle, "Emendatio Vitae"', p. lxxiv.

25 For the history of the dissemination of the two sister manuscripts, see Doyle, 'Books Connected with the Vere Family and Barking Abbey', esp. pp. 222–23, pp. 228–29, and pp. 233–34; Hanna, *The English Manuscripts of Richard Rolle*, pp. 154–55; Kempster, 'Richard Rolle, "Emendatio Vitae"', pp. cviii–cix; and Mooney, 'Vernacular Literary Manuscripts and their Scribes', pp. 208–09.

26 Hanna, *The English Manuscripts of Richard Rolle*, p. 28 and Kempster, 'Richard Rolle, "Emendatio Vitae"', pp. xciii–xcv. For the possessors' notes, see Appendix 1 (readers / owners of Version A).

readership of the manuscript, although the fact that both texts are in the vernacular does point towards a lay audience'.[27] Another early fifteenth-century production is Oxford, Bodleian Library, MS Digby 18, about whose provenance nothing is known before the seventeenth century.[28] Finally, the translation of the *EV* in Dublin, Trinity College, MS 432, is the richest in annotations. Nothing is known about the first readers of this manuscript before it came into the collection of Archbishop James Ussher in the seventeenth century.[29] The *EV* translation was copied by two scribes and annotated by at least four fifteenth- and sixteenth-century hands, whose marginal notes represent not only corrections but occasionally also early readers' responses to the crux of Rolle's mysticism.[30]

This chapter will join Cré and Kempster's discussions of the presence and responses of readers in two versions of the Middle English *EV* with the analysis of two other versions containing readers' annotations. I will focus on readers' responses to the Version B and Version E texts with the aim of contrasting the translators' editorial endeavours with their readers' appreciations. In order to grasp where readers responded to the translators' revisions or interpretations, I will first set up the translator profiles for both Versions B and E, then I will look at where the interests of the readers of these two versions lay as witnessed by manuscript evidence, and finally I will point at the intersections of translators' revisions and readers' responses, i.e. passages covertly edited by the translators to which the readers' attention was ostensibly drawn. With this methodology I intend to illustrate the ways in which individual interpretations or revisions of Rolle were incorporated into a 'common' and 'public' image of the mystic in fifteenth-century devotional writing.

Translator Profiles

The Version B Translation (Cambridge, University Library, MS Ff.5.40 and London, British Library, MS Harley 2406)

The two copies of Version B differ only in a few passages that mostly appear in the Cambridge manuscript, but not in Harley.[31] We can see a translator at work who did not seek to openly authorize himself; at the same time, he did not literally translate Rolle. Overall, the translation is idiomatic, heavily simplifying Rolle's syntax and rhetoric. Simplification also involves numerous omissions of

---

27 Kemspter, 'Richard Rolle, "Emendatio Vitae"', p. xcv.

28 Hanna, *The English Manuscripts of Richard Rolle*, p. 147 and Kempster, 'Richard Rolle, "Emendatio Vitae"', p. cxvii.

29 Kempster, 'Richard Rolle, "Emendatio Vitae"', p. lxxxv.

30 Kempster, 'Richard Rolle, "Emendatio Vitae"', pp. lxxxvii–lxxxviii.

31 For the comparison of the two copies of Version B, see Karáth, *Richard Rolle*, pp. 172–79.

phrases and sentences, as attested by the comparison of the English text to Rüdiger Spahl's edition of the Latin.[32]

The translator very infrequently amplifies or enriches Rolle's text, but when such textual accretions occur, they underline the particular interests of the translator who predominantly extended passages by glossing over some practical aspects of the Rollean contemplative ascent. A second instance of the visibility of the translator in Version B is his insistence on marking the technical challenges of translating two Latin terms, central to Rolle's mysticism: *aureola corona* and *iubilus*. While most Middle English translations, with the notable exception of Misyn's self-authored Prologue, would entirely avoid reflecting on the process of translation, the Version B translator adds translator's comments to the expressions where he feels that the English solutions do not make an autonomous counterpart of the original Latin phrase.

The first type of the Version B translator's interventions into Rolle's assumed original is represented by his revisions of the practical details of abstinence. In the *EV*, Rolle himself was oscillating between the more and less permissive statements on abstinence, and this hesitation is also reflected by other writings of his, especially the *Incendium amoris* and the *Form of Living*. Rolle's hesitations derive from the contrasts he perceives between a contemplative ideal based on austere abstinence (asceticism) and his experience-based personal conviction. Rolle expects different degrees of self-discipline from people at different stages of the contemplative life. The only absolute standard he establishes for penitential practice is moderation so that it should never be exaggerated to the extent that it undermines the physical integrity and stability of the penitent. Self-imposed physical suffering should never inhibit the ability of the contemplative to concentrate on his or her spiritual growth:

> [H]aving established himself as a hermit, there are signs that Rolle did not always practise the expected austerities. [...] It seems [from his accounts in *Incendium amoris*] that asceticism interfered with Rolle's experience of *fervor*, *dulcor* and *canor*, which required him to be relaxed, not too tired from manual work or travel, not too hot or cold, and fairly well fed. As a contemplative whose stance was explicitly anti-penitential [...], he had no spiritual reason for the harsh austerities that Aelred enjoins; on the contrary [...] he had practical reasons for avoiding them. His argument is not altogether untraditional: Walter Hilton, for example, writes in a similar vein about the need to avoid excessive fasting as much as excessive eating.[33]

In five out of the seven independent Middle English translations of the *EV* (with the only exception of Versions E and F) the theme of abstinence receives prominent treatment from the translators. The Version B text tames some of the more rigorous formulations of Rolle. In a few instances of Chapter 3 on poverty, the translator is more permissive with the contemplative's worldly attachment than

---

32 Richard Rolle, *De emendatione vitae*, ed. and trans. by Spahl.
33 Watson, *Richard Rolle*, pp. 45–46.

Rolle. On fol. 18ᵛ of the Cambridge manuscript, Version B fails to literally follow Rolle's request of abandoning all secular attachments in order to rise to the contemplation of heavenly things. In the first passage affected by the translator's editing, two minor but substantial modifications entirely alter the original rigour of the sentence: the conditional conjunctive *si* ('if') is replaced for *þogh* ('though'), and the verb of the conditional clause *deserant* ('abandon') for *loue* ('love'):

> Possunt tamen [...] ad contemplacionem supernorum se levare, *si* occupaciones et secularia negocia *deserant* [...] atque ea, que habent, non amando possideant sed possidendo relinquant.[34]

> (ʒeet [...] þei may ben lefted vp to contemplacioune of heuenly thinges *þogh* þei *loue* werdely occupaciouns and besynesses þerof [...] so þat þei may kepe wordeli goodes withouten loue of þem.)[35]

These changes considerably weaken Rolle's original insistence on abandoning all secular ties to become a contemplative. Besides the substitutions on the level of words, resulting in a meaning unprecedented by the Latin text, the omission of the last clause of the quoted passage (*sed possidendo relinquant*) confirms the direction of the changes: the contemplative is not supposed to be attached to possessions, but the requirement of abandoning everything (while possessing) is not voiced by the English translation.

However, turning to Chapter 4 on the institution of life, the translator is again in overall agreement with Rolle's recipe of self-denial. Only on two occasions does the Version B text less literally interpret the instructions on fasting. In the first case the Latin formulates a general prohibition of rejecting any food received through grace (or due thanksgiving); in the English rendering this is transformed into a piece of advice against squeamishness:

> Nichil reiciendum est pro tempore, quod cum graciarum accione percipitur (Richard Rolle, *De emendatione vitae*, ed. by Spahl, p. 184/62–63).

> (þou schal nouth be queymous [squeamish] of metes but eten of alle manere of mete as þe tyme asketh) (Cambridge, University Library, MS Ff.5.40, fol. 20).

In the second case of a loose translation in the same chapter, shortly following the above passage, the translator inserts an original comment on Rolle's praise of charity over all abstinence: 'Et sine dubitacione virtus caritatis omnem abstinenciam vel ieiunium vel alia opera, quae exterius videri possunt, incomparabiliter

---

[34] Richard Rolle, *De emendatione vitae*, ed. and trans. by Spahl, p. 178/51–54, emphasis mine. All further quotes from the Latin *EV* will be taken from Spahl's edition with parenthetical references to page and line numbers.

[35] Cambridge, CUL, MS Ff.5.40, fol. 18ᵛ. All further quotes from the Version B translation of *EV* will be taken from either of the two manuscript copies with parenthetical references to the manuscript and folio numbers.

excedit' (Richard Rolle, *De emendatione vitae*, ed. by Spahl, p. 188/01–03). Instead of the superiority of charity over all visible deeds of mercy and repentance, the translator emphasizes the dependence of abstinence on meekness and charity: 'for if abstinence be nouth vnderborwe [is not undertaken] with mekenesse and charite it es nouth [nothing]' (Cambridge, University Library, MS Ff.5.40, fol. 20ᵛ).

The translator's interest in the practical implications of the Rollean program of contemplative ascent is exclusively restrained to the above passages concerning fasting and abstinence. Otherwise, the translator's presence in the text can be grasped only in his didactic glosses attached to the Latin technical terms of *iubilus* and *aureola*. In a few instances the translator preserves Latin *iubilus* in the vernacular text along with an English gloss:

> ipsa oracio in iubilum commutatur (Richard Rolle, *De emendatione vitae*, ed. by Spahl, p. 200/29–30).
>
> (þanne is his preier turned *in to a song þat is called of latyn iubileus*) (Cambridge, University Library, MS Ff.5.40, fols 23ᵛ–24).

Iubilus is the key word of the climax of contemplation in the *EV*, and its concentration in the last two chapters of the treatise marks an affective turn in Rolle's guide to contemplative ascent.[36] *Iubilus* necessarily connotes praise and music in Rolle's rhetoric. Because of the semantic density of the Latin word, the English translators of the *EV* struggle with rendering the concept with one lexical item. The Version B translator explicates *iubilus* as a song, glossing it over with its Latin original to point out its particular transitory nature linking earth and heaven. In Chapter 12 on the contemplation of God, the translator pursues the same glossing strategy in rendering *iubilus*:

> Alii dicunt, et bene, quod contemplacio est iubilus supernorum. [heuenely songe þat is callede iubilus (Cambridge, University Library, MS Ff.5.40, fol. 30)]. Michi videtur, quod contemplacio sit iubilus divini amoris. [þis heuenly songe of þe loue of god wheche is called iubilus (Cambridge, University Library, MS Ff.5.40, fol. 30)] (Richard Rolle, *De emendatione vitae*, ed. by Spahl, p. 226/18–21)

The same glossing mentality affects the translations of the word *aureola*, that is, the highest heavenly award for the contemplatives who also persevered in preaching. The Version B translator renders it as 'þe aurel þat is a coroun' (Cambridge, University Library, MS Ff.5.40, fol. 32). With the explicitation of *aureola* as crown, the Version B translator creates a textual connection between this episode and all the previous occurrences of the heavenly crown metaphor. Nevertheless, he is sometimes reluctant to grant it where Rolle does. These minor deviations from Rolle's imagery reflect the caution with which the translator read passages on final heavenly rewards.

---

36 *Iubilus* combined notions of wordlessness, pure music, and bursting out in joy. As a musical term, it could denote melismatic attachments to antiphons. Specifically, the term stood for the textless melisma concluding the *Alleluia*. *Lexicon musicum latinum medii aevi*, x, pp. 294–95.

While the challenge of translating the term *aureola* may seem at first glance purely technical, Cré's discussion of Misyn's 'unease' concerning the theological implications of Rolle's *EV* enables us to perceive similar tendencies shared by the Version B and Misyn's translations. Interpreting Misyn's omissions of some strongly affective elements of Rolle's descriptions of the contemplative fire of love, Cré suggests that the omissions, including the sporadic suppressions of the metaphor of the heavenly crown, may evince Misyn's suspicions of too ardent love, of the highest reward of the perfect contemplatives in this life, and of the eternal joys of the perfect and their assumed high(est) status in heaven.[37] While Cré remains sceptical of ascribing Misyn's omissions to the translator's censoring, she maintains the possibility of Misyn's interventions into the theological discourse of the *EV*:

> Though Misyn's translations do contain implicit anxiety about some aspects of Rolle's doctrine, they do not highlight the corrective elements. Thus, because the criticism is embedded in the text and only shows up after close comparison of the Latin and the English versions, it is much less explicit than in the other contemporary critics. Admiration for Rolle outweighs the criticism, and this attitude summarizes the fourteenth- and fifteenth-century assessment of Rolle and his texts: the hermit of Hampole was esteemed by many and criticized by a few. […] Misyn was, on the whole, less suspicious of Rolle's doctrine than of his own mistranslation of it.[38]

The Version B translator's reluctance to translate all of Rolle's references to the highest award and heavenly crown may also form part of a more extended theological speculation of the translation. The omissions of the Version B text together with some other revisions of the theological speculations of the *EV* reveal the translator's doubts in Rolle's formulations of the full vision of God. Chapter 10 on the cleanness of mind starts with the claim that the preceding nine grades of the contemplative ascent lead to the purity of mind, through which God can be seen: 'Per hos novem gradus pretactos ad puritatem mentis ascenditur, qua videtur deus'. (Richard Rolle, *De emendatione vitae*, ed. by Spahl, p. 210/1–2) The Version B translator replaces seeing (*videtur*) for knowing (*is knowe* in Cambridge, University Library, MS Ff.5.40, fol. 26). This is not the only instance of the translator's reluctance to literally translate the vision of God with the most obvious English verb of perception. Instead of the vision, he emphasizes knowledge as a condition for seeing. In Chapter 8 on meditation the cleansed soul is admitted to higher things to be glorified in the love of God: 'ad alciora admittitur, ut in amore deitatis vehementer glorietur' (Richard Rolle, *De emendatione vitae*, ed. by Spahl, p. 204/17–19). This ascent of the soul (not yet possessing the full vision of God) is again translated with the verb *knowe*: 'he schal ben resseyuede for to knowe heigher thinges' (Cambridge, University Library, MS Ff.5.40, fol. 24ᵛ). Also in other contexts where sight implies an

---

37 Cré, *Vernacular Mysticism in the Charterhouse*, pp. 88–96.

38 Cré, *Vernacular Mysticism in the Charterhouse*, pp. 95–96.

access to invisible and impenetrable truths, the Version B translator prefers knowing over seeing or being.

The translator's repeated rewritings of seeing for knowing merge concepts of perception and epistemology. Contemplation is conceived as the simultaneity of both. Chapter 8 defines contemplation (*contemplacione deitatis*, Richard Rolle, *De emendatione vitae*, ed. by Spahl, p. 204/16) as 'þe sigth and þe knowynge of þe godhed' (Cambridge, University Library, MS Ff.5.40, fol. 24^v). The translation of the closing chord of Rolle's ecstatic Chapter 12 reiterates this idea with the coordination of knowing and seeing in the translation of the phrase *deum vere cognoscere* (Richard Rolle, *De emendatione vitae*, ed. by Spahl, 236/131): 'for to sen god to knowen god' (Cambridge, University Library, MS Ff.5.40, fol. 32^v). If the translator was initially suspicious of Rolle's direct claims of the full vision of God, he reconciled this tension by a gradual blending of the meaning of 'seeing' into 'knowing'.

The Version E Translation (London, British Library, MS Lansdowne 455)

The Version E translation is considerably closer to the Latin than Version B. The copy in MS Lansdowne 455 evinces a thorough care both on the part of the translator and the copyists. The translator occupies the literal end of the spectrum of translation strategies. The text reveals hardly any intervention or editorial incursion. One of the few inconsistencies of the translator is illustrated by his endeavour to merge *cogitacio* and *cor* into 'heart' in Chapter 4 on the institution of life. Also, in this chapter, additional interest in the theology of sin is attested by the relatively more frequent revisions into the catalogue of sins, but such alterations do not seem to have any theological consequence.

The respect for the original is contradicted only by the translations of the vocabulary of melody and joy, in whose rendering the translator shows incomparable creativity. The Version E translator displays an astonishingly rich variation in expressions related to melody, more particularly to *iubilus*, translated as *hevenli melodie* (MS Lansdowne 455, fol. 45), *heuenli ioiynge* (fol. 46), *gostli ioie* (fol. 46 twice), *heuenli ioie* (fol. 46 twice, fol. 48^v), *heuenli syngen* (fol. 47), and *heuenli to synge* (fol. 47^v). The flow of variations on the same theme comes closest to the imitation of Rolle's effusion of song and joy.

Early Reader Profiles on the Basis of Manuscript Evidence[39]

Version B

The two copies of the Version B translation appear in devotional anthologies of Rolle and Hilton's texts. The first booklet of CUL, MS Ff.5.40, contains Hilton's

---

[39] The table in Appendix 1 summarizes the contents and the early readers (if known) of four versions of the Middle English *EV*: Richard Misyn's translations and Versions A, B, and E.

Medled Life followed by the English *EV*. Hilton's *Scale of Perfection I*, in a second hand, fills the entire second booklet and is carried on into Booklet 3. After one and a half leaves a third hand took over all the rest of Booklet 3, which includes Rolle's *Commandment, Of Proper Will* (otherwise attributed to Hilton), Hilton's *Of Angels' Song*, an extract from the *Prick of Conscience*, and further sixteen short prose texts. No owner or reader is identifiable from manuscript evidence.[40]

The later representative of the Version B translation, BL, MS Harley 2406, is a composite codex of three manuscripts, the first two of which have an obvious catechetical design. They gather the basics of religious instruction both in English and Latin. The third manuscript of the codex is more devotional than instructional in its composition. This part contains the English *EV* followed by a unique English exposition of a lost letter by Walter Hilton beginning 'Noviter militanti nova congruit milicia', *The Abbey of the Holy Ghost*, *The Charter of the Abbey*, a Latin exposition of the *Pater noster*, a distich, and a *Dialogue between Jesus and Anima*.[41] A possessor's note on fol. 11ᵛ (the last leaf of Manuscript 1) reveals that at one point of its history this part of the Harley manuscript belonged to *domine Matilde Stuerd*.[42] Two further notes on fols 1 and 83ᵛ associate the manuscript with the Leventhorpe family, loyal servants of the Lancastrians. The two notes mentioning the name *Tho[mas] Leuenthorp* and the date of 1557 (certainly not the date of the manuscript's composition) frame the codex.[43] This implies that the originally three separate manuscripts had been bound together by the time it came into the possession of Thomas Leventhorpe.

BL, MS Harley 2406 contains sporadic marginal notes and almost invisible corrections of the otherwise very neat text. Most of these indicate biblical sources and key-word labels of the major themes of certain passages. Otherwise hardly anything attests to the early readers' interests and interpretations. Three marginal notes comment on the extract from *The Abbey of the Holy Ghost*, which all make claims about the age of the created world.[44]

More particularly, the English *EV* in BL, MS Harley 2406 attests to readers' use only through its scribal corrections and the marginal notes indicating chapter

---

40 *The Index of Middle English Prose*, xix, ed. by Connolly, items 9–20, pp. 138–40.

41 Hanna, *The English Manuscripts of Richard Rolle*, p. 101; *A Catalogue of the Harleian Manuscripts in the British Museum*, ii, pp. 688–89; *A New Index of Middle English Verse*, ed. by Boffey and Edwards, no. 1771, p. 119.

42 Hanna, *The English Manuscripts of Richard Rolle*, p. 102.

43 *A Catalogue of the Harleian Manuscripts in the British Museum*, ii, p. 689.

44 London, British Library, MS Harley 2406, fol. 70ᵛ, bottom of the page: 'Nota. ffyue thousand hundreþ & xxxiii ȝere were from þat tyme þat adam & eue had synned vn to þat tyme þat þe [*sic!*] were bouȝt aȝeyn';

fol. 72, top of the page: 'adam lyued 4 hundreþ and þrytty ȝeres'; underneath: 'quater millenis sexcentum quatuor annis [...] in inferno fuit adam crimine primo'.

Ibid., fol. 72, bottom of the page: 'adam was in hell 4 thousande 6 hundreþ & iiii ȝeres' (translation of the Latin passage on top of the same page; Roman numerals are given above the Arabic '4' and '6').

numbers and chapter themes. The scribe-corrector punctuated obvious confusions in spelling, errors in syntax, and dialect features perceived as errors with a great deal of modesty, as most of his/her corrections remain almost invisible for the less attentive reader, because the punctuation for mistakes can easily be mistaken for intratextual punctuation marks. He/she dotted problematic letters and also placed a dot before (or eventually after) the respective line on the outer margin. Supposedly, the reviser of the text had all reasons to keep his/her corrections almost unnoticeable.[45]

The scribe-corrector scanned only fols 36ᵛ–46ᵛ, leaving his/her corrections evenly spread all throughout the first eight chapters of the English *EV*, from Chapter 1 on conversion to Chapter 8 on meditation. The corrections end before Chapter 9 on reading. The distribution of the corrections is not related to the quiring of the manuscript.[46] The only marginal correction can be found on fol. 51 (in Chapter 10 on the purity of mind, but actually in a long excerpt from Chapter 11 on the love of God inserted in fols 50–52), where the word 'but' appears in the right-hand margin to indicate that it is to be inserted in the line at the place marked with a wedge ('it may nouth be ^ if þu receyue hym'). Non-corrective marginal notes appear on two pages (fol. 70ᵛ and fol. 72), displaying mathematical calculations of the time elapsed from Adam's fall to the Harrowing of Hell and to the duration of Adam's stay in Hell.

Both the neat handwriting and layout of the manuscript and the careful scribal corrections, as well as the lack of any display of personal interpretations by individual readers may indeed underpin the suggestion of the *Index of Printed Middle English Prose* that the text of the *EV* may have been drawn up for the use of nuns.[47] In the context of a communal use (be it private reading in the cell by any member of the community or communal reading in the refectory or some other public space of a religious house), the marginal notes marking chapter numbers and themes are very helpful in orienting the reader and in tracking the sections of the treatise, just as the larger red initials of each chapter and the red underlining of the biblical quotes help the same purpose. Chapter numbers and paraphrased titles are added on the outer margins, and the chapter titles also bespeak (monastic) community use in which a voice of instruction addresses the community in the second person or in the collective first person plural:

London, British Library, MS Harley 2406

Caᵐ pᵐ (fol. 36): no title.
Caᵐ 2ᵐ (fol. 37ᵛ): *How þe worlde schal be dispisede.*
Caᵐ 3ᵐ (fol. 39): *How pouernes schal be hade.*
Caᵐ 4ᵐ (fol. 40ᵛ): *Off þe cettyng and þe rewle off life.*
Caᵐ 5ᵐ (fol. 43ᵛ): *Þat tribulacion schal be suffret paciently.*

---

45 For a full list of the scribe-corrector's notes, see Appendix 2.

46 For details of the quiring, see *A Catalogue of the Harleian Manuscripts in the British Museum*, II, p. 688 and *Index of Printed Middle English Prose*, ed. by Lewis, Blake, and Edwards, p. 219.

47 *Index of Printed Middle English Prose*, ed. by Lewis, Blake, and Edwards, p. 219.

Ca^m 6^m (fol. 44): *How we schul be paciens.*
Ca^m 7^m (fol. 46): *How þu schal prey.*
Ca^m 8^m (fol. 47): *How we schal do in meditacione.*
Ca^m 9^m (fol. 49): *How þu schalt haue þe in redyng.*
Ca^m 10^m (fol. 49^v): Chapter indication appears in the inner margin of the book: *Of þe clennes of herte.*
Ca^m xi^m (fol. 52): *How we schal loue gode.*
[Chapter 12]: No chapter indication on the margin (fol. 54): *How we schal haue vs in contemplacione.*

To conclude on the topic of the readers' presence in the Version B translation of the *EV*, there is not much substantial manuscript evidence to assess the users' appreciations and particular responses to Rolle, let alone to the translator's revisions. Only the Harley manuscript contains corrections and notes to trace the work of its first readers. However, none of these corrections or marginal notes reveals interpretative intentions of the users. Furthermore, the sparse scribal corrections and reader's notes are concentrated on a small range of leaves in the manuscript.

Version E

In the manuscript of the Version E translation of the *EV*, most of the texts are in some relation to the liturgy. The collection may have been used as a liturgical aid by a clergyman. In Booklet 1 of the manuscript, the Old Testament dominical epistles and lessons are followed by the sequence of Rolle's *Form of Living* and the English *EV*.[48] Booklet 2 contains a liturgical calendar and a table of Gospels, epistles, and lessons according to the Sarum use, while Booklet 3 is entirely filled by the Later Version of the Wycliffite New Testament.[49] At least three scribes are identifiable in the entire manuscript, all having (Central) Midland dialects. The first scribe left the copying of Rolle's *Form* incomplete at its two-thirds and a later fifteenth-century hand finished it.[50] The only catchword in the bottom right-hand corner of fol. 47^v indicates that the work was certainly interrupted at this point and taken over by the other copyist. The second hand also corrected the mistakes of the first hand. Only a very few did actually avoid his vigilance. Furthermore, the second copyist not only corrected the translation, but also annotated it. His marginal additions, signs, and notes, witness one of the earliest reader's responses to the vernacular translations of Rolle's *EV*. The annotator used two types of marginal signs. The very infrequent sign ·) in red ink, occurring only twice in the manuscript, marks an error, such as a missing division in the text or the correction of a word.[51] The sign (– expresses emphasis,

---

48 Hanna, *The English Manuscripts of Richard Rolle*, p. 102.

49 Hanna, *The English Manuscripts of Richard Rolle*, pp. 102–03.

50 Hanna, *The English Manuscripts of Richard Rolle*, p. 102.

51 This sign draws attention to a division in the respective passage turning to the description of the third degree of love: 'þat is þe þridde degre whiche is clepid synguler'

but it can occasionally point out errors in copying as well.[52] Four *manicules* in red ink appear at three places of the manuscript. Three of them appear alone, while the fourth one on fol. 46 is accompanied by a note. They more obviously draw the attention of the reader to specific passages. On fol. 42ra a *manicule* highlights a proverbial statement of *EV* which introduces a division of four things that easily deceive those dwelling in temporal abundance: 'when þou schalt wene [believe] for to stonde bi rychesses þou schalt falle in to fyer aȝen [aȝ euer?] þat dwellen in temporal habundaunce ben disceyued bi foure þinges þat þei louen'. Similarly, a *manicule* points at the catalogue of the three kinds of sin (of the heart, of the mouth, and of deeds) in Chapter 4 on the institution of life (fol. 43ra) and at a passage in Chapter 6 on patience consoling the patiently suffering with the promise of a crown in heaven:

> nec cedendum est temptacioni, quamvis gravissima sit, quia quo maior est pugna, eo gloriosior est victoria et sublimior corona (Richard Rolle, *De emendatione vitae*, ed. by Spahl, p. 185/48–49).

> (forwhi whan he [a patient man] is preued he schal take a crowne of lyf whiche god hath bihiȝt to hem þat louen him. þan ne doute þou noȝt þat þou ne art in wei of perfeccioun if dispyt be to þee as prisynge) (fol. 44va).

Besides the signs of correction and the *manicules*, the annotator also left three marginal notes. On fol. 45[v], he corrected the word 'sowen' [to sow] to 'sownen' [to sound] to adjust the translation to what the Latin text says: 'eius laudem sonant' (Richard Rolle, *De emendatione vitae*, ed. by Spahl, p. 197/67). On fol. 46 a note accompanying a *manicule* next to the passage on the three degrees of love in Chapter 11 on the love of God says: 'of iij degr'' and 'loue of crist'. On fol. 48 'Nota aur'' appears next to the line where the meaning of *aureola* is explained.

(BL, MS Lansdowne 455, fol. 46[va]). On fol. 47[rb] the same mark indicates the correction of 'redinge' for 'meditacion'. The Version E translation literally translates the most common Latin variant: 'in meditacione angeli ad nos descendunt' (Richard Rolle, *De emendatione vitae*, ed. by Spahl, 219/3), but as Spahl notes, many Latin manuscript variants amend this obvious mistake to 'leccione'. The careful corrector noticed that the right word in the context should be 'meditation'; the original of the copy may have contained the mistaken version ('reading') at this point: 'in redinge [marginal correction: meditacion] aungels comen doun to vs' (fol. 47rb).

52 The sign stands next to the following lines:
fol. 41va: *alwei in my siȝt not atte on one as þeir done.*
fol. 43va: the sign marks the doubling of a word in the text ('also also').
fol. 43va: the sign with an X marks the redundant repetition of the word 'nought'.
fol. 45va: *þe þouȝtes of hem which if þei knowen.*
fol. 47ra: *þat he schulde ony tyme stonde and ferþermore.*
fol. 47va: the sign marks the divisions in the definition of contemplation.
fol. 48ra: three signs next to three different lines about the cleansing of the eye, of the heart, tears, and ravishing in contemplation. There are no visible errors seen in the respective lines.

What do the annotations of this user amount to? First of all, the corrector's annotations and marks bespeak a very respectful use of the text. Secondly, three of the sparse annotations drawing attention to the importance of a passage reveal a reader's interest in using Rolle's *EV* as a compendium offering handy material for pastoral or catechetical work, such as the lists of four things that deceive worldly persons, the catalogue of three kinds of sin, and the three degrees of love. Finally, two of the notes are anchored on the image of the crown, promised as the ultimate award for those patiently suffering and resisting temptations, even if the English translation slightly attenuates the rhetoric of the Latin, as it omits to translate adjectives referring to the glory of victory and the sublimity of the crown (see the above quote). The second instance of the reader's highlighting the image of the crown on fol. 48 ascribes significance to the passage in which the translator silently glossed over his/her English rendering by giving the Latin equivalent of the English term:

> aureolam propter predicationem suam merentur (Richard Rolle, *De emendatione vitae*, ed. by Spahl, p. 231/111).

> (þei deseruen a special worschip *þat is clepid aureola*) (London, British Library, MS Lansdowne 455, fol. 48rb).

As I have noted earlier, the Version E translator seems to have been preoccupied by the term *aureola* both as a translation challenge and as a theologically suspicious element of Rolle's discourse. While a comparison of the Version E translation and the Latin texts attests to the unease of the translator about the golden crown as a heavenly reward of various ranks of contemplatives and the recurring omissions of these motifs in the English version, the reader of the Lansdowne manuscript marked it as one of the most emblematic images of the *EV*. This ultimately permits us to grasp one particular interference between the editorial activity of a translator and a reader of this translator's work. One of the few but major perceivable endeavours of the Version E translator (i.e. to attenuate the rhetoric of the golden crown) was frustrated by the early reader of the Lansdowne manuscript marking his presence with annotations. As for the theological speculations concerning the heavenly rewards, this reader resisted the new emphases suggested by the translator's strategies. This also reveals that readers unaware of the ways in which the *EV* was affected by the translator's editorial strategies still perceived the tamed rhetoric of the translator as one of the central and most affective elements of Rolle's contemplative guide.

Conclusion

The Version B and E translations of Rolle's *EV* represent the 'clerical' end of the late medieval reader spectrum, which is why the fifteenth-century readers of these manuscripts may share important aspects of their uses of, and attitudes to, the text. While no certainty can be established for the users of the Version B manuscript, cumulative manuscript evidence suggests the probability of the use of the text by a female religious community. As for Version E, the contents of the manuscript strongly suggest a liturgical context of use. This is also confirmed by the tendency of its early reader to scan the *EV* for passages easily applicable in pastoral work, as e.g. materials for preaching. This underlying 'clerical' re-use of Rolle's English *EV* may ultimately explain the lack of any personalized or individualized reader's response and interpretation. The few traces of the readers in the manuscript, manifested in form of scribal corrections, marginal signs, and very few marginal notes, frustrate any attempt to pin down palpable intersections between the translators' editorial strategies and shifted emphases on the one hand and the readers' sensitivities on the other. All manuscript copies of the Version B and E translations reveal a high respect for the author and authority of the text and read the English Rolle with the preliminary assumption of what constitutes the authority and the 'gist' of Rolle. If the non-corrective marginal annotations add anything more to the text than the themes of the twelve chapters of the *EV*, it is a short key-word summary of what Rolle meant as an authority for fifteenth-century clerical readers: resisting temptation, advancing through the three degrees of love, and the promise of obtaining the highest heavenly reward after the vicissitudes of contemplative ascent.

Bibliography

Primary Sources

Richard Rolle, *De emendatione vitae: Eine kritische Ausgabe des lateinischen Textes von Richard Rolle mit einer Übersetzung ins Deutsche und Untersuchungen zu den lateinischen und englischen Handschriften*, ed. and trans. by Rüdiger Spahl, Super Alta Perennis, 7 (Bonn: V & R Unipress, Bonn University Press, 2009)

———, *The Fire of Love, and The Mending of Life or The Rule of Living*, trans. by Richard Misyn, ed. by Ralph Harvey, Early English Text Society, 106 (London: Kegan Paul, Trench, Trübner, 1896; repr. New York: Cosimo Classics, 2010)

Secondary Works

Allen, Hope Emily, *Writings Ascribed to Richard Rolle, Hermit of Hampole and Materials for his Biography*, The Modern Language Association of America Monograph Series, 3 (New York: D. C. Heath & Co., 1927)

Brady, Mary Teresa, 'The Seynt and his Boke: Rolle's "Emendatio Vitae" and "The Pore Caitif"', *14th-Century English Mystics Newsletter*, 7 (1981), pp. 20–31

Catalogue of Additions to the Manuscripts in the British Museum in the Years 1906–1910 (London: Trustees of the British Museum, 1912)

A Catalogue of the Harleian Manuscripts in the British Museum, 4 vols (London: The British Museum, 1808–12), II (1808)

Cré, Marleen, *Vernacular Mysticism in the Charterhouse: A Study of London, British Library, MS Additional 37790*, The Medieval Translator / Traduire au Moyen Âge, 9 (Turnhout: Brepols, 2006)

Doyle, Anthony Ian, 'Books Connected with the Vere Family and Barking Abbey', *Transactions of the Essex Archaeological Society*, 25/2 (1958), pp. 222–43

Hanna, Ralph, *The English Manuscripts of Richard Rolle*, Exeter Medieval Texts and Studies (Exeter: University of Exeter Press, 2010)

Index of Printed Middle English Prose, ed. by Robert E. Lewis, Norman F. Blake, and Anthony S. G. Edwards (London: Garland, 1985)

Karáth, Tamás, 'The Re-Invention of Authority in the Fifteenth-Century Translations of Richard Rolle's "Emendatio Vitae"', in *Translation and Authority – Authorities in Translation*, ed. by Pieter de Leemans and Michele Goyens, The Medieval Translator / Traduire au Moyen Âge, 16 (Turnhout: Brepols, 2016), pp. 255–74

——, *Richard Rolle: The Fifteenth-Century Translations*, Medieval Church Studies, 40 (Turnhout: Brepols, 2018)

Kempster, Hugh, 'Richard Rolle, "Emendatio Vitae: Amendinge of Lyf", A Middle English Translation, Edited from Dublin, Trinity College MS 432' (unpublished doctoral thesis, University of Waikato, 2007)

Lagorio, Valerie M. and Michael G. Sargent (with Ritamary Bradley), 'English Mystical Writings', in *A Manual of the Writings in Middle English 1050–1500*, ed. by Albert E. Hartung and J. Burke Severs, 11 vols (New Haven, CT: Connecticut Academy of Arts and Sciences, 1967–2005), IX, ed. by Albert E. Hartung (1992), pp. 3049–137

Laing, Margaret, 'Linguistic Profiles and Textual Criticism: The Translations by Richard Misyn of Rolle's "Incendium Amoris" and "Emendatio Vitae"', in *Middle English Dialectology: Essays on Some Principles and Problems,* ed. and intr. by Margaret Laing (Aberdeen: The University of Aberdeen Press, 1989), pp. 188–223

Lexicon musicum latinum medii aevi: Dictionary of Medieval Latin Musical Terminology to the End of the 15th Century, ed. by Michael Bernhard (Munich: Verlag der Bayerischen Akademie der Wissenschaften, 1992–), X: *Gutturalis – Lichanos* (2009)

Mooney, Linne R., 'Vernacular Literary Manuscripts and their Scribes', in *The Production of Books in England 1350–1500*, ed. by Alexandra Gillespie and Daniel Wakelin, Cambridge Studies in Palaeography and Codicology, 14 (Cambridge: Cambridge University Press, 2011), pp. 192–211

A New Index of Middle English Verse, ed. by Julia Boffey and Anthony S. G. Edwards (London: British Library, 2005)

Sargent, Michael G., *James Grenehalgh as Textual Critic*, 2 vols, Analecta Cartusiana, 85 (Salzburg: Institut für Anglistik und Amerikanistik, Universität Salzburg, 1984)

Shailor, Barbara A., *Catalogue of Medieval and Renaissance Manuscripts in the Beinecke Rare Book and Manuscript Library, Yale University,* 4 vols (Binghamton, NY: Medieval and Renaissance Texts & Studies, 1984–2004), II: *MSS 251–500* (1987)

The Index of Middle English Prose, 24 vols (Cambridge: Brewer, 1984–2017), *Handlist* XIX: *Manuscripts in the University Library, Cambridge (Dd – Oo)*, ed. by Margaret Connolly (2009)

Thomson, R. M., *A Descriptive Catalogue of the Medieval Manuscripts of the Corpus Christi College Oxford* (Cambridge: Brewer, 2011)

Watson, Nicholas, *Richard Rolle and the Invention of Authority*, Cambridge Studies in Medieval Literature, 13 (Cambridge: Cambridge University Press, 1991)

Appendix 1: Summary Table of Manuscript Contents and Early Readers Containing All Copies of Richard Misyn's and the Version A, B, and E: Translations of Richard Rolle's *EV*[53]

MS	Date	Contents	Readers/Owners
Richard Misyn, O.Carm.			originally translated for Margaret Kirkby in 1434–35
Oxford, Corpus Christi College, MS 236	1435–50	Rolle's EV and Fire	'Wyllyam Ienkins' (pen-trial) John Dee, Elizabethan astrologer
New Haven, Yale University, Marston MS 331	mid-15th c. (after 1435)	EV, verse by Richard Hutton, Fire, verse life of St John of Bridlington	'Richard Hennage' (late 15th c., partially erased) the book was given by William Garleke, rector of 'Marowe', to Richard Hutton in 1508
London, British Library, MS Add. 37790 (Amherst MS)	mid-15th c. (after 1435)	a rich anthology of devotional, contemplative and mystical writing;	Carthusian origin and dissemination
Version A			
Cambridge, University Library, MS Ff.5.30	early 15th c.	Deguileville, The Pilgrimage of the Lyfe of the Manhode	'Iohannes bysshop', 'Thomas hows', 'Liber Iohannes Malet', 'Wille Crane' (all 15th c.)
Oxford, Bodleian Library, MS Digby 18	early 15th c.	Latin liturgical material (calendar and litany) and English devotional texts (Rolle's EV and Form, Maidstone)	not known before the 17th c.
Dublin, Trinity College, MS 432	1400–50	separate MS or part of a booklet together with a treatise derived from the pseudo-Augustinian Visitatio infirmorum and Anselm's Admonitio morienti	used by a priest? ownership not known until the 17th c.

53 Information concerning manuscript contents and users is drawn from the respective manuscript catalogues, as referred to in this chapter, as well as from Cré and Kempster's studies on the Amherst MS and the Version A translation.

MS	Date	Contents	Readers/Owners
Oxford, Bodleian Library, MS Douce 322	1470s–80s	anthology of popular devotional texts [sister MS of MS Harley 1706]	gift of William Baron Esq. to the Dominican nunnery of Dartford, Kent, especially to the use of Dame Pernelle Wrattisley, his granddaughter
London, British Library, MS Harley 1706 [sister MS of MS Douce 322]	c. 1500	2 separate MSS bound in one (similar contents) MS 1: EV, Councils of St Isidore, Aug., 'Cur mundus militat', Contemptus mundi [pseudo-Bernard], The ABC of Aristotle, Anselm on the degrees of pride and humility	Elizabeth (Beaumont) Vere; her nephew: Edmund Jernyngham; 'maiden Elizabeth Rokewood'; 'my wyfe gayne w<expunged>' 'Mysterys Margaret Etwell'

Version B

MS	Date	Contents	Readers/Owners
Cambridge, University Library, MS Ff.5.40	1425–50	devotional anthology of Rolle (EV, The Commandment) and Hilton (Mixed Life, Scale I, Of Proper Will, Of Angels' Song)	unknown
London, British Library, MS Harley 2406	1450–75	originally, 3 separate MSS bound together by the time they came into the possession of Thomas Leventhorpe; MSS 1–2: catechetical; MS 3: devotional anthology of Rolle and Hilton	MS 1: 'domine Matilde Stuerd' MSS 1–3: Thomas Leventhorpe

Version E

MS	Date	Contents	Readers/Owners
London, British Library, MS Lansdowne 455	mid-15th c.	Booklet 1: Old Testament, dominical epistles and lessons, Rolle's Form and English EV Booklet 2: liturgical calendar, table of gospels, epistles and lessons Booklet 3: Wycliffite New Testament (LV)	liturgical aid

Appendix 2: Scribal Corrections in London, British Library, MS Harley 2406

fol. 36ᵛ: a dot appears before a line in the middle of the page but no indication of error can be seen in the respective line; a few lines below an error of spelling is indicated: 'p̣iutteth'.

fol. 37: a dot marks a redundant word in the line: 'of b̲e̲ whom it was seide'.

fol. 37ᵛ: a dot marks that a wrong pronoun is used in the line: 'turnede away fro he̲m̲ [i.e. the devil]'. It suggests that the form 'him/hym' should be used here. The text usually but not regularly distinguishes between the singular masculine form of the pronoun 'him' and the plural 'hem' form.

fol. 38: a redundant word is indicated after a line: 'sathanas i̲s̲ sete is'; a few lines below three dots in a triangular arrangement mark a dialect variant, which may have caused a disturbing interpretation: 'þo þat le̲uet in temporel habundance'. Obviously the meaning of the marked word is 'live' and not 'leave'; the corrector proposed to replace this equivocal form probably for 'liuet/lyuet'.

fol. 39: a dot marks a bizarre spelling for the verb 'give': 'i̲f̲ it to pouer men'. Probably the pronunciation of both the conjunction and the verb was the same in the dialect of the scribe or the copyist. Another dot later on this page can be found on the margin, but no evident mistake is indicated or found in the respective line.

fol. 40: An error in spelling is indicated: 'verto̲u̲s'. The suggested solution would probably be 'vertuous' / 'vertuus'.

fol. 41: 'w̲'tyng': the mark of abbreviation makes it clear that the word is 'writing'. Two dots after the penultimate line indicate a problem: 'qwhat beth þo þat drawi̲t̲ ws to þe vnhede of god'. Such third-person plural suffixes occur in the text elsewhere. The corrector does not seem to have identified it as a suffix. As this is a dialectal form (Norfolk, East Midlands), it can be assumed that the dialect of the corrector was not the same. But at other instances the corrector does not indicate error in case of these dialectal forms.

fol. 41ᵛ: 'þan we sa̲w̲reth [?] gostly thinges' and 'he schall deme no man but he̲m̲'. Again it is implied that the singular form 'him' should be used consistently. A correction in the ensuing line overwrites the plural pronoun form for 'hem'.

fol. 42: A grotesque image is corrected with the suppression of a redundant article: 'whan þu etest and drinkest b̲e̲ mynde of god'. The object of eating and drinking is not the mind of god, but 'mind' is a verb in the imperative starting a new clause: 'When you eat and drink, be mindful of God'.

fol. 42ᵛ: A correction within the line is marked; the two central letters of the word 'tweyn' are written over erasure.

fol. 43: For the first two dots no obvious errors can be found in the respective lines; two further dots indicate problems of spelling for the corrector: 'prye' and 'I mourne and feblet'.

fol. 43ᵛ: The penultimate letter of the word 'lest' is dotted. It cannot be decided if the dotted letter is an <f> or an <s>; the phrase makes meaning with <s>: 'thinke on gode but if slepe lest ye take kepe þat [...]'. Further down three dots shape a triangle, but no error is indicated in the line. Thirdly, the vowel of 'hem' is underlined probably to mark pronoun confusion as in some previous cases of correction.

fol. 44ᵛ: Letter <g> in the word 'glensede' is dotted as an evident case of misspelling for 'clensede'. The mistake is also marked by a dot before the respective line. On the same folio, letter <y> in the word 'brynte' is dotted implying that the correct spelling is 'brente'.

fol. 46ᵛ: The vowel of the pronoun 'hem' is underlined for similar reasons as before. In the phrase 'be flerte [*sic!*] of flesch' the word 'flerte' is marked by one dot underneath letter <e>, and another dot appears before this line on the margin.

A couple of further insignificant corrections appear on fol. 47ᵛ (three times) and fol. 48ᵛ. The only apparent marginal correction can be found on fol. 51, where the word 'but' appears in the right-hand margin to indicate that it is to be inserted in the line at the place marked with a wedge ('it may nouth be ^ if þu receyue hym').

Predestination and Free Will in the Old French and Middle English Versions of the *Elucidarium* and in the Middle English *Chastising of God's Children*

Takami Matsuda

Professor, Faculty of Letters, Keio University, Japan

The relationship between the operation of divine grace and individual merit in human salvation and the extent in which the omniscient God pre-ordained those who would be saved appear on the agenda of almost all representative Church fathers and medieval theologians. This aspect of the doctrine of predestination is, however, one of the more difficult issues to be explained to readers with no or limited theological training; it might be misunderstood as predestination contradicting free will (*liberum arbitrium*), a gift from God bestowed on the human being, unless accompanied with the careful explanation of the theological assumptions behind it. The difficulty comes to surface with the Middle English religious writings intended for a wide readership including the laity; these writings do not often discuss predestination as such in the first place, but in some instructional or devotional writings of a compilatory nature, namely the Middle English versions of the *Elucidarium* and the *Chastising of God's Children*, it is treated at some length. In this paper, I will look at these examples, comparing them with related Old French, Latin and Middle English versions, to argue that in these, predestination was simplified (or explained away) to serve a didactic purpose, being made more readily compatible with the human free will that strives for salvation.

A brief survey of the doctrine reveals that medieval thinkers were not unanimous in the understanding of the extent in which the fate of human soul depends on divine grace rather than on free will. Refuting the Pelagian view of salvation solely through merits, Augustine claimed in *De praedestinatione sanctorum* that one is made worthy of salvation not by human will but by divine grace or predestination: 'Non enim quia credidimus, sed ut credamus elegit nos: [...] Nec quia credidimus, sed ut credamus vocamur'.[1] It is because the elect are predestined to grace according to providence that they may have faith in God and be

---

[1] Augustine, *De praedestinatione sanctorum* 19. 38, ed. by Migne, col. 988 (Augustine, *On the Predestination of the Saints*, trans. by Holmes and Wallis: 'He chose us, not because

saved. Similarly, election precedes free will, which is itself variable.[2] Augustine is aware that the precedence of election before merit can cause an anxiety among believers and insists on the exercise of caution and discretion in preaching.[3]

In *De consolatione Philosophiae*, Lady Philosophy contradicts Boethius's anxiety about divine foreknowledge destroying the freedom of will and rendering human endeavour useless, by pointing out the mistake of regarding necessity as the consequence of foreknowledge.[4] Philosophy explains that foreknowledge is not so much 'foreknowledge of the future but knowledge of a never-passing instant', *providentia* rather than *praevidentia*, because God is outside the temporal sequence and sees all at once, looking 'forward on all things as though from the highest peak of the world'.[5] There are two types of necessity: simple necessity (such as the mortality of man) and conditional necessity which is 'not caused by a thing's proper nature but by the addition of the condition'.[6] But because

---

we believed, but that we might believe [...] Neither are we called because we believed, but that we may believe').

2 Cf. Augustine, *De praedestinatione sanctorum* 5. 10, ed. by Migne, col. 968: 'non quia credere vel non credere non est in arbitrio voluntatis humanae, sed in electis praeparatur voluntas a Domino. Ideo ad ipsam quoque fidem, quae in voluntate est, pertinet' (Augustine, *On the Predestination of the Saints*, trans. by Holmes and Wallis: 'not because it is not in the choice of man's will to believe or not to believe, but because in the elect the will is prepared by the Lord'); Augustine, *De gratia et libero arbitrio* 15. 31, ed. by Migne, cols 899–900: 'Semper est autem in nobis voluntas libera, sed non semper est bona. [...] Gratia vero Dei semper est bona, et per hanc fit ut sit homo bonae voluntatis, qui prius fuit voluntatis malae' (Augustine, *On Grace and Free Will*, trans. by Holmes and Wallis: 'There is, however, always within us a free will — but it is not always good; [...] But the grace of God is always good; and by it it comes to pass that a man is of a good will, though he was before of an evil one').

3 See Augustine, *De dono perseverantiae* 22. 57–62, ed. by Migne, cols 1928–31; cf. Goldstein, 'Future Perfect', p. 98.

4 Boethius, *De consolatione Philosophiae* V pr. 3, ed. by Tester, p. 396, ll. 41–51, pp. 398–400, ll. 81–87, and V pr. 4, p. 408, ll. 60–68.

5 Boethius, *De consolatione Philosophiae* V pr. 6, ed. by Tester, p. 426, ll. 66–72: 'Itaque si praescientiam pensare velis qua cuncta dinoscit, non esse praescientiam quasi futuri sed scientiam numquam deficientis instantiae rectius aestimabis; unde non praevidentia sed providentia potius dicitur, quod porro ab rebus infimis constituta quasi ab excelso rerum cacumine cuncta prospiciat' (Boethius, *The Consolation of Philosophy*, trans. by Tester, p. 427: 'So if you should wish to consider his foreknowledge, by which he discerns all things, you will more rightly judge it to be not foreknowledge as it were of the future but knowledge of a never-passing instant. And therefore it is called not prevision (*praevidentia*) but providence (*providentia*), because set far from the lowest of things it looks forward on all things as though from the highest peak of the world').

6 Boethius, *De consolatione Philosophiae* V pr. 6, ed. by Tester, pp. 428–30, ll. 104–13: 'Duae sunt etenim necessitates, simplex una, veluti quod necesse est omnes homines esse mortales, altera condicionis, ut si aliquem ambulare scias, eum ambulare necesse est; [...] sed haec condicio minime secum illam simplicem trahit. Hanc enim necessitatem non

God beholds 'future events which happen because of the freedom of the will, as present', they 'become necessary through the condition of the divine knowledge, but considered in themselves do not lose the absolute freedom of their nature'.[7] Everything that God foreknows must necessarily come to be, but that does not hinder some of them being initiated by free will.

In order to reconcile free will with the predestination, Hugh of St Victor also uses the idea of conditionality, distinguishing between 'God's active and permissive will'.[8] While God actively wills and predestines grace to the elect, he also permits something which he foreknows to happen.[9] This view of 'single-particular election' in which God actively wills to save particular individuals, was 'a consensus concerning predestination' arrived at by the thirteenth century.[10]

---

propria facit natura sed condicionis adiectio; nulla enim necessitas cogit incedere voluntate gradientem, quamvis eum tum cum graditur incedere necessarium sit' (Boethius, *De consolatione Philosophiae*, trans. by Tester, pp. 429–31: 'For there are really two necessities, the one simple, as that it is necessary that all men are mortal; the other conditional, as for example, if you know that someone is walking, it is necessary that he is walking. [...] but conditional necessity by no means carries with it that other simple kind. For this sort of necessity is not caused by a thing's proper nature but by the addition of the condition; for no necessity forces him to go who walks of his own will, even though it is necessary that he is going at the time when he is walking').

7 Boethius, *De consolatione Philosophiae*, ed. by Tester, V pr. 6, p. 430, ll. 115–20: 'Atqui deus ea futura quae ex arbitrii libertate proveniunt praesentia consuetur. Haec igitur ad intuitum relata divinum necesssaria fiunt per condicionem divinae notionis; per se vero considerata ab absoluta naturae suae libertate non desinunt' (Boethius, *De consolatione Philosophiae*, trans. by Tester, p. 431: 'But God beholds those future events which happen because of the freedom of the will, as present; they therefore, related to the divine perception, become necessary through the condition of the divine knowledge, but considered in themselves do not lose the absolute freedom of their nature').

8 Levy, 'Grace and Freedom in the Soteriology of John Wyclif', p. 327.

9 Hugh of Saint Victor, *De sacramentis Christianae fidei* 1. 2. 21, ed. by Migne, cols 213D–214A: 'Praedestinatio est gratiae praeparatio. Propositum ergo Dei in quo gratiam electis suis dare disposuit ipsum est praedestinatio, quae idcirco praedestinatio vocatur; quoniam in ea quod faciendum fuit, dispositum est priusquam fuit. Potest autem praedestinatio generaliter aliquando intelligi ipsa faciendorum dispositio; ut dicatur Deus quidquid sic facturus fuit ab aeterno praedestinasse. Quod autem facturus non fuit sed permissurus non praedestinasse, sed praescisse solum' (Hugh of St Victor, *On the Sacraments of the Christian Faith*, trans. by Deferrari, p. 38: 'Predestination is the preparation of grace. Therefore, God's design, in which He disposed to give grace to His elect, is itself predestination; and this is called predestination for this reason, because in it what was to be made was disposed before it was. Yet, in general, predestination can at times be understood to be the disposition itself of the things to be made, so that God may be said to have predestined from eternity whatever He was thus to make, but not to have predestined, but only to have foreknown, what He was not to make but was to permit').

10 Halverson, 'Franciscan Theology and Predestinarian Pluralism in Late-Medieval Thought', p. 1. Also cf. Augustine, *De praedestinatione sanctorum* 17. 34, ed. by Migne, cols 985–86.

Thomas Aquinas, the most popular proponent of this view, basically follows Augustine's distinction between predestination and foreknowledge and argues that 'the direction of a rational creature towards the end of life eternal is called predestination', whereas reprobation can be defined as the divine will to permit a person to fall into sin as it is also 'part of providence to permit some to fall away from that end'.[11] He also distinguishes between the two types of divine will: antecedent will, by which God wills the salvation of all as the supreme 'giver of being', and consequent will, which permits the reprobate to sin by their free will and be punished in consequence.[12] This consensus view, however, was challenged by two alternatives:

> In 1317 Peter Aureol, claiming that SPE [single-particular election] is deterministic, argued for general election (GE). According to GE, God offers grace to all, and an individual's salvation or damnation follows according to that person's response to the offer. In 1344 Gregory of Rimini, judging GE to be Pelagian, reacted by advocating double-particular election (DPE), whereby God not only wills to save some individuals but actively wills to damn others.[13]

Thus in the fourteenth century, the nature of the relationship between predestination and free will remained unresolved, or became more controversial. In

---

11 Thomas Aquinas, *Summa theologica* I, q.23, a.1, p. 271: 'Unde ratio praedictae transmissionis creaturae rationalis in finem vitae aeternae, *praedestinatio* nominatur: nam *destinare* est mittere. Et sic patet quod praedestinatio, quantum ad obiecta, est quaedam pars providentiae'. (Thomas Aquinas, *Summa theologica*, trans. by Fathers of the English Dominican Province: 'Hence the type of the aforesaid direction of a rational creature towards the end of life eternal is called predestination. For to destine, is to direct or send. Thus it is clear that predestination, as regards its objects, is a part of providence'); Thomas Aquinas, *Summa theologica* I, q.23, a.3, p. 274: 'Unde, cum per divinam providentiam homines in vitam aeternam ordinentur, pertinet etiam ad divinam providentiam, ut permittat aliquos ab isto fine deficere. Et hoc dicitur *reprobare*. Sic igitur, sicut praedestinatio est pars providentiae respectu eorum qui divinitus ordinantur in aeternam salutem; ita reprobatio est pars providentiae respectu illorum qui ab hoc fine decidunt' (Thomas Aquinas, *Summa theologica*, trans. by Fathers of the English Dominican Province: 'Thus, as men are ordained to eternal life through the providence of God, it likewise is part of that providence to permit some to fall away from that end; this is called reprobation. Thus, as predestination is a part of providence, in regard to those ordained to eternal salvation, so reprobation is a part of providence in regard to those who turn aside from that end').

12 Levering, *Predestination*, p. 81. See Thomas Aquinas, *Summa theologica* I, q.23, a.4, p. 275: 'Deus vult omnes homines salvos fieri *antecedenter*, quod non est simpliciter velle, sed secundum quid, non autem *consequenter*, quod est simpliciter velle' (Thomas Aquinas, *Summa theologica*, trans. by Fathers of the English Dominican Province: 'God wishes all humans to be saved antecedently; he does not "wish" this in a simple sense but under the condition in which he does not wish (that is "to wish" in a simple sense) wish this consequently').

13 Halverson, 'Franciscan Theology and Predestinarian Pluralism in Late-Medieval Thought', p. 2.

Middle English, Chaucer's *Nun's Priest's Tale* makes a playful reference to such a controversy when he refers to Augustine, Boethius, and also to Thomas Bradwardine who insisted on absolute supremacy of grace over human will.[14]

In the late medieval discussions of the issue in Middle English, the difficulty of explaining how predestination is compatible with free will is more readily apparent. Julian of Norwich speaks positively of predestination. As J. P. H. Clark points out in Julian's argument, though the soul of the elect is not 'impeccable', it is never separated from God and 'though sin be committed on the way, God will ensure that the soul which is destined to salvation will direct its final choice to himself'.[15] Despite this hopeful message, however, Julian does not say 'how God's timeless foreknowledge and predestination are to be reconciled with the contingency of the world and the liberty of human choices made in time'.[16]

Predestination is also an important issue in Wycliffite ecclesiology. According to Wyclif, the Church consists of the congregation of the predestined (*congregatio predestinatorum*), which remains distinct from those foreknown to damnation (*congregatio prescitorum*), even though their members mingle in this life. Free will needs to be accommodated in this dualistic distinction and because 'the moral responsibility of those foreknown to damnation for their predetermined evil acts' presented the greatest difficulty, there was a 'gradual departure from strict predestinarianism' which led 'to a watering down of the doctrine in several texts'.[17] Levy points out that 'Wyclif is even more accommodating to human free will than some of his orthodox contemporaries'.[18] In one of the Wycliffite sermons, the contextualization of the free will comes dangerously close to Pelagianism in its emphasis on human will although the concept of God's mercy seems to be different:

> For ȝif man haue mercy on his soule, and vnbynde it or bynde it, God by his iugement in heuene iugeþ þe sowle such; for eche man þat schal be dampned, is dampned for his owne gylt, and eche man þat schal be saued, is saued by his owne meryȝt.[19]

The brief survey so far shows that selective salvation by divine providence has always proved a difficult argument. In Middle English religious texts intended

---

14 See *The Canterbury Tales* VII. 3234–52, in *The Riverside Chaucer*, ed. by Benson. Bradwardine maintains that God's will is the coefficient of human will and the two act jointly without being distinguished; see Leff, *Bradwardine and the Pelagians*, p. 94. See also Payne 'Foreknowledge and Free Will', for the reading of the tale based on the different views on predestination of the three named authors.

15 Clark, 'Predestination in Christ According to Julian of Norwich', p. 80.

16 Clark, 'Predestination in Christ According to Julian of Norwich', p. 80.

17 Hudson, *The Premature Reformation*, p. 320, p. 324 (see also pp. 314–25); cf. *English Wycliffite Sermons*, IV, ed. by Gradon and Hudson, pp. 57–65.

18 Levy, 'Grace and Freedom in the Soteriology of John Wyclif', p. 330.

19 *English Wycliffite Sermons*, II, ed. by Gradon and Hudson, p. 250 (ll. 80–84), IV, p. 62.

for lay and untrained readers, such 'watering down' of the doctrine is often observed. The major issue here seems to be how to explain the relationship between providence and predestination so that the extent of free will and merits drawn from human deeds can be accommodated without a paradox. The human freedom to choose between salvation and damnation is an almost ubiquitous message repeated without any theological complications in such writings. For example, in the moral poems in MS Digby 102 compiled around 1413/4, it is stated on several occasions that the choice of heaven or hell is the consequence of free will.[20] Predestination may appear to contradict such a plain admonition, so it must be properly contextualized if one is to introduce this topic to the laity. In the examples below, we can observe attempts at the exposition which succumb in some cases to a simpler message of the human free will striving for salvation.

One of the most detailed expositions of predestination can be found in the late eleventh-century *Elucidarium*, a compendium of Christian doctrine usually attributed to Honorius Augustodunensis, translated into both Old French and Middle English.[21] There are two principal versions in Old French: the one based on the Latin original and the so-called *Second Lucidaire*, which is an early fourteenth-century abridged version based on one of the Old French versions.[22] Extant Middle English versions include translations of the Latin original as well as of the *Second Lucidaire*.[23]

In the *Elucidarium*, the exposition of predestination is preceded by a passage on two types of necessities, *naturalis* and *voluntaria*, in answer to the question of what the providence of God signifies, apparently inspired by the Boethian idea of two necessities.[24] Predestination is then defined as divine disposition in

---

20 On the date of a series of moral and religious poems in Oxford, Bodleian Library, MS Digby 102, see *The Digby Poems*, ed. by Barr, p. 18. For references to free will, see 'God & man ben made atte on' (*The Digby Poems*, ed. by Barr, p. 186, ll. 61–62) as well as the note to these lines for other references to free will in the *Digby Poems*. Cf. also John the Blind Audelay, *Poems and Carols*, ed. by Fein, p. 30 (ll. 201–07), p. 66 (ll. 64–70), p. 122 (ll. 216–22), p. 179 (ll. 9–12); *Memoriale Credencium*, ed. by Kengen, p. 160 (ll. 10–11): 'god haþ y ȝeue swich powere to man: þat he may not synny aȝen his owne will'.

21 See for the original Latin text, Lefèvre, *L'Elucidarium et les Lucidaires*.

22 Old French versions are available in the following editions: Türk, *'Lucidaire de grant sapientie'*; Kleinhans, *'Lucidere Vault Tant a Dire Comme Donnant Lumiere'*; *Eine altfranzösische Übersetzung des Elucidarium*, ed. by Düwell; Ruhe, *Gelehrtes Wissen, 'Aberglaube' und pastorale Praxis im französischen Spätmittelalter*.

23 The *Elucidarium* survives in Middle English as a partial translation and an abbreviated paraphrase in the following versions: *Early English Homilies from the Twelfth Century MS. Vesp. D. XIV*, ed. by Warner, pp. 140–45; Marx, 'An Abbreviated Middle English Prose Translation of the "Elucidarius"'; *Die mittelenglische Version des Elucidariums des Honorius Augustodunensis*, ed. by Schmitt; *The Late Middle English Lucydarye*, ed. by Morrison.

24 *Elucidarium*, II. 23, ed. by Lefèvre, p. 413: 'Duae necessitates sunt: una naturalis, ut solem in oriente oriri vel diem noctem sequi; altera voluntaria, ut aliquem ambulare vel sedere. Quae Deus vult ut fiant, ut caelum et terra, inevitabile est non evenire,

which some are predestined to salvation, while God foreknows others to be damned, even though the reference to the latter is missing in some manuscripts (II. 28). Throughout the exposition of predestination, there is a consistent tendency to balance the *predestinati* and the *reprobi*, while it is clearly stated that the *reprobi* sin by free will (II. 29). Neither of them rejoices or suffers more than preordained, and actions of the individuals in this world correspond directly to what awaits them in the afterlife, in both heaven and hell. It is also said that both the *predestinati* and the *reprobi* receive recompense according to what they did (II. 73). Such explanation, although fundamentally based on single-particular election, simplifies the issue perhaps for a better understanding but inadvertently can place a more than due emphasis on freedom of choice in individuals.

The same tendency is also seen in the French versions. In the version in Paris, Bibliothèque nationale de France, MS fr. 19920, *praedestinatio* is rephrased as 'esgardement Nostre Seigneur', probably to avoid a theological term, and the passage on the reprobate that follows is not translated.[25] Because the previous section on two necessities is also omitted in this translation, there is no context in which one can link free will to predestination. As a result, the passage on the reprobate, stating that it is only natural for them to perish because they chose vice by their own will, sounds more like a didactic warning than an exposition of the doctrine. Similarly, a version in London, Lambeth Palace Library, MS 431 does not refer to the reprobate either except for the mention that their only function is to provide the occasion for the *predestinati* to be repentant.[26] It altogether avoids a theological argument and turns to morality.

We can find the evidence of a similar simplified dichotomy in the Middle English versions even though only indirectly. The abbreviated version in Aberystwyth, National Library of Wales, Peniarth MS 12 omits the argument on predestination altogether, but there is a fifteenth-century partial translation which survives in two manuscripts (St John's College, Cambridge, MS G.25 and Cambridge University Library, MS Ii. 6. 26) that seems to be an original rendition of the *Elucidarium* with lay education in view. This is probably a Lollard text, as Kleinhans and Giordano have shown, although Lewis offers a different opinion, regarding it as a piece of orthodox self-criticism.[27] The section on free

---

sed per omnia necesse est ita contingere. Quae autem tantum fieri permittit, ut homines per liberum arbitrium bonum vel malum facere, non est necesse evenire' ('There are two necessities: the one "natural", such as the sun rising in the east or the day following the night; the other is "voluntary", such as whether to walk or to sit. What God wishes to be done, either in heaven or on earth, inevitably cannot but happen and is thus contingent to all. However what God permits to be done, so that humans do either good or bad by free will, needs not to happen'). Cf. Boethius, *De consolatione Philosophiae*, ed. by Tester, V pr. 6, pp. 426–28, ll. 83–91, pp. 428–30, ll. 104–13.

25 Türk, '*Lucidaire de grant sapientie*', pp. 302–04 (Version A).

26 *Eine altfranzösische Übersetzung des Elucidarium*, ed. by Düwell, p. 58.

27 Kleinhans, 'Zwischen Orthodoxie und Häresie', pp. 291–324; Giordano, 'Tradurre e adattare'; Lewis, 'Rethinking the Lollardy of the "Lucidarie"'.

will (II. 7) is expanded with an additional dialogue on the availability of grace to everyone who desires. This is illustrated by a simple metaphor:

> þe disciple axiþ. may eche man haue grace þat wole haue it?
> þe maistir answereþ. ȝe forsoþe, lo ensaumple here is: a lord of a toun doth make a crye þat what needeful & poore man wole come & aske a good meelis mete, he schal haue it. þanne manye poore men comen & asken þat, & ben weel holpun in her myscheef, & strengþed up to lijf. & oþere þer ben as needeful as þei, but for proude herte or disdeyne wil not come þere & dyen for defaute. is þis lord cause of her deeþ?[28]

The disciple answers with no to the question. The metaphor of a free meal highlights the ability and responsibility of free will either to accept or deny divine grace. Although the extant manuscripts end soon after this section and the part on predestination is not translated (or has not survived), the basic tenor seems to be didactic, emphasizing free will at the expense of predestination.

The exposition of predestination in the *Second Lucidaire* betrays both simplification and difficulty in explaining the doctrine in the vernacular. The *Second Lucidaire* was compiled, according to its editor, for parish priests to be used in the instruction of the laity after the Fourth Lateran Council.[29] Admitting that no one can be saved unless predestined by God, it introduces the two manners of divine will after the Thomistic distinction between antecedent and consequent will: the *volenté simple* in which God wishes the salvation of all and the will that is actually executed after particular circumstances were taken into consideration. This is preceded by the distinction between 'povoir acompli et parfait' and 'povoir de simple nature': All reasonable creatures by default can be saved, according to simple natural ability ('povoir de simple nature') but what is actually accomplished ('povoir acompli') is different. This is explained by the analogy of a man who has the potential to run twenty leagues but can actually accomplish much less because of a chain attached to his feet. Similarly, one can speak about divine will in two manners:

> Et tout ensement puet on dire de la volenté Dieu que de sa volenté simple, sans prendre les circonstances, il vouldroit que tuit fussent sauvés; mes de sa voulenté en tant comme elle embrace toutez circonstances, il ne vouldroit que nul fust sauvé fors ceulz qui le seront, non pas qu'il ait en Dieu deulx volentés, mes l'en puet parler de sa volenté en .ij. manieres.[30]

---

28 *Die mittelenglische Version des Elucidariums des Honorius Augustodunensis*, ed. by Schmitt, p. 34. The twelfth-century version in London, British Library, MS Cotton Vesp. D. XIV, copied at Rochester in the second quarter of the twelfth century (Richards, 'On the Date and Provenance of MS Cotton Vespasian D. XIV ff. 4–169', p. 34), also includes the translation of the passage on free will roughly corresponding to *Elucidarium* II. 2–16 (*Early English Homilies from the Twelfth Century MS. Vesp. D. XIV*, ed. by Warner, pp. 140–43), but does not include this metaphor.

29 Ruhe, 'Savoir des doctes et pratique pastorale à la fin du moyen âge', p. 37.

30 Ruhe, *Gelehrtes Wissen*, pp. 236–38 (Version A, 114M; Engl. trans.: 'Similarly, one can say about the will of God that with regard to the simple will, without taking circum-

Predestination and Free Will 307

In answer to the question why, if God has preordained everything, it is still necessary to do good and avoid bad, the *Second Lucidaire* explains that because humans, unlike beasts, have *franc arbitre*, the simple ability to judge and choose between good and bad, what one does voluntarily according to free will, rather than by nature, will be subject to judgement.[31] The passage is an attempt to make free will compatible with predestination, and there is perhaps a certain reluctance in taking up this issue since the passage starts with the warning against inquiring into the subtlety of the divine plan and judgement.[32] The entire argument, while trying to explain the apparent paradox in predestination, ends by shifting its emphasis to individual moral duties.

An interesting further change and the use of a new analogy can be observed in some of the printed editions. There are as many as ten editions in French published by 1623 while we also have two Middle English translations attributable to Andrew Chertsey, both probably printed by Wynkyn de Worde, in 1502–04 and 1523(?) according to STC.[33] Both editions are fairly literal translations of the printed French version, presumably of the Lyon edition published by Jean de la Fontaine around 1500.[34] In these French and English editions, the passage on predestination corresponding to the above is revised completely with a new analogy. In answer to the question 'Mayster, knoweth God whether that a man shall be saued or dampned before that he be borne?' the Master answers yes and continues with the explanation of free will that has no close parallel in the manuscript versions:

> Not that God it dothe in entencyon for to dampne hym, for God ne dampnyth hym, but þe man dampnith hymselfe without ony constraynt, but of his owne wyll, the whiche is at his own lyberall arbytre or fre wyll. As we se the boterflye, the whiche of hymselfe and of his propre wyll hym brenneth in the candell. And how be it that the sayde boterflye is sometyme scalded with the fyre of the candell in suche wyse that often he falleth vnto þe erthe, also he ryseth agayn the best wyse he can, and with all his power he putteth hymselfe agayne in þe fyre of the candell all holly that he there abydeth, not withstandynge that he seeth well the daungere. Also done those the whiche dampneth themselfe, for how be it that they se and knowe the daunger that therin is, and also that they ben often scalded by trybulacyo[n]s and aduersytees to thende that they

---

stances into consideration, he wishes that all be saved. But in his will that embraces all circumstances, he only wishes salvation of those who will be saved; it is not that there are two wills in God, but one can speak of the will in two manners').

31 Ruhe, *Gelehrtes Wissen*, p. 241 (Version H 116D). Versions A and B are slightly different, asking who, since God has arranged everything, is to accuse man whether he does good or bad.

32 Ruhe, *Gelehrtes Wissen*, pp. 240–42 (Version A/B 116M).

33 STC 13685.5, 13686. Ruhe, *Gelehrtes Wissen*, pp. 136–39; *The Late Middle English Lucydarye*, ed. by Morrison, pp. xi–xii.

34 *The Late Middle English Lucydarye*, ed. by Morrison, pp. xxi–xxxi.

conuert them and that by inspyracyon dyuyne they haue some remors, how be it for that they cease not tyll vnto that that of theyr owne wyll and without ony constraynt they put them so depe in þe fyre that they there abyde and shall neuer go forthe.[35]

The analogy of a butterfly flying into the flame of the candle is employed not to delineate the inevitable fate of the reprobates but to indicate that they damn themselves by their own free will even if they are aware of the consequences. Immediately after this, the Master mentions the simple will of God that wishes all to be saved, with further emphasis placed on the part of free will in choosing one's fate:

> And how be it that God wyll of symple wyll þat all men be saued [...] and hath one so grete a gyfte as the realme of paradys without ony meryte. And by suche wyse, my chylde, knowe thou þat God hath made þe man not to thende that he be dampned, but to thende that by his holy operacyons in suffryng pacyentlye trybulacyons and aduersytees, and in resystynge and fyghtynge valyauntlye ayenst the deuyll, the worlde and the flesshe, he may meryte to be saued.[36]

Once again, the Master's answer reminds the readers of moral duties, as it ends with a warning against the three enemies of man.

Moreover, on the question whether the predestined can be saved without labour, whereas both the *Elucidarium* and the manuscript versions of the *Second Lucidaire* spell out that they will be saved through tribulations (of death for innocent infants and of hardship in life for adults) as is ordained by God, here it is simply stated that they will be saved 'by theyr merytes and trauayles' and that this applies to the reprobates as well ('And in lyke wyse may a man say of the dampnyd').[37] This reads like a reductive explanation of the relationship between predestination and individual merits, which can lead to a Pelagian misunderstanding. In these printed editions, the idea of prevenient grace or two manners of divine will is lost in the plainer didactic context more readily than in the manuscript versions.[38]

Another Middle English text which includes a fairly substantial discussion of predestination is the late fourteenth-century *Chastising of God's Children*, a devotional compilation written at the request of a female religious, whose com-

---

35 *The Late Middle English Lucydarye*, ed. by Morrison, p. 35/526–39 (113D, 114M).

36 *The Late Middle English Lucydarye*, ed. by Morrison, p. 35/540–45. Cf. Ruhe, *Gelehrtes Wissen*, pp. 237–45.

37 *The Late Middle English Lucydarye*, ed. by Morrison, p. 35/548–49 (115M). Cf. 'car Dieu scet bien par leurs meritez et travaulx ilz seront sauvez, et parailllement peut on dire des damnés'. (*The Late Middle English Lucydarye*, ed. by Morrison, p. 34/515–16, Ruhe, *Gelehrtes Wissen*, p. 241 [Druck I]).

38 This may be related to the possible change of scope in the printed version. Morrison (*The Late Middle English Lucydarye*, p. xxxi, p. xxxvi) argues that unlike the *Second Lucidaire* which was compiled originally as a clerical manual, 'the *Lucydarye* may have appealed as much to a devout lay reading public' as it includes materials that 'meet both general and specific needs in the area of basic religious education'.

plete text survives in nine fifteenth-century manuscripts attributable to male and female religious houses.[39] It should, however, be noted that there is a reluctance in dealing with this topic, perhaps due to the difficulty of handling it for the theologically untrained audience. The author says at the beginning of Chapter 15 ('Of predestinacion and prescience of god; and of remedie for hem þat bien trauelid wiþ suche maner matiers'), he cannot convey its Latin terms adequately in English and in one manuscript (London, British Library, MS Harley 2415), the chapter is omitted altogether.[40]

The understanding of predestination agrees with Thomas Aquinas, but the role of free will is duly emphasized with the Boethian metaphor:

> Oure lord haþ forsent or made his predestinacion tofore þe bigynnyng of þe world. But ȝit þis predestinacioun puttiþ nat ne concludiþ nat a needeful goode worchynge to hem þat shullen be saued, ne his prescience, þat is to seie on ynglisshe his forknowynge, puttiþ nat a needeful yuel worchynge to hem þat shul be dampned, for god haþ ȝouen a man a fre wil boþe for to wilne to do and to performe þat will in dede, as þus: whan a man goth in þe feldys, while he gothe he muste go þer, and ȝit he gothe but at his owne fre wil.[41]

With quotations from the Pauline Epistles (Philippians 2. 13–15 and Romans 8. 30), it is then said that if we leave off good works by our own will, we will be counted among the reprobates, whereas if we continue in good works, we will be among the predestined.[42]

The later part of the chapter turns to the danger of unbridled imagination or fantasizing, incorporating a lengthy passage from the *Stimulus amoris* of James of Milan, commonly attributed to Bonaventure in the Middle Ages.[43] Earlier in

---

39 *The Chastising of God's Children*, ed. by Bazire and Colledge, pp. 37–41.

40 *The Chastising of God's Children*, ed. by Bazire and Colledge, p. 156: 'I seide also in þe sixte chapitle þat sum bien soore trauelid in ymagynaciouns and þouȝtis of predestinacioun and of þe prescience of god, of þe which matier I drede soore to write, for þese teermes han oþer sentence in latyn þanne I can shewe in ynglisshe; naþeles sumwhat wol I shewe shortli'. In London, British Library, MS Harley 2415, fol. 104ᵛ, the rubric states that the section is lacking: 'hic deficit capitlum cuius Rubrica talis est ¶ hou temptacioun of predestinacioun or of dispeir may be ouercomen'.

41 *The Chastising of God's Children*, ed. by Bazire and Colledge, pp. 156/16–57/2. See note 23 above for the Boethian metaphor.

42 *The Chastising of God's Children*, ed. by Bazire and Colledge, p. 157/10–16: 'For if we lyuen in goode werkis and contynue, þanne bi the ordynaunce of god we shullen be accompted amonge þe children of þe whiche poule spekiþ þus: Oure lord haþ clepid hem whiche he haþ ordeyned bi predestinacion, and he haþ made riȝtful hem þat he haþ clepid, and he haþ magnified hem in euerlastynge lijf whiche he made heere riȝtful. Þus þan is predestinacion bigonne of þe ordynance of god'.

43 With the mention of 'an hooli clerk bonauenture', the rest of the chapter (from p. 158/16) is based on *Stimulus Amoris* III. 13. See *The Chastising of God's Children*, ed. by Bazire and Colledge, p. 281 (note to p. 158/14).

Chapter 6, it is said that there are some that 'wolen imagyne of predestinaciouns, and of the prescience or of þe foreknowynge of god' and fall into despair, dreading the sins they committed.[44] Here, referring back to this, the author presents a lengthy model speech against the devil that tries to tempt one to despair by convincing him that he is a reprobate. It stresses the complete trust in providence, but also urges one to persevere in virtue even if he is foreknown to damnation. Such a person should speak as follows, defying the devil:

> Houeuere it be of me, sooþ it is þat þou art dampned, and þouȝ it be sooþ be þe prescience of god þat I shal nat haue my lord god aftir þis lijf, ȝit wil I traueil wiþ al my strengþis þat I mowe haue hym heere; for heere I wol haue hym as moche as I may, þat I faile nat ne lacke nat so moche goodenesse booþ in þis lijf and aftir þis lijf. If I shal haue but wrecchidnesse aftir þis lijf, I wol nat leue ne leese þe litel tyme þat I shal haue heere, but aftir my powere I wil sette my ioie and al my delite in my lord god. A grete woodenesse it were, if I shuld be turmentid wiþ euerlastyng peyne, to take me now into myn enemyes hondis, and so forþ to be wiþ hem for euermore.[45]

It is madness to place oneself in the enemy's hand while alive, even if (or especially if) he is one of the reprobates.

In the long passage refuting the devil, the humble acceptance of one's ordained fate, however, shifts to the veiled plea for divine mercy that no one who willingly throws himself at God's mercy should be denied. The devotional tone of the work comes to the fore and the exposition on predestination is turned into a fervent message of complete trust in Christ and Mary:

> Houeuere my lord god haþ knowyng what shal fal of me, I woote wele he may nat forsake hymsilf; þerfor I wol hym biclippe wiþ al myn inward wittis, / and faste I wol holde hym, þat he shal nat leue me but ȝif he ȝeue me his blessyng. Also I shal hide me in þe deepe hoolis of his woundis, and þere I wil rest me, for out of þoo he shal nat fynde me; he wil nat compelle me to go out, for he seiþ hymsilf: I shal nat cast hym out þat comeþ to me; and þus he shal nat dampne me, but he wol do aȝens his owne doome.[46]

The passage is followed by an equally desperate but confident expression of trust in the compassion of Mary. Neither Christ nor Mary can turn away the one who clings to them hard enough.

A different translation of the same section is found in the *Prickynge of Love*, the Middle English translation of the *Stimulus amoris*, which survives in sixteen late fourteenth- and early fifteenth-century manuscripts.[47] A version in MS 3084 of the Walker-Heneage Collection, which the editor describes as 'less copying

---

44 *The Chastising of God's Children*, ed. by Bazire and Colledge, pp. 119/19–120/4.

45 *The Chastising of God's Children*, ed. by Bazire and Colledge, pp. 158/24–59/8.

46 *The Chastising of God's Children*, ed. by Bazire and Colledge, p. 159/11–20.

47 *The Prickynge of Love*, I, ed. by Kane, pp. iii–xxii.

Predestination and Free Will 311

than free expatiation from the basic text', includes a particularly vivid additional detail that draws attention to the strength of the speaker's will:[48]

> God may not deyne for to ȝeue hym-selfe to me. but ȝif I wil with a feruent desir of loue continue in þe coueytyng aftir so worþi a lord. so þat in such desire I shal enbrace hym to me, by-twene myne armys. al-þouȝh when þat I haue hym þat he shewe me grisly chere & gretly is displesid wiþme [sic] & semyng to me þat he wil not blesse me ne þat he likeþ not me. Ȝit shal I not leeue hym in noo maner wyse. for with-outyn my wil he may not from me departe. for it is leefsum to me to maistrie hym wiþ strengþe. ¶ For god preisith hem. þat wiþ strengþe arisiþ vp in-to þe blis of heuene. And ȝif I may not ellis do, I shal hide me in þe þrillinges of his woundis [...].[49]

In both the *Prickynge of Love* and the *Chastising of God's Children*, the speech ends with the declaration of the unfailing service to God. In the *Chastising of God's Children*, after this speech of defiance, the section concludes with this warning: 'Þus wiþ besynesse and uertuous lyuenge and deuoute preier shul ȝe wiþstonde and ouercome þis temptacion and traueilyng of þe imagynacion and thynkeng of þe predestinacion and prescience of god'.[50] This final message warns against vain curiosity with regard to one's fate, but in the long retort to the devil, there is a suggestion that those steadfast in divine trust and devotion can attain salvation ultimately by the power of will to submit oneself unconditionally to Christ.[51]

In the above examples, predestination is made to serve a didactic purpose in the end, highlighting the power of free will. In this respect, it is not surprising to find the warning against resignation in relation to predestination. An exem-

---

48 *The Prickynge of Love*, I, ed. by Kane, p. xv. In MS 3084 of the Walker-Heneage Collection, the *Prickynge of Love* is followed immediately by the *Chastising of God's Children*, which is also attributed in its *incipit* to Walter Hilton (cf. Sargent, 'A New Manuscript of the "Chastising of God's Children" with an Ascription to Walter Hilton', p. 52). There are some resemblances between this version of the *Prickynge of Love* and the *Chastising of God's Children* not observed in London, British Library, MS Harley 2254, the base manuscript of Kane's edition, e.g. *The Prickynge of Love*, II, ed. by Kane, p. 575/19–20: 'And so shal y gete þre-foolde helpe. þat is as a þrefolde rope. þat wil not liȝtly breke.'; *The Chastising of God's Children*, ed. by Bazire and Colledge, p. 160/1: 'So þat I shal haue treble help and refute'. The passage is based on *Stimulus Amoris* III. 13 (Bonaventure, *Opera omnia*, XII, ed. by Peltier, p. 689): 'Et sic triplex refugium habeo, quod quasi triplex funiculus difficile confringetur'. ('Thus I have three-hold protection, as a three-hold cord is not easily broken'.) The metaphor is absent in London, British Library, MS Harley 2254 (*The Prickynge of Love*, I, ed. by Kane, p. 169). Cf. also Hilton, *The Goad of Love*, ed. by Kirchberger, p. 181.

49 *The Prickynge of Love*, II, ed. by Kane, pp. 574/27–75/3).

50 *The Chastising of God's Children*, ed. by Bazire and Colldege, p. 160/10–13.

51 The attempt to achieve a balance between the function of human will and predestination by grace is also seen in *A Ladder of Foure Ronges*, the fifteenth-century Middle English translation of the *Scala Claustralium* by the Carthusian Guigo II. See Iguchi, 'Translating Grace', p. 669.

plum found in both the Latin and Middle English versions of the *Alphabetum narrationum*, which was originally taken from Caesarius of Heisterbach's *Dialogus miraculorum*, mentions a case of the tyrannous Landgrave Ludwig, who gave himself to all manner of vices, deceiving himself that his fate was predestined and his hour of death could not be changed. However, when he became ill, he was persuaded by his doctor to seek repentance as the medicine of the soul: 'Fro hens furth be þou þe leche of my sawle; ffor be þi medycynable tong I trow þat God shall delyver me from my moste errour'.[52]

It seems that the topic of predestination is often strategically evaded in didactic writing for the laity or for religious with limited theological training. When it is mentioned, the relationship between predestination and free will is not fully explained, but the two are mingled or linked together in pragmatic didacticism; in spite of or because of the predestined fate, individuals should strive by their own free will for salvation. In trying to explain how free will can function within the predestined plan of God, such writings ultimately turn to a didactic admonition, obscuring finer points of the doctrine.

Bibliography

Manuscript Sources

London, British Library, MS Harley 2415

Primary Sources

An Alphabet of Tales, ed. by M. M. Banks, 2 vols, Early English Text Society: Original Series, 126–27 (1904/5; repr. New York: Kraus, 1975)

Arnoldi Leodiensis Alphabetum Narrationum, ed. by Elisa Brill, Corpus Christianorum: Continuatio Mediaevalis, 160 (Turnhout: Brepols, 2015)

Augustine, *De praedestinatione sanctorum*, ed. by Jacques-Paul Migne, Patrologiae Cursus Completus: Series Latina, 44 (Paris: Migne, 1863), cols 959–92

———,, *On the Predestination of the Saints*, trans. by Peter Holmes and Robert Ernest Wallis, rev. by Benjamin B. Warfield, Nicene, and Post-Nicene Fathers, First Series, 5 (Buffalo, NY: Christian Literature Publishing Co., 1887); rev. and ed. for New Advent by Kevin Knight, online: <https://www.newadvent.org/fathers/15121.htm> [accessed 3 November 2022]

———,, *De gratia et libero arbitrio*, ed. by Jacques-Paul Migne, Patrologiae Cursus Completus: Series Latina, 44 (Paris: Migne, 1863), cols 875–912

---

52 *An Alphabet of Tales*, ed. by Banks, p. 422. Cf. *Arnoldi Leodiensis Alphabetum Narrationum*, ed. by Brill, p. 361; Caesarius of Heisterbach, *Dialogus miraculorum* I. 27 (Caesarius von Heisterbach, *Dialogus miraculorum*, I, trans. by Nösges and Schneider, pp. 280–85). Also in the *Fasciculus morum*, a fourteenth-century handbook for lay preaching, there is an anecdote of an unmarried woman who excuses her pregnancy saying that it was predestined for her from the beginning; see *Fasciculus Morum*, ed. and trans. by Wenzel, p. 476, p. 670.

———,, *On Grace and Free Will*, trans. by Peter Holmes and Robert Ernest Wallis, rev. by Benjamin B. Warfield, from Nicene and Post-Nicene Fathers, first series, v, ed. by Philip Schaff (Buffalo, NY: Christian Literature Publishing Co., 1887); rev. and ed. for New Advent by Kevin Knight, online: <https://www.newadvent.org/fathers/1510.htm> [accessed 3 November 2022]

———,, *De dono perseverantiae*, ed. by Jacques-Paul Migne, Patrologiae Cursus Completus: Series Latina, 45 (Paris: Migne, 1863), cols 993–1034

Boethius, *De consolatione Philosophiae*, ed. and trans. by S. J. Tester, in *The Theological Tractates: The Consolation of Philosophy*, ed. and trans. by H. F. Stewart, E. K. Rand, and S. J. Tester, The Loeb Classical Library, 74 (Cambridge, MA: Harvard University Press, 1973), pp. 130–435

Bonaventure, *Opera omnia*, ed. by A. C. Peltier, 15 vols (Paris: Vivès, 1864–71), XII (1868)

Caesarius von Heisterbach, *Dialogus miraculorum / Dialog über die Wunder*, introd. by Horst Schneider and trans. by Nikolaus Nösges and Horst Schneider, 5 vols (Turnhout: Brepols, 2009), I (2009)

The Chastising of God's Children and the Treatise of Perfection of the Sons of God, ed. by Joyce Bazire and Eric Colledge (Oxford: Basil Blackwell, 1957)

Chaucer, Geoffrey, *The Riverside Chaucer*, 3rd edn, gen. ed. by Larry D. Benson (Oxford: Oxford University Press, 2008)

Die mittelenglische Version des Elucidariums des Honorius Augustodunensis, ed. by Friedrich Schmitt (Burhausen a. S.: Trinkl, 1909)

The Digby Poems: A New Edition of the Lyrics Edited from Oxford, Bodleian Library MS Digby 102, ed. by Helen Barr (Exeter: University of Exeter Press, 2009)

Early English Homilies from the Twelfth Century MS. Vesp. D. XIV, ed. by R. D-N. Warner, Early English Text Society: Original Series, 152 (1917; repr. New York: Kraus, 1981)

Eine altfranzösische Übersetzung des Elucidarium: Edition des Elucidaire der Handschrift Lambeth Palace 431, ed. by Henning Düwell, Beiträge zur romanischen Philologie des Mittelalters, 7 (Munich: Fink, 1974)

English Wycliffite Sermons, ed. by Pamela Gradon and Anne Hudson, 5 vols (Oxford: Clarendon, 1983–96), II (1988), IV (1996)

Fasciculus Morum: A Fourteenth-Century Preacher's Handbook, ed. and trans. by Siegfried Wenzel (University Park, PE: Pennsylvania State University Press, 1989)

Hilton, Walter, *The Goad of Love: An Unpublished Translation of the Stimulus Amoris Formerly Attributed to St Bonaventura, Now Edited from Manuscripts*, ed. by Clare Kirchberger (London: Faber and Faber, 1952)

Hugh of Saint Victor, *De sacramentis Christianae fidei*, ed. by Jacques-Paul Migne, Patrologiae Cursus Completus: Series Latina, 176 (Paris: Migne, 1854), cols 173–617

———,, *On the Sacraments of the Christian Faith*, trans. by Roy J. Deferrari (Cambridge, MA: the Medieval Academy of America, 1951)

John the Blind Audelay, *Poems and Carols (Oxford, Bodleian Library MS Douce 302)*, ed. by Susanna Fein, TEAMS Middle English Texts Series (Kalamazoo, MI: Medieval Institute Publications, Western Michigan University, 2009)

The Late Middle English Lucydarye, ed. by Stephen Morrison, Textes vernaculaires du moyen âge, 12 (Turnhout: Brepols, 2013)

Memoriale Credencium: A Late Middle English Manual of Theology for Lay People edited from Bodley MS Tanner 201, ed. by J. H. L. Kengen (Nijmegen: privately printed, 1979)

The Prickynge of Love, ed. by Harold Kane, 2 vols, Elizabethan and Renaissance Studies 92: 10–11 (Salzburg: Institut für Anglistik und Amerikanistik, Universität Salzburg, 1983)

Thomas Aquinas, *Summa theologica*, in *Sancti Thomae Aquinatis doctoris angelici opera omnia iussu impensaque Leonis XIII P. M. edita* (Rome: Typographia Polyglotta S. C. de Propaganda Fide, 1882–), IV (1888)

Thomas Aquinas, *Summa theologica*, trans. by Fathers of the English Dominican Province (New York: Benziger, 1947), <https://aquinas101.thomisticinstitute.org/st-ia-q-23#F-PQ23OUTP1> [accessed 3 November 2022]

Secondary Works

Clark, J. P. H., 'Predestination in Christ According to Julian of Norwich', *The Downside Review*, 100 (1982), pp. 79–91

Giordano, Carmela, 'Tradurre e adattare: il *Lucidaire* inglese medio fra Onorio d'Autun e Wyclif', *Medioevo e Rinascimento*, 9 (1998), pp. 1–48

Goldstein, R. James, 'Future Perfect: The Augustinian Theology of Perfection and the *Canterbury Tales*', *Studies in the Age of Chaucer*, 29 (2007), pp. 87–140

Halverson, James, 'Franciscan Theology and Predestinarian Pluralism in Late-Medieval Thought', *Speculum*, 70 (1995), pp. 1–26

Hudson, Anne, *The Premature Reformation: Wycliffite Texts and Lollard History* (Oxford: Clarendon Press, 2002)

Iguchi, Atsushi, 'Translating Grace: The "Scala Claustralium" and "A Ladder of Foure Ronges"', *The Review of English Studies*, 59 (2008), pp. 659–76

Kleinhans, Martha, *'Lucidere Vault Tant a Dire Comme Donnant Lumiere': Untersuchung und Edition der Prosaversionen 2, 4 und 5 des Elucidarium*, Beihefte zur Zeitschrift für Romanische Philologie, 248 (Tübingen: Niemeyer, 1993)

——, 'Zwischen Orthodoxie und Häresie: Die englischsprachige Rezeption des Elucidarium', in *Elucidarium und Lucidaires: zur Rezeption des Werks von Honorius Augustodunensis in der Romania und in England*, ed. by Ernstpeter Ruhe, Wissensliteratur im Mittelalter, 7 (Wiesbaden: Reichert, 1993), pp. 291–324

Lefèvre, Yves, *L'Elucidarium et les Lucidaires: Contribution, par l'histoire d'un texte, à l'histoire des croyances religieuses en France au Moyen-Age* (Paris: E. de Boccard, 1954)

Leff, Gordon, *Bradwardine and the Pelagians* (Cambridge: Cambridge University Press, 1957)

Levering, Matthew, *Predestination: Biblical and Theological Paths* (Oxford: Oxford University Press, 2011)

Levy, Ian Christopher, 'Grace and Freedom in the Soteriology of John Wyclif', *Speculum*, 60 (2005), pp. 279–337

Lewis, Anna, 'Rethinking the Lollardy of the "Lucidarie": The Middle English Version of the *Elucidarium* and Religious Thought in Late Medieval England', *Florilegium*, 27 (2010), pp. 209–36

Marx, C. W., 'An Abbreviated Middle English Prose Translation of the "Elucidarius"', *Leeds Studies in English*, 31 (2000), pp. 1–53

Payne, F. Anne, 'Foreknowledge and Free Will: Three Theories in the *Nun's Priest's Tale*', *The Chaucer Review*, 10 (1976), pp. 201–19

Richards, Mary P., 'On the Date and Provenance of MS Cotton Vespasian D. XIV ff. 4–169', *Manuscripta*, 17 (1973), pp. 31–35

Ruhe, Doris, *Gelehrtes Wissen, 'Aberglaube' und pastorale Praxis im französischen Spätmittelalter: Der Second Lucidaire und seine Rezeption (14.–17. Jahrhundert)*, Wissensliteratur im Mittelalter, 8 (Wiesbaden: Reichert, 1993)

———., 'Savoir des doctes et pratique pastorale à la fin du moyen âge', *Cristianesimo nella storia*, 11 (1990), pp. 29–60

Sargent, Michael, 'A New Manuscript of the "Chastising of God's Children" with an Ascription to Walter Hilton', *Medium Aevum*, 46 (1977), pp. 49–65

Türk, Monika, *'Lucidaire de grant sapientie': Untersuchung und Edition der altfranzösischen Übersetzung 1 des 'Elucidarium' von Honorius Augustodunensis*, Beihefte zur Zeitschrift für romanische Philologie, 307 (Tübingen: Niemeyer, 2000)

The *Boke of Gostely Grace* and the *Orcherd of Syon*

Revelations of *approuyd wymmen* and their Readership in Fifteenth-Century England

Naoë Kukita Yoshikawa

Professor of medieval English literature,
Shizuoka University, Japan

In the prologue to *Speculum devotorum* (*Mirror to Devout People*), the anonymous Carthusian author from Sheen declares that he has interspersed some revelations of *approuyd wymmen*.[1] Here he refers to the works of Birgitta of Sweden, Catherine of Siena, Mechthild of Hackeborn, and Elizabeth of Töss, probably because he found their visions orthodox and edifying. In the early fifteenth century, Birgitta of Sweden's *Revelationes*,[2] Catherine of Siena's *Dialogo*, and Mechthild of Hackeborn's *Liber specialis gratiae* were translated into English for the nuns at Syon Abbey in a Carthusian or Birgittine milieu, responding to the monastic reform led by Henry V. The *Dialogo* was entitled *Orcherd of Syon*, while the *Liber specialis gratiae* was disseminated as *Boke of Gostely Grace*, based on the wrongly expanded Latin title *Liber spiritualis gratiae* (*Book of Spiritual Grace*).[3] The Middle English translation of the *Liber specialis gratie* survives in two manuscripts, Oxford, Bodleian Library, MS Bodley 220, written in the London dialect, possibly by a Carthusian monk, John Wells, and London, British Library, MS Egerton 2006, written in a northern dialect and

---

1 I would like to thank Professor Catherine Innes-Parker for her invaluable comments and advice on this essay.

A Mirror to Devout People, ed. by Patterson, p. 6; Gillespie, 'The Haunted Text', p. 141. *The Speculum devotorum* or *Myrowre to Devout Peple* is a prose life of Christ, written in Middle English soon after the foundation of the Carthusian monastery at Sheen by Henry V in 1413. The monastery was located on the other side of the Thames from the Syon Abbey.

2 For the Middle English translation of *Revelationes*, see *The Liber celestis of St Bridget of Sweden*, I, ed. by Ellis; Ellis, 'Flores ad fabricandam... coronam'.

3 Medieval scribes expanded *sp'alis*, the abbreviation of Latin word *specialis* to *spiritualis*.

owned by Richard III and his wife Anne; it is very likely that the two manuscripts share a common antecedent, although the original translation is now lost.[4]

The *Boke* was originally prepared for professional religious. However, like many of the textual productions by or for the nuns of Syon, it found its way to readers outside the enclosure,[5] although the readership was largely restricted to a limited group of wealthy, female aristocrats who associated with the Syon nuns. By the second quarter of the fifteenth century, Mechthild's revelations were circulating in English at Syon Abbey and beyond. It was owned by Eleanor Roos of York as early as 1438 and readers included nobility such as Cecily Neville, Duchess of York, who had a close connection with the Birgittines. According to her household ordinance, dating from 1485–95, Cecily's daily devotional reading included the revelations of St Birgitta and Mechthild of Hackeborn and a life of St Catherine of Siena.[6] Regarding the circulation of the *Orchard*, Jennifer Brown comments that 'the *Orcherd* probably traced a very narrow orbit in and around its home in Syon Abbey' even when in print.[7] Yet, it did circulate within the elite society closely tied to Syon: scholars speculate that besides Birgitta's *Liber celestis* and Mechthild's *Boke*, 'parts of [the *Orcherd*] were staple reading for devout aristocratic laywomen as well as nuns'.[8] Considering the survival of three manuscripts, excerpts in other English manuscripts, and Wynkyn de Worde's printed edition of 1519 (*RSTC* 4815),[9] there was definitely interest and some dissemination of the text.[10]

There are significant similarities between Mechthild's *Liber* and Catherine's *Dialogo*. The *Dialogo* is a series of theological revelations on the mysteries of Holy Church, the Trinity, the Redemption, and the Eucharist. However, it can

---

4 Throughout this essay, *Liber* will refer to the Latin text and the *Boke* to the Middle English translation. The only Latin edition available today is *Revelationes Gertrudianae ac Mechtildianae*, II, ed. by Paquelin, pp. 1–422. Unless otherwise noted, all references to the *Liber* are from this edition, followed by part, chapter, and page number. All quotations of the Middle English translation are from *The Boke of Gostely Grace: The Middle English Translation, A Critical Edition from Oxford, MS Bodley 220* (henceforth *Boke*), ed. by Yoshikawa and Mouron with the assistance of Atherton, followed by part, chapter, and page number. London, British Library, MS Egerton 2006 has been edited by Theresa A. Halligan under the title *The Booke of Gostlye Grace of Mechtild of Hackeborn*.

5 Gillespie, '1412–1534', p. 173; Boffey, 'Women Authors and Women's Literacy in Fourteenth- and Fifteenth-Century England', p. 161.

6 *A Collection of Ordinances and Regulations for the Government of the Royal Household*, pp. 37–39; Armstrong, 'The Piety of Cicely, Duchess of York', pp. 140–42.

7 Brown, 'From the Charterhouse to the Printing House', p. 34. Three manuscripts of the Middle English version are extant: London, British Library, MS Harley 3432; Cambridge, St John's College, MS C 25 (James 75); New York, Pierpont Morgan Library, MS 162. See further *The Orcherd of Syon* (henceforth *Orcherd*), ed. by Hodgson and Liegey, 'Preface', pp. v–xi. All references to the *Orcherd* are from this edition and followed by page number.

8 *The Idea of the Vernacular*, ed. by Wogan-Browne and others, p. 235.

9 *A Short-Title Catalogue of Books*, ed. by Pollard and others.

10 My thanks to Professor Jennifer Brown for discussing this with me.

also be read as a continuation of Helfta spirituality in terms of its orthodox teaching and contemplative aspiration, which would then reinforce the spirituality of fifteenth-century religious reform in England. This essay first explores the historical context of the possible influence of Mechthild's *Liber* on Catherine of Siena. It then examines the orthodox, exemplary qualities embedded in the two texts, focusing on their deployment of heart-centered imagery and architectural tropes that convey the idea of sense experience in relation to the will, in order to consider the textual sisterhood of the two continental mystics to whom late fifteenth-century readership was drawn.

Mechthild of Hackeborn and the *Liber specialis gratiae*[11]

Mechthild of Hackeborn (1240–98), a German mystic and chantress at the Benedictine/Cistercian convent of Helfta, was a daughter of the powerful Baron von Hackeborn-Wippra, who held lands in northern Thuringia and the Harz Mountains. The *Liber* recounts that at the age of seven, Mechthild made a visit with her mother to the nunnery at Rodarsdorf, in the diocese of Halberstadt, which her sister Gertrude of Hackeborn (1231–91) had joined at an early age. On her visit to the nunnery, Mechthild insisted on staying there and eventually attended the convent school under the direction of her own sister, who was elected abbess in 1251 and remained in this position until her death in 1291.[12] During Gertrude's reign as abbess, the community flourished as it housed Mechthild of Hackeborn, Mechthild of Magdeburg (c. 1208–c. 1282/94), a former beguine who entered the community late in her life, and the younger Gertrude later known as Gertrude the Great (1256–1301/2). In the late thirteenth century Helfta thus became a centre of learning and mystical spirituality.[13]

The monastery's library housed many volumes, religious as well as secular, which facilitated the pursuit of the nuns' intellectual activities.[14] When Mechthild of Magdeburg came to live with the Helfta community, she dictated the seventh book of her work, *Das fließende Licht der Gottheit* (*The Flowing Light of the Godhead*), to some of the Helfta nuns. This experience could well have stimulated the nuns to compose their own visionary accounts.[15] When Mechthild

---

11 For a full discussion of this section, see *Boke*, ed. by Yoshikawa and Mouron, 'Introduction'.

12 Because of a shortage of water supply Abbess Gertrude moved the community from Rodarsdorf to Helfta near Eisleben in 1258.

13 Involved in the politico-religious conflicts of the time, the Helfta community gradually diminished until a Lutheran bishop dissolved the monastery in 1546. For the subsequent history, see *The Book of Special Grace*, trans. by Newman, 'Introduction', pp. 6–7.

14 They were highly literate in Latin and were trained in the trivium and the quadrivium, the seven liberal arts taught in medieval universities.

15 In 1289, Gertrude the Great wrote an account of her spiritual experience that later became Book 2 of *Legatus divinae pietatis* (*The Herald of God's Loving-Kindness*).

of Hackeborn was on her sickbed, Gertrude the Great embarked on writing down her revelations with another unknown nun, which was to become the *Liber specialis gratiae*.[16]

The *Liber* is the only Helfta text to have been translated into Middle English. But it is a translation from an abridged version of the Latin text which contains only the first five parts: it concentrates on visions connected with the Church's liturgy, as well as those associated with Mechthild's personal piety, together with her instructions on the religious life and prayers for the deceased. While there is only one extant manuscript containing all the seven parts – Wolfenbüttel (Guelferbytanus), Herzog August Bibliothek, Cod. 1003 Helmst., copied in 1370 from a lost original at Helfta by Albert, Vicar of St Paul in Erfurt, the abridged version was widely circulated throughout Europe, with more than a hundred extant Latin manuscripts and numerous adaptations in six vernaculars – Middle Dutch, Middle High German, Middle English, Italian, Swedish, and French.[17] Its popularity is attested by printed books, such as the anthology printed in 1513 by Jacques Lefèvre d'Étaples, a French theologian and humanist, which includes the *Scivias* of Hildegard of Bingen, the revelations of Elisabeth of Schönau and Mechthild of Hackeborn.[18]

Mechthild of Hackeborn and Catherine of Siena: The Dominican Link

Mechthild is linked to Catherine, among others, by their association with the Dominican Order. For their pastoral care, the nuns at Helfta depended on Dominican friars (probably from Halle or Magdeburg) who were employed as confessors and preachers,[19] and as the General Chapter of the Dominican Order in 1278 had imposed the teachings of Thomas Aquinas on all friars, the sermons heard by the nuns at Helfta would have been essentially Thomist.[20] The Dominicans not only contributed to their pastoral care but also to their education. Dominican authors were known at Helfta: Mechthild's book makes direct references to Albertus Magnus, Thomas Aquinas, and their philosophical source, Aristotle. In her vision concerning the judgement of God on their souls, Aristotle

---

16 The *Liber specialis gratiae* is mentioned in Prologue 2. 43 and 5. 24. According to her own report, Mechthild was initially perturbed at the idea of recording her spiritual experience, but accepted it later as she received divine authorization (*Revelationes Gertrudianae ac Mechtildianae*, II, ed. by Paquelin, 2. 43, p. 193).

17 The transmission of the *Liber* is still understudied. For the most reliable study, see *Het Boek der bijzondere Genade van Mechtild van Hackeborn*, ed. by Bromberg, pp. 105–27; Schmidt, 'Mechthild von Hackeborn', pp. 253–60; Hellgardt, 'Latin and the Vernacular'.

18 *Liber trium virorum et trium spiritualium virginum*, ed. by Lefèvre d'Étaples.

19 See further Finnegan, *The Women of Helfta*, p. 15.

20 Finnegan, *The Women of Helfta*, p. 7.

is uniquely described as having been treated kindly by God,[21] while Albert and Thomas are described as entering Heaven escorted by two angels.[22]

As Barbara Newman argues, 'it is reasonable to suppose that Helfta's Dominican confessors first popularized it [the *Liber*] through the efficient networks of their order'.[23] Although it is not known how early the text reached Italy, its Italian translation is found in a fifteenth-century manuscript in Gubbio.[24] The *Liber* was printed at Venice in 1520, 1522, and 1558, and an Italian version was published there in 1590.[25] Moreover, there is possibly an allusion to Mechthild in *Decameron* (c. 1353). In the first tale of Day Seven, a rich but simple-minded weaver, who is captain of the laud-singers at the Dominican church Santa Maria Novella in Florence, learns a few prayers which include the laud of Lady Matelda, who could have been Mechthild of Hackeborn.[26] Dante, who was strongly influenced by the Dominicans and had connections with their Florentine convent,[27] may have been Mechthild's earliest reader in Italy. As Newman again argues, Mechthild's vision of the seven-story mountain (*Liber* 1. 13) seems to have inspired the whole scheme of the Purgatorio, that is, 'a mountain climbed by penitent souls, its seven terraces each dedicated to the cleansing of a particular vice and acquisition of the corresponding virtue, with the Earthly Paradise at its summit'.[28] A Dominican influence can also be discerned in Catherine's life. She became a member of a female group called the Mantellate (tertiaries) who were affiliated with the Order. The influences of the teachings of Augustine, Gregory the Great, Bernard, Francis, and Thomas are found in her writings as well as in the writings of Mechthild.[29] Therefore, it is not surprising to see a spiritual affinity between the two texts.

---

21 *Revelationes Gertrudianae ac Mechtildianae*, II, ed. by Paquelin, 5. 16, p. 344, n. 1, which transcribes a sentence added in the margin of St Gallen, Stiftsbibliothek, Cod. Sang. 583.

22 *Revelationes Gertrudianae ac Mechtildianae*, II, ed. by Paquelin, 5. 9, pp. 332–33. This revelation is not translated into Middle English.

23 *The Book of Special Grace*, trans. by Newman, 'Introduction', p. 28.

24 Bertini Malgarini and Vignuzzi, 'Matilde a Helfta, Melchiade in Umbria (e oltre)', p. 291.

25 Newman, 'The Seven Storey-Mountain'.

26 Boccaccio, *Decameron* VII. 1, trans. by Musa and Bondanella, p. 418. See Paquelin's note in *Revelationes Gertrudianae ac Mechtildianae*, II, p. 65 n. 1; Gardner, *Dante and the Mystics*, p. 284.

27 Vettori, 'Dominicans', p. 313.

28 Newman, 'The Seven-Storey Mountain', p. 65. The jubilee of 1300 brought to Rome enormous numbers of foreign pilgrims including friars fluent in many languages who acted as pilgrims' confessors. Dante himself was among the visitors as he describes the crowd control in *Inferno* 18. He might have been introduced to Mechthild's *Liber* by a Dominican friar in Rome or in Florence: see further *Book of Spiritual Grace*, trans. by Newman, 'Introduction', p. 28.

29 Catherine could also have had an opportunity to learn about Mechthild, who probably was known in Tuscany by then. Noffke speculates that being 'a tireless conversation-

Catherine's *Dialogo* and Mechthild's *Liber* travelled across the Channel at some point in the early fifteenth century. The Carthusians are commonly assumed to have had a hand in the transmission of Mechthild's *Liber* to England.[30] As for the *Dialogo*, emissaries of Syon, the Birgittine convent in England, went back and forth to Rome, seeking papal approbation for the new foundation between 1415 and 1420. As Mary Denise speculates, they might have returned with 'a copy of Raymond Capua's version of the *Dialogo*'.[31] A link between Catherine and England is also provided by William Flete, an English Augustinian friar, who lived as a hermit at Lecceto near Siena and remained one of Catherine's closest associates: as Alexandra Barratt speculates, 'he may well have been the channel through which her writings made their way to England'.[32]

The reception of the *Liber* and the *Dialogo* by the Birgittines and Carthusians suggests that the readership of the two texts may well have converged from time to time in the milieu of the Birgittine house of Syon and the Carthusian monastery at Sheen,[33] which together formed a centre of contemplative piety in fifteenth-century England. The two texts were eventually selected, along with Birgitta's revelations, for contemporaneous translation into English.[34]

Mechthild's and Catherine's Work in English: Internal Correspondence

The relationship between the *Boke* and the *Orcherd* is centred on their thematic concerns.[35] Both texts engender in their reader a meditative and contemplative state of mind, suitable for the Syon community, which was strictly enclosed and

---

alist', Catherine seems to have gained a variety of information through conversations with the friars: see Catherine of Siena, *The Dialogue*, trans. by Noffke, Introduction, p. 9. All references to the *Dialogo* are from this translation, followed by chapter and page number.

30 Voaden argues that the foundation of Syon in 1415 is responsible for the arrival of Mechthild: see Voaden, 'The Company She Keeps', pp. 68–69. This remains most likely: there is only sparse circumstantial evidence to support this hypothesis, but no tangible proof to contradict it.

31 Denise, 'The Orchard of Syon', p. 291. Raymond's version was in circulation before 1399.

32 *Women's Writing in Middle English*, ed. by Barratt, p. 100.

33 See n. 1 above.

34 Hodgson points out that the *Boke* and the *Orcherd* share a similar ending: see Hodgson, '"The Orcherd of Syon"', p. 77. Compare *Boke*, ed. by Yoshikawa and Mouron, p. 325 and *Orcherd*, ed. by Hodgson and Liegey, p. 421. The similarity suggests that the translator(s) could well have been familiar with both texts. Birgitta's *Liber celestis* was very likely to have circulated among the same readership, but this essay's focus is upon the connection between Mechthild and Catherine, although specific references to Birgitta are made where necessary.

35 In the following section, I concentrate on the vernacular translation of both works to illuminate how such texts were received by lay readers in later medieval England.

partly composed of former anchorites and contemplatives. The *Liber/Boke* represents the Helfta convent as a community characterized by 'intense spirituality, frequent revelations, outstanding virtue, and nuptial intimacy with Christ'.[36] It must have supplied an inspirational model for the Syon nuns. Like the *Boke*, the *Orchard* also provides a model for the nuns. The metaphor of the orchard that structures the Middle English text sets out the contemplative spirituality that the nuns should pursue:

> þis book of reuelaciouns [...] I clepe it a fruytful orcherd [...] to deuyde into seuene parties, and ech party into fyue chapitres [...] In þis orchard, whanne ȝe wolen be conforted, ȝe mowe walke and se boþe fruyt and herbis. And albeit þat sum fruyt or herbis seeme to summe scharpe, hard, or bitter, ȝit to purgynge of þe soule þei ben ful speedful and profitable, whanne þei ben discreetly take and resceyued by counceil.[37]
>
>> (I call this book of revelations a fruitful orchard, to be divided into seven parts, each of which has five chapters. When you wish to be comforted, you can walk in this orchard and see both fruits and herbs. Although some fruit or herbs seem sharp, hard or bitter, still they are helpful and profitable to purge your soul, when they are taken discreetly and received by council.)

At first glance, this allegory defines the work as a refreshment in gardens of aristocratic estates and convents, designed for leisurely walking,[38] but it also contains a moral aspect predicated upon the ancient ideal of *otium* – 'the state of philosophical detachment and refreshment', through which everyday anxieties might give way to 'calm but intense thought – and, in its medieval Christian incarnation, reading, meditation, and prayer'.[39] The second prologue to the *Orchard* explains more explicitly that the text is offered for spiritual learning and comfortable recreation.[40] Moreover, this allegorical framework, supplied by the Middle English translator, is appropriate for what it encloses, for Catherine frequently uses the vineyard/orchard image, which, for example, appears in the discourse of Redemption:

> I sente myn oonly sooþfast sone, Ihesu, into þe world for to take incarnacioun, so for to avoyde the infecundite and bareynesse of mankynde and take fro hym þe þornes of orignal synne, and made of þe man a maner of orcherd sprynged wiþ þe blood of Crist crucifyed, settynge þereynne plauntis of þe seuene ȝiftis of þe holy goost, takynge out of hym deedly synne.[41]

---

36 *Book of Special Grace*, trans. by Newman, 'Introduction', p. 30.

37 *Orcherd*, ed. by Hodgson and Liegey, The Translator's Prologue, p. 1.

38 *The Idea of the Vernacular*, p. 235. As the work's 'gardener', the translator takes some responsibility for the text.

39 Watson, 'Introduction', p. 18.

40 *Orcherd*, ed. by Hodgson and Liegey, pp. 16–17.

41 *Orcherd*, ed. by Hodgson and Liegey, p. 335.

> (I sent my only true son, Jesus, into the world for incarnation, to avoid the infecundity and barrenness of mankind and take the thorns of original sin from him, and made from man an orchard flowing with the blood of the crucified Christ, planting the seven gifts of the Holy Ghost there, taking deadly sin out of him.)

Like the *Orcherd*, the *Boke* is replete with horticultural, flourishing metaphors, based on the powerful image of Christ as a tree for the *helth* of the soul. Mechthild sees that 'ther wex oute of þe feete of our Lord twey trees of a wounderfull grenes, which wer full of feyr fruyte and þat fruyte betokened þe fruyte of penaunce' (1. 56, p. 177) ('two wonderfully green trees grow out of our Lord's feet. They were full of beautiful fruit signifying the fruit of penance'). She also envisions Christ's heart as a tree, feeding souls with a sweet, ghostly drink:[42]

> He had also an ornament on hys breste in maner of a full fayr tree, which he spred and devyd hymsilf. And from hys herte which passyd in swettenes any hony in the which herte all þe tresoures of wysdome and science ben hyd, ranne forth a full pur veyne with þe which veyne all þat come to hym wer full replenyschyd with gostely drynke thorow þat rennyng streme of lykyng of God (I. 66, p. 191).
>
> > (He had also an ornament on his breast shaped like a beautiful tree which he spread and divided himself. From his heart, whose sweetness surpassed any honey and in which all treasures of wisdom and knowledge are hidden, ran forth a vein (of pure liquid) and all that come to him are fully replenished with the spiritual drink through the running stream of pleasure in God.)

The horticultural metaphors deployed by Mechthild and Catherine would not have escaped the attention of any medieval reader. Translated at a time of reform and circulated at Syon, both the *Boke* and the *Orcherd* are politically charged and historically specific: the image of the vineyard in their texts has a resonance with the lexis which the Church deployed to visualise its fifteenth-century reform. It is represented in the arresting image of mending 'the infected vineyard and the damaged city wall',[43] the trope which Thomas Arundel deployed in his decrees to depict the University of Oxford polluted by Lollardy. Moreover, in a pan-European context, it is imagery borrowed from the prophecies of Birgitta of Sweden, who used traditional, biblical metaphors to voice her criticism of the contemporary Church.[44]

---

42 Metaphors of flourishing are predominant in the *Boke*. For example, in a vision Christ gives each nun his divine heart filled with fragrant spices whose savours come out of his heart on every side as if they had been green flourishing flowers (I. 33).

43 Gillespie, 'Chichele's Church', p. 17; *Concilia Magnae Britanniae et Hiberniae*, II, ed. by Wilkins, pp. 314–19 (Constitution 11).

44 Gillespie, 'Chichele's Church', p. 17. See further *Boke*, ed. by Yoshikawa and Mouron, 'Introduction'.

Indeed, the Birgittine Order was founded as an attempt to 'restore features of the ideal monastic community of early Christianity'.[45] The *Regula Salvatoris*, the Birgittine Rule, begins with a vineyard allegory which equates the contemporary church with the vineyard, the walls of which are destroyed by thieves, its roots undermined by moles, and its branches withered. In the prologue, Christ himself declares his decision to found a new religious order by deploying this vineyard allegory: 'I shal plante me a vyne3erde of newe, in which þoue shalt bere the brawnches of my words' ('I shall plant a new vineyard, in which you shall bear the branches of my words').[46] A similar vineyard metaphor is used in Catherine's letter penned to the count of Fondi in central Italy in the course of her efforts to find solutions to the Schism. She writes that the vineyard of the soul is 'infested with the thorns of pride and avarice, with the brambles of anger, impatience, and disobedience; it is full of poisonous weeds',[47] based on moral exegetical interpretations of the vineyard.

This reformist movement had a considerable impact on the English Church. Significantly, it is the Church Council convened at Constance (1414–18) to resolve the Schism that stimulated fifteenth-century monastic reform in England. As Vincent Gillespie argues, it was the experiences and contacts made by the Englishmen at the meetings that 'allowed English church leaders to develop a plan for the reform and renovation of the national church'.[48] Therefore, when Henry V made the decision to break with the monastic past by founding the Birgittine monastery, the nuns and brothers were expected to play a role as guardians of the vineyard for church reform in England. The metaphor of the vineyard deployed by Birgitta, Catherine, and Mechthild fits into this religio-political milieu, although in her revelations Birgitta primarily uses the tropes of a besieged castle or a religious house, the walls of which are undermined by disbelievers but will be rebuilt with new walls through which divine grace is poured onto the contrite religious.[49]

The Sacred Heart in the Vineyard

In both the *Boke* and the *Orchard* the vineyard allegory is also integrated with medical, cardiac tropes to elaborate the image of the vineyard in which Christ's blood, flowing from his heart, sustains both the health of the soul and the health of the church as a social body of Christ. Indeed, the Sacred Heart of Christ signifies what Sabine Spitzlei calls *Erfahrungsraum* ('experiential space'), the

---

45 Morris, *St Birgitta of Sweden*, p. 166.

46 *The Rewyll of Seynt Sauioure*, ed. by Hogg, p. 61; Gillespie, 'The Mole in the Vineyard', pp. 131–32.

47 Blumenfeld-Kosinski, *Poets, Saints, and Visionaries of the Great Schism*, p. 49.

48 Gillespie, 'Culture and History', p. 166.

49 *Liber celestis*, ed. by Ellis, Book 1, Ch. 5, pp. 11–13.

space in which a soul is securely enclosed and nurtured.[50] For Mechthild, the heart is predominantly a space of mutual indwelling that transforms in a variety of ways but which always serves to develop Mechthild's mystical relationship with Christ.[51] In a similar vein, the intimacy between Catherine and Christ culminates in a mystical experience: her *vita* reports that Catherine and Christ exchanged their hearts through her intense devotion to Christ's heart.[52]

As I have argued elsewhere, such heart-centred tropes are illuminated by a late medieval cultural milieu in which medicine and religion converged, creating a discourse community that included theologians, philosophers, anatomists, physicians, and visionaries.[53] The medieval doctrine on the heart was complex, but from the twelfth-century onwards, cardio-centric Aristotelian natural philosophy was disseminated among physicians and theologians through the translations of Avicenna's *Canon*. Albertus Magnus's thirteenth-century *De animalibus* cites Avicenna's view of the heart as the organizing principle of the body.[54] This cardio-centricity was incorporated into the medieval body politic, in which traditional Pauline metaphors of the church as a body, with Christ as its head, were transformed in line with the changed focus on the heart.[55] Here Christ's heart reigns in the centre of the mystical body of the Church, nurturing all the members of the community.

Both Mechthild and Catherine could very well have known this concept through their Dominican links. Mechthild has a vision of her heart as a vineyard, in the middle of which is a well by which Christ stands, sprinkling the water (his blood) from his heart on those who desire 'spiritual regeneration'.[56] There are also direct echoes of this metaphor in Catherine's letter addressed to the ecclesiastical authorities, where Christ's heart not only appears within the individual human soul, but is also compared with a well of blood located in the centre of the vineyard where the soul can take nourishment.[57] Ultimately Christ's blood is envisioned bringing new life to the soul and also to the anaemic Church, which, as Catherine observes, lost blood during the years of the Schism.[58]

---

50 Spitzlei, *Erfahrungsraum Herz*.

51 See further Yoshikawa, 'Mechthild of Hackeborn as Spiritual Authority', pp. 243–44.

52 Raymond of Capua, *The Life of St Catherine of Siena*, trans. by Lamb, pt. ii, Ch. 6, pp. 144–45.

53 Webb, *Medieval Heart*, p. 5. For this medical context, see further Yoshikawa, 'Mechtild of Hackeborn and Cecily Neville's Devotional Reading', pp. 29–30.

54 See Webb, *Medieval Heart*, pp. 19–21.

55 Webb, *Medieval Heart*, p. 34.

56 *Boke*, ed. by Yoshikawa and Mouron, I. 51, p. 170. See further Yoshikawa, 'The Virgin in the "Hortus conclusus"'.

57 *Le lettere di S. Caterina da Siena*, V, ed. by Misciattelli, Letter 313, p. 16, p. 21; Webb, *Medieval Heart*, pp. 35–36.

58 See *Le lettere di S. Caterina da Siena*, V, ed. by Misciattelli, Letter 346, pp. 162–63. In her efforts to find solutions to the Schism, Catherine addressed fourteen letters to Gregory XI.

Furthermore, in Mechthild's *Boke*, the metaphor of the vineyard is instrumental in promoting proper relations between Christ and the faithful. In one vision (II. 2), Christ's heart emerges like a vineyard where some trees stand upright like those who lift up their hearts to heaven, while others bow downward like sinful creatures. As Christ delves the earth like a gardener,[59] he reveals to Mechthild that this vineyard is his *holy chirche* in which he sweated with hard labour, and tells her to help him water the vineyard.[60] In the *Orchard*, the soul is also likened to a tree with its root grounded in the soil of divine love, and this tree bears many-fragranced blossoms of virtue like Mechthild's upright trees.[61] God further identifies men as the workers hired to labour in the vineyard of the Holy Church and exhorts them to serve their neighbours and share the fruits of their own vineyard.[62] Thus, in view of the spirit of reform and revitalization of fifteenth-century England, the vineyard is envisioned as the mystic body of the Holy Church, where each member is encouraged to be a virtuous tiller and to embrace the ideal of contemplation and prayer enforced by the reform. This is in accord with what Maryanne Horowitz argues: 'trees of ascent (often biblical trees of life) redirect the human intellect from sensual concerns upward to contemplation of God'.[63]

The Will and the Senses

In addition to the cardio-centric vineyard tropes, Mechthild's and Catherine's deployment of allegories also explore the idea of sense experience in relation to the will. In the medieval contemplative's encounters with Christ, the senses play a major role. Mystics often describe their sensual appreciation of Christ, whom they not only hear and see, but also taste, smell, and touch. Richard Rolle, for example, understands that the five spiritual senses correspond directly with the five corporeal senses and that the spiritual sensations are received directly from God. In Rolle's contemplative sensorium the senses therefore fully contribute to the spiritual ascent.[64] However, according to the Aristotelian, hierarchical scheme, the primary faculties of the soul consist of will and reason, while the

---

59 The translator of the *Orchard* uses the same metaphor for his work; see n. 37 above.

60 *Boke*, ed. by Yoshikawa and Mouron, II. 2, pp. 215-16. See further Yoshikawa, 'Mechtild of Hackeborn and Cecily Neville's Devotional Reading', pp. 30–31.

61 *Orcherd*, ed. by Hodgson and Liegey, p. 39. *The Mirroure of the Worlde*, a manual of moral instructions for laymen, has a section entitled 'Off the Gardyn with the Treys of Vertu': see *The Mirroure of the Worlde*, ed. by Raymo, Whitaker, and Sternglantz, pp. 207–08.

62 *Orcherd*, ed. by Hodgson and Liegey, p. 191.

63 Horowitz, *Seeds of Virtue and Knowledge*, p. 57.

64 Albin, *Richard Rolle's Melody of Love*, pp. 82–96. For Rolle, spiritual senses do not travel along the traditional perceptual pathways established by Galenic physiology and Aristotelian psychology.

remaining faculties of the soul include the internal and external senses and the concupiscent appetites. In the Christian sensorium, the senses, therefore, bear a strong moral connotation in which sensory perception was regarded as potentially dangerous, leading to perdition.[65] To protect souls from the snares of the external senses, catechetical and pastoral works articulate the conception of guarding the senses which were regarded as potential portals of sin.[66] This concept was also popularized through the allegory of protecting the city or castle of the soul by guarding the gates of the senses.[67]

Indeed, the proper use of senses in accord with divine will would be a prerequisite for a virtuous tiller of the vineyard. Throughout the *Boke*, Mechthild is aware of the vulnerability of the will. In her total surrender to the will of God, she deploys architectural tropes to convey the moral message that one should conform one's will and desire to God. In a vision (I. 39), Christ shows Mechthild a beautiful large house which contains a small house. Mechthild understands that the gate signifies the desire of her soul and that the bar of the gate designates her will. The little chain on the gate, God's desire, always goes ahead of the soul's desire, and excites and draws the desire and will of the soul to God.[68] A similar image of an allegorical door and lock to protect the house of soul appears in one of Birgitta's revelations, in which a heartfelt desire to be with God works as the key which will undo the lock.[69]

In another vision (III. 39), Christ gives Mechthild an allegorical discourse on the sensory gates. Linking her five wits with the gates (and windows of the soul), he bids her to await him at the gates. If she sees fair things, she should think how good He is who made them all, and when she hears a merry melody, she should feel the sweetness of Christ's voice.[70] Echoing Rolle's concept of the contemplative sensorium, this episode portrays the senses of seeing and hearing in a very positive light.

Yet, as mentioned earlier, the Christian sense experience is predicated upon the idea that the senses are often unruly and the will to which they are subject is frail. Mechthild is vigilant against the disordered will and its consequent misuse of the senses. In a revelation, Christ instructs Mechthild about how a person should greet the divine Heart, offer her own heart to God, and offer prayers for the sanctification of the senses of sight, hearing, and of mouth, voice, hands and heart, to guard one's soul from the snares of the external senses.[71]

---

65 See further Woolgar, *The Senses in Late Medieval England*, p. 16.

66 *A Cultural History of the Senses*, ed. by Newhauser, p. 9.

67 See Whitehead, *Castles of the Mind*, p. 103.

68 *Boke*, ed. by Yoshikawa and Mouron, I. 39, pp. 155-56. For a moral, didactic message embedded in this vision, see Yoshikawa, 'Mechtild of Hackeborn as Spiritual Authority', pp. 249–50.

69 *Liber celestis*, ed. by Ellis, Book 2, Ch. 27, p. 189; Whitehead, *Castles of the Mind*, pp. 133–34.

70 *Boke*, ed. by Yoshikawa and Mouron, III. 39, pp. 276-77. In the same way, through the five senses man delights in God and offers praises and worship to God.

71 *Boke*, ed. by Yoshikawa and Mouron, III. 15, pp. 260-61.

This anxiety is also embedded in Catherine's *Orcherd*. In a narrative on the divine providence which raises the soul out of imperfection, she deploys the architectural trope of the will in the city of the soul in a similar vein to Mechthild, although more emphasis is placed on free choice, which allows one to enter:

> þis gate of wille which is fre, I will not suffre goostly enemyes to vndo it […] þe soule haþ a keper, þat is, fre choys, which dwelliþ at þat gate, & for þis cause haue I maad fre choys keper of þat gate.
>
> > (This gate of the will is free. I do not allow spiritual enemies to open it […] The soul has a keeper, that is, free choice, who dwells at this gate, and for this cause, I have made free choice keeper of that gate.)[72]

Further, based on the Augustinian model of the three properties of the mind, Catherine expands on the trope: there are three main gates that possess the attributes of memory, understanding, and will, the last of which is thought to hold firm and guard the others.[73] But if the will gives its consent, selfish love and all the other enemies that follow after it come in, because as soon as these gates are opened, 'þe smale doris of þe bodily wittis ben openyd, whiche ben instrumentis answeringe to þe soule' ('the small doors of the body's senses are opened, which are the instruments that respond to the soul').[74] *Instrumentis* is an English translation of the Latin *organum* ('instrument'), and its meaning is an organ as the tool of one of the senses, of a mental faculty, and the body or part of the body as an instrument.[75] The allegory of gates and small doors work on two levels here: the first level is that of the city and its gates, and the second level is introduced by the 'organ'. As Suzanna Noffke argues, in Catherine's day *organo* in Italian had interrelated layers of meaning: 'the primary sense was that of instrumentality, as in the bodily organs or the senses as organs (instruments) of the soul'. In the musical realm, 'everything that carried music in an instrumental way was *organo*'.[76] In Catherine's vision, the two levels work interchangeably.

If one has a proper will, the senses are useful instruments for devotion, making sweet sounds which come forth from the centre of the city of the soul, as 'the gate of wille is schut to his owne propre loue, & it is openyd for to loue & desire my worschip & loue of nei3boreheed' ('The gate of will is shut to selfishness and opened to love and desire of my honour and love of neighbours').[77] Then, the

---

72 *Orcherd*, ed. by Hodgson and Liegey, p. 347.

73 For Augustine's philosophy of memory, see Teske, 'Augustine's Theory of Soul'.

74 *Orcherd*, ed. by Hodgson and Liegey, p. 348.

75 MED s.v. instrument, 2. a. Hodgson and Liegey speculate that the *Orcherd* follows Cristofano Guidini's translation into Latin from Italian: see Hodgson and Liegey, Preface, p. vii.

76 Catherine of Siena, *The Dialogue*, trans. by Noffke, pp. 299–300, n. 42. Noffke's translation is based on *Il Dialogo della divina provvidenza ovvero libro della divina dottrina*, ed. by Cavallini.

77 *Orcherd*, ed. by Hodgson and Liegey, p. 360.

soul's movements make an exultant sound, with the strings of heart tempered and harmonized with prudence and light.[78] Moreover, the first to sound in the sound of life was the Son of God when he took on human flesh, and made a sweet sound upon the cross with his humanity united with the Godhead.[79] Here, Christ on the cross is allegorized as a model instrument, making the music of life.

Music also emerges as a powerful metaphor in Mechthild's revelations. I have argued elsewhere that Mechthild's personal experience with disease and her role as chantress of her community inform her use of music in the course of compiling medical and liturgical metaphors.[80] But Mechthild's understanding of the power of music reaches beyond its therapeutic functions. Her liturgically-induced musical metaphors show that the liturgy activated all the senses in participation with the power of the divinity. Since Augustine, mystics had understood that music provides direct access to God.[81] It has the capacity to move souls to mystical heights when the devout sing, hear or play an instrument. The power of music to raise the spirits and mitigate emotions would have led mystics to incorporate psychosomatic healing intuitively into their longing for union with God, in which Christ's body becomes the means to salvation.[82]

For example, stimulated by the liturgy of Trinity Sunday, Mechthild sees a vision in which a psaltery with ten strings comes out from the heart of God to her heart. As she touches the first string, she gives worship to God and participates in the heavenly choir.[83] The psaltery was the instrument which David played to rid Saul of the evil spirit. This cure was often regarded as an allegory of the role of Christ in curing the disease of the soul. Augustine further explained that the strings of the psaltery were 'stretched over the sound board like the sinews of Christ's body on the Cross',[84] identifying Christ's suffering body with this musical instrument. Mechthild's vision is similar to a miniature from the *Speculum humanae salvationis*, a devotional treatise in rhymed prose composed in 1324 by the Dominicans of Strasburg, in which the slack strings of the *psalterium* invite the viewer to imagine the Passion as a musical performance.[85] Like Christ on the cross in Catherine's vision, the musical body in pain is envisioned as a redemptive sign, making the music of life through the body's senses as instruments of the soul.

For Mechthild and Catherine, the architectural/instrumental allegory is not merely a conduit metaphor, it also opens up the sensual appreciation of God. Christ's body becomes an arena for the orchestration of sense experience that may ultimately lead to a mystical encounter with the divine. But it is also reciprocal. If the

---

78 See further *Orcherd*, ed. by Hodgson and Liegey, pp. 360–61.

79 *Orcherd*, ed. by Hodgson and Liegey, p. 361.

80 See Yoshikawa, 'Heavenly Vision and Psychosomatic Healing'.

81 Boenig, 'St Augustine's "jubilus" and Richard Rolle's "canor"', p. 77.

82 See Holsinger, *Music, Body, and Desire in Medieval Culture*, pp. 225–53.

83 *Boke*, ed. by Yoshikawa and Mouron, II. 35, pp. 239-40.

84 Boenig, 'St Augustine's "jubilus" and Richard Rolle's "canor"', p. 79.

85 See Darmastadt, Universitäts- und Landesbibliothek, MS 2505, fol. 42^v.

sensory organs of the devout act correctly, they can participate in the formation of divine knowledge enabling the devout to become virtuous members of the Church.

***

Mechthild's *Liber specialis gratiae* and Catherine's *Dialogo* were translated into English in a Carthusian or Birgittine milieu, responding to the monastic reform led by Henry V. Their idiosyncratic array of tropes encourages Mechthild and Catherine's devout vernacular readership to aspire for spiritual reform and rejuvenation in fifteenth-century England. In particular, the complex imagery of the heart in the vineyard foregrounds the criticism directed towards the contemporary church in a pan-European context and in the religio-political milieu in which Henry V enforced church reform in England, whilst the instrumental allegory illuminates the musicality of the rightly directed senses that would facilitate the devout in participating in the spirit of the reform. Thus, through their shared allegories, Mechthild's *Boke* and Catherine's *Orcherd* became vehicles for orthodox understanding of the teaching of the Church for their readers, and provided them with an authorial, inspirational model for devotion to God. Mechthild's and Catherine's textual sisterhood meant that these texts supplied a model both inside and outside Syon Abbey, by illustrating ideals suitable for emulation by mostly female vernacular readers, who embraced the spirit of reform as readers of these *approuyd wymmen*.

Bibliography

Manuscript Sources

Cambridge, St John's College, MS C 25 (James 75)
Darmastadt, Universitäts- und Landesbibliothek, MS 2505
London, British Library, MS Egerton 2006
London, British Library, MS Harley 3432
New York, Pierpont Morgan Library, MS 162
Oxford, Bodleian Library, MS Bodley 220
St Gallen, Stiftsbibliothek, Cod. Sang. 583
Wolfenbüttel, Herzog August Bibliothek, Cod. 1003 Helmst.

Primary Sources

Boccaccio, Giovanni, *Decameron*, trans. by Mark Musa and Peter Bondanella (New York: Penguin, 1982)

Het Boek der bijzondere Genade van Mechtild van Hackeborn, ed. by Richard L. J. Bromberg, Zwolse drukken en herdrukken voor de Maatschappij der Nederlandse Letterkunde te Leiden, 51 (Zwolle: Tjeenk Willink, 1965)

The Boke of Gostely Grace: The Middle English Translation, A Critical Edition from Oxford, MS Bodley 220, ed. by Naoë Kukita Yoshikawa and Anne Mouron with the assistance of Mark Atherton, Exeter Medieval Exeter Medieval Texts and Studies (Liverpool: Liverpool University Press, 2022)

The Booke of Gostlye Grace of Mechtild of Hackeborn, ed. by Theresa A. Halligan, Studies and Texts, 46 (Toronto: Pontifical Institute of Mediaeval Studies, 1979)

The Book of Special Grace, trans. by Barbara Newman, Classics of Western Spirituality (New York: Paulist Press, 2017)

Catherine of Siena, *Il dialogo della divina provvidenza ovvero libro della divina dottrina*, ed. by Giuliana Cavallini, Testi cateriniani, 1 (Rome: Edizioni Cateriniane, 1968)

———, *The Dialogue*, trans. by Suzanne Noffke, Classics of Western Spirituality (New York: Paulist Press, 1980)

A Collection of Ordinances and Regulations for the Government of the Royal Household (London: John Nichols for the Society of Antiquaries, 1790)

Concilia Magnae Britanniae et Hiberniae, ed. by David Wilkins, 3 vols (London: Gosling, 1737), II

Gertrude d'Helfta, *Le Héraut [Legatus divinae pietatis]*, in *Oeuvres spirituelles*, ed. and trans. Pierre Doyère et al., 5 vols, Sources chrétiennes, 127, 139, 143, 255, 331 (Paris: Éditions du Cerf, 1967–86), II

Le lettere di S. Caterina da Siena, ed. by Piero Misciattelli, 6 vols (Florence: Casa Editrice Marzocco, 1940), V

The Liber Celestis of St Bridget of Sweden: The Middle English Version in British Library MS Claudius B i, Together with a Life of the Saint from the Same Manuscript, ed. by Roger Ellis, Early English Text Society: Original Series, 291 (Oxford: Oxford University Press, 1987–), I: *Text* (1987)

Liber trium virorum et trium spiritualium virginum, ed. by Jacques Lefèvre d'Étaples (Paris: Estienne, 1513)

A Mirror to Devout People (Speculum Devotorum), ed. by Paul J. Patterson, Early English Text Society: Original Series, 346 (Oxford: Oxford University Press, 2016

The Mirroure of the Worlde: A Middle English Translation of the 'Miroir de Monde', ed. by Robert R. Raymo, Elaine E. Whitaker, and Ruth E. Sternglantz, Medieval Academy Books (Toronto: Toronto University Press, 2003)

The Orcherd of Syon, ed. by Phyllis Hodgson and Gabriel M. Liegey, Early English Text Society: Original Series, 258 (Oxford: Oxford University Press, 1966)

Raymond of Capua, *The Life of St Catherine of Siena*, trans. by George Lamb (London: Harvill Press, 1960; reprint: Charlotte, NC: Tan Books, 2011)

Revelationes Gertrudianae ac Mechtildianae, ed. by Dom Ludwig Paquelin, 2 vols (Paris: Oudin, 1875–77), II: *Sanctae Mechtildis virginis ordinis sancti Benedicti Liber specialis gratiae* (1877)

The Rewyll of Seynt Sauioure, in *The Rewyll of Seynt Sauioure and a Ladder of Foure Ronges by the Which Men Mowe Clyme to Heven*, ed. by James Hogg, Analecta Cartusiana, 183 (Salzburg: Institut für Anglistik und Amerikanistik, 2003)

Women's Writing in Middle English, ed. by Alexandra Barratt, 2nd edn, Langman Annotated Texts (London: Longman, 2010)

Secondary Works

Albin, Andrew, *Richard Rolle's Melody of Love: A Study and Translation with Manuscript and Musical Contexts*, Studies and Texts, 212 (Toronto: Pontifical Institute of Mediaeval Studies, 2018)

Armstrong, Charles A. J., 'The Piety of Cicely, Duchess of York: A Study in Late Mediaeval Culture', in *England, France and Burgundy in the Fifteenth Century*, ed. by Charles A. J. Armstrong, History Series, 16 (London: Hambledon, 1983), pp. 135–56

Bertini Malgarini, Patrizia and Ugo Vignuzzi, 'Matilde a Helfta, Melchiade in Umbria (e oltre): Un antico volgarizzamento umbro del "Liber specialis gratiae"', in *Dire l'Ineffabile: Caterina da Siena e il linguaggio della mistica*, ed. by Lino Leonardi and Pietro Trifone, La mistica cristiana tra Oriente e Occidente, 5 (Florence: Edizioni del Galluzzo, 2006), pp. 291–307

Blumenfeld-Kosinski, Renate, *Poets, Saints, and Visionaries of the Great Schism, 1378–1417* (University Park, PA: Pennsylvania State University Press, 2006)

Boenig, Robert, 'St Augustine's "jubilus" and Richard Rolle's "canor"', in *Vox Mystica: Essays on Medieval Mysticism in Honor of Professor Valerie M. Lagorio*, ed. by Anne Clark Bartlett and others (Cambridge: Brewer, 1995), pp. 75–86

Boffey, Julia, 'Women Authors and Women's Literacy in Fourteenth- and Fifteenth-Century England', in *Women and Literature in Britain, 1150–1500*, ed. by Carol M. Meale, Cambridge Studies in Medieval Literature, 17 (Cambridge: Cambridge University Press, 1993), pp. 159–82

Brown, Jennifer, 'From the Charterhouse to the Printing House: Catherine of Siena in Medieval England', in *Middle English Religious Writing in Practice: Texts, Readers, and Transformations*, ed. by Nicole R. Rice, Binghamton Medieval and Early Modern Studies, 21 (Turnhout: Brepols, 2013), pp. 17–45

A Cultural History of the Senses: In the Middle Ages, ed. by Richard G. Newhauser (London: Bloomsbury, 2016)

Denise, Mary, 'The Orchard of Syon: An Introduction', *Traditio*, 14 (1958), pp. 269–93

Ellis, Roger, '"Flores ad fabricandam… coronam": An Investigation into the Uses of the Revelations of St Bridget of Sweden in Fifteenth-Century England', *Medium Aevum*, 51 (1982), pp. 163–86

Finnegan, Mary Jeremy, *The Women of Helfta: Scholars and Mystics* (Athens, GA: University of Georgia Press, 1991)

Gardner, Edmund G., *Dante and the Mystics: Study of the Mystical Aspect of the 'Divina Commedia' and its Relations with Some of its Mediaeval Sources* (London: Dent, 1913)

Gillespie, Vincent, '1412–1534: Culture and History', in *The Cambridge Companion to Medieval English Mysticism*, ed. by Samuel Fanous and Vincent Gillespie (Cambridge: Cambridge University Press, 2011), pp. 163–93

———, 'Chichele's Church', in *After Arundel: Religious Writing in Fifteenth-Century England*, ed. by Vincent Gillespie and Kantik Ghosh, Medieval Church Studies, 21 (Turhout: Brepols, 2011), pp. 3–42

———, 'The Haunted Text: Reflections in "The Mirrour to Deuote Peple"', in *Medieval Texts in Context*, ed. by Graham D. Caie and Denis Renevey (London: Routledge, 2008), pp. 136–66

———, 'The Mole in the Vineyard: Wyclif at Syon in the Fifteenth Century', in *Text and Controversy from Wyclif to Bale: Essays in Honour of Anne Hudson*, ed. by Helen Barr and Ann M. Hutchison, Medieval Church Studies, 4 (Turnhout: Brepols, 2005), pp. 131–61

Hellgardt, Ernst, 'Latin and the Vernacular: Mechthild of Magdeburg – Mechthild of Hackeborn – Gertrude of Helfta', in *A Companion to Mysticism and Devotion in Northern Germany in the Late Middle Ages*, ed. by Elizabeth Andersen, Henrike Lähnemann and Anne Simon, Brill's Companions to the Christian Tradition, 44 (Leiden: Brill, 2014), pp. 131–45

Hodgson, Phyllis, '"The Orcherd of Syon" and the English Mystical Tradition', in *Middle English Literature: British Academy Gllancz Lectures*, selected and introduction by J. A. Burrow (Oxford: Oxford University Press, 1989), pp. 71–91

Holsinger, Bruce W., *Music, Body, and Desire in Medieval Culture: Hildegard of Bingen to Chaucer* (Stanford, CA: University of California Press, 2001)

Horowitz, Maryanne Cline, *Seeds of Virtue and Knowledge* (Princeton: Princeton University Press, 1997)

The Idea of the Vernacular: An Anthology of Middle English Literary Theory, 1280–1520, ed. by Jocelyn Wogan-Browne and others, Exeter Medieval Texts and Studies (Exeter: University of Exeter Press, 1999)

Morris, Bridget, *St Birgitta of Sweden*, Studies in Medieval Mysticism, 1 (Woodbridge: Boydell, 1999)

Newman, Barbara, 'The Seven-Storey Mountain: Mechthild of Hackeborn and Dante's Matelda', in *Dante Studies*, 136 (2018), pp. 62–92

Schmidt, Margot, 'Mechthild von Hackeborn', in *Die deutsche Literatur des Mittelalters: Verfasserlexikon*, ed. by Kurt Ruh and others, 14 vols, 2nd edn (Berlin and New York: De Gruyter, 1978–2008), VI: *Marienberger Osterspiel – Oberdeutsche Bibeldrucke* (1987), pp. 253–60

A Short-Title Catalogue of Books Printed in England, Scotland and Ireland, and of Books Printed Abroad, 1475–1640 [*RSTC*], ed. by Alfred W. Pollard and Gilbert R. Redgrave, 2nd rev. edn, ed. by William A. Jackson and others, 3 vols (London: Bibliographical Society, 1976–91)

Spitzlei, Sabine B., *Erfahrungsraum Herz: Zur Mystik des Zisterzienserinnenklosters Helfta im 13. Jahrhundert*, Mystik in Geschichte und Gegenwart, 1: Christliche Mystik, 9 (Stuttgart-Bad Cannstatt: Frommann-Holzboog, 1991)

Teske, Roland, 'Augustine's Theory of Soul', in *The Cambridge Companion to Augustine*, ed. by Eleonore Stump and Norman Kretzmann (Cambridge: Cambridge University Press, 2001), pp. 116–23

Vettori, Alessandro, 'Dominicans', in *The Dante Encyclopedia*, ed. by Richard Lansing, Garland Reference Library of the Humanities, 1836 (New York: Garland, 2000)

Voaden, Rosalynn, 'The Company She Keeps: Mechtild of Hackeborn in Late-Medieval Devotional Compilations', in *Prophets Abroad: The Reception of Continental Holy Women in Late-Medieval England*, ed. by Rosalynn Voaden (Cambridge: Brewer, 1996), pp. 51–69

Watson, Nicholas, 'Introduction', in *The Cambridge Companion to Medieval English Mysticism*, ed. by Samuel Fanous and Vincent Gillespie (Cambridge: Cambridge University Press, 2011), pp. 1–27

Webb, Heather, *The Medieval Heart* (New Haven, CT: Yale University Press, 2010)

Whitehead, Christiania, *Castles of the Mind: A Study of Medieval Architectural Allegory*, Religion and Culture in the Middle Ages (Cardiff: University of Wales Press, 2003)

Woolgar, Christopher M., *The Senses in Late Medieval England* (New Haven, CT: Yale University Press, 2006)

Yoshikawa, Naoë Kukita, 'Heavenly Vision and Psychosomatic Healing: Medical Discourse in Mechtild of Hackeborn's "The Booke of Gostlye Grace"', in *Medicine,*

Religion and Gender, ed. by Naoë Kukita Yoshikawa, Gender in the Middle Ages, 11 (Cambridge: Brewer, 2015), pp. 67–84

———, 'Mechtild of Hackeborn and Cecily of Neville's Devotional Reading: Images of the Heart in Fifteenth-Century England', in *Revisiting the North: Interdisciplinary Approaches to the North of England*, ed. by Anita Auer and others (Cardiff: University of Wales Press, 2019), pp. 25–38

———, 'Mechthild of Hackeborn as Spiritual Authority: The Middle English Translation of the "Liber Specialis Gratiae"', in *Translation and Authority, Authorities in Translation: Proceedings of the Tenth Cardiff Conference on the Theory and Practice of Translation in the Middle Ages, University of Leuven, July 2013*, The Medieval Translator / Traduire au Moyen Âge, 16 (Turnhout: Brepols, 2016), pp. 241–54

———, 'The Virgin in the "Hortus conclusus": Healing the Body and Healing the Soul', *Medieval Feminist Forum: A Journal of Gender and Sexuality*, 50/11 (2014), pp. 11–32

The Social Function of a Translation

Earl Rivers, William Caxton, and the *Dicts and Sayings of the Philosophers*

Omar Khalaf

University of Padova

Earl Rivers's *Dicts and Sayings of the Philosophers*

The *Dicts and Sayings of the Philosophers* is one of the numerous gnomic collections that circulated in medieval England. It gathers proverbs, maxims, and teachings attributed to philosophers and legendary figures of the past on a rather arbitrary basis, as was usual practice in that kind of literature.[1] The origins of the *Dicts* are traced back to Arabic literature: Mubaschschir ben Fatik's *Mokhtâr el-hikam wa mahasin al-kalim* (*The Choicest Maxims and Best Sayings*), written in the eleventh century, was first translated into Spanish (*Bocados the oro*) in the thirteenth century, and about half a century later into Latin and called *Liber philosophorum moralium antiquorum*. In the fourteenth century, the *Liber* was translated into French as *Ditz moraulx des philosophes*. Its success in England was so large that four translations were produced in the second half of the fifteenth century. The first was made by Stephen Scrope in 1450 and revised by William Worcester around 1472. An independent translation was produced anonymously around 1460, followed in 1463 by another produced by George Ashby. Rivers's *Dicts*, published in 1477, marked the beginning of the Earl's patronage of William Caxton.

Despite its importance to the history of printing in England, Rivers's *Dicts* has never been studied in detail, and a comprehensive critical edition of the text has yet to be attempted. The only modern edition is a facsimile by William Blades, which does not include an examination of the textual tradition.[2] Elsewhere, Blades discussed the possible relationship between Rivers's and Scrope-Worcester's translations and concluded that the former 'may have cast a glance' at the work of the latter.[3] In his edition of Scrope-Worcester's version, Curt

---

1 Louis, 'Proverbs, Precepts, and Monitory Pieces', p. 2977.

2 *The Dictes*, ed. by Blades.

3 Blades, *The Biography and Typography of William Caxton*, II, p. 37. This position was later supported by Franceschini, *Il 'Liber philosophorum moralium antiquorum'*, pp. 390–91.

Bühler compared it with Rivers's *Dicts* and the anonymous version and convincingly demonstrated that each one is independent of the others. According to Bühler, the similarities spotted by Blades are ascribed to the fact that 'Rivers and Scrope made their translations from very similar French manuscripts', but some faulty readings of the source recorded in Scrope-Worcester's version and not in Rivers's hint at the fact that the latter did not base his translation on the former.[4] In fact, Rivers himself gives an account of how he came to know of the *Ditz Moraulx*. According to his Prologue to Caxton's edition, on his way to Santiago de Compostela in 1473 the Earl was given a copy of the French text and, once back in England, he started working on a translation that could be useful for the education of his nephew Edward, the Prince of Wales.[5]

Only recently has the *Dicts* been the object of some scholarly attention; Nicholas Orme contextualizes it within the late fifteenth-century English educative background, which benefited greatly from Caxton's press and his investment in the growing market of vernacular books.[6] Anne Coldiron also referred to the work as an example of the cultural dynamics underlying late fifteenth-century patronage, focusing on what she calls the 'recalibration of authority' in Caxton's revision of the text prior to the publication of the first edition at Rivers's request.[7] Noticing that his patron had omitted a misogynistic section attributed to Socrates, Caxton decided to place his own translation of the passage in the epilogue:

> I haue put me in deuoyr to ouersee this hys sayd booke and beholden as nyghe as I coude howe it accordeth wyth thoriygnal being in Frensh. And I finde nothing dyscordaunt therin, sauf onely in the dyctes of Socrates, wherin I fynde that my sayde lord hath left out certain and dyuerce conclusions towchyng women. [...] Therfore in accomplishing his comandement [...] I purpose to wryte the same saynges of theat Greke Socrates.[8]

Coldiron interprets Caxton's intervention as the result of a struggle for authority between the translator-patron and the printer, where the latter prevails as better able to anticipate the tastes of the readers: 'the absence-presence of these misogynies keeps in view the issues of translator-printer rights and roles and the reader's, not the patron's, final sovereignty over the material book'.[9] This position is entirely consistent with the view of the *Dicts* as a work designed for the printing press and addressed to a large public made of members of the gentry.[10] Although Coldiron's assumption is heavily influenced by the general view of

---

4 *The Dicts*, ed. by Bühler, p. li.

5 *The Dictes*, ed. by Blades, pp. [2]–[3].

6 Orme, 'Schools and School-Books'.

7 Coldiron, *Printers without Borders*.

8 The Prologues and Epilogues, ed. by Crotch, p. 20.

9 Coldiron, *Printers without Borders*, pp. 75–76.

10 See Orme, 'Schools and School-Books'.

Caxton as a skilled salesman, the relationship between Caxton and Rivers should rather be considered in that context of patronage characterizing the early stages of printed book production in England. As Lotte Hellinga points out, the risky economic investment that Caxton had to face favoured cases of sponsorship from patrons 'who recognized the power of print in disseminating texts, whatever their practical or spiritual motives'.[11] This is the case of Rivers, who acted as a sponsor for Caxton in his early years at Westminster and encouraged the publication of several works; along with the *Dicts*, the *Moral Proverbs* and the *Cordyal*, which he authored, the Earl is also thought to have prompted the publication of Malory's *Morte Darthur* and the translations of Alain Chartier's *Curial* of works by Cicero, and even the first edition of the *Canterbury Tales*.[12] The *Dicts* represents the first and most ambitious of these undertakings and here Rivers appears to have been fully involved in the editorial process, from the production of the work to its publication. Apart from being the first dated book printed on English soil,[13] the *Dicts* holds the record for the number of editions published in the first years of Caxton's activity at Westminster; the 1477 edition, in fact, was followed by another in c. 1480 and yet another in 1489.[14] Important reasons seem to have prompted Rivers to seek a wider readership, ask for Caxton's help, and sponsor the publication of the *Dicts*, as will be argued below.

Rivers's *Dicts* in Late Fifteenth-Century England

The concept of patronage and its relationship with book production in late medieval and early modern England has been investigated extensively, especially in recent times.[15] In this context, Margaret L. Ford underlines the importance

---

11 *Catalogue of Books Printed in the XVth Century Now in the British Library*, XI, ed. by Hellinga, p. 55.

12 For the *Morte Darthur*, see Hellinga and Kelliher, 'The Malory Manuscript'; Hellinga, 'The Malory Manuscript and Caxton'; Kelliher, 'The Early History of the Malory Manuscript'; Hellinga, *Caxton in Focus*, pp. 89–94; Kato, *Caxton's 'Morte Darthur'*. For the *Curyal*, see Blake, *Caxton and his World*, p. 94 and Kuskin, *Symbolic Caxton*, pp. 156–61. For Cicero, see Painter, *William Caxton*, pp. 113–14. For the *Canterbury Tales*, see Hellinga, *Caxton in Focus*, p. 101.

13 The incunable of the first edition held at Manchester John Ryland's Library, reports a colophon indicating 18 November 1477. However, as Hellinga convincingly demonstrated, this date should be considered as referred to that specific copy and not to the first edition in general, which was probably issued earlier. Hellinga, *Caxton in Focus*, pp. 77–80.

14 They collectively count twenty-five incunables. See Hellinga, *Printing in England in the Fifteenth Century*; another edition was published by Wynkyn De Worde in 1528.

15 See Wakelin, *Humanism, Reading and English Literature 1430–1530* and *Translation and Print Culture in Early Modern Europe*, ed. by Hosington. Furthermore, Hosington and Belle, 'Translation, History, and Print', propose a model for the analysis of

of book ownership as a mark of social prestige, for both those who commissioned the printing and distribution of volumes and their owners.[16] One of those early English books was undoubtedly the *Dicts*. As Hellinga argues, Rivers's interest in having texts circulated in printed form and Caxton's attempted connections with the English court demonstrated by *The Recueyl of the Histories of Troye* and *The Play and Game of the Chess*, dedicated, respectively, to Margaret of York and George, duke of Clarence, could have been the causes of the printer's instalment at Westminster.[17] Of course, Rivers was only the first of Caxton's recognized patrons, but no evidence of the economic involvement by any of them is extant;[18] we do not know if they made financial contributions at the outset of the publication process or committed to buying at least part of the print run. In any case, Rivers's patronage stands out as the longest and most prolific – a patronage that, at least in the case of the *Dicts*, seems to be instigated by reasons that go beyond the Earl's mere philanthropic initiative, but involves dynamics related to his social affirmation and the creation of political networks with gentry members in support of the Woodville's politics.

The gentry has a paramount role in this analysis as it is the readership to whom the *Dicts* was primarily addressed.[19] The role this social class was called to play in the management of the English kingdom from the second half of the

---

earlymodern English printed translations. Based on Robert Darnton's communicative circuit and its subsequent revisions, their model introduces the category of patronage as an activity that was fundamental in late medieval England for both the introduction of ex novo literary instances (such as Duke Humphrey's activity of importation of Humanism) and the consolidation of an already existing canon through the patron's support in the production and distribution of certain texts. A thorough study of Humphrey, Duke of Gloucester, as a patron is offered in Petrina, *Cultural Politics in Fifteenth-Century England*.

16 'Prestigious patronage certainly influenced the ownership of the early English books, both directly through distribution of sponsored books, and indirectly through prestige placed on such ownership. Book ownership was an attribute of high social status'. Ford, 'Private Ownership of Printed Books', p. 218. See also Youngs, 'Cultural Networks', p. 119: 'The book was an important accessory to the gentry lifestyle. Despite the commercialisation of the manuscript/book trade in the fifteenth century, the book remained a luxury good and a symbol of affluence'.

17 *Catalogue of Books Printed in the XVth Century Now in the British Library*, xi, ed. by Hellinga, p. 57.

18 'Fifteen works are either dedicated to royals or were sponsored by aristocrats, three were produced for fellow merchants, and one was commissioned for a high-ranking civil servant'. *Catalogue of Books Printed in the XVth Century Now in the British Library*, xi, ed. by Hellinga, p. 57.

19 On the differentiation of the readership of the *Dicts* according its physical support – prints for the gentry, manuscripts for nobles, see *Catalogue of Books Printed in the XVth Century Now in the British Library*, xi, ed. by Hellinga, p. 57. However, as will be shown below, this distinction is not clear-cut.

fifteenth century is nowadays widely recognized;[20] in particular, critics have underlined the social change prompted by the access of the members of the gentry to positions at court that were previously reserved for the nobility. Edward IV was one of the staunchest supporters of this policy, as he was trying to dismiss nobles who had favoured Henry VI during the War of the Roses and replace them with more loyal people, and the Woodvilles were to benefit the most from this situation.[21]

The shift from agricultural activities to urban commerce and the opening of new positions at court determined an increasing demand for education and, consequently, for books. In this light, the role of the printed book as a *status symbol* and material evidence of social achievement is just one side of the coin. As Ford argues, books were widely sought by members of the gentry as the habit of reading works of edification as well as entertainment had become integral part of their lifestyles.[22] Their social aspirations were also nourished by the access to a kind of literature which was no longer prerogative of the higher nobility or the court circle, but, thanks to their serial production in printed form, had a larger circulation.[23] The *Dicts* is one of the earliest printed books the gentry could access, and, looking at the number of published editions (three by Caxton and, one by De Worde in 1528), one of the most successful. Only the first two editions were produced during Rivers's lifetime. Compared with the other texts published by Caxton during his first years at Westminster, the twenty extant incunables of the *Dicts* represent one of the longest print-runs as they are second only to the abovementioned first edition of the *Canterbury Tales* (1476/77), which counts seventy-six copies, and, despite Rivers's possible back-

20 See, for example, the essays collected in *Gentry Culture in Late Medieval England*, ed. by Radulescu and Truelove; Salter, *Popular Reading in English, c. 1400–1600*, and Johnston, *Romance and the Gentry in Late Medieval England*.

21 After Elizabeth's marriage to Edward IV in 1464, his father Richard was created Earl Rivers and constable of England and entered the royal council. Elizabeth's brother John married the Duchess of Norfolk, aunt of that Richard Neville, Duke of Warwick who would have him and his father beheaded in 1469, after the temporary breakdown of the Yorkists following the battle of Edgecote Moore. Finally, Anthony, who succeeded his father as Earl Rivers, was appointed Lieutenant of Calais and Governor to the Prince of Wales. This position gave Rivers total control of the young Edward. At the king's death in 1483, Richard of York, Duke of Gloucester and brother of the king, took the custody of Edward and had Rivers beheaded. Later in the same year he was crowned Richard III, and, according to the tradition, he was the responsible for the death of Edward and his brother Richard, held in the tower of London.

22 Ford, 'Private Ownership of Printed Books', p. 218.

23 In this respect, Orme writes: 'The medieval gentry […] read about education in didactic literature, meaning literature whose purpose was to instruct. A large category of writings, nowadays known as "mirrors for princes" described how kings and nobles should be educated and what they should learn about. […] Not only royalty read it; its many versions and manuscripts show that it was popular among the nobility and gentry'. Orme, 'Education and Recreation', p. 66.

ing, is generally seen as Caxton's first great investment in the English book market.[24] In the absence of documentary evidence on the expenses for the publication of the *Dicts*, the only available information comes from Caxton's epilogue. The production and distribution of the text seem to be the result of a genuine act of patronage, and Caxton's references to Rivers seem to be different from the promotional strategies adopted by the printer in other circumstances. Caxton himself admits that Rivers acted as a conscious and economically active patron to him, as suggested in the following passage of the epilogue:

> [I managed] to take the labour of thenpryntyng in gre & thanke, whiche gladly haue don my dylygence in thaccomplysshyng of his desire and commandement, in whiche I am bounden so to do for the good reward that I haue resseyuyd of his sayd lordship.[25]

Rivers's activity as translator and his sponsorship of Caxton seem to meet the literacy needs manifested by the gentry, a readership that Caxton privileged over others. The printer, in fact, was barely interested in school and university readers, and preferred to concentrate on the household market. Orme counts thirteen household educational works in English printed by Caxton in several editions. Apart from the *Dicts* we might recall the abovementioned *Game and Play of the Chess*, the *Distichs of Cato*, the translation of the *Stans puer ad mensam*, and the *Book of the Knight of the Tower*, all of which were addressed to an audience made mostly of members of the gentry, rather than school or university students.[26] Easier access to culture made possible by the printing press determined a development of the gentry's self-perception as relevant actors in English society, which was boosted by the feeling that they could own works traditionally reserved to the nobility and the court. As in the case of the *Dicts*, the opportunity to have a copy of an educational work expressly produced for the Prince of Wales served two different purposes: on the one hand, it contributed to infuse useful concepts into the minds of the future managing class of the kingdom; on the other hand, the ownership of that book had an iconic value related to its function as 'social object' as it contains a work that comes, allegedly, from the royal library.

If Rivers really decided to invest in Caxton and his press, it was not for a monetary profit. No mentions of business partnerships between Rivers and Caxton are documented and the information found in the Earl's exchanges with his secretary Andrew Dymmock refers to his investments in timber and other goods, but not in publishing;[27] in this context, rather than being economic, the Earl's venture in book production was symbolic. As Ann Astell points out, the value of a medieval book could also be estimated 'in its symbolic status as a

---

24 See among others Hellinga, *Caxton in Focus*, p. 84. For a count of the extant incunables, see Hellinga, *Printing in England in the Fifteenth Century*.

25 *The Prologues and Epilogues*, ed. by Crotch, p. 20.

26 Orme, 'Schools and School-Books', p. 467.

27 Ives, 'Andrew Dymmock and the Papers of Antony, Earl Rivers, 1482–3', pp. 219.

unique gift between persons'.[28] Based on the assumptions of Derrida and others, Astell argues that the book acquires a value as a gift not just as a material object, but for the wisdom it contains. The donor-recipient transfer involves the book as an artefact, sometimes of high material value, but also as a container of knowledge that the author bestows upon the reader. Although Astell refers to a predominantly religious context, the concept of symbolic value can also be applied to the *Dicts* and Rivers's patronage of Caxton. In 1477 printed books were still seen as a novelty in England; incunables were being largely imported from the continent and Caxton had just installed himself at Westminster after producing a very limited stock of books in English when in Bruges. This means that very few titles published before the *Dicts* circulated in England and this, in addition to the social standing of its author and the alleged recipient of the work, might have exerted a fascination on gentry readers. The use and, more importantly, the possession and exchange of books determined the creation of cultural and social networks among individuals and families, like the circles gravitating around John Fastolf and the Paston and Haute families.[29] The development of such connections determined the creation of spheres of influence that involved all the figures relating to book production: authors (or translators), patrons, printers, and users. In this context, Rivers played an undisputable role as translator-patron and a member of the royal family. Being the first to exploit the potential provided by the printing press in England, the Earl became the centre of this system by promoting – and, perhaps, managing himself? – the distribution of his translations. Rivers's initiative can represent a step in the creation of his own social network and influence sphere.

As the first edition appeared four years after Rivers's reception of the book on the way to Santiago, Rivers might have conceived his plan after producing a translation for Prince Edward. However, the evidence at our disposal tends to discredit the original, 'private' purpose of the *Dicts*. The final passage of the Epilogue is rather telling in this respect; here, Rivers apologizes in advance for any possible faults found by readers familiar with the French or the Latin version of the text:

> I drede that suche as shold liste to rede the translacion & haue veray intelligence of ony of thoos bookes, eyther in latyne or in frenche sholde fynde errours in my werke, whiche I wold not afferme cause of the contrary, but allegge the deffaulte to myn unconnyng, with the dyuersytees of the bookes, humbly desyryng the reformacion therof with mys excuse, and the rather syn after my rudeness not expert.[30]

Rivers's *excusatio* and the account of the genesis of his translation is addressed to a general reading public, certainly not to his nephew. Since the Earl's holograph is lost and the surviving manuscripts are all demonstrably copies of Cax-

---

28 Astell, 'On the Usefulness and Use Value of Books', p. 47.
29 See in particular Ford, 'Private Ownership of Printed Books', p. 213.
30 *The Dictes*, ed. by Blades, p. [3].

ton's editions, it cannot be excluded a priori that Rivers had worked on his translation for a wider readership from the outset.

Moreover, a rather underestimated aspect in the study of the *Dicts* concerns the chronological coincidence of the revision of Scrope's *Dicts* by Worcester and Rivers's own work. Apart from excluding any possible influence of the Scrope-Worcester's translation on Rivers's, Bühler also observed that Scrope, Worcester, and the Earl belonged to the same social and cultural network that gravitated around Edward IV's court.[31] Bühler suggests a personal connection between Rivers and the Fastolf circle through a legal dispute that involved Worcester and Rivers for the possession of the castle of Caister, but he concludes that this had no impact on the making of Rivers's *Dicts*.[32] However, the situation sketched by Bühler has more profound consequences for Rivers's cultural policy and his patronage of Caxton than might appear at a first glance.

The Woodvilles had connections with Fastolf and his household since Lancastrian times. In 1421 both Fastolf and Rivers's grandfather, Richard Woodville, fought in France under the command of the regent John of Lancaster, Duke of Bedford, brother of Henry V.[33] Richard's namesake son also was in debt to Fastolf, as reported in one of John Paston's letters,[34] but the affinity between the two households must have been relatively close if at the death of Fastolf Rivers was a claimant for the castle of Caister. Worcester was one of the executors of Fastolf's will and firmly opposed any alien claims to his former master's properties. This caused Rivers to argue with a number of noble families including the Pastons, and the dispute was resolved only when John Paston became engaged to Rivers's cousin, Anne Haute, in 1469; Rivers then officially withdrew all his claims to the estate and tried to support the Pastons. Although in 1466 the king had secured Caister and other former Fastolf properties for the Pastons, in 1468 Caister was enfeoffed to the Duke of Norfolk. In the face of resistance from the Pastons, in 1469 Norfolk placed the castle under siege and eventually occupied it. John Paston regained possession of Caister only after Norfolk's death in 1476, thanks to Worcester's support, rather than Rivers's, as is clear from Paston's correspondence.[35]

Although no evidence survives of legal disputes between Rivers and Worcester, the Caister affair strongly suggests that they knew each other directly, and textual evidence shows that their relationship was rather unfriendly. Worcester is negative about the Woodvilles in his *Annals*, where he reports that in December 1464 Edward IV held a council at Westminster where Queen Elizabeth was granted lands and goods for the value of 4000 marks. Here Worcester adds

---

31 *The Dicts*, ed. by Bühler, pp. xlvii–lix.

32 *The Dicts*, ed. by Bühler, pp. xxxvii–xxxviii.

33 The Woodvilles' allegiance to Bedford continued with Richard's son Richard. After the Duke's death he married his widow, Jacquetta of Luxemburg, the mother of Anthony, Earl Rivers, and of Elizabeth, who would become Edward IV's queen.

34 *Paston Letters*, ed. by Davis, p. 189.

35 *Paston Letters*, ed. by Davis, p. 322.

laconically: 'et quod ipsa viveret cum familia sua ad expensas domini regis' (and there she will live with her family at the expense of the king);[36] even more revealing is his sarcastic comment about the marriage held in January 1465 between Rivers's brother John Woodville and Katherine Neville, Duchess of Norfolk, thirty-five years older than the groom, which Worcester defined 'maritagium diabolicum' (a diabolic marriage), and the violent criticism of the creation of Richard Woodville as Earl Rivers in the same year, 'ob honorem reginae et displicentiam communis regni' (for the Queen's honour and the discontent of the kingdom).[37]

The hostility between Rivers and Worcester seems also to involve the literary sphere. The existence of a common cultural environment in which Rivers, Caxton, and Worcester worked has already been hinted at by William Kuskin, who identifies some parallels between Rivers and what he calls 'the Caister's circle' in terms of the authors they chose to translate, as both privileged Christine de Pizan and Alain Chartier.[38] What might be branded as a mere coincidence, in fact, was rooted in a more complex socio-political situation that saw the main intellectual representatives of both households – Rivers and Worcester – committed in a literary standoff that had seemingly important consequences for the first phases of printed book production in England. May Rivers's *Dicts* have worked as a 'cultural weapon' for the Earl to claim his *auctoritas* over the Fastolf circle, and more specifically over Worcester, where he was unable to exert political authority?

The Caister affair underlines Rivers's lack of political power, despite his prominent position at court and his family connections. From the accession of Queen Elizabeth Woodville to the throne he took part directly in the management of the kingdom as a member of the Royal Council and as Guardian of his nephew the Prince of Wales, but he appears never to have succeeded in acquiring the political influence that could have helped him to secure his own position and further his interests.[39] Rivers did not always enjoy the king's full trust; for example, in 1471 Edward IV revoked his control of Calais in favour of Lord Hastings and forced him to resign from his post as Constable of England. Moreover, Rivers was not as skilled as his father and sister in advancing through marriages.

---

36 *Letters and Papers*, ed. by Stevenson, p. 783.

37 *Letters and Papers*, ed. by Stevenson, pp. 783, 785.

38 'Both translate a version of the *Dictes*, texts by Christine de Pizan (Woodville translates the *Morale Prouerbes*; Scrope, the *L'Epitre d'Othéa à Hector*, and Worcester, selections of *Le livre des faits d'armes et de chevalerie*) and Chartier (Scrope, *La belle dame sans merci*; Caxton, the *Curial*)'. Kuskin, *Symbolic Caxton*, p. 173.

39 Caister was not the only unsuccessful claim by Rivers. He charged Dymmock with exploring the possibility of laying claims to Lady Roos's lands and to the rights of Lord Dudley and Henry Porpoynt. The scarcity of personal properties and incomes heavily jeopardized his economic situation: his letter exchanges with Dymmock clearly demonstrate that he was continually in need of raising money. See Pidgeon, 'Anthony Woodville, Part 1', Pidgeon, 'Anthony Woodville, Part 2', and Ives, 'Andrew Dymmock and the Papers of Antony, Earl Rivers, 1482–3'.

After the death of his former wife, from whom he inherited the title of Baron Scales, he was involved by King Edward in marriage negotiations with Mary of Burgundy and Margaret of Scotland. Probably the king had intended to use him as a mere diplomatic pawn, as both proposals eventually failed.[40]

On the other hand, Rivers had the opportunity to cultivate more spiritual and intellectual interests. Apart from pilgrimages to Santiago in 1473 and Rome in 1476[41] and chivalric exploits – his tournament with the Bastard of Burgundy was celebrated both in England and in the Continent – literature was one of his major accomplishments, as demonstrated by his activity as translator.[42] Worcester also had literary interests. Daniel Wakelin describes him as a major representative of humanism in the third quarter of the fifteenth century.[43] His interests ranged from astronomy, to history, to geography. Apart from the extensive revision of Scrope's translation of the *Dicts* and his abovementioned *Annals*, he also helped edit a chronicle in French of the Hundred Years War, compiled for Fastolf in 1459. His own writings also include a lost life of Fastolf, known as *Acta domini Johannis Fastolf*. However, his most ambitious work was *The Boke of Noblesse*, begun in 1451 and revised between 1472 and 1475, and dedicated to Edward IV, urging him to resume the campaign to conquer France started by his Lancastrian predecessors, and in which Fastolf had himself seen action. As this demonstrates Worcester's connections to the cultural circle that gravitated around the English court, the possibility that Rivers had heard about – and perhaps even had access to – Worcester's literary endeavours, including his version of the *Dicts*, should be considered realistic.

Rivers's *Dicts*: Social Weapon and Political Token

If Rivers was acquainted with Fastolf and his kinsmen, the same can be said of Caxton. A hint of the connection between the printer and Worcester is given by the publication in 1481 of Worcester's *Tullius of Olde Age*, a translation of Cicero's *De senectute*. In the Prologue, Caxton presents this work as being translated from French at Fastolf's request but he does not reveal the identity of the translator;[44] catalogue entries of the incunables argue that, as happened with the *Dicts*, it was translated by Scrope and then revised by Worcester. If that is the case, Caxton might have deliberately omitted the identity of the translators for

---

40 See Pidgeon, 'Antony Wydevile, Part 2', p. 4.

41 On that occasion the pope appointed him 'Defendeur and directour of the siege apostolique for our Holy Father the Pope in this Royaume of Englond', as Caxton reports in the epilogue to the *Dicts*; *The Prologues and Epilogues*, ed. by Crotch, p. 18.

42 In the epilogue to the *Cordyal*, Caxton also attributes to Rivers the composition of 'diuerse balades ayenst the seuen dedely synnes' which are now lost. *Prologues and Epilogues*, ed. by Crotch, p. 39.

43 Wakelin, *Humanism, Reading and English Literature*, pp. 93–125.

44 *Prologues and Epilogues*, ed. by Crotch, pp. 41–44.

Rivers's sake. However, the publication of this work raises some questions concerning the nature of the relationship between Caxton and Rivers from 1481. The 1480 edition of the *Dicts*, in fact, is the last evidence of their collaboration. Might the printed *Tullius* suggest a loosening of their professional relationship? The information provided in the prologue inhibits any possible speculation that the work was among those Ciceronian texts of which Rivers allegedly encouraged the publication. In fact, Caxton makes clear that it had no patronage, as he had trouble in obtaining the book and personally bore the expenses for the supervision and the printing of the work:

> For as moche as this book thus reduced in to our englyssh is with grete instaunce, labour & coste comen in to myn honde, which I aduysed to haue seen, ouer redde [...] I haue endevoured me to gete it with grete difficulte, and so goten, haue put it in enprynte.[45]

The fact that Worcester was still alive in 1481, on the contrary, implies that he had contacts with Caxton and that both might be involved in difficult negotiations concerning the print and publication of the work. Besides possible controversies between Caxton and Worcester, if the printer knew that Worcester was the author of the *Tullius*, he might also be aware of other works of his, including his revision of Scrope's *Dicts*. In this regard, other passages from Rivers's prologue of the *Dicts* deserve attention. Here, Rivers recounts that he was unaware of the *Ditz moraulx* until it was given to him ('whiche book I had neuer seen before') and that he decided to translate it because it had never been turned into English before then ('I [...] concluded in my self to translate it in thenglyssh tonge, whiche in my iugement was not before').[46] Although this phrase may express a well-established cliché,[47] there is no similar statement in the prologues to the other texts of Rivers's – the *Cordyal* and the *Moral Proverbs* – all of them translated into English for the very first time. In the epilogue, Caxton also makes this point:

> I fonde many grete, notable & wyse sayengis of the philosophres acordyng unto the bookes made in Frenshe whiche I had ofte afore redd, *but certaynly I had seen none in English til that tyme* [my emphasis].

Caxton's comment refers in general to all the collections of *dicta philosophorum* circulating in Europe, including the *Ditz Moraulx*. In the *Recueyl*, too, Caxton insists on the novelty of his book in both the prologue and the epilogue and, curiously enough, in the *Tullius* itself.[48] In the former case, if associated with the

---

45 *The Prologues and Epilogues*, ed. by Crotch, p. 42.

46 *The Dictes*, ed. by Blades, pp. [2]–[3].

47 See Ellis, 'Patronage and Sponsorship of Translations', p. 101.

48 In the Prologue to the *Recueyl* we read: 'And for so moche as as this booke was newe and late maad and drawen in to Frensshe and neuer had seen it in oure Englissh tongue, I thought in myself hit shold be a good besynes to translate hyt in to oure Englissh, to thende that hyt myght be had as well in the royame of Englond as in other lands'. Similarly, in the *Tullius* Caxton states: 'By cause I haue not seen ony of the same here to

probably fake patronage of the book by Margaret of York, this claim reveals an obvious marketing move, which would be typical of Caxton's activity as publisher. Regarding the *Tullius*, Caxton simply wrote the truth, as this was the first English translation of that work. In the case of the *Dicts*, however, this statement arguably acquires a different meaning. If Caxton was aware of Scrope-Worcester's *Dicts*, the printer could have used an already-tested marketing strategy for the benefit of his magnate in an attempt to outshine Worcester's literary activity.

Consequently, what Bühler mentioned as a mere coincidence might be the result of specific sociocultural dynamics. If Rivers was too weak politically to assert himself against Fastolf's household and especially Worcester in the Caister matter, he had the upper hand when it came to literary production and dissemination, where he prevailed thanks to his closeness to the royal family and his patronage of Caxton. Print technology gave Rivers the opportunity to consolidate his social position through the circulation of his own work. Rather than economic, this was a political investment made by Rivers. The circulation of his *Dicts* and, consequently, the overshadowing of Worcester's version might represent a suitable element of affirmation for the Earl, lacking the influence and power to succeed in the claim for Caister, but superior to his opponent from a social and economical point of view to afford the expenses for the publication of printed copies of his work. Caxton's serial production and distribution of the books among the gentry benefited both the reading audience and Rivers himself, who was guaranteed a position of undisputed *auctoritas* in the court of Edward IV.

Apart from the rivalry with Worcester, Rivers's patronage of Caxton could also find a more pragmatic explanation, related to the consolidation of political connections favourable to the Woodvilles. What Rutter considered 'a vanity press, for printing [Rivers's] own translations and other favourite books',[49] could, in fact, become an instrument of propaganda exploited for the Earl's household interests. As a member of a much-hated family, he needed political support also outside the court; several letters to Dymmock reveal Rivers's concern to influence the elections of Norfolk members of parliament,[50] and one cannot exclude that his patronage of Caxton and the distribution of copies of the *Dicts* was also aimed at creating a cultural-political network based on his prestige that could favour political support by members of the gentry.

If the above speculations are true, the *Dicts* turned into a formidable symbolic weapon for Rivers to assert his social position and literary authority against

---

fore, I haue ende[u]ored to gete it [...] and so goten, haue put it in enprynte'. *The Prologues and Epilogues*, ed. by Crotch, respectively p. 2, p. 42.

49 Rutter, 'William Caxton and Literary Patronage', p. 448.

50 Ives, 'Andrew Dymmock and the Papers of Antony, Earl Rivers, 1482–3', p. 222. Apart from John Woodville's marriage to Katherine Neville, further evidence of the family's interests in Norfolk is suggested by Rivers's marriage to his second wife Mary, the heiress of Henry FitzLewis, a Norfolk tenant, which probably favoured the spreading of the influence of the Woodvilles in that area.

Worcester and the Caister circle, and, at the same time, a token to be exploited for the creation of favourable social and political connections. The evidence relating to the early owners of the *Dicts* seems to confirm this view. Following Ford's statement that 'many owners of Caxton's books were related or acquainted',[51] one should expect that those who possessed copies of the *Dicts*,[51] can be connected to Rivers or his family. In fact, an incunable copy of the second edition was owned by Oliver St John, Baron Bletsoe of Bedfordshire, who was related to Eleanor, wife of Thomas Grey, another of Queen Elizabeth's sons from her first marriage.[52] A copy of the second edition held at the Huntington Library, San Marino, California, contains the signature of a certain 'Joh[ann]es Sherman', who can be identified with John Sherman, 'fyshemonger of Norwyche' mentioned in one of John Paston III's letters to his father in 1469.[53] Although no further evidence of him is extant, Sherman's ownership of one of the copies of the *Dicts* suggests his involvement in Rivers's political network as one of the Woodvilles' possible candidates to the House of Commons.

In addition, some of the seven existing manuscripts,[54] all copied from the printed editions, bear valuable information about the widespread circulation of Rivers's text, either as abridgements or full reproductions. One of them is extant in New York, Columbia University Library, MS Plimpton 259 (fols 54^r–61^v), a multilingual collection compiled by Robert Gottes, who was also the first owner of the manuscript. Gottes was a member of the Norfolk gentry contemporary with Rivers, as recorded in documents dating 1475, 1477, and 1478,[55] which might suggest that he was, too, part of the abovementioned political circle. This version

---

51 Ford, 'Private Ownership of Printed Books', p. 213.

52 London, British Library, C.10.b. 2. See *Catalogue of Books Printed in the XVth Century Now in the British Library*, XI, ed. by Hellinga, pp. 115–16; Ford, 'Private Ownership of Printed Books', p. 214. A copy of the *Dicts* also appears among the books owned by James Morice, clerk to Lady Margaret Beaufort, in a list he wrote in his copy of the 1481 edition of Worcester's translation of *De senectute*, now held at Cambridge University Library. The catalogue includes a Life of Christ, the *Stans puer ad mensam* (probably in translation), Lydgate's *Temple of Glass* and the *Canterbury Tales*. Unfortunately, it is not possible to determine which edition of the *Dicts* Morice owned and whether it was purchased or bequeathed. As the list dates *c.* 1506, the copy may be any of Caxton's three editions. However, the case is interesting as it demonstrates that the owners of these incunables were involved in social and cultural networks connected, albeit indirectly, with the Woodvilles. After King Henry VII's accession, Lady Margaret became Queen Elizabeth of York's mother-in-law and, consequently, in-law of late queen Elizabeth Woodville. See Oates, 'English Bokes Concernyng to James Morice'.

53 *Paston Letters*, ed. by Davis, p. 549.

54 London, Lambeth Palace Library, MS 265; London, British Library, MS Add. 60577, fols 38^r–44^v; London, British Library, MS Add. 22718; Chicago, Newberry Library, MS f. 36 Ry 20, fols 208–41; Dublin, Trinity College Library, MS 213, fols 70^v–72^r; New York, Columbia University Library, MS Plimpton 259, fols 79^r–86^v; New York, Pierpont Morgan Library, MS B.11.

55 Khalaf, 'An Epitome', 3–4; Acker, 'The "Crafte of Nombrynge"', pp. 78–79, n. 7.

of the *Dicts* does not exclude the fact that Gottes had a printed version of it, donated by Rivers, in his library. As the manuscript is a typical commonplace book which collects proverbs in Latin, some accounts of Gottes himself, *The words of a good horse to his master*, a Latin poem on the seven ages of man, an incomplete copy of Gerald of Wales' *De regimine mundi* and Saint Bernard's *De contemptu mundi*, three short religious poems and a mathematical treatise,[56] the epitome could be the result of Gottes' desire to dispose of texts he deemed interesting or necessary in the same place and have them handy, perhaps when travelling.

Another abridgement of the *Dicts* is extant in Chicago, Newberry Library, Vault Folio Case MS 36 (fols 208^r–41^r).[57] Produced in Lincoln 'per dominum J. Clynton priorem' around 1480,[58] the manuscript could be linked to an unrecorded member of the family of John, sixth baron Clinton (*c.* 1429–88). His father John was a Yorkist and after the re-establishment of Edward IV in 1461 he was restored to the family's title.[59] The common allegiance in the War of the Roses makes Rivers's acquaintance with John the elder and John the younger certain. One might speculate that prior Clinton had had access to an incunable of the *Dicts* in the family library possibly bestowed by Rivers himself, and, once in Lincoln, he wanted a copy to be kept in his diocese.

The full copies were made for nobler readers. The one held in London, British Library, MS Add. 22718 includes several entries of birth dates of members of the Hill family of Spaxton, Somerset. The most relevant is Maud Hill, born in 1505. Her mother Alice was a member of the Stourton household, a gentry family that was related to the court due to the kinship of Alice's uncle William and John de la Pole, Duke of Suffolk and husband of Elizabeth, Edward IV's sister. However, the more interesting manuscript is London, Lambeth Palace Library, MS 256. The text is still imperfect, as it is a copy of Caxton's first edition containing only a small number of the emendations and revisions present in the second. Presented to the royal family as a New Year's gift on Christmas Eve, 1477, this book still claims the greater prestige of manuscripts over printed books, at least in court;[60] in fact, like MS Add. 22718, it reproduces Caxton's edition in full and even reports the epilogue with the printer's addition of the Socrates passages and all references made to the printing process. The famous illumination on the first

---

56 Bühler, 'New Manuscripts of the "Dicts and Sayings of the Philosophers"'. See also Ives, 'Corrigenda and Addenda to the Descriptions of the Plimpton Manuscripts as Recorded in the De Ricci Census', p. 45.

57 *Olim* Chicago, Newberry Library, MS f. 36 Ry 20.

58 A Catalogue of the Pre-1500 Western Manuscript Books at the Newberry Library, ed. by Saenger, p. 66.

59 Burke, A Genealogical and Heraldic Dictionary of the Peerage and Baronetage of the British Empire, p. 223.

60 'The introduction of printing into England, as elsewhere, did not lead to any swift and decisive displacement of the manuscript. [...] And there are grounds for believing that, at least in the eyes of some, the manuscript was perceived to possess the higher status'. Edwards and Meale, 'The Marketing of Printed Books in Late Medieval England', p. 95.

leaf depicting Rivers kneeling before the royal family and handing them the manuscript provides a pictorial, concrete representation of his literary *auctoritas*, intended to be recognized at all social layers, from the gentry to the king.

Favouring the circulation of his translation in both manuscript and printed form, Rivers was able to reach as broad an audience as possible: the gentry through his patronage of Caxton and, using a more traditional mode of textual transmission, the court – the circle Worcester was craving to be part of. The official presentation of his own work to the king in his capacity as Governor to his heir, the Prince of Wales, represented one of the highest accomplishments for a person more versed in literature than in politics, and perhaps (or just for this reason) the most emphatic response to Worcester.

The connections between owners of incunables and manuscripts of the *Dicts* and its author justify the existence of a 'Rivers circle', whose extent is rather difficult to appreciate, but which, at least in the Earl's intentions, could compete with Fastolf and other individuals or households. In this sense, his investment in Caxton's press proved successful. Whether a cultural weapon or a political token, the extensive circulation of the *Dicts* outshone all previous versions, including Worcester's, which is only found in two manuscripts.[61] The incidents of 1483 and the political overturn following Richard III's coup did not allow Rivers and his household to reap the benefits of this initiative, but Rivers's patronage of Caxton had important consequences for the development of printing in late medieval and early modern England.

Bibliography

Manuscripts Sources

Cambridge, Cambridge University Library, MS Gg.I.34.2
Cambridge, Trinity College Library, MS O.5.6
Chicago, Newberry Library, Vault Folio Case MS 36 (*olim* MS f. 36 Ry 20)
Dublin, Trinity College Library, MS 213
London, British Library, MS Add. 60577
———, MS Add. 22718
London, Lambeth Palace Library, MS 265
New York, Columbia University Library, MS Plimpton 259
New York, Pierpont Morgan Library, MS B.11

Primary Sources

Letters and Papers Illustrative of the of the Wars of the English in France under the Reign of Henry the Sixth, King of England, ed. by Joseph Stevenson, 2 vols, Rerum Britannicarum Medii Aevi Scriptores, 22 (London: Longman, 1861–64), II/ii (1864)

---

61 Cambridge, Cambridge University Library, MS Gg.I.34.2 and Cambridge, Trinity College Library, MS O.5.6.

The Dictes and Sayings of the Philosophers: A Facsimile Reproduction of the first Book Printed in England, ed. by William Blades (London: Stock, 1877)

The Dicts and Sayings of the Philosophers: The Translations Made by Stephen Scrope, William Worcester, and an Anonymous Translator, ed. by Curt Bühler, Early English Text Society: Original Series, 211 (London: Oxford University Press, 1941)

Paston Letters and Papers of the Fifteenth Century, ed. by Norman Davis, Early English Text Society: Supplementary Series, 20 (Oxford: Oxford University Press, 1971; repr. 2004)

The Prologues and Epilogues of William Caxton, ed. by Walter J. B. Crotch, Early English Text Society: Original Series, 176 (London: Oxford University Press, 1929)

Secondary Works

Acker, Paul, 'The "Crafte of Nombrynge" in Columbia University Library, Plimpton MS 259', *Manuscripta*, 37/1 (1933), pp. 71–83

Blades, William, *The Biography and Typography of William Caxton*, 2 vols (London: Trübner, 1877), II

Bühler, Curt F., 'New Manuscripts of the "Dicts and Sayings of the Philosophers"', *Modern Language Notes* 63/1 (1948), pp. 26–30

Burke, John, B., *A Genealogical and Heraldic Dictionary of the Peerage and Baronetage of the British Empire*, 8th edn (London: Henry Colburn, 1845)

Catalogue of Books Printed in the XVth Century Now in the British Library, 13 pts (London: The British Library, 1908–2007), XI: *England*, ed. by Lotte Hellinga (2007)

A Catalogue of the Pre-1500 Western Manuscript Books at the Newberry Library, ed. by Paul Saenger (University of Chicago Press, 1989)

Coldiron, Anne E. B., *Printers without Borders: Translation and Textuality in the Renaissance* (Cambridge: Cambridge University Press, 2015)

Edwards, Anthony S. G. and Carol M. Meale, 'The Marketing of Printed Books in Late Medieval England', *The Library*, 6th series, 15 (1993), pp. 95–124

Ellis, Roger, 'Patronage and Sponsorship of Translations', in *The Oxford History of Literary Translation in English*, ed. by Roger Ellis and others (Oxford: Oxford University Press, 2008), I: *To 1550* (2008), ed. by Roger Ellis, pp. 98–115

Ford, Margaret Lane, 'Private Ownership of Printed Books', in *The Cambridge History of the Book in Britain*, ed. by Richard Gameson and others, 7 vols (Cambridge: Cambridge University Press, 1999–2019), III: *1400–1557*, ed. by Lotte Hellinga and Joseph Burney Trapp (1999), pp. 205–28

Franceschini, Ezio, *Il 'Liber philosophorum moralium antiquorum': Testo critico* (Padua: Atti del Reale Istituto Veneto di Scienze, Lettere ed Arti, 1932)

Gentry Culture in Late Medieval England, ed. by Raluca Radulescu and Alison Truelove, Manchester Medieval Studies (Manchester: Manchester University Press, 2005)

Hellinga, Lotte, *Caxton in Focus: The Beginning of Printing in England* (London: The British Library, 1982)

——, *Printing in England in the Fifteenth Century: E. Gordon Duff's Bibliography with Supplementary Descriptions, Chronology and a Census of Copies* (London: The British Library, 2009)

——, 'The Malory Manuscript and Caxton', in *Aspects of Malory*, ed. by Toshiyuki Takamiya and Derek Brewer, Arthurian Studies, 1 (Cambridge: Brewer, 1981), pp. 127–41 and pp. 213–14

―――, and Hilton Kelliher, 'The Malory Manuscript', *The British Library Journal*, 3 (1977), pp. 91–113

Hosington, Brenda and Marie-Alice Belle, 'Translation, History, and Print: A Model for the Study of Printed Translations in Early Modern Britain', *Translation Studies*, 29/1 (2016), pp. 2–21

Ives, Eric William, 'Andrew Dymmock and the Papers of Antony, Earl Rivers, 1482–3', *Bulletin of the Institute of Historical Research*, 41 (1968), pp. 216–29

Ives, Samuel A., 'Corrigenda and Addenda to the Descriptions of the Plimpton Manuscripts as Recorded in the De Ricci Census', *Speculum*, 17/1 (1942), pp. 33–49

Johnston, Michael, *Romance and the Gentry in Late Medieval England* (Oxford: Oxford University Press, 2014)

Kato, Takako, *Caxton's 'Morte Darthur': The Printing Process and the Authenticity of the Text*, Medium Aevum Monographs: New Series, 22 (Oxford: The Society for the Study of Medieval Languages and Literature, 2002)

Kelliher, Hilton, 'The Early History of the Malory Manuscript', in *Aspects of Malory*, ed. by Toshiyuki Takamiya and Derek Brewer, Arthurian Studies, 1 (Cambridge: Brewer, 1981), pp. 143–58 and pp. 215–18

Khalaf, Omar, 'An Epitome of Earl Rivers's *Dicts and Sayings of the Philosophers* in New York, Columbia University Library, MS Plimpton 259', *Philological Quarterly* 101 (2022), 1–22

Kuskin, William, *Symbolic Caxton: Literary Culture and Print Capitalism* (Notre Dame, IN: Notre Dame University Press, 2008)

Louis, Cameron, 'Proverbs, Precepts, and Monitory Pieces', in *A Manual of the Writings in Middle English, 1050–1500*, ed. by Burke Sievers and others, 11 vols (New Haven: The Connecticut Academy of Arts and Sciences, 1967–2005), IX (1967), pp. 2957–3375

Oates, J. C. T., 'English Bokes Concernyng to James Morice', *Transactions of the Cambridge Bibliographical Society*, 3 (1960), pp. 124–32

Orme, Nicholas, 'Schools and School-Books', in *The Cambridge History of the Book in Britain*, ed. by Richard Gameson and others, 7 vols (Cambridge: Cambridge University Press, 1999–2019), III: *1400–1557*, ed. by Lotte Hellinga and Joseph Burney Trapp (1999), pp. 449–69

―――, 'Education and Recreation', in *Gentry Culture in Late Medieval England*, ed. by Raluca Radulescu and Alison Truelove, Manchester Medieval Studies (Manchester: Manchester University Press, 2005), pp. 63–83

Painter, George Duncan, *William Caxton: A Quincentenary Biography of England's First Printer* (London: Chatto and Windus, 1976)

Petrina, Alessandra, *Cultural Politics in Fifteenth-Century England: The Case of Humphrey, Duke of Gloucester*, Brill's Studies in Intellectual History, 124 (Leiden: Brill, 2004)

Pidgeon, Linda, 'Anthony Woodville, Lord Scales and Earl Rivers: Family, Friends and Affinity: Part 1', *The Ricardian*, 15 (2005), pp. 1–19

―――, 'Anthony Woodville, Lord Scales and Earl Rivers: Family, Friends and Affinity: Part 2', *The Ricardian*, 16 (2006), pp. 15–45

Rutter, Russell, 'William Caxton and Literary Patronage', *Studies in Philology*, 84 (1987), pp. 440–70

Salter, Elisabeth, *Popular Reading in English, c. 1400–1600* (Manchester: Manchester University Press, 2012)

Translation and Print Culture in Early Modern Europe, ed. by Brenda Hosington, *Renaissance Studies* [Special Issue], 29/1 (2015)

Wakelin, Daniel, *Humanism, Reading and English Literature 1430–1530* (Oxford: Oxford University Press, 2007)

Youngs, Deborah, 'Cultural Networks', in *Gentry Culture in Late Medieval England*, ed. by Raluca Radulescu and Alison Truelove, Manchester Medieval Studies (Manchester: Manchester University Press, 2005), pp. 119–33

Index

Authors and Texts

Abélard, *Letters* 257
Acta Sanctorum 48
Aegidius Romanus 187
Ælfric 29
 De falsis diis 29
Ælfric of Eynsham 82
Aelred of Rievaulx 256
 De institutione inclusarum 256
Agnesar Saga 46, 48, 50, 51, 53, 54, 58
Agnesar saga meyjar 51
Albertus Magnus / the Great 148, 320, 326
 De animalibus 326
 Paradisus animae 208
Alcuin 36
Alphabetum narrationum 312
Ambrose of Milan 48
 De virginibus 48
 Agnes beatae virginis 48
Ambrosiaster 23
 Commentarius (Commentaries) 23
Ancrene Wisse 255, 267
Anonymus Pisanus 122
Antonius saga 53
Aristotle 92, 198, 216, 296, 320
 Metaphysics 92
 [Pseudo], *Secretum secretorum* 115
Arius 25
Arnulfus de Boeriis 257
 Speculum monachorum 257
Ashby, George 337
Aspasius Paternus 46
Augustine 24, 149, 157, 196, 216, 257, 299, 300, 320
 Confessiones 159
 Contra Faustum 77

Enarrationes in Psalmos 92
 De praedaestinatione sanctorum 299, 300, 301
 [Pseudo], *Speculum peccatoris* 208, 226
 Soliloquia 208
Ave Maria 169
Avicenna, *Canon* 326

Basilius Magnus 226
Bartoloměj of Chlumec (*Claretus*) 99
Beck, Konrad 132
Beneš of Hořovice 209
Bernard of Breydenbach 127, 130, 131
 Peregrinatio in Terram Sanctam 130, 131, 132, 136, 137, 140, 141, 143
Bernard of Clairvaux 14, 148, 149, 152, 187, 206, 212, 218, 253, 256
 [Pseudo], *De contemptu mundi* 259, 265, 350
 Meditationes piisimae de cognitione humanae conditionis 14, 206
Boccaccio, Giovanni 322
 Decameron 322
Boke of Gostely Grace 16, 317, 318
Books of Blessed Bernard the Abbot (*Books*) (*Knige blaženago Brnarda Opata*) 15, 253, 255, 256, 257, 261
Berthold of Regensburg 153
Birger Pettersson 84
Birgitta of Sweden 16, 69, 178, 210, 254, 317, 326

Revelations 16, 69, 178, 210, 318
Regula Salvatoris/Birgittine
    Rule 325
Bishop Hólar 50
Bishop Laurence 45
Bishop Páll Jóhnsson 45, 49
Bishop Theophilius 22
Blasíus saga 44
Blanche of Namur 84
Bocados the oro 338
Boethius 300, 301, 303, 305
    De consolatione Philosophiae 300, 301, 305
Bonaventure, [Pseudo-] 148, 191, 208, 226, 309, 311
    De triplici via 226
    Imago vitae 208
    Meditationes de interiori homine 208
    Meditationes vitae Christi 94
Bradwardine, Thomas 303

Caesarius of Heisterbach 312
    Dialogus miraculorum 312
Cassiodorus 226
Catherine of Siena 16, 317, 320, 322, 326, 329
    Dialogo 16, 317, 318, 322, 330, 331
Caxton, William 337–52
    Dicts 337–52
    Book of the Knight of the Tower 342
    Distichs of Cato 342
    Stans puer ad mensam 342, 349
    The Play and Game of the Chess 340
    The Recueyl of the Histories of Troye 340, 347
Chartier, Alain 339, 345
    Curial 339, 345
    La belle dame sans merci 345
Chastising of God's Children 178, 299, 308–11

Chaucer, Geoffrey 313
    Canterbury Tales 303, 339, 341, 349
    Prodesse et delectare 10
    Nun's Priest's Tale 303
Chertsey, Andrew 308
Christine de Pizan 345
    L'Epitre d'Othéa à Hector 345
    Le livre des faits d'armes et de chevalerie 345
    Morale Prouerbes 345
Cato 342
    Disticha (Distich's of Cato) 342
Charles of Orléans 121
Cicero 149, 329, 346
    De senectute 346, 349
Codex Argenteus 31
Codex Brixianus 35
Codex Carolinus 34
Conrad of Ammenhausen 188
    Schachzabelbuch 188
Conrad of Brundelsheim 147
    Sermones socci 13, 147, 148, 149, 150, 152, 156, 159, 160, 161
Credo (in Deum) 45, 193
Cyprian of Carthage 46, 189
Cyril of Thessaloniki, St 256
Czech New Testament 96, 104

Dante 195, 322
    Devine Comedy 195
David of Augsburg 152
    Seven Stages of Prayer 152
De institutione inclusarum 255
De libris hereticorum legendis 232
De sacra scriptura et de veritatibus catholicis 94
De statu, conditione ac regimine magnis Canis 111
Depositio Martyrum 46, 47
Decem gradus amoris 147, 148, 149, 150, 151, 153, 154, 155, 156, 157, 158, 159, 160

Desiderii mei 95, 96
Deus caritas est, sermon 147, 149, 150, 152, 154, 155, 156, 157, 158, 159, 160, 161
Dicts and Sayings of the Philosophers 16, 337, 350
Dieta salutis 191, 192, 195
Ditz moraulx des philosophes 337, 338, 347
Dionysius the Areopagite 152
Discipulus 148
  see Johannes Herolt OP. 148
Doctrine of the Hert 255, 326
Dominicanus, translator 91, 92, 93
Dresden Bible 90, 91, 93

Eckhart, Meister 153, 154, 160
Elisabeth of Schönau 320
Elizabeth of Töss 317
Elsbeth of Oye 157
Emperor Diocletian 46, 47
Engelberger Predigten 150, 152, 154
Elucidarium 16, 299, 304, 305, 306, 308
Eufemiavisor (*Songs of Eufemia*) 70

Fabri, Felix 132
Faucon, Nicole 111
First Grammatical Treatise (FGT) 44
Four Things Needs Man to Know 178
Frater Ambrosius 96, 102

Galen
Gaytring/Gaitrik, J. de 170, 173, 177, 178
Gerald of Wales 350
  De regimine mundi 350
Gertrude the Great 319, 320
Giovanni da Pian del Carpine 112
  Historia Mongalorum 112
Gizurr 49

Glagolitic Gršković's Miscellany 256, 259, 270
Glagoljica 256
Glossa ordinaria 88, 98
Gottes, Robert 349
  The Words of a Good Horse to his Master 350
Grenehalgh, James 280
Grágás 45, 49, 50
Gregory of Rimini 302
Gregory the Great, St 150, 152, 157, 160, 216, 257, 258, 321
Guðmundar saga 49
Guidini, Cristofano 329
Guigo II 312
  Scala Claustralium 312
Guyart des Moulin 70, 84
  Bible historiale 70, 84
Gylfaginning 53
Gzel, Petr 98

Hákon Hákonarson 58
Hákonar saga Hákonarson 58
Halla, Bishop Páll's daughter 45
hapax legomenon g fganarmenn 56
Hayton of Coricus, 111
  La Flor des estoires de la terre d'Orient 111
Heilagra Manna Søgur 43
Helwicus Theutonicus 149, 155, 160, 162
  De dilectione Dei et proximi 13, 149, 260, 264
  De decem gradibus amoris 150
Henry Totting of Oyta 94
Howard Fabing 32
Herman of Carinthia 123
  Doctrina Muhamet 123
Hildegard of Bingen 320
  Scivias 320
Hilton, Walter 283, 287, 288, 296, 312
Historia Lombardica, see Jacobus de Voragine 48

Honorius of Autun (Honorius
  Augustodunensis) 198, 208,
  304, 306
  Elucidarius 208, 304
Hugh of Saint Victor 92, 301
  *De sacramentis Christianae
  fidei* 301
Hus, Jan 14, 94, 127, 206–20, 223,
  224, 229, 231, 237, 239
  On Simony 221, 224
  *On the Six Errors (O šesti
  bludiech)* 207
  *On the Understanding of the
  Right Way to Salvation (O
  poznání cesty pravé k spasení)
  = Dcerka (The Daughter)* 14, 205–20
  *Czech Festival Sermons (Česká
  sváteční kázání)* 224, 225
  *Czech Sunday Postil (Česká
  nedělní postila)* 206, 207,
  211, 224–48
  Expositions (Výklady) 206
  Expositions on Faith, Ten Commandments, and Pater Noster 224
  *The Nine Pieces of Gold (Devět
  kusóv zlatých)* 208, 210, 211
Hymn from the Roman Breviary 263
Hynek of Roupov 209

Ignis ante ipsum praecedit 153
  see Psalm 96. 3.
Ingold of Basel, Master 185, 188,
  190
  *Puechlein vom Guldin Spil (Book
  of the Golden Game)* 14,
  185, 188, 198, 199, 200
  *Interpretationes Hebraicorum
  nominum (Interpretations of
  Hebrew Names)* 88, 98
interpretatio norroena 53, 54
interpretatio romana 53

Isidore of Seville 208, 296
  Synonyma de lamentatione animae peccatricis 208

Jacobus de Cessolis 187, 188, 190,
  199,
  *Book of Chess / Liber de moribus hominum et officiis nobilium ac popularium super ludo
  scacchorum* 15, 187, 188,
  199
Jacob of Teramo 209
  *Consolatio peccatorum seu processus Luciferi contra Iesum
  Christum = Liber Belial* 209
Jan of Mýto 94, 95,
Jesus 25, 66, 72, 93, 113, 114, 133,
  141, 194, 196, 197, 198, 208, 212,
  213, 217, 228, 233, 237, 241, 242,
  245, 246, 262, 263, 264, 265, 266,
  288, 324
  *Liber philosophorum moralium
  antiquorum* 338
Jacobus de Saraponte 226
  Aurissa sive de arte predicandi 226
Jacobus de Voragine 93
  Legenda aurea 48, 93
  Historia scholastica 93
James of Milan 309, 310, 311
  Stimulus amoris 309, 310, 311
Jan of Jesenice 208
Jan of Příbram 220
Jean d'Arras 121, 123
  Roman de Mélusine 121, 123
Jean de Joinville 112
  Life of Saint Louis 112
Jean le Long 13, 112–24
  Flos historiarum 111, 115
  Chronicon monasterii sancti Bertini 112
Jerome, St, [Pseudo] 95, 97, 196,
  210,
Johannes Herolt OP 198

Index

Discipulus de eruditione christifidelium, De chorea 198
Johannes Nider 198
  Die vierundzwanzig goldenen Harfen (*The Twenty-Four Golden Harps*) 198
Johannes of Indersdorf 158, 159
  Prayer Book I for Elisabeth Ebran 158, 159, 161
  The Three Kinds of Man 158
Johannes of Jenstein 94
Johannes of Rheinfelden 198
  Ludus cartularum moralisatus 198
John Chrysostom, 22, 23, 38, 119
  Epistulae 38
  Homiliae 38
Johannes of Werden 148
  Sermones dormi secure 148
John Fastolf 343, 344, 345, 346, 348, 351
John of Salisbury 187, 188
  Policraticus 188
John of Castiglione 123
  Exhortatio in Turchos 123
John of Mandeville 121
  Livre des merveilles or *Livre des voyages* 121
John of Neumarkt 210
  Letters of St Jerome 210
  O svatém Jeronýmovi knihy troje (*Three Books on St Jerome*) 210
Jón Qgmundarson, *Jóns saga Helga* 60
Josephus Flavius 231
Julian of Norwich 303

Kabátník, Martin 143
King Edom 81
King Hákon V Magnússon 69
King Wenceslas IV 94, 100, 127
Klaudyán, Mikuláš (*Claudianus*) 104, 105

Konungs skuggsjá (King's Mirror) 83
Kralice Bible 98, 105,

La Court de Paradis 195, 196
Latinitatis medii aevi lexicon Bohemorum 234
Lay Folk's Catechism 14, 167–82
Laurentius saga 44
Letters of Abelard and Heloise 255
Liber de modo bene vivendi ad sororem (*Liber*) 15, 253–67
Liber trium virorum et trium spiritualium virginum 320
Life of Adam and Eve 209
Livre des merveilles (*Book of Wonders*) 121, 122, 123
Litoměřice Prologues 96, 98, 100
Litoměřice-Třeboň Bible 90, 93, 94, 98, 100, 102, 103
Lokasenna 53
Lukáš of Prague 105
Lupáč, Martin 208
Lydgate, John 349
  Temple of Glass 349

Magnus Eriksson 65, 69, 84
Maître de l' Épître d' Othéa 120
máldagar 50
Malory, Thomas 339
  Morte Darthur 339
Manere of Good Lyvyng 253, 254
Marco Polo 112, 121, 122, 123
  Devisement du monde 121, 122, 123
Margaret Heslington 278
Marie de Clèves 121
Martin of Troppau 209
Martyrdom of Thane 115
Martyrologium Hieronymianum 47
Mattheus saga postola 44
Mattias Tveitane 53
Maximus of Turin 48

Mechthild of Hackeborn 317–31
  Liber specialis gratiae (*Book of Spiritual Grace*) 16, 317, 319, 320, 331
  Das fließende Licht der Gottheit (*The Flowing Light of the Godhead*) 319
Medeltidens bibelarbeten (*MB, Medieval Bible Works*) 66–86
Medled Life 288
Meditations on Sixty Five Woes of Christ 210
Meditations Upon the Passion 178
Mikuláš Bakalář (Štětina) 129, 130, 132, 133, 136, 137, 138, 142, 143, 144,
  The Treatise on the Holy Land (*Traktát o zemi svaté; The Treatise*) 129, 130, 134, 135, 136, 138
  The Life of Mohamed (*Život Mohamedův*) 129, 131, 136, 137, 138, 143, 144
Mubaschschir ben Fatik's *Mokhtâr el-hikam wa mahasin al-kalim* (*The Choicest Maxims and Best Sayings*) 337
Misyn, Richard 278–87
  Fire of Love 278, 280, 286

National Museum Glossed Psalter 89
Nicolas of Cusa 122
  De pace fidei 122
  Cribratio Alcorani 122
Nicolas of Lyra, 94
  Postilla litteralis 94
Nikolaus saga 54
Nine Divisions of Christians 143, 144

Odorico da Pordenone 111
  Relatio 111
Old Czech Annals 209

Old Czech Collection of Biblical Prologues (*The Collection*) 96, 98–102
On Divine Love 150, 158
Optát, Beneš 98
Orcherd of Syon 16, 317, 318, 322, 323, 324, 325, 327, 329, 331
Ovid 149

Pascentius 24
Paris Bible/exemplar Parisiense 88, 90, 96, 98, 106
Passio Agnetis 48, 49, 51, 52, 59
Paston Letters 344, 349
Paul, Apostle 27, 28, 270
Paradisus anime intelligentis 153
Paul the Deacon 48
Paul Walther von Güglingen 135
Pentateuch 65–84, 87, 91, 95, 96
Peregrinus of Opole 148
Peter Andreas Munch 32
Peter Aureol 302
Peter the Venerable 123
Petr Chelčický 210, 211,
Petr Zmrzlík of Svojšín 100
Petrus Alphonsi 136, 138, 140
  Dialogus contra Judeos 136
Petrus Comestor, *Historia scholastica* 69, 78
Perrin, Jean 191
Philostorgius, *The Ecclesiastical History* 25, 38
Plácidús saga 44
Pope Damasus 23, 47
Pore Caitif 277
Prague Bible 91, 96, 97
Predigt von der Minne zu Gott (*Sermon on the Love of God*) 150, 160
Predigt von den zehn Graden der Liebe (*Sermon on the Ten steps of Love*) 154, 155, 160
Prickynge of Love 310, 311

Index

Prudentius, Christian poet, *Peristephanon* 48
Psalterium iuxta Hebraeos 97

Rath, Martin 136
Riccoldo da Monte di Croce 111, 113, 114, 117, 123
   Liber peregrinationis 111, 112, 113, 114, 115, 116, 123
   Contra legem Sarracenorum 123
Rivers, Earl 337, 341, 342, 344, 345, 348
   Dicts 337–51
   Cordyal 339, 346, 347
   Moral Proverbs 339, 347
Robert of Ketton 123
Rolle, Richard 15, 278–93, 327, 330
   Emendatio vite (*EV*) 15
   Form of Living 283, 290
   Incendium amoris 279, 280, 283
Roman Breviary 263
Rupert of Deutz 196

Saga af Fídes, Spes ok Karítas 54
Saga heilagrar Önnu 44
Salvian of Marseilles 33, 34, 38
   De gubernatione Dei 24
   On the Government of God 34
Schedel, Hartmann 131, 132
   Rezeptbuch 131
   Weltchronik 132
Schwarzwälder Predigten 153
Scrope, Stephen 337, 338, 346
Second Lucidaire 304, 306, 307, 308
Seitenstetten Evangeliary 89
Suso, Henry 153, 210
   Horologium sapientiae 210
Sigmund of Domažlice 207
Sixt of Ottersdorf 104
Socrates 338, 350
Sophista 94

Speculum Christiani 172
Speculum devotorum (*Mirror to Devout People, Myrowre to Devout Peple*) 317
Speculum humanae salvationis 330
Speculum maius see Vincent of Beauvais, *Speculum historiale* 122, 136
Speculum virginum 254, 255, 257
St. Agnes 46–62, 196
St Cecilia 49, 50, 196
Staffel göttlicher Lieb (*Stages of Divine Love*) 150, 158, 159
Stans puer ad mensam 342, 349
Stjórn 54
St Georgener Predigten 153
St Vitus Metropolitan Chapter Prologues 98

Tacitus, Publius Cornelius, *Germania* 53
Tauler, Johannes 153, 154, 160
Teachings that Saint Bernard Gave to his Sister (*Nauci svetog Bernarda sestri svojoj*) 256
The Abbey of the Holy Ghost 288
Theoderic the Great 31, 36
Theodoret of Cyrus 22
Theodulf of Orléans 36
Thomas Aquinas 66, 70, 150. 198, 302, 309, 320
   Summa theologiae 66, 67, 70
   Summa theologica 302
Thomas Hemerken of Kempen 158
   Imitatio Christi 158
Thomas of Froidmont 253
   Vitae of Thomas 253
Thomas Leventhorpe 288, 296
Thomas of Štítné 210, 219
Thoresby, John 168–69, 170, 172–73, 175, 177
Twinger of Königshofen, Jakob 209

Þorgils saga skarða 58
Þorláks saga 49, 50, 51
Tomas saga erkibyskups 58
Tucher, Hans 132–33
   *Die Reise ins Gelobte
      Land* 131–32, 134–36
*Treatise Upon the Value of Time
  and its Proper Employment* 178
Tretise of Miraclis Pleying 181

Uiliaric 34
Ulf Abjörnsson 84
Upon the Love of God 178

Veni creator spiritus 151
Vespucci, Amerigo 129, 133
Vetus Latina 35
Vienna Evangeliary 89
Vigilius Tapsensis 24, 38
Vincent de Beauvais 122, 136
   Speculum historiale 122, 136
Vitae Patrum 54
Vulgate 35, 67–68, 78, 87–88, 98,
   100, 237–38

Walter of Châtillon 115
   Alexandreis 115
Wells, John 318

Wilhelm von Boldensele 111
   *Liber de quibusdam ultramarinis
     partibus et praecipue de Terra
     Sancta* 111
Wilhering Sermons 224–48
William Briton (*Guillelmus
   Brito*) 99
   *Expositiones prologorum Bib-
     liae* 99
William of Lavicea 191
Wittenberg Psalter 89
Worcester, William 337, 338, 344,
   345, 346, 347, 348, 349, 351
   *Acta domini Johannis Fas-
     tolf* 346
   Dicts 337–51
   The Boke of Noblesse 346
   Tullius of Olde Age 346–47
Wulfila 12, 24, 25, 26, 28, 29, 30,
   32, 33,
Wyclif, John 14, 96, 127, 205–19,
   223, 232, 301, 303,

X trapkijns vander mynnen (*Ten
   Steps of Love*) 150, 156, 157,
   158, 161

Ynglinga saga 53

Bible References

Apocryphal texts
   Baruch   88
   Epistle of Jeremiah   88
   Ezra 3   88
Acts 2   93
Acts of the Apostles   91, 93
   Acts of the Apostles 2.4–11   25
Apocalypse
   Apocalypse 5.8–10   193
   Apocalypse 6.1–2   197
   Apocalypse 7.12   193
   Apocalypse 14.3   195
Corinthians 100

I Corinthians 11.6   26
I Corinthians 13.1–2   27
I Corinthians 15.15   30
I Corinthians 10.19–21   28, 29
II Corinthians 11.13   30
II Corinthians 11.26   30
Deuteronomy   67, 68, 69, 70
   Deuteronomy 4.2   104
Ecclesiasticus   103, 270
Epistles   87, 91, 151, 290, 296, 309
Esther   66
Exodus   67
   Exodus 2.11–12   77

Index

Exodus 3.13 and 15	193
Exodus 8.12	73
Exodus 12	69
Exodus 12.35–36	78
Exodus 12.36	79
Exodus 14	74
Exodus 15.27	72
Exodus 17.8–16	72
Exodus 18	69
Exodus 19	69, 70
Exodus 19.4 and 6	193
Exodus 22.1	238
Exodus 34	75
Four Books of the Kings	87
Genesis	66, 67, 69, 70, 76, 82, 91, 103
Genesis 1.1	75
Genesis 12.11–16	75
Genesis 13.18	74
Genesis 15.29–33	71
Genesis 18	73
Genesis 22	72
Genesis 27.18–19	80
Genesis 50.1–3	73
Genesis-Exodus	18 69, 70
Gospel of John/Skeireins	33
Gospel of Luke	90
Gospel of Matthew	91, 94
Isaiah 6.3	195
James	103
James 75	318
John	103
I John 4.16	147, 151, 153
John 2.4	30, 192
John 6.69–70	193
John 11.4	155, 159
Joshua	66, 68, 69
Jude	103
Judges	66
Judith	66
Kings	69, 73, 87,
Leviticus	67, 68, 70, 82
Leviticus 19.29–32	81
Luke	
Luke 1.1–4	90
Luke 1.45–46	192
Luke 3.14	26,
Luke 6.26	30
Luke 8.27	31
Luke 19.2	238
Luke 19.5	238
Luke 22.28–30	193
Luke 24.13	14, 206, 213, 214
I and II Maccabees	66, 103, 231
Mark	
Mark 13.22	30
Mark 16	93
Mark 16.15	93
Matthew	
Matthew 5.10–14	194
Matthew 6.9–10	25
Matthew 7	240
Matthew 7.2	271
Matthew 8.28–31	31
Matthew 11.28	194
Matthew 13.23	195
Matthew 25.32–34	195
New Testament	12, 22, 26, 72, 73, 93, 96, 97, 98, 102, 104, 105, 216, 269, 290, 296
Numbers	67
Numbers 10.1–10	81
Numbers 13.17–20	73
Numbers 17.10	74
Numbers 20.21	81
Old Testament	12, 67, 68, 72, 74, 76, 82, 83, 89, 91, 264, 290, 296
Pentateuch	13, 65–84, 87, 91, 95, 96
Paul's First Epistle to the Corinthians	23, 28, 100
I Peter 2.9	194
Philippians 2.13–15	309
Proverbs	103, 270
Proverbs 8.21	195
Proverbs 9.10	271
Psalms	97, 226, 270
Psalm 32	18
Psalm 41	151
Psalm 44.1	206

Psalm 65.12	194	Song of Solomon 1.1	195
Psalm 87.10	155, 159	Song of Songs 2.1	269
Psalm 96.3	153	Song of Songs 3.1	154
Psalm 102.20	193	Song of Songs 3.1–2	154
Psalm 126.4	197	Song of Songs 5.8	155, 159
Revelation	66	Timothy	
Romans	8.17 195	I Timothy 1.17	195
Romans 8.30	309	II Timothy 2.11	194
Ruth	66, 103	Wisdom	270
Sirach	270	Wisdom of Solomon 4.1	195

Song of Solomon (Song of Songs)
253, 260, 262, 263, 264, 272